Webster's Essential Mini Dictionary

CAMBRIDGE
UNIVERSITY PRESS

CAMBRIDGE
UNIVERSITY PRESS

32 Avenue of the Americas, New York, NY 10013, USA

Cambridge University Press is part of the University of Cambridge.

It furthers the University's mission by disseminating knowledge in the pursuit of education, learning and research at the highest international levels of excellence.

www.cambridge.org
Information on this title: www.cambridge.org/9780521133135

© Cambridge University Press 2011

First published 2011
3rd printing 2014

Printed in the United States of America

A catalog record for this publication is available from the Library of Congress.

ISBN 978-0-521-13313-5 Paperback

Webster's Essential Mini Dictionary

Senior Commissioning Editor
Colin McIntosh

Commissioning Editor
Wendalyn Nichols

Development Editor
Helen Waterhouse

Editorial contributors
Constance Baboukis
Sarah Hilliard
Katherine M. Isaacs
Diane Nicholls
Marina Padakis
Enid Pearsons
Jane Solomon

Global Corpus Manager
Ann Fiddes

Pronunciations
Constance Baboukis
Enid Pearsons

Design
Adventure House
Boag Associates
Claire Parson

Typesetting
Grapevine Publishing Services LLC

Production
Alan Kaplan
Christopher Rice
Clive Rumble
Chris Williams

Illustrators
Oxford Designers and Illustrators
Corinne Burrows
Ray Burrows
David Shenton

Contents

Guide to the dictionary

What is an entry?

A dictionary entry tells you what a word means and how to use it. At the beginning of each entry in this dictionary is the main form of the word, in color. This is the **headword**. A headword can be one word (**light**) or it can be more than one word (**light bulb**).

This guide will help you to use the entries in this dictionary. It will show you how to look for the entry you want and what information you will find in the entry.

Alphabetical order

The English alphabet has 26 letters. The order of the letters is:

Small letters: a b c d e f g h i j k l m n o p q r s t u v w x y z
Capital letters: A B C D E F G H I J K L M N O P Q R S T U V W X Y Z

The entries in the dictionary are in alphabetical order. We ignore spaces and punctuation marks when putting words in alphabetical order. For example, **fairy tale** is found between the words **fairy** and **faith**.

If you are trying to decide the alphabetical order of two words with the same first letter, look at the second letter. Go through each letter of the word from left to right until you find a letter that is different. The first letter that is different shows you what order the words should be in.

To help you remember the alphabetical order of English, the alphabet is shown down the side of each page of the dictionary.

1   **Put these words in alphabetical order.**

table   book   light   pencil   chair   sock   hair

1 _____   2 _____   3 _____   4 _____
5 _____   6 _____   7 _____

2   Put these words in alphabetical order.

talk   take   thank   teacher   tall   today   Thursday

1 _____   2 _____   3 _____   4 _____
5 _____   6 _____   7 _____

Finding an entry

When you open the dictionary, you will see a word at the top of each
page. These help you to find the page that the word you are looking for
is on. The word at the top of the left page is the first entry on that page,
and the word at the top of the right page is the last entry on that page. If
the word you are looking for comes in alphabetical order between these
two words, it will be on the two pages you are looking at.

3   Draw a line from the headword to the words that it will appear
    between.

1 good	port...	...praise
2 police	we'd...	...which
3 early	goal...	...grandchild
4 whale	point...	...population
5 poster	DVD...	...easy

4   Which of these words will you find on the pages that start with
    mouse and end with must? Draw a line under the words that will
    be on these two pages.

<u>mouth</u>   more   much   mood   my   mug
move   Mr.   mother   mustn't   music   Ms.

Spelling

The dictionary entries show the correct spellings of words. Sometimes
words can be spelled in more than one way, or another word can be used
with exactly the same meaning. These different spellings or different
words are shown in parentheses at the beginning of the entries:

adviser /ədˈvaɪ·zər/ noun (also **advisor**)
someone whose job is to give advice
about a subject: *a financial adviser*

bye /baɪ/ exclamation (also **bye-bye**)
A1 goodbye: *Bye, see you tomorrow.*

everyone /ˈev·riˌwʌn/, /ˈev·ri·wən/ **pronoun** (also **everybody**) **A2** every person: *I've received a reply from everyone now.* ○ *Everyone agreed with the decision.*

eyelash /ˈaɪˌlæʃ/ **noun** (also **lash**) one of the short hairs that grow from the edge of your eyelids: *false eyelashes*

Vocabulary levels **A1** **A2** **B1**

In the dictionary entries you will see the numbers and letters A1, A2, and B1. These are symbols that show you which words or meanings of words are most important for you to learn first. A1 words are the most basic words and should be learned first, followed by A2 words, then B1 words. You can use these levels to decide what the important words are that you need to study.

5 **Look up these words and write down the level for each one.**

  1 bread _____
  2 home (noun) _____
  3 home (adverb) _____
  4 lucky _____
  5 fast (adjective) _____
  6 fast (adverb) _____
  7 rainforest _____

Pronunciations

Pronunciations are shown after the headword. For example, the pronunciation for the word **dog** is shown like this: /dɔg/. The pronunciations are written using the symbols of the International Phonetic Alphabet (IPA). The list on the inside front cover of the dictionary tells you how to read the pronunciation symbols. The most difficult symbols are also shown at the bottom of each page, with an example of a word that contains that sound.

The symbols ' and ˌ show you which part of the word to say strongly. The high symbol ' shows you the part of the word that you should say in the strongest voice. The low symbol ˌ shows you the part of the word that you should say in a strong voice, but not as strong as '.

The dictionary entries do not show pronunciation for abbreviations used only in writing, such as **Dr., in.,** and **lb.**.

6   Look up these words. Draw a line from the word to its
    pronunciation.

    1   fish   /læf/
    2   dictionary   /θruː/
    3   island   /saɪn/
    4   knee   /hwɪtʃ/
    5   through   /fɪʃ/
    6   sign   /ˈdɪkˌʃəˌnerˑi/
    7   laugh   /ˈaɪˑlənd/
    8   which   /niː/

7   Put a line under the part of the word that has the strongest stress.

    1   doctor   2   incorrect   3   award
    4   question   5   record (noun)   6   record (verb)

Parts of speech

A part of speech is one of the grammatical groups into which words
are divided, such as noun, verb, and adjective. It shows what job each
word does in a sentence. In the dictionary, each word has a part of
speech label that is shown at the beginning of the entry, after the
pronunciation. The names of the parts of speech used in this dictionary
are: *noun, verb, auxiliary verb, adj, adv, pronoun, preposition, conjunction,
quantifier,* and *exclamation. Phrasal verbs* also have a part of speech label.

When two words have the same spelling but different parts of speech,
they have separate entries. For example, **bite¹** and **bite²** have the same
spelling but are separate because **bite¹** is a verb and **bite²** is a noun.

8   Look up these words. How many parts of speech do they have?

    1   light   ___3___   2   chat   _____
    3   milk   _____   4   hot   _____
    5   tax   _____   6   home   _____

9   What part of speech are these words? Look them up in the
    dictionary to find out.

    1   opinion   __noun__   2   curious   _____
    3   tent   _____   4   frighten   _____
    5   together   _____ 6   within   _____

noun

A noun is a word that refers to a person, object, place, event, substance, idea, feeling, or quality. For example, the words **teacher**, **book**, and **beauty** are nouns.

10 Look up these words. Draw a line under the words that are nouns.

hat   happy   actor   between   luck

<u>chair</u>   read   awful   compare   house

Some nouns have only a plural form and cannot be used with **a** or **an**. These nouns are called *plural nouns* and are always used with plural verbs. Nouns such as **scissors** and **glasses** are plural nouns.

scissors /ˈsɪz·ərz/ **plural noun** **B1** a tool for cutting paper, hair, etc. that you hold in your hand and that has two blades: *a pair of scissors*

glasses /ˈɡlæs·ɪz/ **plural noun** **A1** a piece of equipment with two transparent parts that you wear in front of your eyes to help you see better: *a pair of glasses* ○ *She was **wearing glasses**.*

11 Look up these words to see if they are plural nouns, then draw a circle around the correct verb form in the sentences.

1 Where is/are my **pajamas**?
2 The computer **graphics** is/are very good.
3 The **furniture** has/have arrived.
4 My **pants** is/are dirty.
5 I think **politics** is/are very boring.

Some nouns do not have a plural form and cannot be used with **a** or **an**. These nouns have [no plural] after the part of speech label:

knowledge /ˈnɑl·ɪdʒ/ **noun** [no plural] **B1** information and understanding that you have in your mind: *His **knowledge** of history is amazing.*

12 Look up the words that have a line under them. Are the sentences correct?

	correct	incorrect
1 I need an <u>advice</u>.	_____	✓
2 Can you send me some <u>informations</u>?	_____	_____
3 They bought some new <u>equipment</u>.	_____	_____

4 I have some <u>sand</u> in my shoe.   _____ _____
5 Someone has stolen my <u>luggages</u>.   _____ _____
6 We have a good <u>news</u> for you.   _____ _____

pronoun
A pronoun is a word that is used instead of a noun that has already been
talked about. For example, **she**, **it**, and **mine** are pronouns.

determiner
A determiner is a word that is used before a noun or adjective to show
which person or thing you are referring to. For example, **my** in *my old
car* and **that** in *that man* are determiners.

adjective
An adjective is a word that describes a noun or pronoun. For example,
small, **interesting**, and **blue** are all adjectives.

13 **Look up these words. Draw a line under the words that are
adjectives.**

<u>afraid</u>   nibble   bag   react   broken
adventure   narrow   honest   immediately   deep

preposition
A preposition is a word that is used before a noun or pronoun to show
place, direction, or time. For example, **on** in *Your keys are on the table* is
a preposition.

verb, auxiliary verb
A verb is a word that is used to say what someone does or what happens.
For example, the words **go**, **read**, **make**, and **feel** are verbs. An auxiliary
verb is a verb that is used together with another verb to make a new
tense or other grammatical form. For example, **have** in *They have arrived*
and **be** in *to be called* are auxiliary verbs.

phrasal verb
A phrasal verb is a verb that has two or three words. Together these
words have a meaning that is different from each of the separate words.
For example, **count on** and **count up** are phrasal verbs.

count¹ /kaʊnt/ **verb** **1** to see how many people or things there are: *I counted the money on the table.* **2** to say numbers in their correct order: *Can you count to twenty in French?* **3** to be important: *Doesn't my opinion count for anything?*

count on *someone* **phrasal verb** to be certain that you can depend on someone: *I can always count on my parents to help me.*
count *someone/something* **up phrasal verb** to add together all the people or things in a group

In this dictionary, phrasal verbs are in alphabetical order at the end of the entry for the verb. There is also a list of the most important phrasal verbs in the middle of the dictionary.

14 How many phrasal verbs can you find in the dictionary formed from these verbs?

1 get   2 stand   3 look   4 read

15 Choose a meaning from the box and write it next to the correct phrasal verb.

to start a trip
to break into pieces
to say or write something that is not true
to wait for a short time
to return to a place

1 fall apart   _____
2 make up   _____
3 set off   _____
4 get back   _____
5 hang on   _____

adverb
An adverb is a word that gives more information about a verb, adjective, phrase, or other adverb. In the sentence *He ate quickly*, **quickly** is an adverb.

conjunction
A conjunction is a word that is used to connect phrases or parts of a sentence. For example, the words **and** and **because** are conjunctions.

Irregular forms

Some forms of nouns, verbs, and adjectives have special forms or spellings. These are *irregular* forms. Irregular forms are shown at the beginning of the entry:

break[1] /breɪk/ **verb** (present participle **breaking**, past tense **broke**, past participle **broken**)

good[1] /gʊd/ **adj** (comparative **better**, superlative **best**)

Irregular forms of verbs

Past tenses that are not regular are shown at the entry for the verb. There is also a list of irregular verbs at the back of the book that shows the infinitive form of the verb, its past tense, and the past participle.

Irregular forms have their own entries, which tell you to go to the main form of the word:

went /went/ past tense of **go**

16 Write the past tense and past participle of these verbs.

		past tense	past participle
1	break	_____	_____
2	make	_____	_____
3	get	_____	_____
4	swim	_____	_____
5	take	_____	_____

Irregular forms of nouns

To make most nouns plural, you normally add **–s**, for example, **book**, **books**. Some nouns do not have this regular plural form. If a plural form of a noun is not regular, it is shown in parentheses after the headword:

shelf /ʃelf/ **noun** (plural **shelves**) **A2** a board used to put things on, often attached to a wall:
Please put that book on the shelf over there.

17 Look up these nouns. Write down their plural form.

1	bookshelf	bookshelves
2	child	_____
3	foot	_____
4	man	_____

5 mouse _____
6 potato _____
7 sheep _____
8 wife _____

18 Look up these nouns. Put a line under the correct plural form.

1 city   <u>cities</u>   citys   cityes
2 life   lifes   lifs   lives
3 fireman   firemans   firemen   firemens
4 tomato   tomatoes   tomatos   tomates

Irregular forms of adjectives

Adjectives can have different forms. The comparative form is used to
show that someone or something has more of a particular quality than
someone or something else. To make the regular comparative form, you
either add **–er** to the end of the adjective or use the word **more** before it.

The superlative form of adjectives is used to show that someone or
something has more of a particular quality than anyone or anything
else. To make the regular superlative form, you either add **–est** to the
end of the adjective or use the word **most** before it.

Comparative and superlative forms that are not regular are shown at the
beginning of the entry:

far^2 /fɑr/ **adj** (comparative **farther** or
  further, superlative **farthest** or **furthest**)
  describing the part of something that is
  most distant from you: *His office is at the
  far end of the hallway.*

**19 Look up these words. Write their comparative and superlative
forms.**

		comparative	superlative
1	bad	_____	_____
2	heavy	_____	_____
3	lazy	_____	_____
4	good	_____	_____
5	well	_____	_____

Definitions

The definition tells you what a word or phrase means. Many words and phrases have more than one meaning. Each different meaning has a number.

All the definitions in this dictionary use simple words. Words that are more difficult than usual are explained in parentheses:

camel /ˈkæm·əl/ noun **B1** a large animal that lives in hot, dry places and has one or two humps (= raised parts) on its back

20 **Look up the words in dark letters and answer these questions.**

1 How many meanings does the verb **light** have?
2 What is the number of the meaning of **light** that is connected with being able to see?
3 How many meanings does the adjective **bright** have?
4 What is the number of the meaning of **bright** that is connected with being intelligent?
5 Look at the entry for **present** (noun). How many meanings does the phrase **the present** have?

21 **What types of things are the dark words? Look the words up and complete the sentences with a word from the box.**

> sport   tree   shoe   animal   food

1 A **kangaroo** is a type of _____
2 **Lettuce** is a type of _____
3 **Boxing** is a type of _____
4 A **sandal** is a type of _____
5 An **oak** is a type of _____

Phrases

A phrase is a group of words that are often used together and have a particular meaning. Phrases are shown in colored letters.

In the entry for the noun **minute** there are five meanings. Three of them are for phrases:

minute¹ /ˈmɪn·ət/ *noun* **1** **A2** a period of time equal to 60 seconds: *It'll take you thirty minutes to get to the airport.* ○ *She was ten minutes late for her interview.* **2** **A1** a very short period of time: *I'll be with you in a minute.* **3** **wait/just a minute** **A2** used when asking someone to wait for a short time: *Just a minute – I left my coat in the restaurant* **4** **at the last minute** at the latest time possible: *The concert was canceled at the last minute.* **5** **(at) any minute** very soon: *Her train will be arriving any minute.*

If there are parentheses around part of a phrase, for example **(at) any minute**, it means that you can leave that part out. So you can say *Her train will arrive at any minute* or *Her train will arrive any minute*.

If there is a slash / in a phrase, for example **wait/just a minute**, it means that the phrase can be used with either the part before the slash or the part after the slash. So you can say *wait a minute* or *just a minute*.

Some phrases have **etc.** at the end of them. This means that you can use the phrase with one of the words in the list, or a similar word:

5 save money, space, time, etc. **B1** to reduce the amount of money, space, time, etc. that you have to use: *You'll save time by doing it yourself.*

Some phrases have … after the words. This means that the phrase is the start of a sentence and you can add words to the phrase to make a complete sentence:

3 would you like…? **A1** used to offer someone something: *Would you like a drink?* ○ *Would you like to eat now?*

If you are looking for a phrase in the dictionary, you will usually find it at the entry for the first important word in the phrase. For example, **take it easy** is found at the entry for **easy** (adverb).

22 **Look up these phrases. Where did you find them? Write the headword of the entry where you found the phrase.**

1 standard of living   standard
2 lose your temper (with somebody)   _____
3 fold your arms   _____
4 cross your mind   _____
5 look like   _____

6 let someone know   _____
7 for good   _____
8 feel bad   _____

Example sentences
Example sentences help you to understand a word and show you how to use the word.

Words that are often used together are shown in dark letters in examples:

*He has had a lot of **bad luck** in his life.*

Words that are more difficult than usual are explained in brackets:

*Did you **take** many **pictures** (= photograph many things) while you were at the Grand Canyon?*

23 **Look at the example sentences at the entries for the words in dark letters. Use the example sentences to answer the questions.**

1 What type of container do you drink **tea** from?
2 What verb is normally used with the noun **shelter**?
3 What prepositions are used with the verb **reach**?
4 What are two types of things you can put in a **stack**?
5 What verb is used with **money** that means "to use money to buy things"?
6 What do you use with a **needle** to sew?
7 Write the correct word after **need**: *I **need** ___ leave at five o'clock.*

Formal and informal

The labels informal and formal tell you about how a word is used. Informal means that a word is used with people you know and is not usually used in serious writing.

okay[1] (also **OK**, /ˌoʊˈkeɪ/, /ˌoʊˈkeɪ/) /ˈoʊˌkeɪ/, /ˌoʊˈkeɪ/ **exclamation** informal

Formal means that the word is used in serious writing or for communicating with people you do not know well, for example in a store or in a work situation.

cease /sis/ **verb** (present participle **ceasing**, past tense and past participle **ceased**) formal
to stop: *The soldiers ceased firing.*

Words without a formal or informal label are used in general English.

24 Are these words formal, informal, or general? Use the dictionary to find out.

1 gig   informal
2 freezing   _____
3 clean   _____
4 acquire   _____
5 guy   _____
6 attend   _____
7 terror   _____
8 snooze   _____
9 frequently   _____
10 kin   _____

Related words

Some words that are related to the headword and that you can easily understand if you know the headword are shown at the end of entries. Example sentences show you how to use the word:

beautiful /ˈbjuː·ʈɪ·fəl/ **adj 1** **A1** very attractive: *a beautiful woman* ○ *beautiful scenery* **2** **A1** very pleasant: *beautiful music* ○ *It's a beautiful day* (= the sun is shining).
• **beautifully** adv **B1** *She sings beautifully.*

Pictures

The dictionary contains pictures to help you understand the meanings of words. There are color pictures in the middle of the dictionary and black and white pictures at some entries. If there is a color picture for the entry you are looking at, a note at the bottom of the entry will tell you to look at the color picture:

• **skiing** noun [no plural] **B1** *I'd like to go skiing in Vermont.*
→ See **Sports 1** on page C15

Opposites

An opposite is a word that is as different as possible from another word. Opposites are given at the end of some entries to give you help in learning vocabulary and to show you the differences between words.

In this entry you can see that both **small** and **little** are opposite of **big**:

big /bɪg/ **adj** (comparative **bigger**, superlative
biggest) **1** **A1** large in size or amount:
I come from a big family. ◦ *We're looking
for a bigger house.* → Opposite **small adj** (1),
little adj (1)

25 Look up these words. Write down their opposites.

1	heavy	light
2	happy	_____
3	friendly	_____
4	guilty	_____
5	high	_____
6	major	_____
7	noisy	_____
8	rich	_____
9	smooth	_____
10	weak	_____

Common mistake notes

Throughout the dictionary you will see notes about common mistakes that people make when using English. These are based on the *Cambridge Learner Corpus*, which is a large collection of students' written work. They give extra information about words that often cause problems, to help you avoid making mistakes.

26 Look up the words in **bold letters** and read the common mistake note at the entry. Now write the correct versions of these sentences.

1 He gave me an **advice**.
2 I did a **mistake** on my test.
3 He **said** me a story.
4 The house is **quite** when the children go away.
5 What time did you come to **home**?

Exercise answer key

1 **1** book **2** chair **3** hair **4** light **5** pencil **6** sock **7** table

2 **1** take **2** talk **3** tall **4** teacher **5** thank **6** Thursday **7** today

3 **1** good: goal … grandchild **2** police: point … population **3** early: DVD … easy
4 whale: we'd … which **5** poster: port … praise

4 <u>mouth</u>, more, <u>much</u>, mood, my, <u>mug</u>, <u>move</u>, Mr., mother, mustn't, <u>music</u>, Ms.

5 **1** A1 **2** A1 **3** A2 **4** A2 **5** A1 **6** A2 **7** B1

6 **1** fish /fɪʃ/, **2** dictionary /ˈdɪk·ʃəˌner·i/, **3** island /ˈaɪ·lənd/, **4** knee /ni/,
5 through /θru/, **6** sign /saɪn/, **7** laugh /læf/, **8** which /hwɪtʃ/

7 **1** <u>doc</u>tor **2** in<u>cor</u>rect **3** <u>a</u>ward **4** <u>ques</u>tion **5** <u>rec</u>ord **6** re<u>cord</u>

8 **1** 3 **2** 2 **3** 2 **4** 1 **5** 2 **6** 3

9 **1** noun **2** adjective **3** noun **4** verb **5** adverb **6** preposition

10 hat, happy, <u>actor</u>, between, <u>luck</u>, <u>chair</u>, read, awful, compare, <u>house</u>

11 **1** Where are my pajamas? **2** The computer graphics are very good. **3** The
furniture has arrived. **4** My pants are dirty. **5** I think politics is very boring.

12 **1** incorrect **2** incorrect **3** correct **4** correct **5** incorrect **6** incorrect

13 <u>afraid</u>, nibble, bag, react, <u>broken</u>, adventure, <u>narrow</u>, <u>honest</u>, immediately, <u>deep</u>

14 **1** 1 **2** 7 **3** 3 **4** 2

15 **1** fall apart – to break into pieces **2** make up – to say or write something that is
not true **3** set off – to start a trip **4** get back – to return to a place **5** hang on –
to wait for a short time

16 **1** break: broke/broken **2** make: made/made **3** get: got/gotten
4 swim: swam/swum **5** take: took/taken

17 **1** bookshelves **2** children **3** feet **4** men **5** mice **6** potatoes **7** sheep **8** wives

18 **1** cities **2** lives **3** firemen **4** tomatoes

19 **1** bad: worse/worst **2** heavy: heavier/heaviest **3** lazy: lazier/laziest
4 good: better/best **5** well: better/best

20 **1** 2 **2** 2 **3** 4 **4** 3 **5** 2

21 **1** animal **2** food **3** sport **4** shoe **5** tree

22 **1** standard **2** temper **3** fold **4** mind **5** look **6** know **7** good **8** bad

23 **1** a cup **2** take **3** for, out **4** books, CDs **5** spend **6** thread **7** need <u>to</u>

24 **1** informal **2** informal **3** general **4** formal **5** informal **6** formal **7** general
8 informal **9** formal **10** formal

25 **1** light **2** unhappy **3** unfriendly **4** innocent **5** low **6** minor **7** quiet
8 poor **9** rough **10** strong

26 **1** He gave me ~~an~~ some **advice**. **2** I ~~did~~ **made** a **mistake** in my exam. **3** He ~~said~~
told me a story. **4** The house is ~~quite quiet~~ **quiet** when the children go away. **5** What
time did you come ~~to~~ **home**?

Aa

A, a /eɪ/ the first letter of the alphabet

a /ə/, /eɪ/ (also **an**) determiner **1** 🅐 used before a noun to mean one thing or person: *I need a car.* ○ *Can I have an apple?* **2** 🅐 every or each: *Take one pill three times a day.* **3** 🅐 used to say what job someone does: *She's a mechanic.*

> **⚠ Common mistake: a or an?**
>
> Remember to use **an** in front of words that begin with a vowel sound. These are words that start with the letters a, e, i, o, or u, or with a sound like those letters.
>
> *a car, an orange, an hour*

abandon /əˈbæn·dən/ verb **1** to leave someone or something somewhere: *Dad had to abandon the car on the side of the road.* **2** to stop doing something before it is finished: *We abandoned the picnic when it started to rain.*

abbreviation /əˌbri·viˈeɪ·ʃən/ noun a shorter form of a word or phrase, especially used in writing: *"St." is an abbreviation of the word "street."*

ability /əˈbɪl·ə·t̬i/ noun (plural **abilities**) 🅑 the skill or qualities that you need to do something: *He had the **ability to** explain things clearly.*

able /ˈeɪ·bəl/ adj 🅐 If you are able to do something, you can do it: *He'll **be able to** help you.*

abnormal /æbˈnɔr·məl/ adj not normal: *abnormal behavior*

aboard /əˈbɔrd/ adv, preposition on or onto a plane, ship, bus, or train: *Welcome aboard flight 109 to Paris.*

abolish /əˈbɑl·ɪʃ/ verb to end a law or system: *Slavery was abolished in the U.S. in 1865.*

about[1] /əˈbaʊt/ preposition **1** 🅐 relating to a particular subject: *What was she talking about?* **2** what/how about...? 🅐 used to suggest something: *What about some pizza for lunch?* **3** what/how about...? 🅑 used to ask for someone's opinion on a particular subject: *How about this restaurant? Is it good?*

about[2] /əˈbaʊt/ adv **1** 🅐 close to a particular number or time, although not exactly that number or time: *It happened about two months ago.* **2** about to do *something* going to do something very soon: *I'm about to leave.*

above /əˈbʌv/ adv, preposition **1** 🅐 in a higher position than something else: *Look on the shelf above your head.* **2** 🅐 more than an amount or level: *a camp for children age eight and above* **3** 🅑 higher on the page: *Please send the items to the address shown above.* **4** above all 🅑 most important of everything: *Above all, I'd like to thank my family.*

abroad /əˈbrɔd/ adv 🅑 in or to a different country: *I would like to study abroad next year.*

abrupt /əˈbrʌpt/ adj sudden: *The conversation came to an abrupt end.*

absence /ˈæb·səns/ noun **1** a time when you are not in a place: *His absence was noticed.* **2** [no plural] the fact that something does not exist: *the absence of proof*

absent /ˈæb·sənt/ adj 🅑 not in a place, especially school or work: *He has been **absent from** school all week.*

absolute /ˈæb·səˌlut/ adj complete: *Our trip to Hawaii was an **absolute disaster**.*

absolutely /ˈæb·səˌlut·li/ adv **1** 🅑 completely: *The food was absolutely delicious.* **2** used to strongly agree with someone: *"Do you agree?" "Absolutely."*

absorb /əbˈzɔrb/, /əbˈsɔrb/ verb **1** to take in liquid, gas, or heat and hold it: *Cook the rice until all the liquid has been absorbed.* **2** to understand and remember something: *It's hard to absorb so much information.*

absorbent /əbˈzɔr·bənt/, /əbˈsɔr·bənt/ adj able to take in liquids: *an absorbent sponge*

a
b
c
d
e
f
g
h
i
j
k
l
m
n
o
p
q
r
s
t
u
v
w
x
y
z

|æ cat|ɑ hot|e get|ɪ sit|i see|ɔ saw|ʊ book|u too|ʌ cut|ə about|ɑr mother|ɜr turn|ɔr for|aɪ my|aʊ how|eɪ say|ɔɪ boy|

abstract /æbˈstrækt/ adj   **1** relating to ideas and not real things: *Truth and beauty are abstract concepts.*   **2** abstract art involves shapes and colors and not images of real things or people: *abstract paintings*

absurd /əbˈsɜrd/ adj   very silly: *Your argument is completely absurd.*

abuse¹ /əˈbjus/ noun   **1** the act of using something for the wrong purpose in a way that is bad: *drug abuse*   **2** [no plural] the act of being violent or cruel to another person: *child abuse*

abuse² /əˈbjuz/ verb (present participle **abusing**, past tense and past participle **abused**)   **1** to be cruel and violent with someone: *Some of the women were abused by their husbands.*   **2** to use something for the wrong purpose in a way that is bad: *He abused drugs for many years.*

abusive /əˈbjuˌsɪv/ adj   using rude language or violence to be cruel to someone: *an abusive phone call*

academic /ˌækəˈdɛmɪk/ adj   related to education, schools, universities, etc.: *academic standards*

accelerate /əkˈsɛləˌreɪt/ verb   to start to move or drive faster: *I accelerated to pass the bus.*

accelerator /əkˈsɛləˌreɪtər/ noun   the part of a car that you push with your foot to make it go faster
→ See **Car** on page C3

accent /ˈækˌsɛnt/ noun   **B1** the way that someone speaks, showing where he or she comes from: *a British accent ○ a French accent*

accept /əkˈsɛpt/ verb   **1** **B1** to take something that someone offers you: *He accepted the job. ○ He won't accept advice from anyone.*   **2** to say that something is true, often something bad: *He refuses to accept that he made a mistake.*   **3** **accept responsibility/blame** to admit that you caused something bad that happened: *I accept full responsibility for the accident.*

> ⚠ **Common mistake: accept or agree?**
>
> When you accept an invitation, job, or offer, you say yes to something that is offered. **Accept** is never followed by another verb.
>
> *They offered me the job, and I accepted it.*
>
> ~~They offered me the job, and I accepted to take it.~~
>
> When you **agree** to do something, you say that you will do something that someone asks you to do.
>
> *They offered me the job and I agreed to take it.*

acceptable /əkˈsɛptəbəl/ adj   **B1** good enough: *A grade of 63 is not acceptable in this class.*

access¹ /ˈækˌsɛs/ noun [no plural]   **1** **B1** the fact of being able to use or see something: *Do you have access to a computer? ○ Internet access*   **2** **B1** the way that you reach or go into a place: *The only access to the island is by boat.*

access² /ˈækˌsɛs/ verb   to be able to find and see information, especially using a computer: *You will need a password to access those files.*

accessory /əkˈsɛsəˌri/ noun [usually plural] (plural **accessories**)   something added to something else to make it more attractive or useful: *a green suit with matching accessories (=hat, belt, bag, etc.) ○ The camera isn't expensive, but all the accessories to go with it cost extra. ○ car accessories like leather seats and DVD players*

accident /ˈækˌsəˌdənt/ noun   **1** **A2** something bad that happens that is not wanted or planned, and that hurts someone or damages something: *a car accident ○ She had an accident in the kitchen.*   **2** **by accident** without wanting to or planning to: *I deleted the wrong file by accident.*

accidental /ˌækˌsəˈdɛnˌtᵊl/ adj   happening without being wanted or planned: *accidental damage*

|oʊ go|ɑɪɑr fire|aʊər hour|ear hair|ɪər ear|ʊər poor|j yet|ʒ measure|ʃ ship|dʒ judge|tʃ chin|ð that|θ thin|ŋ hang|

accidentally /ˌæk·sə'den·t̬ºl·i/ adv If you do something bad accidentally, you do it without wanting to or planning to: *I accidentally knocked over a glass of water.*

accommodations /əˌkɑm·ə'deɪ·ʃºnz/ plural noun a place where travelers can stay: *The price includes airfare, **hotel accommodations**, and tickets to the theater.*

accompany /ə'kʌm·pə·ni/ verb (present participle **accompanying**, past tense and past participle **accompanied**) **1 B1** formal to go to a place with someone: *All children must be accompanied by an adult.* **2** to play a musical instrument with someone else who is playing or singing

accord /ə'kɔrd/ noun [no plural] **of your own accord** because you decide to, and not because someone tells you to: *She left of her own accord.*

according to /ə'kɔr·dɪŋ tu/ preposition **1 B1** as said by someone or as shown by something: *According to the weather report, it will rain tomorrow.* **2** based on a particular system or plan: *Students are put in groups according to their ability.*

account¹ /ə'kaʊnt/ noun **1 A1** an arrangement with a bank to keep your money there: *I put the money into my account.* **2** a description of something that happened: *They **gave** different **accounts** of the event.* **3 take something into account/take account of something** to think about something when judging a situation: *We will take everyone's opinion into account before making a decision.* ○ *A good architect takes account of the building's surroundings.*

account² /ə'kaʊnt/ verb **account for something** phrasal verb to explain something: *Can she account for the missing money?*

accountant /ə'kaʊn·t̬ºnt/ noun **B1** someone whose job is keeping records of all the money that people or companies spend and earn

accounting /ə'kaʊn·t̬ɪŋ/ noun [no plural] the job of being an accountant: *She works in accounting.*

accounts /ə'kaʊnts/ plural noun a set of official records of all the money a company spends and earns

accuracy /'æk·jər·ə·si/ noun [no plural] how correct or exact something is: *All reports must be checked for accuracy.*

accurate /'æk·jər·ət/ adj **B1** correct or exact: *accurate information*
  → Opposite **inaccurate** adj
  • **accurately** adv

accusation /ˌæk·ju'zeɪ·ʃən/ noun a statement that you think someone has done something bad: *Her manager **made** several **accusations against** her.*

accuse /ə'kjuz/ verb (present participle **accusing**, past tense and past participle **accused**) to say that you think someone has done something bad: *She **accused** him **of** stealing from her.*

accustomed /ə'kʌs·təmd/ adj **be accustomed to something** to have done something so often or have had it so long that it is normal or comfortable for you: *He was accustomed to public speaking.*

ace /eɪs/ noun a playing card with one symbol on it, which has the highest or lowest value in many card games: *the ace of hearts*

ache¹ /eɪk/ noun **B1** pain that continues for a long time: *I have a **stomach ache**.*

ache² /eɪk/ verb (present participle **aching**, past tense and past participle **ached**) to hurt continuously: *My legs are aching after all that exercise.*

achieve /ə'tʃiv/ verb (present participle **achieving**, past tense and past participle **achieved**) **B1** to succeed in doing something difficult: *We finally achieved our goal of buying a house.*

achievement /ə'tʃiv·mənt/ noun **1 B1** something good that you have done that was difficult: *Winning a gold medal is the greatest achievement in sports.* **2** how well a student has learned what he or she is expected to know: *a plan to improve **academic/student** achievement*

acid /'æs·ɪd/ noun a liquid that burns or dissolves things: *hydrochloric acid*

acne /'æk·ni/ noun [no plural]   a skin problem that causes a lot of red spots on the face

acorn /'eɪ·kɔrn/ noun
a nut that grows on oak trees

acquaintance /ə'kweɪn·tᵊns/ noun   someone whom you have met, but do not know well: *He's a business acquaintance.*

acquainted /ə'kweɪn·tɪd/ adj formal   If you are acquainted with someone, you have met him or her but do not know him or her well: *I'd like to get better acquainted with her.*

acquire /ə'kwɑɪər/ verb (present participle **acquiring**, past tense and past participle **acquired**) formal   **1** to get something: *My grandfather acquired several valuable paintings.*   **2** to learn something: *I've acquired some useful skills in this job.*

acre /'eɪ·kər/ noun   a unit for measuring area, equal to 4,840 square yards

across /ə'krɔs/ adv, preposition   **1** ⒶⒶ from one side to the other: *They walked across the road.*   **2** ⒶⒶ on the opposite side of: *There's a bank just across the street.* ○ *The library is across from the school.*

act¹ /ækt/ verb   **1** ⒷⒷ to behave in a particular way, usually a bad way: *Stop acting like a child!*   **2** ⒷⒷ to perform in a play or movie   **3** to do something to stop a problem: *We have to act now to stop the spread of this disease.*

act as something phrasal verb   to do a job for a short time: *She acts as an interpreter for our French clients.*

act² /ækt/ noun   **1** ⒷⒷ one of the parts in a play   **2** something that someone does: *an act of kindness*   **3** a law made by a government: *an act of Congress*   **4** a way of behaving in which someone pretends to feel or feel something: *She's not really upset – it's just an act.*

acting /'æk·tɪŋ/ noun [no plural]   the job of performing in plays and movies

action /'æk·ʃən/ noun   **1** ⒷⒷ [no plural]   exciting or important things that are

happening: *He likes movies with a lot of action.*   **2** something that you do: *We must take action before the problem gets worse.*   **3 out of action** damaged or hurt and not able to operate or move: *My car's out of action.*

active /'æk·tɪv/ adj   **1** ⒷⒷ busy doing a lot of things: *She's still very active, even at the age of 87.*   **2** ⒷⒷ In an active verb or sentence, the subject of the verb is the person or thing doing the action. For example, "Andy drove the car" is an active sentence.   **3** very involved in an organization or planned activity: *He is an active member of his church.*

actively /'æk·tɪv·li/ adv   in a way that involves intentional effort: *I've been actively looking for a job for six months.*

activity /æk'tɪv·ə·t̬i/ noun   ⒶⒶ (plural **activities**) something that you do, especially for enjoyment: *We enjoy outdoor activities like hiking and fishing.*   **2** [no plural] the actions of people when they are moving around and doing things: *There was no sign of activity outside.*

actor /'æk·tər/ noun   ⒶⒶ someone who performs in plays, in movies, or on television

actress /'æk·trəs/ noun   a woman who performs in plays, in movies, or on television

---

⚠ Common mistake: actual or current?

Actual means "real." It does not mean "happening now."
> *His friends call him Jo-Jo, but his actual name is John.*

Use current to talk about things that are happening or that exist now.
> *She started her current job two years ago.*

---

actual /'æk·tʃu·əl/ adj   **1** real, not guessed or imagined: *We were expecting about fifty people, but the actual number was higher.*   **2 in actual fact** used to show what is really true, or to give more information: *I thought she was Portuguese, but in actual fact she's Brazilian.*

actually /ˈæk·tʃu·ə·li/ *adv* **1** A2 used when you are saying what is true about a situation: *He didn't actually say anything important.* ○ *So what actually happened?* **2** used to politely correct or say no to someone: *She's Mexican, actually, not Puerto Rican.* ○ *"Can I borrow $20?" "Actually, no, sorry."* **3** B1 used to emphasize that something surprising is true: *A friend from college was actually at the same concert – I hadn't seen her in years!*

acute /əˈkjut/ *adj* An acute problem is very bad: *There's an acute shortage of doctors in the area.*

ad /æd/ *noun* short form of advertisement

A.D. /ˈeɪˈdi/ (also **AD**) used to show that a particular year or period came after the birth of Jesus Christ: *the 11th century A.D.*

adapt /əˈdæpt/ *verb* **1** to change something to fit a different use or situation: *The original book has been adapted for television.* **2** to change the way that you behave or think to fit a new situation: *It took time to adapt to having a different boss.*

adaptable /əˈdæp·tə·bəl/ *adj* able to change for a different situation or use: *Frogs are highly adaptable and live in many environments.*

adapter /əˈdæp·tər/ *noun* an object that connects two pieces of electrical equipment that were not designed to work together: *a power adapter*

add /æd/ *verb* **1** A2 to put something together with something else, making the whole thing bigger: *Mix the sugar and butter, then add the eggs.* ○ *Do you have anything to add to the list?* **2** A2 to put two or more numbers together to get a total: *Don't forget to add the cost of postage.* **3** B1 to say another thing: *She said she liked him but added that he was difficult to work with.*

add something up *phrasal verb* B1 to put two or more numbers together to get a total: *Have you added up the figures?*

addict /ˈæd·ɪkt/ *noun* someone who cannot stop taking a drug or doing something as a habit: *a drug addict*

addicted /əˈdɪk·tɪd/ *adj* not able to stop taking a drug or doing something as a habit: *Sam is addicted to computer games.*

addition /əˈdɪʃ·ən/ *noun* **1** in addition (to *something*) B1 added to what already exists, happens, or is true: *In addition to teaching, she works in a restaurant in the summer.* **2** [no plural] the act of adding numbers together to get a total **3** a new or extra thing that is added to something: *Baby Eva is the latest addition to the family.*

additional /əˈdɪʃ·ə·nˀl/ *adj* more than what already exists: *We need additional information.*

address¹ /əˈdres/, /ˈæd·res/ *noun* **1** A1 the number of a building and the name of the street, city, etc. where it is **2** A1 a group of letters and signs used to send email to someone or to find information on the Internet: *an email address* ○ *a Web address*

address² /əˈdres/ *verb* **1** to write a name or address on an envelope or package: *A package arrived addressed to Emma.* **2** to do something in order to stop a problem: *We have to address the problem now.*

address book /əˈdres ˌbʊk/ *noun* a book or electronic file in which you keep a list of names, addresses, and phone numbers: *She put his new phone number in her address book.*

adequate /ˈæd·ɪ·kwət/ *adj* **1** enough: *I didn't have adequate time to prepare.* **2** good enough, but not very good: *It's not a fancy computer, but it's adequate for my needs.*

• **adequately** *adv*

adjective /ˈædʒ·ɪk·tɪv/ *noun* A2 a word that describes a noun or pronoun. The words "big," "boring," and "blue" are all adjectives.

adjust /əˈdʒʌst/ *verb* **1** to change something slightly to make it fit or work better: *You can adjust the heat with this switch.* **2** to change the way you behave or think and become comfortable in a new situation: *They found it difficult to adjust to life in a new country.*

adjustment /əˈdʒʌstˈmənt/ noun
a small change that you make to something so that it works better, fits better, or is more suitable: *We've made a few adjustments to the schedule.*

administration /ədˌmɪnˈəˈstreɪˈʃən/ noun **1** [no plural] the things that you have to do to manage the work of an organization **2** the government of a particular president, governor, or mayor: *the Obama administration*

admiration /ˌædˈməˈreɪˈʃən/ noun [no plural] the feeling of liking something or of liking and respecting someone for the good qualities that he, she, or it has: *I have great admiration for my professor.*

admire /ədˈmaɪər/ verb (present participle **admiring**, past tense and past participle **admired**) **1** 🅱🅱 to look at something or someone and think that he, she, or it is attractive: *I was just admiring your shirt.* **2** to like something or to like and respect someone for the good qualities that he, she, or it has: *I admire him for being so determined.*

admission /ədˈmɪʃˈən/ noun **1** 🅱🅱 [no plural] the money that you pay to enter a place: *The museum doesn't charge admission for children.* **2** the act of agreeing that you did something bad: *Her departure was seen by many as an admission of guilt.* **3** permission to attend a school or to be a member of an organization: *admission requirements*

admissions /ədˈmɪʃˈənz/ plural noun
the people who have been accepted as students or as members of an organization, or the process of accepting them: *the college admissions office*

admit /ədˈmɪt/ verb (present participle **admitting**, past tense and past participle **admitted**) **1** 🅱🅱 to agree that you did something bad, or that something bad

is true: *Both men admitted to taking illegal drugs.* ○ *I was wrong – I admit it.*
2 to allow someone to enter a place: *No one will be admitted to the club without a valid ID.*

adolescence /ˌædˈəˈlesˈəns/ noun [no plural] the period of time in someone's life between being a child and being an adult

adolescent /ˌædˈəˈlesˈənt/ noun
a young person who is between being a child and being an adult

adopt /əˈdɑpt/ verb **1** to take someone else's child into your family and legally become the parent of that child: *He was adopted as a baby.* **2** to start doing or using something new: *We've adopted a different approach to solving the problem.*

adopted /əˈdɑpˈtɪd/ adj An adopted child has legally become part of another family: *They have two adopted children.*

adoption /əˈdɑpˈʃən/ noun the process of legally becoming the parents of someone else's child: *They couldn't have children, so they were considering adoption.*

adore /əˈdɔr/ verb (present participle **adoring**, past tense and past participle **adored**) to love someone or something very much: *Sarah adored her father.*

adult¹ /əˈdʌlt/ noun 🅰🅰 a person or animal that has finished growing and is not now a child

adult² /əˈdʌlt/ adj **1** having finished growing: *an adult rat* **2** 🅰🅰 for or relating to adults: *adult education*

advance¹ /ədˈvænsˈmənt/ noun **1** in advance 🅱🅱 before a particular time: *We bought tickets in advance.* **2** new discoveries and inventions: *scientific advances*

advance² /ədˈvæns/ verb (present participle **advancing**, past tense and past participle **advanced**) **1** to develop or progress, or to make something develop or progress: *Research has advanced our understanding of the virus.* **2** to move forward, especially while fighting

advanced /ədˈvænst/ adj **1** 🅰🅰 at a higher, more difficult level: *an advanced English course* **2** 🅱🅱 having developed to a more modern stage: *advanced technology*

| ou go | aɪər fire | auər hour | eər hair | ɪər ear | ʊər poor | j yet | ʒ measure | ʃ ship | dʒ judge | tʃ chin | ð that | θ thin | ŋ hang |

advantage /əd'væn·tɪdʒ/ noun
1 **B1** something good that helps you: *One advantage of living in town is being close to the stores.* → Opposite **disadvantage** **2** take advantage of *something* **B1** to use the things that are good or that can help you in a situation: *Take advantage of the fitness center while you're here.* **3** take advantage of *someone/something* to treat someone or something badly in order to get what you want: *She takes advantage of his generosity.*

adventure /əd'ven·tʃər/ noun **A2** an exciting and sometimes dangerous experience: *Our trip to Africa was an amazing adventure.*

adventurous /əd'ven·tʃər·əs/ adj
An adventurous person likes to try new or difficult things: *I'm going to be more adventurous with my cooking.*

adverb /'æd‚vɜrb/ noun **A2** a word that gives more information about a verb, adjective, phrase, or other adverb. In the sentence "He ate quickly," "quickly" is an adverb.

advertise /'æd·vər‚taɪz/ verb (present participle **advertising**, past tense and past participle **advertised**) **1** **B1** to tell people about a product or service, on television, on the Internet, in newspapers, etc., so that people will buy it: *Companies are not allowed to advertise cigarettes on television.* **2** **B1** to put information in a newspaper, on the Internet, etc., asking for someone or something that you need: *My company is advertising for a new receptionist.*

advertisement /‚æd·vər'taɪz·mənt/ noun **A2** a picture, short movie, etc. that is designed to persuade people to buy something: *a newspaper/television/online advertisement*

advertising /'æd·vər‚taɪ·zɪŋ/ noun [no plural] the business of persuading people to buy products or services: *Sarah works in advertising.*

advice /əd'vaɪs/ noun [no plural]
A2 suggestions about what you think someone should do: *This book gives advice on saving money.* ○ *I took your advice and went home early.* ○ *Can I give you a piece of advice?*

> ⚠️ **Common mistake: advice**
>
> Remember that this word is not countable.
>
> I need some advice.
> ~~I need an advice.~~
>
> To make **advice** singular, say a piece of advice.

> ⚠️ **Common mistake: advice or advise?**
>
> Be careful not to confuse the noun **advice** with the verb **advise**.
>
> I advise you to see a lawyer.
> ~~I advice you to see a lawyer.~~

advise /əd'vaɪz/ verb (present participle **advising**, past tense and past participle **advised**) **B1** to tell someone that he or she should do something: *I would advise him to see a doctor.*

adviser /əd'vaɪ·zər/ noun (also **advisor**) someone whose job is to give advice about a subject: *a financial adviser*

aerobics /eə'roʊ·bɪks/ noun [no plural] physical exercises that you do to music, especially in a class

aerosol /'eər·ə‚sɔl/ noun
a metal container that forces liquid out in small drops when you press a button

aerosol

affair /ə'feər/ noun
1 a sexual relationship between two people when one or both of them is married to someone else: *He had an affair with a woman at work.*
2 a situation, especially a bad one: *The way the mayor's office is handling the affair is being criticized.*

affairs /ə'feərz/ plural noun situations that involve a particular subject or a particular type of person: *an expert on foreign affairs* ○ *the university office of student affairs*

| æ cat | ɑ hot | e get | ɪ sit | i see | ɔ saw | ʊ book | u too | ʌ cut | ə about | ər mother | ɜr turn | ɪr for | aɪ my | aʊ how | eɪ say | ɔɪ boy |

a b c d e f g h i j k l m n o p q r s t u v w x y z

affect /əˈfekt/ verb **1** to cause a change in someone or something: *How will the new road affect the community?* **2** If an illness affects someone, the person becomes ill: *The disease affects older people.* **3** to cause a strong emotion, especially sadness: *Try not to let her mood affect you.*

> ⚠ **Common mistake: affect or effect?**
>
> Be careful not to confuse these two words.
>
> **Affect** is a verb that means to cause a change.
>
> *Pollution seriously affects the environment.*
>
> Use the noun **effect** to talk about the change, reaction, or result caused by something.
>
> *Global warming is one of the effects of pollution.*

> ⚠ **Common mistake: affect someone or something**
>
> Remember that you do not need a preposition after the verb **affect**.
>
> *The problem affects everyone.*
> ~~The problem affects to everyone.~~

affection /əˈfek·ʃən/ noun [no plural] a feeling of liking or loving someone, or the things you do to show this: *Mom gave us lots of love and affection.*

affectionate /əˈfek·ʃə·nət/ adj often showing that you like or love someone: *an affectionate little girl*
• **affectionately** adv

> ⚠ **Common mistake: afford to do something**
>
> When **afford** is followed by a verb, it is always in the **to** + **infinitive** form.
>
> *We can't afford to go on vacation this year.*
> ~~We can't afford going on vacation this year.~~

afford /əˈfɔrd/ verb **B1** to have enough money to buy something or enough time to do something: *Can we afford a new car?* ○ *I can't afford to wait.*

afraid /əˈfreɪd/ adj **1** **A2** feeling fear or worry: *I'm afraid of big dogs.* ○ *They were afraid that their son would get hurt.* **2 I'm afraid** **A2** used to politely tell someone something bad or to politely disagree with someone: *I'm afraid that we can't come to your party.*

African American /ˈæf·rɪ·kən əˈmer·ɪ·kən/ noun an American person whose family came from Africa in the past
• **African-American** adj *the African-American community*

after[1] /ˈæf·tər/ preposition **1** **A1** following something that has happened: *We went swimming after lunch.* **2** **A2** following in order: *H comes after G in the alphabet.* **3** used to say how many minutes past the hour it is: *It's five after three.* **4** **A2** once you have passed a particular place: *Turn left after the hotel.* **5** **B1** following someone or something: *We ran after him.* **6 after all** **B1** used to add an explanation to something that you have just said: *You can't expect to be perfect – after all, it was only your first lesson.* **7 day after day, year after year, etc.** **B1** happening every day, year, etc., over a long period: *We go to the same place on vacation year after year.* **8** because of something that happened: *I'll never trust her again after what she did to me.* **9** although something happened or is true: *I can't believe he was so rude to you after all the help you gave him!*

after[2] /ˈæf·tər/ conjunction **B1** at a later time than something else happens or happened: *We arrived after the game had started.*

after[3] /ˈæf·tər/ adv **A2** later than someone or something else: *Hilary got here at noon and Matt arrived soon after.*

afternoon /ˌæf·tərˈnun/ noun **A1** the time between the middle of the day and the evening: *I played tennis on Saturday afternoon.*

| oʊ go | aɪər fire | aʊər hour | eər hair | ɪər ear | ʊər poor | j yet | ʒ measure | ʃ ship | dʒ judge | tʃ chin | ð that | θ thin | ŋ hang |

⚠ Common mistake: afternoon

If you talk about what happens during the afternoon, use the preposition **in**.

In the afternoon I called my girl-friend.

~~In the afternoon I called my girl-friend.~~

If you say a day of the week before "afternoon," use the preposition **on**.

I'm going to see the dentist on Tuesday afternoon.

afterward /'æf·tər·wərd/ **adv** (also **afterwards**) **A2** at a later time, after something else has happened: *I did my homework and went swimming afterward.*

again /ə'gen/ **adv** **1 A2** once more: *Ask her again.* **2 A2** as before: *Get some rest and you'll feel better again soon.*
3 again and again B1 many times: *He played the same song again and again.*
4 all over again repeated from the beginning: *I'm not starting my story all over again.* **5 yet again** another time after something has happened or been done many times before: *The bus was late yet again.*

against /ə'genst/ **preposition**
1 A2 competing with someone or something: *The Cowboys are playing against the Steelers on Sunday.* **2 A2** touching something: *Push the bed against the wall.*
3 disagreeing with a plan or activity: *Andrew wants to buy a motorcycle, but I'm against it.* **4 against the law/the rules** not allowed by a law or rule: *It's against the law to sell alcohol to teenagers.*

age /eɪdʒ/ **noun 1 A1** the number of years that someone has lived, or that something has existed: *Mozart died at the age of 35.* ○ *a child under/over the age of five* ○ *Redwood trees live to a great age.* ○ *Their son is your age (=as old as you are).* **2 B1** a period of history: *the Ice Age* **3** [no plural] the state of being old: *Some wines improve with age.*

⚠ Common mistake: describing age

If you describe someone's age by saying "Tom is eight years old," you always write the age as three separate words.

My son is eight years old.

You can use also use **eight-year-old**, etc., as an adjective. When you do this, the words are written together using hyphens (-).

I have a twelve-year-old son.

You can also do the same with days, weeks, and months.

My rabbit is ten weeks old.
I have a ten-week-old rabbit.
The baby is three months old.
a three-month-old baby

aged /eɪdʒd/ **adj** **A2** having a particular age: *They have one daughter, aged three.*

agency /'eɪ·dʒən·si/ **noun** (plural **agencies**) **B1** a business that provides a service: *an advertising agency*

agenda /ə'dʒen·də/ **noun** a list of subjects that people will discuss at a meeting: *There are several items on the agenda.*

agent /'eɪ·dʒənt/ **noun 1** someone whose job is to deal with business for someone else: *To make reservations, contact your travel agent.* **2** someone who tries to find out secret information, especially about another country: *a secret agent*

aggressive /ə'gres·ɪv/ **adj** angry and violent toward another person: *aggressive behavior*
• **aggressively adv** *These dogs sometimes behave aggressively.*

ago /ə'goʊ/ **adv** **A2** in the past: *It happened a long time ago.*

agony /'æg·ə·ni/ **noun** (plural **agonies**) very bad pain: *She was in agony after her operation.*

agree /ə'gri/ **verb** (present participle **agreeing**, past tense and past participle **agreed**) **1 A2** to have the same opinion as someone: *I agree with you.* ○ *We all agreed that mistakes had been made.*

○ *They have finally **agreed on** a name for their new dog.* → Opposite **disagree**
2 🔵 to decide something with someone: *They **agreed to** meet on Sunday.*
3 to say you will do something that someone asks you to do: *She **agreed to** help him.*

agree with *something* phrasal verb to think that something is morally right: *I don't agree with hunting.*

agreement /əˈgriˑmənt/ noun
1 a promise or decision made between two or more people: *The company and the union **reached an agreement**.* **2** [no plural] a situation in which all the people involved in something have the same opinion: *Not everyone was **in agreement**.*

agriculture /ˈæɡˑrɪˌkʌl·tʃər/ noun [no plural] the work of growing plants and taking care of animals that are used for food
• **agricultural** adj *agricultural machinery*

ahead /əˈhed/ adj, adv **1** 🔵 in front: *She walked **ahead of** us.* **2** 🔵 in the future: *He has a difficult time **ahead of** him.* **3** with more points than someone else in a competition: *The Giants were ahead in the first half of the game.* **4** go **ahead** informal said to allow someone to do something: *"Can I use your phone?" "Sure, go ahead."*

aid /eɪd/ noun help, or something such as food or equipment that gives help: *Emergency aid was sent to the flood victims.* ○ *teaching aids*

AIDS /eɪdz/ noun [no plural] a serious illness that stops the body from fighting other illnesses

aim[1] /eɪm/ noun **1** 🔵 a result that you try to achieve: *The **aim** of the movie was to make people laugh.*

aim[2] /eɪm/ verb **1** 🔵 to try to do something: *We're **aiming** for a 10% increase in sales.* **2** to point a weapon toward someone or something: *He **aimed** the gun **at** the target.* **3** be **aimed at** *someone* to be intended to influence a particular person or group: *These commercials are aimed at teenagers.*

air /ear/ noun **1** 🔵 [no plural] the mixture of gases around the Earth that we

breathe: *I love the smell of the air in the mountains.* **2** 🔵 [no plural] used especially before another noun about activities that involve planes: *air travel* **3** the **air** the space above and around things: *He hit the ball high into the air.*

air conditioner /ˈear kənˌdɪʃ·ə·nər/ noun a machine that keeps the air cool in a building or car

air conditioning /ˈear kənˌdɪʃ·ə·nɪŋ/ noun [no plural] 🔵 a system that keeps the air cool in a building or car

aircraft /ˈear.kræft/ noun (plural **aircraft**) a vehicle that can fly

airfare /ˈear.fear/ noun the price of a ticket to fly on a plane

air force /ˈear.fɔrs/ noun 🔵 the part of a country's military organization that uses aircraft to fight wars

airline /ˈear.laɪn/ noun 🔵 a company that takes people and things to places in planes

airmail /ˈear.meɪl/ noun [no plural] the system of sending letters or packages by plane

airplane /ˈear.pleɪn/ noun a vehicle that flies and has an engine and wings

airport /ˈear.pɔrt/ noun 🔵 a place where planes take off and land

aisle /aɪl/ noun **1** a passage between the lines of seats in a plane, church, theater, etc. **2** a passage between the shelves in a store

aisle

alarm[1] /əˈlɑrm/ noun **1** 🔵 a loud noise that tells you there is danger: *a fire alarm* **2** 🔵 a clock that makes a noise to wake you: *The alarm went off at 5:30.* **3** [no plural] a sudden feeling of fear that something bad might happen: *There's no need for alarm – we're completely safe.*

alarm[2] /əˈlɑrm/ *verb* to worry someone: *I didn't want to alarm him by saying that she was sick.*

alarm clock /əˈlɑrm ˌklɑk/ *noun* **A2** a clock that makes a noise to wake you

album /ˈæl·bəm/ *noun*
1 **A2** a group of songs or pieces of music on a CD, disk, etc. **2** **A2** a book in which you keep photographs, stamps, etc.

alcohol /ˈæl·kəˌhɔl/ *noun* [no plural]
1 **A2** drinks such as wine and beer that can make you drunk **2** **A2** the substance that can make you drunk that is produced in the process of making wine, beer, etc.

alcoholic /ˌæl·kəˈhɔ·lɪk/ *adj* **B1** containing alcohol: *alcoholic drinks*

alert /əˈlɜrt/ *adj* quick to notice things around you

algebra /ˈæl·dʒə·brə/ *noun* [no plural] a type of mathematics in which numbers are shown by letters and symbols

alien /ˈeɪ·li·ən/ *noun* **1** a creature from a planet other than Earth **2** someone who was not born in the United States but who lives there: *a resident alien*

alike /əˈlɑɪk/ *adj, adv* **B1** similar, or in a similar way: *My mother and I look alike.* ∘ *We think alike about politics.*

alive /əˈlɑɪv/ *adj* **B1** living, not dead: *Are your grandparents still alive?*

all[1] /ɔl/ *pronoun, determiner* **1** **A1** every person or thing in a group: *We were all dancing.* **2** **A1** for the whole of a period of time: *It rained all day.* **3** **A2** the whole amount of something: *He spends all of his money on clothes.* **4** **B1** the only thing: *All I want is a new car.* **5** **at all** **B1** in any way: *He hasn't changed at all.* **6 in all** used to show the total amount of something: *There were twenty people at the meeting in all.*

> **!** Common mistake: **all** + period of time
>
> You do not say "the" when you use **all** + a period of time.
>
> *all day/morning/week/year/summer*
> ~~all the day/morning/week/year/summer~~

all[2] /ɔl/ *adv* **1** **A2** completely or very: *You're all wet!* **2 all along** from the beginning of a period of time: *I knew all along that it was a mistake.* **3 all in all** considering everything: *All in all, it was a great vacation.* **4 all over (somewhere)** everywhere in a particular place: *He traveled all over the world.*

allergic /əˈlɜr·dʒɪk/ *adj* having an allergy: *I'm allergic to nuts.*

allergy /ˈæl·ər·dʒi/ *noun* (plural **allergies**) a medical problem in which you get sick if you eat, breathe, or touch something: *He has an allergy to cats.*

alley /ˈæl·i/ *noun* a narrow street between buildings

alligator /ˈæl·ɪˌgeɪ·tər/ *noun* an animal with a long tail, a long mouth, and sharp teeth, that lives in hot areas and spends a lot of its time in water

alligator

allow /əˈlɑʊ/ *verb* **A2** to say that someone can do something: *They didn't allow me to finish what I was doing.* ∘ *Smoking is not allowed in the restaurant.* ∘ *You're not allowed to walk on the grass here.*

> **!** Common mistake: **allow** or **let**?
>
> Allow and let have similar meanings.
> **Allow** is used in more formal or official situations, especially when talking about rules and laws.
> *The new law allows companies to charge for this service.*
> *We can't allow this situation to continue.*
> **Let** is used in more informal and spoken situations.
> *Dad never lets anyone drive his car.*
> *She let her hair grow longer.*

---

allowance /əˈlau·əns/ *noun*
1 an amount of something such as money that you are allowed to have every day, week, month, etc.: *a clothing allowance* ○ *the **recommended daily allowance** of vitamin C* **2** an amount of money that parents give to a child each week

all right[1] /ˌɔl ˈrait/ *adj, adv* **1 A1** happening successfully or without problems: *Did the interview go all right?* **2 A2** safe or well: *You look pale – are you all right?* **3 A2** used to ask if you can do something or to say that someone can do something: *Is it all right if I put some music on?* **4 that's all right A2** something you say when someone says sorry to show that you are not angry: *"I'm sorry, I forgot all about your party." "That's all right."* **5 that's all right A2** used as an answer when someone thanks you: *"Thanks for cleaning the kitchen." "That's all right."* **6 B1** good enough, although not excellent: *The hotel wasn't great, but it was all right.*

all right[2] /ˌɔl ˈrait/ *exclamation* **A1** used to say yes to a suggestion: *"How about going out for dinner?" "All right."*

ally /ˈæl·ai/ *noun* (plural **allies**) a person or country that helps you when you are arguing or fighting with another person or country

almond /ˈɑ·mənd/, /ˈæl·mənd/ *noun* a flat, oval nut, often used in cooking

almost /ˈɔl·moust/ *adv* **A2** nearly: *I almost missed the bus.* ○ *We're almost finished.* ○ *She's almost 18 years old.*

alone /əˈloun/ *adj, adv* **A2** without other people: *She lives alone.* ○ *I don't like being alone.* **2** without any more or anything else: *Last year alone the company made a million dollars.* **3 leave someone alone** to stop talking to someone or annoying them: *Leave him alone – he's tired.* **4 leave something alone** to stop touching something: *Leave your hair alone!*

⚠ Common mistake: alone or lonely?

Alone means without other people. If you feel sad because you are alone, you are **lonely**.

Sometimes I like to be alone to think.
She has been very lonely since her husband died.

along[1] /əˈlɔŋ/ *preposition* **1 A2** from one part of a road, river, etc. to another: *a walk along the beach* **2 B1** in a line next to something long: *There is a row of new houses along the river.*

along[2] /əˈlɔŋ/ *adv* **1 B1** forward: *We were just walking along, talking.* **2 come along** to arrive somewhere: *Three buses came along at the same time.* **3 bring/take someone along** to take someone with you to a place: *Can I bring some friends along to the party?*

alongside /əˈlɔŋˌsaid/ *adv, preposition* next to someone or something: *A car pulled up alongside ours.*

aloud /əˈlaud/ *adv* **B1** in a way that other people can hear: *I laughed aloud.*

alphabet /ˈæl·fə·bet/ *noun* **A2** a set of letters used for writing a language: *The English alphabet starts with A and ends with Z.*

alphabetical /ˌæl·fəˈbet·ɪ·kəl/ *adj* in the same order as the letters of the alphabet: *Put the names **in alphabetical order**.*
• **alphabetically** *adv* *The books are arranged alphabetically.*

already /ɔlˈred·i/ *adv* **1 A2** before now, or before a time in the past: *I've already seen that movie.* **2 B1** used to say that something has happened earlier than you expected: *I can't believe you're already done!*

also /ˈɔl·sou/ *adv* **A1** in addition: *She speaks French and also a little Spanish.*

alter /ˈɔl·tər/ *verb* to change, or to make someone or something change: *A new haircut can really alter your appearance.*

alteration /ˌɔl·təˈreɪ·ʃən/ noun
a change: We've **made** a few **alterations to** the kitchen.

alternate[1] /ˈɔl·tər·nət/ adj **1** available as a different possibility: an alternate plan **2** one out of every two days, weeks, years, etc.: I work alternate Saturdays.
• **alternately** adv

alternate[2] /ˈɔl·tərˌneɪt/ verb (present participle **alternating**, past tense and past participle **alternated**) If two things alternate, one thing happens, then the other thing happens, then the first thing happens again, etc.: She easily **alternates between** speaking Spanish and English. ○ Alternate layers of fruit and yogurt in a tall glass.

alternative[1] /ɔlˈtɜr·nə·t̬ɪv/ noun one of two or more things that you can choose between: Olive oil is a healthy **alternative to** butter.

alternative[2] /ɔlˈtɜr·nə·t̬ɪv/ adj **1** different: We can make alternative arrangements if necessary. **2** different from what is usual or traditional: an alternative lifestyle

alternatively /ɔlˈtɜr·nə·t̬ɪv·li/ adv used to give a second possibility: You can buy tickets by phone or, alternatively, place your order online.

although /ɔlˈðoʊ/ conjunction
1 despite the fact that: She walked home by herself, although she knew it was dangerous. **2** 🅱1 but: He's coming tomorrow, although I don't know what time.

altogether /ˌɔl·təˈɡeð·ər/ adv **1** 🅱1 in total: There were twenty people there altogether. **2** completely: The train slowed down and then stopped altogether.
3 used to make a statement about several things you have mentioned: Altogether, the party was a great success.

aluminum /əˈlu·mə·nəm/ noun [no plural]
a light, silver-colored metal

always /ˈɔl·weɪz/ adv **1** 🅰1 every time, or at all times: I always walk to work.
2 🅰2 at all times in the past: We've always lived here. **3** forever: I will always

remember you. **4** 🅱1 used to suggest something: You can always stay with us if you miss your flight.

am /æm/, /əm/ present simple of be, used with "I": I am not happy about this.

a.m. /ˈeɪˈem/ 🅰1 in the morning: We're open from 9 a.m. to 5 p.m. daily.

amateur[1] /ˈæm·əˌtʃər/, /ˈæm·ə·tər/ adj
doing something as a hobby: an amateur photographer

amateur[2] /ˈæm·əˌtʃər/, /ˈæm·ə·tər/ noun
someone who does something as a hobby

amaze /əˈmeɪz/ verb (present participle **amazing**, past tense and past participle **amazed**) to make someone very surprised: **It amazes me** how much energy you have.

amazed /əˈmeɪzd/ adj 🅱1 very surprised: I was **amazed at** the price.

amazement /əˈmeɪz·mənt/ noun
[no plural] the state of being very surprised: I watched **in amazement**.

amazing /əˈmeɪ·zɪŋ/ adj **1** 🅰2 very good: My trip to Thailand was really amazing. **2** 🅱1 very surprising: **It's amazing that** they survived the crash.
• **amazingly** adv 🅱1 She played amazingly well.

ambassador /æmˈbæs·ə·dər/ noun
an important person who officially represents his or her country in a different country: the American **ambassador to** Brazil

ambition /æmˈbɪʃ·ən/ noun
1 🅱1 something that you want to do in your life: My ambition is to become a doctor. **2** [no plural] a strong feeling that you want to be successful or powerful: He has no ambition.

ambitious /æmˈbɪʃ·əs/ adj **1** wanting to be successful or powerful: an ambitious young lawyer **2** An ambitious plan will need a lot of work and will be difficult to achieve: This is our most ambitious project so far.

ambulance /ˈæm·bjə·ləns/ *noun*
A2 a vehicle that takes people to the hospital when they are ill or hurt

ambulance

among /əˈmʌŋ/ *preposition* **1** **A2** in or from a group: *He got lost among the crowds.* ○ *Among the options, which is your favorite?* **2** **A2** used to talk about the people in a particular group: *The decision will not be popular among students.* **3** into shares for each one in a group: *She divided the cake among the children.*

amount¹ /əˈmaʊnt/ *noun* **B1** how much there is of something: *He ate a huge amount of food.*

amount² /əˈmaʊnt/ *verb*
amount to *something* *phrasal verb* to have a particular total: *The cost of repairing the roof amounted to $900.*

> **❗ Common mistake: amount of or number of?**
>
> **Amount of** is used with uncountable nouns.
> *I should reduce the amount of coffee I drink.*
> *Did you use the right amount of flour?*
> **Number of** is used with countable nouns.
> *We don't know the number of people involved yet.*
> *They received a large number of complaints.*

amuse /əˈmjuz/ *verb* (present participle **amusing**, past tense and past participle **amused**) **1** to make someone smile or laugh: *I thought this article might amuse you.* **2** to keep someone interested and help that person to enjoy himself or herself: *Be sure to pack car toys for the children to amuse themselves with.*

amusement /əˈmjuz·mənt/ *noun* [no plural] the feeling that you have when something makes you smile or laugh:

I watched the performance with great amusement.

amusement park /əˈmjuz·mənt ˌpark/ *noun* a large park where you can ride on machines and have fun

amusing /əˈmjuz·zɪŋ/ *adj* **B1** funny: *an amusing letter*

an /ən/, /æn/ *determiner* **A1** used instead of "a" when the next word starts with a vowel sound: *an apple* ○ *an hour*

analysis /əˈnæl·ə·sɪs/ *noun* (plural **analyses**) the process of analyzing something: *A sample of soil was sent for analysis.*

analyze /ˈæn·əˌlaɪz/ *verb* (present participle **analyzing**, past tense and past participle **analyzed**) to look at and think about something carefully, in order to understand it: *to analyze data*

ancestor /ˈænˌses·tər/ *noun* a person in your family who lived a long time ago: *My ancestors came from Ireland.*

anchor /ˈæŋ·kər/ *noun*
a heavy metal object that is dropped into water to stop a boat from moving

anchor

ancient /ˈeɪn·ʃənt/ *adj* **B1** from a very long time ago: *ancient Greece* ○ *an ancient statue*

> **❗ Common mistake: ancient, former, or old?**
>
> Ancient cannot be used to describe someone or something that existed in the recent past, but not now. Use **former** instead.
> *He is a former student of mine.*
> ~~He is an ancient student of mine.~~
> Ancient means thousands or hundreds of years old. It should not be used for people.
> *We need to provide care for old people.*
> ~~We need to provide care for ancient people.~~

and /ænd/ *conjunction* **1** **A1** used to join two words or two parts of a sentence: *tea and coffee* ○ *We were tired and hungry.* **2** **A1** used to say that one thing happens after another thing: *I got dressed and had breakfast.* **3** **B1** used between two words that are the same to make their meaning stronger: *We laughed and laughed.*

anesthetic /ˌæn·əsˈθet̬·ɪk/ *noun* a drug that stops you from feeling pain during an operation: *The operation is done under anesthetic* (= using anesthetic).

angel /ˈeɪn·dʒəl/ *noun* **B1** a creature like a human with wings, who some people believe lives with God in heaven

angel

anger /ˈæŋ·ɡər/ *noun* [no plural] the feeling that you want to shout at someone or hurt him or her because he or she has done something bad

angle /ˈæŋ·ɡəl/ *noun* **1** a space between two lines or surfaces that meet at one point, which you measure in degrees: *an angle of 90 degrees* **2** the way you think about a situation: *Try looking at the problem from another angle.*

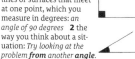
angles

angrily /ˈæŋ·ɡrɪ·li/ *adv* **B1** in a way that shows anger: *He said it angrily.*

angry /ˈæŋ·ɡri/ *adj* (comparative **angrier**, superlative **angriest**) **A2** feeling that you want to shout at someone or hurt him or her because he or she has done something bad: *He's really angry with me for upsetting Sophie.*

animal /ˈæn·ə·məl/ *noun* **1** **A1** something that lives and moves but is not a person, bird, fish, or insect: *a wild animal* **2** anything that lives and moves, including people, birds, etc.: *Are humans the only animals that use language?*

animated /ˈæn·əˌmeɪ·t̬ɪd/ *adj* Animated drawings or models look as if they move: *animated computer graphics*

ankle /ˈæŋ·kəl/ *noun* **B1** the part of your leg that is just above your foot
→ See **The Body** on page C2

anniversary /ˌæn·əˈvɜr·sə·ri/ *noun* (plural **anniversaries**) **B1** a day on which you remember or celebrate something that happened on that day in the past: *a wedding anniversary* ○ *the 50th anniversary of Kennedy's death*

> ❗ **Common mistake: announce or advertise?**
>
> Announce means to tell people about something. If you want to talk about telling people about a product or service so that they will buy it, for example in newspapers or on television, you should use advertise.

announce /əˈnaʊns/ *verb* (present participle **announcing**, past tense and past participle **announced**) **B1** to tell people new information, especially officially: *The company has announced plans to open six new stores.*

announcement /əˈnaʊns·mənt/ *noun* **B1** something that someone says officially, giving new information about something: *The president made an unexpected announcement this morning.*

announcer /əˈnaʊn·sər/ *noun* someone who describes what is happening on a live radio or television program: *a sports announcer*

annoy /əˈnɔɪ/ *verb* **B1** to make someone a little angry: *He's always late and it's starting to annoy me.*

annoyed /əˈnɔɪd/ *adj* **B1** a little angry: *I was annoyed with Jack for being late.*

annoying /əˈnɔɪ·ɪŋ/ *adj* **B1** making you feel a little angry: *He has an annoying habit of interrupting people.*

annual /ˈæn·ju·əl/ *adj* **1** **B1** happening once a year: *an annual meeting* **2** **B1** measured over a period of one year: *What is your annual income?*
• **annually** *adv* *The festival takes place annually.*

anonymous /əˈnɑn·ə·məs/ *adj* from or by someone who does not say or write his or her name: *an anonymous phone call*

| æ cat | ɑ hot | e get | ɪ sit | i see | ɔ saw | ʊ book | u too | ʌ cut | ə about | ər mother | ɑr turn | ɔr for | ɑɪ my | aʊ how | eɪ say | ɔɪ boy |

• **anonymously** adv *He made the complaint anonymously.*

another /əˈnʌð·ər/ pronoun, determiner
1 🔵 one more: *Would you like another drink?* ○ *They're having another baby.*
2 🔵 a different thing or person: *I'm going to look for another job.* ○ *The disease spreads easily from one person to another.*

⚠ Common mistake: another or other?

Another means "one other" and is used with a singular noun. It is written as one word.

Would you like another cup of coffee?
~~Would you like another cup of coffee?~~

Other is used with a plural noun and means different things or people than the ones you are talking about.

She had other ambitions.
~~She had another ambitions.~~

---

answer¹ /ˈæn·sər/ verb **1** 🔵 to speak or write back to someone who has asked you a question: *I asked her what time it was, but she didn't answer.* ○ *I must answer his letter.* **2** 🔵 to say hello to someone who has telephoned you: *Could someone answer the phone?* **3** 🔵 to write or say something as a reply to a question in a test **4** to open the door to someone who has arrived: *I knocked several times, but no one answered.*

answer² /ˈæn·sər/ noun **1** 🔵 something that you say or write back to someone who has asked you a question: *I asked him if he was young, but I didn't hear his answer.* **2** 🔵 the act of picking up a telephone or opening a door: *I rang the bell, but there was no answer.* **3** 🔵 the correct information given as a reply to a question in a test: *Did you get the answer to question six?* **4** 🔵 a way of stopping a problem: *It's a big problem, and I don't know what the answer is.*

answering machine /ˈan·sə·rɪŋ məˌʃin/ noun a machine that records your message if you telephone someone and he or she does not answer: *I left a message on her answering machine.*

ant /ænt/ noun 🔵 a small insect that lives in groups in the ground
→ See picture at **insect**

antenna /ænˈten·ə/ noun **antenna**
1 (antennae) one of two long, thin parts on the head of an insect or ocean creature, used for feeling things **2** (plural antennas) a piece of metal that is used for receiving television or radio signals
→ See **Car** on page C3

anti- /ˈæn·ti/, /ˌæn·taɪ/ prefix **1** opposed to or against: *anti-pollution laws* ○ *an anti-war march* **2** fighting or preventing: *powerful antibiotics* ○ *an anti-theft device*

antibiotic /ˌænt·i·baɪˈɒt·ɪk/ noun a medicine that cures infections by destroying bad bacteria: *He is taking antibiotics for an ear infection.*

antique¹ /ænˈtik/ noun 🔵 an object that is old, and often rare or beautiful: *I enjoy shopping for antiques.*

antique² /ænˈtik/ adj 🔵 old and often rare or beautiful: *antique furniture*

antiseptic /ˌæn·tɪˈsep·tɪk/ noun a substance that you put on an injury to prevent infection
• **antiseptic** adj *a bottle of antiseptic lotion*

anxiety /æŋˈzaɪ·ɪ·ti/ noun (plural anxieties) the feeling of being very worried

anxious /ˈæŋk·ʃəs/ adj **1** 🔵 worried and very nervous: *She's very **anxious** about her exams.* **2** wanting something to happen soon: *He's **anxious** to get home.*
• **anxiously** adv *We waited anxiously by the phone.*

any¹ /ˈen·i/ determiner, pronoun
1 🔵 used in questions and negative statements to mean "some": *Is there any cake left?* ○ *I haven't read any of his books.* **2** 🔵 used to mean "one" when it is not important which one: *Any of those shirts would be fine.*

any² /ˈen·i/ adv 🔵 used in questions and negative statements before a comparative adjective to make the sentence stronger: *Do you feel any **better**? ∘ I can't walk any **faster**.*

anybody /ˈen·ɪˌbɑd·i/, /ˈen·ɪˌbʌd·i/ **pronoun** **A2** another word for anyone

anyhow /ˈen·iˌhɑʊ/ **adv** another word for anyway

anymore /ˌen·iˈmɔr/ **adv** used to say that something is different now from what it was in the past: *This coat doesn't fit me **anymore**.*

anyone /ˈen·iˌwʌn/ **pronoun** **1** **A2** used in questions and negative statements to mean "a person or people": *I didn't know anyone at the party.* **2** **B1** any person or any people: ***Anyone** could do that – it's easy.*

anyplace /ˈen·iˌpleɪs/ **adv** another word for anywhere

anything /ˈen·iˌθɪŋ/ **pronoun** **1** **A1** used in questions and negative statements to mean "something": *I don't have **anything** to wear.* ∘ *Was there **anything** else you wanted to say?* **2** **A1** any object, event, or situation: *Tom will eat almost **anything**.*

anytime /ˈen·iˌtɑɪm/ **adv** at a time that is not decided or agreed: *Come to my house **anytime** tomorrow.*

anyway /ˈen·iˌweɪ/ **adv** **1** **A2** although something happened or is true: *I hate carrots, but I ate them **anyway**.* **2** **A2** used when you are returning to an earlier subject: ***Anyway**, as I said, I'll be away next week.* **3** **B1** used to give a more important reason for something that you are saying: *I don't need a car, and can't afford one **anyway**.*

anywhere /ˈen·iˌhweɑr/ **adv** **1** **A2** in or to any place: *Just sit anywhere.* ∘ *I couldn't find a post office **anywhere**.* **2** **A2** used in questions and negative statements to mean "a place": *He doesn't have **anywhere** to stay.* ∘ *Is there **anywhere** else you'd like to go while you're here?*

apart /əˈpɑrt/ **adv** **1** **B1** separated by a space or period of time: *Stand with your feet wide **apart**.* ∘ *Our children were born eighteen months **apart**.* **2** into separate, smaller pieces: *My jacket is so old, it's falling **apart**.* **3** not with someone else: *It was my first time traveling **apart** from my family.*

apartment /əˈpɑrt·mənt/ **noun** **A2** a set of rooms for someone to live in on one level of a building or house

apartment building /əˈpɑrt·mənt ˌbɪl·dɪŋ/ **noun** a large building that is divided into apartments

ape /eɪp/ **noun** a hairy animal like a monkey but with no tail and long arms

apologize /əˈpɑlˌəˌdʒɑɪz/ **verb** (present participle **apologizing**, past tense and past participle **apologized**) **B1** to say sorry for something bad you have done: *He **apologized for** being rude.* ∘ *I **apologized to** her.*

> ### ⚠ Common mistake: apologize to someone
>
> Remember to use **to** when you mention the person who receives the apology.
>
> *I **apologized to** them immediately.*
> ~~I apologized them immediately.~~

apology /əˈpɑlˌəˌdʒi/ **noun** (plural **apologies**) **B1** something that you say or write to say sorry for something bad you have done: *a letter of apology*

apostrophe /əˈpɑsˌtrəˌfi/ **noun** **1** a mark (') used to show that letters or numbers are not there: *I'm (=I am) hungry.* **2** a punctuation mark (') used before the letter "s" to show that something belongs to someone or something: *I drove my brother's car.*

app /æp/ **noun** short form of application: *a computer app*

apparent /əˈpær·ənt/ **adj** easy to notice: *It soon became **apparent that** she had lost interest.*

apparently /əˈpær·ənt·li/ **adv** used to say that you have read or been told something: *Apparently it's going to rain today.*

appeal[1] /ə'piːl/ noun [no plural] the quality that makes you like someone or something: *I've never understood the appeal of skiing.*

appeal[2] /ə'piːl/ verb **1** to attract or interest someone: *Smoking has never **appealed** to me.* **2** to ask people to give money, information or help: *The police have **appealed for** more information.*

appear /ə'pɪər/ verb **1** 🔵 to seem: *He appeared calm and relaxed.* **2** 🔵 to start to be seen: *She suddenly appeared in the doorway.* → Opposite **disappear** verb **3** 🔵 to perform in a movie, play, etc.: *She appears briefly in the new James Bond movie.* **4** to start to exist or become available: *Laptop computers first appeared in the 1980s.*

appearance /ə'pɪərəns/ noun **1** 🔵 the way a person or thing looks: *She's very concerned with her appearance.* **2** an occasion when someone is seen in public: *a public appearance* **3** [no plural] the fact of something starting to exist or becoming available: *The appearance of cell phones has changed the way people communicate.*

appetite /'æpɪˌtaɪt/ noun the feeling that makes you want to eat: *All that walking has **given** me an **appetite**.*

appetizer /'æpɪˌtaɪzər/ noun something that you eat as the first part of a meal: *We had soup as an appetizer.*

applaud /ə'plɔːd/ verb to hit your hands together to show that you have enjoyed a performance, speech, etc.: *The audience applauded loudly.*

applause /ə'plɔːz/ noun [no plural] the noise or action of people hitting their hands together to show that they have enjoyed something: *There was loud applause at the end of her speech.*

apple /'æpəl/ noun 🔵 a hard, round fruit with a green or red skin: *apple pie* → See **Fruits and Vegetables** on page C8

appliance /ə'plaɪəns/ noun a piece of electrical equipment with a particular purpose in the home: *They sell refrigerators, dishwashers, and other appliances.*

application /ˌæplɪ'keɪʃən/ noun **1** 🔵 an official request for something, usually in writing: *an **application for** a bank loan* **2** a computer program with a particular purpose

application form /ˌæplɪ'keɪʃən ˌfɔːrm/ noun a form that you use to officially ask for something, for example a job

apply /ə'plaɪ/ verb (present participle **applying**, past tense and past participle **applied**) **1** 🔵 to officially ask for something: *I **applied for** a job.* **2** to affect a particular person or situation: *This law only **applies to** married people.* **3** to spread something on a surface: *Apply the paint to a clean, dry surface.*

appoint /ə'pɔɪnt/ verb to officially choose someone for a job: *A new judge will be **appointed to** the court this fall.*

appointment /ə'pɔɪntmənt/ noun 🅰2 a time when you have arranged to see someone: *I **made** a doctor's **appointment** for next week.*

appreciate /ə'priːʃiˌeɪt/ verb (present participle **appreciating**, past tense and past participle **appreciated**) **1** to understand how good something or someone is: *He wouldn't appreciate an expensive wine.* **2** to feel grateful for something: *I really appreciate all your help.* **3** would appreciate used when you are politely requesting something: *I **would appreciate it** if you didn't smoke in the house.*

appreciation /əˌpriːʃi'eɪʃən/ noun [no plural] **1** an understanding of how good something or someone is: *His **appreciation** of art increased as he grew older.* **2** a feeling of being grateful for something: *To show our appreciation, we bought you a little present.*

> ⚠ **Common mistake: approach**
>
> The verb **approach** is not normally followed by a preposition.
> *He approached the door.*
> ~~He approached to the door.~~

approach[1] /ə'proʊtʃ/ verb **1** 🔵 to come close in distance or time: *The* crowd cheered as she approached the finish line. ○ The new school year is fast approaching. **2** to deal with something: I'm not sure how to approach the problem.

approach[2] /əˈprəʊtʃ/ noun **1** a way of doing something: Neil has a different **approach to** the problem. **2** [no plural] movement closer to someone or something in distance or time: the approach of winter

appropriate /əˈprəʊpriˈət/ adj right for a particular situation or person: Is this movie **appropriate for** children?
→ Opposite **inappropriate** adj

approval /əˈpruːvəl/ noun [no plural] **1** the belief that something or someone is good or right: Alan always tries hard to **win** his father's **approval**. → Opposite **disapproval** noun **2** official permission: The project has received approval from the government.

approve /əˈpruːv/ verb (present participle **approving**, past tense and past participle **approved**) **1** 🅱1 to allow something: The committee approved the new budget. **2** to think that something is good or right: I don't **approve of** smoking.
→ Opposite **disapprove** verb

approximate /əˈprɒksəmət/ adj not completely accurate but close: What is the approximate cost of a taxi to the airport?

approximately /əˈprɒksəmətli/ adv 🅱1 close to a particular number or time, but not exactly that number or time: The college has approximately 700 students.

April /ˈeɪprəl/ noun 🅰1 the fourth month of the year

arch

arch /ɑːtʃ/ noun a curved structure that usually supports something, for example a bridge or wall

architect /ˈɑːrkɪˌtekt/ noun 🅱1 someone who designs buildings

architecture /ˈɑːrkɪˌtekˈtʃər/ noun [no plural] 🅱1 the design and style of buildings: modern architecture

are /ɑːr/, /ər/ 🅰1 present simple of be, used with "you," "we," and "they"

area /ˈeərˈiˈə/ noun **1** 🅰2 a part of a country or city: a poor area **2** 🅱1 a part of a building or piece of land used for a particular purpose: a picnic area **3** a part of a subject or activity: What area of art does the course cover? **4** the size of a flat surface

aren't /ɑːrnt/, /ˈɑːrˈənt/ **1** 🅰1 short form of are not: We aren't going to the party. **2 aren't I?** 🅰1 short form of am I not?: I am invited, aren't I?

argue /ˈɑːrˈgjuː/ verb (present participle **arguing**, past tense and past participle **argued**) **1** 🅱1 to speak angrily to someone, telling the person that you disagree with him or her: My parents are always **arguing about** money. **2** to give reasons to support or oppose an idea, action, etc.: She **argued that** it would be cheaper to travel by bus.

argument /ˈɑːrˈgjəˈmənt/ noun **1** 🅱1 an angry discussion with someone in which you both disagree: They **had** an **argument** about who should clean the house. **2** a reason or reasons why you support or oppose an idea, action, etc.: There are many **arguments against** raising taxes.

arise /əˈraɪz/ verb (present participle **arising**, past tense **arose**, past participle **arisen**) If a problem arises, it starts to happen: The whole problem **arose from** a lack of communication.

arithmetic /əˈrɪθˈməˌtɪk/ noun [no plural] the part of mathematics that deals with the adding, multiplying, etc. of numbers

arm /ɑːrm/ noun 🅰1 the long part at each side of the human body, ending in a hand: She held the baby in her arms.
→ See **The Body** on page C2

arm

elbow

armchair /'ɑrm.tʃeər/ noun   armchair
A2 a comfortable chair
with sides that support
your arms

armed /ɑrmd/ adj   carrying
or using weapons: *armed
guards*

the armed forces /'ɑrmd 'fɔr·sɪz/
plural noun a country's military forces,
for example the army and the navy

armpit /'ɑrm.pɪt/ noun the part of your
body under your arm, where your arm
meets your body

arms /ɑrmz/ plural noun weapons: *the
sale of arms*

army /'ɑr·mi/ noun (plural **armies**)
B1 a military force that fights wars on
the ground: *the U.S. army*

arose /ə'rouz/   past tense of arise

around /ə'raund/ adv, preposition
1 A2 on all sides of something: *They sat
around the table.* **2 A2** in a circular
movement: *This switch makes the wheels
turn around.* **3 A2** to or in different
parts of a place: *I spent a year traveling
around Asia.* **4 A2** here, or near this
place: *Is there a grocery store around here?
○ Will you be around next week?* **5 A2** used
before a number or amount to mean
"close to, but not exactly": *They will arrive around four o'clock.* **6 A2** to someone's home: *Wendy's coming around this
afternoon.* **7 B1** to the opposite direction: *He turned around and looked at her.*
8 B1 from one place or person to another: *Could you pass these forms around,
please?*

arrange /ə'reɪndʒ/ verb (present participle
arranging, past tense and past participle
arranged) **1 B1** to make plans for
something to happen: *I arranged for a
car to pick us up.* **2** to put objects in a
particular order or position: *Arrange the
books alphabetically by author.*

arrangement /ə'reɪndʒ·mənt/ noun
1 B1 plans for how something will happen: *I made arrangements to meet her
on Saturday.* **2** an agreement between
two people or groups: *She has an arrangement with the bank to pay the loan.*

arrest[1] /ə'rest/ verb **B1** If the police
arrest someone, they take the person
away to ask him or her about a crime
that he or she might have done: *He was
arrested for possession of illegal drugs.*

arrest[2] /ə'rest/ noun the act of arrest-
ing someone: *Police made twenty ar-
rests at yesterday's demonstration.*

arrival /ə'raɪ·vəl/ noun [no plural]
B1 the act of someone or something
coming to a place: *We waited for her
arrival at the airport.*

arrive /ə'raɪv/ verb (present participle
arriving, past tense and past participle
arrived) **A2** to get to a place: *We arrived in Dallas at noon.* ○ *We arrived at
the airport early.*

> **! Common mistake: arrive**
> somewhere
>
> Be careful to choose the correct prep-
> osition after **arrive**.
> You **arrive at** a place such as a build-
> ing.
> *We arrived at the hotel just after 12
> o'clock.*
> You **arrive in** a town, city or country.
> *They arrived in Tokyo on Wednesday.
> When did David arrive in Australia?*
> You **arrive** home, here, or there. You
> do not use a preposition when **arrive**
> is used before these words.
> *We arrived home yesterday.
> I had a lot of problems when I first ar-
> rived here.*

arrogance /'ær·ə·gəns/ noun [no plural]
behavior that shows you believe you are
better than other people

arrogant /'ær·ə·gənt/ adj believing
that you are better than other people

arrow /'ær·ou/ noun   arrows
1 a symbol used on signs   arrow
to show a direction **2** a
long stick with a sharp
point at one end that is
shot from a bow (=curved
piece of wood)

art /ɑrt/ noun **1 A2** [no
plural] the making of things such as

paintings or drawings, or the things that are made: *modern art* ○ *an art gallery* **2** a skill: *the art of conversation*

article /ˈɑr·tɪ·kəl/ noun **1** 🅑1 a piece of writing in a magazine or newspaper: *I read an **article on** astrology.* **2** 🅑1 in grammar, used to mean the words "the," "a," or "an" **3** an object: *articles of clothing*

artificial /ˌɑr·təˈfɪʃ·əl/ adj not natural, but made by people: *artificial flowers*
• **artificially** adv *artificially colored drinks*

artist /ˈɑr·tɪst/ noun 🅐2 someone who makes art, especially paintings and drawings

artistic /ɑrˈtɪs·tɪk/ adj **1** good at making things, such as paintings and drawings **2** relating to art: *the artistic director of the theater*

arts /ɑrts/ plural noun **1** subjects of study that are not sciences, for example history and languages: *an arts degree* **2** the arts activities such as painting, music, film, dance, and writing

as /æz/ preposition, conjunction **1** 🅐1 used to describe something's purpose or someone's job: *She **works as a** waitress.* ○ *They **use** their spare bedroom **as** an office.* **2** as ... as 🅐2 used to compare two things, people, amounts, etc.: *He's not as tall as his brother.* ○ *She earns three times as much as I do.* **3** 🅑1 while: *I saw James as I was leaving.* **4** 🅑1 in the same way: *This year, as in previous years, tickets sold very quickly.* **5** as if /as though 🅑1 used to describe how a situation seems to be: *It looks as if it might rain.* **6** as for used to talk about how another person or thing is affected by something: *I'm satisfied. As for Kyle, I don't care what he thinks.*

ash /æʃ/ noun (plural **ash, ashes**) the soft, gray powder that remains after something has burned: *cigarette ash*

ashamed /əˈʃeɪmd/ adj 🅑1 feeling angry and disappointed about someone or something, or because you have done something wrong: *You should be **ashamed of** yourself for lying to her!*

ashtray /ˈæʃˌtreɪ/ noun a small, open container used to put cigarette ash in

aside /əˈsaɪd/ adv **1** in a direction to one side: *Step aside, please.* **2** If you put or set something aside, you do not use it now, but keep it to use later: *We put some money aside for our vacation.*

ask /æsk/ verb **1** 🅐1 to say something to someone as a question: *I **asked** him **about** his hobbies.* ○ *I **asked** why the plane was so late.* **2** 🅐2 to invite someone to do something: *She asked him to lunch.* **3** 🅑1 to say to someone that you would like something from him or her: *He **asked for** a bike for his birthday.* **4** 🅑1 to say something to someone because you want him or her to do something: *They **asked** me to feed their cat while they're away.* **5** 🅑1 to say something to someone because you want to know if you can do something: *Ask your dad if you can come.*

ask *someone* **out** phrasal verb to invite someone to go out with you: *Jack asked me out to dinner on Friday.*

> ⚠ **Common mistake: ask for** something
>
> When you use **ask** to mean that you want someone to give you something, remember to use the preposition **for** before the thing that is wanted.
> *I'm writing to ask for information about your products.*
> ~~I'm writing to ask information about your products.~~

asleep /əˈslip/ adj 🅑1 sleeping: *The children are asleep.* ○ *He **fell asleep** in front of the TV.*

aspect /ˈæs·pekt/ noun one part of a situation, problem, or subject: *His illness affects every aspect of his life.*

aspirin /ˈæs·pə·rɪn/, /ˈæs·prɪn/ noun (plural **aspirin, aspirins**) 🅑1 a common drug used to stop pain and fever

assault /əˈsɔlt/ noun an attack: *There was an **assault on** a police officer.*
• **assault verb**

a
b
c
d
e
f
g
h
i
j
k
l
m
n
o
p
q
r
s
t
u
v
w
x
y
z

assembly /əˈsem·bli/ **noun** (plural **assemblies**) **1** a meeting of a large group of people, especially one that happens regularly for a particular purpose: *Our school **has assembly** (= when all the classes in the school meet for special activities)on Fridays.* **2** one of the two parts of the government in many states in the U.S. that make laws

assess /əˈses/ **verb** to decide how good, important, or serious something is: *The tests are designed to assess a child's reading skills.*
• **assessment** noun

assignment /əˈsaɪn·mənt/ **noun** a piece of work or a job that someone gives you to do: *a written assignment*

assist /əˈsɪst/ **verb** to help: *The army arrived to **assist** in the search for survivors.*

assistance /əˈsɪs·təns/ **noun** [no plural] formal help: *financial assistance*

assistant /əˈsɪs·tənt/ **noun** **B1** someone whose job is to help a person who has a more important job: *assistant manager*

associate /əˈsoʊ·ʃiˌeɪt/, /əˈsoʊ·siˌeɪt/ **verb** (present participle **associating**, past tense and past participle **associated**) to relate two things or people in your mind: *Most people **associate** this brand **with** good quality.*

be associated with *something* **phrasal verb** to be caused by something: *There are many health problems associated with smoking.*

associate's degree /əˈsoʊ·ʃiˌɪts dɪˌɡri/, /əˈsoʊ·siˌɪts/ **noun** (also **associate's**) a college degree that is given after a course of study that typically takes two years

association /əˌsoʊ·siˈeɪ·ʃən/, /əˌsoʊ·ʃiˈeɪ·ʃən/ **noun** an organization of people with the same interests or purpose: *an alumni association*

assume /əˈsum/ **verb** (present participle **assuming**, past tense and past participle **assumed**) to think that something is true, although you have no proof: *You didn't call, so I assumed you were OK.*

assure /əˈʃʊər/ **verb** (present participle **assuring**, past tense and past participle **assured**) to stop someone from worrying by telling him or her that something is certain: *She **assured** me **that** she would be safe.*

asterisk /ˈæs·tə,rɪsk/ **noun** the symbol *

asthma /ˈæz·mə/ **noun** [no plural] an illness that makes it difficult to breathe: *an asthma attack*

astonished /əˈstɑn·ɪʃt/ **adj** very surprised: *I was **astonished** at the news.*

astonishing /əˈstɑn·ɪ·ʃɪŋ/ **adj** very surprising: *The team had an astonishing victory after losing five games.*

astonishment /əˈstɑn·ɪʃ·mənt/ **noun** [no plural] a feeling of great surprise: *I tried to hide my astonishment.*

astrologer /əˈstrɑl·ə·dʒər/ **noun** someone who studies astrology

astrology /əˈstrɑl·ə·dʒi/ **noun** [no plural] the study of the positions and movements of stars, and the belief that they change people's lives

astronaut
/ˈæs·trə,nɔt/ **noun** someone who travels into space

astronaut

astronomer /əˈstrɑn·ə·mər/ **noun** a scientist who studies astronomy

astronomy /əˈstrɑn·ə·mi/ **noun** [no plural] the scientific study of stars and planets

at /æt/ **preposition** **1** **A1** in a particular place or position: *We met at the station.* ○ *She was sitting at the table.* **2** **A1** used to show the time something happens: *The meeting starts at three.* **3** **A1** toward: *I threw the ball at him.* **4** **A2** used to show the cause of something, especially a feeling: *We were surprised at the news.* **5** **B1** used after an adjective to show a person's ability to do something: *He's good at making friends.* **6** used to show the price, speed, or level of something: *He was driving at 80 miles per hour.* **7** **A1** the symbol @, used in email addresses to separate the name of a person from the name of the organization

ate /eɪt/ **A1** past tense of eat

athlete /ˈæθ·liːt/ noun **B1** someone who is good at sports and other types of exercise

athletic /æθˈlet·ɪk/ adj **1** strong, healthy, and good at sports **2** relating to athletes

athletics /æθˈlet·ɪks/ noun [no plural] sports, for example football and baseball: *a college athletics program*

atlas /ˈæt·ləs/ noun a book of maps: *a road atlas*

ATM /ˌeɪˌtiːˈem/ noun short form of automated teller machine: a machine that you get money from using a plastic card

atmosphere /ˈæt·məˌsfɪər/ noun
1 **B1** [no plural] the feeling that exists in a place or situation: *The atmosphere in the office is very relaxed.* **2** the atmosphere the gases around the Earth

atom /ˈæt·əm/ noun the smallest unit that an element can be divided into

atomic /əˈtɑm·ɪk/ adj **1** relating to atoms **2** using the energy created when an atom is divided: *atomic power/weapons*

attach /əˈtætʃ/ verb **1** **B1** to join one thing to another: *She attached a picture to her letter.* **2** to join a file, such as a document, picture, or computer program, to an email: *The information is in the attached document.*

attached /əˈtætʃt/ adj be attached to someone/something to like someone or something very much: *I'm really attached to my old car.*

attachment /əˈtætʃ·mənt/ noun
1 a computer file that is sent together with an email message: *Have you opened the attachment?* **2** a feeling of love or liking for someone or something

attack[1] /əˈtæk/ noun **1** **B1** a violent act intended to hurt or damage someone or something: *There was a terrorist attack on the capital.* **2** a sudden, short illness: *He had a terrible allergy attack.*

attack[2] /əˈtæk/ verb **1** **B1** to use violence to hurt or damage someone or something: *He was attacked by a bully.* **2** to say that someone or something is bad: *She attacked the government's new education policy.*

attempt[1] /əˈtempt/ verb **B1** to try to do something: *He attempted to escape through a window.*

attempt[2] /əˈtempt/ noun an act of trying to do something: *This is his second attempt at passing the exam.*

attend /əˈtend/ verb formal **1** **B1** to go to an event: *He attended a meeting.*
2 **B1** to go regularly to a place such as a school or church: *Which school does your daughter attend?*

attendance /əˈten·dəns/ noun the number of people who go to an event or a place such as a school or church, or how often they go there: *They want to increase attendance at their meetings.*

attendant /əˈten·dənt/ noun someone whose job is to help the public in a public place: *a parking attendant*

attention /əˈten·ʃən/ noun [no plural]
1 **B1** the act of watching or listening to something carefully: *I wasn't paying attention (= listening) to what she was saying.* ○ *Ladies and gentlemen, could I have your attention, please? (= please listen to me)* **2** catch/get someone's attention to make someone notice you: *I waved at him to get his attention.* **3** draw (someone's) attention to something/someone to make someone notice something or someone: *She jumped and shouted to draw attention to herself.*

> ⚠ **Common mistake: attention**
>
> **Attention** is usually followed by the preposition **to**.
> *You should pay attention to what she tells you.*
> *We want to draw people's attention to the risks involved.*

attic /ˈæt·ɪk/ noun a room at the top of a house under the roof

attitude /ˈæt·ɪˌtud/ noun **B1** how you think or feel about something: *He has a very bad attitude toward work.*

attorney /əˈtɜr·ni/ noun a lawyer, especially one who represents someone in court

attract /əˈtrækt/ verb **1** 🅱1 to make people come to a place or do a particular thing: *The museum attracts more than 300,000 visitors a year.* **2 attract attention, interest, etc.** 🅱1 to cause people to pay attention, be interested, etc.: *Her ideas have attracted a lot of attention.* **3** to cause someone to be interested, especially sexually: *So what attracted you to Joe in the first place? ○ I was attracted to him right away .*

attraction /əˈtræk·ʃən/ noun **1** 🅱1 something that makes people come to a place: *a tourist attraction* **2** [no plural] a feeling of liking someone because of the way he or she looks or behaves: *physical attraction*

attractive /əˈtræk·tɪv/ adj **1** 🅰2 beautiful or pleasant to look at: *an attractive woman* **2** interesting or useful: *a very attractive offer*

auction[1] /ˈɔk·ʃən/ noun a sale in which things are sold to the person who offers the most money

auction[2] /ˈɔk·ʃən/ verb to sell something at an auction

audience /ˈɔ·di·əns/ noun 🅱1 the people who sit and watch a performance at a theater or concert

audio /ˈɔ·di·oʊ/ adj relating to the recording or playing of sound: *audio equipment*

audiovisual /ˌɔ·di·oʊˈvɪʒ·u·əl/ adj using sounds and pictures: *audiovisual equipment*

audition /ɔˈdɪʃ·ən/ noun a short performance that someone has to try to get a job as an actor, musician, dancer, etc.: *I have an audition for the play tomorrow.*

August /ˈɔ·ɡəst/ noun 🅰1 the eighth month of the year

aunt /ænt/, /ɑnt/ noun 🅰2 the sister of someone's mother or father, or the wife of someone's uncle: *I'm going to visit my aunt next week.*

authentic /ɔˈθen·tɪk/ adj real and not false: *authentic Italian food*

author /ˈɔ·θər/ noun 🅱1 someone who writes a book, article, etc.: *a popular author of children's fiction*

authority /əˈθɔr·ɪ·ti/ noun **1** [no plural] the official power to make decisions or control people **2** (plural **authorities**) an official group with the power to control a particular public service: *a city's transportation authority*

autobiography /ˌɔ·tə·baɪˈɑg·rə·fi/ noun (plural **autobiographies**) a book that someone has written about his or her own life

autograph /ˈɔ·tə·ɡræf/ noun a famous person's name, written by that person

automated /ˈɔ·tə·meɪ·tɪd/ adjective made to operate by machines or computers in order to reduce the work done by humans

automatic /ˌɔ·təˈmæt·ɪk/ adj **1** An automatic machine works by itself or with little human control: *automatic doors* **2** done without thinking: *After lots of practice, driving becomes automatic.*

automatically /ˌɔ·təˈmæt·ɪ·kli/ adv **1** If a machine does something automatically, it does it without being controlled by anyone: *The camera automatically puts the time and date on the photo.* **2** without thinking about what you are doing: *I automatically put my hand out to catch it.*

automobile /ˈɔ·tə·mə·bil/ noun (also **car**) a vehicle with an engine, four wheels, and seats for a few people

autumn /ˈɔ·təm/ noun (also **fall**) the season of the year between summer and winter, when leaves fall from the trees: *autumn leaves*

auxiliary verb /ɑɡˈzɪl·jə·ri ˈvɜrb/ noun a verb that is used with another verb to form tenses, negatives, and questions, for example "do" and "must"

available /əˈveɪ·lə·bəl/ adj 🅰2 If something is available, you can use it or get it: *This information is available free on the Internet.*

avenue /ˈæv·əˌnu/ noun a wide road in a town or city: *Park Avenue*

average[1] /ˈæv·rɪdʒ/ adj **1** 🅱1 An average amount is calculated by adding some amounts together and then dividing by the number of amounts: *The average*

age of the students is 18. **2** usual and like the most common type: *an average day* **3** not excellent, although not bad: *The food was pretty average.*

average[2] /ˈæv·rɪdʒ/ **noun** **1** 🔒 an amount calculated by adding some amounts together and then dividing by the number of amounts: *They work an average of 30.5 hours per week.* **2** 🔒 the usual or typical amount: *An eight-hour day at work is about the average.* **3** **on average** usually, or based on an average: *On average, people who don't smoke are healthier than people who do.*

> ⚠ **Common mistake: avoid doing** something
>
> When **avoid** is followed by a verb, the verb is always in the **-ing** form.
> *I avoided seeing him for several days.*
> ~~I avoided to see him for several days.~~

avoid /əˈvɔɪd/ **verb** **1** 🔒 to stay away from a person or place: *Try to avoid Main Street.* **2** to prevent something from happening: *I braked to avoid hitting a deer.* **3** to not do something because you do not want to: *She managed to avoid answering my question.*

awake /əˈweɪk/ **adj** 🔒 not sleeping: *I was awake half the night.*

award[1] /əˈwɔrd/ **noun** a prize given to someone for something good he or she has done: *the award for best actress*

award[2] /əˈwɔrd/ **verb** to officially give someone something such as a prize or an amount of money: *He was awarded the Nobel Prize for Physics.*

aware /əˈwear/ **adj** knowing about something: *Were you aware of the problem?*
→ Opposite **unaware** adj

away /əˈweɪ/ **adv** **1** 🔒 to a different place: *Go away and leave me alone.* ○ *We moved away from the city.* **2** 🔒 at a particular distance from a place: *The nearest town is ten miles away.* **3** 🔒 not at the place where someone

usually lives or works: *Sophie is feeding the cat while we're away.* **4** 🔒 at a particular time in the future: *My exam is only a week away.* **5** 🔒 in or into the usual or a suitable place, especially one that can be closed: *Please put your toys away.* **6** gradually disappearing until mostly or completely gone: *All the snow has melted away.*

awesome /ˈɔ·səm/ **adj** **1** very big or special and making you feel respect, admiration, or fear: *an awesome responsibility* **2** *informal* very good: *You look awesome in those jeans.*

awful /ˈɔ·fəl/ **adj** **1** 🔒 very bad: *an awful place* ○ *The play was absolutely awful.* **2** **an awful lot (of** *something***)** a very large amount: *It costs an awful lot of money.*

awfully /ˈɔ·fli/ **adv** very: *We had to get up awfully early.*

awkward /ˈɔk·wərd/ **adj** **1** difficult or causing problems: *an awkward question* **2** embarrassing and not relaxed: *an awkward silence* **3** moving in a way that is not attractive: *His movements were slow and awkward.*

axe /æks/ **noun** (also **ax**) a tool with a sharp piece of metal at one end, used for cutting trees or wood

axe

Bb

B, b /bi/ the second letter of the alphabet

baby /ˈbeɪ·bi/ **noun** (plural **babies**) 🔒 a very young child or animal: *a baby girl*

baby

babysit /ˈbeɪ·bi.sɪt/ **verb** (present participle **babysitting**, past tense and past participle **babysat**) 🔒 to take care of children while their parents are not at home

• **babysitting** noun [no plural] **B1** *He earns extra money by babysitting.*

babysitter /'beɪ·bi ˌsɪt·ər/ noun **B1** someone who takes care of children while their parents are not at home

bachelor /'bætʃ·ə·lər/ noun a man who has never been married

bachelor's degree /'bætʃ·ə·lərz dɪ ˌgri/ noun (also **bachelor's,** /'bætʃ·ə·lərz/) a college or university degree that is given after a course of study that typically takes four years

back¹ /bæk/ adv **1** **A1** to the place where someone or something was before: *When do you go back to college?* ∘ *I put it back in the cupboard.* **2** **A2** as a reply or reaction to something: *Can I call you back later?* **3** **B1** in a direction behind you: *She stepped back.* **4** **B1** to the state something or someone was in before: *Try to go back to sleep.* **5** to an earlier time: *Looking back, I think we did the right thing.* **6** **back and forth** in one direction then the opposite way, many times: *She goes back and forth between the U.S. and Canada often.*

> **! Common mistake: back to**
>
> Remember to use the preposition **to** when you are talking about returning to a place.
>
> *I haven't seen her since she went back to Korea.*
>
> ~~I haven't seen her since she went back Korea.~~

back² /bæk/ noun **1** **A1** the part of something that is away from the front: *Our seats were in the back of the theater.* **2** **A2** the part of your body from your shoulders to your bottom: *He was lying on his back.* → See **The Body** on page C2 **3** **in back of** behind: *They sat in back of us on the plane.*

back³ /bæk/ verb **1** to give support to a person or plan: *He backed Clark in the recent election.* **2** to move or drive backward: *It's best to **back into** a parking space.* ∘ *Everyone please **back up**.*

back *something* **up** phrasal verb **1** to prove that something is true: *He hasn't backed his statement up with facts.* **2** to make an extra copy of computer information

back *someone* **up** phrasal verb to say that someone is telling the truth: *That's exactly what happened – Cleo will back me up.*

back⁴ /bæk/ adj **A2** at the back of something: *the back door*

backache /'bæk·eɪk/ noun **B1** a pain in your back: *Gardening gives me a backache.*

background /'bæk·graʊnd/ noun **1** **B1** a person's education and family: *He was from a poor background.* **2** the things at the back of a picture or view: *He had a photo of Paul with his children in the background.* **3** [no plural] sounds you can hear that are not the main sounds that you are listening to: *background music/noise* ∘ *If you listen carefully to this piece of music, you can hear a flute in the background.* **4** [no plural] the things that have happened in the past that affect a situation: *Can you give me some background on the issue?*

backpack /'bæk·pæk/ noun **B1** a bag that you carry on your back, with two straps that go over your shoulders

backpacker /'bæk·pæk·ər/ noun **B1** someone who travels, carrying the things he or she needs in a backpack

backpacking /'bæk·pæk·ɪŋ/ noun [no plural] **B1** the activity of traveling around an area without spending much money, carrying the things you need in a backpack: *He wants to **go backpacking** this summer.*

backup /'bæk·ʌp/ noun **1** an extra copy of computer information: *Have you **made a backup** of that document?*

2 extra help, support, or equipment that is available if you need it: *Keep extra batteries for emergency backup.*

backward[1] /ˈbæk·wərd/ adj   in the direction behind you: *a backward glance*

backward[2] /ˈbæk·wərd/ adv (also **backwards**)   **1** **B1** toward the direction behind you: *She took a couple of steps backward.*   **2** in the opposite order from what is usual: *"Erehwon" is "nowhere" spelled backward.*   **3** with the part that is usually at the front at the back: *You have your skirt on backward.*

backwards /ˈbæk·wərdz/ adv   another form of backward

backyard /ˈbæk·ˈjɑrd/ noun   the area behind a house

bacon /ˈbeɪ·kən/ noun [no plural]
B1 meat from a pig that has been treated with salt or smoke, often cut into long, thin slices

bacteria /bækˈtɪər·i·ə/ plural noun   very small living things that can cause disease

bad /bæd/ adj (comparative **worse**, superlative **worst**)   **1** not good or pleasant: *bad weather* ○ *bad news*   **2** of low quality and not acceptable: *The movie was so bad we couldn't watch it.* ○ *I'm very **bad at** cooking.*   **3** serious: *a bad injury* ○ *bad flooding*   **4** evil or morally unacceptable: *Stealing is a bad thing to do.*   **5** not lucky, or not happening in a way that you would like: *It was just **bad luck** that she heard us.* ○ *I'll call you later if this is a **bad time** for you.*   **6** Food that is bad is not fresh and cannot be eaten.   **7** not bad fairly good: *"How was your sandwich?" "Not bad."*   **8** be bad for *someone* to be harmful for someone: *Too much fat is bad for you.*   **9** feel bad to feel guilty: *I felt **bad about** leaving her by herself.*   **10** too bad used to say that you are sorry about a situation: *"He didn't get the job." "Oh, that's too bad."*

badge /bædʒ/ noun   a small piece of metal, plastic, cloth, etc., with words or a picture on it, that is pinned or sewn to your clothes: *a name badge*

badly /ˈbæd·li/ adv   **1** **A2** not well: *You're behaving very badly.* ○ *The team played badly in the first half.* ○ *Nurses are **badly paid** (= do not earn much money).*   **2** **A2** seriously: *He was badly injured in the accident.*   **3** **A2** very much: *He needs the money badly.*   **4** in an unpleasant way: *I think they treated her very badly.*

badminton /ˈbæd·mɪn·t°n/ noun [no plural]   **A2** a sport in which two or four people hit a small object that looks like a ball with feathers on it over a net

bags

sandwich bag

plastic bag   shopping bag

bag /bæg/ noun   **A1** a container made of paper, plastic, cloth, or other material, used for carrying things: *a paper bag* ○ *I was carrying three **bags of** groceries.*
→ See picture at **container**

bagel /ˈbeɪ·gəl/ noun
a type of bread for one person to eat that is made in the shape of a ring

bagel

baggage /ˈbæg·ɪdʒ/ noun [no plural]
B1 all the cases and bags that you take with you when you travel: *I waited at the baggage claim* (= the place where you get your baggage at the airport).

baggy /ˈbæg·i/ adj (comparative **baggier**, superlative **baggiest**)   Baggy clothes are big and loose.

bait /beɪt/ noun [no plural]   food that is used to attract and catch animals or fish

bake /beɪk/ verb (present participle **baking**, past tense and past participle **baked**)   **A2** to cook something such as bread or a cake in an oven: *I baked a cake for the party.*
→ See picture at **cook**

baked beans /ˈbeɪkt ˈbɪnz/ plural noun   beans cooked in a thick, slightly sweet sauce, often sold in cans

a
b
c
d
e
f
g
h
i
j
k
l
m
n
o
p
q
r
s
t
u
v
w
x
y
z

baker /ˈbeɪ·kər/ *noun* **B1** someone who makes and sells bread, cakes, etc.

bakery /ˈbeɪ·kə·ri/ *noun* (plural **bakeries**) a store or part of a store where you can buy bread, cakes, etc.

balance¹ /ˈbæl·əns/ *noun* **1** [no plural] a state in which weight is spread in such a way that something does not fall over: *I lost my balance and fell off the bike.* **2** [no plural] a state in which the correct amount of importance is given to each thing so that a situation is successful: *It's hard to find the **right balance between** doing too much exercise and not doing enough.* **3** the amount of money that you still have to pay, or that you have left to use: *I always pay off the balance on my credit card each month.*

balance² /ˈbæl·əns/ *verb* (present participle **balancing**, past tense and past participle **balanced**) **1** to be in a position where you will not fall to either side, or to put something in this position: *She was trying to balance a book on her head.* **2** to give the same amount of attention to each thing: *I try to balance work and family commitments.*

balcony /ˈbæl·kə·ni/ *noun* (plural **balconies**) **B1** an area with a wall or bars around it that is on the outside wall of building on an upper level

bald /bɔld/ *adj* **B1** with little or no hair: *John started to **go bald** at an early age.*
→ See **Hair** on page C9

balls

baseball · soccer ball · tennis ball · football · golf ball · basketball

ball /bɔl/ *noun* **A1** a round object that you throw, kick, or hit in a game, or

something with this shape: *a tennis ball* ○ *a ball of string*

ballet /bæˈleɪ/ *noun* [no plural] **B1** a type of dancing that is done in a theater and tells a story, usually with music: *She wants to be a ballet dancer.*

balloon /bəˈlun/ *noun* **A2** a thin rubber bag that you blow air into or fill with light gas until it is round and can float, used as a decoration or a toy

ballot /ˈbæl·ət/ *noun* a secret written vote

ballpoint pen /ˈbɔlˌpɔɪnt ˈpen/ *noun* a pen with a small ball in the end that rolls ink onto paper

bamboo /bæmˈbu/ *noun* [no plural] a tall plant with hard, hollow stems, often used for making furniture

bamboo

ban¹ /bæn/ *verb* (present participle **banning**, past tense and past participle **banned**) to officially stop a person or many people from doing something: *Mom thinks plastic bags should be banned.*

ban² /bæn/ *noun* an official rule that people must not do or use something: *There is a **ban on** smoking in restaurants.*

banana /bəˈnæn·ə/ *noun* **A1** a long, white fruit with a yellow skin
→ See **Fruits and Vegetables** on page C8

band /bænd/ *noun* **band** **1** **A1** a group of musicians who play modern music together: *a jazz band* **2** a line of a different color or design **3** a piece of material put around something: *a rubber band*

bandage¹ /ˈbæn·dɪdʒ/ *noun* **1** **A2** a long piece of cloth that you wrap around a part of the body that is hurt **2** a thin piece of material that you stick to the skin to cover a small cut

bandage² /ˈbæn·dɪdʒ/ *verb* (present participle **bandaging**, past tense and past participle **bandaged**) to put a bandage around a part of the body

Band-Aid /ˈbændˌeɪd/ **noun** trademark a small plastic bandage

bang[1] /bæŋ/ **noun 1** a sudden, loud noise: *The door shut with a bang.* **2** an act of suddenly hitting part of your body on something hard: *She had a painful **bang on** her head.*

bang[2] /bæŋ/ **verb 1** to make a loud noise by hitting something against something hard: *We heard the door bang.* **2** to hit part of your body against something hard: *Ted fell and banged his head.*

bangs /bæŋz/ **plural noun** hair that is cut short and straight at the top of someone's face

banish /ˈbænɪʃ/ **verb** to send someone away from a place as a punishment

banister

banister

/ˈbæn·ə·stər/ **noun** a long piece of wood that you hold as you go up or down stairs

bank[1] /bæŋk/ **noun 1** **A1** a place where you can keep or borrow money: *I need to go to the bank on my way home.* **2** **B1** the land along the side of a river

bank[2] /bæŋk/ **verb** to put or keep money in a bank: *Who do you **bank** with?*

bank account /ˈbæŋk əˌkaʊnt/ **noun** **B1** an arrangement with a bank to keep your money there and take it out when you need it

banker /ˈbæŋ·kər/ **noun** someone who has an important job in a bank

banking /ˈbæŋ·kɪŋ/ **noun** [no plural] the business of operating a bank

bankrupt /ˈbæŋk·rəpt/ **adj** not having enough money to pay what you owe to others: *He **went bankrupt** after only a year in business.*

banner /ˈbæn·ər/ **noun** a long piece of cloth, often stretched between poles, with words or a sign written on it

banquet /ˈbæŋ·kwɪt/ **noun** a dinner for many people, usually for a special occasion: *a wedding banquet*

baptism /ˈbæp·tɪz·əm/ **noun** a Christian ceremony in which water is put on someone to show that he or she has become a member of the Church

baptize /bæpˈtaɪz/, /ˈbæp·taɪz/ **verb** (present participle **baptizing**, past tense and past participle **baptized**) to do a baptism ceremony for someone

bar[1] /bɑr/ **noun 1** **A1** a place where alcoholic drinks are sold and drunk: *I met him in a bar in Soho.* **2** **B1** a small block of something solid: *a chocolate bar* → See **Quantities** on page C14 **3** a long, thin piece of metal or wood: *There were bars on the windows.*

bar[2] /bɑr/ **verb** (present participle **barring**, past tense and past participle **barred**) to officially stop someone from doing something or going somewhere: *The court **barred** him **from** driving.*

barbecue /ˈbɑr·bɪˌkju/ **noun 1** **A2** a party at which you cook food over a fire outdoors **2** **A2** a piece of equipment with a metal frame for cooking food over a fire outdoors
• **barbecue verb** **B1** *barbecued steaks*

barbed wire /ˈbɑrbd ˈwaɪər/ **noun** [no plural] strong wire with short, sharp points on it to keep people out of a place: *a barbed wire fence*

barbed wire

barber /ˈbɑr·bər/ **noun** someone whose job is to cut men's hair

bare /beər/ **adj 1** not covered by clothes: *bare legs* **2** not covered by anything: *The walls were bare.*

barefoot /ˈbeər·fʊt/ **adj, adv** not wearing any shoes or socks: *They ran barefoot along the beach.*

barely /ˈbeər·li/ **adv** only just: *He was barely alive when they found him.*

bargain[1] /ˈbɑr·gən/ **noun** something that is sold for less than its usual price: *At $8.95, it's a bargain.*

bargain[2] /ˈbɑr·gən/ **verb** to try to agree how much you will pay for something: *We **bargained over** the price.*

a
b
c
d
e
f
g
h
i
j
k
l
m
n
o
p
q
r
s
t
u
v
w
x
y
z

a
b
c
d
e
f
g
h
i
j
k
l
m
n
o
p
q
r
s
t
u
v
w
x
y
z

barge /bɑrdʒ/ noun   a long, narrow boat with a flat bottom that is used to carry things

bark¹ /bɑrk/ noun   **1** [no plural] the hard substance that covers the surface of a tree   **2** the sound that a dog makes

bark² /bɑrk/ verb   If a dog barks, it makes loud, short sounds.

barley /'bɑr·li/ noun [no plural]   a type of grain used for making food and alcoholic drinks

barn /bɑrn/ noun   a large building on a farm where crops or animals are kept

barracks /'bær·əks/ noun   a building or group of buildings where soldiers live: *an army barracks*

barrel /'bær·əl/ noun
1 a large, round container for storing liquids such as oil or wine   **2** the tube in a gun that the bullet shoots out of

barrel

barrier /'bær·i·ər/ noun
1 a wall that stops people from going into an area: *Police put up barriers to hold back the crowd.*   **2** something that prevents people from doing what they want to do: *Shyness is one of the biggest barriers to making friends.*

bartender /'bɑr·ten·dər/ noun   someone who serves drinks in a bar

base¹ /beɪs/ noun   **1** the bottom part of something: *We started climbing at the base of the mountain.*   **2** the main place where a person lives or works, or from where he or she does things: *The hotel is an excellent base for exploring the city.*   **3** a place where people in the armed forces live and work: *an American Air Force base*

base² /beɪs/ verb (present participle **basing**, past tense and past participle **based**)
be based at/in If you are based at or in somewhere, that is where you live or work: *The company is based in Geneva.*
base something on something phrasal verb **B1** If you base something on facts or ideas, you use those facts or ideas to develop it: *This book is based on a true story.*

baseball /'beɪs‚bɔl/ noun   **1** [no plural] a game in which two teams try to win points by hitting a ball and running around four fixed points → See **Sports 2** on page C12   **2** **A1** the ball used in this game → See picture at **ball**

baseball cap /'beɪs‚bɔl ‚kæp/ noun   a hat with a curved piece of stiff material at the front
→ See **Clothes** on page C5

basement /'beɪs·mənt/ noun   part of a building that is under the level of the ground

bases /'beɪ·siz/   plural of basis

basic /'beɪ·sɪk/ adj   **1** **B1** being the main or most important part of something: *These are basic needs, such as food and water.*   **2** **B1** very simple, with nothing special added: *The software is very basic.*

basically /'beɪ·sɪk·li/ adv   **1** in the most important ways: *The two computers are basically the same.*   **2** used before you explain something simply: *Basically, there aren't enough people.*

basics /'beɪ·sɪks/ plural noun   the most important facts, skills, or needs: *I need to learn the basics of first aid.*

basil /'bæz·əl/, /'beɪ·zəl/ noun [no plural]   a plant whose leaves are used to add flavor to food

basis /'beɪ·sɪs/ noun (plural **bases**)
1 a way or method of doing something: *We are living here on a temporary basis.*   **2 on a daily/monthly/regular basis** how often something is done: *Meetings are held on a weekly basis.*   **3** a situation or idea from which something can develop: *Dani's essay can serve as **a basis for** our discussion.*

basket /'bæs·kɪt/ noun **B1** a container for carrying things, made of thin strips of plastic, metal, or wood: *a shopping basket*

baskets

basketball /ˈbæs·kɪt̩ˌbɔl/ *noun* **1** 🅐 [no plural] a game in which two teams try to win points by throwing a ball through a high net → See **Sports 2** on page C16 **2** 🅐 the ball used in this game → See picture at **ball**

bass /beɪs/ *adj* producing low musical notes: *a bass guitar*

bat¹ /bæt/ *noun* **1** 🅐 a piece of wood used to hit the ball in sports such as baseball **2** 🅑 a small animal like a mouse with wings that flies at night

bat² /bæt/ *verb* (present participle **batting**, past tense and past participle **batted**) to try to hit a ball with a bat

bath /bæθ/ *noun* 🅐 an act of washing your body when sitting in water: *I'll just take a quick bath.*

bathe /beɪð/ *verb* (present participle **bathing**, past tense and past participle **bathed**) **1** to wash yourself in a bathtub **2** to swim

bathing suit /ˈbeɪ·ðɪŋ ˌsut/ *noun* (also **swimsuit**) 🅐 a piece of clothing that you wear for swimming

bathrobe /ˈbæθˌroʊb/ *noun* a loose piece of clothing, like a soft coat, that you wear before or after you take a bath

bathroom /ˈbæθˌrum/, /ˈbæθˌrʊm/ *noun* **1** 🅐 a room with a toilet, sink (=bowl for washing), and often a bathtub (=container you sit in to wash) **2 go to the bathroom** to use the toilet → See **The Bathroom** on page C1

bathtub /ˈbæθˌtʌb/ *noun* 🅐 the container that you fill with water and sit in to wash your body

bathtub

battery /ˈbæt̬·ə·ri/ *noun* (plural **batteries**) 🅐 an object that provides electricity for things such as radios, toys, or cars

battery

battle¹ /ˈbæt̬·ᵊl/ *noun* **1** 🅑 a fight between two armies in a war: *the Battle of Gettysburg* **2** a fight against something

that is very difficult, or that is hurting you: *a long battle with cancer*

battle² /ˈbæt̬·ᵊl/ *verb* (present participle **battling**, past tense and past participle **battled**) to try very hard to do something difficult: *Both teams **are battling for** a place in the finals.*

bay /beɪ/ *noun* 🅑 an area of coast where the land curves in: *a sandy bay*

B.C. /ˈbiˈsi/ used to show that a particular year came before the birth of Christ: *331 B.C.*

be¹ /bi/ *verb* (present participle **being**, past tense **was**, past participle **been**) **1** 🅐 used to describe someone or something: *I'm Maria (=I am Maria).* ∘ *I'm sixteen.* ∘ *He's German (=He is German).* ∘ *They were sick.* ∘ *Be quiet!* **2 there is/there are** 🅐 used to show that someone or something exists: *There are three of us.* ∘ *Is there a bank near here?* **3** 🅐 used to show where someone or something is: *She's in the kitchen.* **4 it is, it was, etc.** used to give a fact or your opinion about something: *It's a good idea.* ∘ *It's a big problem.*

be² /bi/ *auxiliary verb* (present participle **being**, past tense **was**, past participle **been**) **1** 🅐 used with the -ing form of other verbs to describe actions that are or were still happening: *Are you leaving?* ∘ *He was talking to Andrea.* **2** 🅐 used with other verbs to describe actions that will happen in the future: *I'm going to Florida next week.* ∘ *I'll be coming back on Tuesday.* **3** 🅐 used with the past participle of other verbs to show that something happens to someone or something: *He was injured in a car crash.* ∘ *The results will be announced next week.*

beach /bitʃ/ *noun* 🅐 an area of sand or rocks next to the ocean

beak /bik/ *noun* the hard part of a bird's mouth

beam /bim/ *noun* **1** a line of light that shines from something: *a laser beam* → See picture at **light noun** **2** a long, thick

| æ cat | ɑ hot | e get | ɪ sit | i see | ɔ saw | ʊ book | u too | ʌ cut | ə about | ɑr mother | ɜr turn | ɔr for | aɪ my | aʊ how | eɪ say | ɔɪ boy |

piece of wood that supports weight in a building

bean /biːn/ noun **1** (A2) a seed or seed case of some climbing plants, that is used as food: *lima beans* **2** A plant seed used to make coffee and chocolate: *coffee beans*

bear[1] /beər/ verb (present participle **bearing**, past tense **bore**, past participle **borne**) **1** to accept someone or something bad: *I can't bear her* (= I dislike her very much). ○ *The pain was too much to bear.* **2** to support something: *I don't think that chair will bear his weight.*

bear[2] /beər/ noun
(A2) a large, strong, wild animal with thick fur

bear

beard /bɪərd/ noun
(A1) the hair that grows on a man's chin (= the bottom of his face)
→ See **Hair** on page C9

beast /biːst/ noun formal an animal, especially a large or wild one

beat[1] /biːt/ verb (present participle **beating**, past tense **beat**, past participle **beaten**) **1** (B1) to defeat someone in a competition: *Our team beat the Yankees 3–1.* **2** (B1) When your heart beats, it makes regular movements and sounds: *By the time the doctor arrived, his heart had stopped beating.* **3** to hit a person or animal repeatedly: *They saw him beating his dog with a stick.* **4** to hit against something hard, making a regular sound: *Rain beat against the windows.*

beat someone up phrasal verb to hit or kick someone until he or she is hurt: *He beat up one of the other prisoners.*

beat[2] /biːt/ noun **1** a regular sound that is made by your heart or by something hitting a surface: *the beat of a drum* **2** the main rhythm of a piece of music: *I like music with a strong beat.*

beautiful /ˈbjuː.tɪ.fəl/ adj **1** (A1) very attractive: *a beautiful woman* ○ *beautiful scenery* **2** (A1) very pleasant: *beautiful music* ○ *It's a beautiful day* (= the sun is shining).
• **beautifully** adv (B1) *She sings beautifully.*

> **! Common mistake: beautiful**
>
> People often spell **beautiful** wrong. Remember that it starts with **beau** and has one **l** at the end.

beauty /ˈbjuː.ti/ noun [no plural] (B1) the quality of being beautiful: *The area is famous for its natural beauty.*

became /bɪˈkeɪm/ past tense of become

because /bɪˈkɒz/, /bɪˈkʌz/ conjunction (A1) used to give a reason for something: *I'm calling because I need to ask you something.*

> **! Common mistake: because**
>
> People often spell **because** wrong. Remember that it has **au** in the middle, like **cause**.

because of /bɪˈkɒz əv/, /bɪˈkʌz əv/ preposition (B1) as a result of someone or something: *She is coughing because of her sore throat.*

become /bɪˈkʌm/ verb (present participle **becoming**, past tense **became**, past participle **become**) (A2) to begin to be something: *They became great friends.*

bed /bed/ noun **1** (A1) a piece of furniture that you sleep on: *What time did you go to bed last night?* ○ *She's still in bed.* ○ *Did you make the bed* (= arrange the bed neatly after you slept in it)? **2** the ground at the bottom of the sea or a river: *the sea bed*

bed and breakfast /ˈbed ən ˈbrek.fəst/ noun a house or small hotel where you pay for a room to sleep in for the night and a meal in the morning

bedclothes /ˈbed.kləʊðz/, /ˈbed.kləʊz/ plural noun the sheets and other pieces of cloth that cover you and keep you warm in bed

bedroom /ˈbed.ruːm/, /ˈbed.rʊm/ noun (A1) a room used for sleeping in

bedspread /ˈbed.spred/ noun a cloth cover that is put over a bed

bedtime /ˈbed.taɪm/ noun the time that you usually go to bed

bee /biː/ noun **B1** a yellow and black insect that makes honey (=sweet, sticky food)

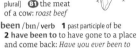
bee

beef /biːf/ noun [no plural] **B1** the meat of a cow: *roast beef*

been /bɪn/ verb **1** past participle of be **2 have been** to have gone to a place and come back: *Have you ever been to Thailand?*

beep /biːp/ verb If a machine beeps, it makes a short, high noise.
• beep noun

beer /bɪər/ noun **A1** an alcoholic drink made from grain: *a bottle of beer*

beetle /ˈbiː.tᵊl/ noun an insect with a hard, usually black, shiny body

beet /ˈbiːt/ noun a round, dark red vegetable, that is usually cooked

before¹ /bɪˈfɔːr/ preposition **1 A1** earlier than something or someone: *a week before Christmas* ○ *She arrived before me.* **2 A1** at a place where you arrive first when going toward another place: *The hospital is just before the bridge.* **3 B1** in front of someone or something in an order or a list: *K comes before L in the English alphabet.* **4 B1** in a position in front of someone or something: *I've never performed this before an audience.*

before² /bɪˈfɔːr/ conjunction **1 A2** earlier than the time when something happens: *He was a teacher before he became famous.* **2 B1** in order to avoid something bad happening: *Put that stick down before you hurt someone!* **3 B1** until: *It took a few moments before I realized that he was joking.*

before³ /bɪˈfɔːr/ adv **A2** at an earlier time: *I've never seen her before.*

beg /beg/ verb (present participle **begging**, past tense and past participle **begged**) **1** to ask someone for food or money, because you do not have any: *Young children were begging on the streets.* **2** to

ask for something in a strong and emotional way: *I begged him not to leave.*

began /bɪˈgæn/ past tense of begin

beggar /ˈbeg.ər/ noun a poor person who asks other people for money and food

begin /bɪˈgɪn/ verb (present participle **beginning**, past tense **began**, past participle **begun**) **1 A1** to start to happen: *What time does the movie begin?* **2 A2** to start to do something: *She began to cry.* **3 begin with** *something* **B1** to have something at the start: *Local phone numbers begin with 212.* **4 to begin with B1** at the start of a situation: *To begin with, I was very nervous.*

beginner /bɪˈgɪn.ər/ noun **A2** someone who is learning or doing something for the first time: *a Spanish class for beginners*

beginning /bɪˈgɪn.ɪŋ/ noun **A2** the start of something: *We met at the beginning of 2008.*

begun /bɪˈgʌn/ past participle of begin

behalf /bɪˈhæf/ noun **on behalf of** *someone* for someone or instead of someone: *I accept this prize on behalf of Ms. Jones, who could not be here tonight.*

behave /bɪˈheɪv/ verb (present participle **behaving**, past tense and past participle **behaved**) **1 B1** to do or say things in a particular way: *He behaved very badly.* ○ *You're behaving like a child!* **2 behave** *yourself* **B1** to be polite and not make a situation difficult: *Did the children behave themselves?*

behavior /bɪˈheɪv.jər/ noun [no plural] **B1** the way that you behave: *good/bad behavior*

behind¹ /bɪˈhaɪnd/ preposition **1 A1** at or to the back of someone or something: *Close the door behind you.* ○ *There's a hotel behind the train station.* **2 B1** slower or less successful than someone or something: *Our team is three points behind the winners.* **3 B1** giving your help or support to someone: *The group is 100 percent behind her.*

behind² /bɪˈhaɪnd/ adv **1 A2** at or to the back of someone or something:

a b c d e f g h i j k l m n o p q r s t u v w x y z

Somebody pulled me from behind.
2 A2 in the place where someone or something was before: *When we got to the restaurant, I realized that I had left my purse **behind**.*

beige[1] /beɪʒ/ *adj* being a pale brown color

beige[2] /beɪʒ/ *noun* the color beige
→ See **Colors** on page C6

being[1] /'biː·ɪŋ/ A1 present participle of be

being[2] /'biː·ɪŋ/ *noun* a living person or imaginary creature: *human beings*

belief /bɪ'liːf/ *noun* **1** an idea that you are certain is true: *political beliefs* **2** a strong feeling that something is true or real: *my belief in God* **3 beyond belief** too bad, good, difficult, etc. to be imagined: *Her kindness is beyond belief.*

believable /bɪ'liː·və·bəl/ *adj* If something is believable, you can believe that it could be true or real.

believe /bɪ'liːv/ *verb* (present participle **believing**, past tense and past participle **believed**) **1** A2 to think that something is true, or that what someone says is true: *She says she's only thirty, but I don't believe it.* ○ *Do you believe him?* **2** A2 to think something, although you are not completely sure: *The murderer is believed to be in his thirties.* **3 believe it or not** B1 used to say that something surprising is true: *He even remembered my birthday, believe it or not.* **4 not believe your eyes/ears** B1 to be very surprised when you see someone or something, or when you hear what someone says: *I couldn't believe my ears when Dan said they were getting married.*
believe in *something phrasal verb* B1 to be certain that something exists: *Do you believe in ghosts?*
believe in *something/in doing something phrasal verb* to be confident that something is good and right: *They don't believe in living together before marriage.*

> ⚠️ **Common mistake: believe**
>
> People often spell **believe** wrong. Remember that the **i** comes before the **e**.

bell /bel/ *noun* **1** B1 an electrical object that makes a ringing sound when you press a switch: *Please **ring the bell** for service.* **2** a hollow metal object, shaped like a cup, that makes a ringing sound: *church bells*

bells

belong /bɪ'lɔŋ/ *verb* **1** to be in the right place: *That chair belongs in the dining room.* **2** to feel happy or comfortable in a situation: *I spent two years in New York, but I never felt that I belonged there.*
belong to *someone phrasal verb* If something belongs to you, you own it: *This necklace belonged to my grandmother.*
belong to *something phrasal verb* B1 to be a member of an organization: *We belong to the same health club.*

belongings /bɪ'lɔŋ·ɪŋz/ *plural noun* the things that you own: *I took a few personal belongings with me.*

below /bɪ'loʊ/ *adv, preposition* **1** A1 in a lower position than someone or something else: *He could hear people shouting below his window.* **2** B1 less than an amount or level: *The temperature there rarely drops below 70 degrees.*

belt /belt/ *noun* A2 a thin piece of leather or cloth that you wear around the middle of your body
→ See **Clothes** on page C5

bench /bentʃ/ *noun* a long seat for two or more people, usually made of wood: *a park bench*

bend[1] /bend/ *verb* (past tense and past participle **bent**) **1** to move your body or part of your body so that it is not straight: *Bend your knees when lifting heavy objects.* **2** to become curved, or to make something become curved: *The road bent to the left.*

bend[2] /bend/ noun   a curved part of something: *a bend in the road/river*

beneath /bɪˈniːθ/ adv, preposition
B1 under something, or in a lower position than something: *He hid the letter beneath a pile of papers.*

benefit[1] /ˈben·ə·fɪt/ noun   **1** **B1** something good that helps you: *I've had the benefit of a happy childhood.*   **2** for someone's benefit in order to help someone: *We bought the piano for the children's benefit.*

benefit[2] /ˈben·ə·fɪt/ verb   to help someone: *These changes will benefit the whole company.*

bent[1] /bent/   past tense and past participle of bend

bent[2] /bent/ adj   Something that is bent has a curve or angle in it instead of being straight or flat: *The metal bars were bent and twisted.*

berry /ˈber·i/ noun (plural **berries**)   a small, round fruit on some plants and trees

beside /bɪˈsaɪd/ preposition   **A2** next to someone or something: *She sat down beside him.*

besides[1] /bɪˈsaɪdz/ preposition   **B1** in addition to: *Do you play any other sports besides football?*

besides[2] /bɪˈsaɪdz/ adv   **1** **B1** used to give another reason for something: *She won't mind if you're late – besides, it's not your fault.*   **2** **B1** in addition to: *Besides taking care of the children, she also runs a successful business.*

best[1] /best/ adj   **A1** superlative of good: better than any other: *She's one of our best students.* ∘ *Susie is my best friend.*

best[2] /best/ adv   **A1** superlative of well: most, or more than any other: *Which of the songs did you like best?*   **2** **B1** in the most suitable or satisfactory way: *I sleep best with the windows open.*

best[3] /best/ noun   **1** all the best! **A2** used to say that you hope someone will be

happy, healthy, successful, etc.: *All the best for the game tomorrow!*   **2** at its best **B1** at the highest level of achievement or quality: *The new building is an example of architecture at its best.*   **3** the best **B1** someone or something that is better than any other: *He's the best of the new players.*   **4** do/try your best **B1** to try very hard to do something: *I did my best to persuade him.*   **5** make the best of *something* to try to be positive about a situation you do not like but cannot change: *Our hotel room is small, but we'll just have to make the best of it.*

bestseller /ˈbestˈsel·ər/ noun   a very popular book that many people have bought: *The "Harry Potter" novels are all bestsellers.*

• **best-selling** adj *It's the best-selling book of the year.*

bet[1] /bet/ verb (present participle **betting**, past tense and past participle **bet**)   **1** to risk money on the result of a game or competition: *I bet him a dollar that I was right.*   **2** I bet informal **B1** something you say to show that you are certain something is true or will happen: *I bet he'll be late.*

bet[2] /bet/ noun   an act of risking money on the result of a game or competition: *She won her bet.*

betray /bɪˈtreɪ/ verb   to behave in a dishonest way to someone who trusts you

better[1] /ˈbet·ər/ adj   **1** **A1** comparative of good: of a higher quality or more enjoyable than someone or something else: *He got a better job in Chicago.* ∘ *Her English is getting better (=improving).*   **2** **A1** less ill than before: *I feel much better.* ∘ *I hope you get better soon.*   **3** be better off richer: *We're better off now that we're both working.*   **4** be better off in a better situation: *Steve's an idiot – you'd be better off without him.*

better[2] /ˈbet·ər/ adv   **1** **A1** comparative of well: more, or in a more successful way: *I'd like to get to know him better.* ∘ *Helen did much better than I did on the exam.*   **2** you had better do *something* **A2** used to say that someone should do: *You'd better hurry or you'll miss the train.*

between[1] /bɪˈtwin/ **preposition** **1** 🄐 in the space that separates two places, people, or things: *The town lies halfway between Dallas and Houston.* **2** 🄐 in the period of time that separates two events or times: *Please call back between the hours of 9 a.m. and 5 p.m.* **3** 🄐 involving two or more groups of people: *Tonight's game is between the New Orleans Saints and the Los Angeles Rams.* **4** 🄐 connecting two or more places or things: *the train service between Boston and New York* **5** 🄐 used when comparing two people or things: *What's the **difference** between these two cameras?* **6** 🄐 If something is between two amounts, it is larger than the first amount but smaller than the second: *The temperature will be between 20 and 25 degrees today.* **7** 🄑 shared by a particular number of people: *We shared the cake between us.*

between[2] /bɪˈtwin/ **adv** **1** 🄑 in the space that separates two places, places, or things: *The houses were built without much room **in between**.* **2** 🄑 in the period of time that separates two events or times: *There are trains at 6:15 and 10:30, but nothing **in between**.*

beware /bɪˈwɛər/ **verb** used in order to warn someone to be careful: ***Beware** of the dog.*

beyond /biˈɑnd/ **preposition** **1** 🄑 on the other side of something: *Our house is just beyond the bridge.* **2** 🄑 continuing after a particular time or date: *Not many people live beyond the age of a hundred.*

the Bible /ˈbaɪ·bəl/ **noun** **1** the holy book of Christianity **2** the holy book of Judaism

bicycle /ˈbaɪ·sɪ·kəl/ **noun** **bicycle** 🄐 a vehicle with two wheels that you sit on and move by turning the two pedals (=parts you press with your feet)
→ See **Sports 2** on page C16

bicycle lane /ˈbaɪ·sɪ·kəl ˌleɪn/ **noun** (also **bike lane**) a part of a road or a special path that only people riding bicycles can use

bid[1] /bɪd/ **noun** **1** an attempt to do something good: *a successful **bid for** re-election* **2** an offer to pay a particular amount of money for something: *I made a **bid of** $150 **for** the painting.*

bid[2] /bɪd/ **verb** (present participle **bidding**, past tense and past participle **bid**) to offer to pay an amount of money for something: *They **bid** $500 million **for** the company.*

big /bɪɡ/ **adj** (comparative **bigger**, superlative **biggest**) **1** 🄐 large in size or amount: *I come from a big family.* ○ *We're looking for a bigger house.* → Opposite **small adj** (1), **little adj** (1) **2** 🄐 important or serious: *Buying that car was a big mistake.* **3 your big brother/sister** informal 🄐 your older brother or sister

bike[1] /baɪk/ **noun** informal **1** 🄐 short form of bicycle → See **Sports 2** on page C16 **2** 🄑 short form of motorcycle: *He came **on** his **bike**.*

bike[2] /baɪk/ **verb** informal to ride a bicycle • **biking noun** [no plural]

bikini /bəˈki·ni/ **noun** a piece of clothing with two parts that women wear for swimming
→ See **Clothes** on page C5

bilingual /ˌbaɪˈlɪŋ·ɡwəl/ **adj** using or able to speak two languages: *a bilingual dictionary* ○ *She's bilingual in English and Spanish.*

bill /bɪl/ **noun** **1** 🄐 a piece of paper that tells you how much you must pay for something: *Have you **paid** the electricity **bill**?* **2** a piece of paper money: *a five-dollar bill*

billion /ˈbɪl·jən/ 🄑 the number 1,000,000,000

bin /bɪn/ **noun** a large container that is used to store things: *a recycling bin*

bind /baɪnd/ **verb** (past tense and past participle **bound**) to tie something together with string, rope, etc.: *His hands were bound behind his back.*

binder /ˈbaɪn·dər/ **noun** a stiff cover that can hold loose papers, often one that has metal rings in it
→ See **The Classroom** on page C4

binoculars /bɪˈnɑk·jə·lərz/ **binoculars**
plural noun a piece of
equipment for looking at
things that are far away,
made from two tubes with
glass at the ends

biography /baɪˈɑg·rə·fi/ **noun** (plural
biographies) **B1** the story of a person's life written by another person

biological /ˌbaɪ·əˈlɑdʒ·ɪ·kəl/ **adj** connected with the natural processes of living things, such as plants and animals:
the biological sciences

biologist /baɪˈɑl·ə·dʒɪst/ **noun**
B1 a scientist who does work that involves biology

biology /baɪˈɑl·ə·dʒi/ **noun** [no plural]
A2 the study of living things

bird /bɜrd/ **noun**   **bird**
A1 an animal that has
wings and feathers and is
usually able to fly

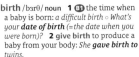

birth /bɜrθ/ **noun**   **1** **B1** the time when
a baby is born: *a difficult birth* ○ *What's
your **date of birth** (= the date when you
were born)?*   **2** **give birth** to produce a
baby from your body: *She **gave birth** to
twins.*

birthday /ˈbɜrθ·deɪ/ **noun**   **A1** the day
of the year on which someone was born:
Her birthday is on March eighteenth.
○ *Happy Birthday!*

biscuit /ˈbɪs·kɪt/ **noun** a small, round
bread that is light and soft

bishop /ˈbɪʃ·əp/ **noun** an important
priest in some Christian churches: *the
Bishop of Newark*

bit[1] /bɪt/ past tense of bite

bit[2] /bɪt/ **noun**   **1** **A2** a small amount or
piece of something: *There's a little bit
more pasta left.*   **2 a bit** **A2** slightly: *It
was a bit too expensive.*   **3 a bit** informal a
short period of time: *I'll see you **in a bit**.*
4 quite a bit informal **B1** a lot: *He does
quite a bit of traveling.*   **5 bit by bit** gradually: *She saved up the money, bit by bit.*
6 a unit of information in a computer

bite[1] /baɪt/ **verb** (present participle **biting**,
past tense **bit**, past participle **bitten**) **B1** to
cut something using your teeth: *She **bit**
into an apple.* ○ *He was bitten by a dog.*

bite[2] /baɪt/ **noun**   **1** a piece taken from
food when you bite it: *She **took a bite**
from her pizza.*   **2** an injury caused
when an animal or insect bites you:
mosquito bites

bitten /ˈbɪt·ən/ past participle of bite

bitter /ˈbɪt·ər/ **adj**   **1** **B1** having a strong,
unpleasant taste   **2** angry and upset:
*She is still very **bitter about** the way she
was treated.*   **3** very cold   **4** making
you feel very unhappy or angry: *Failing
the test was a bitter disappointment for me.*
• **bitterness** noun [no plural]

bizarre /bɪˈzɑr/ **adj** very strange and
surprising: *bizarre behavior*
• **bizarrely** adv

black[1] /blæk/ **adj**   **1** **A1** being the color
of the sky on a dark night: *a black jacket*
2 **A2** Someone who is black has the
dark skin typical of people from Africa:
black Americans   **3** funny about unpleasant or frightening subjects: *black
comedy*
• **blackness** noun [no plural]

black[2] /blæk/ **noun** **A2** the color of the
sky on a dark night: *She always dresses
in black.*
→ See **Colors** on page C6

blackberry /ˈblæk·ber·i/ **noun** (plural
blackberries) a small, soft, purple fruit
with seeds

blackboard /ˈblæk·bɔrd/ **noun** (also
chalkboard) **A2** a large, black or green
board that teachers write on with chalk
(= soft, white rock)

blackmail /ˈblæk·meɪl/ **noun** [no plural]
a situation in which someone forces you
to do something, or to pay him or her-
money, by saying he or she will tell another person something secret
• **blackmail verb**

blade /bleɪd/ **noun**   **1** the flat, sharp,
metal part of a knife, tool, or weapon
2 a long, thin leaf of grass: *a blade of
grass*

|æ cat|ɑ hot|e get|ɪ sit|i see|ɔ saw|ʊ book|u too|ʌ cut|ə about|ɚ mother|ɑr turn|ɔr for|ɑɪ my|ɑʊ how|eɪ say|ɔɪ boy|

a b c d e f g h i j k l m n o p q r s t u v w x y z

blame¹ /bleɪm/ **verb** (present participle **blaming**, past tense and past participle **blamed**) **B1** to say that someone or something has done something bad: *She still **blames** him **for** Tony's death.*

blame² /bleɪm/ **noun** [no plural] **take the blame** to be the person that everyone thinks has done something bad: *When a team loses, it's always the manager who takes the blame.*

bland /blænd/ **adj** **1** boring and without excitement **2** If food is bland, it has no taste.

blank /blæŋk/ **adj** **1** **B1** with no writing, pictures, or sound: *a blank page* ∘ *a blank CD* **2 go blank** If your mind goes blank, you suddenly cannot remember or think of something.

blanket /ˈblæŋ·kɪt/ **noun** **1** **A2** a thick, warm cover that you sleep under **2** a thick layer of something: *a blanket of snow*

blast /blæst/ **noun** **1** an explosion: *a bomb blast* **2** a sudden, strong movement of air: *a blast of cold air*

blaze¹ /bleɪz/ **verb** (present participle **blazing**, past tense and past participle **blazed**) to burn or shine very brightly or strongly: *the blazing sun*

blaze² /bleɪz/ **noun** **1** a large fire: *The blaze started in the hall.* **2 a blaze of color** a lot of bright colors: *The flowers were a blaze of color outside her window.*

bled /bled/ past tense and past participle of bleed

bleed /blid/ **verb** (past tense and past participle **bled**) **B1** to have blood coming out from a cut in your body

blend¹ /blend/ **verb** **1** to mix two or more things together completely: *Blend the sugar and butter till smooth.* **2** to look, sound, or taste good together: *The flavors blend very nicely.*

blend² /blend/ **noun** two or more things that are put together: *Their music is a blend of jazz and African rhythms.*

blender /ˈblen·dər/ **noun** an electric machine that turns soft foods into a smooth liquid

bless /bles/ **verb** **1** to ask God to help or protect someone or something: *The priest blessed their marriage.* **2 Bless you!** something you say when someone sneezes

blew /blu/ past tense of blow

blind¹ /blaɪnd/ **adj** **B1** not able to see: *She **went blind** after an accident.*
• **blindness noun** [no plural]

blind² /blaɪnd/ **noun** a cover that you pull down over a window

blink /blɪŋk/ **verb** to quickly close and open your eyes
• **blink noun**

blister /ˈblɪs·tər/ **noun** a raised area of skin that hurts, caused by rubbing or burning

blizzard /ˈblɪz·ərd/ **noun** a storm with strong winds and snow

block¹ /blak/ **noun** **1** **B1** the distance from one street to the next in streets: *They only live two blocks away from school.* **2** a solid piece of something, in the shape of a square or rectangle: *a block of wood*

block² /blak/ **verb** to stop someone or something from passing through a place: *A fallen tree blocked the road.*
block something up/block up *something* **phrasal verb** to fill a narrow space with something so that nothing can pass through: *In the fall, leaves block the drains up.*

blog¹ /blɔɡ/, /blɑɡ/ **noun** **B1** a record of your activities or opinions that you put on the Internet for other people to read and that you change regularly: *There are two or three blogs that I read daily.*

blog² /blɔɡ/, /blɑɡ/ **verb** **B1** to write a blog: *He blogs about traveling around the world.*

blogger /ˈblɔ·ɡər/, /ˈblɑɡ·ər/ **noun** **B1** someone who writes a blog: *Bloggers everywhere are commenting on the issue.*

blonde /blɑnd/ (also **blond**) **adj** **A2** Blonde hair is yellow.
→ See **Hair** on page C9

|oʊ go|ɑɪɑr **fire**|ɑʊər **hour**|eər **hair**|ɪər **ear**|ʊər **poor**|j **yet**|ʒ **measure**|ʃ **ship**|dʒ **judge**|tʃ **chin**|ð **that**|θ **thin**|ŋ **hang**|

blood /blʌd/ *noun* [no plural] **A2** the red liquid that flows around your body

bloom /blum/ *verb* If a plant blooms, its flowers open.

blossom /ˈblɒs·əm/ *noun* a small flower, or the small flowers on a tree or plant: *cherry blossom*

blouse /blaʊs/ *noun* a shirt that women wear

blow[1] /bloʊ/ *verb* (present participle **blowing**, past tense **blew**, past participle **blown**) **1** **B1** If the wind blows, it moves and makes currents of air: *The wind blew hard during the storm.* **2** **B1** to force air out through your mouth: *I blew on my coffee to cool it.* **3** **B1** to make a sound by forcing air out of your mouth and through a musical instrument: *Ann blew a few notes on the trumpet.* **4** If the wind blows something somewhere, it makes it move in that direction: *The storm blew a tree across the road.* **5 blow your nose** **B1** to clear your nose by forcing air through it into a piece of paper

blow (*something*) **away** *phrasal verb* **B1** If something blows away, or if the wind blows something away, that thing moves because the wind blows it: *The letter blew away and I had to run after it.*

blow (*something*) **down** *phrasal verb* **B1** If something blows down, or if the wind blows something down, that thing falls to the ground because the wind blows it: *The wind blew our fence down last night.*

blow *something* **out** *phrasal verb* **B1** to stop a flame burning by blowing on it: *Emma blew out the candle.*

blow *something* **up** *phrasal verb* **1** **B1** to destroy something with a bomb: *Terrorists blew up an office building.* **2** to fill something with air: *blowing up balloons*

blow[2] /bloʊ/ *noun* **1** a hard hit with a hand or heavy object: *He received a blow on the head.* **2** a shock or disappointment: *Losing his job was a terrible blow to him.*

blown /bloʊn/ past participle of blow

blue[1] /blu/ *adj* **A1** being the same color as the sky when there are no clouds: *a dark blue jacket*

blue[2] /blu/ *noun* **1** **A2** the color of the sky when there are no clouds **2 out of the blue** If something happens out of the blue, you did not expect it.
→ See Colors on page C6

blunt /blʌnt/ *adj* **1** not sharp: *a blunt knife* **2** saying exactly what you think without caring if you upset people
• **bluntness** *noun* [no plural]

blurred /blɜrd/ *adj* **1** not clear: *a blurred photograph* **2** If your sight is blurred, you cannot see clearly: *My eyes were blurred with tears.* ○ *blurred vision*

blush /blʌʃ/ *verb* If you blush, your face becomes red because you are embarrassed: *He blushed with shame.*
• **blush** *noun*

board[1] /bɔrd/ *noun* **1** **A1** a surface on the wall of a classroom that a teacher writes on: *The teacher wrote her name on the board.* **2** **A2** a piece of wood, plastic, etc. on a wall where information can be put: *I put the notice up on the bulletin board.* **3** **A2** a flat piece of wood, cardboard, etc. for playing games on: *a chess board* **4** **B1** a flat object or surface used for a particular purpose: *an ironing board* ○ *a cutting board* ○ *a chess board* **5** a long, thin, flat piece of wood: *He put some boards across the broken window.* **6** a group of people who control a company: *The board approved the sales plan.* **7 on board** **B1** on a boat, train, or plane **8** [no plural] meals that are provided to the students who live at a school or university: *Tuition fees do not include the price of **room and board** (=a place to live and food).*

board[2] /bɔrd/ *verb* **1** **B1** to get on a bus, boat, or plane **2** If a plane or train is boarding, passengers are getting onto it: *The plane is now boarding at gate 26.*

board game /ˈbɔrd ˌgeɪm/ *noun* **A2** a game such as chess that is played on a board: *It rained all day so we played lots of board games.*

æ cat | ɑ hot | e get | ɪ sit | i see | ɔ saw | ʊ book | u too | ʌ cut | ə about | ɑr mother | ɜr turn | ɔr for | ɑɪ my | aʊ how | eɪ say | ɔɪ boy

boarding pass /'bɔr·dɪŋ ˌpæs/ *noun*
a piece of paper you must show to get
on a plane or ship

boat /boʊt/ *noun* **A1** a vehicle for traveling on water: *a fishing boat*

body /'bɑd·i/ *noun* (plural **bodies**)
1 A1 all of a person or animal: *the human body* → See **The Body** on page C2
2 A2 a dead person: *Police found the
body in a field.* **3 B1** the main part of a
person or animal's body, not the head,
arms, or legs: *a dog with a thin body and
short legs*

boil /bɔɪl/ *verb* **1 A2** If a liquid boils, or
if you boil it, it reaches the temperature
where bubbles rise up in it and it produces steam: *Could you boil some water
for the pasta?* ∘ *boiling water* **2 B1** to
cook food in water that is boiling: *Boil
the eggs for three minutes.* → See picture at
cook 3 B1 If a container of liquid
boils, or if you boil it, it reaches the temperature where bubbles rise up in it and
it produces steam: *Could you boil the kettle for me?* ∘ *The pot is boiling.*

boiled /bɔɪld/ *adj* **A2** cooked in water
that is boiling: *boiled potatoes*

boiling /'bɔɪ·lɪŋ/ *adj informal* very hot:
It's boiling in this room!

bold /boʊld/ *adj* **1 B1** strong in color
or shape: *a bold design* **2** brave: *It was
a bold decision to go and live overseas.*
• **boldly** *adv*

bolt[1] /boʊlt/ *noun* **1** a metal bar that
you push across a door or window to
lock it **2** a piece of metal that is used
to attach things together by going
through a nut (=piece of metal with a
hole in it)

bolt[2] /boʊlt/ *verb* to lock a door or window with a bolt: *I bolted the door before
going to bed.*

bomb[1] /bɑm/ *noun* **B1** a weapon that
explodes and causes damage: *The bomb
went off (=exploded), destroying the
building.*

bomb[2] /bɑm/ *verb* **B1** to attack a place
using bombs: *Factories were bombed
during the war.*

bomber /'bɑm·ər/ *noun* a person who
puts a bomb somewhere to cause an explosion: *The bombers escaped by car.*

bone /boʊn/ *noun* **B1** one
of the hard, white pieces
inside the body of a per-
son or animal: *He broke a
bone in his hand.*

bone

bonus /'boʊ·nəs/ *noun*
1 a pleasant thing in addition to something you
were expecting: *The sunny
weather was an **added bonus**.* **2** money
you receive in addition to the usual
amount, often because you have
worked hard: *an annual bonus*

book[1] /bʊk/ *noun* **1 A1** a set of pages
with writing on them fastened together
in a cover: *I just read a really good book.*
∘ *Open your books to page 154.* → See picture
at **open verb (1) 2** a set of pages fastened together in a cover and used for
writing on: *an address book*

book[2] /bʊk/ *verb* **A2** to arrange to use
or do something at a time in the future:
We booked two seats for the show.

bookcase /'bʊk·keɪs/ *noun* **A2** a piece
of furniture with shelves for putting
books on
→ See **The Living Room** on page C11

bookshelf /'bʊk·ʃelf/ *noun* (plural **bookshelves**) **A2** a shelf that you put books
on: *There's a bookshelf above our bed.*

bookstore /'bʊk·stɔr/ *noun* **A1** a store
that sells books

boom /bum/ *noun* **1** a loud, deep
sound: *We heard a boom in the distance.*
2 a period when there is a big increase
in sales or profits: *an economic boom*

boost[1] /bust/ *verb* to increase or improve something: *We hope that lower
prices will boost house sales.*

boost[2] /bust/ *noun* [usually no plural]
something that makes you feel more
confident and happy, or that helps
something increase or improve: *Passing
my test was a **boost to** my **confidence**.*

bounce

boot /but/ noun **A2** a shoe that covers your foot and part of your leg: *a pair of boots*
→ See **Clothes** on page C5

border /'bɔr·dər/ noun **1** **B1** the line that separates two countries or states: *the border between California and Nevada* **2** a line around the edge of something: *white plates with a blue border*

bore[1] /bɔr/ past tense of bear

bore[2] /bɔr/ verb (present participle **boring**, past tense and past participle **bored**) to make someone feel bored

bore[3] /bɔr/ noun a person or a situation that is boring: *That professor can be a bore sometimes.*

bored /bɔrd/ adj **A1** tired and unhappy because something is not interesting or because you are doing nothing: *I'm **bored with** doing homework.*

> ⚠ **Common mistake: bored or boring?**
>
> **Bored** is used to describe how someone feels.
>
> *He didn't enjoy the class because he was bored.*
>
> ~~He didn't enjoy the class because he was boring.~~
>
> If someone or something is **boring**, he, she, or it makes you feel bored.
>
> *The book was long and boring.*

boredom /'bɔr·dəm/ noun a state of feeling bored: *the boredom of a long car trip*

boring /'bɔr·ɪŋ/ adj **A1** not interesting or exciting: *a boring job* ∘ *The movie was so boring that I fell asleep.*

born /bɔrn/ verb **be born** **A2** When a person or animal is born, he or she comes out of his or her mother's body and start to exist: *She was born in Chicago in 1973.*

borne /bɔrn/ past participle of bear

borrow /'bɑr·oʊ/ verb **1** **A2** to use something that belongs to someone

else and then return it to them: *Can I borrow a pen, please?* **2** to take money from a person or bank and pay it back over a period of time

boss[1] /bɔs/ noun **A2** someone who is responsible for employees and tells them what to do

boss[2] /bɔs/ verb (also **boss around**) to tell someone what he or she should do all the time: *She's always bossing her little brother around.*

bossy /'bɔ·si/ adj (comparative **bossier**, superlative **bossiest**) always telling other people what to do

both /boʊθ/ pronoun, determiner **A1** used to talk about two people or things: *Both her parents are dead.* ∘ *Both of my sisters are teachers.*

bother /'bɑð·ər/ verb **1** **A2** to annoy someone by talking to him or her when he or she is busy: *Don't bother your father when he's working.* **2** to worry or upset someone: *I'm used to living by myself – it doesn't bother me.* **3** to make the effort to do something: *He didn't even **bother to** call.* **4** **can't be bothered** informal If you can't be bothered to do something, you are too lazy or tired to do it: *I can't be bothered to iron my clothes.*

bottle /'bɑt̬·əl/ noun **A2** a container for liquids, usually made of glass or plastic, with a narrow top: *a bottle of wine*

bottled /'bɑt̬·əld/ adj contained, stored, or sold in bottles: *bottled water*

bottom /'bɑt̬·əm/ noun **1** **A1** the lowest part of something: *Click on the icon at the bottom of the page.* **2** **A2** the flat surface on the lowest side of something: *Something is stuck to the bottom of my shoe.* **3** **A2** the lowest position in a group or organization: *His team is at the bottom of the league.* **4** **B1** the part of your body that you sit on **5** **B1** [no plural] the ground under a river, lake, or sea: *The ship sank to the bottom of the sea.*

bought /bɔt/ past tense and past participle of buy

bounce /baʊns/ verb (present participle **bouncing**, past tense and past participle

bounced) 1 to hit a surface and then move quickly away, or to make something do this: *The ball bounced high into the air.* **2** to jump up and down many times on a soft surface: *The children love to bounce on the bed.*

bound¹ /baʊnd/ past tense and past participle of bind

bound² /baʊnd/ adj **bound to do** *something* certain to do something, or certain to happen: *You're bound to feel nervous before a test.*

bow¹ /baʊ/ verb to bend your head or body forward in order to show respect or to thank an audience

bow² /baʊ/ noun an act of bending your head or body forward: *The actors came back on stage and took a bow.*

bow³ /boʊ/ noun **1** a knot with two circles that is used to tie shoes or as a decoration **2** a piece of curved wood with string attached to both ends, used for shooting arrows **3** a long, thin piece of wood with hair stretched between the ends, used to play some musical instruments

bowl /boʊl/ noun **A2** a round, deep dish used for holding soup and other food

box /bɑks/ noun **1** **A1** a square or rectangular container: *a cardboard box* ○ *a box of chocolates* → See picture at **container 2** **A2** a small square on a page that gives you information or where you write information: *If you would like more information, check this box.*

boxer /ˈbɑk·sər/ noun someone who does the sport of boxing

boxers /ˈbɑk·sərz/ plural noun (also **boxer shorts**) loose underwear for men
→ See **Clothes** on page C5

boxing /ˈbɑk·sɪŋ/ noun [no plural]
B1 a sport in which two people hit each other while wearing big, leather gloves (= pieces of clothing for your hands)
→ See **Sports 1** on page C15

boy /bɔɪ/ noun **A1** a male child or young man: *We have three children – a boy and two girls.*

boyfriend /ˈbɔɪˌfrend/ noun **A2** a man or boy whom someone is having a romantic relationship with

bra /brɑ/ noun a piece of underwear for women that supports the breasts
→ See **Clothes** on page C5

bracelet /ˈbreɪs·lɪt/ noun **B1** a piece of jewelry that you wear around your wrist
→ See picture at **jewelry**

braces /ˈbreɪ·sɪz/ plural noun a set of wire objects that some people wear on their teeth to make them straight

brackets /ˈbræk·ɪts/ noun a pair of marks [ ] used in text around information that is separate from the main part

brag /bræg/ verb (present participle **bragging**, past tense **bragged**) to talk too proudly about something good that you have done or that you own: *He's always bragging about how much money he earns.*

braid /breɪd/ verb to twist three pieces of hair, rope, etc. together so that they form one long piece
• **braid** noun *She wore her hair in braids.*
→ See **Hair** on page C9

brain /breɪn/ noun
A2 the part inside your head that controls your thoughts, feelings, and movements: *brain damage*

brain

brake¹ /breɪk/ noun **B1** the part of a vehicle that makes it stop or go more slowly
→ See **Car** on page C3

brake² /breɪk/ verb (present participle **braking**, past tense and past participle **braked**) **B1** to make a car stop by using its brake

branch /bræntʃ/ noun **1** **B1** one of the many parts of a tree that grows out from the main part → See picture at **tree 2** **B1** one of many stores or offices that

---

|oʊ go|aɪər fire|aʊər hour|ear hair|ɪər ear|ʊər poor|j yet|ʒ measure|ʃ ship|dʒ judge|tʃ chin|ð that|θ thin|ŋ hang|

are part of a company: *a bank with branches all over the country* **3** a part of a subject: *Geometry is a **branch of** mathematics.*

brand /brænd/ *noun* a product that is made by a particular company: *Which brand of toothpaste do you use?*

brand new /ˌbrænd ˈnuː/, /ˌbræn ˈnuː/ *adj* **B1** completely new: *a brand new car*

brandy /ˈbræn·di/ *noun* (plural **brandies**) a strong alcoholic drink made from wine

brass /bræs/ *noun* [no plural] a shiny yellow metal: *a door with a brass handle*

brave /breɪv/ *adj* **B1** Not afraid of dangerous or difficult situations: *He died after a brave fight against cancer.*
• **bravely** *adv*

bravery /ˈbreɪ·və·ri/ *noun* [no plural] actions or behavior that show someone is brave

bread /bred/ *noun* [no plural] **A1** a basic food made by mixing and baking flour and water: *a slice of bread* ○ *a loaf of white bread*
→ See **Quantities** on page C14

break¹ /breɪk/ *verb* (present participle **breaking**, past tense **broke**, past participle **broken**) **1** **A2** to separate into two or more pieces, or to make something separate into two or more pieces: *They had to break a window to get in.*
2 **A2** to damage a part in your body: *She broke her leg in the accident.*
3 **A2** to stop working or to make something stop working: *Who broke the TV?*
4 **B1** to stop an activity and have a short rest: *Let's **break for** five minutes and have some coffee.* **5** to come to an end or make something come to an end: *Eventually someone spoke, breaking the silence.* **6** to not do something that you should do: *I don't like to **break promises.*** **7 break the law** to do something that the law says you must not do
break down *phrasal verb* **B1** If a car or machine breaks down, it stops working: *My car broke down on the way to work.*
break into *something phrasal verb* **B1** to get into a building or car using

force, usually to steal something: *Someone broke into the office and stole some computers.*
break off *phrasal verb* to become separated from something by force: *A large piece of ice had broken off from the iceberg.*
break *something* **off** *phrasal verb* **1** to separate something from something else by breaking it: *He broke off a piece of chocolate.* **2** to end something suddenly: *She broke off the engagement two weeks before the wedding.*
break out *phrasal verb* If something dangerous or unpleasant breaks out, it suddenly starts: *The fire broke out in the early morning.* ○ *War broke out in 1914.*
break up *phrasal verb* **B1** to stop having a relationship: *He just **broke up with** his girlfriend.*

break

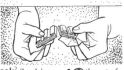

break² /breɪk/ *noun* **1** **A2** the act of stopping an activity for a short time, usually to rest: *a coffee break* **2** **B1** a vacation or period of time away from work or school: *spring break* **3** **B1** a place where something has broken: *The x-ray shows a bad break in her arm.*

breakdown /ˈbreɪk·daʊn/ *noun* **1** (also **nervous breakdown**) a short period of mental illness **2** an occasion when a car or machine stops working

breakfast /ˈbrek·fəst/ *noun* **A1** the food you eat in the morning after you wake up

breast /brest/ *noun* **B1** one of the two soft, round parts on a woman's chest

breath /breθ/ *noun* **1** **B1** [no plural] the air that comes out of your lungs: *His* *breath smells like garlic.* **2** an amount of air that goes into or out of your lungs: *She took a deep breath before she started.* **3 be out of breath** to be breathing quickly because you have been doing exercise **4 hold your breath** to keep air in your lungs and not let it out: *How long can you hold your breath under water?*

⚠ Common mistake: breath or breathe?

Be careful not to confuse the noun **breath** with the verb **breathe**.
I was so excited, I could hardly breathe.

---

breathe /briːð/ **verb** (present participle **breathing**, past tense and past participle **breathed**) **B1** to take air into and out of your lungs: *breathe in/out ∘ breathe deeply*

bred /bred/ past tense and past participle of breed

breed¹ /briːd/ **noun** a type of dog, sheep, pig, etc.: *a rare breed of cattle*

breed² /briːd/ **verb** (past tense and past participle **bred**) **1** If animals breed, they produce babies. **2** to keep animals in order to produce baby animals

breeze /briːz/ **noun** **B1** a gentle wind: *a cool breeze*

bribe /braɪb/ **noun** money or a present that you give to someone so that he or she will do something for you: *The politician was accused of **accepting bribes** from companies.*
• **bribe verb**

brick /brɪk/ **noun** a hard, rectangular block used for building walls: *a brick wall*

bride /braɪd/ **noun** **B1** a woman who is getting married or has just been married

bridegroom /ˈbraɪdˌɡruːm/ **noun** a man who is getting married

bridesmaid /ˈbraɪdzˌmeɪd/ **noun** a woman or girl who helps the bride on her wedding day

bridge /brɪdʒ/ **noun** **A2** a structure that is built over a river or road so that people can go across it: *Brooklyn Bridge*

bridge

brief /briːf/ **adj** **1** **B1** lasting only for a short time: *a brief visit* **2** **B1** using only a few words: *a brief description* • **briefly adv** *They discussed the matter briefly.*

briefcase /ˈbriːfˌkeɪs/ **noun** a flat, rectangular case with a handle for carrying documents or books → See picture at **luggage**

briefs /briːfs/ **plural noun** a type of men's underwear that fits tightly → See **Clothes** on page C5

bright /braɪt/ **adj** **1** **A2** having a strong, light color: *bright yellow/blue* **2** **B1** full of light or shining strongly: *bright sunshine* **3** intelligent: *He's a bright boy.* **4** happy or full of hope: *You're very **bright and cheerful** this morning!* ∘ *She's an excellent student with a **bright future**.*
• **brightly adv**
• **brightness noun** [no plural]

brilliant /ˈbrɪlˌjənt/ **adj** **1** **B1** very intelligent: *a brilliant scholar* **2** **B1** full of light or color: *The sky was a brilliant blue.*
• **brilliantly adv** *He played the piano brilliantly.*

bring /brɪŋ/ **verb** (past tense and past participle **brought**) **1** **A2** to take someone or something with you when you go somewhere: *Did you bring an umbrella with you?* ∘ *He brought me some flowers.* **2 bring** (*someone*) **happiness, luck, peace, etc.** **B1** to cause happiness, luck, peace, etc.: *She's brought us so much happiness over the years.*

bring something back phrasal verb **A2** to return from somewhere with

---

something: *Look at what I brought back from my trip.*

bring *someone* **up** phrasal verb
B1 to take care of a child until he or she becomes an adult: *Her grandparents brought her up.*

bring *something* **up** phrasal verb to start to talk about a particular subject: *She's always bringing up her health problems.*

❗ Common mistake: bring or take?

Use **bring** to talk about moving something or someone toward the speaker or toward the place where you are now.
    Did you bring any money?
    I brought you a present.
Use **take** to talk about moving something or someone away from the speaker or away from the place where you are now.
    I can take you home.
    Don't forget to take your umbrella.

---

broad /brɔd/ adj **1** **B1** wide: *broad shoulders* **2** **B1** including many different things: *a broad range of subjects*

broadband /ˈbrɔdˌbænd/ noun [no plural] a type of Internet connection that allows large amounts of information to be sent or received very quickly: *We have broadband at home.*

broadcast[1] /ˈbrɔdˌkæst/ noun a television or radio program: *a news broadcast*

broadcast[2] /ˈbrɔdˌkæst/ verb (past tense and past participle **broadcast**) to send out a program on television or radio: *The concert will be broadcast live next week.*

broccoli /ˈbrɑk·ə·li/ noun [no plural] **B1** a vegetable that looks like a small green bush

brochure /brouˈʃʊər/ noun **B1** a thin book with pictures and information, usually advertising something: *a travel brochure*

broil /brɔɪl/ verb to cook food using heat from above: *Broil the fish for 8 minutes.*
→ See picture at **cook**

broiler /ˈbrɔɪ·lər/ noun a piece of equipment used for cooking food under heat from above, or the part of the oven that produces this heat

broke /brouk/ past tense of break

broken[1] /ˈbrou·kən/ past participle of break

broken[2] /ˈbrou·kən/ adj **1** **A2** damaged and separated into pieces: *broken glass* **2** **B2** with a damaged bone: *a broken leg* **3** **A2** not working: *The TV is broken.* **4** a **broken heart** a feeling of sadness because of the end of a relationship

bronze /brɑnz/ noun [no plural] a shiny orange-brown metal

broom /brum/ noun a brush with a long handle used for cleaning the floor
→ See picture at **brush**

brother /ˈbrʌð·ər/ noun **A1** a boy or man who has the same parents as you: *an older/younger brother* ∘ *my little brother* (= younger brother) ∘ *my big brother* (= older brother)

brother-in-law /ˈbrʌð·ər·ɪnˌlɔ/ noun (plural **brothers-in-law**) the man married to someone's sibling, or the brother of someone's husband or wife: *My sister and brother-in-law have two kids.*

brought /brɔt/ past tense and past participle of bring

brown[1] /braʊn/ adj **A1** being the same color as chocolate: *dark brown hair*

brown[2] /braʊn/ noun **A2** the color brown → See **Colors** on page C6

browser /ˈbraʊ·zər/ noun a computer program that allows you to look at pages on the Internet

bruise /bruz/ noun a dark area on your skin where you have been hurt: *I have cuts and bruises from falling off my bike.*
• **bruise** verb (present participle **bruising**, past tense and past participle **bruised**) *He was badly bruised in the accident.*

brush[1] /brʌʃ/ noun **A2** an object made of short, thin pieces of plastic, wire, etc. attached to a handle and used to arrange hair, to clean, or to paint: *a stiff brush*

brushes

toothbrush

hairbrush

paintbrush

dustpan and brush

broom

brush[2] /brʌʃ/ verb **1** Ⓐ2 to use a brush to clean something or make something neat: *to brush your hair/teeth* **2** to lightly touch someone or something as you move past: *Charlotte brushed against him as she left the room.* **3** brush *something* away, off, etc. to move something somewhere using a brush or your hand: *Jackie brushed the hair out of her eyes.* ○ *He brushed away a tear.*

brutal /ˈbruː.t̬əl/ adj very violent or cruel: *a brutal murder*
• **brutally** adv

bubble /ˈbʌb.əl/ noun a ball of air or gas with liquid around it: *an air bubble*

bucket /ˈbʌk.ɪt/ noun (also **pail**)
Ⓑ1 a round, open container with a handle, used for carrying liquids: *a bucket of water*

bucket

buckle /ˈbʌk.əl/ noun a metal object used to fasten the ends of a belt or strap: *a silver buckle*
→ See **Clothes** on page C5

bud /bʌd/ noun a part of a plant that develops into a leaf or a flower: *In spring the trees are covered in buds.*

Buddhism /ˈbuː.dɪz.əm/ noun [no plural] a religion based on the ideas that Buddha taught

Buddhist /ˈbuː.dɪst/ noun someone whose religion is Buddhism
• **Buddhist** adj

budget /ˈbʌdʒ.ɪt/ noun a plan that shows how much money you have and how you will spend it

buffalo /ˈbʌf.ə.loʊ/ noun (plural **buffaloes**, **buffalo**) a large wild animal similar to a cow: *a herd of buffalo*

buffet /bəˈfeɪ/ noun a place where dishes of food are arranged on a table and you serve yourself, or a meal served this way: *a wedding buffet*

bug /bʌɡ/ noun **1** Ⓑ1 a small insect **2** a bacteria or virus, or the illness that it causes: *a stomach bug* **3** a mistake in a computer program

build /bɪld/ verb (past tense and past participle **built**) Ⓐ2 to make something by putting materials and parts together: *He built his own house.*

builder /ˈbɪl.dər/ noun Ⓑ1 someone who makes or repairs buildings as a job

building /ˈbɪl.dɪŋ/ noun **1** Ⓐ2 a structure with walls and a roof, such as a house or school: *an office building* **2** [no plural] the activity of putting together materials and parts to make structures

built /bɪlt/ Ⓑ1 past tense and past participle of build

bulb /bʌlb/ noun Ⓑ1 a glass object containing a wire that produces light from electricity: *an electric light bulb*

bulky /ˈbʌl.ki/ adj (comparative **bulkier**, superlative **bulkiest**) too big and taking up too much space

bull /bʊl/ noun Ⓑ1 a male cow

bullet /ˈbʊl.ɪt/ noun a small metal object that is fired from a gun

bulletin board /ˈbʊl.ə.tɪn ˌbɔːrd/ noun Ⓑ1 a board on a wall where you put pieces of paper telling people about things: *a sign on a bulletin board*
→ See **The Classroom** on page C4

bully[1] /ˈbʊl.i/ verb (present participle **bullying**, past tense and past participle

bullied) to try to frighten someone who is smaller or weaker than you: *He was bullied by some older boys.*
• **bullying** noun [no plural] *Bullying is a problem in many schools.*

bully² /ˈbʊl·i/ noun (plural **bullies**) someone who intentionally frightens a person who is smaller or weaker than him or her

bump¹ /bʌmp/ verb to hurt part of your body by hitting it against something hard: *I bumped my head on the door.*

bump into *something* phrasal verb to hit something with force: *She bumped into his tray, knocking the food onto his lap.*

bump into *someone* phrasal verb to meet someone you know without planning it: *I bumped into an old school friend in town today.*

bump² /bʌmp/ noun **1** a round, raised area on a surface: *My bike hit a bump in the road.* **2** a raised area on your body where it has been hurt: *a painful bump on the head*

bumper /ˈbʌm·pər/ noun a bar attached to the front and back of a car to protect it in an accident

bun /bʌn/ noun a small, round piece of bread: *a hamburger bun*

bunch /bʌntʃ/ noun **1** 🅱🄻 a number of things of the same type that are joined together: *a bunch of flowers* → See **Quantities** on page C14 **2** 🅱🄻 informal a group of people: *His friends are a nice bunch.*

bundle /ˈbʌn·dəl/ noun a number of things that are tied together: *a bundle of letters/clothes*

buoy /ˈbuː·i/ noun a floating object used in water to mark dangerous areas for boats

burger /ˈbɜr·gər/ noun 🄰🄿 short form of hamburger

burglar /ˈbɜr·glər/ noun someone who gets into buildings illegally and steals things

burglarize /ˈbɜr·glə‚raɪz/ verb (present participle **burglarizing**, past tense and past participle **burglarized**) to get into a building

illegally and steal things: *Their house was burglarized when they were on vacation.*

burglary /ˈbɜr·glə·ri/ noun (plural **burglaries**) the crime of going into a building illegally and stealing things

burn¹ /bɜrn/ verb **1** 🅱🄻 to destroy something with fire, or to be destroyed by fire: *I burned all his letters.* ∘ *The factory burned to the ground.* **2** 🅱🄻 to produce flames: *The fire is burning well.* **3** 🅱🄻 to be hurt by fire or heat: *He burned his hand on the iron.* **4** to copy music, information, or images onto a CD: *He burned all his favorite songs onto a CD.* **5** to use fuel to produce heat or energy: *to burn fuel*

burn down phrasal verb to be destroyed by fire: *Their house burned down while they were away on vacation.*

burn² /bɜrn/ noun a place where fire or heat has damaged or hurt something: *She has a painful burn on her arm.*

burning /ˈbɜr·nɪŋ/ adj **1** 🅱🄻 on fire: *Firefighters rushed into the burning house.* **2** very hot: *the burning heat of the desert sun*

burnt /bɜrnt/ another form of the past tense and past participle of burn

burp /bɜrp/ verb to let air from your stomach come out of your mouth in a noisy way
• **burp** noun

burst /bɜrst/ verb (past tense and past participle **burst**) **1** If a container bursts, or if you burst it, it breaks suddenly, so that what is inside it comes out: *A water pipe burst and flooded the cellar.* ∘ *He burst all the balloons.* **2** **burst into flames** to suddenly start burning **3** **burst into tears** to suddenly start crying: *She burst into tears and ran away.* **4** **burst out laughing** to suddenly start laughing

bury /ˈber·i/ verb (present participle **burying**, past tense and past participle **buried**) **1** 🅱🄻 to put a dead body into the ground: *He was buried next to his wife.* **2** 🅱🄻 to hide something in the ground or under something: *buried treasure*

a
b
c
d
e
f
g
h
i
j
k
l
m
n
o
p
q
r
s
t
u
v
w
x
y
z

bus /bʌs/ **noun** **A1** a large vehicle that carries passengers by road, usually along a fixed route: *a school bus*
→ See picture at **vehicle**

bush /buʃ/ **noun** a short, thick plant with a lot of branches: *a rose bush*

bush

tree   bush

business /ˈbɪznəs/ **noun** **1** **A1** [no plural] the buying and selling of goods or services: *We do a lot of business with China.* **2** **A2** an organization that sells goods or services: *He runs a small cleaning business.* **3** [no plural] work that is part of your job: *a business trip/lunch* **4 be none of** *someone's* **business** to be something private that another person should not be interested in **5 mind your own business** used to rudely tell someone that a subject is private and he or she should not ask you about it

businessman, businesswoman /ˈbɪznəsˌmæn/, /ˈbɪznəsˌwʊmən/ **noun** (plural **businessmen, businesswomen**) **A2** someone who works in business, usually having an important job

bus station /bʌs ˌsteɪʃən/ **noun** **A2** the place where a bus starts or ends its trip: *The bus station is in the center of town.*

bus stop /ˈbʌs ˌstɑp/ **noun** a place where a bus stops to allow passengers to get on and off: *Wait for me at the bus stop.*

busy /ˈbɪz·i/ **adj** (comparative **busier**, superlative **busiest**) **1** **A2** working hard, or giving your attention to a particular activity: *Mom was busy in the kitchen.* ◦ *I've got plenty of jobs to keep you busy.* **2** **A2** full of activity or people: *a busy restaurant*

3 **A2** In a busy period, you have a lot of things to do: *I've had a busy day.*

but[1] /bʌt/ **conjunction** **A1** used to introduce something new, especially something that is different from what you have just said: *I'd drive you there, but I don't have my car.* ◦ *The food was good but very expensive.*

but[2] /bʌt/ **preposition** **B1** except: *Everyone but Andrew knows.*

butcher /ˈbʊtʃ·ər/ **noun** **B1** someone who prepares and sells meat

butter /ˈbʌt·ər/ **noun** [no plural] **A1** a soft, yellow food made from cream that you put on bread
→ See **Food** on page C7

butterfly /ˈbʌt̬·ər·ˌflaɪ/ **noun** (plural **butterflies**) **B1** an insect with large, colored wings
→ See picture at **insect**

buttock /ˈbʌt̬·ək/ **noun** one of the two sides of your bottom

button /ˈbʌt̬·ən/ **noun** **1** **B1** a small, round object that you push through a hole to fasten clothes: *There are buttons down the front of her jacket.* **2** **B1** a switch that you press to control a piece of equipment: *Press the play button to listen to your recording.*

buy /baɪ/ **verb** (present participle **buying**, past tense and past participle **bought**) **A1** to get something by giving money for it: *I went to the store to buy some milk.*

buyer /ˈbaɪ·ər/ **noun** **B1** someone who buys something expensive, such as a house: *He's still looking for a buyer for his house.*

buzz /bʌz/ **verb** to make a continuous sound like a bee: *I can hear something buzzing.*

by[1] /baɪ/ **preposition** **1** **A2** used to show the person or thing that does something: *a painting by Van Gogh* ◦ *The building had been destroyed by fire.* **2** **A2** through doing or using something: *I sent it by email.* ◦ *We'll get there by car.* **3** **A2** before a particular time or date: *Applications have to be in by the 31st.* **4** 🔵 near or next to: *I'll meet you by the post office.* **5** holding a particular part of someone or something: *She grabbed me by the arm.* **6** past: *He sped by me on a motorcycle.* **7** used to show measurements or amounts: *twelve by ten feet of floor space* ○ *I'm paid by the hour.*

by[2] /baɪ/ **adv** past: *I sat there, watching people walk by.*

bye /baɪ/ **exclamation** (also **bye-bye**) 🔵 goodbye: *Bye, see you tomorrow.*

byte /baɪt/ **noun** a unit for measuring the amount of information a computer can store

Cc

C, c /siː/ the third letter of the alphabet

c. written abbreviation for cup: a measurement used in cooking

C written abbreviation for Celsius or centigrade: *30°C*

cab /kæb/ **noun** informal 🔵 a taxi (=car that you pay to travel in): *We took a cab to the theater.*

cabbage /ˈkæb·ɪdʒ/ **noun** 🔵 a large, round vegetable with a lot of green or white leaves

cabin /ˈkæb·ɪn/ **noun** **1** 🔵 the area where most people sit on a plane **2** a small house made of wood: *a log cabin* **3** a small room to sleep in on a ship

cabinet /ˈkæb·ə·nət/ **noun** **1** a cupboard with shelves or drawers: *kitchen cabinets* **2** a group of people in a government who advise the leader: *a member of the Cabinet*
→ See **The Kitchen** on page C10

cable /ˈkeɪ·bəl/ **noun** **1** 🔵 [no plural] the system of sending television programs or telephone signals along wires in the

ground: *cable TV* **2** a wire that carries electricity or telephone signals **3** a metal rope

cactus /ˈkæk·təs/ **noun** (plural **cacti, cactuses**) a plant with thick leaves and sharp points that grows in deserts

café /kæˈfeɪ/ **noun** (also **cafe**) 🔵 a small restaurant where you buy drinks and small meals

cafeteria /ˌkæf·əˈtɪər·i·ə/ **noun** a restaurant where you pick up and pay for your food and drink before you eat it: *a school cafeteria*

cage /keɪdʒ/ **noun** 🔵 a container made of wire or metal bars used for keeping birds or animals in: *a bird cage*

cake /keɪk/ **noun** 🔵 a sweet food made from flour, butter, sugar, and eggs mixed together and baked: *a chocolate cake*
→ See **Food** on page C7

layer

calculate /ˈkæl·kjəˌleɪt/ **verb** (present participle **calculating**, past tense and past participle **calculated**) to discover an amount or number using mathematics: *I'm trying to calculate the cost of the trip.*

calculation /ˌkæl·kjəˈleɪ·ʃən/ **noun** the use of mathematics to find a number or amount

calculator /ˈkæl·kjəˌleɪ·t̬ər/ **noun** 🔵 a small machine that you use to do mathematics

calendar /ˈkæl·ən·dər/ **noun** 🔵 something that shows all the days, weeks, and months of the year

calf /kæf/ **noun** (plural **calves**) **1** 🔵 a young cow **2** the back of your leg below your knee
→ See **The Body** on page C2

cactus

cage

cake

| æ cat | ɑ hot | e get | ɪ sit | i see | ɔ saw | ʊ book | u too | ʌ cut | ə about | ər mother | ɜr turn | ɪr for | aɪ my | aʊ how | eɪ say | ɔɪ boy |

call[1] /kɔl/ verb **1** Ⓐ1 to telephone someone: *Call the police.* **2** be called *something* Ⓐ1 to have a particular name: *a boy called Adam* ∘ *Their latest album is called "Shine."* **3** Ⓑ1 to shout: *I heard someone call my name.* **4** Ⓑ1 to give someone a name: *They called their first son Joshua.* **5** to describe someone or something in a particular way: *Are you calling me a liar?* **6** to ask someone to come somewhere: *She called me into her office.*

call (someone) back phrasal verb Ⓐ2 to telephone someone a second time, or to telephone someone who telephoned you earlier: *I'll call back later.*

call someone up phrasal verb Ⓑ1 to telephone someone: *Call Paul up and ask what he's doing tonight.*

call something off phrasal verb to decide that something that is planned will not happen: *The game was called off because of bad weather.*

call[2] /kɔl/ noun **1** Ⓐ2 the act of using the telephone: *Give me a call* this weekend. ∘ *I got a call* from Sue this morning. **2** Ⓑ1 the act of shouting something **3** a sound made by a bird or other animal

caller /ˈkɔ·lər/ noun someone who makes a telephone call

call-in /ˈkɔlˌɪn/ noun a television or radio program in which members of the public can ask questions or give opinions over the telephone

calm[1] /kɑm/, /kɑlm/ adj **1** Ⓑ1 relaxed and not showing worry or fear: *a calm voice* **2** Ⓑ1 If the weather or the sea is calm, it is quiet and peaceful.
• **calmly** adv in a relaxed way: *He spoke slowly and calmly.*

calm[2] /kɑm/, /kɑlm/ verb

calm down phrasal verb to stop feeling angry, upset, or excited: *Calm down and tell me what's wrong.*

calorie /ˈkæl·ə·ri/ noun a unit for measuring the amount of energy food provides: *I try to eat about 2,000 calories a day.*

calves /kævz/ plural of calf

camcorder /ˈkæmˌkɔr·dər/ noun a camera that you hold in your hand and that records moving pictures

came /keɪm/ past tense of come

camel /ˈkæm·əl/ noun Ⓑ1 a large animal that lives in hot, dry places and has one or two humps (=raised parts on its back)

camel

camera /ˈkæm·ər·ə/, /ˈkæm·rə/ noun Ⓐ1 a piece of equipment used to take photographs

camp[1] /kæmp/ noun **1** Ⓑ1 an area where people stay in tents for a short time, usually on vacation: *We set up camp near a stream.* **2** a place where people, especially children, can go to visit or live for a short time to enjoy nature or do organized activities: *Are you going to summer camp?* **3** an area containing temporary buildings or tents used for soldiers, prisoners, etc.

camp[2] /kæmp/ verb Ⓐ2 to stay in a tent or other temporary shelter: *We camped on the beach for two nights.*

campaign[1] /kæmˈpeɪn/ noun **1** a group of activities that are planned to get a result: *an election campaign* **2** a lot of military attacks: *a bombing campaign*

campaign[2] /kæmˈpeɪn/ verb to organize a group of activities to try to make something happen

camper /ˈkæm·pər/ noun **1** a vehicle, or a structure that is pulled by a vehicle, that people stay in when they are on vacation **2** someone, especially a child, who attends a summer camp **3** someone who stays in a tent or camper on vacation

campfire /ˈkæmpˌfaɪər/ noun a fire that is made and used outside, especially by people who are staying in tents or other temporary shelters

campground /ˈkæmpˌɡraʊnd/ noun an area of land that has space for many

a
b
c
d
e
f
g
h
i
j
k
l
m
n
o
p
q
r
s
t
u
v
w
x
y
z

people to put up tents and stay while they are traveling or on vacation

camping /'kæm·pɪŋ/ noun [no plural] **A2** living in a tent for a vacation

> **⚠ Common mistake: camping or campsite?**
>
> Be careful not to use **camping**, the activity of staying in a tent, when you mean **campsite**, the area of ground where you do this.

campsite /'kæmp·saɪt/ noun **B1** a space where someone has put up a tent or other temporary shelter, especially on vacation

campus /'kæm·pəs/ noun the land and buildings belonging to a college or university

can[1] /kæn/ noun **A2** a metal container for food or liquids: *a can of soup*
→ See picture at **container**

can[2] /kæn/ modal verb **1 A1** to be able to do something: *Can you drive?* ○ *I can't swim.* **2 A1** used to request something: *Can I have a glass of water?* **3 A1** used in polite offers of help: *Can I help you with those bags?* **4 A1** to be allowed to do something: *You can't park here.* ○ *Can I go now?* **5 A2** used to talk about what is possible: *You can get stamps from the post office.* **6 B1** used to show surprise or lack of belief: *You can't possibly be hungry already!* ○ *Can you believe it?*

canal /kə'næl/ noun **B1** a river made by people

cancel /'kæn·səl/ verb (present participle **canceling**, past tense and past participle **canceled**) **B1** to say that an organized event will not happen: *The meeting has been canceled.*

cancellation /ˌkæn·səˈleɪ·ʃən/ noun a decision that an event will not happen

cancer /'kæn·sər/ noun **B1** a serious disease that is caused when some cells in the body grow too much and damage other cells: *lung cancer*

candidate /'kæn·dəˌdeɪt/ noun a person who takes part in an election or tries to get a job: *a presidential candidate*

candle /'kæn·dəl/ noun **B1** a stick of wax with string inside that you burn to make light
→ See **The Living Room** on page C11

candlestick /'kæn·dəlˌstɪk/ noun (also **candle holder**) a base in which you set a candle so it can burn safely

candy /'kæn·di/ noun (plural **candies**) **A2** a small piece of sweet food: *a candy bar* ○ *a bag of hard candies*

cane /keɪn/ noun a long stick with a handle, which a person can lean on while walking

canned /kænd/ adj Canned food is sold in metal containers: *canned tomatoes*

cannon /'kæn·ən/ noun a very large gun

cannot /'kæn·ɑt/, /ˌkænˈnɑt/ modal verb **A1** the negative form of "can": *I cannot say what will happen.*

> **⚠ Common mistake: cannot**
>
> Remember that the negative form of **can** is written as one word.
> *They cannot decide what to do.*
> ~~They can not decide what to do.~~

canoe /kəˈnu/ noun a small, thin boat with pointed ends for one or two people

canoe

can opener /'kæn ˌoʊ·pə·nər/ noun a piece of kitchen equipment for opening metal food containers
→ See **The Kitchen** on page C10

can't /kænt/ modal verb short form of cannot: *I can't drive.*

canteen /kænˈtin/ noun a small container used to carry water or other liquids to drink

canvas /'kæn·vəs/ noun [no plural] strong cloth used for tents and paintings

canyon /'kæn·jən/ noun a deep valley with very steep sides

cap /kæp/ noun **1 A2** a hat with a flat part at the front: *a baseball cap*
→ See picture at **baseball cap** **2** the top part of a bottle or tube that you take off

| æ cat | ɑ hot | e get | i sit | i see | ɔ saw | ʊ book | u too | ʌ cut | ə about | ɑr mother | ɜr turn | ɔr for | ɑɪ my | ɑʊ how | eɪ say | ɔɪ boy |

capable /ˈkeɪ·pə·bəl/ *adj* **1** able to do things well: *She's a very capable young woman.* **2 capable of** able to do something: *I know the quality of work she is capable of.* → Opposite **incapable** *adj*

capacity /kəˈpæs·ɪ·t̬i/ *noun* (plural **capacities**) **1** the largest amount that a container or building can hold: *The restaurant has a capacity of about 200.* **2** the ability to do or feel something: *She has a great capacity for love.*

capital /ˈkæp·ɪ·t̬əl/ *noun* **1** 🅰🅰 the most important city in a country or state: *Paris is the capital of France.* **2** 🅰🅰 (also **capital letter**, /ˈkæp·ɪ·t̬·əl ˈlet·ər/) a large letter of the alphabet used at the beginning of sentences **3** [no plural] money used in business

captain /ˈkæp·tən/ *noun* **1** 🅱🅱 the leader of a team **2** the person who controls a ship or plane **3** an officer in the army, navy, or air force

captive /ˈkæp·tɪv/ *noun* a prisoner

captivity /kæpˈtɪv·ɪ·t̬i/ *noun* [no plural] the state of being kept somewhere and not allowed to leave: *lion cubs born in captivity*

capture /ˈkæp·tʃər/ *verb* (present participle **capturing**, past tense and past participle **captured**) **1** to catch someone and make him or her your prisoner: *Two soldiers were captured by the enemy.* **2** to show or describe something successfully using words or pictures: *The painting captures the beauty of the landscape.*

car /kɑr/ *noun* **1** 🅰 a vehicle with an engine, four wheels, and seats for a few people → See **Car** on page C3 **2** one of the separate parts of a train where people sit → See picture at **vehicle**

carbon /ˈkɑr·bən/ *noun* [no plural] a chemical element that exists in all animals and plants and in coal and oil

carbonated /ˈkɑr·bəˌneɪ·t̬əd/ *adj* A carbonated liquid has lots of bubbles of gas in it: *carbonated soda*

carbon dioxide /ˌkɑr·bən daɪˈɑk·saɪd/ *noun* [no plural] a gas that is produced when people or animals breathe out, or when carbon is burned

card /kɑrd/ *noun* **1** 🅰🅰 a piece of folded paper with a picture on the front and some writing inside: *a birthday card* **2** 🅰🅰 (also **playing card**) a piece of hard paper with numbers and pictures used for playing games: *We spent the evening playing cards (=playing games using cards).* **3** 🅱🅱 a piece of hard paper or plastic with information on it: *a library card* **4** 🅱🅱 a part inside a computer that controls how the computer operates: *a sound card*

cardboard /ˈkɑrdˌbɔrd/ *noun* [no plural] thick, hard paper that is used for making boxes

cardigan
/ˈkɑr·dɪ·ɡən/ *noun*
a piece of clothing like a jacket, often made of wool, that fastens at the front

cardigan

care[1] /keər/ *verb* (present participle **caring**, past tense and past participle **cared**) **1** 🅱🅱 to feel interested in something or worried about it: *I don't care what she thinks.* **2** 🅱🅱 to love someone: *I only worry about him because I care about him.* **3 who cares?** *informal* used to emphasize that you do not think something is important: *"We're going to be late." "Who cares?"*

care for someone *phrasal verb* 🅱🅱 to provide for the needs of someone who is young, old, or ill: *The children are being cared for by a relative.*

care[2] /keər/ *noun* **1** 🅱🅱 [no plural] the process of protecting or providing for the needs of someone or something: *A small baby requires constant care.* ∘ *My parents take care of our house while we're away.* **2 take care** 🅱🅱 to give a lot of attention to what you are doing, especially something dangerous: *The roads are very icy so take care when you drive home.* **3 take care!** *informal* 🅰🅰 used when saying goodbye to someone: *See you soon, Bob – take care!*

career /kə'rɪər/ **noun** **B1** a job that you do for a lot of your life, especially one for which you are trained: *a successful career in marketing*

careful /'keər·fəl/ **adj** **A2** giving a lot of attention to what you are doing so that you do not have an accident or make a mistake: ***Be careful**, Michael – that knife is sharp.*
• **carefully adv** **A2** *He carefully lifted the baby.*

careless /'keər·ləs/ **adj** **B1** not giving enough attention to what you are doing: *He was fined $100 for littering.*
• **carelessly adv**

cargo /'kɑr·gou/ **noun** (plural **cargoes**) things that are carried in a vehicle or ship: *a cargo of oil*

caring /'keər·ɪŋ/ **adj** describes someone who is kind and who helps other people: *She's a very caring person.*

carnival /'kɑr·nə·vəl/ **noun** a public event where people wear special clothes and dance in the streets

carol /'kær·əl/ **noun** a song that people sing at Christmas

carpet /'kɑr·pɪt/ **noun** **A2** thick material for covering floors, often made of wool

carrot /'kær·ət/ **noun** **A2** a long, thin, orange vegetable that grows in the ground
→ See **Fruits and Vegetables** on page C8

carry /'kær·i/ **verb** (present participle **carrying**, past tense and past participle **carried**) **1** **A1** to hold something or someone with your hands or on your back and take them somewhere: *He was carrying my bags.* **2** **B1** to have something with you all the time: *She still carries his photo in her wallet.* **3** to move someone or something from one place to another: *The plane was carrying 30 passengers.* **4** If a person or animal carries a disease, it can be given to others: *Mosquitoes can carry malaria.* **5** If a store carries something, people can buy it there: *We don't carry that brand of jeans.*

be/get carried away phrasal verb to be so excited about something that you cannot control what you say or do: *There's far too much food – I'm afraid I got carried away!*

carry something out phrasal verb **B1** to do or complete something, especially something that you have said you would do or that you have been told to do: *The plan may not be easy to carry out.*

carryall /'kær·i·ɔl/ **noun** a large, strong, cloth bag used for carrying things when you travel
→ See picture at **luggage**

carry-on[1] /'kær·i·ɑn/, /'kær·i·ɔn/ **adj** small enough to bring onto a plane with you when you travel: *carry-on luggage*

carry-on[2] /'kær·i·ɑn/, /'kær·i·ɔn/ **noun** a bag that is small enough to be taken onto a plane with you

cart /kɑrt/ **noun** a metal structure on wheels that is used for carrying things: *a shopping cart*

carts

carton /'kɑr·tᵊn/ **noun** a container for food and drink that is made from strong paper or plastic: *a carton of milk*
→ See picture at **container**

cartoon /kɑr'tun/ **noun** **1** **A2** a movie made using characters that are drawn and not real: *Mickey Mouse and other famous cartoon characters* **2** **A2** a funny drawing, especially in a newspaper or magazine

carve /kɑrv/ **verb** (present participle **carving**, past tense and past participle **carved**) **1** to make an object or shape by cutting wood or stone: *The statue was **carved***

out of stone. **2** to cut a piece of cooked meat into thin pieces

case /keɪs/ *noun* **1** 🅐🅑 a large bag with a handle that you use for carrying clothes in when you are traveling **2** 🅐🅑 a container for storing or protecting something: *a pencil case* **3** 🅑🅒 a particular situation or example of something: *We usually ask for references, but in your case it will not be necessary.* **4** something that is decided in a court of law: *a divorce case* **5** a crime that the police are trying to solve: *a murder case* **6 in case** 🅑🅒 because something might happen: *I don't think it will rain, but I'll bring an umbrella just in case.* **7 in case of** *something* 🅑🅒 so you are ready if something happens: *Here is my number in case of an emergency.* **8 be the case** 🅑🅒 to be true: *A poor diet can make you tired, but I don't think that's the case here.* **9 in any case** used to give another reason for something you are saying, or that you have done: *I don't want to go, and in any case, I wasn't invited.* **10 in that case** because that is the situation: *"Peter will be there." "Oh, in that case, I'll come too."*

cash[1] /kæʃ/ *noun* [no plural] **1** 🅐🅑 money in the form of coins or bills (= paper money): *I'm paying her $50 in cash.* **2** 🅑🅒 informal money in any form: *I'm short on cash* (= I don't have much money).

cash[2] /kæʃ/ *verb* **cash a check** to get money in return for a check (= piece of paper printed by a bank and used to pay for things): *I need to cash a check.*

cashier /kæˈʃɪr/ *noun* someone whose job is to take and pay out money in a store or bank

cash machine /ˈkæʃ məˌʃin/ *noun* (also **ATM**) 🅑🅒 a machine that you get money from using a plastic card

cash register /ˈkæʃ ˌrɛdʒ·ə·stər/ *noun* a machine that is used in stores for keeping money in, and for recording everything that is sold

cast[1] /kæst/ *verb* (past tense and past participle **cast**) **1 cast a spell on** *someone* to use

magic to make something happen to someone: *The witch cast a spell on him and turned him into a frog.* **2** to choose an actor for a particular part in a movie or play: *Why is he always cast as a criminal?*

cast[2] /kæst/ *noun* all the actors in a movie, play, or show: *The play has a cast of twenty actors.*

castle /ˈkæs·əl/ *noun* 🅐🅑 a large, strong building that was built in the past to protect the people inside from being attacked

casual /ˈkæʒ·u·əl/ *adj* **1** 🅑🅒 Casual clothes are comfortable and not formal. **2** not planned: *a casual remark* **3** relaxed and not very interested in someone or something: *a casual attitude*
• **casually** *adv* *She was dressed casually in shorts and a T-shirt.*

cat /kæt/ *noun* 🅐🅑 a small animal with fur, four legs, and a tail that is kept as a pet

catalog /ˈkæt·əlˌɔg/, /ˈkæt·əlˌɑg/ *noun* (also **catalogue**) a magazine that lists all the things that you can buy from a store or company: *a children's clothing catalog*

catastrophe /kəˈtæs·trə·fi/ *noun* an extremely bad event that causes a lot of suffering or destruction: *The country is facing an environmental catastrophe.*

catch /kætʃ/ *verb* (present participle **catching**, past tense and past participle **caught**) **1** 🅐🅑 to stop something that is moving through the air by getting it in your hands: *Try to catch the ball.* **2** 🅐🅑 to get on a bus, train, etc.: *I caught the last train home.* **3** 🅐🅑 to get an illness or disease: *I think I caught a cold from her.* **4** 🅑🅒 to find and stop a person or animal who is trying to escape: *He ran after the dog, but couldn't catch him.* **5** to stick somewhere, or to make something stick somewhere: *My dress got caught on a nail and tore.* **6 catch fire** 🅑🅒 to start burning **7 catch someone's attention, interest, etc.** to make someone notice something and feel interested: *A noise in the street caught his attention.* **8** to discover someone who is doing something wrong or something secret: *She was caught cheating on the test.*

catch up phrasal verb **1** ⓑ1 to reach the same level or quality as someone or something else: *She's doing extra work to* ***catch up*** *with the rest of the class.* **2** to learn and discuss the newest facts about something: *Let's go out for lunch – I want to* ***catch up on*** *all your news.* **3** to reach someone or something that is in front of you by moving faster: *We soon* ***caught up*** ***with*** *the car in front.*

category /ˈkæt·ɪˌɡɔr·i/ noun (plural **categories**) a group of people or things of a similar type: *Our customers fall into two main categories.*

catering /ˈkeɪ·tə·rɪŋ/ noun [no plural] providing food and drinks for people: *Who* ***did the catering*** *for the party?*

caterpillar /ˈkæt·ərˌpɪl·ər/ noun a small, long animal with many legs that eats leaves

caterpillar

cathedral /kəˈθi·drəl/ noun ⓐ2 the largest and most important church in an area

Catholic /ˈkæθ·lɪk/ noun (also **Roman Catholic**) a member of the part of the Christian religion whose leader is the Pope
• **Catholic** adj

cattle /ˈkæt̬·əl/ plural noun ⓑ1 cows kept on a farm for their milk and meat

caught /kɔt/ past tense and past participle of catch

cauliflower /ˈkɑl·ɪˌflɑʊ·ər/,/ˈkɔ·lɪˌflɑʊ·ər/ noun a round, white vegetable with green leaves around the outside
→ See **Fruits and Vegetables** on page C8

cause[1] /kɔz/ verb (present participle **causing**, past tense and past participle **caused**) to make something happen, especially something bad: *What caused the fire?*

cause[2] /kɔz/ noun **1** someone or something that makes something happen: *They still don't know the* ***cause of the***

accident. **2** [no plural] a reason to feel something: *There is no* ***cause for*** *alarm.* **3** a reason for doing something, especially one that involves helping other people: *The money will go to charity – it's a good cause.*

caution /ˈkɔ·ʃən/ noun [no plural] great care to avoid danger or bad situations: *Caution! Wet floor.*

cautious /ˈkɔ·ʃəs/ adj taking care to avoid danger or bad situations: *a cautious driver*
• **cautiously** adv

cave /keɪv/ noun ⓑ1 a large hole in the ground or in the side of a mountain

CD /ˈsiˈdi/ noun ⓐ1 a small disc on which music or information is recorded
→ See **The Office** on page C12

CD player /ˈsiˈdi ˌpleɪ·ər/ noun ⓐ1 a machine that is used for playing music CDs

CD-ROM /ˈsiˌdiˈrɑm/ noun ⓑ1 a CD that holds large amounts of information that can be read by a computer: *Cambridge dictionaries are available* ***on CD-ROM.***

cease /sis/ verb (present participle **ceasing**, past tense and past participle **ceased**) formal to stop: *The soldiers ceased firing.*

ceiling /ˈsi·lɪŋ/ noun ⓐ2 the top surface of a room

celebrate /ˈsel·əˌbreɪt/ verb (present participle **celebrating**, past tense and past participle **celebrated**) ⓑ1 to have a party or a nice meal because it is a special day or something good has happened: *We went out to celebrate Richard's birthday.*

celebration /ˌsel·əˈbreɪ·ʃən/ noun ⓑ1 an occasion or party that celebrates a special event: *You passed your test? This* ***calls for*** *a celebration.*

celebrity /səˈleb·rɪ·t̬i/ noun (plural **celebrities**) ⓑ1 a famous person

celery /ˈsel·ə·ri/ noun [no plural] a vegetable with long green stems that can be eaten raw or cooked
→ See **Fruits and Vegetables** on page C8

cell /sel/ **noun 1** the smallest living part of an animal or a plant: *brain cells* **2** a small room where a prisoner is kept **3** short form of cell phone

cellar /'sel·ər/ **noun** a room under the bottom floor of a building

cello /'tʃel·oʊ/ **noun** a large, wooden musical instrument that you hold between your knees to play

cell phone /'sel ˌfoʊn/ **noun** (also **cell, mobile phone**) **A1** a telephone that you can carry everywhere with you: *I was talking on my cell phone.*

cell phone

Celsius /'sel·si·əs/ **noun** [no plural] (written abbreviation **C**) a measurement of temperature in which water freezes at 0° and boils at 100°

cement /sɪ'ment/ **noun** [no plural] a powder used in building that is mixed with water to make a hard substance

cemetery /'sem·ɪˌter·i/ **noun** (plural **cemeteries**) a place where dead people are buried: *She went to the cemetery where her grandfather was buried.*

cent /sent/ **noun** **A2** a coin 1/100 of a dollar and some other types of money, or a coin of this value

center /'sen·tər/ **noun 1** **A2** the middle point or part of something: *the center of a circle* **2** **A2** a building used for a particular activity: *a shopping center* **3 be the center of attention** to get more attention than anyone else

centigrade /'sen·tɪˌɡreɪd/ **noun** [no plural] (written abbreviation **C**) a measurement of temperature in which water freezes at 0° and boils at 100°

centimeter (written abbreviation **cm**) /'sent·əˌmi·tər/ **noun** a unit for measuring length, equal to 0.01 meters

central /'sen·trəl/ **adj** **B1** in or near the center of a place or thing: *central America*
• **centrally** adv

century /'sen·tʃə·ri/ **noun** (plural **centuries**) **A2** a period of 100 years: *the twentieth century*

cereal /'sɪər·i·əl/ **noun 1** a plant that is grown to produce grain for food **2** **A2** a food that is made from grain and eaten with milk, especially in the morning: *breakfast cereals*
→ See **Food** on page C7

ceremony /'ser·əˌmoʊ·ni/ **noun** **B1** (plural **ceremonies**) a set of actions that are performed on formal social or religious occasions: *a wedding ceremony*

certain /'sɜr·tᵊn/ **adj 1** **B1** definite: *I am certain that you're doing the right thing.* ○ *It now looks certain that she will resign.*
→ Opposite **uncertain** adj **2** **B1** some: *The museum is only open at certain times of the day.*

certainly /'sɜr·tᵊn·li/ **adv 1** **A2** definitely: *They certainly deserved to win.* ○ *"Do you regret what you said?" "Certainly not!"* **2** **A2** used to politely agree to do something: *"Could you pass the salt, please?" "Certainly."*

certificate /sər'tɪf·ɪ·kət/ **noun** **B1** an official document that gives details to show that something is true: *a birth certificate*

chain¹ /tʃeɪn/ **noun 1** **A2** a line of metal rings connected together: *She wore a gold chain around her neck.* **2** **B1** a number of similar stores, restaurants, etc. owned by the same company: *a chain of hotels* **3** a series of things that happen one after the other: *His arrival set off a surprising chain of events.*

chain

chain² /tʃeɪn/ **verb** to tie someone or something using a chain: *I chained my bike to a fence.*

chair¹ /tʃeər/ **noun** **A1** a seat for one person, with a back and usually four legs
→ See **The Classroom** on page C4

chair² /tʃeər/ **verb** to control a meeting or organization: *Would you like to chair the meeting tomorrow?*

chairman, chairwoman /ˈtʃeər·mən/, /ˈtʃeərˌwʊm·ən/ *noun* (plural **chairmen, chairwomen**) (also **chair**)   a man or woman who controls a meeting or company

chalk /tʃɔk/ *noun* **1** [no plural] a soft, white rock **2** a small stick of this rock used for writing

challenge¹ /ˈtʃæl·əndʒ/ *noun* **1** 🔵 something difficult that tests your ability: *Managing a large team is quite a challenge.* **2** an invitation to compete in a game or a fight

challenge² /ˈtʃæl·əndʒ/ *verb* (present participle **challenging**, past tense and past participle **challenged**) **1** to tell someone you do not accept his or her rules or you think he or she is wrong: *The election results are being challenged.* **2** to ask someone to compete in a game or fight: *He challenged me **to** a game of tennis.*

challenging /ˈtʃæl·ən·dʒɪŋ/ *adj* 🔵 difficult, in a way that tests your ability or determination: *This has been a challenging time for all of us.*

champagne /ʃæmˈpeɪn/ *noun* [no plural] 🔵 French white wine with a lot of bubbles in it

champion /ˈtʃæm·pi·ən/ *noun* 🔵 a person or animal that wins a competition

championship /ˈtʃæm·pi·ən·ʃɪp/ *noun* 🔵 a competition to find the best team or player in a game or sport

chance /tʃæns/ *noun* **1** 🔵 the possibility that something will happen: *There's a chance that she'll still be there.* ○ *She has a small chance of passing the exam.* **2** 🔵 the opportunity to do something: *I didn't get a chance to talk to you at the party.* **3** 🔵 [no plural] the way something happens because of luck, or without being planned: *I saw her by chance in the store.* **4 stand a chance** to have a chance of success or of doing something good: *He stands a good chance of winning the election.*

change¹ /tʃeɪndʒ/ *verb* (present participle **changing**, past tense and past participle

changed) **1** 🔴 to stop having or doing one thing, and start having or doing another: *I changed jobs to make more money.* **2** 🔴 to become different, or to make something or someone become different: *She's changed a lot in the last few years.* ○ *That book changed my life.* **3** 🔴 to take off your clothes and put on different ones: *Is there somewhere I can get changed?* **4 change buses, planes, etc.** 🔴 to get off one bus, plane, etc. and get on a different one: *I have to change planes in Atlanta.* **5 change the subject** to start talking about a different subject: *I'd tried to explain my feelings, but he just changed the subject.*

change² /tʃeɪndʒ/ *noun* **1** 🔴 the process or result of something becoming different: *We need to **make** a few **changes to** the design.* **2** 🔴 the process of stopping one thing and starting to have or do another thing: *a **change of** address* **3** 🔴 [no plural] the money that you get back when you pay more for something than it costs: *Here's your receipt and change.* **4** 🔴 [no plural] coins, not paper money: *Do you have any change for the parking meter?* **5 a change of clothes** 🔴 a set of clean clothes you can put on if you need to take off the ones you are wearing: *Make sure you bring a change of clothes.* **6** 🔵 a different experience from what is usual: *You know, I'm really ready for a change.* **7** 🔵 something that is pleasant or interesting because it is unusual or new: *It's nice to see her smile **for a change**.*

channel /ˈtʃæn·ᵊl/ *noun* **1** 🔴 a number on a television that you choose in order to watch a program **2** a long passage for water or other liquids to move along

chaos /ˈkeɪ·ɑs/ *noun* [no plural]   a state in which there is confusion and no organization: *The city was in chaos after the earthquake.*

chapel /ˈtʃæp·əl/ *noun*   a small church, or a room used as a church in a building

chapter /ˈtʃæp·tər/ *noun* 🔵 one of the parts that a book is divided into

character /'kær·ək·tər/ noun **1** 🅱1 the qualities that make one person or thing different from another: *The whole character of the neighborhood changed after the road was built.* **2** 🅱1 a person in a book, movie, etc.: *a cartoon character*

characteristic /ˌkær·ək·tə'rɪs·tɪk/ noun a typical or noticeable quality of someone or something: *A long neck is a common characteristic of the giraffe.*

charge¹ /tʃɑrdʒ/ noun **1** 🅱1 the price of something, especially a service: *delivery charges* **2** be in charge 🅱1 to be responsible for something: *She's in charge of the team.* **3** something written by the police saying that someone has done a crime

charge² /tʃɑrdʒ/ verb (present participle **charging**, past tense and past participle **charged**) **1** 🅱1 to ask for money for something: *How much do you charge for delivery?* **2** to officially say that someone has done a crime: *He has been charged with murder.* **3** to run: *The children charged out of the school.* **4** to attack someone or something by moving forward quickly: *The bull charged at the boy.* **5** to put electricity into something: *My cell phone needs charging.*

charger /'tʃɑr·dʒər/ noun a piece of equipment used for putting electricity in a battery: *a phone charger*

charity /'tʃær·ɪ·ti/ noun **1** 🅱1 (plural **charities**) an official organization that gives money, food, or help to people who need it: *We're raising money for charity.* **2** [no plural] money, food, or other help that is given to people

charm /tʃɑrm/ noun **1** a quality that makes you like someone or something: *Part of his charm is his sense of humor.* **2** something that brings you good luck: *a lucky charm*

charming /'tʃɑr·mɪŋ/ adj 🅱1 nice and attractive: *a charming smile*

chart /tʃɑrt/ noun **1** a drawing that shows information in a simple way: *a sales chart* **2** the charts an official list of the most popular songs each week: *It's been number one on the charts for six weeks.*

chase /tʃeɪs/ verb (present participle **chasing**, past tense and past participle **chased**) to run after someone or something to catch him, her, or it: *The dog was chasing a rabbit.*

chase

chat¹ /tʃæt/ verb (present participle **chatting**, past tense and past participle **chatted**) **1** 🅰2 to talk with someone in a friendly way **2** 🅰2 to communicate with someone on the Internet by sending messages that you can read and reply to immediately

chat² /tʃæt/ noun 🅰2 a friendly conversation: *We had a long chat on the phone.*

chat room /'tʃæt ˌrum/, /'tʃæt ˌrʊm/ noun a place on the Internet where people can have a conversation by writing to each other

cheap /tʃip/ adj 🅰1 not expensive, or costing less than usual: *a cheap flight*
• **cheaply** adv *You can buy a used car very cheaply.*

cheat /tʃit/ verb to do something that is not honest, in order to get something: *She cheated on the exam.*

check¹ /tʃek/ verb **1** 🅰1 to put a mark [√] by an answer to show that it is correct **2** 🅰2 to look at something to make sure that it is right or safe: *Check that you locked the door.* **3** 🅱1 to find out information from something or about something: *I need to check my email before we go.*

check in phrasal verb 🅱1 to show your ticket at an airport so they can give you your seat number

check in/check into something phrasal verb 🅱1 to say who you are when you arrive at a hotel so that you can be given a key for your room: *Please **check in at** the reception desk.*

check out phrasal verb **1** 🅑1 to leave a hotel after paying **2** to go to an area to pay for the things you have chosen to buy in a store or on a website: *I had already checked out when I remembered we were out of milk.* **3** to borrow a book, CD, etc. from a library: *You can check out up to six items at a time.*

check² /tʃek/ noun **1** 🅐2 a piece of paper printed by a bank that you use to pay for things **2** 🅐2 a mark [√] that shows that an answer is correct **3** 🅑1 the act of looking at something to make sure it is right or safe: *We run safety **checks on** all our equipment.* **4** a piece of paper that shows how much you must pay for a meal in a restaurant: *Could I have the check, please?* **5** a pattern of squares of different colors

checkbook /ˈtʃekˌbʊk/ noun a book of papers printed by a bank that you use to pay for things

checked /tʃekt/ adj with a pattern of squares of different colors: *a checked shirt*

check-in /ˈtʃekˌɪn/ noun [no plural] **1** 🅑1 the place at an airport where you go to say that you have arrived for your flight: *We went straight to check-in.* **2** the act of showing your ticket at an airport to say that you have arrived for your flight: *There was a line at the **check-in counter**.*

checkout /ˈtʃekˌaʊt/ noun **1** 🅑1 a place in a large store where you pay for things: *a supermarket checkout* **2** 🅑1 [no plural] the place on a website where you order and pay for goods: *Click here to go to checkout.*

checkup /ˈtʃekˌʌp/ noun a general medical examination to see if you are healthy: *I'm going to the doctor for a checkup.*

cheek /tʃik/ noun 🅑1 one of the two soft parts of your face below your eyes: *Tears ran down his cheeks.*

cheer¹ /tʃɪər/ verb to shout loudly at someone whom you like or want to

encourage: *The crowd was cheering as he ran into the stadium.*

cheer up phrasal verb to stop feeling sad: *Cheer up. It will be OK!*

cheer² /tʃɪər/ noun a shout that shows you like someone or want to encourage him or her

cheerful /ˈtʃɪərfəl/ adj **1** 🅑1 happy: *She seemed fairly cheerful.* **2** describes a place or thing that is bright and pleasant and makes you feel happy: *Her bedroom was bright and cheerful with yellow walls and curtains.*

• **cheerfully** adv *He walked down the road, whistling cheerfully.*

cheers! /tʃɪərz/ exclamation 🅑1 something friendly that you say before you start to drink alcohol with someone

cheese /tʃiz/ noun 🅐1 a yellow or white solid food made from milk: *a slice of cheese* ○ *a cheese sandwich* ○ *French cheeses*

→ See **Food** on page C7

cheeseburger /ˈtʃizˌbɜr·gər/ noun a hamburger (=meat cooked in a round, flat shape) eaten between round pieces of bread with a slice of cheese

chef /ʃef/ noun 🅐2 someone who cooks food in a restaurant

chemical¹ /ˈkem·ɪ·kəl/ adj relating to chemistry or chemicals

chemical² /ˈkem·ɪ·kəl/ noun a substance that is used in chemistry or produced by chemistry

chemistry /ˈkem·ə·stri/ noun [no plural] 🅐2 the scientific study of substances and how they change when they combine

cherry /ˈtʃer·i/ noun (plural **cherries**) a small, round red or black fruit with a large seed inside

chess /tʃes/ noun [no plural] 🅐2 a game that two people play by moving specially shaped pieces around a board of black and white squares

chest /tʃest/ noun **1** the front of your body between your neck and your

a b c d e f g h i j k l m n o p q r s t u v w x y z

stomach → See **The Body** on page C2 **2 a** big wooden box for keeping things in

chest of drawers /ˈtʃest əv ˈdrɔːz/ noun (also **bureau**) **B1** a piece of furniture with drawers for keeping clothes in

chew /tʃuː/ verb to break food between your teeth as a part of eating

chewing gum /ˈtʃuː·ɪŋ ˌɡʌm/ noun [no plural] **B1** a sweet substance that you chew but do not eat

chick /tʃɪk/ noun a baby bird, especially a baby chicken

chicken /ˈtʃɪk·ən/ noun **1 A2** a bird kept on a farm for its meat and eggs **2 A2** [no plural] the meat of a chicken

chief[1] /tʃiːf/ adj most important: The low pay was my chief reason for quitting.

chief[2] /tʃiːf/ noun the leader of a group

child /tʃaɪld/ noun (plural **children**) **1 A1** a young person who is not yet an adult **2** a son or daughter of any age

childcare /ˈtʃaɪldˌkeər/ noun [no plural] the care of children, especially while their parents are working: The office has **childcare** facilities.

childhood /ˈtʃaɪldˌhʊd/ noun **B1** the part of your life when you are a child: She **had** a happy **childhood**.

childish /ˈtʃaɪl·dɪʃ/ adj silly, like the behavior of a child: Don't be so childish! • **childishly** adv

children /ˈtʃɪl·drən/ noun plural of child

chili /ˈtʃɪl·i/ noun (plural **chilies**) **1** a small, thin, red or green vegetable that tastes very hot: chili pepper **2** [no plural] a spicy dish of beans, meat, and chilies

chilly /ˈtʃɪl·i/ adj (comparative **chillier**, superlative **chilliest**) too cold: It's chilly outside.

chimney /ˈtʃɪm·ni/ noun a pipe that takes smoke from a fire out through a roof

chimney
roof

chimpanzee /ˌtʃɪm·pænˈziː/ noun

an African animal like a large monkey with no tail

chin /tʃɪn/ noun **B1** the bottom part of your face, below your mouth → See **The Body** on page C2

china /ˈtʃaɪ·nə/ noun [no plural] **1** the hard substance that plates, cups, bowls, etc. are made from: a china teapot **2** cups, plates, bowls, etc. that are made from china: I use the best china when we have company.

chip[1] /tʃɪp/ noun **1** a very small part of a computer that stores information **2** a thin, dry slice of fried potato → See **Food** on page C7

chip[2] /tʃɪp/ verb (present participle **chipping**, past tense and past participle **chipped**) to break a small piece off something that is hard: She chipped her tooth when she fell off her bike.

chocolate /ˈtʃɔk·lət/, /ˈtʃɔ·kə·lət/ noun **1 A1** [no plural] a sweet, brown food that is usually sold in a block: a bar of chocolate ○ milk chocolate → See **Quantities** on page C14 **2** a small piece of sweet food covered in chocolate: a box of chocolates

choice /tʃɔɪs/ noun **1 B1** the possibility of choosing between two or more things: If I had a choice, I'd stop working. **2** the decision to choose one thing or person and not someone or something else: In the past women had to **make a choice between** a career or marriage. **3 B1** the things or people you can choose from: The dress is available in a **choice of** colors. **4 B1** the person or thing that someone has chosen: Harvard was his **first choice** of schools.

choir /kwaɪər/ noun a group of people who sing together: a church choir

choke /tʃoʊk/ verb (present participle **choking**, past tense and past participle **choked**) to stop breathing because something is in your throat: Small children can **choke on** peanuts.

choose /tʃuːz/ verb (present participle **choosing**, past tense **chose**, past participle **chosen**) **1 A1** to decide which thing you want: *Have you chosen a name for the baby?* ○ *There were lots of books to* **choose from.** **2** **choose to do something** to decide to do something: *She chose to take a job in Denver.*

chop[1] /tʃɑp/ **verb** (present participle **chopping**, past tense and past participle **chopped**) to cut something into small pieces: *Chop the onion and pepper.*

chop

chop[2] /tʃɑp/ **noun** a flat piece of meat with a bone in it: *a lamb chop*

chord /kɔrd/ **noun** two or more musical notes that are played at the same time

chore /tʃɔr/ **noun** a boring job that you must do: *the household chores*

chorus /ˈkɔr·əs/ **noun** the part of a song that is repeated many times

chose /tʃoʊz/ past tense of choose

chosen /ˈtʃoʊ·zən/ past participle of choose

christening /ˈkrɪs·ə·nɪŋ/ **noun** a ceremony in which a baby is given a name and made a member of the Christian Church

Christian /ˈkrɪs·tʃən/ **noun** someone whose religion is Christianity
• **Christian adj**

Christianity /ˌkrɪs·tʃiˈæn·ɪ·ti/ **noun** [no plural] a religion based on belief in one God and the ideas that Jesus Christ taught

Christmas /ˈkrɪs·məs/ **noun** the period of celebration around December 25,

when Christians celebrate the birth of Jesus Christ and people give each other presents: *Merry Christmas!*

chunk /tʃʌŋk/ **noun** a large piece of something: *a chunk of cheese*
→ See **Quantities** on page C14

church /tʃɜrtʃ/ **noun** **A2** a building where Christians go to pray: *We go to church every Sunday morning.*

cider /ˈsɑɪ·dər/ **noun** [no plural] the juice of crushed apples, used as a drink or to make vinegar

cigar /sɪˈgɑr/ **noun** a thick tube made from rolled tobacco leaves, which people smoke

cigarette /ˌsɪg·əˈret/ **noun** **A2** a thin tube of paper filled with tobacco, which people smoke

cinnamon /ˈsɪn·ə·mən/ **noun** [no plural] a spice that has a hot taste and is used especially in sweet foods

circle /ˈsɜr·kəl/ **noun** **A2** a round, flat shape like the letter O: *We all sat on the floor* **in a circle.**
→ See picture at **shape noun** (1)

circular /ˈsɜr·kjə·lər/ **adj** shaped like a circle

circulate /ˈsɜr·kjəˌleɪt/ **verb** (present participle **circulating**, past tense and past participle **circulated**) to move around: *Hot water circulates through the pipes.*

circulation /ˌsɜr·kjəˈleɪ·ʃən/ **noun** [no plural] the movement of blood around the body

circumference /sərˈkʌm·fər·əns/ **noun** the distance around a circle

circumstances /ˈsɜr·kəmˌstæn·sɪz/ **plural noun** **1** the facts or events of a situation: *I think they coped very well* **under the circumstances** (= that difficult situation). **2** **under no circumstances** used to say that something must never happen: *Under no circumstances should you approach the bear.*

circus /ˈsɜr·kəs/ **noun** **B1** a show in which a group of people and animals perform in a large tent

citizen /ˈsɪt̬·ə·zən/ **noun** **1** someone who lives in a particular town or city: *the*

citizens of Berlin **2** someone who has a legal right to live in a particular country: *He applied to become an American citizen.*

citizenship /ˈsɪt·ə·zənˌʃɪp/ **noun** [no plural] the legal right to be a citizen of a particular country: *American citizenship*

city /ˈsɪt·i/ **noun** (plural **cities**) **A1** a large town

civilization /ˌsɪv·ə·ləˈzeɪ·ʃən/ **noun** the way that people live together, with laws to control their behavior, education, and a government: *Nuclear war could mean the end of civilization.*

civilized /ˈsɪv·əˌlaɪzd/ **adj** a civilized society is advanced and has laws, education, and a government

civil war /ˈsɪv·əl ˈwɔr/ **noun** a war between groups of people who live in the same country

claim[1] /kleɪm/ **verb 1** to say that something is true: *She claimed that the dog attacked her.* **2** to ask for something because it belongs to you or you have the right to have it: *She claimed $2,500 in travel expenses.*

claim[2] /kleɪm/ **noun 1** a statement that something is true: *There were claims that he had lied.* **2** an official demand for something you think you have a right to: *a claim for compensation*

clap /klæp/ **verb** (present participle **clapping**, past tense and past participle **clapped**) **B1** to hit your hands together to show that you have enjoyed a performance, talk, etc.: *The crowd clapped and cheered.*

clap

clash[1] /klæʃ/ **verb 1** to fight or argue: *Protesters clashed with police outside the courthouse.* **2** If colors clash, they do not look good together

clash[2] /klæʃ/ **noun 1** a fight or argument: *a clash of different cultures* **2** a loud sound that is made when metal objects hit each other

clasp /klæsp/ **verb** to hold something or someone tightly: *He clasped his daughter in his arms.*

class /klæs/ **noun 1** **A1** a group of students who have lessons together: *We were in the same class in school.* **2** **A1** a period of time in which students are taught something: *My first class starts at 8:30.* **3** **A2** a group into which products, services, or people are put according to their standard: *a business-class fare* ○ *a first-class ticket* **4** one of the groups in a society with the same social and economic position **5** a group of similar or related things, especially plants and animals

> **⚠ Common mistake: class or classroom?**
>
> A **class** is a group of students who have lessons together.
> *The whole class arrived late.*
> A **classroom** is a room where lessons happen.
> *There are computers in every classroom.*

classic[1] /ˈklæs·ɪk/ **adj 1** A classic book, movie, etc. is one that has been popular for a long time and is very good: *the classic movie "The Wizard of Oz"* **2** typical: *He's a classic example of a child who's smart but lazy.*

classic[2] /ˈklæs·ɪk/ **noun** a classic book, movie, etc.

classical /ˈklæs·ɪ·kəl/ **adj** classical music **A2** serious music by people like Mozart and Stravinsky

classmate /ˈklæsˌmeɪt/ **noun** **A2** someone who is in your class in school or college

---

| oʊ go | aɪər fire | aʊər hour | eər hair | ɪər ear | ʊər poor | j yet | ʒ measure | ʃ ship | dʒ judge | tʃ chin | ð that | θ thin | ŋ hang |

classroom /ˈklæsˌrum/, /ˈklæsˌrum/ noun
A1 a room in a school where students have lessons
→ See **The Classroom** on page C4

clause /klɔz/ noun a group of words containing a subject and a verb, that is usually only part of a sentence

claw /klɔ/ noun
one of the sharp, curved nails on the feet of some animals and birds

claws

clay /kleɪ/ noun
[no plural] a heavy soil that is hard when it is dry, used for making bricks and containers

clean[1] /klin/ adj **A1** not dirty: *clean hands* ∘ *Please keep your room clean.*

clean[2] /klin/ verb **A1** to remove the dirt from something: *I spent the morning cleaning the house.*

cleaner /ˈkli·nər/ noun **A2** someone whose job is to clean houses, offices, and other places

clear[1] /klɪr/ adj **1 A2** easy to understand: *clear instructions* **2 A2** easy to hear, read, or see: *These photos are very clear.* **3 A2** easy to see through: *clear glass* **4 B1** obvious; not possible to doubt: *It was **clear that** she didn't like him.* **5 B1** not covered or blocked by anything: *a clear road* ∘ *a clear sky*

clear[2] /klɪr/ verb **1 B1** to take away all the things or people from a place: *They completely cleared the room.* **2** If the sky or weather clears, the clouds and rain disappear.

clear *something* **out** phrasal verb
to make a place clean by throwing away things that you do not want: *If we clear out the attic, we can use it as a study.*

clear up phrasal verb **1** to improve: *If the weather clears up, we'll go out.* **2** to give an explanation for something, or to deal with a problem or argument: *I'm glad we cleared up the misunderstanding.*

clearly /ˈklɪr·li/ adv **1 A2** in a way that is easy to see, hear, or understand: *He*
spoke very clearly. **2 A2** in a way that is not confused: *I had only two hours of sleep and wasn't thinking clearly.* **3 B1** in a way that you cannot doubt: *He's clearly not interested.*

clerk /klɜrk/ noun someone who works in an office but does not have an important job: *a bank clerk*

clever /ˈklev·ər/ adj **B1** showing intelligence and skill: *a clever idea*
• **cleverly** adv

click[1] /klɪk/ verb **1** to make a short, sharp sound: *The door clicked shut behind him.* **2 A2** to push part of a computer mouse (=small computer control) to make the computer do something: *To start the program, **click on** its icon.*

click[2] /klɪk/ noun **1 A2** a short, sharp sound: *the click of a switch* **2 A2** the action of pressing on part of a computer mouse: *You can get the information with a single click.*

client /ˈklaɪ·ənt/ noun someone who pays for services or advice

cliff /klɪf/ noun
B1 a high area of rock with a very steep side, often next to a coast

cliff

climate /ˈklaɪ·mət/ noun **B1** the weather conditions of an area: *a hot, dry climate* ∘ *climate change* (=the way the Earth's weather is changing)

climax /ˈklaɪ·mæks/ noun the most exciting or important time: *The **climax of** her career was winning a gold medal.*

climb /klaɪm/ verb **1 A2** to go up something: *Slowly we climbed the hill.* **2** to move into or out of a small space, often with difficulty or effort: *The baby had managed to climb out of his crib.*
• **climb** noun *a long climb*

a b c d e f g h i j k l m n o p q r s t u v w x y z

climber   64

climb

clockwise   counterclockwise

that point to the numbers) on a clock move

→ Opposite **counterclockwise**

climber /ˈklaɪ·mər/ *noun* someone who climbs mountains, hills, or rocks as a sport

climbing /ˈklaɪ·mɪŋ/ *noun* [no plural] **A2** the sport of climbing mountains, hills, or rocks: *mountain climbing* ○ *climbing boots*

cling /klɪŋ/ *verb* (past tense and past participle **clung**) to hold someone or something tightly: *I clung on to his hand in the dark.*

clinic /ˈklɪn·ɪk/ *noun* **B1** a place where people go for medical treatment or advice: *an eye clinic*

clip¹ /klɪp/ *noun* **1** a small metal object used for holding things together: *a paper clip* **2** a short part of a film: *They showed clips from his new movie.* **3** a short video recording that you can see on a website: *The site has thousands of TV and movie clips.*

clip² /klɪp/ *verb* (present participle **clipping**, past tense and past participle **clipped**) **1** to fix things together with a clip: *Clip the microphone to the collar of your jacket.* **2** to cut small pieces from something

clipping /ˈklɪp·ɪŋ/ *noun* an article or picture that has been cut out of a newspaper or magazine: *She keeps all her press clippings.*

clock /klɑk/ *noun* **A1** a piece of equipment that shows you what time it is: *There was a clock on the wall.* → See **The Living Room** on page C11

clockwise /ˈklɑk·waɪz/ *adj, adv* in the same direction as the hands (= parts

close¹ /kloʊz/ *verb* (present participle **closing**, past tense and past participle **closed**) **1** **A1** If something closes, it moves so that it is not open. If you close something, you move it so that it is not open: *Jane closed the window.* ○ *Suddenly the door closed.* **2** **A2** If a store, restaurant, etc. closes, people cannot go in it: *The supermarket closes at 8 p.m.* **3** If a business closes, it stops operating.

close down *phrasal verb* If a business closes down, it stops operating: *So many stores are closing down.*

close² /kloʊs/ *adj* **1** **A1** near in distance: *His house is close to the beach.* **2** near in time: *It was close to lunchtime when we arrived.* **3** **A2** If people are close, they know each other well and like each other: *close friends* **4** **B1** A close relative is someone who is directly related to you, for example your mother, father, or brother: *There weren't many people at the funeral – just close family.* **5** A close competition is one in which people's scores are very similar. **6** looking at or listening to someone or something very carefully: *Keep a close watch on the children* (= watch them carefully).
• **closely** *adv*

close³ /kloʊs/ *adv* **B1** near in distance: *They sat close together.*

close⁴ /kloʊz/ *noun* [no plural] the end of something: *They finally reached an agreement at the close of a week of negotiations.* ○ *The year was drawing to a close.*

closed /kloʊzd/ *adj* **1** **A1** not open for business: *We went to the library but it*

|oʊ go|aɪər fire|aʊər hour|ear hair|ɪər ear|ʊər poor|j yet|ʒ measure|ʃ ship|dʒ judge|tʃ chin|ð that|θ thin|ŋ hang|

was closed. **2** A1 not open: *Her eyes were closed.*

closet /ˈklɑz·ɪt/ *noun* B1 a small room or space in a wall where you can store things, often with a door on it: *a clothes/linen closet*

cloth /klɔθ/ *noun* **1** [no plural] material made from cotton, wool, etc., and used, for example, to make clothes or curtains **2** a piece of material used for cleaning or drying things

> ⚠ **Common mistake: cloth, clothes, or clothing?**
>
> The most usual word for the things you wear is **clothes. Clothing** is slightly more formal, and often used for particular types of clothes.
> **Cloth** is the material that clothes are made from. Do not try to make a plural "cloths," because **cloth** is an uncountable noun.
> *I put my clothes on.*
> ~~I put my cloth on.~~
> *They gave us money for food and clothing.*
> ~~They gave us money for food and cloths.~~

clothes /kloʊðz/, /kloʊz/ *plural noun* A1 things such as shirts and pants that you wear on your body: *She always wears nice clothes.*
→ See **Clothes** on page C5

> ⚠ **Common mistake: clothes**
>
> Remember that **clothes** is plural. If you want to talk about one particular thing that you wear, use **a piece of clothing** or **an item of clothing.**
> *I need some new clothes.*
> *He bought two or three pieces of clothing.*

clothing /ˈkloʊ·ðɪŋ/ *noun* [no plural] clothes, especially of a particular type: *outdoor clothing*

cloud /klaʊd/ *noun*
1 A2 one of the white or gray things in the sky

cloud

that are made of small water drops: *rain clouds* **2** a mass of something such as dust or smoke that looks like a cloud: *A huge cloud of smoke spread across the sky.*

cloudy /ˈklaʊ·di/ *adj* (comparative **cloudier,** superlative **cloudiest**) A2 with many clouds in the sky: *a cloudy day*

clown /klaʊn/ *noun* A2 someone with funny clothes and a painted face, who makes people laugh by being silly

club /klʌb/ *noun* **1** A2 a group of people who do a sport or other activity together: *a drama club* **2** a long, thin stick used to hit the ball in golf **3** a place where people listen to music or dance, usually late at night: *a jazz club*

clubs /klʌbz/ *plural noun* one of the four suits (=groups) of playing cards: *the four of clubs*

clue /klu/ *noun* **1** something that helps you to solve a problem or answer a question: *Police are searching the area for **clues to** the murder.* **2 not have a clue** *informal* to know nothing about something: *I don't have a clue what you're talking about.*

clumsy /ˈklʌm·zi/ *adj* (comparative **clumsier,** superlative **clumsiest**) Clumsy people move in a way that is not controlled or careful, and often knock or damage things.

clung /klʌŋ/ past tense and past participle of cling

clutch[1] /klʌtʃ/ *verb* to hold something tightly: *She clutched a coin in her hand.*

clutch[2] /klʌtʃ/ *noun* [no plural] the part of a car that you press with your foot when you change gears (=the parts that control how fast the wheels turn)

cm written abbreviation for centimeter: a unit for measuring length

coach[1] /koʊtʃ/ *noun* B1 someone who gives lessons, especially in a sport: *a tennis coach*

coach[2] /koʊtʃ/ *verb* to give someone lessons, especially in a sport or school subject
• **coaching** *noun* [no plural]

coal /koʊl/ *noun* [no plural] a hard, black substance that is found in the ground and burned as fuel: *a lump of coal*

coast /koʊst/ *noun* **B1** the land next to the ocean: *the east coast of Florida*

coastline /ˈkoʊstˌlaɪn/ *noun* the land next to the ocean, or the shape of this land on a map: *a rocky coastline*

coat /koʊt/ *noun* **1 A1** a piece of clothing that you wear over your other clothes when you are outside: *a winter coat* → See **Clothes** on page C5 **2** the fur that covers an animal's body **3** a layer of a liquid over a surface: *a coat of paint*

coatroom /ˈkoʊtˌrum,/ ˈkoʊtˌrʊm/ *noun* a room where you leave your coat at a theater, school, etc.

cocoa /ˈkoʊ·koʊ/ *noun* [no plural] **1** the dark brown powder used to make chocolate **2** a drink made by mixing cocoa powder with hot milk

coconut /ˈkoʊ·kə·nʌt/ *noun* **B1** a large nut with a hard shell, a white part that you eat, and liquid in the center

code /koʊd/ *noun* a set of letters, numbers, or signs that are used instead of ordinary words to keep a message secret: *It was written in code.*

coffee /ˈkɔ·fi/ *noun* **1 A1** a hot drink made from dark beans that are made into a powder, or a cup of this drink: *a cup of coffee* **2 A1** [no plural] the beans from which coffee is made, or the powder made from these beans: *instant coffee*

coffee shop /ˈkɔ·fi ˌʃɑp/ *noun* a small restaurant where you can buy coffee drinks and light food such as cake or sandwiches

coffee table /ˈkɔ·fi ˌteɪ·bəl/ *noun* a low table in a living room on which people set magazines, drinks, etc.
→ See **The Living Room** on page C11

coffin /ˈkɔ·fɪn/ *noun* a box in which a dead body is buried

coin /kɔɪn/ *noun* **B1** a flat, round piece of metal used as money: *a gold coin*

coincidence /koʊˈɪn·sɪ·dəns/ *noun* an occasion when two very similar things happen at the same time by

chance: *It was just a coincidence that we were traveling on the same train.*

cola /ˈkoʊ·lə/ *noun* **A2** a sweet, dark brown drink with lots of bubbles, or a glass or can of this drink: *a can of cola*

colander /ˈkɑl·ən·dər/ *noun* a large bowl with holes in it, used for washing food or pouring liquid off cooked food

cold[1] /koʊld/ *adj* **1 A1** having a low temperature: *cold water/weather*
→ Opposite **hot** **2 B1** unfriendly or showing no emotion: *a cold stare*

cold[2] /koʊld/ *noun* **1 A2** a common illness that makes your nose produce liquid: *I have a cold.* **2 the cold** **B1** cold weather: *Don't go out in the cold!*

collapse /kəˈlæps/ *verb* (present participle **collapsing**, past tense and past participle **collapsed**) to fall down, sometimes breaking into pieces: *The roof collapsed under the weight of the snow.* ○ *He collapsed and died of a heart attack.*
• **collapse** *noun* [no plural]

collar /ˈkɑl·ər/ *noun* **1 B1** the part of a shirt or coat that goes around your neck → See picture at **jacket** **2** a thin piece of leather that goes around the neck of a dog or a cat

colleague /ˈkɑl·ig/ *noun* **A2** someone whom you work with

collect[1] /kəˈlekt/ *verb* **1 A2** to get and keep things of one type, such as stamps or coins, as a hobby: *She collects dolls.* **2 B1** to get things from different places and bring them together: *The police collected a lot of information during the investigation.* **3** to gradually increase in amount in a place: *Dust had collected on top of the refrigerator.*

collect[2] /kəˈlekt/ *adj, adv* If you call collect or make a collect telephone call, the person you telephone pays for the call: *She called her parents collect.*

collection /kəˈlek·ʃən/ *noun* **1 B1** a group of objects of the same type that have been brought together: *a private art collection* **2** the act of removing something from a place: *garbage collection*

collector /kəˈlek·tər/ noun someone who collects objects because they are interesting or beautiful: *an art collector*

college /ˈkɑl·ɪdʒ/ noun a place where students study at a high level to get a degree (=type of qualification): *Where did you go to college?*

collision /kəˈlɪʒ·ən/ noun an accident in which vehicles hit each other

colon /ˈkoʊ·lən/ noun a mark [:] used before a list, an example, an explanation, etc.

colony /ˈkɑl·ə·ni/ noun (plural **colonies**) a country or area controlled by a more powerful country

color[1] /ˈkʌl·ər/ noun **1** Ⓐ red, blue, green, yellow, etc.: *What color should I paint the kitchen?* → See **Colors** on page C6 **2** [no plural] the color of a person's skin, which shows his or her race

color[2] /ˈkʌl·ər/ verb Ⓐ to make something a particular color: *He drew a heart and colored it red.*

colorful /ˈkʌl·ər·fəl/ adj **1** Ⓑ having bright colors: *a large, colorful painting* **2** interesting and unusual: *The town has a very colorful history.*

column /ˈkɑl·əm/ noun **1** a tall stone post that supports a roof **2** a long, vertical line of something **3** one of the blocks of print into which a page of a newspaper, magazine, or dictionary is divided: *I didn't have time to read the whole article – just the first column.*

comb[1] /koʊm/ noun Ⓐ a tool used for making your hair neat, made of a flat piece of metal or plastic with a line of long, narrow parts along one side

comb[2] /koʊm/ verb Ⓑ to make your hair neat using a comb

combination /ˌkɑm·bəˈneɪ·ʃən/ noun a mixture of different people or things: *Strong passwords are a combination of letters, numbers, and symbols.*

combine /kəmˈbaɪn/ verb (present participle **combining**, past tense and past participle **combined**) to become mixed or joined, or to mix or join things together: *Combine the sugar and the butter.*

come /kʌm/ verb (present participle **coming**, past tense **came**, past participle **come**) **1** Ⓐ to move or travel toward a person who is speaking: *Come here.* ○ *Can you come to my party?* ○ *Here comes Adam* (=Adam is coming). **2** Ⓐ to arrive somewhere: *I came to see Mr. Curtis.* ○ *Did the paper come yet?* **3** Ⓐ to go somewhere with the person who is speaking: *Come with us later.* **4** Ⓐ to be available to buy in a particular color, size, etc.: *Do these socks come in any other color?* **5** Ⓑ to have a particular position in a competition or list: *Our team came in third.* **6 come true** Ⓑ If something you want comes true, it happens: *My dream of owning my own home has come true.* **7** to happen: *Spring came early this year.* **8 come apart/off** to become separated or removed from something: *The book came apart in my hands.* ○ *The handle came off.* **9 how come** used to ask why something has happened: *How come you didn't go to the party?*

come along phrasal verb Ⓐ to go somewhere with someone: *We're going to the zoo. Do you want to come along?*

come back phrasal verb Ⓐ to return to a place: *We just came back from vacation.*

come down phrasal verb If a price or a level comes down, it becomes lower: *House prices have come down recently.*

come from *something* phrasal verb Ⓐ to be born, gotten from, or made somewhere: *She comes from Poland.* ○ *Milk comes from cows.*

come in phrasal verb Ⓐ to enter a room or building: *Come in and have a seat.*

come on phrasal verb Ⓑ said to encourage someone to do something, especially to hurry or try harder: *Come on, the taxi's waiting.*

come out phrasal verb **1** Ⓑ If a book, movie, etc. comes out, it becomes available for people to buy or see: *When does their new album come out?* **2** Ⓑ If the sun, the moon, or a star comes out, it appears in the sky.

come over phrasal verb ⒜ to visit someone at his or her house: *You should come over for dinner sometime.*

come up phrasal verb **1** to move toward someone: *A young girl came up to me and asked for money.* **2** to be mentioned or talked about in conversation: *What issues came up at the meeting?*

come up with *something* phrasal verb to suggest or think of an idea or plan: *We need to come up with a great idea to make money.*

comedian /kə·ˈmi·di·ən/ noun someone who entertains people by telling jokes

comedy /ˈkɑm·ɪ·di/ noun (plural **comedies**) ⒝ a funny movie or play

comfort[1] /ˈkʌm·fərt/ noun [no plural] ⒝ a nice feeling of being relaxed and without pain: *Now you can watch the latest movies in the comfort of your living room.*

comfort[2] /ˈkʌm·fərt/ verb to make someone feel better when he or she is sad: *We comforted Sasha after her dog died.*

comfortable /ˈkʌm·fər·tə·bəl, ˈkʌmf·tər·bəl/ adj **1** ⒜ making you feel relaxed and free from pain: *comfortable shoes ○ a comfortable bed* **2** ⒝ relaxed and without pain: *Make yourself comfortable while I get you a drink.* **3** If you are comfortable in a situation, you do not have any worries about it: *I don't feel comfortable about leaving the children here alone.*
→ Opposite **uncomfortable** adj
• **comfortably** adv

> **⚠ Common mistake:**
> **comfortable**
>
> People often spell **comfortable** wrong. Remember that it begins with **com**.

comic[1] /ˈkɑm·ɪk/ adj ⒝ funny: *a comic novel*

comic[2] /ˈkɑm·ɪk/ noun ⒜ a magazine with stories told in pictures

comma /ˈkɑm·ə/ noun ⒝ a mark [,] used to separate parts of a sentence, or to separate the items in a list

command[1] /kə·ˈmænd/ noun **1** an order to do something **2** [no plural] control over someone or something and responsibility for them: *Jones was in command (= the leader).* **3** an instruction to a computer

command[2] /kə·ˈmænd/ verb formal to order someone to do something: *The officer commanded his men to shoot.*

comment[1] /ˈkɑm·ent/ noun something that you say or write that shows your opinion: *He read my essay and made a few comments.*

comment[2] /ˈkɑm·ent/ verb to make a comment: *My mom always comments on what I'm wearing.*

commentary /ˈkɑm·ən,ter·i/ noun (plural **commentaries**) a spoken description of an event while the event is happening: *election commentary*

commerce /ˈkɑm·ərs/ noun [no plural] the activities involved in buying and selling things

commercial[1] /kə·ˈmɜr·ʃəl/ adj **1** relating to buying and selling things **2** done in order to make a profit: *a commercial success (= something that makes a profit)*

commercial[2] /kə·ˈmɜr·ʃəl/ noun ⒝ an advertisement on the radio or television

commit /kə·ˈmɪt/ verb (present participle **committing**, past tense and past participle **committed**) **1** to do something bad or illegal: *He went to prison for a crime he didn't commit.* **2** to make a definite decision to do something: *I said I might be interested in the job but I haven't committed myself yet.*

commitment /kə·ˈmɪt·mənt/ noun **1** a promise to do something: *Players must make a commitment to daily training.* **2** [no plural] the willingness to give a lot of time and energy to something

committed /kə·ˈmɪt·ɪd/ adj loyal and giving a lot of your time and energy to something: *She's committed to the job.*

committee /kə·ˈmɪt·i/ noun a group of people who represent a larger organization and make decisions for it

common[1] /'kɑm·ən/ adj **1** 🔵 happening often or existing in large numbers: *Injuries are common in sports such as hockey.* **2** 🔵 shared by two or more people or things: *We don't have any common interests.*

common[2] /'kɑm·ən/ noun **have something in common** 🔵 to have the same interests, experiences, or qualities as someone or something else: *Sue and I don't have much in common.*

common sense /'kɑm·ən 'sens/ noun [no plural] 🔵 the ability to use good judgment in making decisions: *The kids will be fine as long as they use their common sense.*

communicate /kə'mju·nɪ‚keɪt/ verb (present participle **communicating**, past tense and past participle **communicated**) 🔵 to talk or write to someone in order to share information with them: *I usually **communicate with** him by email.*

communication /kə‚mju·nɪ'keɪ·ʃən/ noun [no plural] 🔵 the act of communicating with other people: *The school is improving **communication between** teachers and parents.*

communications /kə‚mju·nɪ'keɪ·ʃənz/ plural noun the different ways of sending information between people and places, such as mail, telephones, computers, and radio: *the communications industry*

community /kə'mju·nɪ·t̬i/ noun (plural **communities**) **1** the people living in a particular area: *the local community* **2** a group of people with the same interests, religion, or nationality: *the Chinese community in Chicago*

community college /kə'mju·nɪ·t̬i 'kɑl·ɪdʒ/ noun a place where students study at a higher level after high school, usually for two years, to prepare to enter a university

commute /kə'mjut/ verb (present participle **commuting**, past tense and past participle **commuted**) to travel regularly between work and home

commuter /kə'mju·t̬ər/ noun someone who regularly travels between work and home: *The train was full of commuters.*

companion /kəm'pæn·jən/ noun someone whom you spend a lot of time with or go somewhere with: *a travel companion*

company /'kʌm·pə·ni/ noun **1** 🅰 (plural **companies**) an organization that sells things or services: *a software company* **2** [no plural] a state of having a person or people with you: *I enjoy his company.* **3** **keep someone company** to stay with someone so that he or she is not alone: *I keep Grandma company every Saturday.* **4** [no plural] visitors to your home: *We **have company** coming for dinner.*

comparative /kəm'pær·ə·t̬ɪv/ noun 🅰 the form of an adjective or adverb that is used to show that someone or something has more of a particular quality than someone or something else. For example, "better" is the comparative of "good," and "smaller" is the comparative of "small."

compare /kəm'peər/ verb (present participle **comparing**, past tense and past participle **compared**) **1** 🔵 to examine the ways in which two people or things are different or similar: *The teachers are always **comparing me with** my sister.* **2** **compared to/with** someone/something used when saying how one person or thing is different from another: *Her room is very clean compared to mine.*

comparison /kəm'pær·ə·sən/ noun the act of comparing two or more people or things: *She's so tall that he looks tiny **by/in comparison**.*

compartment /kəm'pɑrt·mənt/ noun **1** a separate part of a container, bag, etc.: *a refrigerator with a small freezer compartment* **2** one of the separate areas inside a train

compass /'kʌm·pəs/, /'kɑm·pəs/ noun a piece of equipment that shows you which direction you are going in

compass

| a |
| b |
| **c** |
| d |
| e |
| f |
| g |
| h |
| i |
| j |
| k |
| l |
| m |
| n |
| o |
| p |
| q |
| r |
| s |
| t |
| u |
| v |
| w |
| x |
| y |
| z |

æ cat | ɑ hot | e get | ɪ sit | i see | ɔ saw | ʊ book | u too | ʌ cut | ə about | ɑr mother | ɜr turn | ɔr for | ɑɪ my | ɑʊ how | eɪ say | ɔɪ boy

a
b
c
d
e
f
g
h
i
j
k
l
m
n
o
p
q
r
s
t
u
v
w
x
y
z

compatible /kəmˈpæt̬·ə·bəl/ adj happy or successful when together or combined: *This keyboard is **compatible with** all of our computers.*

compensation /ˌkɑm·pənˈseɪ·ʃən/ noun [no plural] money that you give someone because you have hurt him or her or damaged something that he or she owns

compete /kəmˈpit/ verb (present participle **competing**, past tense and past participle **competed**) 1 **B1** to try to win a competition: *She's **competing for** a place in next year's Olympics.* 2 to try to be more successful than someone or something else: *It's difficult for a small grocery store to **compete against/with** the big supermarkets.*

competition /ˌkɑm·pəˈtɪʃ·ən/ noun 1 **A2** an event in which people try to win something by being the best, fastest, etc. 2 [no plural] a situation in which people or companies try to be more successful than others: *There's a lot of **competition between** computer companies.*

competitive /kəmˈpet̬·ɪ·t̬ɪv/ adj 1 wanting to win or be better than other people: *She's very competitive.* 2 involving competition: *competitive sports* 3 as good as or better than other prices, services, etc.: *They offer high-quality products at competitive prices.*

competitor /kəmˈpet̬·ɪ·t̬ər/ noun **B1** someone who is trying to win a competition

> ⚠ **Common mistake: complain about** something
>
> Be careful to choose the correct preposition after **complain**.
> *I am writing to **complain about** the trip.*
> ~~I am writing to complain for the trip.~~
> ~~I am writing to complain on the trip.~~

complain /kəmˈpleɪn/ verb **B1** to say that something is wrong or that you are angry about something: *Lots of people have **complained about** the noise.* ∘ *She **complained** that no one listened to her.*
complain of *something* phrasal verb

B1 to tell other people that something is making you feel sick: *She's been complaining of a headache all day.*

complaint /kəmˈpleɪnt/ noun **B1** a statement that someone makes to say something is wrong or not good enough: *I wish to **make a complaint**.*

complete¹ /kəmˈplit/ adj 1 **B1** with all parts: *the complete works of Mark Twain* 2 **B1** used to make what you are saying stronger: *The meeting was a complete waste of time.*

complete² /kəmˈplit/ verb (present participle **completing**, past tense and past participle **completed**) 1 **A2** to finish doing or making something: *The palace took 15 years to complete.* 2 **A2** to provide the last part needed to make something whole: *Complete the sentence with one of the adjectives provided.* 3 **A2** to write all the necessary details on a form or other document: *Have you completed your application form yet?*

completely /kəmˈplit·li/ adv **B1** in every way or as much as possible: *I completely forgot that you were coming.* ∘ *The two sisters are completely different.*

complex /kəmˈpleks/ adj made of a lot of different but connected parts; difficult to understand: *a complex network of roads* ∘ *The story was so complex that I couldn't understand it.*

complicated /ˈkɑm·plɪˌkeɪ·t̬ɪd/ adj **B1** with many different parts and difficult to understand: *The instructions were too complicated.*

complication /ˌkɑm·plɪˈkeɪ·ʃən/ noun something that makes a situation more difficult

compliment /ˈkɑm·plə·mənt/ noun something good that you say about someone, showing that you admire him or her

compose /kəmˈpoʊz/ verb (present participle **composing**, past tense and past participle **composed**) 1 If something is composed of other things, it has those things in it: *The committee is composed of three men and six women.* 2 to write a piece of music

composition /ˌkɑm·pəˈzɪʃ·ən/ noun
1 **B1** a short piece of writing about a particular subject, done by a student: *a 500-word composition* **2** a piece of music that someone has written: *The children played their own compositions in the concert.*

compromise /ˈkɑm·prəˌmaɪz/ noun
the act of agreeing to something that is not exactly what you want in order to end an argument or solve a problem: *We need to **reach a compromise** on this issue.*

compulsory /kəmˈpʌl·sə·ri/ adj If something is compulsory, you must do it because a rule or law says you must.

computer /kəmˈpju·tər/ noun **A1** an electronic machine that can store and arrange large amounts of information: *We keep all our records on the computer.*
→ See **The Office** on page C12

computer game /kəmˈpju·tər ˌɡeɪm/ noun a game that is played on a computer, in which the pictures on the screen are controlled by pressing keys

conceal /kənˈsil/ verb to hide something: *I couldn't conceal my anger.*

concentrate /ˈkɑn·sənˌtreɪt/ verb (present participle **concentrating**, past tense and past participle **concentrated**) **B1** to think very hard about the thing you are doing and nothing else: *Be quiet – I'm trying to concentrate.* ○ *I can't **concentrate on** my work. It's too noisy.*

concentration /ˌkɑn·sənˈtreɪ·ʃən/ noun [no plural] the ability to think only about something you are doing

concept /ˈkɑn·sept/ noun an idea or principle: *It is very difficult to define **the concept** of beauty.*

concern¹ /kənˈsɜrn/ verb **1** to be important to someone: *Environmental issues concern us all.* **2** to worry or upset someone: *What concerns me is her lack of experience.* **3** If a story, movie, etc. concerns a particular subject, it is about that subject.

concern² /kənˈsɜrn/ noun **1** a feeling of worry about something: *I have **concerns***

about his health. **2** something that involves or affects you or is important to you: *Our primary concern is safety.*

concerned /kənˈsɜrnd/ adj **1** worried: *I'm a little **concerned about** her health.* **2 as far as someone is concerned** used to show what someone thinks about something: *He can do what he wants as far as I'm concerned.* **3 as far as something is concerned** used to say what you are talking about: *As far as money is concerned, we're doing very well.*

concerning /kənˈsɜr·nɪŋ/ preposition about something: *I got a letter concerning my tax payments.*

concert /ˈkɑn·sɑrt/ noun **A2** a performance of music, with or without singing: *a rock/jazz/classical concert*

conclusion /kənˈklu·ʒən/ noun **1** **B1** your opinion after considering all the information about something: *I have **come to the conclusion that** we'll have to sell the car.* **2 in conclusion** used to begin the last part of a speech or a piece of writing: *In conclusion, I would like to thank our speaker for her interesting talk.*

concrete /ˈkɑn·krit/ noun [no plural] a wet mixture that is used in building and that becomes hard when it dries: *concrete blocks*

condemn /kənˈdem/ verb to say very strongly that you think something is very bad: *The president was quick to condemn the terrorists.*

condition /kənˈdɪʃ·ən/ noun **1** **B1** the state that something or someone is in: *My bike is a few years old but it's **in really good condition**.* **2 conditions** **B1** the situation in which people live, work, or do things: *What are their **living conditions** like?* ○ *The prisoners were kept **in terrible conditions**.* **3** an illness: *a heart condition* **4** something that must happen or be agreed before something else can happen: *We'll let you get a dog, **on one condition**: that you take care of it.*

conduct¹ /ˈkɑn·dʌkt/ noun [no plural] the way someone behaves

a
b
c
d
e
f
g
h
i
j
k
l
m
n
o
p
q
r
s
t
u
v
w
x
y
z

conduct[2] /kənˈdʌkt/ verb **1** to organize or do something: *We are conducting a survey.* **2** to stand in front of a group of musicians and control how they play

conductor /kənˈdʌk·tər/ noun someone who stands in front of a group of musicians and controls how they play

cone /koʊn/ noun **1** a solid shape with a round bottom and a pointed top **2** a sweet, hard food shaped like a cone or cup that holds ice cream
→ See picture at **ice cream**

conference /ˈkɑn·fər·əns/ noun **B1** a large meeting, often lasting a few days, where people talk about a subject: *the annual sales conference*

confess /kənˈfes/ verb to say that you have done something wrong: *He finally **confessed to** the murder.*

confession /kənˈfeʃ·ən/ noun a statement someone makes to say that he or she has done something wrong: *The thief **made a full confession** to the police.*

confidence /ˈkɑn·fɪ·dəns/ noun [no plural] the belief that you are able to do things well or be successful: *He's a good player, but he **lacks confidence**.*

confident /ˈkɑn·fɪ·dənt/ adj
1 **B1** certain about your ability to do things well **2** certain that something will happen: *I am **confident that** we can win this.*
• **confidently** adv *Try to act confidently, even if you feel nervous.*

confirm /kənˈfɜrm/ verb **1** **B1** to make sure an arrangement or meeting will happen, often by telephone or in writing: *They offered me the job, but they haven't **confirmed** it **in writing** yet.* **2** to say or show that something is true: *His wife **confirmed that** he left the house at 8:00.*

confirmation /ˌkɑn·fərˈmeɪ·ʃən/ noun [no plural] a statement or document that shows something is true or certain

conflict[1] /ˈkɑn·flɪkt/ noun disagreement or fighting: *The **conflict between** the two sides lasted for years.*

conflict[2] /kənˈflɪkt/ verb to be different: *Her views on raising children **conflict with** mine.*

confuse /kənˈfjuz/ verb (present participle **confusing**, past tense and past participle **confused**) **1** to stop someone from understanding something: *My explanation just confused her.* **2** to think that one person or thing is another person or thing: *People often **confuse** me **with** my brother.*

confused /kənˈfjuzd/ adj **1** **B1** not able to think clearly or to understand something: *Sorry, I'm completely confused.* ◦ *Even the politicians are **confused about** what to do.* **2** not clear: *The witnesses gave confused accounts of what happened.*

confusing /kənˈfju·zɪŋ/ adj **B1** difficult to understand: *These instructions are really confusing.*

confusion /kənˈfju·ʒən/ noun [no plural] **1** a state in which people do not understand what is happening or what they should do: *The new system has caused a lot of confusion.* **2** a situation, with a lot of activity and noise, in which people do not know what to do: *I lost my bag **in the confusion** after the explosion.*

congratulate /kənˈɡrætʃ·əˌleɪt/ verb (present participle **congratulating**, past tense and past participle **congratulated**) to tell someone that you are happy about something good that he or she has done: *I **congratulated** Lulu **on** passing her exam.*

congratulations! /kənˌɡrætʃ·əˈleɪ·ʃənz/ exclamation **A2** something that you say to show someone you are happy about an event or achievement: *I hear you're getting married. Congratulations!*

congregation /ˌkɑŋ·ɡrɪˈɡeɪ·ʃən/ noun a group of people who worship together regularly

conjunction /kənˈdʒʌŋk·ʃən/ noun a word that is used to connect phrases or parts of a sentence. For example, the words "and" and "because" are conjunctions.

connect /kəˈnekt/ verb **B1** to join two things or places together: *A small bridge connects the two parts of the building.*

connection /kəˈnek·ʃən/ noun **1** **B1** something that joins things together: *Many*

a
b
c
d
e
f
g
h
i
j
k
l
m
n
o
p
q
r
s
t
u
v
w
x
y
z

companies now offer free connection to the Internet. **2** a relationship between people or things: *The connection between smoking and heart disease is well known.* **3 in connection with something** used to say what something is about: *A man has been arrested in connection with the murder.* **4** a train, bus, or plane that leaves a short time after another arrives, so that people can continue their trip: *The train was ten minutes late and I missed my connection.*

conquer /'kaŋ·kər/ verb to take control of a country or to defeat people in a war: *Peru was conquered by the Spanish in 1532.*

conquest /'kaŋ·kwest/ noun the act of taking control of a country, area, or situation: *the Spanish conquest of Mexico*

conscience /'kan·ʃəns/ noun the part of your mind that makes you feel bad when you have done something wrong: *a guilty conscience*

conscious /'kan·ʃəs/ adj awake and able to think and notice things: *He's still conscious, but he's very badly injured.*
→ Opposite **unconscious adj**

consciousness /'kan·ʃəs·nəs/ noun [no plural] the state of being awake and being able to think and notice things: *He lost consciousness (= stopped being conscious) for several minutes.*

consent /kən'sent/ noun [no plural] permission to do something: *You can't come without your parents' consent.*

consequence /'kan·sɪ·kwəns/ noun the result of an action, especially a bad result: *If you make him angry, you'll have to suffer the consequences.*

consequently /'kan·sɪ·kwənt·li/ adv as a result: *I had car trouble and was consequently late.*

conservation /ˌkan·sər'veɪ·ʃən/ noun [no plural] the protection of nature: *wildlife conservation*

conservative /kən'sɜr·və·tɪv/ adj not liking sudden changes or new ideas: *Older people tend to be more conservative.*

consider /kən'sɪd·ər/ verb **B1** to think carefully about something: *We're considering buying a new car.* **2 consider someone/something (to be) something** to have a particular opinion about someone or something: *We don't consider her (to be) right for the job.*

considerable /kən'sɪd·ər·ə·bəl/ adj large or important enough to be noticed: *a considerable amount of money*
• **considerably** adv *He's considerably fatter than he was the last time I saw him.*

consideration /kənˌsɪd·ə'reɪ·ʃən/ noun **1** something that you have to think about when you make decisions: *Safety is our main consideration.* **2** [no plural] the quality of thinking about other people's feelings and trying not to upset them: *They always treated me with consideration.* **3** [no plural] careful thought and attention: *After **careful consideration**, we decided to offer her the job.* ◦ *It may be cheap to buy a used car, but you've got to **take into consideration** the money you'll spend on repairs.*

consist /kən'sɪst/ verb
consist of *something* phrasal verb **B1** to be made from two or more things: *The dessert consisted of fruit and cream.*

console[1] /kən'soʊl/ verb to make someone who is sad feel better: *I tried to console her, but she just kept crying.*

console[2] /'kan·soʊl/ noun an object that contains the controls for a piece of equipment: *a video game console*

consonant /'kan·sə·nənt/ noun **B1** a letter of the alphabet that is not a vowel. (The vowels are a, e, i, o, and u.)

constant /'kan·stənt/ adj happening a lot or all the time: *She's in constant pain.*
• **constantly** adv *She has the television on constantly.*

construct /kən'strʌkt/ verb to build something from many parts: *The building was constructed in 1930.*

construction /kən'strʌk·ʃən/ noun **1** [no plural] the work of building houses, offices, bridges, etc.: *highway construction* **2** something that is built: *a large steel construction*

| æ cat | a hot | e get | ɪ sit | i see | ɔ saw | ʊ book | u too | ʌ cut | ə about | ər mother | ɜr turn | ɔr for | aɪ my | aʊ how | eɪ say | ɔɪ boy |

consul /'kɑn·səl/ *noun* someone whose job is to work in a foreign country and help people from their own country who go there

consult /kən'sʌlt/ *verb* **1** to go to a person or book to get information or advice: *For more information, consult your travel agent.* **2** to talk with someone before you decide something: *Why didn't you consult me about this?*

consume /kən'sum/ *verb* (present participle **consuming**, past tense and past participle **consumed**) **1** to use something: *These lights consume a lot of electricity.* **2** formal to eat or drink something: *People generally consume too much sugar.*

consumer /kən'su·mər/ *noun* someone who buys or uses goods or services: *These price cuts are good news for consumers.*

consumption /kən'sʌmp·ʃən/ *noun* [no plural] the amount of something that someone uses, eats, or drinks: *China's total energy consumption*

contact¹ /'kɑn·tækt/ *noun* **1** A2 someone you know who can help you because of his or her job: *business contacts* **2** B1 [no plural] communication with someone: *We keep in close contact with our grandparents.* **3** [no plural] the condition of two people or things touching each other: *Wash your hands if they come into contact with chemicals.*

contact² /'kɑn·tækt/ *verb* A2 to telephone someone or write to him or her: *I've been trying to contact him.*

contact lens /'kɑn·tækt ˌlenz/ *noun* a small piece of plastic that you put on your eye to make you see more clearly

contain /kən'teɪn/ *verb* B1 If one thing contains another, it has that thing inside it: *a box containing a diamond ring*

> ⚠ **Common mistake: contain or include?**
>
> Use **contain** to talk about objects that have something else inside them.

> *This folder contains important letters.*
> *This soup contains garlic and onions.*
>
> Use **include** to say that something or someone is a part of something else.
>
> *The team includes two new players.*
> *The price of the ticket includes insurance and tax.*

container /kən'teɪ·nər/ *noun* an object such as a box or a bottle that is used for holding something

containers

tube

cans

boxes

cartons

bags

jars

content¹ /kən'tent/ *adj* happy: *I was content to stay home and read.*

content² /'kɑn·tent/ *noun* [no plural] the ideas that are talked about in a piece of writing, a speech, or a movie: *the content of the article*

contented /kən·ten·tɪd/ adj   happy: *a contented smile*

contents /ˈkɑn·tents/ plural noun
1 all of the things that are contained inside something: *Please empty out the contents of your pockets.* **2** a list in a book that tells you what different parts the book contains: *a table of contents*

contest /ˈkɑn·test/ noun   **B1** a competition; used especially when individuals rather than groups are competing

contestant /kən·tes·tənt/ noun
someone who tries to win a competition: *a game show contestant*

context /ˈkɑn·tekst/ noun   all the facts, opinions, etc. relating to a particular thing or event: *This battle is very important in the context of American history.*

continent /ˈkɑn·tⁿn·ənt/ noun   **B1** one of the seven main areas of land on the Earth, such as Asia, Africa, or Europe

continual /kən·tɪn·ju·əl/ adj   happening again and again over a long period of time: *I can't work with these continual interruptions.*
• **continually** adv *Dad continually complains about money.*

continue /kən·tɪn·ju/ verb (present participle **continuing**, past tense and past participle **continued**) **1** **B1** to keep happening or doing something: *It continued to snow for three days.* ○ *Ava continued working until June.* **2** **B1** to start doing or saying something again, after stopping: *We'll continue this discussion tomorrow.* **3** to go farther in a particular direction: *Continue down the road until you reach Elm Street.*

continuous /kən·tɪn·ju·əs/ adj   **1** not stopping: *continuous pain* **2** in grammar, the continuous form of a verb is used to show that an action is continuing to happen: *the present continuous*
• **continuously** adv *Their baby cried continuously all afternoon.*

contract /ˈkɑn·trækt/ noun   **B1** a legal agreement between two people or organizations

contrary /ˈkɑn·trer·i/ adj   **contrary to something** opposite to what someone said or thought: *Contrary to popular belief, he is not a stupid man.*

contrast¹ /ˈkɑn·træst/ noun   an obvious difference between two people or things: *The contrast between their lifestyles couldn't be greater.*

contrast² /kən·træst/ verb   to compare two people or things: *If you contrast his early novels with his later work, you can see how his writing has developed.*

contribute /kən·trɪb·jut/ verb (present participle **contributing**, past tense and past participle **contributed**) to give something, especially money: *I contributed $20 towards Andrea's present.*

contribution /ˌkɑn·trə·bju·ʃən/ noun
an amount of money that is given to help pay for something: *a generous contribution to charity*

control¹ /kən·troul/ noun   **1** [no plural] the power to make a person or thing do what you want: *The new teacher has no control over the class.* ○ *He lost control of the car.* **2** **under control** If a situation is under control, things are happening in the way that you want them to: *Don't worry – everything's under control.* **3** **out of control** behaving very badly and not stopped by anyone: *The children were out of control.* **4** **beyond your control/out of control** If something is beyond your control or out of control, nothing you do can change what is happening: *There's nothing we can do – the situation is beyond our control.* ○ *The car skidded and went out of control.* **5** a switch or other device used to operate a machine: *Where's the volume control on your phone?* **6** **take control** to start to rule or govern an area: *The dictator took control of the country in 1933.*

control² /kən·troul/ verb (present participle **controlling**, past tense and past participle **controlled**) **1** **B1** to make a person or thing do what you want: *Can't you control your dogs?* **2** **B1** to stop yourself from expressing strong emotions or behaving in a silly way: *You're going to have to learn to control your temper.* **3** to limit the number, amount, or increase of something: *They couldn't control the spread of the disease.* **4** to rule or govern an area: *The police controlled the country during the civil war.*

controversial /ˌkɑn·trəˈvɜr·ʃəl/ *adj* causing disagreement or discussion: *The book was very controversial.*

convenience /kənˈvin·jəns/ *noun* **1** [no plural] the quality of being easy to use or suitable for what you want to do: *the convenience of credit cards*
→ Opposite **inconvenience** *noun*
2 something that makes life easier: *The house has every modern convenience.*

convenient /kənˈvin·jənt/ *adj* **1** 🔵 easy and helpful: *What would be a convenient time to meet?* **2** 🔵 near or easy to get to: *The new supermarket is very convenient for me.*
• **conveniently** *adv*

convent /ˈkɑn·vent/ *noun* a building where women live as a religious group

conversation /ˌkɑn·vərˈseɪ·ʃən/ *noun* 🔵 a talk between two or more people: *a telephone conversation* ∘ *We **had a conversation** about football.*

convert /kənˈvɜrt/ *verb* to change something into something else: *The old factory was **converted into** offices.*

convict /kənˈvɪkt/ *verb* to decide officially in a court of law that someone has done a crime: *He was **convicted of** murder.*

convince /kənˈvɪns/ *verb* (present participle **convincing**, past tense and past participle **convinced**) 🔵 to make someone believe that something is true: *He tried to **convince** me **that** I needed a new car.*

convinced /kənˈvɪnst/ *adj* completely certain about something: *I'm **convinced that** he's wrong.*

cook[1] /kʊk/ *verb* 🔵 to make food ready to eat: *Who's cooking this evening?* ∘ *She cooked the meat in a hot pan.*

cook

cook[2] /kʊk/ *noun* 🔵 someone who prepares food for people to eat

cookbook /ˈkʊk.bʊk/ *noun* a book that explains how to make many different kinds of things to eat

cookie /ˈkʊk·i/ *noun* 🔵 a thin, flat cake that is sweet and dry
→ See **Food** on page C7

cookies

cookie sheet /ˈkʊk·i ˌʃit/ *noun* a rectangular sheet of metal used for baking food

cooking /ˈkʊk·ɪŋ/ *noun* [no plural] 🔵 preparing food for people to eat: *I **do** all the **cooking**.*

cool[1] /kul/ *adj* **1** 🔵 slightly cold: *a cool drink* **2** 🔵 informal good or fashionable: *Cool hat, Maria!* **3** calm and not worried: *She seemed very cool before her exam.*
• **coolness** *noun* [no plural]

cool[2] /kul/ *verb* to become less hot, or make something become less hot: *Allow the bread to cool before you eat it.*

cool down *phrasal verb* to become less hot: *We went for a swim to cool down.*

cool[3] /kul/ *exclamation* informal 🔵 used when you like something or agree to something: *"I'll meet you there at 6:00." "Cool!"*

cooperate /koʊˈɑpəˌreɪt/ *verb* (present participle **cooperating**, past tense and past participle **cooperated**) **1** to work together with someone: *Witnesses are **cooperating with** detectives.* **2** to do what someone asks you to do: *We will get there on time as long as the children cooperate.*

cooperation /koʊˌɑpəˈreɪ·ʃən/ *noun* [no plural] the activity of working together with someone or doing what he or she asks you to do: *international cooperation*

cooperative /koʊˈɑp·ər·ə·t̬ɪv/ *adj* willing to help or do what people ask: *She is usually very cooperative when I need help.*

cop /kɑp/ *noun* informal a police officer

cope /koʊp/ *verb* (present participle **coping**, past tense and past participle **coped**) to do something well in a difficult situation: *She has a lot of work but somehow she **copes** with it.*

copper /ˈkɑp·ər/ *noun* [no plural] a soft, red-brown metal

copy[1] /ˈkɑp·i/ *noun* (plural **copies**) **1** 🔵B1 something that is made to look exactly like something else: *Please **make** ten **copies** of the report.* **2** a single book, newspaper, etc. of which many have been made: *a copy of the New York Times*

copy[2] /ˈkɑp·i/ *verb* (present participle **copying**, past tense and past participle **copied**) **1** 🔵A2 to make something that is the same as something else: *Copy the file onto a disk.* **2** to behave like someone else: *He likes to copy his older brother.* **3** to cheat by using someone else's work: *She copied his answers.*

cord /kɔrd/ *noun* **1** thick string, or a piece of this **2** a piece of wire covered in plastic, used to connect electrical equipment to a power supply: *a telephone cord*

core /kɔr/ *noun* **1** the most important part of something: *Lack of money is **at the core of** the problem.* **2** the hard central part of fruits such as apples, which contains the seeds

cork /kɔrk/ *noun* **1** [no plural] a light material that comes from the outside of a particular tree **2** a small piece of this material put in the top of a wine bottle to close it

corkscrew /ˈkɔrkˌskru/ *noun* a piece of equipment used for pulling corks out of wine bottles

corn /kɔrn/ *noun* [no plural] **1** 🔵B1 a tall plant with yellow seeds that are eaten as food **2** the sweet, yellow seeds of corn that are eaten as a vegetable
→ See **Fruits and Vegetables** on page C8

corner /ˈkɔr·nər/ *noun* 🔵A2 the point or area where two lines, walls, or roads meet: *the corner of the table* ◦ *There was a television **in the corner** of the room.* ◦ *The store is **at the corner** of Ross Street and Mill Road.*

corporation /ˌkɔr·pəˈreɪ·ʃən/ *noun* a large company or group of companies

corpus /ˈkɔr·pəs/ *noun* (plural **corpora**) an electronic collection of many millions of words that can be studied to show how language works

correct[1] /kəˈrekt/ *adj* **1** 🔵A2 accurate, or having no mistakes: *Check that you have the correct information.* ◦ *Was that the correct answer?* **2** 🔵B1 right for a particular situation: *We have the correct number of players for the game.*
• **correctly** *adv* 🔵B1

> **❗ Common mistake: correct or right?**
>
> **Correct** means "accurate" or "without mistakes."
> *All the details were correct.*
> **Right** is another word for "correct." It also means "suitable" or "morally acceptable."
> *Be careful to choose the right word.*
> *I don't think it's right for parents to hit their children.*
> Remember that **correct** does not mean "good."
> *The hotel was cheap but good.*
> ~~The hotel was cheap but correct.~~

correct[2] /kəˈrekt/ verb to show or tell someone that something is wrong and to make it right: *The teacher corrected the students' pronunciation.*

correction /kəˈrek·ʃən/ noun
B1 a change to make something right or better: *She made some corrections before giving the essay to her teacher.*

correspond /ˌkɔr·əˈspɑnd/, /ˌkɑr·əˈspɑnd/ verb 1 to be the same or very similar: *The newspaper story does not correspond with/to what really happened.* 2 to communicate with someone by writing letters: *They corresponded for many years.*

correspondence /ˌkɔr·əˈspɑn·dəns/, /ˌkɑr·əˈspɑn·dəns/ noun [no plural] letters from one person to another: *business correspondence*

corridor /ˈkɔr·ɪ·dər/, /ˈkɑr·ɪ·dər/ noun a passage in a building or train with rooms on one or both sides

corruption /kəˈrʌp·ʃən/ noun [no plural] dishonest or immoral behavior, usually by people who have important positions: *There is widespread corruption in the government.*

cosmetics /kɑzˈmet·ɪks/ plural noun substances that you put on your face or body to make you look better

cost[1] /kɔst/ noun 1 **A2** the amount of money that you need to buy or do something: *The cost of fuel has been rising.* 2 **at all costs** If something must be done at all costs, it is very important that it is done: *We have to win at all costs.*

cost[2] /kɔst/ verb (past tense and past participle **cost**) 1 **A2** If something costs a particular amount of money, you have to pay that in order to buy or do it: *How much do these shoes cost?* ◦ *It costs $20 per ticket.* 2 to cause someone to lose something valuable: *Drinking and driving costs lives (= can cause accidents in which people die).* ◦ *His affairs cost him his marriage.*

costume /ˈkɑs·tum/ noun 1 a set of clothes worn in order to look like someone else, especially for a party, or in a movie or play: *Halloween costumes*

2 the set of clothes typical of a particular country or period of history: *Japanese national costume*

cottage /ˈkɑt·ɪdʒ/ noun **B1** a small house, usually in the country

cotton /ˈkɑt·ən/ noun [no plural] 1 **B1** cloth that is made from the cotton plant: *a cotton shirt* 2 a plant that produces a soft, white substance used for making thread and cloth, or the substance itself

cotton ball /ˈkɑt·ən ˌbɔl/ noun a small, soft ball of cotton used especially for cleaning your skin
→ See **The Bathroom** on page C1

couch /kaʊtʃ/ noun **A2** a long, comfortable piece of furniture that two or more people can sit on
→ See **The Living Room** on page C11

cough[1] /kɔf/ verb **B1** to make air come out of your throat with a short sound: *He's been coughing and sneezing all day.*

cough[2] /kɔf/ noun **B1** the action or sound of coughing, or an illness that makes you cough: *I have a bad cough.*

could /kʊd/, /kəd/ modal verb 1 **A2** used as the past form of "can" to talk about what someone or something was able or allowed to do: *I couldn't see him.* ◦ *But you said I could go!* 2 **A2** used as a more polite form of "can" when asking for permission: *Excuse me, could I just say something here?* ◦ *Could I speak to Mr. Davis, please?* 3 **B1** used to talk about what is possible or might happen: *She could arrive any time now.* 4 **B1** used as a more polite form of "can" when asking someone to give you something or do something: *Could you lend me $5?* ◦ *Could you turn the music down a little, please?* 5 **B1** used for making a suggestion: *We could go for a drink after work tomorrow, if you like.*

couldn't /ˈkʊd·ənt/ **A2** short form of could not: *I couldn't understand what he was saying.*

council /ˈkaʊn·səl/ noun a group of people who are chosen to control a town, city, or area: *the town council*

councilman /ˈkoun·səl·mən/ *noun* (plural **councilmen**) a man who is chosen to be a member of a town, city, or area council

councilwoman /ˈkoun·səlˌwʊm·ən/ *noun* (plural **councilwomen**) a woman who is chosen to be a member of a town, city, or area council

counselor /ˈkaʊn·sə·lər/ *noun* someone whose job is to provide help or advice: *a **guidance counselor** (=someone who helps students choose what kind of work or study to do)*

count[1] /kaʊnt/ *verb* **1** 🔵 to see how many people or things there are: *I counted the money on the table.* **2** 🔵 to say numbers in their correct order: *Can you count to twenty in French?* **3** to be important: *Doesn't my opinion **count** for anything?*

count on *someone* phrasal verb to be certain that you can depend on someone: *I can always count on my parents to help me.*

count *someone/something* **up** phrasal verb to add together all the people or things in a group

count[2] /kaʊnt/ *noun* **1** the action of counting something, or the total number you get after counting: ***At the last count** the club had 410 members.* **2 lose count** to forget how many of something there is: *I've lost count of the number of times she's arrived late.*

countable noun /ˈkaʊn·tə·bəl ˈnaʊn/ *noun* 🔵 a noun that can be used in the singular and the plural: *"House" is a countable noun.*

counter /ˈkaʊn·tər/ *noun* **1** the place in a store, bank, etc. where people are served: *The woman **behind the counter** took his money.* **2** a flat surface in a kitchen where you prepare food

counterclockwise /ˌkaʊn·tərˈklɑk·waɪz/ *adj, adv* in the opposite direction from the way the hands (=parts that point to the numbers) of a clock move
→ Opposite **clockwise**
→ See picture at **clockwise**

country /ˈkʌn·tri/ *noun* **1** 🔴 (plural **countries**) an area of land that has its own government, army, etc.: *African countries* **2** 🔵 [no plural] land that is not in towns or cities, and that can have fields and farms on it or be wild: *It's nice to get out in **the country** on weekends.* ○ *This whole area is **bear country** (=where many bears live).*

> ⚠ **Common mistake: country, land, nation,** or **state**?
>
> **Country** is the most general word that means "an area of land." It usually means an area of land with its own government and people.
>
> *China, Japan, and other countries in Asia*
>
> **Nation** is used to talk about a country, especially when you mean the people or the culture of that country.
>
> *The nation celebrated the 100th anniversary of its independence.*
>
> **State** is used to talk about a country as a political or official area. Some countries are divided into political units that are also called **states**.
>
> *Belgium became an independent state in 1830.*
> *America has 50 states.*
> *the State of Florida*
>
> **Land** means an area of ground, not an area with its own government.
>
> *We bought some land to build a house on.*

> ⚠ **Common mistake: country** or **countryside**?
>
> The **country** is land that is not part of a town or city. It can have buildings on it or be wild.
>
> *They have a cabin out in the country.*
>
> **Countryside** is often used to talk about what an area in the country looks like.
>
> *The countryside in the valley is beautiful.*

countryside /ˈkʌn·triˌsaɪd/ *noun* [no plural] 🔵 land that is not in towns or cities and may have farms, fields, etc.

county /'kaʊn·ti/ noun (plural **counties**) an area of a state that has its own government

couple /'kʌp·əl/ noun **1** 🅱️ two or a few: *I went to New York with **a couple of** friends.* **2** 🅱️ two people who are married or having a romantic relationship: *a married couple*

coupon /'ku·pɑn/ noun a piece of paper that you can use to buy something at a lower price

courage /'kɜr·ɪdʒ/, /'kʌr·ɪdʒ/ noun [no plural] the quality that makes you able to do dangerous or difficult things: *The soldiers fought with great courage.* ○ *She didn't have the courage to tell him the truth.*

courageous /kə'reɪ·dʒəs/ adj brave: *He was a courageous soldier.*

course /kɔrs/ noun **1 of course** 🅰️ used to say "yes" strongly, often to be polite: *"Can you help me?" "Of course!"* **2 of course** 🅱️ used to show that what you are saying is obvious: *Of course, the Olympics are not just about money.* **3 of course not** 🅰️ used to say "no" strongly: *"Do you mind if I borrow your pen?" "Of course not."* **4** 🅰️ a set of lessons about a particular subject: *She took a ten-week computer course.* **5** 🅰️ a part of a meal: *a three-course dinner* **6** 🅱️ an area used for horse races or playing golf: *a golf course* **7** the direction in which a ship, plane, etc. is moving: *The storm blew the boat **off course** (= in the wrong direction).* **8** the way something develops, usually over a long time: *Nuclear weapons have changed the course of modern history.*

coursebook /'kɔrs·bʊk/ noun a book used by students when they take a particular course of study

court /kɔrt/ noun **1** the place where a judge decides if someone has done a crime: *The suspect appeared in court charged with robbery.* **2** 🅱️ an area for playing a sport: *a tennis court*

courteous /'kɜr·ti·əs/ adj polite and showing respect

courtesy /'kɜr·tə·si/ noun [no plural] behavior that is polite and shows respect

courthouse /'kɔrt·haʊs/ noun a building with one or more rooms in it where legal trials happen

courtroom /'kɔrt·rum/, /'kɔrt·rʊm/ noun a room where legal trials happen

cousin /'kʌz·ɪn/ noun 🅰️ the child of someone's aunt or uncle: *He comes from a big family and has a lot of cousins.*

cover¹ /'kʌv·ər/ verb **1** 🅰️ to put something over something else: *They **covered** him **with** a blanket.* ○ *He **covered** his face **with** his hands.* **2** 🅱️ to form a layer on the surface of something: *Snow covered the trees.* **3** 🅱️ to include or deal with a subject or piece of information: *The book covers European history from 1789-1914.* **4** to travel a particular distance: *We covered 300 miles in four days.* **5** to be a particular size or area: *The town **covers an area** of 15 square miles.* **6** to report the news about a particular important event: *She's covering the election for local TV.*

cover something up phrasal verb to put something over something else, in order to hide it: *We used a picture to cover up a hole in the wall.*

cover² /'kʌv·ər/ noun **1** 🅱️ the outer part of a book, magazine, etc. that protects the pages: *Her picture was on the cover of Vogue magazine.* **2** 🅱️ something you put over something else, usually to protect it: *an ironing board cover*

covering /'kʌv·ə·rɪŋ/ noun [no plural] a layer that covers something: *a thick covering of snow*

cow /kaʊ/ noun 🅰️ a large female farm animal kept for milk or meat

coward /'kaʊ·ərd/ noun someone who is not brave and does not do dangerous things

cowboy /'kaʊ·bɔɪ/ noun a man whose job is to take care of cows, and who rides a horse

cozy /'koʊ·zi/ adj (comparative **cozier**, superlative **coziest**) 🅱️ comfortable and warm: *It's nice and cozy in this room.*

crab /kræb/ noun a sea animal with ten legs and a shell

crack[1] /kræk/ **verb 1** to break something so that thin lines appear on its surface, or to become broken in this way: *Linda cracked her tooth when she fell.* ○ *The glass cracked in my hand.* **2** to make a sudden, short noise

crack[2] /kræk/ **noun 1** a line on the surface of something that is damaged: *Several cups had cracks in them.* **2** a narrow space between two parts of something or between two things: *I could see sunlight through a crack in the curtains.*

cracker /'kræk·ər/ **noun** **A1** a type of small, dry, flat bread that is usually salty: *a plate of cheese and crackers*

cradle /'krei·d°l/ **noun** a baby's bed, especially one that moves from side to side

craft /kræft/ **noun 1** an activity in which you make something using a lot of skill, especially with your hands: *traditional crafts such as weaving* **2** (plural **craft**) a boat: *The wind is too strong for small craft.*

cram /kræm/ **verb** (present participle **cramming**, past tense and past participle **crammed**) **cram** *something* **in, into,** etc. to force too many things into a small space: *Thousands of people were crammed into the stadium.*

crane /krein/ **noun** a large machine used for lifting and moving heavy things

crash[1] /kræʃ/ **noun 1** **B1** an accident in which a vehicle hits something: *a car/ plane crash* **2** a sudden, loud noise made when something falls or breaks: *I heard a crash and ran into the kitchen.*

crash[2] /kræʃ/ **verb 1** **B1** If a vehicle crashes, it hits something by accident: *The van skidded and **crashed into** a tree.* **2** If a computer or computer system crashes, it suddenly stops working. **3** to hit something and make a loud noise: *wave crashing onto rocks*

crash helmet /'kræʃ ˌhel·mət/ **noun** a hard hat that protects your head when you ride a motorcycle

crate /kreit/ **noun** a large wooden box used for carrying or storing things

crawl /krɔl/ **verb** to move on your hands and knees: *I crawled under the desk to plug the lamp in.*

crawl

crayon /'krei·ɑn/ **noun** a stick of colored wax used for drawing

crazy /'krei·zi/ **adj** (comparative **crazier**, superlative **craziest**) **1** **A2** stupid or strange: *a crazy idea* **2** annoyed or angry: *Dad **went crazy** when I told him what had happened.* **3** **be crazy about** *someone/ something* **A2** to love someone very much, or to be very interested in something: *Mia's crazy about baseball.*

creak /krik/ **verb** If something such as a door or a piece of wood creaks, it makes a long noise when it moves: *The floorboards creaked under my feet.*

cream[1] /krim/ **noun 1** **A2** [no plural] a thick, white liquid that is taken from milk **2** **A2** [no plural] a yellow-white color **3** **B1** a soft substance that you put on your skin: *face/hand cream*

cream[2] /krim/ **adj** **A2** being a yellow-white color: *cream paint*

create /kri'eit/ **verb** (present participle **creating**, past tense and past participle **created**) **B1** to make something happen or exist: *The project will create more than 500 jobs.* ○ *The snow created traffic delays.*

creation /kri'ei·ʃən/ **noun 1** [no plural] the act of making something happen or exist: *the creation of a new political party* **2** something that someone has made: *The museum has some of his best creations.*

creative /kri'ei·tɪv/ **adj** **B1** good at thinking of new ideas and making interesting things: *Her book is full of creative ways to decorate your home.*
• **creatively adv** *We have to think creatively about this problem.*

creature /'kri·tʃər/ **noun** **B1** anything that lives but is not a plant: *Dolphins are intelligent creatures.*

credit /'kred·ɪt/ **noun 1** [no plural] a way of buying something in which you

a b c d e f g h i j k l m n o p q r s t u v w x y z

arrange to pay for it at a later time: *He bought most of the furniture **on credit**.* **2** **B1** an amount of money in your bank account: *I didn't have enough credit in my account to pay the bill.* **3** [no plural] praise that is given to someone for something he or she has done: *I did most of the work, but Dan **got all the credit**!* **4** a unit that shows you have completed part of a college course: *I got three credits for the class.*

credit card /'kred·ɪt ˌkard/ noun **A1** a small plastic card that allows you to buy something and pay for it later: *He paid **by credit card**.*

creep /krip/ verb (past tense and past participle **crept**) to move very quietly and carefully: *I crept out of the room.*

crept /krept/ past tense and past participle of creep

crescent /'kres·ənt/ noun a curved shape that is narrow at each end and wider in the middle: *the pale crescent of the moon*

crew /kru/ noun **1** **B1** the people who work together on a ship, plane, or train: *a crew member* **2** a team of people with special skills who work together: *an ambulance crew*

crib /krɪb/ noun a bed with high sides for a baby

crib

cricket /'krɪk·ɪt/ noun an insect that jumps and makes a noise by rubbing its wings together

crime /kraɪm/ noun **1** **B1** [no plural] illegal activities: *violent crime* **2** **B1** something someone does that is illegal: *He **committed** a serious crime.*

criminal /'krɪm·ə·nᵊl/ noun **B1** someone who has done a crime

crisis /'kraɪ·sɪs/ noun (plural crises) a situation or time that is very dangerous or difficult: *The country's leadership is **in crisis**.*

crisp /krɪsp/ adj Crisp food is hard and pleasant: *a crisp apple* ○ *crisp crackers*

critic /'krɪt·ɪk/ noun **1** someone who says that he or she does not approve of someone or something: *a critic of the government* **2** someone whose job is to give his or her opinion of a book, play, movie, etc.: *a theater critic*

critical /'krɪt·ɪ·kəl/ adj **1** saying that someone or something is bad or wrong: *He is very **critical of** the way I work.* **2** very important for the way things will happen in the future: *a critical decision* **3** very serious or dangerous: *The doctors said her condition was critical.*
• **critically** adv *They were both critically injured in the crash.*

criticism /'krɪt·ə.sɪz·əm/ noun remarks about the faults of someone or something: *You have to learn to **take criticism**.*

criticize /'krɪt·ə.saɪz/ verb (present participle **criticizing**, past tense and past participle **criticized**) to say that something or someone is bad: *The movie was criticized for being too violent.*

crocodile /'krak·ə.daɪl/ noun a big reptile with a long mouth and sharp teeth, that lives in lakes and rivers

croissant /krə'sant/ noun a soft, curved piece of bread, eaten for breakfast

crooked /'krʊk·ɪd/ adj not straight: *crooked teeth*

crop /krap/ noun **B1** a plant such as a grain, fruit, or vegetable that is grown in large amounts by farmers

cross[1] /krɔs/ verb **1** **A2** to go from one side of something to the other side: *This is not a good place to cross the street.* **2** **cross your mind** If an idea crosses your mind, you think about it for a short time. **3** If two lines, roads, etc. cross, they go over or across each other. **4** **cross your arms/fingers/legs** to put one of your arms, fingers, or legs over the top of the other

cross something out phrasal verb to draw a line through something that you have written, usually because it is wrong: *Cross out that last sentence.*

cross[2] /krɔs/ noun **1** **A1** a written mark [x], used for showing that something is wrong **2** **B1** an object in the shape of a cross, used as a symbol of the Christian religion

crossing /'krɒ·sɪŋ/ noun **B1** a place where people can go across a road, river, etc.

crosswalk /'krɒs,wɔk/ noun a special place on a road where traffic must stop to allow people to walk across

crossword /'krɒs,wɜrd/ noun (also **crossword puzzle**) a game in which you write words that are the answers to questions in a pattern of black and white squares

crouch /kraʊtʃ/ verb to move your body close to the ground by bending your knees: *I crouched behind the chair to hide.*

crow /kroʊ/ noun a large black bird that makes a loud noise

crowd[1] /kraʊd/ noun **A2** a large group of people who are together in one place: *A large crowd had gathered to wait for the mayor.*

crowd[2] /kraʊd/ verb
crowd around (*someone/something*) phrasal verb to stand in a group around someone or something: *Everyone crowded around my desk.*

crowded /'kraʊ·dɪd/ adj **A2** very full of people: *a crowded train*

crown /kraʊn/ noun a round object made of gold and jewels (= valuable stones) that a king or queen wears on his or her head

crucial /'kru·ʃəl/ adj extremely important or necessary: *a crucial decision*

crude /krud/ adj **1** simple and made without skill: *It's a fairly crude device.* **2** rude: *a crude remark*

cruel /'kru·əl/ adj **B1** very unkind, or causing people or animals to suffer: *a cruel joke* ○ *Many people think hunting is* ***cruel to*** *animals.*
• **cruelly** adv *They treated her cruelly.*

cruelty /'kru·əl·ti/ noun [no plural] cruel behavior or a cruel action: *laws against cruelty to animals*

cruise /kruz/ noun **B1** a vacation on a ship, sailing from place to place

crumb /krʌm/ noun a very small piece of bread, cake, etc.
→ See **Quantities** on page C14

crumble /'krʌm·bəl/ verb (present participle **crumbling**, past tense and past participle **crumbled**) to break into small pieces, or to make something break into small pieces: *Buildings crumbled as the earthquake struck.*

crunch /krʌntʃ/ verb **1** to make a noise by chewing hard food: *She was crunching on an apple.* **2** to make a sound as if something is being crushed: *The gravel crunched under our feet.*

crush /krʌʃ/ verb to press something so hard that it is made flat or broken into pieces: *Her car was crushed by a falling tree.*

crust /krʌst/ noun the hard part on the outside of bread or other baked foods

crutch /krʌtʃ/ noun a stick that you put under your arm to help you walk if your leg is hurt: *Charles was* ***on crutches*** *(= walking with crutches) for six weeks.*

cry[1] /kraɪ/ verb (present participle **crying**, past tense and past participle **cried**) **1** **A2** to produce tears from your eyes because you are sad: *My baby brother cries all the time.* **2** **B1** to speak or say something loudly: *"Look at this!" cried Raj.*

cry

cry[2] /kraɪ/ noun (plural **cries**) **B1** a shout: *I could hear the cries of children playing in the street.*

crystal /'krɪs·tᵊl/ noun **1** a piece of a substance that has become solid, with a regular shape: *ice crystals* **2** [no plural] a type of glass of high quality: *a crystal vase*

cub /kʌb/ noun a young animal, such as a bear, fox, or lion

cube /kjub/ noun a solid object with six square sides of the same size
→ See picture at **shape**

a
b
c
d
e
f
g
h
i
j
k
l
m
n
o
p
q
r
s
t
u
v
w
x
y
z

cucumber /ˈkjuˈkʌmˌbər/ **noun**
B1 a long, green vegetable that you eat in salads
→ See **Fruits and Vegetables** on page C8

cuddle /ˈkʌd·əl/ **verb** (present participle **cuddling**, past tense and past participle **cuddled**) to put your arms around someone to show the person that you love him or her: *Her mother cuddled her until she stopped crying.*
• **cuddle noun**

cuff /kʌf/ **noun** the bottom part of a sleeve that goes around your wrist
→ See picture at **jacket**

cultivate /ˈkʌl·təˌveɪt/ **verb** (present participle **cultivating**, past tense and past participle **cultivated**) to prepare land and grow crops on it
• **cultivation noun** [no plural]

cultural /ˈkʌl·tʃər·əl/ **adj 1** **B1** relating to the habits, traditions, and beliefs of a society: *cultural differences ○ Greek cultural traditions* **2** **B1** relating to music, art, theater, literature, etc.: *cultural events*
• **culturally adv** *The two countries are culturally very different.*

culture /ˈkʌl·tʃər/ **noun 1** **B1** the habits, traditions, and beliefs of a country or group of people: *American/Japanese culture* **2** **B1** [no plural] music, art, theater, literature, etc.: *popular culture*

cunning /ˈkʌn·ɪŋ/ **adj** skillful at getting what you want, especially by tricking people

cup /kʌp/ **noun 1** **A1** a small, round container with a handle on the side, used to drink from: *a cup of coffee* **2** A small container with a handle used to measure dry or liquid food for cooking, or the amount this container holds: *Add two cups of flour, an egg, and half a cup of milk. ○ a measuring cup* **3** **B1** a prize given to the winner of a competition

cupboard /ˈkʌb·ərd/ **noun** **B1** a piece of furniture with a door on the front and shelves inside, used for keeping things

curb /kɜrb/ **noun** the edge of the raised path at the side of the road

cure[1] /kjʊər/ **noun** **B1** something that makes someone with an illness healthy again: *They are trying to find **a cure for** cancer.*

cure[2] /kjʊər/ **verb** (present participle **curing**, past tense and past participle **cured**) **B1** to make someone with an illness healthy again

curiosity /ˌkjʊər·iˈɑs·ɪ·t̬i/ **noun** [no plural] the feeling of wanting to know or learn about something: *Just out of curiosity, how did you get my address?*

curious /ˈkjʊər·i·əs/ **adj** **B1** wanting to know or learn about something: *I was curious about his life in India.*

curiously /ˈkjʊər·i·əs·li/ **adv** **B1** in a way that shows you want to know more about something: *"What are you doing?" she asked curiously.*

curl[1] /kɜrl/ **noun** something with a small, curved shape, especially a piece of hair: *a child with blonde curls*

curl[2] /kɜrl/ **verb** to make something into the shape of a curl, or to be this shape: *The cat curled its tail around its body.*
curl up phrasal verb to sit or lie in a position with your arms and legs close to your body: *She curled up on the couch.*

curly /ˈkɜr·li/ **adj** (comparative **curlier**, superlative **curliest**) **B1** with many curls: *curly hair*
→ See **Hair** on page C9

currency /ˈkɜr·ən·si/, /ˈkʌr·ən·si/ **noun** (plural **currencies**) **B1** the units of money used in a particular country: *foreign currency*

current[1] /ˈkɜr·ənt/, /ˈkʌr·ənt/ **adj** happening or existing now: *What is your current address?*
• **currently adv** *The factory currently (=now) employs 750 people.*

current[2] /ˈkɜr·ənt/, /ˈkʌr·ənt/ **noun 1** the natural flow of air or water in one direction: *a current of air* **2** the flow of

cup

saucer

electricity through a wire: *an electrical current*

current events /ˈkɜr·ənt ɪˈvents /, /ˈkʌr·ənt ɪˈvents / **plural noun** important political or social events that are happening in the world now

curriculum /kəˈrɪk·jə·ləm/ **noun** (plural **curricula**) **B1** all the subjects taught in a school, college, etc., or in an educational course: *the school curriculum*

cursor /ˈkɜr·sər/ **noun** a symbol on a computer screen that shows the place where you are working

curtain /ˈkɜr·t²n/ **noun** **A2** a piece of material that hangs down to cover a window, stage, etc.
→ See **The Living Room** on page C11

curve[1] /kɜrv/ **noun** a line that bends around like part of a circle: *a road with gentle curves*

curve[2] /kɜrv/ **verb** (present participle **curving**, past tense and past participle **curved**) to move in a curve or form a curve: *The road curves to the left.*

curved /kɜrvd/ **adj** bent in a shape like part of a circle: *a curved handle*

cushion /ˈkʊʃ·ən/ **noun** **B1** a cloth bag filled with something soft that you put on a chair
→ See **The Living Room** on page C11

custom[1] /ˈkʌs·təm/ **noun** **B1** a habit or tradition

custom[2] /ˈkʌs·təm/ **adj** made for a particular person to buy: *custom furniture*

customer /ˈkʌs·tə·mər/ **noun** **A2** a person or organization that buys things or services from a store or business

customs /ˈkʌs·təmz/ **noun** [no plural] **B1** the place where your bags are examined when you are going into a country

cut[1] /kʌt/ **verb** (present participle **cutting**, past tense and past participle **cut**) **1** **A2** to use a knife or other sharp tool to divide something or make a hole in something: *Cut the meat into small pieces.* ∘ *He cut the piece of wood in half.* ∘ *I got my hair cut last week.*

cut

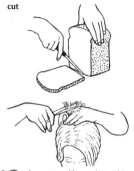

2 **B1** to hurt yourself on a sharp object that makes you bleed: *She cut her finger on some broken glass.* **3** to reduce the size or amount of something: *Prices have been cut by 25%.* **4** to remove part of a movie or piece of writing: *The movie was too long, so they cut some scenes.*

cut across *something* **phrasal verb** to go from one side of an area to the other, instead of going around it: *If we cut across this field, it will save time.*

cut back (*something*) **phrasal verb** to reduce the amount of money being spent on something: *We have had to **cut back on** training this year.*

cut *something* **down** **phrasal verb** to make a tree or other plant fall to the ground by cutting it near the bottom

cut down on (*something*) **phrasal verb** to eat or drink less of a particular thing, usually in order to improve your health: *I'm trying to cut down on the amount of sugar I eat.*

cut *something* **off** **phrasal verb** to stop providing something such as electricity or water: *If we don't pay the bill, the gas will be cut off.*

cut *something* **out** **phrasal verb** to cut a shape from cloth or paper, or to cut a piece of information from something that is printed: *She cut his picture out of the magazine.*

a b c d e f g h i j k l m n o p q r s t u v w x y z

cut *something* **up** *phrasal verb*
B1 to cut something into pieces

cut² /kʌt/ *noun* **1** **B1** an injury made when the skin is cut with something sharp: *He got some cuts and bruises in the accident.* **2** a reduction in the number or amount of something: *job cuts* ◦ *The workers were angry about the **cut** in pay.* **3** an opening made with a sharp tool: *She made a cut in the material.*

cycle /'saɪ·kəl/ *verb* (present participle **cycling**, past tense and past participle **cycled**)
B1 to ride a bicycle

cycling /'saɪ·klɪŋ/ *noun* [no plural]
A2 the activity of riding a bicycle
→ See **Sports 2** on page C16

cyclist /'saɪ·klɪst/ *noun* **B1** someone who rides a bicycle

cylinder /'sɪl·ən·dər/ *noun* a shape with circular ends and long, straight sides
→ See picture at **shape**

Dd

D, d /di/ the fourth letter of the alphabet

dab¹ /dæb/ *verb* (present participle **dabbing**, past tense and past participle **dabbed**) to touch something quickly and lightly, or to put a substance on something with quick, light touches: *She dabbed a drop of perfume behind her ears.*

dab² /dæb/ *noun* a small amount of a cream or liquid
→ See **Quantities** on page C14

dad /dæd/ *noun* informal **A1** father: *My dad has curly brown hair.*

daddy /'dæd·i/ *noun* (plural **daddies**) a word for "father," used mainly by children

daffodil /'dæf·ə,dɪl/ *noun* a yellow flower that usually grows in the spring

daffodil

daily /'deɪ·li/ *adj, adv* **A2** happening or made every day or once a day: *a daily newspaper* ◦ *He exercises daily.*

dairy /'deər·i/ *adj* relating to milk or to foods made using milk: *dairy products*

daisy /'deɪ·zi/ *noun* (plural **daisies**) a small flower with white petals and a yellow center

dam /dæm/ *noun* a strong wall built across a river to stop the water and make a lake

damage¹ /'dæm·ɪdʒ/ *noun* [no plural]
B1 harm or injury: *The strong wind caused serious **damage to** the roof.*

damage² /'dæm·ɪdʒ/ *verb* (present participle **damaging**, past tense and past participle **damaged**) **B1** to harm or break something: *Many buildings were damaged in the storm.*

damaged /'dæm·ɪdʒd/ *adj* **B1** harmed or broken: *Both cars involved in the accident looked **badly damaged**.*

damn¹ /dæm/ *exclamation* (also **damn it**) impolite **B1** used to express anger or disappointment: *Damn! I forgot the tickets.*

damn² /dæm/ *adj* (also **damned**) impolite used to express anger: *He didn't listen to a damn thing I said.* ◦ *That dog's a damned nuisance.*

damn³ /dæm/ *adv* (also **damned**) impolite very: *He worked damn hard to pass that test.* ◦ *It was a damned good movie.*

damn⁴ /dæm/ *noun* impolite to not be interested in or worried about someone or something: *I don't give a damn what people think.*

damn⁵ /dæm/ *verb* **1** impolite used to express anger about someone or something: *Stop complaining, damn it!* **2** to strongly criticize someone or something: *He was damned by the media.*

damp /dæmp/ *adj* slightly wet, usually in a bad way: *It was cold and damp outside.* ◦ *damp socks*

dance¹ /dæns/ *verb* (present participle **dancing**, past tense and past participle

danced) **A1** to move your feet and body to the rhythm of music: *She's dancing with Steven.*

dance² /dæns/ noun **1 A1** an occasion when you dance: *the bride and groom's first dance* **2 A2** [no plural] the activity or skill of dancing: *a dance class* **3 B1** a set of movements that you do to music **4** a social event where people dance to music

dancer /ˈdæn·sər/ noun **1 A2** someone who dances either as a job or for pleasure: *He's a dancer in the San Francisco Ballet.* **2** someone who is dancing or who dances in a particular way: *The dancers looked strong and graceful.* ○ *I'm not a good dancer.*

dancing /ˈdæn·sɪŋ/ noun [no plural] **A1** the activity of moving your feet and body to the rhythm of music: *Let's go dancing on Friday night.*

dandelion /ˈdæn·dəˌlaɪ·ən/ noun a yellow wild flower that often grows where people do not want it to

dandruff /ˈdæn·drəf/ noun [no plural] small pieces of dead skin in someone's hair or on his or her clothes

danger /ˈdeɪn·dʒər/ noun **1 A2** the possibility that someone will be harmed or killed: *the dangers of rock climbing* ○ *The soldiers were in serious danger.* **2 B1** something or someone that may harm you: *Icy roads are a danger to drivers.*

dangerous /ˈdeɪn·dʒər·əs/ adj **A2** If someone or something is dangerous, the person or thing could harm you: *It's dangerous to ride a bike without a helmet.*
• **dangerously** adv **B1** *dangerously close to the edge*

dare /deər/ verb (present participle **daring**, past tense and past participle **dared**) **1** dare (to) do *something* to be brave enough to do something: *I didn't dare tell Dad that I'd scratched his car.* **2** dare *someone* to do *something* to try to make someone do something dangerous: *She dared her friend to climb onto the roof.* **3 Don't you dare!** used to tell someone angrily not to do something: *Don't you*

dare hit him! **4 How dare she, you, etc.** said when you are very angry about something someone has done: *How dare you talk to me like that!*

dark¹ /dɑrk/ adj **1 A1** nearer to black than white in color: *dark blue/green* **2 A2** with no light or not much light: *It doesn't get dark until nine at night.* **3** having black or brown hair or brown skin: *A short, dark woman arrived.*
→ See **Hair** on page C9

dark² /dɑrk/ noun **1 the dark B1** a lack of light in a place: *He's scared of the dark.* **2 before/after dark B1** before or after it becomes night: *She doesn't let her children out after dark.*

darkness /ˈdɑrk·nəs/ noun [no plural] a state in which there is little or no light: *He stumbled around in the darkness looking for the light switch.*

darling /ˈdɑr·lɪŋ/ noun used when you speak to someone you love: *Are you feeling all right, darling?*

dart /dɑrt/ verb to move somewhere quickly and suddenly: *A cat darted across the street.*

darts /dɑrts/ noun [no plural] a game played by throwing small arrows at a round board

dash¹ /dæʃ/ verb to run somewhere suddenly: *She dashed back into the house to grab her sunglasses.*

dash² /dæʃ/ noun **1** a mark [-] used to separate parts of sentences **2** the action of running somewhere suddenly: *We made a dash for shelter from the rain.*

dashboard /ˈdæʃˌbɔrd/ noun the part at the front of a car with equipment to show things such as how fast you are going and how hot it is
→ See **Car** on page C3

data /ˈdeɪ·t̬ə/ noun [no plural] **1** information or facts about something: *financial data* **2** information in the form of text, numbers, or symbols that can be used by or stored in a computer: *He transferred the data to a disk.*

database /ˈdeɪ·t̬əˌbeɪs/ noun information stored in a computer in an organized

a
b
c
d
e
f
g
h
i
j
k
l
m
n
o
p
q
r
s
t
u
v
w
x
y
z

structure so that it can be searched in different ways: *The library has a database of newspaper articles.*

date¹ /deɪt/ *noun* **1** **A1** a particular day of the month or year: *"What's the date today?" "It's June fifth."* ○ *Please give your name, address, and date of birth.* **2** **B1** a romantic meeting when two people go out somewhere: *He asked her out on a date.* **3** **B1** a time when something has been arranged to happen: *Let's make a date to have lunch.* **4 out of date** **B1** old and no longer useful, correct, or fashionable: *I have a map, but I think it's out of date.* **5 up to date** **B1** modern, recent, or containing the latest information: *Is the information in your files up to date?*

date² /deɪt/ *verb* **B1** to write or print the day's date on something: *Thank you for your letter dated August 30.*

daughter /ˈdɔ·tər/ *noun* **A1** someone's female child: *Their daughter is seven years old.*

daughter-in-law /ˈdɔ·tər·ɪnˌlɔ/ *noun* (plural **daughters-in-law**) the wife of someone's child: *Our son and daughter-in-law are coming to visit.*

dawn /dɔn/ *noun* [no plural] the early morning when light first appears in the sky: *We woke at dawn.*

day /deɪ/ *noun* **1** **A1** a period of 24 hours: *the days of the week* ○ *I saw her the day before yesterday.* **2** **A2** the period during the day when there is light from the sun: *a bright, sunny day* **3** **A2** the time that you usually spend at work or school: *It's been a very busy day at the office.* ○ *I have a day off (= when I am not at work) tomorrow.* **4 one day** **A2** used to talk about something that happened in the past: *One day, I came home to find my windows smashed.* **5 these days** **A2** used to talk about the present period of time: *I don't go out much these days.* **6 for days** **B1** for a long time: *I haven't seen Jack for days.* **7 one day/one of these days** **B1** used to talk about something you think will happen in the future: *One of these days*

I'll tell her what really happened. **8 the other day** **B1** a few days ago: *I saw Ann in the post office the other day.* **9 day after day** every day for a long period of time: *Day after day they marched through the mountains.*

daycare center /ˈdeɪ.keərˌsen·tər/ *noun* a place where parents pay to leave their children while the parents work

daydream /ˈdeɪ.drim/ *verb* to spend time thinking good thoughts about something you wish would happen

daylight /ˈdeɪ.laɪt/ *noun* [no plural] the natural light from the sun during the day

daytime /ˈdeɪ.taɪm/ *noun* [no plural] the period of the day when there is light from the sun, or the period when most people are at work: *a daytime telephone number*

dead /ded/ *adj* **1** **A2** not now alive: *She's been dead for ten years.* ○ *There were two firefighters among the dead.* **2** If a piece of equipment is dead, it is not working: *a dead battery* ○ *The phone suddenly went dead.* **3** informal If a place is dead, it is too quiet and nothing interesting is happening there.

deadline /ˈded.laɪn/ *noun* a time by which something must be done: *The deadline for entering the competition is tomorrow.*

deadly /ˈded·li/ *adj* causing death: *a deadly virus*

deaf /def/ *adj* **B1** not able to hear: *Many deaf people use sign language.* ○ *He goes to a school for the deaf.*
• **deafness** *noun* [no plural]

deal¹ /dil/ *noun* **1** an arrangement or an agreement, for example in business or politics: *a business deal* ○ *I'll make a deal with you – you wash the car, and I'll let you use it tonight.* **2 a good/great deal** if something is a good or great deal, it is of good quality or you think the amount of money you spent on it was right: *That dress is a really good deal.* **3 a great deal** **B2** a lot: *A great deal of* *time and effort went into organizing this party.*

deal[2] /diːl/ **verb** (past tense and past participle **dealt**) to give cards to players in a game: *Whose turn is it to deal?*

deal with *someone* **phrasal verb** to find a way to talk to someone or work with someone, especially as part of your job: *She's good at dealing with children.*

deal with *something* **phrasal verb** **B1** to do something to make a situation work or to solve a problem: *How will we deal with the issue of immigration?*

dealer /ˈdiːlər/ **noun** a person or company that buys and sells things for profit: *a car dealer*

dealt /delt/ past tense and past participle of **deal**

dear[1] /dɪər/ **adj** **1 A1** used at the beginning of a letter, before the name of the person you are writing to: *Dear Amy* ○ *Dear Sir/Madam* **2** liked very much: *She is a very dear friend.*

dear[2] /dɪər/ **exclamation Oh dear!** **A2** used to express surprise and disappointment: *Oh dear! I forgot my keys!*

death /deθ/ **noun** **1 B1** the end of life: *After the death of her husband she lost interest in life.* ○ *We need to reduce the number of deaths from heart attacks.* **2 bored, frightened, etc. to death** extremely bored, frightened, etc.: *She's scared to death of dogs.*

debate[1] /dɪˈbeɪt/ **noun** talk or arguments about a subject: *There has been a lot of public debate on the safety of food.*

debate[2] /dɪˈbeɪt/ **verb** (present participle **debating**, past tense and past participle **debated**) **1** to talk about a subject in a formal way: *These issues need to be debated.* **2** to try to make a decision about something: *I'm still debating whether to go out tonight or not.*

debit card /ˈdeb·ɪt ˌkɑrd/ **noun** a plastic card used to pay for things directly from your bank account

debt /det/ **noun** **1** an amount of money that you owe someone: *She's working in*

*a bar to try to **pay off** her debts.* **2** [no plural] the situation of owing money to someone: *We don't want to **get into debt**.* ○ *He's over $4,000 **in debt**.*

decade /ˈdek·eɪd/ **noun** a period of ten years

decaffeinated /diˈkæf·əˌneɪ·t̬ɪd/ **adj** Decaffeinated coffee or tea does not contain caffeine (= a chemical that makes you feel more awake).

decay /dɪˈkeɪ/ **verb** to gradually become bad or be destroyed: *Sugar makes your teeth decay.*
• **decay noun** [no plural] *tooth decay*

deceive /dɪˈsiːv/ **verb** (present participle **deceiving**, past tense and past participle **deceived**) to make someone believe something that is not true: *The company deceived customers by selling old computers as new ones.*

December /dɪˈsem·bər/ **noun** **A1** the twelfth month of the year

decent /ˈdiː·sənt/ **adj** **1** of a quality or level that is good enough: *a decent meal* **2** honest and good: *He seemed like a very decent man.*

decide /dɪˈsaɪd/ **verb** (present participle **deciding**, past tense and past participle **decided**) **A2** to choose something after thinking about the possibilities: *She decided to take the job.* ○ *Have you decided what to wear?*

decision /dɪˈsɪʒ·ən/ **noun** **B1** a choice that you make about something after thinking about many possibilities: *What was their decision – are they coming or not?* ○ *We need to **make a decision**.*

deck /dek/ **noun** **1** one of the floors of a ship, bus, or plane: *The kids like going out on the deck when we ride the ferry.* **2** a wooden floor outside a house, usually with a low fence around it and without a roof: *In the summer, we eat on the deck whenever we can.* **3** a set of cards used for playing games

declaration /ˌdek·ləˈreɪ·ʃən/ **noun** something that someone says officially, giving information about something: *a declaration of independence*

a b c d e f g h i j k l m n o p q r s t u v w x y z

declare /dɪˈkleər/ **verb** (present participle
declaring, past tense and past participle
declared) **1 B1** to officially tell someone the value of something, for example at an airport, because you might
have to pay tax: *Do you have anything to
declare?* **2** to announce something
publicly or officially: *Scientists have declared that the process is safe.* ○ *The
country declared war on its neighbor.*

decline[1] /dɪˈklaɪn/ **noun** [no plural] (present
participle **declining**, past tense and past participle **declined**)   a reduction in the amount,
importance, quality, or strength of something: *a steady decline in sales*

decline[2] /dɪˈklaɪn/ **verb**   to become less
in amount, importance, quality, or
strength: *Sales of CDs have declined.*

decorate /ˈdek·əˌreɪt/ **verb** (present particip-
ple **decorating**, past tense and past participle
decorated) **1 B1** to make something
look more attractive by putting things
on it: *They decorated the room with balloons for her party.* **2 B1** to put paint or
paper on the walls of a room or building: *The whole house needs decorating.*

decoration /ˌdek·əˈreɪ·ʃən/ **noun**   the
act or process of making something
look more attractive by putting things
on it, or something that you use to do
this: *Christmas decorations* ○ *She hung
some pictures around the room for decoration.*

decrease /dɪˈkris/ **verb** (present participle
decreasing, past tense and past participle
decreased) **B1** to become less, or to
make something become less: *Prices
have decreased.* → Opposite **increase verb**
• **decrease noun B1** *There has been a
decrease in the number of violent crimes.*

deed /did/ **noun** formal   something that
you do: *good deeds*

deep[1] /dip/ **adj** **1 A2** having a long distance from the top to the bottom or the
front to the back: *The water is a lot
deeper than it seems.* **2 B1** A deep color
is strong and dark: *deep brown eyes*
3 one inch, six feet, etc. deep one inch,
six feet, etc. from the top to the bottom,

or from the front the back: *This end of
the pool is eight feet deep.* **4** A deep
feeling is very strong: *deep affection*
5 a deep sleep the action of someone
sleeping in a way that makes it difficult
to wake them up **6** A deep sound is
low: *a deep voice*

deep

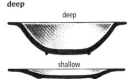

deep[2] /dip/ **adv** **B1** a long way into
something from the top or outside:
They traveled deep into the forest.

deeply /ˈdip·li/ **adv**   very much: *I have
fallen deeply in love with her.*

deer /dɪər/ **noun**
(plural **deer**)
a large, wild animal
that has antlers
(=long horns) if it
is male

deer

defeat[1] /dɪˈfit/ **verb**
B1 to win against someone in a fight or
competition: *She was defeated in the first
round of the tournament.*

defeat[2] /dɪˈfit/ **noun** **B1** the action of
someone losing a fight or competition

defend /dɪˈfend/ **verb** **1 B1** to protect
someone or something from being attacked, especially by fighting: *She tried
to defend herself with a knife.* **2** to support someone or something that is being criticized: *They are fighting to defend
their rights.*

defender /dɪˈfen·dər/ **noun**   someone
on a sports team who tries to prevent
the other team from scoring points,
goals, etc.

defense[1] /dɪˈfens/ **noun** **A2** protection,
or something that provides protection
against an attack or criticism: *the body's
defenses against infection* ○ *She argued
strongly in defense of her actions.*

defense[2] /'di·fens/ **noun** 🅱1 the part of a sports team that tries to prevent the other team from scoring points: *The team's defense needs to practice more.*

define /dɪˈfaɪn/ **verb** (present participle **defining**, past tense and past participle **defined**) to say exactly what something means: *Your duties are clearly defined in the contract.*

definite /'def·ə·nɪt/ **adj** certain, clear, and not likely to change: *We need a definite answer by tomorrow.*

definite article /'def·ə·nɪt 'ɑr·tɪ·kəl/ **noun** 🅱1 in grammar, used to mean the word "the"

definitely /'def·ə·nɪt·li/ **adv** 🅱1 without any doubt: *This book is definitely worth reading.*

definition /ˌdef·əˈnɪʃ·ən/ **noun** an explanation of the meaning of a word or phrase: *a dictionary definition*

defrost /dɪˈfrɔst/ **verb** If frozen food defrosts, or if you defrost it, it becomes warmer and no longer frozen: *You need to defrost the fish before you cook it.*

defy /dɪˈfaɪ/ **verb** (present participle **defying**, past tense and past participle **defied**) to refuse to obey someone or something

degree /dɪˈgri/ **noun** **1** 🅰2 a unit for measuring temperatures or angles, shown by the symbol [°] written after a number **2** 🅱1 a document that proves you have completed a course of study at a college or university: *He has a degree in physics.* **3** an amount or level of something: *There was some degree of truth in what she said.*

delay[1] /dɪˈleɪ/ **verb** **1** 🅰2 to make something happen at a later time than you planned: *Can you delay your trip until next week?* **2** 🅱1 to make someone or something late: *I was delayed by traffic.*

delay[2] /dɪˈleɪ/ **noun** **1** 🅰2 a situation in which you have to wait longer than expected: *An accident caused long delays on the highway.* **2** **without delay** 🅱1 immediately: *We need to deal with this problem without delay.*

delete /dɪˈlit/ **verb** (present participle **deleting**, past tense and past participle **deleted**) 🅱1 to remove something, especially on a computer: *I deleted the file by mistake.*

deli /'del·i/ **noun** (plural **delis**) short form of **delicatessen**

deliberate /dɪˈlɪb·ər·ət/ **adj** If an action is deliberate, you wanted or planned to do it: *This was a deliberate attempt by them to deceive us.*

deliberately /dɪˈlɪb·ər·ət·li/ **adv** If you do something deliberately, you wanted or planned to do it: *He deliberately lied to the police.*

delicate /'del·ɪ·kət/ **adj** **1** easy to damage or break: *a delicate shell* **2** soft, light, or gentle: *a delicate shade of pink*

delicatessen /ˌdel·ɪ·kəˈtes·ən/ **noun** (short form **deli**) a store or part of a store that sells foods such as cheeses, cold cooked meats, salads, and often sandwiches

delicious /dɪˈlɪʃ·əs/ **adj** 🅱1 very good to eat or drink: *This soup is really delicious.*

delight[1] /dɪˈlaɪt/ **noun** [no plural] happiness and excited pleasure: *The children screamed with delight.*

delight[2] /dɪˈlaɪt/ **verb** to make someone feel very pleased: *The new discovery has delighted scientists everywhere.*

delighted /dɪˈlaɪ·tɪd/ **adj** 🅱1 very pleased: *They are delighted with their new car.*

delightful /dɪˈlaɪt·fəl/ **adj** very pleasant or attractive: *We had a delightful evening.*

deliver /dɪˈlɪv·ər/ **verb** **1** 🅱1 to take letters or things to a person or place: *They can deliver the couch on Wednesday.* **2 deliver a baby** to help take a baby out of its mother when it is being born

delivery /dɪˈlɪv·ə·ri/ **noun** (plural **deliveries**) 🅱1 the act of taking letters or things to a person or place: *Is there a charge for delivery?*

demand[1] /dɪˈmænd/ **noun** **1** 🅱1 a strong request or need for something:

a
b
c
d
e
f
g
h
i
j
k
l
m
n
o
p
q
r
s
t
u
v
w
x
y
z

| æ cat | ɑ hot | e get | ɪ sit | i see | ɔ saw | ʊ book | u too | ʌ cut | ə about | ər mother | ɑr turn | ɔr for | aɪ my | aʊ how | eɪ say | ɔɪ boy |

There was not much **demand for** ice cream in the winter. **2 in demand** wanted or needed in large numbers: *Good teachers are always in demand.*

demand² /dɪˈmænd/ verb **1** 🔵 to ask for something in an angry way: *I demanded an explanation.* **2** to need something such as time and effort: *This work demands a lot of concentration.*

demanding /dɪˈmæn·dɪŋ/ adj needing a lot of time, attention, or effort: *This is a very demanding job.*

demo /ˈdem·oʊ/ noun an example of a product, given or shown to someone to try to make him or her buy it: *a software demo*

democracy /dɪˈmɑk·rə·si/ noun (plural **democracies**) a system of government in which all the people choose their leaders, or a country with this system

democrat /ˈdem·əˌkræt/ noun **1** someone who supports democracy **2 Democrat** someone who supports the Democratic Party

democratic /ˌdem·əˈkræt·ɪk/ adj following or supporting the political system of democracy: *a democratic society*

demolish /dɪˈmɑl·ɪʃ/ verb to destroy something such as a building: *The factory is dangerous, and will have to be demolished.*

demonstrate /ˈdem·ənˌstreɪt/ verb (present participle **demonstrating**, past tense and past participle **demonstrated**) **1** to show someone how to do something: *She demonstrated how to use the new software.* **2** to show that something exists or is true: *The experiment clearly **demonstrates that** there are positive benefits.* **3** to walk or stand with a group of people to show that you have a strong opinion about something: *Thousands of people gathered to **demonstrate against** the new proposals.*

demonstration /ˌdem·ənˈstreɪ·ʃən/ noun **1** an event at which a group of people walk or stand together to show that they have a strong opinion about some-

thing: *They're taking part in a **demonstration against** nuclear weapons.* **2** an act of showing how to do something: *A salesman gave us a demonstration.*

demonstrator /ˈdem·ənˌstreɪ·tər/ noun someone who takes part in a demonstration to show their opinion about something: *Police arrested several of the demonstrators.*

den /den/ noun the home of some kinds of wild animals

denim /ˈden·əm/ noun [no plural] thick, strong cotton cloth, used to make clothes: *denim jeans*

dense /dens/ adj **1** with a lot of people or things close together: *dense forest* **2** thick and difficult to see through: *dense fog*
• **densely** adv

dent¹ /dent/ noun an area in a hard surface that has been hit and pushed inward: *The car door had a dent in it.*

dent² /dent/ verb to push an area of a hard surface inward by hitting it with something: *The side of the car was dented in the accident.*

dental /ˈden·t̬əl/ adj relating to the teeth: *a dental appointment*

dentist /ˈden·tɪst/ noun 🔵 someone who looks at and repairs teeth: *I have a **dentist appointment** tomorrow.*

dentures /ˈden·tʃərz/ plural noun artificial teeth that fit inside the mouth of someone who does not have their own teeth: *Grandma wears dentures.*

deny /dɪˈnaɪ/ verb (present participle **denying**, past tense and past participle **denied**) to say that something is not true, or that you have not done something: *She denies any involvement in the attack.*

deodorant /diˈoʊ·dər·ənt/ noun something that you put on your body to stop bad smells

depart /dɪˈpɑrt/ verb formal 🔵 to leave a place: *The train to Lincoln will **depart from** platform 9.*

department /dɪˈpɑrt·mənt/ noun 🔵 a part of an organization that does a particular type of work: *the sales department*

| ou go | aɪər **fire** | aʊər **hour** | eər **hair** | ɪər **ear** | ʊər **poor** | j **yet** | ʒ **measure** | ʃ **ship** | dʒ **judge** | tʃ **chin** | ð **that** | θ **thin** | ŋ **hang** |

department store /dɪˈpɑrt·mənt ˌstɔr/ noun **A2** a large store that sells different types of things

departure /dɪˈpɑr·tʃər/ noun **B1** the action of someone or something leaving a place: *the departure of flight BA117*

depend /dɪˈpend/ verb **it/that depends** **B1** used to say that you are not certain about something because other things affect your answer: *"Are you coming out tonight?" "It depends where you're going."*

depend on someone/something phrasal verb **1 B1** to need the help of someone or something: *Our economy depends on the car industry.* **2** to be affected by someone or something: *What you buy depends on what you can spend.* **3** to trust someone or something and know that he, she, or it will help you or do what you want or expect: *You can always depend on her in a crisis.*

> **❗ Common mistake: depend on something**
>
> Be careful to choose the correct preposition after **depend**.
>
> I might go on Friday – it depends on the weather.
> ~~I might go on Friday – it depends of the weather.~~
> ~~I might go on Friday – it depends from the weather.~~

dependent[1] /dɪˈpen·dənt/ adj needing the help of someone or something: *She's completely **dependent on** her parents for money.*

dependent[2] /dɪˈpen·dənt/ noun someone, usually a child, who needs your money to live: *The insurance is for him and all his dependents.*

deposit[1] /dɪˈpɑz·ɪt/ noun **1 B1** a payment that you make immediately when you decide to buy something: *They put down a **deposit on** a house.* **2** money that you pay into a bank: *to **make a deposit*** **3** money that you pay when you rent something, and that is returned to you if you do not damage anything

deposit[2] /dɪˈpɑz·ɪt/ verb **1** to put something down somewhere: *He **deposited**

his books **on** the table.* **2** to put money into a bank: *She **deposited** $150,000 **in** a Swiss bank account.*

depot /ˈdi·poʊ/ noun a place where vehicles or goods are kept

depress /dɪˈpres/ verb to make someone feel very sad: *This place really depresses me.*

depressed /dɪˈprest/ adj **B1** very sad, often for a long time: *She's been very depressed since her marriage broke up.*

depressing /dɪˈpres·ɪŋ/ adj making you feel sad and without any hope for the future: *The news is very depressing.*

depression /dɪˈpreʃ·ən/ noun a feeling of sadness, or a mental illness that makes you feel very sad: *Millions of people suffer from depression.*

deprive /dɪˈpraɪv/ verb (present participle **depriving**, past tense and past participle **deprived**) to take something, especially something necessary or pleasant, away from someone: *They were **deprived of** food for long periods of time.*

depth /depθ/ noun **1 B1** the distance from the top of something to the bottom: *Dig a hole 2 ft. **in depth**.* **2** the quality of having a lot of knowledge or of being able to think seriously about something: *Her writing shows astonishing depth.* **3 in depth** in a very detailed way: *I have studied this subject in depth.*

deputy /ˈdep·jə·t̬i/ noun (plural **deputies**) someone who has the second most important job in an organization: *the deputy mayor ○ a sheriff's deputy*

descend /dɪˈsend/ verb formal to move down or go down: *We descended four flights of stairs (=series of steps).*

descendant /dɪˈsen·dənt/ noun someone who is related to someone who lived a long time ago

describe /dɪˈskraɪb/ verb (present participle **describing**, past tense and past participle **described**) **A2** to say what someone or something is like: *I tried to describe what I had seen.*

description /dɪˈskrɪp·ʃən/ noun
B1 words that tell you what someone or something is like: *I **gave** the police a **description of** the stolen jewelry.*

desert[1] /ˈdez·ərt/ noun **A2** a large, hot, dry area of land with very few plants: *the Sahara Desert*

desert[2] /dɪˈzɜrt/ verb **1** to leave a place, so that it is empty: *People desert the city on summer weekends and go to the beaches.* **2** to leave the military, or a job you have when you are in the military, without permission: *He deserted his post.* **3** to leave someone and never come back

deserted /dɪˈzɜr·t̬ɪd/ adj A deserted place has no people in it: *The street was completely deserted.*

deserve /dɪˈzɜrv/ verb (present participle **deserving**, past tense and past participle **deserved**) **B1** If you deserve something good or bad, it should happen because of the way you have behaved: *He deserves to be locked up for life.*

design[1] /dɪˈzaɪn/ noun **1** **B1** the way in which something is planned or made: *Engineers are working on the new designs.* **2** **B1** a pattern or decoration: *a design of fish and sea shells* **3** **B1** [no plural] the art of making plans or drawings for something: *He's studying fashion design in college.*

design[2] /dɪˈzaɪn/ verb **1** **B1** to draw or plan something before making it: *She designs furniture.* **2** **be designed for/to do something** to have been planned or done for a particular purpose: *These light bulbs are designed to use less energy.*

designer[1] /dɪˈzaɪ·nər/ noun **B1** someone who draws and plans how something will be made: *a fashion designer*

designer[2] /dɪˈzaɪ·nər/ adj **designer jeans, sunglasses, etc.** expensive clothes or things

desire /dɪˈzaɪər/ noun wanting something very much: *the desire to have children*

desk /desk/ noun
A1 a table that you sit at to write or work

→ See **The Office** on page C12

desk

desktop /ˈdesk·tɑp/ noun a computer screen that shows the files, programs, etc. that are available to be used

despair /dɪˈspeər/ noun [no plural] a feeling of having no hope: *She shook her head in despair.*
• **despair** verb

desperate /ˈdes·pər·ət/ adj **1** feeling that you have no hope and will do anything to change the situation you are in: *He was **desperate to** get home.* **2** needing or wanting something very much: *By two o'clock I was **desperate for** something to eat.*
• **desperately** adv
• **desperation** noun [no plural]

despise /dɪˈspaɪz/ verb (present participle **despising**, past tense and past participle **despised**) to hate someone or something and have no respect for him, her, or it: *The two groups despise each other.*

despite /dɪˈspaɪt/ preposition **B1** although something happened or is true: *I'm still pleased with the house despite all the problems we've had.* ○ *The company has been forced to close, **despite the fact that** sales have been strong.*

dessert /dɪˈzɜrt/ noun **A2** sweet food that is eaten at the end of a meal

desserts

destination /ˌdes·təˈneɪ·ʃən/ noun
B1 the place where someone or something is going: *Florida is a very popular vacation destination.*

destroy /dɪˈstrɔɪ/ verb **B1** to damage something so badly that it cannot be used or does not exist: *Many works of art were destroyed in the fire.*

destruction /dɪˈstrʌk·ʃən/ noun [no plural] the act or process of destroying something: *We are all responsible for the **destruction** of the forest.*

detach /dɪˈtætʃ/ verb to take a part of something off so that it is separate: *Please complete and detach the form below.*

detail /ˈdiːteɪl/,/dɪˈteɪl/ noun **1 A2** a piece of information about something: *Please send me **details** of your training courses.* **2 in detail** **B1** including every part of something: *He explained it all in great detail.* **3 go into detail** to tell or include all the facts about something: *I won't go into detail over the phone, but I've had a few problems recently.*

detailed /ˈdiːteɪld/,/dɪˈteɪld/ adj giving a lot of information: *a detailed description*

detect /dɪˈtekt/ verb to discover or notice something: *This special camera can detect bodies by their heat.*

detective /dɪˈtek·tɪv/ noun **B1** someone whose job is to discover information about a crime

detergent /dɪˈtɜr·dʒənt/ noun a liquid or powder that is used to clean things

determination /dɪˌtɜr·məˈner·ʃən/ noun [no plural] the action of continuing to try to do something, although it is very difficult: *He'll need great determination and skill to win the competition.*

determined /dɪˈtɜr·mənd/ adj wanting so much to do something that you keep trying very hard: *He's **determined to** succeed.*

determiner /dɪˈtɜr·mə·nər/ noun in grammar, a word that is used before a noun to show which person or thing you mean: *In the phrases "my first apartment" and "that red car," the words "my" and "that" are determiners.*

detest /dɪˈtest/ verb to hate someone or something: *They used to be friends, but now they absolutely detest each other.*

detour /ˈdiː·tʊər/ noun a different route that must be used while a road is closed
• **detour** verb *All traffic will be detoured during the parade.*

devastate /ˈdev·əˌsteɪt/ verb to destroy or damage something very badly: *The hurricane devastated the city.*

develop /dɪˈvel·əp/ verb **1 B1** to change and become better, or to make someone or something become better: *He's **developing into** a very good tennis player.* **2 B1** to make something new, such as a product: *Scientists are developing new drugs all the time.* **3** to start to have a problem or feeling: *Soon after takeoff the plane developed engine trouble.* **4** to use special chemicals on a piece of film to make photographs appear

developed /dɪˈvel·əpt/ adj describes a country or region of the world with an advanced level of technology, industry, etc.: *a developed country*

developing /dɪˈvel·ə·pɪŋ/ adj describes a country or region of the world that is poor and has few industries: *the developing countries*

development /dɪˈvel·əp·mənt/ noun **1 B1** the action of someone or something changing and becoming better: *There have been some major developments in technology recently.* **2 B1** [no plural] the process of developing something new: *the development of new drugs* **3** something new that happens and changes a situation: *Have there been any more developments since I left?*

device /dɪˈvaɪs/ noun a piece of equipment: *an electronic device for sending messages*

devil /ˈdev·əl/ noun **1 the Devil** the most powerful evil spirit, according to the Christian and Jewish religions **2** an evil spirit

devote /dɪˈvoʊt/ verb (present participle **devoting**, past tense and past participle **devoted**) **1** to use time or energy for a particular person: *She devotes most of her free time to charity work.* **2** to use a space or area for a particular purpose: *Most of the magazine is devoted to photos.*

a
b
c
d
e
f
g
h
i
j
k
l
m
n
o
p
q
r
s
t
u
v
w
x
y
z

dew /du/ **noun** [no plural] drops of water that form on surfaces outside during the night

diabetes /ˌdaɪ·ə·ˈbiː·t̬ɪs/ **noun** [no plural] a serious medical condition in which your body cannot control the amount of sugar in your blood

diabetic /ˌdaɪ·ə·ˈbet̬·ɪk/ **noun** a person who has diabetes
• **diabetic adj** *a diabetic patient*

diagonal /daɪˈæg·ə·nᵊl/ **adj** going from the top corner of a square to the bottom corner on the other side
• **diagonally adv**

diagram /ˈdaɪ·ə·græm/ **noun** **B1** a simple picture showing what something looks like or explaining how something works

dial¹ /daɪl/, /ˈdaɪ·əl/ **noun** a round part on a clock or piece of equipment that shows you the time or other measurement

dial² /daɪl/, /ˈdaɪ·əl/ **verb** **B1** to make a telephone call to a particular number: *Dial 0 for the operator.*

dialect /ˈdaɪ·əˌlekt/ **noun** a form of a language that people speak in a particular part of a country

dialogue /ˈdaɪ·əˌlɔg/, /ˈdaɪ·əˌlɑg/ **noun** (also **dialogue**) the talking in a book, play, or movie

diameter /daɪˈæm·ɪ·t̬ər/ **noun** a straight line that goes from one side of a circle to the other side and through the center: *The cake was about 10 inches in diameter.*

diamond /ˈdaɪ·mənd/ **noun** **diamonds**
1 a very hard, transparent stone that is very valuable and is often used in jewelry: *a diamond ring* **2** a shape with four straight sides of equal length that join to form two large angles and two small angles

diamonds /ˈdaɪ·məndz/ **plural noun** one of the four suits (=groups) of playing cards: *the three of diamonds*

diaper /ˈdaɪ·pər/ **noun** a thick piece of paper or cloth worn by a baby on its bottom: *I need to change her diaper.*

diarrhea /ˌdaɪ·əˈriː·ə/ **noun** [no plural] an illness that makes a person go to the toilet more often

diary /ˈdaɪ·ə·ri/ **noun** (plural **diaries**) **A2** a book in which you write about what you have done and your thoughts and feelings: *She kept a diary of her vacation.*

dice /daɪs/ **noun** (singular **die**) **dice** small objects with six equal square sides, each with between one and six spots on it, used in games

dictate /ˈdɪk·teɪt/ **verb** (present participle **dictating**, past tense and past participle **dictated**) to say or read something for someone to write down

dictation /dɪkˈteɪ·ʃən/ **noun** **1** [no plural] the act of saying something for someone else to write down **2** a test in which a teacher reads something for students to write down

dictator /ˈdɪk·teɪ·t̬ər/ **noun** a leader who has complete power in a country

dictionary /ˈdɪk·ʃəˌner·i/ **noun** (plural **dictionaries**) **A1** a book that contains a list of words in alphabetical order with their meanings explained and sometimes written in another language: *Use your dictionary to look up any words you don't understand.*

did /dɪd/ past tense of do

didn't /ˈdɪd·ᵊnt/ short form of did not

die /daɪ/ **verb** (present participle **dying**, past tense and past participle **died**) **1** **A1** to stop living: *Many of the refugees died of hunger.* **2** be dying for *something*; be dying to do *something* informal **B1** to want to have or do something very much: *I'm dying for something cold to drink.*

> **⚠ Common mistake: die**
>
> Be careful to choose the correct preposition.
>
> He **died of** *a heart attack.*
> ~~He died by a heart attack.~~

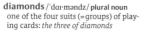

> ## ❗ Common mistake: **died** or **dead**?
>
> Be careful not to confuse the verb and adjective forms of these words. **Died** is the past of the verb "to die," which means "to stop living."
>
> *My cat died last week.*
>
> **Dead** is an adjective and is used to talk about people or things that are not alive.
>
> *My cat is dead.*

die out phrasal verb to become more and more rare and then disappear completely: *Dinosaurs died out about 65 million years ago.*

diesel /'di·zəl/ **noun** [no plural] fuel used in the engines of some vehicles

diet /'daɪ·ɪt/ **noun** 1 **B1** the type of food that someone usually eats: *His diet isn't very healthy.* 2 **B1** the practice of someone eating a particular type or amount of food for a special reason, such as being sick or wanting to become thinner: *No cake for me, thanks – I'm on a diet.*

difference /'dɪf·rəns/ **noun** 1 **A2** the way in which two people or things are not the same: *What's the difference between an ape and a monkey?* 2 **B1** the amount by which one thing is different from another: *There's a big difference in age between them.* 3 **make any difference** to have an effect on a situation: *Do what you want; it doesn't make any difference.* 4 **tell the difference** to notice the way in which two things are different: *This coffee is half the price of that one, but I can't tell the difference.*

> ## ❗ Common mistake: **difference**
>
> When you want to talk about how something or someone has changed, use the preposition **in**.
>
> *The graph shows the difference in sales this year.*
>
> ~~The graph shows the difference of sales this year.~~

different /'dɪf·rənt/ **adj** 1 **A1** not the same as someone or something else:

Jo's very different from her sister, isn't she? 2 **B1** used to talk about separate things or people of the same type: *eight different flavors of ice cream*
• **differently adv**

> ## ❗ Common mistake: different
>
> **Different** is usually followed by the preposition **from**. In American English, people also use **than**.
>
> *The United States is very different from/than my country.*

difficult /'dɪf·ɪ·kəlt/ **adj** 1 **A1** not easy to do or understand: *Japanese is a difficult language to learn.* 2 **B1** not friendly or easy to deal with: *a difficult teenager*

difficulty /'dɪf·ɪ·kəl·ti/ **noun** (plural **difficulties**) **B1** a problem: *I had difficulty finding somewhere to park.*

dig /dɪg/ **verb** (present participle **digging,** past tense and past participle **dug**) 1 to make a hole in the ground by moving some of the ground or soil away: *They dug a huge hole in the road.* 2 **B1** to break up and move soil using a tool, a machine, or your hands: *Digging in the garden is good exercise.*

dig

digest /dɪˈdʒest/, /daɪˈdʒest/ **verb** to change food in your stomach into substances that your body can use
• **digestion noun**

digit /'dɪdʒ·ɪt/ **noun** any of the numbers from 0 to 9, especially when they form part of a longer number: *a seven-digit telephone number*

digital /'dɪdʒ·ɪ·t̬ᵊl/ **adj** 1 **A2** using an electronic system that changes sounds or images into numbers before it stores or sends them: *digital television* 2 **B1** A digital clock or watch shows the time in the form of numbers.

digital camera /'dɪdʒ·ɪ·t̬ᵊl 'kæm·rə/ **noun** **A2** a type of camera that records images that you can use and store on a computer

Sidebar letters: a b c **d** e f g h i j k l m n o p q r s t u v w x y z

dilute /dɪˈlut/, /ˈdaɪˈlut/ **verb** (present participle **diluting**, past tense and past participle **diluted**) to make a liquid thinner by adding another liquid to it: *You need to dilute this juice before you drink it.*

dim /dɪm/ **adj** (comparative **dimmer**, superlative **dimmest**) not bright or clear: *He could hardly see her in the dim light.*
• **dimly adv** *a **dimly** lit room*

dime /daɪm/ **noun** a coin with a value of ten cents (=10/100 of a dollar)

dimension /dəˈmen·ʃən/ **noun** a measurement of the length, width, or height of something: *The **dimensions** of the photo should be no larger than ten inches by six inches.*

dinghy /ˈdɪŋ·i/ **noun** (plural **dinghies**) a small boat

dining room /ˈdaɪ·nɪŋ ˌrum/, /ˈdaɪ·nɪŋ ˌrum/ **noun** **A1** a room where you eat your meals

dinner /ˈdɪn·ər/ **noun** **A1** the main meal of the day that people eat in the evening

dinosaur /ˈdaɪ·nəˌsɔr/ **noun** **A2** a very large animal that used to live millions of years ago

dinosaurs

dip /dɪp/ **verb** (present participle **dipping**, past tense and past participle **dipped**) to put something into a liquid for a short time: *She dipped the brush into the paint.*

diploma /dɪˈploʊ·mə/ **noun** **A2** an official document showing that someone has completed a course of study: *a high school diploma*

direct /dəˈrekt/, /daɪˈrekt/ **adj, adv** **1** **B1** going straight from one place to

another without turning or stopping: *We went by the most direct route.* **2** with no other person or thing involved or between: *direct sunlight* → Opposite **indirect adj**

direct /dəˈrekt/, /daɪˈrekt/ **verb** **1** **B1** to tell the actors in a movie or play what to do: *a movie directed by Alfred Hitchcock* **2** **B1** to show or tell someone how to get to a place: *Can you direct me to the manager's office, please?*

direction /dəˈrek·ʃən/, /daɪˈrek·ʃən/ **noun** **1** **B1** the way that someone or something is going or facing: *The car sped away in the direction of the airport.* **2** in someone's direction toward someone: *She keeps looking in my direction.*

directions /dəˈrek·ʃənz/, /daɪˈrek·ʃənz/ **plural noun** **A2** instructions that tell you how to get to a place, or how to do something: *Did you ask for directions?*

directly /dəˈrekt·li/, /daɪˈrekt·li/ **adv** **B1** with no other person or thing involved or between: *Why don't you speak to him directly?*

director /dəˈrek·tər/, /daɪˈrek·tər/ **noun** **1** **B1** an important manager in an organization or company: *Meet the new sales director.* **2** **B1** someone who tells the actors in a movie or play what to do

directory /dəˈrek·tə·ri/, /daɪˈrek·tə·ri/ **noun** (plural **directories**) a book or list of names and numbers: *a phone directory*

dirt /dɜrt/ **noun** [no plural] **B1** a substance that makes something not clean: *You've got some dirt on your pants.*

dirty /ˈdɜr·ṭi/ **adj** (comparative **dirtier**, superlative **dirtiest**) **1** **A2** not clean: *dirty dishes* ○ Try not to **get** your clothes **dirty**. **2** Dirty words or jokes relate to sex or going to the toilet.

disability /ˌdɪs·əˈbɪl·ɪ·ṭi/ **noun** (plural **disabilities**) an illness, injury or condition that makes it difficult for someone to do the things that other people do: *a physical disability*

disabled /dɪsˈeɪ·bəld/ **adj** **B1** having an illness or condition that makes it difficult to do the things that other people do: *equal rights for the disabled*

disadvantage /ˌdɪs·əd'væn·tɪdʒ/ noun
B1 something that makes a situation more difficult: *One disadvantage of living in the country is the lack of public transportation.* → Opposite **advantage** noun (1)

disagree /ˌdɪs·ə'gri/ verb (present participle **disagreeing**, past tense and past participle **disagreed**) **B1** to have a different opinion from someone else: *I disagree with most of what he said.* ∘ *Experts disagree about/on the causes of the disease.* → Opposite **agree** verb (1)

disagreement /ˌdɪs·ə'gri·mənt/ noun a situation in which people have a different opinion about something or have an argument: *They had a disagreement about money.*

disappear /ˌdɪs·ə'pɪər/ verb **1 B1** to suddenly go somewhere and become impossible to see or find: *She watched him disappear into the crowd.* ∘ *Amelia Earhart's plane disappeared in 1937.* **2** to no longer exist: *Frogs are disappearing from many parts of the world.*

disappearance /ˌdɪs·ə'pɪər·əns/ noun the fact of someone or something suddenly going somewhere and becoming impossible to see or find: *Police are investigating the girl's disappearance.*

disappoint /ˌdɪs·ə'pɔɪnt/ verb **B1** to make someone feel sad because someone or something was not as good as he or she had expected: *We don't want to disappoint the fans.*

disappointed /ˌdɪs·ə'pɔɪn·tɪd/ adj **B1** sad because something was not as good as you expected, or because something did not happen: *I was very disappointed that he didn't come.*

disappointing /ˌdɪs·ə'pɔɪn·tɪŋ/ adj **B1** making you feel disappointed: *a disappointing performance*

disappointment /ˌdɪs·ə'pɔɪnt·mənt/ noun **1 B1** [no plural] the feeling of being disappointed **2 B1** someone or something that disappoints you: *I'm sorry I'm such a disappointment to you.*

disapproval /ˌdɪs·ə'pru·vəl/ noun [no plural] a feeling of thinking that someone or something is bad or wrong

disapprove /ˌdɪs·ə'pruv/ verb (present participle **disapproving**, past tense and past participle **disapproved**) to think that someone or something is bad or wrong: *Her family disapproved of the marriage.*

disaster /dɪ'zæs·tər/ noun **1** a very bad situation, especially something that causes a lot of harm or damage: *floods and other natural disasters* **2** something that is a failure or negative result: *His idea was a total disaster.*

disastrous /dɪ'zæs·trəs/ adj bad and causing big problems: *a disastrous week*

disc /dɪsk/ noun **1 B1** a record or CD **2** a flat, round shape or object

discipline /'dɪs·ə·plən/ noun [no plural] the action of controlling people's behavior using rules and punishments: *There should be better discipline in schools.*

disconnect /ˌdɪs·kə'nekt/ verb to separate an electrical machine from the electricity supply or from another machine: *Switch off the machine before disconnecting it from the power supply.*

discount /'dɪsˌkaʊnt/ noun **B1** a reduction in the price of something: *a 10 percent discount on travel for students*

discourage /dɪ'skɜr·ɪdʒ/, /dɪ'skʌr·ɪdʒ/ verb (present participle **discouraging**, past tense and past participle **discouraged**) **1** to try to persuade someone to stop doing something: *a campaign to discourage people from smoking* **2** to make someone less confident or enthusiastic about something: *The thought of how much work she had to do discouraged her.*

discover /dɪ'skʌv·ər/ verb **B1** to find something or get information about something for the first time: *The body was discovered in a river.* ∘ *She discovered that he was already married.*

discovery /dɪ'skʌv·ə·ri/ noun (plural **discoveries**) finding something or someone for the first time: *Scientists have made some important discoveries about genetics recently.*

discrimination /dɪˌskrɪm·ə'neɪ·ʃən/ noun [no plural] unfair treatment because of a person's sex, race, age, etc.

discuss /dɪˈskʌs/ verb **A2** to talk about something with someone and tell each other your ideas or opinions: *Have you discussed this matter with anyone else?*

> **⚠ Common mistake: discuss**
>
> **Discuss** is not followed by a preposition.
>
> *We discussed the plans for the wedding.*
>
> ~~We discussed about the plans for the wedding.~~
>
> You can **discuss something with someone.**
>
> *Can I discuss this report with you?*

discussion /dɪˈskʌʃ·ən/ noun **B1** a talk in which people tell each other their ideas or opinions about someone or something: *They were having a discussion about football.*

disease /dɪˈziz/ noun **B1** an illness: *heart disease*

disgrace /dɪsˈgreɪs/ noun [no plural] **1** the action of someone doing something very bad that makes people stop respecting him or her: *They were sent home in disgrace.* **2** be a disgrace to be very bad: *It's a disgrace that money is being wasted like this.*

disgraceful /dɪsˈgreɪs·fəl/ adj very bad: *disgraceful behavior*

disguise[1] /dɪsˈgaɪz/ noun things that you wear to change the way you look so that people cannot recognize you: *She usually goes out in disguise to avoid being bothered by the public.*

disguise[2] /dɪsˈgaɪz/ verb (present participle **disguising**, past tense and past participle **disguised**) to change the way you look so that people cannot recognize you: *He managed to escape by disguising himself as a woman.*

disgust /dɪsˈgʌst/ noun [no plural] a very strong feeling of dislike: *She walked out in disgust.*
• **disgust** verb

disgusted /dɪsˈgʌs·tɪd/ adj feeling extreme dislike of something: *I'm totally disgusted with your behavior.*

disgusting /dɪsˈgʌs·tɪŋ/ adj **B1** extremely unpleasant: *a disgusting smell*

dish /dɪʃ/ noun **1** **A2** a container for food that you eat from and cook food in **2** **A2** part of a meal: *She cooked a very nice chicken dish.* **3** the dishes **A2** dirty plates and other objects that have been used for cooking or eating food: *Who's going to do the dishes (= wash them)?*

dishcloth /ˈdɪʃˌklɔθ/ noun a cloth used for washing dirty dishes

dishonest /dɪsˈɑn·əst/ adj not honest and likely to lie

dishwasher /ˈdɪʃˌwɑʃ·ər/ noun **B1** a machine that washes plates, glasses, and other kitchen equipment → See **The Kitchen** on page C10

disinfectant /ˌdɪs·ɪnˈfek·tənt/ noun a chemical substance that destroys bacteria

disk /dɪsk/ noun **B1** a piece of computer equipment that records and keeps information: *How much free space is there on the disk?*

dislike /dɪsˈlaɪk/ verb (present participle **disliking**, past tense and past participle **disliked**) **B1** to not like someone or something: *Why do you dislike her so much?*
• **dislike** noun *He has a strong dislike of perfume.*

dismal /ˈdɪz·məl/ adj very bad or unpleasant and making you feel sad: *What dismal weather!*

dismay /dɪsˈmeɪ/ noun [no plural] a feeling of sadness and disappointment: *To our dismay, it started raining.*
• **dismayed** adj

dismiss /dɪsˈmɪs/ verb **1** to officially make someone leave his or her job: *Anyone who breaks company rules will be dismissed.* **2** to give someone official permission to leave: *The bell rang and the teacher dismissed the class.*

disobedient /ˌdɪs·əˈoʊ·bi·ənt/ adj refusing to do what someone in authority tells you to do: *a disobedient child*

disobey /ˌdɪs·əˈbeɪ/ verb to not do what you are told to do by someone in authority: *How dare you disobey me!*

disorganized /dɪsˈɔːrɡəˌnaɪzd/ **adj**
not good at planning or organizing
things: *She's extremely disorganized.*

dispenser /dɪˈspenˌsər/ **noun** a container or device that gives out measured
amounts of something: *a liquid soap dispenser* ○ *a tape dispenser*
→ See **The Classroom** on page C4

display[1] /dɪˈspleɪ/ **noun** **1** 🔵 a performance or a collection of things for people to look at: *a fireworks display* ○ *a
display of children's paintings* **2 on display** 🔵 If something is on display, it is
there for people to look at: *Many old
planes are on display at the museum.*
3 🔵 the part of a piece of electronic
equipment that shows information,
such as a computer screen: *The display
shows the time and date.*

display[2] /dɪˈspleɪ/ **verb** **1** 🔵 to arrange
something somewhere so that people
can see it: *There were some family photographs displayed on his desk.* **2** to show
something on a computer screen: *The
text can be displayed on screen.*

disposal /dɪˈspoʊzəl/ **noun** [no plural]
1 the act of getting rid of something:
waste disposal **2 at** *someone's* **disposal**
available for someone to use at any
time: *You will have a car at your disposal
for the whole trip.*

dispose /dɪˈspoʊz/ **verb** (present participle
disposing, past tense and past participle
disposed)
dispose of *something* **phrasal verb** to
get rid of something: *the proper way to
dispose of old paint*

dispute /dɪˈspjut/ **noun** a disagreement, especially one that lasts a long
time: *A man stabbed his neighbor in a
dispute over noise.*

disrespect[1] /ˌdɪsrɪˈspekt/ **noun** [no plural]
impolite behavior to someone, especially
a person who is older or more important than you: *They show* **disrespect for**
their teachers. ○ *I don't mean any disrespect.*

disrespect[2] /ˌdɪsrɪˈspekt/ **verb** to not
accept that someone is important or
has rights, and behave badly toward

him or her: *How dare you disrespect your
mother that way!*

disrupt /dɪsˈrʌpt/ **verb** to interrupt
something and stop it from continuing
as it should: *He got in trouble for disrupting the class.*

dissatisfied /dɪsˈsæt̬əsˌfaɪd/ **adj**
not happy with something: *Were you
dissatisfied with our service?*

dissertation /ˌdɪsərˈteɪʃən/ **noun**
a very long piece of writing done as
part of a doctorate (= advanced university course): *She's writing her* **dissertation** *on American poetry.*

dissolve /dɪˈzɑlv/ **verb** (present participle
dissolving, past tense and past participle
dissolved) If a solid dissolves, it becomes part of a liquid, and if you dissolve it, you make it become part of a
liquid: *Stir until the sugar dissolves.*

distance /ˈdɪstəns/ **noun** **1** 🔵 the
length of the space between two places:
We're only a short **distance from** *my
house.* **2** [no plural] somewhere that is far
away: *I could see Mary* **in the distance**.

distant /ˈdɪstənt/ **adj** far away in space
or time: *distant galaxies* ○ *We hope to see
you in the not too distant future* (= soon).

distinct /dɪˈstɪŋkt/ **adj** **1** different and
separate: *This word has three distinct
meanings.* **2** clear and easy to see or
hear: *The voices gradually became louder
and more distinct.*
• **distinctly adv**

distinguish /dɪˈstɪŋɡwɪʃ/ **verb** **1** to see
or understand the differences between
two people, ideas, or things: *Children
must learn to* **distinguish between** *right
and wrong.* **2** to make one person or
thing seem different from another: *His
great skill* **distinguishes** *him* **from** *the
rest of the team.* **3** to be able to see, hear
or understand something: *I couldn't distinguish anything in the dark.*

distinguished /dɪˈstɪŋɡwɪʃt/ **adj** famous
or admired: *a distinguished writer*

distract /dɪˈstrækt/ **verb** to make someone stop giving his or her attention to
something: *Stop distracting me – I'm trying to finish my essay.*

a
b
c
d
e
f
g
h
i
j
k
l
m
n
o
p
q
r
s
t
u
v
w
x
y
z

distress /dɪˈstres/ **noun** [no plural] **1** the feeling of being very upset or worried: *The newspaper reports caused her a great deal of distress.* **2** the fact of someone or something being in danger and needing help: *an aircraft **in distress***
• **distress verb** *The news distressed her.*
• **distressing adj** *a distressing experience*

distribute /dɪˈstrɪbjut/ **verb** (present participle **distributing**, past tense and past participle **distributed**) to give something out to a lot of people or places: *The books will be **distributed to** local schools.*
• **distribution noun**

district /ˈdɪstrɪkt/ **noun** 🔵 a part of a city or country: *New York's fashion district*

disturb /dɪˈstɜrb/ **verb** **1** to stop what someone is doing or make problems for him or her, often by making a noise: *Georgia is working, so try not to disturb her.* **2** to upset someone or make him or her feel worried: *He was disturbed by the violence in the movie.*

ditch /dɪtʃ/ **noun** a long, narrow hole in the ground next to a road or field that water can flow through

dive /daɪv/ **verb** (present participle **diving**, past tense and past participle **dived** /daɪvd/ or **dove** /doʊv/) **1** 🔵 to jump into water with your head and arms going in first: *He dived off the dock into the lake.*

dive

2 🔵 to swim under water, usually with breathing equipment

diver /ˈdaɪvər/ **noun** 🔵 someone who swims under water, usually with breathing equipment

divide /dɪˈvaɪd/ **verb** (present participle **dividing**, past tense and past participle **divided**) **1** 🔵 to separate into parts or groups, or to make something separate into parts or groups: *We **divided up into** teams of six.* **2** to separate a place into two areas: *There's a narrow alley that **divides** our house **from** the one next door.* **3** **divide** *something* (up) among/between *someone* to separate something into parts and give a part to each person in a group: *The prize money will be divided equally among the winners.* **4** to calculate how many times a number can go into another number: *12 **divided by** 6 equals 2.*

divine /dɪˈvaɪn/ **adj** relating to or coming from God or a god

diving /ˈdaɪvɪŋ/ **noun** [no plural] **1** 🔵 the activity or sport of swimming under water, usually using special breathing equipment: *We **went diving** in the Bahamas.* **2** the activity or sport of jumping into water with your arms and head going in first

diving board /ˈdaɪvɪŋ ˌbɔrd/ **noun** a raised board next to a swimming pool that you jump from into the water

division /dɪˈvɪʒən/ **noun** **1** [no plural] the act of separating something into parts or groups: *the equal division of wealth* **2** one of the groups in an organization: *the sales division* **3** one of the groups of teams in a league: *the Second Division swimming team* **4** [no plural] the process of dividing one number by another number

divorce /dɪˈvɔrs/ **noun** 🔵 the legal ending of a marriage: *My parents are **getting a divorce**.*
• **divorce verb** (present participle **divorcing**, past tense and past participle **divorced**) 🔵 *She's divorcing her husband.*

divorced /dɪˈvɔrst/ **adj** **1** 🔵 married before but not married now **2** **get divorced** to officially stop being married: *My parents got divorced when I was two.*

dizzy /ˈdɪz·i/ adj (comparative **dizzier**, superlative **dizziest**) feeling like everything is turning around and as if you might fall

DJ /ˈdiːˌdʒeɪ/ noun 🔵 short for disc jockey: someone who plays music on the radio or in dance clubs

do[1] /duː/ auxiliary verb (present participle **doing**, past tense **did**, past participle **done**) **1** 🔵 used with another verb to form questions and negative phrases: *Do you need any help?* ○ *I don't know.* **2** 🔵 used at the end of a sentence to make it into a question: *Sarah lives near here, doesn't she?* **3** 🔵 used to avoid repeating a verb that has just been used: *"I hate that song." "So do I."* **4** used to make the main verb stronger: *He does like you – he's just shy.*

do[2] /duː/ verb (present participle **doing**, past tense **did**, past participle **done**) **1** 🔵 to perform an action: *Go upstairs and do your homework.* s **2** 🔵 to perform a sports activity: *She does yoga every week.* **3** 🔵 to make or prepare something: *Max's Diner does great sandwiches.* **4** 🔵 used for talking or asking about someone and whether he or she is healthy, happy, or succeeding: *"How is your niece doing?" "She's doing really well, thanks."* **5 do the cleaning, cooking, etc.** 🔵 to perform a job in the house: *I do the cooking, but Joe does most of the cleaning.* **6 what does someone do?** used to ask what someone's job is: *"What do you do?" "I'm a doctor."* **7 do badly/well** 🔵 to not succeed, or to succeed: *Sam did very well on his test.* **8 do your best** 🔵 to make the greatest effort possible: *I did my best on the exam.* **9 do your hair, makeup, etc.** 🔵 to make your hair, makeup, etc. look nice: *I need to do my hair before we go out.* **10 have to do with something** to be related to something: *Our profits are down, which has to do with poor sales.* **11 do someone good** to have a good effect on someone: *A vacation would do you good.* **12 will do** will be satisfactory: *You don't have to pay now; next week will do.*

do without (someone/something) phrasal verb to do something well without having someone or something: *Jack's the kind of player we can't do without.*

do with something phrasal verb used to ask where something might be: *What did you do with my keys?*

do with someone/something phrasal verb could do with someone/something to need or want someone or something: *I could do with a few days off work.*

> ⚠ **Common mistake: do or make?**
>
> Do generally means to perform an activity or job.
> You need to do your homework.
> ~~You need to make your homework.~~
> Make generally means to create or produce something.
> Did you make the dress yourself?
> ~~Did you do the dress yourself?~~

dock /dɑk/ noun the place where ships stop and goods are taken off or put on
• **dock** verb *Dock your boat at the pier.*

doctor /ˈdɑk·tər/ noun 🔵 a person whose job is to treat people who are sick or hurt

doctorate /ˈdɑk·tər·ət/ noun the highest degree that a college or university gives: *She has a **doctorate** in physics.*

document /ˈdɑk·jə·mənt/ noun **1** 🔵 a piece of paper with official information on it **2** 🔵 a piece of text produced on a computer: *How do you save a document?*

documentary /ˌdɑk·jə'men·tə·ri/ noun (plural **documentaries**) 🔵 a movie or television program that gives facts about a real situation

dodge /dɑdʒ/ verb (present participle **dodging**, past tense and past participle **dodged**) **1** to move quickly to avoid someone or something: *He managed to **dodge past** the security guard.* **2** to avoid doing something you should do: *The senator dodged questions about his relationship with the actress.*

does /dʌz/ present simple of do, used with "he," "she," and "it"

doesn't /'dʌz·ənt/ short form of does not:
Keith doesn't like mushrooms or garlic.

dog /dɔg/ noun **A1** an animal with fur, four legs, and a tail, that is kept as a pet

doghouse
/'dɔg,haʊs/ noun
a small building for
a dog to sleep in

doghouse

doll /dɑl/ noun
A1 a child's toy
that looks like a
small person

dollar /'dɑl·ər/ noun **A1** the unit of
money used in the U.S., Canada, and
some other countries. The symbol is [$]

dolphin /'dɑl·fɪn/
noun **B1** an intelli-
gent sea animal
that breathes air
and looks like a
large, gray fish

dolphin

dome /doʊm/ noun a curved, round
roof of a building

domestic /də'mes·tɪk/ adj **1** relating to
the home and family relationships: *domestic violence* **2** inside one country: *a
domestic flight* **3** A domestic animal is
kept as a pet.

dominate /'dɑm·ə,neɪt/ verb (present participle **dominating**, past tense and past participle **dominated**) to control or have
power over someone or something: *One
person often dominates at a meeting.*

dominoes /'dɑm·ə,noʊz/ noun [no plural]
a game played with small, flat, rectangular objects that have spots on them

donate /'doʊ·neɪt/ verb (present participle
donating, past tense and past participle
donated) to give something, mainly
money, to a person or organization that
needs help: *Four hundred new computers
were donated to the college.*

donation /doʊ'neɪ·ʃən/ noun something such as money that is given to
help a person or organization: *I would
like to **make a donation**.*

done[1] /dʌn/ past tense and past participle of
do

done[2] /dʌn/ adj finished or completed:
Did you get your essay done in time?

donkey /'dɑŋ·ki/ noun
B1 an animal that looks
like a small horse with
long ears

donkey

donor /'doʊ·nər/ noun
someone who gives some-
thing to a person or organization that
needs help

don't /doʊnt/ short form of do not: *Please
don't talk during the exam.*

donut /'doʊ·nʌt/ noun another spelling of
doughnut (= a small fried cake)

doodle /'du·dəl/ verb (present participle **doodling**, past
tense and past participle
doodled) to draw little
pictures or patterns on
something without think-
ing about it
• **doodle** noun

doodles

door /dɔr/ noun
A1 the part of a
building or room
that you open or
close to get inside it
or out of it: *Please
shut the door.*

door

doorbell /'dɔr,bel/ noun a button next
to a door that you press to make a noise
to let someone know that you are there
→ See picture at **bell**

doorknob /'dɔr,nɑb/ noun a round
object on a door that you use to open or
close it

doormat /'dɔr,mæt/ noun a piece of
thick material on the floor by a door,
used to clean your shoes before entering a building

doorway /'dɔr,weɪ/ noun an entrance
to a building or room through a door

dorm /dɔrm/ noun short form of dormitory: a large building containing many
bedrooms, especially at a college, university, or boarding school (=high
school where students live and study)

dormitory /'dɔr·mɪ,tɔr·i/ *noun* (plural **dormitories**) **1** a large bedroom with a lot of beds, especially in a school **2** the full form of dorm

dosage /'doʊ·sɪdʒ/ *noun* how much medicine you should take and how often you should take it: *the recommended daily dosage*

dose /doʊs/ *noun* a measured amount of medicine that is taken: *Do not take more than four doses in a 24-hour period.*

dot /dɑt/ *noun* **1** a small, round mark or spot: *a pattern of blue and green dots* **2** 🔵 [no plural] the spoken form of "." in an Internet address: *dot com (=.com)* **3 on the dot** at that exact time: *We have to leave at 7:30 on the dot.*

double[1] /'dʌb·əl/ *adj* **1** 🔵 twice the amount, number, or size of something: *a double hamburger* **2** made to be used by two people: *a double bed* ○ *a double stroller*

double[2] /'dʌb·əl/ *determiner* 🔵 twice as much or as many: *Our new house is double the size of the old one.*

double[3] /'dʌb·əl/ *verb* (present participle **doubling**, past tense and past participle **doubled**) to increase and become twice the original size or amount, or to make something do this: *Our house has almost doubled in value.*

double-click /'dʌb·əl'klɪk/ *verb* to quickly press a button twice on a mouse (=small computer control) to make something happen on a computer screen: *Double-click on the icon to start the program.*

doubt[1] /daʊt/ *noun* **1** 🔵 a state of being uncertain about something, or not trusting someone or something: *I have some doubts about his ability to do the job.* **2 have no doubt** 🔵 to be certain: *I have no doubt that I made the right decision.* **3 there is no doubt** 🔵 it is certain: *There is no doubt that he's a good player.* **4 be in doubt** to not be certain: *The future of the project is in doubt.* **5 without (a) doubt** certainly: *She is without doubt a great writer.* **6 no**

doubt used to say that something is very likely: *No doubt she'll spend the money on her son.*

doubt[2] /daʊt/ *verb* to not feel certain about something or think that something will not happen: *I doubt that I'll get the job.*

doubtful /'daʊt·fəl/ *adj* **1** If something is doubtful, it probably will not happen: *It's doubtful whether he'll be able to come.* **2** not feeling certain about something: *The teacher is doubtful about having parents working as classroom assistants.*

doubtless /'daʊt·ləs/ *adv* probably: *He will doubtless be criticized by journalists.*

doughnut
/'doʊ·nʌt/ *noun*
a small, round,
fried cake, some-
times with a hole
in the middle

doughnut

dove[1] /dʌv/ *noun* a white bird, sometimes used as a symbol of peace

dove[2] /doʊv/ a past tense and past participle of dive

down[1] /daʊn/ *adv, preposition* **1** 🔵 moving from above and onto a surface: *Put that box down on the floor.* **2** 🔵 toward or in a lower place: *I bent down to have a look.* **3** 🔵 toward or at a lower level or amount: *Can you turn the music down?* **4 down the road, river, etc.** 🔵 along or further along the road, river, etc.: *There's another gas station down the street.* **5 note/write something down** 🔵 to write something on a piece of paper: *Can I just write down your phone number?*

down[2] /daʊn/ *adj* unhappy or unable to feel excited or energetic about anything: *She's been really down since her husband died.*

downhill /'daʊn'hɪl/ *adv* toward the bottom of a hill or slope: *It's so much easier biking downhill.*

download[1] /'daʊn,loʊd/ *verb* 🔵 to copy computer programs, music, or information electronically, usually from the Internet or from a larger computer: *You can download this software free from their website.*

download[2] /ˈdaʊn.loʊd/ *noun*
B1 a computer program, music, or other information that has been or can be downloaded: *a free download*

downstairs[1] /ˈdaʊnˈsteɑrz/ *adv* **A2** on or to a lower level of a building: *She went downstairs to see who was at the door.*

downstairs[2] /ˈdaʊnˈsteɑrz/ *adj* **B1** on or at a lower level of a building, especially the ground floor: *The burglars had gotten in through a downstairs window.*

downtown /ˈdaʊnˈtaʊn/ *adj, adv* in or to the central part or main business area of a city: *downtown Chicago ○ I work downtown.*

downward /ˈdaʊn·wərd/ *adv* toward a lower place or level: *The road slopes downward to the river.*

downwards /ˈdaʊn·wərdz/ *adv* another form of downward

doze /doʊz/ *verb* (present participle **dozing**, past tense and past participle **dozed**) to sleep lightly
doze off *phrasal verb* to gradually start sleeping, usually during the day: *He dozed off during the movie.*

dozen /ˈdʌz·ən/ *noun, determiner*
1 **B1** twelve, or a group of twelve: *There were about **a dozen** people at the party.*
2 *dozens* informal a lot: *She has **dozens of** friends.*

Dr. **A2** written abbreviation for doctor: *Dr. Anna Prescott*

draft /dræft/ *noun* **1** cold air coming into a room: *There's a terrible draft coming from under the door.* **2** a piece of writing or a plan that is not yet in its finished form: *He made several changes to the **first draft**.*

drag /dræg/ *verb* (present participle **dragging**, past tense and past participle **dragged**) **1** to pull something or someone along the ground somewhere, usu-

ally with difficulty: *The table was too heavy to lift, so we had to drag it across the room.* **2** **B1** to move something somewhere on a computer screen using a mouse (=small computer control)
3 **drag and drop** **B1** to move something on a computer screen using a mouse and place it where you want it to be: *You can drag and drop photos from one folder to another.* **4** (also **drag on**) to continue for too much time in a boring way: *The talks dragged on for months.*

dragon /ˈdræg·ən/ *noun* a big imaginary creature that breathes out fire

dragonfly /ˈdræg·ən.flaɪ/ *noun* an insect with long wings and a thin, colorful body, often seen near water

drain[1] /dreɪn/ *verb* **1** to remove the liquid from something, usually by pouring it away: *Drain the pasta and add the tomatoes.* **2** If something drains, liquid flows away or out of it.

drain[2] /dreɪn/ *noun* a pipe or hole that takes away waste liquids or water: *She poured the dirty water down the drain.*

drama /ˈdrɑ·mə/ *noun* **1** **B1** a play in a theater or on television or radio: *a historical drama* **2** **B1** [no plural] plays and acting generally: *modern drama* **3** **B1** the fact of something exciting or unusual happening, or an exciting or unusual event: *There was a lot of drama at work today.*

dramatic /drəˈmæt.ɪk/ *adj* **1** very sudden or exciting: *a dramatic change/ improvement* **2** relating to plays and acting
• **dramatically** *adv Your life changes dramatically when you have a baby.*

drank /dræŋk/ past tense and past participle of drink

draw /drɔ/ *verb* (past tense **drew**, past participle **drawn**) **1** **A1** to make a picture with a pen or pencil: *She drew a picture of a tree.* **2** to attract someone to a

place or person: *He's an excellent speaker who always draws a crowd.* **3** to move somewhere, usually in a vehicle: *The train drew into the station.* **4** to pull something or someone in a particular direction: *He took her hand and drew her toward him.* **5 draw near/close** to become nearer in space or time: *Her wedding is drawing nearer every day.*
6 draw attention (to) to make someone notice something or someone: *We think she wears those strange clothes to draw attention to herself.* **7 draw the curtains** to pull curtains open or closed **8** (also **draw out**) to take money from your bank account

draw back phrasal verb to move away from someone or something: *She drew back in fear when she saw the snake.*

draw *something* **up** phrasal verb to prepare something by writing it: *He drew up some plans for the new office.*

drawer /drɔːr/ noun **A2** a container like a box that is part of a piece of furniture and moves in and out

drawing /ˈdrɔːɪŋ/ noun **1** a picture made with a pencil or pen: *There were some children's drawings pinned up on the wall.* **2 A2** [no plural] the skill or activity of making pictures using a pencil or pen: *Do you want to do some drawing?*

drawn /drɔːn/ past tense and past participle of draw

dreadful /ˈdredfəl/ adj very bad

dream¹ /driːm/ noun **1 A2** events and images in your mind while you are sleeping: *I had a very strange dream last night.* **2 B1** something that you want to happen although it is not very likely: *It was his dream to become an actor.*

dream² /driːm/ verb **1 A2** to experience events and images in your mind while you are sleeping: *Last night I dreamed that I was flying.* **2 B1** to imagine something that you would like to happen: *I dream of living on a desert island.*

dress¹ /dres/ verb **1 A2** to put clothes on yourself or someone else: *I usually get dressed before having breakfast.*

→ Opposite **undress** verb **2 B1** to wear a particular type, style, or color of clothes: *She was dressed in black.*

> ⚠ **Common mistake: be/get dressed**
> Be careful to use the correct preposition. You do not always need one.
> *I got dressed and went to school.*
> *Are you dressed yet?*
> *He was dressed in a black suit.*
> ~~He was dressed with a black suit.~~

dress up phrasal verb **1** to wear formal clothes for a special occasion: *Weddings are a great opportunity to dress up.* **2** to wear special clothes for a game or party: *He dressed up as Superman for the party.*

dress² /dres/ noun **1 A1** a piece of clothing for women that covers the top of the body and hangs down over the legs → See **Clothes** on page C5 **2** [no plural] a particular style of clothes: *casual dress*

dress³ /dres/ adjective **dress shirt/pants/shoes** a nice shirt or pair of pants or shoes worn for work or for a formal occasion → See **Clothes** on page C5

dressed /drest/ adj **1 A2** wearing clothes and not naked: *I usually get dressed before I eat breakfast.* ○ *He was dressed in a gray suit.* **2 B1** wearing clothing of a particular type: *a well-dressed man*

dressing /ˈdresɪŋ/ noun **1** a sauce, especially a mixture of oil and vinegar for salad **2** a covering that protects an injury **3** a type of food made from pieces of bread, vegetables, and spices that is cooked inside a large piece of meat

dressing room /ˈdresɪŋ ˌrʊm/, /ˈdres-ɪŋ ˌrʊm/ noun **1** a room where actors get dressed before a performance **2** a room in a store where you can try on clothes

drew /druː/ past tense and past participle of draw

dried /draɪd/ past tense and past participle of dry

drift /drɪft/ verb to be moved slowly somewhere by wind or water: *The boat drifted toward the beach.*

drill /drɪl/ noun a machine for making holes in a hard substance: *an electric drill*
• **drill** verb

drink¹ /drɪŋk/ verb (past tense **drank**, past participle **drunk**) **1** **A1** to put liquid into your mouth and swallow it: *He was drinking a glass of milk.* **2** **A2** to drink alcohol, usually regularly: *She doesn't smoke or drink.*

drink² /drɪŋk/ noun **1** **A1** a liquid or an amount of liquid that you drink: *a cold drink* **2** **A2** alcoholic liquid: *Let's have a drink to celebrate.*

drip /drɪp/ verb (present participle **dripping**, past tense and past participle **dripped**) **1** to fall in drops: *There was water dripping from the ceiling.* **2** to produce drops of liquid: *The candle's dripping.*

drive¹ /draɪv/ verb (present participle **driving**, past tense **drove**, past participle **driven**) **1** **A1** to make a car, bus, or train move, and control what it does: *She's learning how to drive.* **2** **A1** to travel somewhere in a car, or to take someone somewhere in a car: *Annie drove me home last night.* **3** **drive someone crazy, nuts, etc.** to make someone extremely annoyed: *He leaves dirty clothes all over the floor and it's driving me crazy.*

> **⚠ Common mistake: drive or ride?**
>
> You **drive** a car, truck, or bus.
> *She drives an expensive sports car.*
> You **ride** a bicycle, motorcycle, or horse.
> *My brother is learning to ride a bicycle.*
> ~~My brother is learning to drive a bicycle.~~

drive² /draɪv/ noun **1** **B1** a trip in a car: *The drive from Boston to New York took four hours.* **2** **B1** a part of a computer that can keep information: *Save your work on the C: drive.*

driven /'drɪv·ən/ past participle of drive

driver /'draɪ·vər/ noun **A1** someone who drives a vehicle: *a bus/train driver*

driver's license /'draɪ·vərz ˌlaɪ·səns/ noun **A2** an official document that allows you to drive a car

driveway /'draɪv·weɪ/ noun the area of the ground that you drive on to get from your house to the road: *Please don't park in the driveway.*

droop /drup/ verb to hang down in a weak way: *drooping eyelids*

drop¹ /drɑp/ verb (present participle **dropping**, past tense and past participle **dropped**)

drop

1 **B1** to fall or let something fall: *He tripped and dropped the vase.* **2** If you drop a plan, activity, class, or idea, you stop doing or planning it: *Plans for a new supermarket have been dropped.* ○ *Is it too late to drop your art class?* **3** If a level or amount drops, it becomes less: *Unemployment has dropped from 8% to 6% in the last year.* **4** (also **drop off**) to take someone or something to a place, usually by car as you travel somewhere else: *I can drop you at the station on my way to work.*

drop by/in phrasal verb to visit someone for a short time, usually without arranging it before: *I dropped in on George on my way home.*

drop someone/something off phrasal verb to take someone or something to a place, usually by car

drop out phrasal verb to stop doing something before you have completely finished: *He dropped out of school at 14.*

drop² /drɑp/ noun **1** **B1** a small, round-shaped amount of liquid: *I felt a few drops of rain.* → See **Quantities** on page C14 **2** a fall in the level or amount of something: *There has been a drop in crime recently.*

drought /draʊt/ *noun* a long period when there is no rain and people do not have enough water: *A severe drought ruined the crops.*

drove /droʊv/ past tense of drive

drown /draʊn/ *verb* to die because you are under water and cannot breathe, or to kill someone in this way

drowsy /'draʊ·zi/ *adj* (comparative **drowsier**, superlative **drowsiest**) feeling tired and wanting to sleep

drug /drʌg/ *noun* **1** a chemical substance used as a medicine: *Scientists are developing a new drug to treat cancer.* **2** an illegal substance that people take to make them feel happy: *a drug dealer*

drug addict /'drʌg ˌæd·ɪkt/ *noun* someone who cannot stop taking drugs

drugstore /'drʌgˌstɔr/ *noun* **B1** a store that sells medicines and also things such as soap and beauty products

drum /drʌm/ *noun*
1 **A2** a round, hollow musical instrument that you hit with your hands or with sticks

drum

2 a large, round container for holding things such as oil or chemicals

drunk[1] /drʌŋk/ past participle of drink

drunk[2] /drʌŋk/ *adj* not able to behave or speak normally because you have drunk too much alcohol: *He often **gets drunk** at parties.*

dry[1] /draɪ/ *adj* (comparative **drier**, superlative **driest**) **1** **A2** without water or liquid on the surface: *dry paint ○ Is your hair dry yet?* **2** **A2** without rain: *a dry summer* **3** Dry wine is not sweet.

dry[2] /draɪ/ *verb* (present participle **drying**, past tense and past participle **dried**) **A2** to become dry, or to make something become dry: *He dried his hands on a towel.*

dry-clean /'draɪˈklin/ *verb* to clean clothes using a special chemical, not water: *This dress has to be dry-cleaned.*

dryer /'draɪ·ər/ *noun* **B1** a machine that dries clothes

duck[1] /dʌk/ *noun* **A2** a bird with short legs that lives in or near water, or the meat from this bird

ducks

duck[2] /dʌk/ *verb* to move your body down quickly to avoid being hit or seen: *Billy ducked behind a car when he saw his teacher.*

duckling /'dʌk·lɪŋ/ *noun* a young duck

due /du/ *adj* **1** **B1** expected or planned: *When is the baby due (=expected to be born)? ○ He was **due to** fly back this morning.* **2 due to** *something* **B1** because of something: *The train was late due to snow.* **3** owed to someone: *The rent is due today. ○ He didn't get the praise and recognition that was **due to** him.* **4 be due for** *something* If you are due for something, it should happen very soon: *She's due for a pay raise.*

duet /du'et/ *noun* a piece of music for two people to perform together

duffel bag /'dʌf·əlˌbæg/ *noun* a very large, strong, cloth bag used for carrying things when you travel

dug /dʌg/ past tense and past participle of dig

dull /dʌl/ *adj* **1** **B1** not interesting: *a dull place* **2** not bright: *dull colors* **3** A dull sound is not loud or clear: *a dull thud*

dumb /dʌm/ *adj* **1** informal stupid or silly: *That was a dumb thing to do.* **2** not able to talk

dummy /'dʌm·i/ *noun* (plural **dummies**) informal a stupid person

dump[1] /dʌmp/ *verb* **1** to put something somewhere to get rid of it: *The company was fined for illegally dumping toxic chemicals.* **2** to quickly put something somewhere: *He dumped his bag on the table.*

dump[2] /dʌmp/ *noun* a place where people take things that they do not want

dune /dun/ *noun* a hill of sand in the desert or on the coast

during /'dʊər·ɪŋ/ *preposition* **1** **A2** for the whole of a period of time: *Emma's*

a
b
c
d
e
f
g
h
i
j
k
l
m
n
o
p
q
r
s
t
u
v
w
x
y
z

usually at home during the day. **2 A2** at a particular moment in a period of time: *We'll arrange a meeting some time during the week.*

> **⚠ Common mistake: during or for?**
>
> Use **during** to talk about a period of time when something happens.
>
> *I'm at work during the day, so it's better to call in the evening.*
> *Please don't take photos during the performance.*
>
> Use **for** to say how long something happens or continues, for example "for two hours" or "for three days."
>
> *I've been in Montreal for six months now.*
> *We waited for an hour and then left.*
> ~~We waited during an hour and then left.~~

dusk /dʌsk/ noun [no plural] the time in the evening when it starts to become dark

dust[1] /dʌst/ noun [no plural] **B1** a powder of dirt that you see on a surface or in the air: *The shelves were covered in a thick layer of dust.*

dust[2] /dʌst/ verb to remove dust from something: *I straightened and dusted the shelves.*

duster /'dʌs·tər/ noun an object consisting of a handle with feathers or cloth strips on the end, used for removing dust from furniture and other objects

dustpan /'dʌst,pæn/ noun a flat container with a handle, used with a brush for removing dirt from a floor
→ See picture at **brush noun**

dusty /'dʌs·ti/ adj (comparative **dustier**, superlative **dustiest**) **B1** covered with dust

duty /'du·ti/ noun (plural **duties**)
1 B1 something you must do because the law says you must or because it is right: *The police have a duty to protect the public.* **2** something you do as part

of your job or because of your position: *professional duties* **3 on/off duty** If a doctor, police officer, etc. is on duty, he or she is working, and if he or she is off duty, he or she is not working: *I'm on duty tomorrow night.*

DVD /ˌdiˌviˈdi/ noun **A1** a small disk for storing movies, games, or other information: *Is this movie available on DVD?* ○ *I just bought a new DVD player.*
→ See **The Living Room** on page C11

dwarf /dwɔrf/ noun an imaginary creature like a little man, in children's stories

dye[1] /daɪ/ noun a substance that is used to change the color of something

dye[2] /daɪ/ verb (present participle **dyeing**, past tense and past participle **dyed**) to change the color of something by using a dye: *I dyed my hair blonde.*

dying /'daɪ·ɪŋ/ present participle of die

dynamite /'daɪ·nə,maɪt/ noun [no plural] a type of explosive: *a stick of dynamite*

Ee

E, e /i/ the fifth letter of the alphabet

each /itʃ/ pronoun, determiner **A1** every one in a group: *Each of the teams has four players.* ○ *Each student received a new pen.* ○ *The check comes to $79, so that's about $10 each.*

each other /ˌitʃ ˈʌð·ər/ pronoun **A2** used to show that each person in a group of two people does something to or with the other: *My cousin and I haven't seen each other in weeks.*

eager /'i·gər/ adj wanting to do or have something very much: *Sam was eager to go home and play on his computer.*
• **eagerly** adv *The results were eagerly awaited.*
• **eagerness** noun [no plural]

eagle /ˈi·gəl/ **noun** a large wild bird with a big, curved beak, that hunts smaller animals

eagle

ear /ɪər/ **noun** **1** A1 one of the two parts of the body on your head that you hear with: *She whispered in his ear.* → See **The Body** on page C2 **2** the part of the corn plant that the small pieces of corn grow on: *an ear of corn* → See **Fruits and Vegetables** on page Center 8

earache /ˈɪərˌeɪk/ **noun** B1 pain in your ear: *I have an earache.*

early /ˈɜr·li/ **adj, adv** (comparative **earlier**, superlative **earliest**) **1** A1 near the beginning of a period of time, process, etc.: *the early 1980s* **2** A2 before the usual time or the time that was planned: *The plane arrived ten minutes early.* **3 early on** in the first stage or part of something: *I lost interest really early on in the book.*

earn /ɜrn/ **verb** **1** A2 to get money for doing work: *She earns about $40,000 a year.* **2 earn a/your living** to work to get money for the things you need **3** to get something good that you deserve: *As a teacher you have to earn the respect of your students.*

earphones /ˈɪərˌfoʊnz/ **plural noun** a piece of electronic equipment that you put on your ears so that you can listen to radio, recorded music, etc.

earring /ˈɪər·ɪŋ/ **noun** A2 a piece of jewelry that you wear on your ear: *silver earrings* → See picture at **jewelry**

earth /ɜrθ/ **noun** **1** B1 (also **the Earth**) the planet that we live on **2** [no plural] soil or ground: *a pile of earth* **3 how, what, why, etc. on earth** informal used when you are extremely surprised, confused, or angry about something: *How on earth did this happen?* ○ *Why on earth didn't you tell me before?*

earthquake /ˈɜrθˌkweɪk/ **noun** a sudden movement of the Earth's surface, often causing damage

ease[1] /iz/ **noun** **1** [no plural] If you do something with ease, it is very easy for you to do it: *Luca passed his classes **with ease**.* **2 at ease** feeling relaxed: *I felt completely at ease with him.*

ease[2] /iz/ **verb** (present participle **easing**, past tense and past participle **eased**) to become less bad, or to make something become less bad: *The pain eased after a while.*

easily /ˈi·zə·li/ **adv** A2 with no difficulty: *She makes friends very easily.*

east, East /ist/ **noun** [no plural] **1** A2 the direction that you face to see the sun rise: *Which way is east?* **2 the east** A2 the part of an area that is farther toward the east than the rest: *It rains less in the east of the region.*
- **east, East adj** A2 *the east side of the city* ○ *the East China Sea*
- **east adv** A2 *They sailed east.*

Easter /ˈi·stər/ **noun** a holiday in March or April when Christians celebrate the return to life of Jesus Christ

Easter egg /ˈi·stər ˌeg/ **noun** an egg with a painted or decorated shell

eastern, Eastern /ˈi·stərn/ **adj** B1 in or from the east part of an area: *eastern Europe*

easy[1] /ˈi·zi/ **adj** (comparative **easier**, superlative **easiest**) A1 not difficult: *The exam was easy.* ○ *It's easy to see why he's so popular.*
→ Opposite **difficult adj, hard adj**

> **! Common mistake: easy or easily?**
>
> Remember, **easy** is an adjective and usually describes a noun.
>
> *an easy question*
> *The test was easy.*
>
> **Easily** is an adverb and usually describes a verb.
>
> *You should pass the test easily.*
> ~~*You should pass the test easy.*~~

easy[2] /ˈi·zi/ **adv** **take it easy** B1 to relax and not work hard: *I'm going to take it easy this weekend.*

a b c d e f g h i j k l m n o p q r s t u v w x y z

easygoing /ˈiːˈziˈɡoʊ·ɪŋ/ adj **B1** able to stay calm about things that make other people worried or upset

eat /iːt/ verb (past tense **ate**, past participle **eaten**) **1 A1** to put food into your mouth and then swallow it: *Who ate all the cake?* ∘ *Let's have something to eat* (= some food). **2 A1** to have a meal: *We usually eat at about 7 o'clock.*

eat out phrasal verb **B1** to eat at a restaurant: *Let's eat out tonight.* → See **Phrasal Verbs** on page C13

eat *something* **up** phrasal verb to eat all the food you have been given: *Be good and eat up your dinner.*

echo[1] /ˈek·oʊ/ verb If a sound echoes, you hear it again and again, usually because you are in a large, empty space: *Their voices echoed around the room.*

echo[2] /ˈek·oʊ/ noun (plural **echoes**) a sound that you hear more than once because you are in a big, empty space

eclipse /ɪˈklɪps/ noun an occasion when the sun is covered by the moon, or the moon is covered by the Earth's shadow (= dark area)

ecological /ˌiː·kəˈlɑdʒɪ·r·kəl/ adj relating to ecology or to the environment: *an ecological disaster*
• **ecologically** adv

economic /ˌiː·kəˈnɑm·ɪk/ adj relating to trade, industry, and money: *economic policies*
• **economically** adv *The country would benefit economically.*

economical /ˌiː·kəˈnɑm·ɪ·kəl/ adj using little money, fuel, etc.: *an economical car*
• **economically** adv

economics /ˌiː·kəˈnɑm·ɪks/ noun [no plural] **B1** the study of the way in which trade, industry, and money are organized: *She's studying economics at Yale University.*

economy /ɪˈkɑn·ə·mi/ noun (plural **economies**) the system by which a country makes and uses goods and money: *the U.S. economy* ∘ *effects on the global economy*

economy class /ɪˈkɑn·ə·mi ˌklæs/ noun [no plural] the cheapest and least comfortable type of seats on a plane: *We are traveling in economy class.*

edge /edʒ/ noun **B1** the part around something that is furthest from the center: *Rick was sitting on the edge of the bed.* ∘ *She ran down to the water's edge.*

edible /ˈed·ə·bəl/ adj safe to eat: *edible berries*

edition /ɪˈdɪʃ·ən/ noun one of many books or newspapers that are the same and were made at the same time: *a new edition*

editor /ˈed·ɪ·t̬ər/ noun someone who is in charge of a newspaper or magazine

educate /ˈedʒ·ə₁keɪt/ verb (present participle **educating**, past tense and past participle **educated**) **1** to teach someone at a school or college: *She was educated at Duke University.* **2** to give people information about something: *Kids must be educated about the dangers of smoking.*

education /ˌedʒ·əˈkeɪ·ʃən/ noun **B1** teaching and learning in a school or college: *More money should be spent on education.*
• **educational** adj *the educational system*

eel /iːl/ noun a fish that looks like a snake

effect /ɪˈfekt/ noun **1 B1** a change or result that is caused by something: *The accident had a huge effect on her life.* ∘ *We don't know the long-term effects of this drug.* **2 take effect** to start to produce results or changes: *They had to wait for the anesthetic to take effect.*

effective /ɪˈfek·tɪv/ adj getting the result that you want: *What is the most effective way of teaching grammar?*

effectively /ɪˈfek·tɪv·li/ adv in a way that gets what you want: *Teachers need to communicate ideas effectively.*

efficient /ɪˈfɪʃ·ənt/ adj **B1** working well and not wasting time or energy: *Email is a quick and efficient way of contacting people.*
• **efficiently** adv

effort /ˈef·ərt/ noun **1 B1** an attempt to do something: *He was making an effort to be sociable.* **2 B1** [no plural] the energy that you need to do something: *I put a lot of **effort into** organizing the party.*

EFL noun [no plural] abbreviation for English as a Foreign Language: the teaching of English to students whose first language is not English

e.g. (also **eg**) used to give an example of what you mean: *green vegetables, e.g., spinach and cabbage*

egg /eg/ noun

egg
yolk
shell
white

1 Ⓐ1 an oval object made by a female chicken, that you eat as food: *a boiled/fried egg* → See **Food** on page C7 **2** Ⓐ1 An oval object with a hard shell that contains a baby bird, insect, or other creature: *The bird **lays** its **eggs** in a nest.*

eggplant /'eg,plænt/ noun an oval, purple vegetable that is white inside → See **Fruits and Vegetables** on page C8

eggshell /'eg,ʃel/ noun the hard outer covering of an egg

eight /eɪt/ Ⓐ1 the number 8

eighteen /'eɪ'tin/ Ⓐ1 the number 18

eighteenth /'eɪ'tinθ/ 18th written as a word

eighth[1] /eɪtθ/ Ⓐ2 8th written as a word

eighth[2] /eɪtθ/ noun one of eight equal parts of something; 1/8

eighties /'eɪ,tiz/ plural noun **1** the eighties the years from 1980 to 1989: *CDs became popular **in the eighties**.* **2** be **in your eighties** to be aged between 80 and 89: *My grandma is **in her eighties**.*

eighty /'eɪ,ti/ Ⓐ2 the number 80
• **eightieth** 80th written as a word

either[1] /'i·ðər/, /'aɪ·ðər/ conjunction **either ... or** Ⓑ1 used when you are giving a choice of two or more things: *Either you or I can go.*

either[2] /'i·ðər/, /'aɪ·ðər/ pronoun, determiner **1** Ⓑ1 one of two people or things, when it is not important which:

"A hot or a cold drink?" – "Oh, either." **2** both: *There are trees on either side of the house.*

either[3] /'i·ðər/, /'aɪ·ðər/ adv Ⓑ1 used in negative sentences to mean that something else is also true: *The food was bad and it wasn't cheap either.*

elaborate /ɪ'læb·ər·ət/ adj complicated or with many details: *elaborate designs*
• **elaborately** adv

elastic /ɪ'læs·tɪk/ adj Something that is elastic can stretch and return to its original size: *Your skin is more elastic when you are young.*

elbow /'el·boʊ/ noun Ⓑ1 the part in the middle of your arm where it bends
→ See picture at **arm**
→ See **The Body** on page C2

elder[1] /'el·dər/ adj **elder brother, daughter, sister, etc.** Ⓑ1 the older of two brothers, daughters, sisters, etc.: *Their elder daughter lives in Florida.*

elder[2] /'el·dər/ noun **1** the elder the older of two people: *He's the elder of two sons.* **2** **your elders** people older than you: *You should respect your elders.*

elderly /'el·dər·li/ adj Ⓑ1 Elderly people are old: *an elderly man*

eldest /'el·dəst/ adj **eldest child, daughter, brother, etc.** Ⓑ1 the oldest child, daughter, brother, etc.: *My eldest brother is a doctor.*

elect /ɪ'lekt/ verb to choose someone for a particular job or position by voting: *He was elected president in 2008.*

election /ɪ'lek·ʃən/ noun Ⓑ1 a time when people vote in order to choose someone for a political or official job

electric /ɪ'lek·trɪk/ adj Ⓐ2 using or giving electricity: *an electric heater* ○ *an electric socket*

electrical /ɪ'lek·trɪ·kəl/ adj Ⓑ1 using or relating to electricity: *electrical goods* ○ *an electrical engineer*

electrician /ɪ,lek'trɪʃ·ən/ noun someone whose job is to put in or repair electrical equipment

a
b
c
d
e
f
g
h
i
j
k
l
m
n
o
p
q
r
s
t
u
v
w
x
y
z

electricity /ɪˌlekˈtrɪs·ə· t̬i/ noun [no plural]
A2 a type of energy that can produce
light and heat, or make machines work:
The electricity has been turned off.

electronic /ɪˌlekˈtrɑn·ɪk/ adj **1** **B1** Electronic equipment consists of things
such as computers, televisions, and radios.
2 **B1** done by computers: *electronic
communication*
• **electronically** adv *electronically controlled gates*

electronics /ɪˌlekˈtrɑn·ɪks/ noun [no plural]
the science of making electronic equipment: *the electronics industry*

elegant /ˈel·ɪ·ɡənt/ adj stylish and attractive: *an elegant dining room* ∘ *She's a
very elegant woman.*
• **elegantly** adv *She was elegantly
dressed.*

element /ˈel·ə·mənt/ noun **1** a part of
something: *This book has all the elements
of a good story.* **2** an element of something a small amount of something:
*There's an element of truth in what she
says.* **3** a simple substance that you
cannot reduce to smaller chemical
parts: *Iron is one of the elements of the
Earth's crust.*

elementary /ˌel·əˈmen·tri/ adj **B1** relating to the early stages of studying a
subject: *students at elementary level*

elementary school /ˌel·əˈmen·tri ˈskul/
noun **B1** a school where children begin their education, usually for children
between five and eleven years old

elephant /ˈel·ə·fənt/
noun **A2** a very
large, gray animal
with big ears and a
very long nose

elephant

elevator
/ˈel·əˌveɪ·t̬ər/ noun
A2 a machine that carries people up
and down in tall buildings

eleven /ɪˈlev·ən/ **A1** the number 11

eleventh[1] /ɪˈlev·ənθ/ 11th written as a
word

eleventh[2] /ɪˈlev·ənθ/ noun one of
eleven equal parts of something; 1/11

else /els/ adv **1** **A2** in addition to someone or something: *Would you like **anything else** to eat?* ∘ *What else did he say?*
2 **A2** different from someone or something: *I don't like it here. Let's go somewhere else.* **3** **A2** Other things or
people: *I forgot my toothbrush, but I remembered **everything else**.* **4** or else
used to say what will happen if another
thing does not happen: *We must be there
by six, or else we'll miss the beginning.*

elsewhere /ˈelsˌhwear/ adv in or to
another place: *If we can't find it here,
we'll have to **go elsewhere**.*

email[1] /ˈiˌmeɪl/ (also e-mail) noun **1** **A1**
[no plural] a way of sending messages
electronically, from one computer to another: *What's your **email address**?*
2 **A2** a message sent to a computer: *I
got an email from Danielle yesterday.*

email[2] /ˈiˌmeɪl/ (also e-mail) verb **A2** to
send a message using email: *I'll email
you tomorrow.* ∘ *Has he emailed you that
list of addresses yet?*

embarrass /ɪmˈbær·əs/ verb to make
someone feel ashamed or shy: *My dad
embarrassed me in front of my friends.*

embarrassed /ɪmˈbær·əst/ adj
B1 feeling ashamed or shy: *I was too
embarrassed to admit that I was scared.*

embarrassing /ɪmˈbær·ə·sɪŋ/ adj
B1 making you feel embarrassed: *I forgot his name – it was very embarrassing.*

embarrassment /ɪmˈbær·əs·mənt/
noun [no plural] shy, ashamed, or uncomfortable feelings: *He blushed with embarrassment.*

embassy /ˈem·bə·si/ noun (plural
embassies) **B1** the official group of
people who live in a foreign country
and represent their government there,
or the building where they work

embrace /ɪmˈbreɪs/ verb (present participle
embracing, past tense and past participle
embraced) to put your arms around
someone: *They embraced and kissed each
other.*

embryo /ˈem·briˌoʊ/ noun a human or
an animal that is starting to grow inside
its mother

emerald /ˈem·ər·əld/ *noun* a valuable bright green stone that is used in jewelry

emerge /ɪˈmɜrdʒ/ *verb* (present participle **emerging**, past tense and past participle **emerged**) to appear from somewhere or come out of somewhere: *A figure **emerged from** the shadows.*

emergency /ɪˈmɜr·dʒən·si/ *noun* (plural **emergencies**) **B1** a serious or dangerous situation that needs immediate action: *In an emergency, call this number.* ∘ *an emergency exit*

emergency brake /ɪˈmɜr·dʒən·si ˌbreɪk/ *noun* a stick inside a car that you pull up to stop the car from moving: *You should **put the emergency brake on** whenever you stop on a hill.*
→ See **Car** on page C3

emergency room /ɪˈmɜr·dʒən·si ˌrum/, /ɪˈmɜr·dʒən·si ˌrum/ *noun* the part of a hospital where people go when they need treatment quickly: *She was taken to the emergency room.*

emigrate /ˈem·ɪˌɡreɪt/ *verb* (present participle **emigrating**, past tense and past participle **emigrated**) to leave your own country to live in a different one: *He **emigrated to** New Zealand.*
• **emigration** *noun* [no plural]

emotion /ɪˈmoʊ·ʃən/ *noun* a strong feeling such as love or anger: *He finds it hard to express his emotions.*

emotional /ɪˈmoʊ·ʃə·n³l/ *adj* **1** relating to emotions: *a child's emotional development* **2** showing strong feelings: *an emotional speech*
• **emotionally** *adv* *She spoke emotionally about her experiences as a nurse.*

emphasis /ˈem·fə·sɪs/ *noun* (plural **emphases**) the particular importance or attention that you give to something: *Her family **places** great **emphasis on** getting a good education.*

emphasize /ˈem·fəˌsɑɪz/ *verb* (present participle **emphasizing**, past tense and past participle **emphasized**) to show that something is important or needs special attention: *He emphasized the importance of learning foreign languages.*

empire /ˈem·pɑɪər/ *noun* a group of countries that is ruled by one person or government

employ /ɪmˈplɔɪ/ *verb* **B1** to pay someone to work for you: *The company employs 2,500 workers.*

employee /ɪmˌplɔɪˈi/ *noun* **B1** someone who is paid to work for a person or company: *How many employees work here?*

employer /ɪmˈplɔɪ·ər/ *noun* **B1** a person or company that pays people to work for him, her, or it

employment /ɪmˈplɔɪ·mənt/ *noun* [no plural] **B1** work that a person or company pays you to do: *It is not easy to **find employment** in this part of the state.*

empty[1] /ˈemp·ti/ *adj* (comparative **emptier**, superlative **emptiest**) **A2** with nothing or no one inside: *an empty house* ∘ *empty bottles*
• **emptiness** *noun* [no plural]

empty[2] /ˈemp·ti/ *verb* (present participle **emptying**, past tense and past participle **emptied**) (also **empty out**) to remove everything that is inside something: *Where can I empty this ashtray?*
→ See picture at **full adj**

enable /ɪˈneɪ·bəl/ *verb* (present participle **enabling**, past tense and past participle **enabled**) to make someone able to do something: *This money enabled me to buy a new computer.*

enclose /ɪnˈkloʊz/ *verb* (present participle **enclosing**, past tense and past participle **enclosed**) to send something in the same envelope or package as something else: *I enclosed a map of the area.*

encourage /ɪnˈkɜr·ɪdʒ/, /ɪnˈkʌr·ɪdʒ/ *verb* (present participle **encouraging**, past tense and past participle **encouraged**) **1** **B1** to say good things to someone that will make them confident about doing something: *My parents **encouraged** me **to** try new things.* **2** **B1** to make something more likely to happen: *We hope the new hotel will encourage tourism.*

encouragement /ɪnˈkɜr·ɪdʒ·mənt/, /ɪnˈkʌr·ɪdʒ·mənt/ *noun* [no plural] good

a
b
c
d
e
f
g
h
i
j
k
l
m
n
o
p
q
r
s
t
u
v
w
x
y
z

| æ cat | ɑ hot | e get | ɪ sit | i see | ɔ saw | ʊ book | u too | ʌ cut | ə about | ər mother | ɜr turn | ɔr for | ɑɪ my | ʊ how | eɪ say | ɔɪ boy |

things that you say to someone in order to make them more confident: *Kids need lots of encouragement from their parents.*

end¹ /end/ noun **1** 🔵 the final part of something: *I'll pay you at the end of next month.* **2** 🔵 the farthest part: *They live at the other end of the street.* **3** in the end 🔵 finally: *We thought we might go away for Christmas, but in the end we stayed home.* **4** a situation in which something stops happening or existing: *They are calling for an end to the violence.* **5** put an end to something to make something stop: *We must put an end to this violence.*

end² /end/ verb 🔵 to stop, or to make something stop: *What time does the concert end?* ○ *These talks are not likely to end the war.*

end up phrasal verb 🔵 to finally be in a particular place or situation: *He ended up in prison.*

endangered /ɪnˈdeɪn·dʒərd/ adj used to describe animals and plants that may soon disappear from the world because there are very few left alive: *Tigers are now an endangered species.*

ending /ˈen·dɪŋ/ noun **1** 🔵 the last part of a story: *I hope this movie has a happy ending.* **2** 🔵 a part added to the end of a word: *To make the plural of "dog," you add the ending "-s."*

endless /ˈend·ləs/ adj never seeming to stop: *We used to have endless arguments about politics.*
• **endlessly** adv

endure /ɪnˈdʊər/ verb (present participle **enduring**, past tense and past participle **endured**) formal to experience something difficult or unpleasant: *She endured two painful heart operations.*

enemy /ˈen·ə·mi/ noun (plural **enemies**) 🔵 a person or country that you are arguing or fighting with: *I try not to make enemies.*

energetic /ˌen·ərˈdʒet·ɪk/ adj having or needing a lot of energy: *an energetic young woman*

energy /ˈen·ər·dʒi/ noun [no plural] **1** 🔵 the ability to be very active

without becoming tired: *Taking care of children takes up a lot of time and energy.* ○ *I didn't even have the energy to get out of bed.* **2** 🔵 the power that comes from electricity, gas, etc.: *nuclear energy*

engaged /ɪnˈgeɪdʒd/ adj 🔵 If two people are engaged, they have agreed to marry each other: *When did you get engaged?*

engagement /ɪnˈgeɪdʒ·mənt/ noun **1** an agreement to get married to someone: *an engagement ring* **2** an arrangement to meet someone

engine /ˈen·dʒɪn/ noun 🔵 the part of a vehicle that uses oil, electricity, or steam to make it move

engineer /ˌen·dʒəˈnɪər/ noun 🔵 someone whose job is to design, build, or repair machines, engines, roads, bridges, etc.: *a mechanical engineer*

engineering /ˌen·dʒəˈnɪər·ɪŋ/ noun [no plural] 🔵 the work of an engineer, or the study of this work

English /ˈɪŋ·glɪʃ/ noun **1** [no plural] the language that is spoken in the U.K., the U.S., and in many other countries **2** the English the people of England

⚠ Common mistake: English

Remember that **English** is always written with a capital letter.

enjoy /ɪnˈdʒɔɪ/ verb **1** 🔵 If you enjoy something, it makes you feel happy: *I hope you enjoy your meal.* ○ *I enjoyed being with him.* **2** **enjoy yourself** 🔵 to like something that you are doing: *It was a great party – I really enjoyed myself.*

⚠ Common mistake: enjoy doing something

When **enjoy** is followed by a verb, the verb must be in the -ing form.
We enjoy hiking in the mountains.
~~We enjoy to hike in the mountains.~~

enjoyable /ɪnˈdʒɔɪ·ə·bəl/ adj 🔵 If something is enjoyable, it makes you feel happy: *We had an enjoyable evening.*

enjoyment /ɪnˈdʒɔɪ·mənt/ **noun** [no plural]
the feeling of enjoying something: *She gets a lot of enjoyment from music.*

enlarge /ɪnˈlɑrdʒ/ **verb** (present participle **enlarging**, past tense and past participle **enlarged**) to make something become bigger: *I want to get this photo enlarged.*

enormous /ɪˈnɔr·məs/ **adj** **B1** very large: *They have an enormous house.*

enough[1] /ɪˈnʌf/ **pronoun, quantifier**
1 **A2** as much as you need: *Have you had enough to eat?* ○ *She brought enough clothes for the trip.* **2** as much as or more than is wanted: *Stop. You've made enough of a mess already.* ○ *You've eaten more than enough already.*

enough[2] /ɪˈnʌf/ **adv** **1** **A2** as much as you need: *Are you old enough to vote?* ○ *You're not going fast enough.* **2** funnily, strangely, etc. **enough** although it may seem funny, strange, etc.: *Strangely enough, I was just speaking to him the other day.*

enquiry /ɪnˈkwaɪər·i/ **noun** (plural **enquiries**) another spelling of inquiry

enter /ˈen·tər/ **verb** **1** **A2** to go into a place: *The police entered by the back door.* **2** **B1** to put information into a computer, book, or document: *You have to enter a password to access this information.* **3** **B1** to do a competition: *Are you going to enter the photography competition?*

> **⚠ Common mistake: enter a place**
>
> You do not need to use a preposition after **enter**.
> *I entered the classroom.*
> ~~I entered in the classroom.~~
> Be careful not to use **enter** with vehicles.
> *The children got on the bus.*
> ~~The children entered the bus.~~

entertain /ˌen·tərˈteɪn/ **verb** **1** **B1** to keep someone interested and help them to have an enjoyable time: *We hired a clown to entertain the children.* **2** to

invite someone to be your guest and give them food and drink: *We don't entertain as much as we used to.*

entertainer /ˌen·tərˈteɪ·nər/ **noun** someone whose job is to make people laugh and enjoy themselves by singing, telling jokes, etc.

entertaining /ˌen·tərˈteɪ·nɪŋ/ **adj** interesting and helping someone to have an enjoyable time: *an entertaining and informative book*

entertainment /ˌen·tərˈteɪn·mənt/ **noun** [no plural] **B1** shows, movies, television, or other performances or activities that entertain people: *There is live entertainment in the bar every night.*

enthusiasm /ɪnˈθuˈziˌæz·əm/ **noun** [no plural] a feeling of interest and excitement about something: *She has always had a lot of enthusiasm for her work.*

enthusiastic /ɪnˌθuˈziˈæs·tɪk/ **adj** showing enthusiasm: *The teacher was very enthusiastic about my project.*
• **enthusiastically adv** *Everyone cheered enthusiastically.*

entire /ɪnˈtaɪr/ **adj** whole or complete: *She spent her entire life caring for other people.*

entirely /ɪnˈtaɪr·li/ **adv** completely: *It was entirely my fault.*

entrance /ˈen·trəns/ **noun** **1** **A2** a door or other opening that you use to go in somewhere: *I'll meet you at the main entrance.* **2** **B1** [no plural] the right to enter a place or join an organization: *Entrance is free, but you have to pay for your drinks.* **3** the act of going into a place: *Everyone got quiet when he made his entrance* (=came in).

entry /ˈen·tri/ **noun** **1** **B1** (plural **entries**) a piece of work that you do to try to win a competition: *The first ten correct entries will receive a prize.* **2** **B1** (plural **entries**) a separate piece of information that is recorded in a dictionary, diary, or list: *Dictionary entries are arranged in alphabetical order.* **3** **B1** [no plural] the right or ability to come into or go into a place:

There's free entry to the exhibition for students after 6 p.m. **4 B1** [no plural] the act of joining an organization or taking part in a competition: *Have you filled in your **entry form** yet?*

envelope /ˈen·vəˌloʊp/, /ˈɑn·vəˌloʊp/ **noun** **A2** a flat paper container for a letter → See **The Office** on page C12

envious /ˈen·vi·əs/ **adj** wanting something that someone else has: *She was **envious of** his successful career.*

environment /ɪnˈvɑɪ·rən·mənt/ **noun** **1 B1** the air, land, and water where people, animals, and plants live: *The new road may cause damage to the environment.* **2** the situation that you live or work in, and how it changes how you feel: *We are working in a very competitive environment.*

environmental /ɪnˌvɑɪ·rənˈmen·tᵊl/ **adj** **B1** relating to the environment: *environmental issues*
• **environmentally adv environmentally friendly** products (= that do not harm the environment)

envy[1] /ˈen·vi/ **noun** [no plural] the feeling of wanting something that someone else has: *I watched with envy as he climbed into his brand new sports car.*

envy[2] /ˈen·vi/ **verb** (present participle **envying**, past tense and past participle **envied**) to want something that someone else has: *I envy her good looks.*

epic /ˈep·ɪk/ **noun** a story or movie that is very long and has a lot of action

epidemic /ˌep·ɪˈdem·ɪk/ **noun** a situation in which a large number of people get the same disease at the same time: *the AIDS epidemic*

episode /ˈep·əˌsoʊd/ **noun** one of the parts into which a story is divided, mainly on television or radio: *I didn't see last week's episode.*

equal[1] /ˈi·kwəl/ **adj** **1 B1** the same in amount, number, or size: *The sides are of equal length.* ○ *One meter is **equal to** 39.37 inches.* **2** the same in importance and deserving equal treatment: *All people are equal.*

equal[2] /ˈi·kwəl/ **verb** to have the same value, size, etc. as something else, often shown using a symbol [=]: *Two plus two equals four.*

equal[3] /ˈi·kwəl/ **noun** someone who has the same ability or rights as someone else: *The teacher treats us all as equals.*

equality /ɪˈkwɑl·ɪ·t̬i/ **noun** [no plural] a situation in which everyone is equal and has the same rights: *racial/sexual equality*

equally /ˈi·kwə·li/ **adv** fairly and in the same way: *Everyone should be treated equally.*

equator /ɪˈkweɪ·t̬ər/ **noun** [no plural] the imaginary line around the Earth that divides it into equal north and south parts

equip /ɪˈkwɪp/ **verb** (present participle **equipping**, past tense and past participle **equipped**) **be equipped with** *something* to include the things that are needed for a particular purpose: *The new trains are equipped with all the latest technology.*

equipment /ɪˈkwɪp·mənt/ **noun** **1 B1** [no plural] the things that are used for an activity or purpose: *kitchen/office equipment* **2 a piece of equipment** a tool or object used for an activity or purpose

---
⚠ Common mistake: equipment

Remember you cannot make **equipment** plural. Do not say "equipments."
The computer room has all the equipment you need.

---

era /ˈɪər·ə/, /ˈer·ə/ **noun** a period of time in history that is special for a particular reason: *the Victorian era* ○ *a new era of peace*

eraser /ɪˈreɪ·sər/ **noun** a small object that is used to remove pencil marks from paper
→ See **The Classroom** on page C4

erotic /ɪˈrɑt̬·ɪk/ **adj** making you feel strong sexual feelings: *an erotic movie*

errand /'er·ənd/ *noun* a short trip to a place such as a store to buy or do something for yourself or someone else: *I need to **run a few errands** this morning.*

error /'er·ər/ *noun* a mistake: *a computer error* ○ *an accident caused by human error* ○ *to **make an error***

erupt /ɪ'rʌpt/ *verb* If a volcano erupts, it suddenly throws out fire and melted rocks.
• **eruption** *noun a volcanic eruption*

escalator
/'es·kə,leɪ·t̬ər/ *noun*
moving stairs that
take people from
one level of a build-
ing to another: *We
took the escalator
down to the lobby.*

escalator

escape[1] /ɪ'skeɪp/ *verb* (present participle **escaping**, past tense and past participle **escaped**) **1** 🅱1 to succeed in getting away from a place where you do not want to be: *The two killers **escaped from** prison last night.* **2** to avoid a dangerous or unpleasant situation: *She was lucky to escape serious injury.*

escape[2] /ɪ'skeɪp/ *noun* a successful attempt to get out of a place or a dangerous or bad situation: *He made his escape while no one was watching.*

ESL *noun* [no plural] abbreviation for English as a Second Language: the teaching of English to students whose first language is not English

especially /ɪ'speʃ·ə·li/ *adv* **1** 🅰2 more than other things or people: *I liked all the food but I especially liked the dessert.* **2** for one particular person, purpose, or reason: *I made cookies **especially for** you.*

essay /'es·eɪ/ *noun* 🅱1 a short piece of writing about a subject, especially one written by a student: *He wrote an **essay on** modern Japanese literature.*

essential /ɪ'sen·ʃəl/ *adj* 🅱1 very important and necessary: *Computers are an essential part of our lives.* ○ *It is absolutely **essential that** she gets this message.*

establish /ɪ'stæb·lɪʃ/ *verb* to start a company or organization that will continue for a long time: *The company was established in 1822.*

estimate[1] /'es·tə·mət/ *noun* a guess of what the size, value, amount, cost, etc. of something might be: *This is only a **rough estimate**.*

estimate[2] /'es·tə,meɪt/ *verb* (present participle **estimating**, past tense and past participle **estimated**) to guess the cost, size, or value of something: *They **estimate that** fifty people were killed in the accident.*

etc. used after a list of words to show that other similar words could be added: *This shelf is for pens, paper, etc.*

eternal /ɪ'tɜr·nᵊl/ *adj* continuing forever: *eternal youth*

euro /'jʊər·oʊ/ *noun* 🅰2 A unit of money that is used in many European countries. The symbol is [€].

eve /iv/ *noun* **Christmas Eve/New Year's Eve** the day or night before Christmas Day or New Year's Day

even[1] /'i·vən/ *adj* flat, level, or smooth: *Find an even surface to work on.*
→ Opposite **uneven adj**

even[2] /'i·vən/ *adv* **1** 🅰2 used to emphasize something that is surprising: *Everyone danced, even Mike.* ○ *I said hello, but he didn't even look at me.* **2 even better, faster, smaller, etc.** 🅱1 used when comparing things, to emphasize the difference: *Alex will be even taller than his father.* **3 even if** used to say that nothing will change if something happens: *Even if you take a taxi, you'll still miss your train.* **4 even though** although: *He went to work even though he wasn't well.*

evening /'iv·nɪŋ/ *noun* 🅰1 the part of the day between the afternoon and the night: *What are you doing this evening?*

evenly /'i·vən·li/ *adv* into equal amounts: *They divided the prize money evenly between them.*

even number /'i·vən 'nʌm·bər/ *noun* a number that can be exactly divided by two, for example four, six, or eight
→ Opposite **odd number noun**

a b c d e f g h i j k l m n o p q r s t u v w x y z

event /ɪˈvent/ **noun** **1** B1 something that happens, especially something important or strange: *Local people have been shocked by recent events in the town.* **2** B1 a race, party, competition, etc. that has been organized for a particular time: *They organize a lot of* ***social events****.*

eventually /ɪˈven·tʃu·ə·li/ **adv** in the end, especially after a long time: *We all hope that an agreement can be reached eventually.*

ever /ˈev·ər/ **adv** **1** A2 at any time: *Have you ever been skiing?* ◦ *No one ever calls me anymore.* **2 ever since** B1 always since that time: *We met in high school and have been friends ever since.* **3 hardly ever** B1 almost never: *We hardly ever go out these days.* **4 ever so** very: *He smiled ever so slightly.*

→ See also **forever**

every /ˈev·ri/ **determiner** **1** A1 each one of a group of people or things: *He knows the name of every child in the school.* **2** A1 used to show that something is repeated regularly: *They go camping every summer.*

> **! Common mistake: every**
>
> When **every** is followed by **body**, **one**, **thing**, or **where**, you write the words together.
>
> *Everybody needs to bring something to eat.*
> *Can everyone see that?*
> *Do you have everything you need?*
> *I've looked everywhere for it.*
>
> In other situations you use **every** as a separate word.
>
> *You have to show your membership card every time you go.*
> *Do you go jogging every morning?*

everybody /ˈev·riˌbɑd·i/, /ˈev·riˌbʌd·i/ **pronoun** A2 another word for everyone

everyone /ˈev·riˌwʌn/, /ˈev·ri·wən/ **pronoun** (also **everybody**) A2 every person: *I've received a reply from everyone now.* ◦ *Everyone agreed with the decision.*

everything /ˈev·riˌθɪŋ/ **pronoun** **1** A2 all things or each thing: *They lost everything in the fire.* ◦ *What's the matter, Nick, is everything all right?* **2 everything else** all the other things: *The meat tasted weird, but everything else was okay.*

everywhere /ˈev·riˌhweər/ **adv** A2 in or to every place: *I've looked everywhere, but I still can't find that letter.*

evidence /ˈev·ɪ·dᵊns/ **noun** [no plural] **1** something that makes you believe that something is true or exists: ***evidence of*** *global warming* ◦ *There is no scientific evidence that the drug is harmful.* **2** information that is given or things that are shown in a court of law to help to prove that someone has done a crime: *He was arrested despite the lack of* ***evidence against*** *him.*

evident /ˈev·ɪ·dᵊnt/ **adj** formal obvious to everyone and easy to see or understand: *It was evident from his voice that he was upset.*

evil[1] /ˈi·vəl/ **adj** very bad and cruel: *an evil monster*

evil[2] /ˈi·vəl/ **noun** [no plural] a force that is very bad or makes bad things happen: *The theme of the play is the battle between good and evil.*

evolution /ˌev·əˈlu·ʃən/ **noun** [no plural] **1** the way in which living things gradually change and develop over millions of years: *Darwin's theory of evolution* **2** a gradual process of change and development: *the* ***evolution of*** *language* ◦ *the painter's artistic evolution*

ex- /eks/ **prefix** used to show that someone is no longer what he or she was: *my ex-girlfriend*

exact /ɪgˈzækt/ **adj** B1 completely correct: *I don't know the exact price.*

exactly /ɪgˈzækt·li/ **adv** **1** A2 used when you are giving or asking for information that is completely correct: *What exactly is the problem?* ◦ *The train got in at exactly ten o'clock.* **2** B1 used to make stronger what you are saying: *I found a dress that's exactly the same color as my shoes.* **3** something you say when you agree completely with someone: *"Surely* *they should have told us about this problem sooner?" "Exactly."* **4 not exactly** used to say that something is not completely true: *"Did you give her your book?" "Not exactly, I lent it to her."*

exaggerate /ɪɡˈzædʒ.ə.ˌreɪt/ **verb** (present participle **exaggerating**, past tense and past participle **exaggerated**) to make something seem larger, better, or worse than it really is: *Don't exaggerate – it didn't cost that much!*

exam /ɪɡˈzæm/ **noun** **A2** an official test of how much you know about something, or how well you can do something: *a final exam* ∘ *to fail/pass an exam*

examination /ɪɡˌzæm.ɪˈneɪ.ʃən/ **noun** **1 A2** formal an exam: *a written examination* **2** the process of looking at something very carefully: *a medical examination*

examine /ɪɡˈzæm.ɪn/ **verb** (present participle **examining**, past tense and past participle **examined**) **1** to look at someone or something very carefully, especially to try to discover something: *She picked up the knife and examined it carefully.* **2** formal to test someone to see how much he or she knows or how well he or she can do something: *You'll be examined in three main areas: speaking, listening, and reading.*

example /ɪɡˈzæm.pəl/ **noun** **1 A1** something that is typical of the group of things that you are talking about: *This is a good example of the architecture of the period.* **2 for example A1** used to give an example of what you are talking about: *Some people, students for example, can get cheaper tickets.*

excellent /ˈek.sə.lənt/ **adj** **A2** very good, or of a very high quality: *That was an excellent meal.*

except /ɪkˈsept/ **preposition, conjunction A2** not including a particular fact, thing, or person: *He works every day except Sunday.* ∘ *Everyone passed the test except for Steve.* ∘ *So nothing changed, except that Anna saw her son less often.*

exception /ɪkˈsep.ʃən/ **noun** **1** someone or something that is not included in a

rule, group, or list: *There are exceptions to every rule.* ∘ *I like all kinds of movies, with the exception of horror movies.* **2 make an exception** to treat someone differently from all other people: *I don't usually accept credit cards, but for you I'll make an exception.*

exceptional /ɪkˈsep.ʃə.nəl/ **adj** very good, and better than most other people or things: *an exceptional student* • **exceptionally adv** *an exceptionally intelligent child*

excess /ɪkˈses/, /ˈek.ses/ **noun** more of something than is usual or needed: *There's a charge for excess baggage on a plane.*

exchange[1] /ɪksˈtʃeɪndʒ/ **noun** **1 B1** an occasion when you give something to someone and he or she gives you something else: *an exchange of ideas* ∘ *They were given food and shelter in exchange for work.* **2 B1** a period when students and teachers from one country go to stay with students and teachers in another: *I have happy memories of going on an exchange to France.*

exchange[2] /ɪksˈtʃeɪndʒ/ **verb** (present participle **exchanging**, past tense and past participle **exchanged**) **1 B1** to give something to someone and get something similar from them: *The two teams usually exchange shirts after the game.* **2** to take something back to the store where you bought it and get something else: *Could I exchange this shirt for a larger size?* **3 exchange looks, opinions, views, etc.** If two people exchange looks, opinions, views, etc., they look at each other, talk to each other, etc.: *The group meets every month to exchange views on a book they have all read.*

exchange rate /ɪksˈtʃeɪndʒ ˌreɪt/ **noun** **B1** how much of a country's money you can buy with a particular amount of another country's money

excited /ɪkˈsaɪ.tɪd/ **adj** **A1** feeling very happy and interested, or showing this: *happy, excited faces* ∘ *The kids are getting really excited about the party.* • **excitedly adv B1** *She ran excitedly to meet her cousins.*

a b c d e f g h i j k l m n o p q r s t u v w x y z

a
b
c
d
e
f
g
h
i
j
k
l
m
n
o
p
q
r
s
t
u
v
w
x
y
z

> ⚠ **Common mistake: excited or exciting?**
>
> **Excited** is used to describe how someone feels.
>
> *She was very excited about the visit.*
> ~~She was very exciting about the visit.~~
>
> **Exciting** is used to describe the thing that makes you excited.
>
> *I have some exciting news!*

excitement /ɪkˈsaɪt.mənt/ **noun** [no plural] **B1** a feeling of happiness and interest: *There's a lot of excitement about the competition.*

exciting /ɪkˈsaɪ.tɪŋ/ **adj** **A1** making you feel very happy and interested: *an exciting football game* ○ *You're going to Africa? How exciting!*

exclamation /ˌek.skləˈmeɪ.ʃən/ **noun** something that you say loudly and suddenly because you are surprised or angry: *an exclamation of delight*

exclamation point /ˌek.skləˈmeɪ.ʃən ˌpɔɪnt/ **noun** a symbol [!] used at the end of a sentence to show surprise or excitement

exclude /ɪkˈsklud/ **verb** (present participle **excluding**, past tense and past participle **excluded**) **1** to not allow someone or something to do an activity or enter a place: *Women are still **excluded from** the club.* **2** to not include something: *The insurance coverage excludes particular medical conditions.*

excluding /ɪkˈsklu.dɪŋ/ **preposition** not including: *That's $600 per person for seven days, excluding travel costs.*

exclusive /ɪkˈsklu.sɪv/ **adj** expensive and only for people who are rich or important: *an exclusive private club*

excuse[1] /ɪkˈskjuz/ **verb** (present participle **excusing**, past tense and past participle **excused**) **1** **B1** to forgive someone for something that is not very serious: *Please excuse my appearance – I've been painting.* **2** to say that someone does not have to do something: *Could I be*

excused from football practice today? **3 excuse me** **A1** used to politely get someone's attention: *Excuse me, does this bus go downtown?* **4 excuse me** **A2** used to say sorry for something that you have done: *Oh, excuse me, did I take your seat?*

excuse[2] /ɪkˈskjus/ **noun** **1** **B1** a reason that you give to explain why you did something wrong: *I hope he has a good **excuse for** being so late.* **2** **B1** a false reason that you give to explain why you do something: *Nick was just looking for an excuse to call her.*

execute /ˈek.sɪˌkjut/ **verb** (present participle **executing**, past tense and past participle **executed**) to kill someone as a legal punishment: *He was executed for murder.*

execution /ˌek.sɪˈkju.ʃən/ **noun** the killing of someone as a legal punishment

executive /ɪgˈzek.jə.tɪv/ **noun** someone who has an important job in a business

exercise[1] /ˈek.sərˌsaɪz/ **noun** **1** **A2** activity that you do with your body to make it strong: *Swimming is my favorite form of exercise.* **2** **A2** a piece of written work that helps you learn something: *For your homework, please do exercise 3 on page 24.*

exercise[2] /ˈek.sərˌsaɪz/ **verb** (present participle **exercising**, past tense and past participle **exercised**) **A2** to do activities with your body to make it strong and healthy: *I try to exercise every day.*

exhausted /ɪgˈzɔs.tɪd/ **adj** **B1** very tired: *He looks exhausted.*

exhausting /ɪgˈzɔs.tɪŋ/ **adj** making you feel very tired: *What an exhausting day!*

exhibit /ɪgˈzɪb.ɪt/ **noun** **B1** a special collection of things that is shown to the public: *There's a new sculpture exhibit at the art museum.*

exile /ˈeg.zaɪl/ **noun** [no plural] a situation in which someone has to leave his or her home and live in another country, often for political reasons: *He spent many years **in exile**.*

exist /ɪgˈzɪst/ **verb** **B1** to be real or present: *Poverty still exists in this country.*

existence /ɪgˈzɪs·təns/ *noun* [no plural]
the fact of something or someone exist-ing: *The theater company that we started is still **in existence** today.*

exit[1] /ˈeg·zɪt/, /ˈek·sɪt/ *noun* **1** ⒜ a door, window, or other opening that allows you to leave a structure or a vehicle: *a fire exit* ◦ *an airplane's emergency exits* **2** ⒜ a road that you use to leave an-other, larger road such as a freeway: *Take the next **exit**.*

exit[2] /ˈeg·zɪt/, /ˈek·sɪt/ *verb* **1** Ⓑ to stop using a program on a computer: *Press "escape" to exit the game.* **2** to leave a place: *Please exit by the side doors.*

exotic /ɪgˈzɑt̬·ɪk/ *adj* unusual, interest-ing, and often foreign: *exotic fruit*

expand /ɪkˈspænd/ *verb* to get larger, or to make something get larger: *The company has expanded in recent years.*

expansion /ɪkˈspæn·ʃən/ *noun* [no plural] the action of getting larger: *the rapid expansion of the software industry*

expect /ɪkˈspekt/ *verb* **1** Ⓑ to think that something will happen: *He didn't **expect to** see me.* ◦ *I **expect that** she'll be very angry about this.* **2** **be expecting someone/something** to be waiting for someone or something to arrive: *We've been expecting you.* **3** to think that someone should do a particular thing: *You will be **expected to** work some weekends.* **4** **be expecting** to be going to have a baby: *I'm expecting my first baby in May.*

expedition /ˌek·spəˈdɪʃ·ən/ *noun* Ⓑ an organized journey, especially a long one for a particular purpose: *Peary led the first expedition to the North Pole.*

expel /ɪkˈspel/ *verb* (present participle **expelling**, past tense and past participle **expelled**) to make someone leave a school, organization, or country: *He was **expelled from** school **for** fighting.*

expense /ɪkˈspens/ *noun* the money that you spend on something: *You have to pay your own medical expenses.*

expensive /ɪkˈspen·sɪv/ *adj* ⒜ costing a lot of money: *expensive jewelry*
→ Opposite **cheap adj**
• **expensively** *adv* *expensively dressed*

experience[1] /ɪkˈspɪr·i·əns/ *noun* **1** Ⓑ [no plural] knowledge that you get from doing a job, or from seeing, doing, or feeling something: *You've obviously had **experience with** babysitting.* ◦ *He knows **from experience** how difficult she can be.* **2** Ⓑ something that happens to you that affects how you feel: *My trip to Australia was an amazing experience.*

experience[2] /ɪkˈspɪr·i·əns/ *verb* (present participle **experiencing**, past tense and past participle **experienced**) Ⓑ If you experi-ence something, it happens to you, or you feel it: *It was the worst pain I had ever experienced.*

experienced /ɪkˈspɪr·i·ənst/ *adj* Ⓑ having skill and knowledge because you have done something many times: *She's a very experienced ski instructor.*
→ Opposite **inexperienced adj**

experiment[1] /ɪkˈsper·ə·mənt/ *noun* Ⓑ a test, especially a scientific one, that you do in order to discover whether something is true: *We **do** lots of **experiments** in class.*

experiment[2] /ɪkˈsper·əˌment/ *verb* **1** to try something in order to discover what it is like: *Did he ever **experiment with** drugs?* **2** to do an experiment: *He's against **experimenting on** animals.*

expert[1] /ˈek·spərt/ *noun* Ⓑ someone who has a lot of skill in something or a lot of knowledge about something: *He's **an expert on** Japanese literature.*

expert[2] /ˈek·spərt/ *adj* having a lot of knowledge or skill: *He's an expert fisher-man.*

explain /ɪkˈspleɪn/ *verb* ⒜ to make something clear or easy to understand by giving reasons for it: *Can you **explain** why you did this?* ◦ *Can you **explain** to me how this phone works?* ◦ *He **explained** that he was looking for a job.*

a
b
c
d
e
f
g
h
i
j
k
l
m
n
o
p
q
r
s
t
u
v
w
x
y
z

❗ Common mistake: explain something

Explain is followed by the thing you are explaining.
I'll explain the situation.
Remember to use the preposition **to** before a person.
I'll explain the situation to my parents.
~~I'll explain my parents the situation.~~

explanation /ˌek·splə'neɪ·ʃən/ *noun*
B1 the details or reasons that someone gives to make something clear or easy to understand: *What's your **explanation for** the team's poor performance? ○ Could you give me a quick **explanation of** how it works?*

explode /ɪk'sploud/ *verb* (present participle **exploding**, past tense and past participle **exploded**) **B1** If a bomb explodes, it bursts (= breaks suddenly from inside) with noise and force

explore /ɪk'splɔːr/ *verb* (present participle **exploring**, past tense and past participle **explored**) **1** **B1** to go around a place where you have never been in order to find out what is there: *The children love exploring. ○ The best way to explore the countryside is on foot.* **2** to find out more about something, especially something that you might do in the future: *We're exploring the possibility of buying a house at the beach.*
• **exploration** *noun She's always loved travel and exploration.*

explosion /ɪk'splou·ʒən/ *noun*
the action of something such as a bomb exploding: *Forty people were killed in the explosion.*

explosive /ɪk'splou·sɪv/ *adj* able to cause an explosion: *The explosive device was hidden in a suitcase.*

export[1] /'ek·spɔːrt/ *noun* a product that one country makes that is sold in other countries: *American beef exports to Japan*
→ Opposite **import**

export[2] /ek'spɔːrt/ *verb* to send products to other countries in order to sell

them there: *Singapore exports large quantities of rubber.*
→ Opposite **import verb**
• **exporter** *noun Brazil is the world's largest exporter of coffee.*

expose /ɪk'spouz/ *verb* (present participle **exposing**, past tense and past participle **exposed**) **1** to show something by removing its cover: *He removed the bandage to expose the wound.* **2 be exposed to *something*** to experience something or be affected by something: *It was the first time I'd been exposed to violence.*

express /ɪk'spres/ *verb* to show what you think or how you feel using words or actions: *I'm simply expressing my opinion.*

expression /ɪk'spreʃ·ən/ *noun* **1** the look on someone's face showing what he or she feels or thinks: *He had a sad expression on his face.* **2** a group of words that has a special meaning: *"A can of worms" is an expression meaning "a difficult situation."*

extend /ɪk'stend/ *verb* **1** to make something bigger or longer: *We're going to extend our kitchen.* **2** to make an activity, agreement, etc. last for a longer time: *They extended the deadline by one week.*

extension /ɪk'sten·ʃən/ *noun* **1** a telephone that is connected to the main telephone in an office or other large building: *Call me **at extension** 3104.* **2** extra time that you are given to do or use something: *I applied for an **extension** to my visa.* **3** something that is added on to something else to make it longer or bigger: *hair extensions ○ an extension to the subway line*

extent /ɪk'stent/ *noun* [no plural] **1** the size or importance of something: *They are just beginning to realize the full extent of the damage.* **2 to a great, large, etc. extent** mainly: *Her book is based to a large extent on real events.* **3 to some extent/to a certain extent** used to say that something is true, but is not the whole truth: *To some extent she was responsible for the accident. ○ I agree with you to a certain extent.*

exterior /ek'stɪər·i·ər/ noun the outside part of something or someone: *The exterior of the house was painted white.*
• **exterior adj** *an exterior wall*
→ Opposite **interior noun**

external /ek'stɜr·n°l/ adj **1** relating to the outside part of something: *the external walls of the house* **2** coming from or relating to another country, group, organization, etc.: *We don't want any external interference in our affairs.*
→ Opposite **internal adj**
• **externally adv** *The cream should only be applied externally* (=on the skin).

extinct /ɪk'stɪŋkt/ adj If a type of animal is extinct, it does not now exist.

extinguish /ɪk'stɪŋ·gwɪʃ/ verb to make something stop burning: *The fire took two hours to extinguish.*

extra¹ /'ek·strə/ adj **A2** more, or more than usual: *Can I invite extra people?*

extra² /'ek·strə/ adv **B1** more: *They pay her extra for working late.*

extra³ /'ek·strə/ noun **B1** something that you can get with something else if you pay a little more money: *The car comes with optional extras such as a CD player.*

extract¹ /ɪk'strækt/ verb formal to remove or take something out, especially using force: *to extract a tooth*

extract² /'ek·strækt/ noun a short part taken from a book, poem, etc.: *The newspaper printed extracts from the court documents.*

extraordinary /ɪk'strɔr·d°n̩er·i/ adj **B1** very special or strange: *She was an extraordinary young woman.*
• **extraordinarily adv**

extreme /ɪk'strim/ adj **1** the worst or most serious: *extreme weather conditions* **2** very large in amount or degree: *extreme pain* **3** at the furthest point of something: *the extreme east of the island*

extremely /ɪk'strim·li/ adv **B1** very: *extremely beautiful* ○ *He works extremely hard.*

extreme sports /ɪk'strim 'spɔrts/ noun **B1** activities that are exciting and dangerous: *extreme sports like snowboarding*

eye /ɑɪ/ noun **eye**
1 **A1** one of the two organs in your face that you use to see with: *Sara has black hair and brown eyes.* ○ *She closed her eyes and fell asleep.*
→ See **The Body** on page C2 **2** the small hole at the end of a needle that you put the thread through **3 keep an eye on** *someone/something* to watch or take care of someone or something: *Could you keep an eye on the kids for a little while?* **4 in** *someone's* **eyes** in someone's opinion: *In my parents' eyes, I'll always be a child.*

eyebrow /'ɑɪ.brɑʊ/ noun the thin line of hair that is above each eye
→ See **The Body** on page C2

eyelash /'ɑɪ.læʃ/ noun (also **lash**) one of the short hairs that grow from the edge of your eyelids: *false eyelashes*

eyelid /'ɑɪ.lɪd/ noun the piece of skin that covers your eyes when you close them

eyesight /'ɑɪ.sɑɪt/ noun [no plural] the ability to see: *My eyesight is getting worse.*

Ff

F, f /ef/ the sixth letter of the alphabet

F written abbreviation for Fahrenheit: a measurement of temperature: *a body temperature of 98.6°F*

fable /'feɪ·bəl/ noun a short story that shows people how to behave

fabric /'fæb·rɪk/ noun cloth: *a light cotton fabric*

a b c d e **f** g h i j k l m n o p q r s t u v w x y z

| æ cat | ɑ hot | e get | ɪ sit | i see | ɔ saw | ʊ book | u too | ʌ cut | ə about | ər mother | ɜr turn | ɔr for | ɑɪ my | ɑʊ how | eɪ say | ɔɪ boy |

fabulous /ˈfæb·jə·ləs/ *adj* very good: *They have a fabulous house.*

face[1] /feɪs/ *noun*

face

1 [A1] the front part of the head where the eyes, nose, and mouth are: *She has a long, thin face.* **2** the front or surface of something: *the north face of the mountain* ○ *a clock face* **3 face to face** [B1] being with someone in the same place: *We need to talk face to face.* **4 make a face** [B1] to show with your face that you do not like someone or something: *Joe made a face when he saw what was for lunch.* **5** to **someone's face** If you say something to someone's face, you say it to the person directly, when you are with him or her: *I would never say that to her face.*

face[2] /feɪs/ *verb* (present participle **facing**, past tense and past participle **faced**) **1** [B1] to be or turn in a particular direction: *The room faces south.* ○ *She turned to face him.* **2** to have a problem: *Passengers could face long delays.* **3** to accept that something unpleasant is true and start to deal with the situation: *I think he has to face the fact that she no longer loves him.* **4 let's face it** used before you say something that is bad but true: *Let's face it, we are not going to win this game.* **5 can't face (doing)** *something* to not want to do something or deal with something because it is difficult or unpleasant: *I can't face walking up all those steps again.*

face up to *something phrasal verb* to accept that a difficult situation exists and is something you must deal with: *Eventually he faced up to his money problems.*

face-to-face /ˈfeɪs·tə·ˈfeɪs/ *adj* [B1] between people who are in the same place: *a face-to-face meeting*

facilities /fəˈsɪl·ə·t̬iz/ *plural noun* [B1] equipment or services that are provided for a particular purpose: *childcare/ exercise facilities*

facility /fəˈsɪl·ə·t̬i/ *noun* a building or set of rooms that is designed or used for a particular purpose: *a sports/military facility*

fact /fækt/ *noun* **1** [A2] something that you know is true, exists, or has happened: *No decision will be made until we know all the facts.* ○ *The real problem is the fact that we cannot agree.* **2 in fact/in actual fact** [B1] used to say what is really true: *I was told there were some tickets left, but in actual fact they were sold out.* **3** real events and experiences, not things that are imagined: *The movie is based on historical facts.* **4 the fact is** used to tell someone that something is the truth: *The fact is that we don't have enough money.*

factor /ˈfæk·tər/ *noun* one of the things that has an effect on a particular situation, decision, event, etc.: *Safety is an important factor in car design.*

factory /ˈfæk·tə·ri/ *noun* (plural **factories**) [A1] a building or group of buildings where things are made or put together: *a toy factory*

fade /feɪd/ *verb* (present participle **fading**, past tense and past participle **faded**) If a color or sound fades, it gradually becomes less bright or strong: *The music fades at the end of the song.*

fade away *phrasal verb* to gradually become less strong or clear and then disappear: *As the years passed, her memories of her childhood faded away.*

Fahrenheit /ˈfær·ən·haɪt/ *noun* [no plural] (written abbreviation **F**) a measurement of temperature in which water freezes at 32° and boils at 212°

fail /feɪl/ *verb* **1** [A2] to not pass a test or an exam: *I just failed my driver's test.* **2** to not be successful: *Dad's business failed after just three years.* → Opposite **succeed** *verb* **3 fail to do** *something* to not do what is expected: *He failed to turn in his homework yesterday.* **4** to stop working normally, or to become weaker: *The brakes failed and the car crashed into a tree.*

failure /ˈfeɪl·jər/ *noun* **1** [no plural] a situation in which someone or something does not succeed: *Their attempt to climb*

the mountain ended in failure. **2** someone or something that does not succeed: *I felt like a failure after losing the race.*
→ Opposite **success** noun **3** [no plural] a situation in which you do not do something that you are expected to do: *Failure to pay within 14 days will result in a fine.*

faint[1] /feɪnt/ adj **1** slight and not easy to notice: *a faint smell of smoke* **2** feel **faint** to feel very weak and as if you might fall down: *Seeing all the blood made me feel faint.*

faint[2] /feɪnt/ verb   to suddenly become unconscious for a short time

fair[1] /feər/ adj **1** 🄰🄸 Fair hair or skin, or a person who has it, is pale or light in color: *a boy with fair hair* **2** 🄱🄸 treating or affecting everyone in the same way: *a fair trial* ○ *It's not fair that she gets to go and I don't!* ○ *I'm willing to do my fair share of the work (=an equal part).*
→ Opposite **unfair** **3 a fair price, deal, offer, etc.** 🄱🄸 a price, deal, offer, etc. that is right for a situation and not asking for too much **4 a fair amount, number, etc.** a fairly large amount, number, etc.: *There's still a fair amount of work to be done on the house.* **5** good, but very not good: *He has a fair chance of winning.* **6** sunny and not raining

fair[2] /feər/ noun **1** 🄱🄸 a place outside where you can ride on big machines for pleasure and play games to win prizes **2** an event at which companies, organizations, or groups show what they do or sell their products or services: *a book/craft/job fair*

fairly /ˈfeərli/ adv **1** 🄱🄸 more than average, but less than very: *a fairly large family* **2** done in a fair or honest way: *The company says that all of its workers are treated fairly.*

fairness /ˈfeərnəs/ noun
[no plural]   the fact of treating everyone in the same way

fairy /ˈfeəri/ noun (plural **fairies**)   a small, imaginary person with wings who has magic powers

fairy tale /ˈfeəri ˌteɪl/ noun   a story told to children that has magic in it and a happy ending

faith /feɪθ/ noun **1** [no plural] the belief that someone or something is good and can be trusted: *I have great faith in her ability to do well.* **2** a religion: *the Jewish and Christian faiths* **3** [no plural] strong belief in a god or gods: *Throughout her illness, she never lost her faith in God.*

faithful /ˈfeɪθ·fəl/ adj   always liking and supporting someone or something: *She's a trusted and faithful friend.*

fake[1] /feɪk/ adj   not real, but made to look or seem real: *She was carrying a fake passport.*

fake[2] /feɪk/ noun   a copy of something that is intended to make people think it is real: *Experts say that the painting is a fake.*

fall[1] /fɔl/ verb (past tense **fell**, past participle **fallen**) **1** 🄰🄸 to move down toward the ground: *Huge snowflakes were falling from the sky.* **2** 🄱🄸 to become less in number or amount: *House prices have fallen by 15% this year.* **3 fall asleep** 🄱🄸 to start to sleep: *Dad fell asleep on the couch.* **4 fall in love** 🄱🄸 to start to love someone **5** to suddenly go down and hit the ground: *She fell off her bike.*

fall apart phrasal verb to break into pieces: *These old boots are falling apart.*

fall down phrasal verb 🄱🄸 to fall onto the ground: *The wall is in danger of falling down.*

fall over phrasal verb 🄱🄸 to fall from a standing position: *My glass fell over and spilled.*

> **❗ Common mistake: fall and feel**
>
> Be careful not to confuse the past forms of the verbs **fall** and **feel**.
> The past tense of **fall** is **fell**.
> *He fell off a ladder and broke his arm.*
> The past tense of **feel** is **felt**.
> *I felt really happy and relaxed.*

fall[2] /fɔl/ noun **1** 🄰🄸 (also **autumn**) the season of the year between summer and

fairy

winter, when leaves fall from the trees
2 ⓑ a drop in the number or amount
of something: *There was a sharp fall in
prices this year.* **3** a drop from a higher
level to a lower level: *He was injured in a
fall from a ladder.*

fallen /ˈfɔ·lən/ past participle of fall

false /fɔls/ adj **1** ⓑ not true or correct:
He gave false information to the police.
2 not real: *false teeth*

fame /feɪm/ noun [no plural] a state of
being known by many people

familiar /fəˈmɪl·jər/ adj **1** ⓑ If something is familiar, you know it well or
have seen it before: *This street looks
familiar to me.* **2 be familiar with
something** to know about something or
have done or seen it many times before:
I'm not familiar with his poetry.

family /ˈfæm·ə·li/ noun (plural **families**)
1 ⓐ a group of people who are related
to each other, especially parents and
children: *My family originally came from
Poland.* **2** ⓑ the children of two parents: *They have a large family.*

famine /ˈfæm·ən/ noun a lack of food
for a long time in a particular place

famous /ˈfeɪ·məs/ adj ⓐ known by
many people: *a famous actress*

fan /fæn/ noun **1** ⓐ someone who
likes a person or thing very much: *He's
a big fan of country music.*
2 ⓑ something that is used to move
the air around so it feels cooler: *an electric fan*

fans

fancy /ˈfæn·si/ adj **1** expensive and
fashionable: *a fancy restaurant*
2 complicated or having a lot of decoration: *That dress is too fancy for a little girl.*

fantastic /fænˈtæs·tɪk/ adj informal
ⓐ very good: *He looks fantastic in that
suit.*

fantasy /ˈfæn·tə·si/ noun (plural
fantasies) a pleasant situation or
event that you imagine, which is not
real or true: *Steve's fantasy was to have a
big house and an expensive car.*

FAQ /fæk/ noun a set of questions that
many people ask when they use the Internet or a computer program, or a document containing these questions and
their answers

far¹ /fɑr/ adv **1** ⓐ used to talk about
how distant something is: *How far is it
to the supermarket?* **2** very much:
*Young people are far more independent
these days.* **3 as far as I know** used to
say what you think is true, although you
do not know all the facts: *As far as I
know, they are coming to the party.* **4 by
far** used to say that something is the
biggest, the best, etc.: *This is his best
book by far.* **5 so far** ⓑ until now: *So
far, we haven't made much progress on
the project.*

far² /fɑr/ adj (comparative **farther** or
further, superlative **farthest** or **furthest**)
describing the part of something that is
most distant from you: *His office is at the
far end of the hallway.*

fare /feər/ noun ⓑ the price that you
pay to travel on a plane, train, bus, etc.:
plane/bus fares

farm /fɑrm/ noun ⓐ land and buildings used for growing crops and keeping animals: *a dairy farm* (= where cows
are raised for milk)

farmer /ˈfɑr·mər/ noun ⓐ someone
who owns or takes care of a farm

farming /ˈfɑr·mɪŋ/ noun [no plural]
ⓑ the job of working on a farm

farmyard /ˈfɑrm·jɑrd/ noun an area of
land with farm buildings around it

farther /ˈfɑr·ðər/ adj, adv comparative of
far: more distant: *I can't walk any farther.*

farthest /ˈfɑr·ðəst/ adj, adv superlative of
far: most distant: *Which planet is farthest
from the sun?*

fascinated /'fæs·əˌneɪ·t̬ɪd/ adj
very interested: *They were absolutely fascinated by the video game.*

fascinating /'fæs·əˌneɪ·t̬ɪŋ/ adj
very interesting: *a fascinating story*

fashion /'fæʃ·ən/ noun **1** 🇦🇷 the most popular style of clothes or behavior at a particular time: *Long hair is in fashion now.* ○ *Fur coats have gone out of fashion.* **2** 🇧🇷 [no plural] the business of making and selling clothes: *fashion magazines*

fashionable /'fæʃ·ə·nə·bəl/ adj
🇧🇷 popular at a particular time: *fashionable clothes*
→ Opposite **unfashionable** adj

fast[1] /fæst/ adj **1** 🇦🇷 quick: *fast cars* ○ *a fast swimmer* → Opposite **slow** adj **2** If a clock or watch is fast, it shows a time that is later than the correct time: *My watch is five minutes fast.*

fast[2] /fæst/ adv **1** 🇦🇷 quickly: *We ran as fast as we could.* **2 fast asleep** completely asleep (=sleeping) **3** in a firm or tight way: *He tried to get away, but she held him fast.*

> ⚠ **Common mistake: fast**
>
> Remember that there is no adverb "fastly." Use the adverbs **fast** or **quickly** instead.
> *The situation is changing fast.*
> *Alice got dressed very quickly.*

fasten /'fæs·ən/ verb **1** 🇧🇷 to close or attach something: *Fasten your seat belts.* **2** to attach one thing to another: *He fastened the shelf to the wall.*

fast food /ˈfæst ˈfud/ noun [no plural]
🇦🇷 hot food that is served very quickly in a restaurant because it is already made

fat[1] /fæt/ adj (comparative **fatter**, superlative **fattest**) 🇦🇷 Someone who is fat weighs too much: *He eats a lot but never gets fat.*
→ Opposite **thin** adj

fat[2] /fæt/ noun a solid or liquid substance like oil that is taken from plants or animals and used in cooking: *animal/vegetable fat*

fatal /'feɪ·t̬əl/ adj **1** A fatal accident or illness makes someone die: *a fatal car crash* **2** Fatal actions have very bad effects: *He made the fatal error of deleting the file.*

fate /feɪt/ noun [no plural] **1** a power that some people believe controls what will happen: *I believe it was fate that caused us to meet again.* **2** something that happens to someone, especially something bad: *The election will decide his fate.*

father /'fɑð·ər/ noun 🇦🇷 someone's male parent: *My father and mother met in college.*

father-in-law /'fɑð·ər·ɪnˌlɔ/ noun (plural **fathers-in-law**) the father of someone's husband or wife: *My father-in-law has always been very kind to me.*

faucet /'fɔ·sɪt/ noun 🇧🇷 the part at the end of a pipe that controls the flow of water: *Turn the faucet on/off.* ○ *The faucet in the bathroom sink is leaking.*
→ See **The Bathroom** on page C1

fault /fɔlt/ noun **1** *someone's* **fault**
🇧🇷 If something bad that happened is someone's fault, he or she made it happen: *The accident was not my fault.* **2** something that is wrong with something: *The car has a serious design fault.* **3** something that is wrong with someone's character: *He has many faults, but laziness isn't one of them.*

> ⚠ **Common mistake: fault** or **mistake**?
>
> Use **fault** for explaining who is responsible when something bad happens.
> *It's my fault that the car was stolen. I left the window open.*
> ~~It's my mistake the car was stolen. I left the window open.~~
> Use **mistake** for talking about something that you did or thought that was wrong.
> *I still make lots of mistakes in my essays.*
> ~~I still make lots of faults in my essays.~~

a b c d e f g h i j k l m n o p q r s t u v w x y z

faulty /ˈfɒl·ti/ adj (comparative **faultier**, superlative **faultiest**) not working correctly: *faulty brakes*

favor /ˈfeɪ·vər/ noun **1 B1** something that you do to help someone: *Could you do me a favor, please?* **2** be in favor of *something* to agree with a plan or idea: *Most people are in favor of reducing traffic in cities.*

favorable /ˈfeɪ·və·ə·bəl/ adj **1** showing that you like or approve of someone or something: *We've had a favorable response to the plan so far.* **2** making you support or approve of someone or something: *She made a very favorable impression on us.*

favorite[1] /ˈfeɪ·vər·ɪt/ adj **A1** Your favorite person or thing is the one that you like best: *What's your favorite color?*

favorite[2] /ˈfeɪ·vər·ɪt/ noun **B1** a thing that someone likes best or enjoys most: *These chocolates are my favorites.*

fax /fæks/ noun **1** a document that is sent using a special machine and a telephone line **2** a machine that is used to send and receive faxes
→ See **The Office** on page C12
• **fax** verb **B1** *I faxed the changes to my publisher.*

fear[1] /fɪər/ noun **B1** a strong, bad feeling that you get when you think that something bad might happen: *She was trembling **with fear**.* ○ *There are **fears that** the disease will spread.*

fear[2] /fɪər/ verb **1** to be worried or afraid that something bad might happen or might have happened: *Police **fear that** she drowned in the river.* **2** to be frightened of something or someone unpleasant: *Many older people fear death.*

feast /fist/ noun a large meal, especially to celebrate something special

feather /ˈfeð·ər/ noun one of the soft, light things that cover a bird's skin

feature[1] /ˈfi·tʃər/ noun **1** an important part of something: *This phone has some new features.* **2** a part of a person's face: *His eyes are his best feature.*

feature[2] /ˈfi·tʃər/ verb to include someone or something as an important part: *a new movie featuring Sandra Bullock*

February /ˈfeb·ruˌer·i/, /ˈfeb·juˌer·i/ noun **A1** the second month of the year

fed /fed/ past tense and past participle of feed

federal /ˈfed·ər·əl/ adj **1** A federal system of government consists of a group of regions that can make their own laws, but are also controlled by a national government. **2** relating to the national government of a country such as the United States, and not to the government of one of its states: *the **federal government*** ○ *a federal employee*

fed up /ˈfed ˈʌp/ adj informal bored or annoyed by something that you have done for too long: *I'm **fed up with** my job.*

fee /fi/ noun **B1** an amount of money that you pay to do or use something: *entrance fees*

feeble /ˈfi·bəl/ adj very weak: *She was too feeble to get out of bed.*

feed /fid/ verb (past tense and past participle fed) **B1** to give food to a person, group, or animal: *Did you feed the cat?*

feedback /ˈfid·bæk/ noun (no plural) information or opinions about how well you have done: *The teacher gave us **feedback** on our speeches.*

feel /fil/ verb (past tense and past participle felt) **1 A1** to experience happiness, sadness, fear, etc.: *I feel guilty about shouting at her.* ○ *He's feeling lonely.* ○ *I felt sorry for her.* **2 A1** to experience a touch, a pain, or something else that is physical: *I felt a sharp pain in my foot.* ○ *Do you feel sick?* **3 B1** to have an opinion about something: *I **feel that** she's the best person for the job.* **4** feel like *someone/something* **B1** to seem to be similar to a type of person, thing, or situation: *Your hands feel like ice.* **5** feel as if/feel like **B1** to have a feeling or idea about something that you have experienced, even though it might not be true: *It feels like I've been here forever,* *but it's only been a week.* **6 feel like something** 🔵 to want something: *I feel like a sandwich.* **7 feel like doing something** 🔵 to want to do something: *Jane felt like crying.* **8** to touch something in order to examine it: *He felt her ankle to see if it was broken.* **9 feel different, strange, etc.** If a place, situation, etc. feels different, strange, etc., that is how it seems to you: *It felt strange to see him again after so long.* ○ *The house feels empty without the kids.*

feeling /ˈfiːlɪŋ/ *noun* **1** 🔵 something that you feel in your mind when you are happy, sad, afraid, etc.: *Sitting by the lake gives me a nice, peaceful feeling.* ○ *He tries to hide his feelings.* **2** 🔵 something that you feel in your body: *I had a strange feeling in my fingers.* **3** 🔵 an idea that something is true or exists: *I had the feeling that we had met before.* ○ *I got the feeling that she was unhappy.* **4** an opinion or belief: *My feeling is that we should not hire him.*

feelings /ˈfiːlɪŋz/ *plural noun* **hurt someone's feelings** 🔵 to upset someone by insulting him or her: *Say you like the cake, or you'll hurt her feelings.*

feet /fiːt/ *plural of* foot

fell /fel/ *past tense of* fall

fellow /ˈfeloʊ/ *adj* used to describe people with the same interests or situation: *her fellow students*

felt /felt/ *past tense and past participle of* feel

felt-tip pen /ˌfelt tɪp ˈpen/ *noun* a pen with a soft point and colored ink for coloring pictures

female /ˈfiːmeɪl/ *adj* 🔵 belonging to the sex that can have babies: *a female butterfly*
• **female** *noun*

feminine /ˈfemənɪn/ *adj* showing qualities that people think are typical of women: *feminine beauty*

fence /fens/ *noun* a wood or metal structure that goes around an area: *We put up a fence around the yard.*

fence

fern /fɜːrn/ *noun* a green plant with narrow leaves like feathers and no flowers

ferry /ˈferi/ *noun* (plural **ferries**) 🔵 a boat that regularly carries people and vehicles across an area of water: *a car/passenger ferry*

fern

fertile /ˈfɜːrtl/ *adj* **1** Fertile land or soil produces a lot of healthy plants. **2** If people or animals are fertile, they are able to have babies.

fertilizer /ˈfɜːrtlˌaɪzər/ *noun* something that you put on land in order to make plants grow well

festival /ˈfestəvəl/ *noun* **1** 🔵 a series of special events or performances: *a dance/music festival* **2** 🔵 a special day or period when people celebrate something, especially a religious event: *the Jewish festival of Hanukkah*

fever /ˈfiːvər/ *noun* 🔵 a high body temperature that happens because someone is sick

feverish /ˈfiːvərɪʃ/ *adj* having a fever

few /fjuː/ *quantifier* **1 a few** 🔵 some, or a small number of: *I'm only here for a few days.* ○ *I've met a few of her friends.* **2 quite a few** 🔵 a large number of: *Quite a few people have had the same problem.* **3** 🔵 not many, or only a small number of: *Very few people can afford to pay those prices.*

fiancé /ˌfiːɑːnˈseɪ/, /fiˈɑːnseɪ/ *noun* Someone's fiancé is the man that the person will marry.

fiancée

132

fiancée /ˌfiˌɑnˈseɪ/,/ˈfiˈɑn·seɪ/ noun
Someone's fiancée is the woman that the person will marry.

fiber /ˈfaɪ·bər/ noun **1** [no plural] a substance in foods such as vegetables that helps other foods pass through the body easily: *This cereal is **high in fiber**.* **2** one of the thin threads that cloth is made of: *Cotton fibers can be woven into fabric.*

fiction /ˈfɪk·ʃən/ noun [no plural] **B1** books and stories about imaginary people and events: *She is a writer of children's fiction.*

field /fild/ noun **1** **A2** an area of land used for growing crops or keeping animals **2** **B1** an area of land where you can play a sport: *a football field* **3** an area of study or activity: *He's an expert in the field of chemistry.*

field hockey /ˈfild ˌhɑk·i/ noun [no plural] a game that two teams play on grass, in which players hit a ball with long curved sticks

fierce /fɪərs/ adj **1** violent or angry: *a fierce dog* ○ *a fierce attack* **2** very strong or powerful: *fierce wind* **3** showing strong feeling or energetic activity: *There is fierce competition among computer companies.*

fifteen /ˈfɪfˈtin/ **A1** the number 15

fifteenth /ˈfɪfˈtinθ/ 15th written as a word

fifth¹ /fɪfθ/ **A2** 5th written as a word

fifth² /fɪfθ/ noun **B1** one of five equal parts of something; 1/5

fifties /ˈfɪf·tiz/ plural noun **1** the fifties the years from 1950 to 1959: *He was born **in the fifties**.* **2** be in your fifties to be aged between 50 and 59: *My dad is **in his fifties**.*

fifty¹ /ˈfɪf·ti/ **A2** the number 50
• **fiftieth** 50th written as a word

fifty² /ˈfɪf·ti/ noun a fifty-dollar bill: *Do you have anything smaller than a fifty?*

fig /fɪg/ noun a dark, sweet fruit with lots of seeds

fight¹ /faɪt/ verb (past tense and past participle **fought**) **1** **B1** to try to hurt someone

using your body or weapons: *Two men were fighting outside the bar.* **2** to argue: *Don't fight in front of the children!* **3** to take part in a war: *I'm proud that I fought for my country.* **4** to try hard to stop something bad from happening: *She **fought against** racism.* **5** to try hard to get or achieve something: *They are **fighting for** their freedom.*

fight² /faɪt/ noun **1** **B1** a situation in which people try to hurt each other using their body or weapons: *He gets into a lot of fights with his brother.* **2** an argument: *We had a big fight about money.* **3** a situation in which people try very hard to achieve something or to stop something: *She was brave in her **fight against** cancer.* ○ *a **fight for** freedom*

figure¹ /ˈfɪg·jər/ noun **1** **B1** a symbol for a number: *Write down the amount in words and figures.* **2** **B1** the shape of someone's body, usually an attractive shape: *That big coat hides her figure.* **3** a person that you cannot see clearly: *I could see two figures in the distance.* **4** a particular type of person, often someone important or famous: *Kennedy was a major figure in American politics.*

figure² /ˈfɪg·jər/ verb (present participle **figuring**, past tense and past participle **figured**)

figure something/someone out phrasal verb to think about and then understand something or someone: *I can't figure this map out.*

file¹ /faɪl/ noun **1** **A2** a collection of information stored electronically: *Do you want to download these files?* **2** **A2** a box or folded piece of thick paper used to store documents: *files full of personal papers*
→ See **The Office** on page C12 **3** a small tool with a rough edge that is used to make a surface smooth: *a nail file*

file² /faɪl/ verb (present participle **filing**, past tense and past participle **filed**) **1** to put documents into an ordered system so that you can easily find them: *She filed all her tax returns under T.* **2** to rub something with a rough tool in order to make it smooth

|ou go|aɪər fire|auər hour|eər hair|ɪər ear|uər poor|j yet|ʒ measure|ʃ ship|dʒ judge|tʃ chin|ð that|θ thin|ŋ hang|

file cabinet /ˈfaɪl ˌkæb·ə·nət/ *noun* a piece of office furniture with deep drawers for storing documents

file cabinet

fill /fɪl/ *verb*
1 🔵 to make a container or space full, or to become full: *He filled the bucket with water.* ○ *The bathtub should fill in five minutes.* **2** 🔵 If people or things fill a space, there are a lot of them in it: *The streets were **filled with** tourists.* **3** 🔵 If light, sound, or a smell fills a place, you can easily notice it: *The smell of smoke filled the room.*

fill *something* **in/out** *phrasal verb* 🔵 to write all the information that is needed on a document: *Please fill out this form.*

fill (*something***) up** *phrasal verb* 🔵 to become full, or to make something become full: *The restaurant soon filled up with people.*

filling /ˈfɪl·ɪŋ/ *noun* a hard substance that is put in a hole in a tooth

film[1] /fɪlm/ *noun* **1** 🔵 a movie: *a foreign film* **2** special thin plastic used for making photographs

film[2] /fɪlm/ *verb* 🔵 to record moving pictures with a camera, usually to make a movie: *They filmed for a week in Spain.*

filmmaker /ˈfɪlmˌmeɪ·kər/ *noun* 🔵 someone who makes movies or television shows

filter /ˈfɪl·tər/ *noun* a device that you pass liquid through in order to remove particular substances: *a coffee filter*
• **filter** *verb*

filthy /ˈfɪl·θi/ *adj* (comparative **filthier**, superlative **filthiest**) very dirty: *filthy clothes*

fin /fɪn/ *noun* a thin, flat part on a fish that helps it to swim

final[1] /ˈfaɪ·nºl/ *adj* 🔵 last or coming at the end: *the final paragraph* ○ *They scored a goal in the final minute.*

final[2] /ˈfaɪ·nºl/ *noun* 🔵 (also **finals**) the last part of a competition to decide who will win: *college basketball finals*

finally /ˈfaɪ·nºl·i/ *adv* 🔵 **1** after a long time: *We finally got home at midnight.* **2** 🔵 used before you say the last point or idea: *Finally, I'd like to thank everyone for coming.*

finals /ˈfaɪ·nºlz/ *plural noun* exams that you take at the end of a school course

finance[1] /ˈfaɪ·næns/, /fəˈnæns/ *noun* [no plural] the control of the way large amounts of money are spent: *She wants to get a job in finance.*

finance[2] /ˈfaɪ·næns/, /fəˈnæns/ *verb* (present participle **financing**, past tense and past participle **financed**) to give the money that is needed to do something: *Who is financing the project?*

finances /ˈfaɪ·næn·sɪz/ *plural noun* the money that a person, company, or country earns and spends: *They need to keep better track of their finances.*

financial /faɪˈnæn·ʃəl/ *adj* 🔵 relating to money or how money is used: *financial advice*
• **financially** *adv* *He's still financially dependent on his parents.*

find /faɪnd/ *verb* (past tense and past participle **found**) **1** 🔵 to discover something or someone that you have been looking for: *I can't find my car keys.* **2** 🔵 to discover something by chance: *I found some money in my coat pocket.* **3** 🔵 to become aware of something: *I came home to find the kitchen window had been broken.* **4** 🔵 to think or feel a particular way about someone or something: *I find tests very stressful.* **5 find** *someone* **guilty** to judge that someone is guilty in a court of law: *She was found guilty of murder.* **6 find** *yourself* **somewhere/doing** *something* to become aware that you have gone somewhere or done something without intending to: *I woke up and found myself in a hospital bed.* **7 be found** to exist or be present somewhere: *Many animals are found only in Australia.*

find (*something***) out** *phrasal verb* 🔵 to get information about something: *Did you find out Ruby's phone number?*

a
b
c
d
e
f
g
h
i
j
k
l
m
n
o
p
q
r
s
t
u
v
w
x
y
z

fine¹ /faɪn/ *adj* **1** well, healthy, or happy: *"How are you?" "I'm fine, thanks. And you?"* **2** (that's) fine used to agree with a suggestion: *"Should we meet at eight tonight?" "Yes, that's fine."* **3** good enough: *"Is the soup okay?" "Yes, it's fine."* **4** excellent, or of very good quality: *fine wines* **5** thin: *fine brown hair*

fine² /faɪn/ *noun* **B1** an amount of money that you must pay for doing something wrong: *a library fine (= for bringing a book back late)*

fine³ /faɪn/ *verb* (present participle **fining**, past tense and past participle **fined**) to punish someone by making him or her pay some money

fine⁴ /faɪn/ *adv* very well, or without any problems: *"How did your test go?" "It went fine, I think."*

finger /ˈfɪŋ.ɡər/ *noun* **A2** one of the five long parts at the end of your hand
→ See **The Body** on page C2

finger

fingernail

fingertip

fingernail /ˈfɪŋ.ɡər.neɪl/ *noun* the hard, thin part on the top of the end of your finger
→ See picture at **finger**

fingerprint /ˈfɪŋ.ɡər.prɪnt/ *noun* the mark made on something by the pattern of curved lines on the end of someone's finger: *The police found fingerprints on the murder weapon.*

fingertip /ˈfɪŋ.ɡər.tɪp/ *noun* the end of your finger
→ See picture at **finger**

finish¹ /ˈfɪn.ɪʃ/ *verb* **1** **A1** to stop doing something, because nothing more needs to be done: *Did you finish your homework? ○ We finished planting the garden.* **2** **A1** to end: *The meeting will finish at five o'clock.* **3** **B1** (also **finish off/up**) to eat, drink, or use something completely: *They finished their coffee and left the restaurant.*

finish *something* **off** *phrasal verb* to do the last part of something: *I have to finish off this report by Friday.*

finish² /ˈfɪn.ɪʃ/ *noun* **B1** the end of a race, or the last part of something: *I enjoyed the movie from start to finish.*

fir /fɜr/ *noun* a tree with very thin, straight leaves that do not fall off in the winter

fire¹ /faɪər/ *noun* **1** **A2** heat, light, and flames that are made when something burns: *Three people were killed in the fire.* **2** **catch fire** **B1** to start burning: *Dry grass can catch fire easily.* **3** **be on fire** **B1** to be burning: *That house is on fire.* **4** **set fire to** *something* to make something start burning: *Enemy troops set fire to the village.* **5** **B1** a pile of wood or coal that is burning to produce heat: *He sat close to the fire to keep warm.* **6** **open fire (on** *someone***)** to start shooting with guns, usually at a group of people: *Suddenly, the soldiers opened fire on the enemy.*

fire² /faɪər/ *verb* (present participle **firing**, past tense and past participle **fired**) **1** to shoot a bullet from a gun: *She fired three shots at the target.* **2** to tell someone that he or she must leave his or her job: *She was fired for stealing from the company.*

fire department /ˈfaɪər dɪˌpɑrt.mənt/ *noun* an organization of people whose job is to stop fires

fire engine /ˈfaɪər ˌen.dʒɪn/ *noun* a vehicle for carrying firefighters and equipment for stopping large fires

fire escape /ˈfaɪər ɪˌskeɪp/ *noun* a set of metal stairs on the outside of a building that people can use to leave if there is a fire

fire extinguisher /ˈfaɪər ɪkˌstɪŋ.ɡwɪʃ.ər/ *noun* a piece of equipment that is used to stop small fires

firefighter /ˈfaɪərˌfaɪ.tər/ *noun* **B1** someone whose job is to stop fires from burning

firehouse /ˈfaɪərˌhaʊs/ *noun* another word for fire station

fireman /ˈfaɪər·mən/ **noun** (plural **firemen**) a man whose job is to stop fires from burning

fireplace /ˈfaɪərˌpleɪs/ **noun** the open part of a wall in a room where you can make a fire

fire station /ˈfaɪərˌsteɪ·ʃən/ **noun** a building where fire engines are kept, and firefighters wait when they are not fighting fires

fireworks /ˈfaɪərˌwɜrks/ **plural noun** **B1** small objects that explode and make loud noises and bright colors in the sky: *a fireworks display*

fireworks

firm¹ /fɜrm/ **adj** **1** not soft, but not completely hard: *A firm bed is better for your back.* **2** strongly fixed in place: *Get a firm grip on the ladder before you climb up.* **3** If you are firm, you show people that you are strong and in control: *My parents were always very firm with me.* **4** certain and not likely to change: *We don't have any firm plans yet.*
• **firmly adv** *The door was firmly shut.* ○ *"Let me do it," she said firmly.* ○ *She was firmly convinced that she was right.*

firm² /fɜrm/ **noun** a company that sells goods or services: *a law firm*

first¹ /fɜrst/ **adj** **1** **A1** coming before all others: *Ken was the first person to arrive.*

2 **A2** most important: *Sheila won **first prize** in the photo competition.* **3** **A2** 1st written as a word

first² /fɜrst/ **adv** **1** **A1** before everything or everyone else: *Jason **came in first** in the race (= he won).* **2** **B1** for the first time: *I first met him last year.* **3 at first** **B1** at the beginning of a situation or period of time: *I didn't like her at first, but now we are friends.* **4 first; first of all** **B1** before doing anything else: *First of all, make sure you have permission.*

first³ /fɜrst/ **noun, pronoun** **the first** **B1** the first person or thing: *I liked the second movie more than the first.* ○ *I was the first to arrive at the party.*

first aid /ˈfɜrst ˈeɪd/ **noun** [no plural] basic help that someone who is not a doctor can give to a person who is hurt or sick: *The police officer **gave** him **first aid** before the ambulance arrived.*

first-class /ˈfɜrstˈklæs/ **adj** relating to the best and most expensive quality or service: *a first-class ticket* ○ *first-class wines*
• **first class adv** *I want to travel first class.*

first language /ˈfɜrst ˈlæŋ·gwɪdʒ/ **noun** the language that someone learns to speak first: *Marie's first language is French, but she also speaks German fluently.*

first name /ˈfɜrst ˈneɪm/ **noun** **A2** the name that comes before your family name: *What is Mrs. Jackson's first name?*

fish¹ /fɪʃ/ **noun** (plural **fish, fishes**) **A1** an animal that lives only in water, swims, and can be eaten as food

> **! Common mistake: fish or fishes?**
>
> Fish is the usual plural of fish.
> *I caught six fish in the river.*
> ~~I caught six fishes in the river.~~
> **Fishes** is sometimes used to talk about different types of fish.

fish² /fɪʃ/ **verb** **B1** to try to catch fish

a
b
c
d
e
f
g
h
i
j
k
l
m
n
o
p
q
r
s
t
u
v
w
x
y
z

fisherman /ˈfɪʃ·ər·mən/ *noun* (plural **fishermen**) someone who catches fish as a job or as a hobby

fishing /ˈfɪʃ·ɪŋ/ *noun* [no plural] **A2** the sport or job of catching fish: *Dad loves to go fishing.* ○ *a fishing boat*

fist /fɪst/ *noun*
a hand closed into a ball with the fingers and thumb curled tightly together: *He banged his fist angrily on the table.*

fist

fit[1] /fɪt/ *verb* (present participle **fitting**, past tense and past participle **fitted**) **1** **B1** to be the right shape or size for someone or something: *This shirt doesn't fit me anymore.* **2** **B1** If people or things fit somewhere, that place is big enough for them: *How many people can you fit in your car?*

fit in with *something* phrasal verb
If one thing fits in with another thing, they look pleasant together or are suitable for each other: *It's a very nice couch, but it doesn't fit in with the rest of the room.*

fit[2] /fɪt/ *adj* (comparative **fitter**, superlative **fittest**) **1** **A2** healthy, especially because you exercise a lot: *He's very fit for his age.* → Opposite **unfit** *adj* **2** good enough for a particular purpose: *Is this water fit to drink?*

fitness /ˈfɪt·nəs/ *noun* [no plural] **B1** the condition of being physically strong and healthy: *I'm trying to improve my fitness by biking to work.*

fitness center /ˈfɪt·nəs ˌsen·tər/ *noun* a building or a place in a building with equipment that people can use for exercising: *the hotel's fitness center*

fitting room /ˈfɪt·ɪŋ ˌrum/, /ˈfɪt·ɪŋ ˌrʊm/ *noun* a room in a store where you can try on clothes

five[1] /faɪv/ **A1** the number 5

five[2] /faɪv/ *noun* a five-dollar bill: *Here's a five to pay the tip.*

fix /fɪks/ *verb* **1** **B1** to repair something: *Can you fix my watch?* **2** to prepare a drink or meal: *I'll fix you a sandwich.*

fix *something* **up** phrasal verb **B1** to repair or change something so it can be used or looks better: *She's almost finished fixing up her new apartment.*

flag /flæɡ/ *noun*
B1 a piece of cloth with a special design and colors, that is the symbol of a country or group

flag

flake /fleɪk/ *noun* a small, flat, thin piece of something: *flakes of skin*

flame /fleɪm/ *noun* hot, bright, burning gas made by something on fire: *The car crashed and burst into flames* (=suddenly started burning).

flap[1] /flæp/ *noun* something that hangs over an opening and is attached on one side

flap[2] /flæp/ *verb* (present participle **flapping**, past tense and past participle **flapped**) If a bird flaps its wings, it moves them up and down.

flash[1] /flæʃ/ *verb* **1** to shine brightly and suddenly, or to make something shine in this way: *The doctor flashed a light into my eye.* **2** (also **flash up**) to appear for a short time, or to make something appear for a short time: *An icon flashed up on the screen.*

flash[2] /flæʃ/ *noun* **1** a sudden bright light: *The bomb exploded in a flash of yellow light.* **2** a piece of camera equipment that produces a bright light when you take a photograph in a dark place

flashlight /ˈflæʃ·laɪt/ *noun* a small electric light that you hold in your hand

flashlight

flat[1] /flæt/ *adj* (comparative **flatter**, superlative **flattest**) **1** **B1** smooth and level, with no lumps or curves: *a flat surface* ○ *The land around here is very flat.* **2** If a tire is flat, it does not contain enough air.

|ου go|aɪər fire|aʊər hour|ear hair|ɪər ear|ʊər poor|j yet|ʒ measure|ʃ ship|dʒ judge|tʃ chin|ð that|θ thin|ŋ hang|

flat

flat

curved

round

hollow

flat^2 /flæt/ **adv** in a horizontal or level position: *Lie flat on your back and relax.*

flatter /ˈflæt̬·ər/ **verb** to say nice things to someone to please him or her, or because you want something from that person: *He flattered me with his compliments.*

flattering /ˈflæt̬·ə·rɪŋ/ **adj** making you look more attractive than usual: *a flattering dress*

flavor /ˈfleɪ·vər/ **noun** **B1** the taste of a type of food or drink: *We sell 50 different flavors of ice cream.*

flea /fli/ **noun** a small, jumping insect that lives on animals or people and drinks their blood

flee /fli/ **verb** (present participle **fleeing**, past tense and past participle **fled**) to leave a place quickly because you are in danger: *He fled the country during the war.*

fleece /flis/ **noun** **1** a warm, soft jacket, or the material used to make it **2** the thick covering of wool on a sheep

fleet /flit/ **noun** a group of ships

flesh /fleʃ/ **noun** [no plural] the soft part under the skin of a person's or animal's body

flew /flu/ past tense of fly

flexibility /ˌflek·səˈbɪl·ɪ·t̬i/ **noun** [no plural] the ability to change or be changed easily to suit different situations: *The advantage of this computer system is its flexibility.*

flexible /ˈflek·sə·bəl/ **adj** **1** able to change or be changed easily according to the situation: *I'd like a job with more flexible hours.* **2** able to bend easily without breaking

flight /flaɪt/ **noun** **A2** a trip in a plane

flight attendant /ˈflaɪt əˌten·dənt/ **noun** someone whose job is to take care of passengers on a plane

fling /flɪŋ/ **verb** (present participle **flinging**, past tense and past participle **flung**) to suddenly throw something: *She flung her jacket on the sofa.*

flirt /flɜrt/ **verb** to behave as if you are sexually attracted to someone: *She was **flirting with** a guy at the bar.*

float /floʊt/ **verb** **1** **B1** to stay on the surface of a liquid and not go under: *I like floating on my back in the pool.* **2** **B1** to move gently through the air: *A balloon floated across the sky.*

float

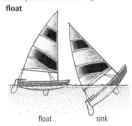

float   sink

flock /flɑk/ **noun** a group of birds or sheep: *a flock of geese*

flood^1 /flʌd/ **verb** **1** **B1** to become covered with water: *Our basement flooded during the storm.* **2** to fill or enter a place in large numbers or amounts: *She opened the curtains and sunlight flooded the room.*

flood^2 /flʌd/ **noun** **B1** a large amount of water that covers an area that is usually dry: *The flood destroyed thousands of homes.*

a
b
c
d
e
f
g
h
i
j
k
l
m
n
o
p
q
r
s
t
u
v
w
x
y
z

flood

floodlights /ˈflʌdˌlaɪts/ noun powerful lights used at night to light up sports fields or the outside of buildings

floor /flɔr/ noun **1** **A1** a surface that you walk on inside a building: *a wooden floor* **2** **A2** a particular level of a building: *the second/third floor* **3** **B1** an area where a particular activity happens: *a dance floor*

florist /ˈflɔrɪst/ noun **1** someone who sells and arranges flowers in a store **2** a store that sells flowers

flour /flaʊər/ noun [no plural] **B1** a powder made from grain that is used to make bread and cakes

flourish /ˈflɜrɪʃ/ verb to grow or develop well: *The tourist industry is flourishing.*

flow /floʊ/ verb **B1** If a liquid flows, it moves somewhere in a smooth, continuous way: *The river flows from the mountains to the ocean.*
• **flow** noun the continuous, smooth movement of something: *the flow of traffic through the town*

flower /ˈflaʊər/ noun **A1** the attractive colored part of a plant where the seeds grow: *a bunch of flowers*
→ See **Quantities** on page C14

flown /floʊn/ past participle of fly

flu /flu/ noun [no plural] **B1** an illness like a very bad cold that causes pains and fever

fluent /ˈfluənt/ adj **1** able to use a language naturally and well: *She is **fluent in** six languages.* **2** produced or done

in a smooth, natural style: *He speaks fluent Korean.*
• **fluency** noun *The job requires fluency in French.*
• **fluently** adv *I'd like to speak English fluently.*

fluff /flʌf/ noun [no plural] small, loose bits of wool or other soft material

fluffy /ˈflʌf·i/ adj (comparative **fluffier**, superlative **fluffiest**) very light and soft to touch: *a fluffy kitten*

fluid /ˈflu·ɪd/ noun a liquid: *Drink plenty of fluids.*

flush /flʌʃ/ verb to clean something, especially a toilet, by sending water through it: *Remember to **flush** the **toilet** when you are done.*

flute /flut/ noun **B1** a musical instrument that you hold out to the side and play by blowing into it

flutter /ˈflʌt̬·ər/ verb to move quickly and gently in the air: *The flag was fluttering in the breeze.*

fly[1] /flaɪ/ verb (present participle **flying**, past tense **flew**, past participle **flown**) **1** **A1** to travel through the air in a plane or other aircraft: *I'm flying to Hawaii tomorrow.* **2** **A2** to move through the air: *The bird flew up into a tree.* **3** to control a plane or other aircraft in the sky: *He learned to fly in the military.* **4** to move somewhere very quickly: *He grabbed some clothes and flew down the stairs.*

fly[2] /flaɪ/ noun **1** **B1** (plural **flies**) a small insect with two wings → See picture at **insect** **2** [no plural] the part where pants open and close at the front

foam /foʊm/ noun [no plural] a lot of small, white bubbles on the surface of a liquid

focus[1] /ˈfoʊ·kəs/ noun **1** in focus If a picture is in focus, it is clear: *Try to get your subject in focus.* **2** out of focus If a picture is out of focus, it is not clear: *The photos were all out of focus.* **3** the person or thing that is getting most attention in a situation or activity: *He is the focus of a police investigation.*

focus² /'fou·kəs/ *verb* to adjust something, such as a camera, so that the picture is clear: *This camera is easy to focus.*

focus on *someone/something* phrasal verb to give most of your attention to someone or something: *Try to focus on the most important facts.*

fog /fɑg/, /fɔg/ *noun* [no plural] **A2** a thick cloud close to the ground that makes it difficult to see: *The fog should lift (= go away) by this afternoon.*
• **foggy** *adj* (comparative **foggier**, superlative **foggiest**) **A2** *a foggy day*

foil /fɔɪl/ *noun* [no plural] metal made into very thin sheets like paper, used mainly for covering food: *aluminum foil*

fold¹ /fould/ *verb* **1** **B1** to bend something so that one part of it lies flat on top of another part: *Can you help me fold the sheets?* **2** **fold your arms** to bend your arms across your chest, with one crossing over the other: *He sat with his arms folded.*

fold² /fould/ *noun* a line made where paper or cloth is folded: ***Make a fold** across the center of the card.*

folder /'foul·dər/ *noun* **1** **A2** a folded piece of plastic or thick paper used to store loose papers → See **The Office** on page C12 **2** **B1** a place on a computer where particular files (= documents, pictures) are kept

folk /fouk/ *adj* **B1** typical of the people of a particular group or country: *folk music/art/dancing*

folks /fouks/ *noun* (also **folk**) informal people: *old folks ○ I'm still living with **my folks** (= my parents).*

follow /'fɑl·ou/ *verb* **1** **A2** to move behind someone or something and go where they go: *She followed me into the kitchen.* **2** **B1** to happen or come after something: *There was a bang, **followed by** a cloud of smoke.* **3** **follow a path/road** **B1** to travel along a path or road: *Follow the main road down to the traffic lights.* **4** **follow instructions/orders** **B1** to do what instructions or orders say you should do: *Did you follow the instructions on the box?* **5** **B1** to understand

something: *Could you say that again? I didn't really follow.* **6** **as follows** used to introduce a list or description: *The main reasons are as follows.*

following¹ /'fɑl·ou·ɪŋ/ *adj* **the following day, morning, etc. B1** the next day, morning, etc.

following² /'fɑl·ou·ɪŋ/ *preposition* after or as a result of: *Following a long illness, he died in October.*

fond /fɑnd/ *adj* **1** **be fond of *someone/something* B1** to like someone or something: *We're very fond of each other.* **2** expressing or causing happy feelings: *I have fond memories of my childhood.*

food /fud/ *noun* **A1** something that people and animals eat to keep them alive: *baby/dog food ○ You should eat healthy foods.*

food processor /'fud ˌprɑ·ses·ər/ *noun* a kitchen machine used for cutting or mixing food very quickly
→ See **The Kitchen** on page C10

fool¹ /ful/ *noun* **1** **B1** a stupid person **2** **make a fool of *yourself*** to behave in a silly or embarrassing way: *He got drunk and made a fool of himself.*

fool² /ful/ *verb* to trick someone: *He fooled the old man into giving him the money.*

fool around phrasal verb to behave in a silly way: *Stop fooling around – this is serious!*

foolish /'fu·lɪʃ/ *adj* silly: *a foolish mistake ○ You'd be foolish to ignore his advice.*
• **foolishly** *adv* *I foolishly didn't write her phone number down.*

foot /fʊt/ *noun* **1** **A1** (plural **feet**) one of the two flat parts on the ends of your legs that you stand on: *bare feet*
→ See **The Body** on page C2 **2** **B1** (plural **foot, feet**) (written abbreviation **ft.**) a unit for measuring length, equal to 12 inches: *Alex is about 6 feet tall.* **3** the **foot of *something*** the bottom of something: *He was standing at the foot of the stairs.* **4** **on foot** **A2** walking: *I usually go to school on foot.*

a
b
c
d
e
f
g
h
i
j
k
l
m
n
o
p
q
r
s
t
u
v
w
x
y
z

football /ˈfʊtˌbɔl/ *noun* **1** **A1** the oval ball used in the game of football
→ See picture at **ball** **2** **A2** [no plural] a game in which two teams of 11 players try to kick, carry, or throw a ball across the other team's line: *a football team*
→ See **Sports 2** on page C16

footprint /ˈfʊtˌprɪnt/ *noun* a mark made by a foot or shoe

footstep /ˈfʊtˌstep/ *noun* the sound of a foot hitting the ground when someone walks: *I heard footsteps behind me and quickly turned around.*

for /fɔr/ *preposition* **1** **A1** to be given to or used by someone or something: *I bought a dress for their new baby.* ○ *We need some curtains for the bedroom.* **2** **A1** used to show an amount of time or distance: *We walked for miles.* ○ *I lived with my parents for a year.* **3** **A2** having a particular purpose: *What are those large scissors for?* **4** **A2** because of something: *New York is famous for its buildings.* **5** **A2** in exchange for something, especially an amount of money: *How much did you pay for your computer?* **6** **A2** on the occasion of: *What did you buy him for his birthday?* **7** **A2** at a particular time: *I reserved a table at the restaurant for nine o'clock.* **8** **A2** toward or in the direction of: *Just follow the signs for the airport.* **9** **A2** meaning or representing something: *What's the German word for "cucumber"?* **10** **B1** in order to help someone: *I'll carry those bags for you.* **11** **B1** representing a country, school, or organization: *He plays football for Michigan.* **12** supporting or agreeing with someone or something: *Who did you vote for?* **13** used when comparing something to a particular fact: *She's very tall for her age.*

forbid /fərˈbɪd/ *verb* (present participle **forbidding**, past tense **forbade**, past participle **forbidden**) to tell someone that he or she must not do something: *The school forbids students to smoke.* ○ *National Park regulations forbid hunting.*
• **forbidden** *adj* *Smoking is forbidden (= not allowed) in this area.*

force¹ /fɔrs/ *noun* **1** [no plural] physical power or strength: *The army has gained power by force.* **2** a group of people who work together for a particular purpose, for example in military service: *the police force* ○ *the United States Air Force*

force² /fɔrs/ *verb* (present participle **forcing**, past tense and past participle **forced**) **1** to make someone do something that he or she does not want to do: *You can't force her to eat.* **2** to make an object move by pushing or pulling it hard: *She forced the window shut.*

forecast¹ /ˈfɔrˌkæst/ *noun* **B1** something that says what will happen in the future: *the weather forecast*

forecast² /ˈfɔrˌkæst/ *verb* (past tense and past participle **forecast**) to say what will happen in the future: *They're forecasting more snow for this area.*
• **forecaster** *noun* *a weather forecaster*

forehead /ˈfɑrˌəd/, /ˈfɔrˌhed/ *noun* **B1** the part of your face between your eyes and your hair
→ See **The Body** on page C2

foreign /ˈfɔrˌən/, /ˈfɑrˌən/ *adj* **A2** from a country that is not yours: *a foreign language/student*

foreigner /ˈfɔrˌə-nər/, /ˈfɑrˌə-nər/ *noun* **B1** a person from another country

foresee /fɔrˈsi/ *verb* (present participle **foreseeing**, past tense **foresaw**, past participle **foreseen**) to think that something will happen in the future: *I don't foresee any problems with the project.*

forest /ˈfɔrˌəst/, /ˈfɑrˌəst/ *noun* **A2** a large area of trees growing close together: *a pine forest*

forever /fərˈevˌər/, /fɔrˈevˌər/ *adv* **B1** for all time in the future: *I want to live here forever.*

forgave /fərˈgeɪv/ past tense of forgive

forge /fɔrdʒ/ *verb* (present participle **forging**, past tense and past participle **forged**) to make an illegal copy of something in order to deceive people: *She forged his signature.*

| oʊ **go** | ɑːr **fire** | aʊər **hour** | eər **hair** | ɪər **ear** | ʊər **poor** | j **yet** | ʒ **measure** | ʃ **ship** | dʒ **judge** | tʃ **chin** | ð **that** | θ **thin** | ŋ **hang** |

forget /fər'ɡet/ **verb** (present participle **forgetting**, past tense **forgot**, past participle **forgotten**) **1** 🅰2 to not bring something with you because you did not remember it: *I forgot my umbrella.* **2** 🅱1 to not remember something: *I forgot his name.* ○ *Don't forget to feed the cat.* **3** 🅱1 (also **forget about**) to stop thinking about someone or something: *Let's try to forget about work.*

> ⚠ **Common mistake: forget or leave?**
>
> With **forget**, you do not mention the place where you left the thing.
>
> ~~I forgot my phone at home.~~
>
> You use **leave** to say that you forgot an object when you left a place or when you got off the bus, train, etc.
>
> *I left my umbrella on the bus.*
> ~~I forgot my umbrella on the bus.~~

forgetful /fər'ɡet·fəl/ **adj** often forgetting things: *She's 84 now and a little forgetful.*

forgive /fər'ɡɪv/ **verb** (present participle **forgiving**, past tense **forgave**, past participle **forgiven**) 🅱1 to decide not to be angry with someone, or not to punish him or her for something bad he or she has done: *Jane never forgave her mother for lying to her.*

forgot /fər'ɡɑt/ past tense of forget

forgotten /fər'ɡɑt·ᵊn/ past participle of forget

fork /fɔrk/ **noun** 🅰2 a small tool with three or four points and a handle, used to eat with: *a knife and fork*

form[1] /fɔrm/ **noun 1** 🅰2 a printed document with spaces for you to write information: *Please fill in the form using black ink.* **2** 🅱1 a way of writing or saying a word that shows if it is singular or plural, past or present, etc.: *"Isn't" is the short form of "is not."* **3** a type of something or way of doing something: *Swimming is the best form of exercise.* **4** the body or shape of someone or something: *paintings of the human form*

form[2] /fɔrm/ **verb 1** 🅱1 to make something by putting different parts together: *In English you form the present participle by adding "-ing" to the verb.* **2** to begin to exist, or to make something begin to exist: *This plant forms new leaves in the spring.* **3** to start an organization or business: *Brown formed her own company last year.* **4** to make a shape: *Hold hands and form a circle.*

formal /'fɔr·məl/ **adj 1** used about clothes, language, and behavior that are serious or very polite: *a formal dinner party* **2** public or official: *a formal announcement*

formation /fɔr'meɪ·ʃən/ **noun** [no plural] the development of something into a particular thing or shape: *the formation of a star*

former /'fɔr·mər/ **adj** 🅱1 happening or existing in the past but not now: *the former Soviet Union*

formerly /'fɔr·mər·li/ **adv** in the past: *Mumbai was formerly called Bombay.*

formula /'fɔr·mjə·lə/ **noun** (plural **formulas, formulae**) a list of the substances that something is made of: *What is the formula for water?*

forth /fɔrθ/ **adv** in a forward direction: used mainly in the phrase "back and forth"

forties /'fɔr·tiz/ **plural noun 1 the forties** the years from 1940 to 1949: *My family left India in the forties.* **2 be in your forties** to be aged between 40 and 49: *She's probably in her early forties.*

fortieth /'fɔr·ti·əθ/ 40th written as a word

fortunate /'fɔr·tʃə·nət/ **adj** lucky: *It was fortunate that our plane was not late.*
→ Opposite **unfortunate** adj

fortunately /'fɔr·tʃə·nət·li/ **adv** 🅱1 happening as a result of good luck: *Fortunately, no one was hurt in the fire.*
→ Opposite **unfortunately** adv

fortune /'fɔr·tʃən/ **noun 1** a lot of money: *Nick's new car must have cost a*

a
b
c
d
e
f
g
h
i
j
k
l
m
n
o
p
q
r
s
t
u
v
w
x
y
z

fortune! **2** the good or bad things that happen to you: *The family's fortunes changed almost overnight.*

forty /ˈfɔr·t̮i/ **A2** the number 40

forward /ˈfɔr·wərd/ *adv* **B1** toward the direction that is in front of you: *She leaned forward to make sure I could hear her.* ○ *Please step forward when I call your name.*

forwards /ˈfɔr·wərdz/ *adv* another form of forward

fought /fɔt/ past tense and past participle of fight

foul /faʊl/ *adj* very dirty or bad: *a foul smell* ○ *The bathrooms were foul.*

found[1] /faʊnd/ past tense and past participle of find

found[2] /faʊnd/ *verb* to start an organization, especially by giving money: *He founded the charity in 1861.*

foundation /faʊnˈdeɪ·ʃən/ *noun* the part of a building that is under the ground and supports it: *The house has a concrete foundation.*

fountain /ˈfaʊn·t̮ən/ *noun* **B1** a structure that forces water up into the air as a decoration

four /fɔr/ **A1** the number 4

fourteen /ˈfɔrˈtin/ **A1** the number 14

fourteenth /ˈfɔrˈtinθ/ 14th written as a word

fourth[1] /fɔrθ/ **A2** 4th written as a word

fourth[2] /fɔrθ/ *noun* one of four equal parts of something; 1/4

the Fourth of July /ˈfɔrθ əv dʒəˈlaɪ/ *noun* (also **Independence Day**) July 4, a public holiday in the U.S.

fox /faks/ *noun* a wild animal like a dog with brown fur and a long thick tail

fraction /ˈfræk·ʃən/ *noun* a number less than 1, such as 1/2 or 3/4

fracture /ˈfræk·tʃər/ *verb* (present participle **fracturing**, past tense and past participle **fractured**) to break a bone: *She fractured her ankle.*
• **fracture** *noun*

fragile /ˈfrædʒ·əl/ *adj* easy to break: *a fragile china cup*

fragment /ˈfræg·mənt/ *noun* a small piece of something larger: *fragments of pottery*

fragrance /ˈfreɪ·grəns/ *noun* a good smell: *the delicate fragrance of roses*

fragrant /ˈfreɪ·grənt/ *adj* with a good smell: *fragrant flowers*

frail /freɪl/ *adj* not strong or healthy: *a frail old lady*

frame[1] /freɪm/ *noun* **1** **B1** a structure that goes around the edge of something, such as a picture or window: *a window frame*

frame

— frame

2 the main structure of a building or vehicle that other parts are added onto: *a bicycle frame*

frame[2] /freɪm/ *verb* (present participle **framing**, past tense and past participle **framed**) to put something such as a picture into a frame: *I am going to frame this picture.*

frank /fræŋk/ *adj* honest and saying what you really think: *We had a frank discussion.*

frankly /ˈfræŋk·li/ *adv* in an honest way: *Quite frankly, I think you're making a big mistake.*

fraud /frɔd/ *noun* [no plural] something illegal a person does in order to get money: *credit card fraud*

fray /freɪ/ verb If material frays, the threads at the edge break and become loose.

freak /frik/ noun **1** informal someone who is very interested in something: *My brother is a computer freak.* **2** someone who looks strange or behaves in a strange way: *They made me feel like a freak.*

freckle /ˈfrek·əl/ noun a light brown spot on a person's skin

freckles

free¹ /fri/ adj **1** 🔵A2 costing no money: *Entry is free for children under 12.* **2** 🔵A2 not busy doing anything: *Are you free on Friday?* ○ *free time* **3** able to do things without being controlled: *People should be free to say what they think.* **4** not in prison or in a cage: *He opened the cage and set the birds free.* **5** not being used by anyone: *Is this seat free?*
• **freely** adv *For the first time in months she could move freely.*

free² /fri/ adv **1** 🔵A2 without paying money: *Children under five travel free.* **2** in a way that is not tied up, limited, or controlled: *Dogs can run free in the park.*

free³ /fri/ verb (present participle **freeing**, past tense and past participle **freed**) to allow someone to leave a prison or place where he or she has been kept: *The hostages were finally freed yesterday.*

freedom /ˈfri·dəm/ noun [no plural] the right to live in the way you want without being controlled by anyone else

freeway /ˈfriˌweɪ/ noun a long, wide road between cities, usually used by cars traveling fast

freeze /friz/ verb (present participle **freezing**, past tense **froze**, past participle **frozen**) **1** 🔵B1 If something freezes, it becomes hard and solid because it is very cold: *The pond froze overnight.* **2** 🔵B1 to make food last a long time by making it very cold and hard: *Freeze any bread that you have left over.* **3** to feel very cold: *You'll freeze if you don't*

wear a coat. **4** to suddenly stop moving, especially because you are frightened: *She saw someone outside the window and froze.*

freezer /ˈfri·zər/ noun 🔵B1 a large electric container in which food can be frozen and stored
→ See **The Kitchen** on page C10

freezing /ˈfri·zɪŋ/ adj informal 🔵B1 very cold: *It's absolutely freezing in here.*

French fries /frentʃ ˈfraɪz/ plural noun long, thin pieces of potato that have been cooked in hot oil
→ See **Food** on page C7

frequency /ˈfri·kwən·si/ noun [no plural] the number of times something is repeated: *Hurricanes have increased in frequency over the last few years.*

frequent /ˈfri·kwənt/ adj 🔵B1 happening often: *He is a frequent visitor to the museum.*

frequently /ˈfri·kwənt·li/ adv formal 🔵B1 often: *I see him very frequently.*

fresh /freʃ/ adj **1** 🔵A2 Fresh food has been made or collected recently and has not been frozen or dried: *fresh fruit/ vegetables* ○ *fresh bread* **2** 🔵B1 new or different from what existed before: *fresh ideas* **3** 🔵B1 smelling clean or feeling cool: *a fresh breeze* ○ *fresh air* **4** recently done and not yet changed by time: *a fresh coat of paint*
• **freshly** adverb *freshly washed sheets*

freshman /ˈfreʃ·mən/ noun (plural **freshmen**) a student in his or her first year of high school or college: *special meetings for new freshmen*
• **freshman** adj *my freshman year*

Friday /ˈfraɪ·deɪ/ noun 🔵A1 the day of the week after Thursday and before Saturday

fridge /frɪdʒ/ noun 🔵A2 a large electric cabinet that keeps food cold

fried /fraɪd/ adj 🔵A2 cooked in hot oil or fat: *a fried egg*

friend¹ /frend/ noun **1** 🔵A1 someone whom you know well and like: *Sarah is my best friend* (= *the friend I like most*). **2** 🔵A2 a person you write to on an Internet site: *I just added Adam as a friend on*

a
b
c
d
e
f
g
h
i
j
k
l
m
n
o
p
q
r
s
t
u
v
w
x
y
z

Facebook). **B1** to begin to know and like someone: *He's shy and finds it difficult to make friends.* **4 be friends (with someone) B1** to know and like someone: *I've been friends with Lynne for years.* **5 old friend B1** someone whom you have known and liked for a long time: *Ricardo and I are old friends.*

friend² /frend/ **verb** to connect with someone on a social website so that you can share information, pictures, etc.: *A lot of people from my old job have friended me.*

friendly /'frend·li/ **adj** (comparative **friendlier**, superlative **friendliest**)
A2 behaving in a pleasant, kind way toward someone: *a friendly face/smile*
→ Opposite **unfriendly adj**
• **friendliness noun** [no plural] *The city is famous for the friendliness of its people.*

friendship /'frend.ʃɪp/ **noun** **B1** a relationship between friends: *a close friendship*

fries /fraɪz/ **plural noun** (also **french fries**) long, thin pieces of potato that have been cooked in hot oil

fright /fraɪt/ **noun** [no plural] a sudden feeling of shock and fear: *She was shaking with fright.*

frighten /'fraɪ·tᵊn/ **verb** to make someone afraid or nervous: *It frightens me when he drives so fast.*

frightened /'fraɪ·tᵊnd/ **adj** **B1** afraid or nervous: *The kids were frightened by the thunder.* ◦ *Don't be frightened of the dog – he won't bite.*

frightening /'fraɪ·tᵊn·ɪŋ/ **adj** **B1** making you feel afraid or nervous: *a frightening movie*

fringe /frɪndʒ/ **noun** loose threads that hang along the edge of cloth as a decoration

frog /frɔg/, /frɑg/ **noun** **B1** a small, green animal with long back legs for jumping, that lives in or near water

from /frʌm/ **preposition** **1 A1** used to show the place where someone or something started: *Did you walk all the way* from the beach? ◦ *I'm flying from Chicago to Boston tomorrow.* **2 A1** used to show the time when something starts or the time when it was made or first existed: *The museum is open from 9:30 to 6:00.* **3 A1** used to say where someone was born, or where someone lives or works: *Steve's father is from Norway.* **4 A1** used to say how far away something is: *The house is about five miles from the city.* **5 A1** used to say who gave or sent something to someone: *Who are your flowers from?* **6 A2** used to say what something is made of: *juice made from oranges* **7** If you take something from a person, place, or amount, you take it away: *He took a knife from the drawer.* **8** used to say what causes something: *Deaths from heart disease continue to rise every year.* ◦ *He suffers from asthma.* **9** used to show a change in the state of someone or something: *Things went from bad to worse.*

front¹ /frʌnt/ **noun** **1 the front A2** the side of something that faces forward: *Write the address on the front of the envelope.* **2 the front A2** the part of something that is farthest forward: *He was standing right at the front.* **3 in front of something A2** close to the front part of something: *He parked the car in front of the house.* **4 in front B1** farther forward than someone or something else: *He sat in front of me.*

front² /frʌnt/ **adj** **B1** in or at the front of something: *the front door/yard*

frontier /frʌn'tɪər/ **noun** a line or border between a known area and an unknown or wild area: *Lewis and Clark were explorers of the American frontier.*

frost /frɔst/ **noun** [no plural] a thin, white layer of ice that forms on very cold surfaces

frosty /'frɔ·sti/ **adj** (comparative **frostier**, superlative **frostiest**) very cold, with a thin layer of white ice covering everything: *a frosty morning*

frown /fraʊn/ **verb** to look angry or worried by moving your eyebrows close together: *She frowned when I mentioned his name.*

froze /frouz/ past tense of freeze

frozen[1] /ˈfrou·zən/ past participle of freeze

frozen[2] /ˈfrou·zən/ adj **1** 🔵 Frozen food has been made very cold so that it will last a long time: *frozen peas* **2** 🔵 turned into ice: *The pond was frozen this morning.* **3** 🔵 informal If a person or a part of his or her body is frozen, he or she is very cold: *Will you turn the heat on? I'm frozen!*

fruit /frut/ noun 🔵 things such as apples or oranges that grow on a tree or a bush, contain seeds, and can be eaten as food: *dried/fresh fruit* ○ *I love summer fruits like berries and peaches.*
→ See **Fruits and Vegetables** on page C8

fruit salad /ˈfrut ˌsæl·əd/ noun a mixture of pieces of different types of fruit, eaten at the end of a meal or with breakfast

frustrated /ˈfrʌsˌtreɪ·tɪd/ adj annoyed because you cannot achieve or do what you want: *Are you feeling **frustrated with** your job?*

frustrating /ˈfrʌsˌtreɪ·tɪŋ/ adj making you feel annoyed because you cannot achieve or do what you want: *a frustrating situation* ○ *It's frustrating to see money being wasted like that.*

frustration /frʌsˈtreɪ·ʃən/ noun the feeling of being annoyed because you cannot achieve or do what you want: *I could sense his **frustration at** not being able to help.*

fry /fraɪ/ verb (present participle **frying**, past tense and past participle **fried**) 🔵 to cook something in hot oil or fat: *Fry the onions for two minutes.*
→ See picture at **cook**

frying pan /ˈfraɪ·ɪŋ ˌpæn/ noun 🔵 a flat, metal pan with a long handle that is used for frying food
→ See **The Kitchen** on page C10

ft. written abbreviation for foot: a unit for measuring length

fuel /ˈfjuːəl/ noun 🔵 a substance that is burned to give heat or power

fulfill /fʊlˈfɪl/ verb (present participle **fulfilling**, past tense and past participle **fulfilled**) to do something that you have promised or planned to do: *I finally fulfilled my ambition.*

full /fʊl/ adj   full

1 🔵 If a container or a space is full, it contains as many things or people as possible: *a full bottle of red wine* **2** 🔵 containing a lot of things or people: *The room was full of people.*

full   empty

3 🔵 complete and including every part: *Please give your full name and address.* **4** 🔵 the greatest possible: *We were driving at full speed all the way.* **5 in full** 🔵 completely and with nothing missing: *The bill must be paid in full by the end of the month.* **6** informal having eaten enough food: *No more for me, thanks, I'm full.*

full-time /ˈfʊlˌtaɪm/ adj 🔵 happening or working for the whole of the work week and not only part of it: *a full-time job/student*

fully /ˈfʊl·i/ adv 🔵 completely: *The restaurant is fully booked this evening.*

fun[1] /fʌn/ noun [no plural] **1** 🔵 enjoyment or pleasure, or something that gives you enjoyment or pleasure: *Did you **have fun** at the party? ○ That was fun!* **2 for fun** 🔵 for pleasure and not for any other reason: *I ran in the race, but it was just for fun.* **3 make fun of someone/something** to make a joke about someone or something in an unkind way: *The other children used to make fun of his red hair.*

fun[2] /fʌn/ adj informal 🔵 enjoyable or entertaining: *There are lots of fun things to do here.*

> ### ❗ Common mistake: **fun** or **funny**?
>
> Use **fun** to talk about something that you enjoy doing.
> *Going to the beach is fun.*
> Use **funny** to describe something that makes you laugh.
> *The movie was really funny.*

function /'fʌŋk·ʃən/ **noun** the purpose of something or someone: *Each button has a different function.*

fund /fʌnd/ **noun** an amount of money that is collected or given for a purpose: *a college fund*

funeral /'fju·nər·əl/ **noun** a ceremony for honoring a person who has died, before the body is buried or burned: *The funeral will be held next Friday.*

fungus /'fʌŋ·ɡəs/ **noun** (plural **fungi**) a type of plant without leaves that gets its food from other living or decaying things: *The mushroom is a fungus.*

funnel /'fʌn·ºl/ **noun** a tube with a wide part at the top that you use to pour liquid into a small opening

funnel

funny /'fʌn·i/ **adj** (comparative **funnier**, superlative **funniest**) **1** **A1** making you smile or laugh: *a funny story* **2** **B1** strange or unusual and not what you expect: *This chicken tastes a little funny.*

fur /fɜr/ **noun** [no plural] **B1** the thick hair that covers the bodies of some animals like cats and rabbits

furious /'fjʊər·i·əs/ **adj** very angry: *My boss was **furious with** me.*
• **furiously adv** *"Get out of here!" she shouted furiously.*

furnace /'fɜr·nəs/ **noun** a large piece of equipment that is used to heat buildings or melt metals

furniture /'fɜr·nɪ·tʃər/ **noun** [no plural] **A2** things like chairs, tables, and beds that you put into a room or building

> ### ❗ Common mistake: **furniture**
>
> Remember that you cannot make **furniture** plural. Do not say "furnitures."
> *I want to buy some new furniture for my bedroom.*

furry /'fɜr·i/ **adj** (comparative **furrier**, superlative **furriest**) covered with fur

further[1] /'fɜr·ðər/ **adv** **1** **B1** comparative of far: at or to a place or time that is a longer distance away: *The library is a little further down the road.* **2** more: *He refused to discuss the matter further.*

further[2] /'fɜr·ðər/ **adj** **A2** more or extra: *For further details about the offer, call this number.*

> ### ❗ Common mistake: **further** or **farther**?
>
> **Farther** can only be used to talk about distance.
> *The bookstore is two blocks farther south.*
> **Further** means the same as **farther** when you are talking about distance.
> *We walked further down the street.*
> *We walked farther down the street.*
> In all other situations you should use **further**.
> *Gas prices have increased further.*
> *For further information, contact our office.*

furthest /'fɜr·ðəst/ **adj, adv** **B1** superlative of far: most distant: *What is the furthest distance you can run?*

fury /'fjʊər·i/ **noun** [no plural] very strong anger: *He could hardly control his fury.*

fuse /fjuz/ **noun** a small object that stops electrical equipment from working if there is too much electricity going through it: *a fuse box*

fuss /fʌs/ **noun** **1** excitement or worry about something that is not important: *What's all the fuss about?* **2 make a fuss** to complain about something: *He made*

a fuss because I was five minutes late.
3 make a fuss over *someone* to give someone a lot of attention and treat him or her well: *My uncle always makes a fuss over the children.*

fussy /'fʌs·i/ *adj* (comparative **fussier**, superlative **fussiest**) very difficult to please and only liking particular things: *She is a fussy eater (=does not like many foods).*

future[1] /'fju·tʃər/ *noun* **1 the future** **A2** in grammar, the form of a verb that is used to talk about something that will happen **2 the future** **B1** the time that is to come: *At some point in the future, we'll probably move.* **3 in the future** **B1** beginning from now: *In the future, I'll be more careful.* **4 B1** things that will happen to someone or something in the time that is to come: *We need to discuss the future of the company.*

future[2] /'fju·tʃər/ *adj* **B1** happening or existing in the time which is to come: *in future years*

Gg

G, g /dʒi/ the seventh letter of the alphabet

g written abbreviation for gram: a unit for measuring weight

gadget /'gædʒ·ɪt/ *noun* a small piece of equipment that does a particular job: *a kitchen gadget*

gain /geɪn/ *verb* **1 B1** to get something good: *You'll gain a lot of experience from working there.* **2 B1** to increase: *He's gained a lot of weight in the last few months.*

gal. written abbreviation for gallon: a unit for measuring liquid

galaxy /'gæl·ək·si/ *noun* (plural **galaxies**) a very large group of stars held together in the universe

gale /geɪl/ *noun* a very strong wind

gallery /'gæl·ə·ri/ *noun* (plural **galleries**) **B1** a room or building that is used for showing paintings and other art to people: *an art gallery*

gallon /'gæl·ən/ *noun* (written abbreviation **gal.**) a unit for measuring liquid, equal to 4 quarts

gallop /'gæl·əp/ *verb* If a horse gallops, it runs very fast.

gamble[1] /'gæm·bəl/ *verb* (present participle **gambling**, past tense and past participle **gambled**) to try to win money by saying who will win a game, race, or competition: *He gambled away all of our savings.*

• **gambler** *noun*

• **gambling** *noun* [no plural] *People can become addicted to gambling.*

gamble[2] /'gæm·bəl/ *noun* the act of doing something that you hope will have a good result, although you know that this might make something bad happen: *Buying this place was a big gamble, but it seems to have paid off.*

game /geɪm/ *noun* **1 A1** an activity or sport that people play, usually with rules and needing skill: *a computer game* ○ *Football is such an exciting game.* ○ *Do you want to **play** a different **game**?* **2 A2** a particular occasion when people play a game: *We **played** a **game** of cards.* ○ *Who won yesterday's game?*

game show /'geɪm ˌʃoʊ/ *noun* a program on television in which people play games to try to win prizes

gang /gæŋ/ *noun* **1** a group of young people who spend time together, often fighting with other groups: *a member of a gang* **2** a group of criminals who work together: *a gang of armed robbers* **3** informal a group of young friends

gangster /'gæŋ·stər/ *noun* one of a group of violent criminals

gap /gæp/ *noun* **1** an empty space or hole in the middle of something, or between two things: *There's a big **gap between** the door and the floor.* ○ *The sun was shining through a **gap** in the curtains.* **2** something that is absent and

a b c d e f **g** h i j k l m n o p q r s t u v w x y z

stops something from being complete: *There are still huge gaps in my knowledge.* **3** a difference between two groups of people or two situations: *an age gap* ○ *The **gap between** rich and poor is increasing.*

garage /gə'rɑʒ/ *noun* **1** 🇦2 a small building where you put your car **2** 🇧1 a place where cars are repaired or sold and sometimes fuel is sold

garbage /'gɑr·bɪdʒ/ *noun* [no plural] **1** 🇧1 things that you throw away because you do not want them: *Could you take out the garbage?* **2** something that is wrong or very bad: *There's so much garbage on TV.*

garbage can /'gɑr·bɪdʒ ˌkæn/ *noun* a large container for garbage, especially one that you keep outside your house

garden[1] /'gɑr·dᵊn/ *noun* 🇦1 an area of ground where flowers, vegetables, or other plants are grown: *a vegetable/ flower garden* ○ *Dad's outside, working **in** the garden.*

garden[2] /'gɑr·dᵊn/ *verb* to work in a garden, growing plants and making it look attractive

gardening /'gɑrd·nɪŋ/ *noun* [no plural] the work that you do in a garden in order to grow plants and keep it attractive

garlic /'gɑr·lɪk/ *noun* [no plural] 🇦2 a vegetable like a small onion with a very strong taste and smell
→ See **Fruits and Vegetables** on page C8

garment /'gɑr·mənt/ *noun* formal a piece of clothing

gas /gæs/ *noun* **1** 🇦2 [no plural] a liquid fuel used in cars: *a tank of gas* **2** 🇧1 [no plural] a substance in a form that is like air, and is used for cooking and burning: *a gas stove* **3** a substance in a form that is like air, and not solid or liquid: *poisonous gases*

gasp /gæsp/ *verb* to make a noise by suddenly breathing in because you are shocked or surprised: *She gasped in amazement.*
• **gasp** *noun* *a gasp of surprise*

gas station /'gæs ˌstei·ʃən/ *noun* 🇦2 a place where you can buy fuel for cars

gate /geɪt/ *noun* **1** 🇦2 a door in a fence or outside wall: *Please shut the gate.* **2** 🇧1 the part of an airport where you get on or off a plane: *The flight to Miami is now boarding at gate 8.*

gather /'gæð·ər/ *verb* **1** to join other people somewhere to make a group: *Crowds of fans gathered at the stadium for the big game.* **2** to collect a lot of things together, often from different places or people: *She **gathered** her things **together** and left.* **3** to think something is true, although you are not completely sure: *I gather they're arriving on Friday.*

gathering /'gæð·ə·rɪŋ/ *noun* a party or a meeting where many people get together as a group: *a family gathering*

gave /geɪv/ *past tense of give*

gay /geɪ/ *adj* 🇧1 attracted to people of the same sex: *a gay couple*

gaze /geɪz/ *verb* (present participle **gazing**, past tense and past participle **gazed**) **gaze at, into, etc.** to look at someone or something for a long time: *They gazed into each other's eyes.*
• **gaze** *noun*

gear /gɪər/ *noun* **1** the parts in a car or bicycle that control how fast the wheels turn: *a mountain bike with 21 gears* ○ *I **changed gears** on the hill.* **2** **first, second, third, etc. gear** a particular position of the gears in a car, bicycle, etc. that controls how fast the wheels turn: *I left the car **in first gear.*** **3** [no plural] the clothes and things that you use for a particular purpose: *sports gear*

gearshift /'gɪər·ʃɪft/ *noun* a metal rod or handle that you use to change from one gear to another in a vehicle
→ See **Car** on page C3

geek /gik/ *noun* informal someone who likes a particular subject a lot, and who is usually uncomfortable around people and not fashionable: *a computer geek*

geese /gis/ *plural of goose*

gel /dʒel/ noun [no plural]   a thick, clear liquid that you use to wash your body or to make you hair stay in the right position: *shower gel ○ hair gel*

gem /dʒem/ noun   a valuable stone, especially one that is used in jewelry

gender /ˈdʒen·dər/ noun   **1** the state of being male or female   **2** the division of words into groups corresponding to masculine, feminine, etc.: *In English, nouns don't have gender, but in French and Spanish, they do.*

gene /dʒin/ noun   a part of a cell that is passed on from a parent to a child and that controls particular characteristics: *Red hair is in my genes.*

general[1] /ˈdʒen·rəl/, /ˈdʒen·ər·əl/ adj   **1** 🔵 with the most basic or necessary information but no details: *These leaflets contain some general information about the school.*   **2** relating to or involving all or most people, things, or places: *There seems to be general agreement on this matter.*   **3 in general** considering the whole of someone or something: *I still have a sore throat, but I feel much better in general.*   **4 in general** 🔵 usually, or in most situations: *In general, the weather here is good.*

general[2] /ˈdʒen·rəl/, /ˈdʒen·ər·əl/ noun   a very important officer in the army or air force

general knowledge /ˈdʒen·rəl ˈnɑl·ɪdʒ/, /ˈdʒen·ər·əl ˈnɑl·ɪdʒ/ noun [no plural]   knowledge of many different subjects

generally /ˈdʒen·rə·li/, /ˈdʒen·ər·ə·li/ adv   **1** 🔵 usually or mostly: *I generally wake up early.* ○ *The children were generally very well-behaved.*   **2** considering the whole of someone or something, and not just a particular part of them: *My health is generally very good.*   **3** by most people, or to most people: *He is generally believed to be their best player.*

generate /ˈdʒen·əˌreɪt/ verb (present participle **generating**, past tense and past participle **generated**)   **1** to make something exist: *This movie has generated a lot of interest.*   **2** to make energy: *Windmills generate electricity.*

generation /ˌdʒen·əˈreɪ·ʃən/ noun   **1** 🔵 all the people who are about the same age: *the older/younger generation* ○ *This is the story of three generations of women.*   **2** a period of about 25 to 30 years; the time it takes for children to become adults and take the place of their parents in society: *Our family has lived in this village for generations.*

generator /ˈdʒen·əˌreɪ·tər/ noun   a machine that produces electricity

generosity /ˌdʒen·əˈrɑs·ə·t̬i/ noun [no plural]   the quality of being generous

generous /ˈdʒen·ər·əs/ adj   🔵 often giving people money or presents: *It was very generous of you to buy her flowers.*
• **generously** adv *He generously offered to pay for dinner.*

genetic /dʒəˈnet̬·ɪk/ adj   relating to genes: *genetic research*

genetics /dʒəˈnet̬·ɪks/ noun [no plural]   the scientific study of genes

genius /ˈdʒin·jəs/ noun   someone who is extremely intelligent or extremely good at doing something: *Einstein was a genius.*

gentle /ˈdʒen·t̬l/ adj   **1** 🔵 kind and careful not to hurt or upset anyone: *My mother was such a gentle, loving person.*   **2** 🔵 not strong or unpleasant: *a gentle breeze*
• **gently** adv *He gently stroked her cheek.*

gentleman /ˈdʒen·t̬l·mən/ noun (plural **gentlemen**)   **1** a very polite man: *He was a perfect gentleman.*   **2** a polite word for "man": *There's a gentleman here to see you.*

genuine /ˈdʒen·ju·ən/, /ˈdʒen·ju·aɪn/ adj   real or true: *a genuine antique* ○ *Was her disappointment genuine?*

genuinely /ˈdʒen·ju·ən·li/, /ˈdʒen·ju·aɪn·li/ adv   used to say that something really is true: *I think she was genuinely concerned.*

geography /dʒiˈɑg·rə·fi/ noun [no plural]   🅰2 the study of all the countries of the world, and of the surface of the Earth such as the mountains and seas

geology /dʒiˈɑl·ə·dʒi/ noun [no plural]   the study of rocks and soil and how they were made

geometry /dʒiˈɑm·ɪ·tri/ **noun** [no plural]
a type of mathematics that deals with
points, lines, angles, and shapes

germ /dʒɜrm/ **noun** a very small living
thing that causes disease: *Wash your
hands often so you don't spread germs.*

gesture[1] /ˈdʒes·tʃər/ **noun** **1** a movement you make with your hand, arm, or
head to show what you are thinking or
feeling: *He made a rude gesture at the
crowd.* **2** something you do to show
people how you feel about a person or
situation: *It would be a nice gesture to
invite her to dinner.*

gesture[2] /ˈdʒes·tʃər/ **verb** (present participle
gesturing, past tense and past participle
gestured) to point at something or
show something using your hand, arm,
or head: *He gestured toward the window.*

get /get/ **verb** (present participle **getting**, past
tense **got**, past participle **gotten**) **1 A1** to
obtain or buy something: *Where did you
get your shoes?* ○ *I got you a ticket.*
2 A1 to receive something: *Did you get
anything nice for your birthday?* ○ *Ben
still hasn't gotten my email yet.* **3 get a
bus, train, taxi, etc. A1** to travel somewhere in a bus, train, or other vehicle:
Should we get a taxi to the station?
4 A1 to arrive somewhere: *What time do
you get home from work?* **5 A2** to go
somewhere and bring back someone or
something: *Wait here while I get the car.*
6 get married A2 to become someone's
husband or wife: *Danielle is getting married on Saturday.* **7** to understand
something: *He never gets any of my
jokes.* **8 get rich, sick, wet, etc. B1** to
become rich, sick, wet, etc.: *Hurry up –
your breakfast is getting cold.* **9 B1** to
become sick: *I feel like I'm getting a cold.*
10 get caught, hurt, killed, etc. B1 to
have something done to you. This is
sometimes used instead of the usual
passive structure: *He got killed in the
war.* **11 get worse B1** to become more
sick, unpleasant, difficult, severe, etc.
than before: *My cold seems to be getting
worse.* **12 get something wrong B1** to
produce an answer or result that is not

correct, or to say or write something
that is not correct: *I got most of the
answers wrong.* **13 get in touch B1** to
contact someone: *I'm trying to get in
touch with my old roommate.* **14 get
down/into/off, etc. B1** to move to a different place or into a different position:
I saw her getting into his car. **15 get rid
of something B1** to throw or give something away because you no longer want
it: *I need to get rid of these old magazines.*
16 B1 used with the past participle of
some verbs to mean to do something,
or to arrange for someone to do something for you: *Could you get the kids
dressed?* ○ *I need to get my hair cut.*
17 B1 to move to a different place or
into a different position: *I saw her getting into his car.* **18 B1** to deal with or
answer a ringing telephone, a knock on
the door, etc.: *Could you get the phone?*
**19 get someone/something to do some-
thing** to make something happen, or
make someone or something do something: *I can't get my computer to work!*
○ *I got my dad to pick me up from the station.* **20 get to do something** to have
the chance to do something: *I never got
to meet her.*

get along phrasal verb **1 A2** If two or
more people get along, they like each
other and are friends: *Karen and Dianne
don't get along.* **2 B1** to manage or
deal with a situation: *How are you getting
along in your new job?*

get around phrasal verb **B1** to move
from place to place: *The subway makes it
easy to get around New York City.*

get at something phrasal verb **B1** to be
able to reach or get something: *Put the
cake on a high shelf where the kids can't
get at it.*

get away phrasal verb **1** to leave or escape from a place or person, often when
it is difficult to do this: *We walked to the
next beach to get away from the crowds.*
2 to go somewhere to take a vacation,
often because you need to rest: *I just
need to get away for a few days.*

get away with something phrasal verb
to do something bad without being

punished for it: *If he's rude to you, don't let him get away with it.*

get back phrasal verb **A2** to return to a place after you have been somewhere else: *We got back home late last night.*

get back *something/***get** *something* **back** phrasal verb **B1** to be given something again that you had before: *Don't lend him money – you'll never get it back.*

get in phrasal verb **1** **B1** to succeed in entering a place, especially a building: *They got in through the bathroom window.* **2** **B1** to arrive at a place at a particular time: *My train gets in at 9:45 p.m.* **3** **B1** to succeed in being chosen or elected: *He wanted to go to Princeton but he didn't get in.*

get into *something* phrasal verb to succeed in being chosen to study at a school or to join an organization: *She got into law school.*

get off (*something***)** phrasal verb **A2** to leave a bus, train, plane, or boat: *We should get off at the next stop.*

get on (*something***)** phrasal verb **A2** to go onto a bus, train, plane, or boat: *I think we got on the wrong bus.*

get out phrasal verb **B1** to move out of a car: *Stop at the corner so I can get out.*

get over *something* phrasal verb to feel better after being sick or sad: *She's just getting over a cold.*

get through *something* phrasal verb to succeed in an exam or competition: *She got through the first test just fine.*

get together phrasal verb **B1** to meet in order to do something or spend time together: *A few of us are getting together next week for a barbecue.*

get (*someone***) up** phrasal verb **A1** to wake up and get out of bed, or to make someone do this: *I had to get up at five o'clock this morning.*

get up phrasal verb to stand up: *The whole audience got up and clapped.*

ghetto /ˈget·oʊ/ *noun* (plural **ghettos**, **ghettoes**) a poor part of a city where many people of the same race or background live

ghost /ɡoʊst/ *noun* **B1** a dead person's spirit, which some people believe they

can see: *Do you believe in ghosts?* ○ *a ghost story*

ghost

giant[1] /ˈdʒaɪ·ənt/ *adj* **B1** very big: *a giant spider*

giant[2] /ˈdʒaɪ·ənt/ *noun* a very big person in children's stories

gift /ɡɪft/ *noun* **1** **A2** something that you give to someone, usually on a special day: *a birthday/wedding gift* **2** a natural ability: *She* **has a gift for** *art.*

gift shop /ˈɡɪft ʃɑp/ *noun* a store that sells things that are suitable for giving as presents

gig /ɡɪɡ/ *noun* informal a concert where music is performed: *Our band has a gig on Friday night.*

gigantic /dʒaɪˈɡæn·tɪk/ *adj* very big: *a gigantic teddy bear*

giggle /ˈɡɪɡ·əl/ *verb* (present participle **giggling**, past tense and past participle **giggled**) to laugh in a nervous or silly way: *She couldn't stop giggling.*
• **giggle** *noun*

ginger /ˈdʒɪn·dʒər/ *noun* [no plural] a root with a strong taste that is used in cooking

giraffe /dʒəˈræf/ *noun* **B1** a large African animal with a very long neck and long, thin legs

giraffe

girl /ɡɜrl/ *noun* **A1** a female child or young woman: *We have three children – a boy and two girls.*

girlfriend /ˈɡɜrl.frend/ *noun* **1** **A2** a woman or girl who someone is having a romantic relationship with: *Have you met Steve's new girlfriend?* **2** a female friend, especially of a woman

give /ɡɪv/ *verb* (present participle **giving**, past tense **gave**, past participle **given**) **1** **A1** to provide someone with something: *I gave her a bike for her birthday.* ○ *Do you* **give** *money* **to** *charity?* **2** **A2** to put something in someone's hand so that he or she can use it or look at it: *Can you give me that pen?* **3** **A2** to tell someone something: *Can you give Jo a* message? **4** *give someone* a call (A2) to telephone someone **5** *give a party* (A2) to have a party: *We gave a party for her 50th birthday.* **6** (B1) to do an action: *He gave her a kiss.* **7** (B1) to produce or cause something: *That book gave me an idea.* **8** (B1) to allow someone or something a particular amount of time: *I'm almost ready – just give me a few minutes.* **9** (B1) to pay someone a particular amount of money for something: *I gave him $20 for his old camera.* **10** to perform or speak in public: *Tony gave a great speech.*

give *something* **away** phrasal verb **1** (B1) to give something to someone without asking for payment: *They're giving away a CD with this magazine.* **2** to tell people something secret, often without intending to: *The party was supposed to be a surprise, but Sharon gave it away.*

give *something* **back** phrasal verb (A2) to give something to the person who gave it to you: *Did she give you those books back yet?*

give in phrasal verb (B1) to finally agree to do something that someone wants: *We won't give in to the terrorists' demands.*

give *something* **out** phrasal verb (B1) to give something to a lot of people: *He gave out copies of the report.*

give up phrasal verb (B1) to accept that you cannot continue trying to do something: *You'll never guess the answer – do you give up?* ○ *I had to give up halfway through the race.*

give up *something* phrasal verb **1** (B1) If you give up something bad, such as smoking, you stop doing it or having it: *I gave up drinking two years ago.* **2** (B1) to stop doing an activity or piece of work before you have completed it, usually because it is too difficult: *I gave up trying to help her.* **3** (B1) to stop doing a regular activity or job: *Are you going to give up work when you have your baby?*

glacier /ˈgleɪ·ʃər/ noun a very large piece of ice that moves very slowly

glad /glæd/ adj **1** (A2) happy about something: *I'm very glad that you like*

your present. **2** very willing to do something: *I'd be glad to help.*

gladly /ˈglæd·li/ adv If you would gladly do something, you would like to do it: *I would gladly pay extra for better service.*

glamorous /ˈglæm·ər·əs/ adj attractive in an exciting and special way: *She's very glamorous.*

glamour /ˈglæm·ər/ noun [no plural] (also **glamor**) the quality of being attractive, exciting and special: *the glamour of Hollywood*

glance[1] /glæns/ verb (present participle **glancing**, past tense and past participle **glanced**) **1** (B1) to look somewhere for a short time: *He glanced at his watch.* **2** to read something quickly: *She glanced through the newspaper.*

glance[2] /glæns/ noun a quick look: *She took a quick glance around the room.*

glare[1] /gleər/ noun a long, angry look

glare[2] /gleər/ verb (present participle **glaring**, past tense and past participle **glared**) to look at someone in an angry way: *She glared at him.*

glass /glæs/ noun **1** (A1) [no plural] a hard, clear substance that objects such as windows and bottles are made of: *broken glass* ○ *glass jars* **2** (A1) a container made of glass that is used for drinking: *Would you like a glass of water?*

glass

The window is made of glass.

glass

glasses

glasses /ˈglæs·ɪz/ plural noun (A1) a piece of equipment with two transparent parts that you wear in front of your eyes to help you see better: *a pair of glasses* ○ *She was wearing glasses.*

gleam /glim/ *verb* to shine in a pleasant, soft way: *Her new car gleamed in the sun.*

glee club /'gli ˌklʌb/ *noun* a group organized to sing together, often at a school or university

glide /glaɪd/ *verb* (present participle **gliding**, past tense and past participle **glided**) to move somewhere smoothly and quietly: *The train slowly glided out of the station.*

glimmer /'glɪm·ər/ *noun* **1 a glimmer of happiness, hope, etc.** a small sign of something good **2** a light that shines in a weak way

glimpse[1] /glɪmps/ *noun* a look at something or someone for a very short time: *He caught a glimpse of her as she got into the car.*

glimpse[2] /glɪmps/ *verb* (present participle **glimpsing**, past tense and past participle **glimpsed**) to see something or someone for a very short time: *She glimpsed him out of the corner of her eye.*

glisten /'glɪs·ən/ *verb* If something glistens, it shines, often because it is wet: *Their faces were **glistening with** sweat.*

glitter /'glɪt·ər/ *verb* to shine with small flashes of light: *Snow glittered on the mountains.*

glittering /'glɪt·ə·rɪŋ/ *adj* **1** shining with small flashes of light: *glittering jewels* **2** successful and exciting: *a glittering career*

global /'gloʊ·bəl/ *adj* relating to the whole world: *global problems*

global warming /'gloʊ·bəl ˈwɔr·mɪŋ/ *noun* [no plural] an increase in the temperature of the air around the world that is caused by pollution

globe /gloʊb/ *noun* **1 the globe** the world: *This event was watched by 200 million people around the globe.* **2** a model of the world

shaped like a ball with a map of all the countries on it

gloomy /'glu·mi/ *adj* (comparative **gloomier**, superlative **gloomiest**) **1** sad or without hope: *a gloomy face* ○ *gloomy predictions* **2** dark in a bad way: *a small, gloomy room*
• **gloomily** *adv*

glorious /'glɔr·i·əs/ *adj* **1** beautiful or very good: *We had four days of glorious sunshine.* ○ *glorious colors* **2** getting praise and respect: *a glorious career*

glory /'glɔr·i/ *noun* [no plural] praise and respect you get from other people for doing something very brave and good

glove /glʌv/ *noun* **A2** a piece of clothing that covers your fingers and hand: *a pair of gloves*
→ See picture at **pair noun**

glow[1] /gloʊ/ *noun* **1** a soft, warm light: *the warm glow of the moon* **2** a pink color on your face that makes it appear happy and healthy: *Sam's face had lost its usual glow.*

glow[2] /gloʊ/ *verb* **1** to produce a soft, warm light: *toys that glow in the dark* **2** to have a warm and healthy appearance: *She glows with health.* **3 glow with happiness, pride, etc.** to feel very happy, proud, etc.: *Glowing with pride, she showed me her painting.*

glue[1] /glu/ *noun* [no plural] a substance used to stick things together: *Put a little glue on both edges and hold them together.*
→ See **The Classroom** on page C4

glue[2] /glu/ *verb* (present participle **glueing**, past tense and past participle **glued**) to stick something to something else with glue: *Do you think you can **glue** this vase back **together**?*

glum /glʌm/ *adj* sad: *Why are you looking so glum today?*
• **glumly** *adv*

go /goʊ/ *verb* (present participle **going**, past tense **went**, past participle **gone**) **1 A1** to move or travel somewhere: *I'd love to go to Florida.* ○ *We went into the house.* ○ *Are you going by train?* **2 A1** to move or travel somewhere in order to do something: *Let's go for a walk.* ○ *We're going*

camping tomorrow. **3 go running, swimming, etc.** *A2* to go somewhere to do a particular activity: *We went skating yesterday.* **4 be going to do/be something** *A2* to intend to do or be something: *I'm going to call her tonight.* ○ *I'm going to be a dancer when I grow up.*
5 be going to do *something* *A2* used to say that something is expected to happen in the future: *It's going to snow tonight.* **6 go to the bathroom** *A2* to use the toilet **7 go badly, well, etc.** *B1* to happen in a particular way: *My vacation went really well.* **8** *B1* to disappear or no longer exist: *When I turned around, the man was gone.* **9** *B1* If two things go, they match each other: *Does the jacket* **go with** *the pants?* **10** to go *B1* If you ask for food to go in a restaurant, you are asking for food that you can take away: *I would like a burger and french fries to go.* **11 go bald/blind/gray, etc.** *B1* to become bald, blind, gray, etc.: *He went bald when he was thirty.* **12** *B1* If a road, path, etc. goes in a particular direction, it leads there: *This road* **goes to** *Springfield.* **13** to work correctly: *I managed to get the car going.* **14** to have a particular tune or words: *I can't remember how that song goes.* **15** If time goes, it passes: *The day went very quickly.*

❗ Common mistake: go, gone, and been

Gone is the usual past participle of the verb **go**. Sometimes you use the past participle **been** when you want to say that you have gone somewhere and come back, or to say that you have visited somewhere.

Paul has gone to the hospital this morning (= he is still there).

Paul has been to the hospital this morning (= he went and has come back).

He has gone to New York (= he is still there).

Have you ever been to New York? (= Have you ever visited New York?)

---

go ahead phrasal verb **1** to start to do something: *We have permission to go ahead with the project.* **2** something that you say to someone to allow him or her to do something: *"Can I borrow your book?" "Sure, go ahead."*
go away phrasal verb **1** *B1* to leave a place: *Just go away and leave me alone.* **2** *B1* to leave your home in order to spend time in a different place: *We're going away for a few weeks this summer.*
go back phrasal verb *B1* to return to a place where you were or where you have been before: *When are you* **going back to** *Las Vegas?*
go by phrasal verb If time goes by, it passes: *The days went by really slowly.*
go down phrasal verb **1** *B1* to become lower in level: *Profits have gone down by about 2%.* **2** *B1* When the sun goes down, it moves down in the sky until it cannot be seen anymore: *I sat on the beach and watched the sun go down.*
go for *something* phrasal verb *B1* to choose something: *I don't know whether to go for the fish or the steak for dinner.*
go in phrasal verb *A2* to enter a place: *I looked in the window, but I didn't go in.*
go into *something* phrasal verb to describe, discuss, or examine something in a detailed way: *She didn't* **go into** *detail about her problems.* ○ *I'd rather not go into it.*
go off phrasal verb **1** *B1* to leave a place and go somewhere else: *She went off with Laurie.* **2** *B1* If a light or machine goes off, it stops working: *The heat goes off at 10 o'clock.* **3** If a bomb or gun goes off, it explodes or fires. **4** If something that makes a noise goes off, it suddenly starts making a noise: *His car alarm goes off every time it rains.*
go on phrasal verb **1** *B1* to last for a particular period of time: *The speech seemed to go on forever.* **2** *B1* to happen: *What's going on?* **3** to continue doing something: *We can't go on living like this.*
go out phrasal verb **1** *A1* to leave a place in order to go somewhere else: *Are you going out tonight?* **2** *B1* If two people go out together, they have a romantic

relationship with each other: *Tina is going out with Peter.* **3 B1** If a light or something that is burning is going out, it stops producing light or heat: *I'm sorry – I let the fire go out.*

go over *something* phrasal verb to examine something, such as a piece of writing or some numbers, in order to make sure that it is correct: *I'm just going over my essay one more time.*

go through *something* phrasal verb to have a difficult or bad situation: *They are going through a difficult divorce.*

go up phrasal verb **B1** to become higher in level: *House prices keep going up.*

goal /goul/ noun **1 A2** a point scored in sports such as soccer by sending a ball into a particular area, such as between two posts: *He scored two goals in the second half.* **2 A2** in some sports, the area between two posts where players try to send the ball → See **Sports 2** on page C16 **3 B1** something that you want to do in the future: *Andy's goal is to run in the New York Marathon.*

goalkeeper /ˈɡoʊlˌki·pər/ noun **B1** the player in a sport such as soccer who tries to stop the ball from going into the goal

goalkeeper

goat /goʊt/ noun **B1** an animal with horns that is kept for the milk it makes

god /gɑd/ noun **1 God A2** in certain religions, the being that made the universe and controls it **2 Oh my God!** *informal* **B1** used to emphasize how surprised, angry, shocked, etc. you are: *Oh my God! The car got stolen.* **3 thank God** *informal* **B1** something you say when you are happy because something bad did not happen: *Thank God nobody was hurt in the accident.* **4** a spirit, especially a male one, that people pray to: *the ancient Greek gods and goddesses*

goddess /ˈɡɑd·əs/ noun a female spirit that people pray to: *the goddess of love*

goggles /ˈɡɑɡ·əlz/ noun special glasses for protecting your eyes: *a pair of goggles*

gold¹ /goʊld/ noun [no plural] **A2** a valuable, shiny, yellow metal used to make coins and jewelry

gold² /goʊld/ adj **1 A2** made of gold: *gold jewelry* **2 A2** being the shiny yellow color of gold: *gold paint*

golden /ˈɡoʊl·dən/ adj **A2** being a bright yellow color: *golden hair*

goldfish /ˈɡoʊldˌfɪʃ/ noun (plural **goldfish**) a small orange fish that is often kept as a pet

golf /ɡɑlf/ noun [no plural] **A2** a game you play by hitting a small ball with a long, thin stick into holes on a large area of grass: *a golf ball*
→ See picture at **ball**
→ See **Sports (2)** on page C16
• **golfer** noun

golf course /ˈɡɑlf ˌkɔrs/ noun an area of land used for playing golf

gone /ɡɔn/, /ɡɑn/ past participle of go

good¹ /ɡʊd/ adj (comparative **better**, superlative **best**) **1 A1** enjoyable or nice: *a good book* ○ *Did you have a good time at the party?* **2 A1** of a high quality: *The food at this restaurant is very good.* **3 A1** able to do something well: *Anna is a good cook.* **4 A1** kind or helpful: *She's a good friend.* **5 A1** something you say when you are happy about something: *Oh good, he finally got here.* **6 B1** having a positive or useful effect: *Fruit is **good** for you.* **7 A1** *informal* something that you say when a person asks how you are or how someone you know is: *"How are you, Emily?" "I'm good, thanks!"* **8 A2** A good child or animal behaves well. **9 A2** suitable or satisfactory: *When would be a good time to call?* **10 B1** morally right: *a good person*

good² /ɡʊd/ noun **1** [no plural] what people think is morally right: *Children don't always understand the difference between good and bad.* **2** something that is an advantage or help to a person or situation: *It's hard work, but it's **for your own***

good. 3 do someone good to be useful or helpful to someone: *A vacation will do you good.* **4 for good** forever: *When he was 20, he left home for good.*

> ⚠ **Common mistake: good or well?**
>
> Good is an adjective and is used to describe nouns.
> *She's a **good** cook.*
> *Her children had a **good** education.*
> Well is an adverb and is used to describe verbs.
> *She cooks **well**.*
> *Her children were **well** educated.*

good afternoon /ˌɡʊd ˌæf·tərˈnʊn/ **exclamation** **A1** something you say to greet someone in the afternoon, especially when speaking on the phone

goodbye /ˌɡʊdˈbaɪ/ **exclamation** **A1** something you say when you leave someone or when he or she leaves you: *Goodbye, Vicki! See you next week.*

good evening /ˌɡʊd ˈiv·nɪŋ/ **exclamation** **A1** something you say to greet someone in the evening

good-looking /ˈɡʊdˈlʊk·ɪŋ/ **adj** **A2** attractive: *a good-looking woman*

good morning /ˌɡʊd ˈmɔr·nɪŋ/ **exclamation** **A1** something you say to greet someone in the morning

goodness /ˈɡʊd·nəs/ **noun 1** [no plural] the quality in people that makes them behave well and treat other people kindly: *She believes in the goodness of human nature.* **2** informal something you say when you are surprised: *My goodness, he's a big baby, isn't he?*

good night /ˌɡʊd ˈnaɪt/ **exclamation** **A1** something you say when you leave someone in the evening or when someone is going to bed

goods /ɡʊdz/ **plural noun** items that are made to be sold: *We sell pies, cakes, and other baked goods.*

goose /ɡus/ **noun** (plural **geese**) a large water bird similar to a duck

gorgeous /ˈɡɔr·dʒəs/ **adj** **B1** very beautiful or pleasant: *You look gorgeous in that dress!*

gorilla /ɡəˈrɪl·ə/ **noun** a big, black, hairy animal, like a large monkey

gorilla

gossip[1] /ˈɡɑs·ɪp/ **noun** [no plural] conversation about other people's private lives that might not be true: *an interesting piece of gossip*

gossip[2] /ˈɡɑs·ɪp/ **verb** to talk about other people's private lives

got /ɡɑt/ past tense and past participle of get

govern /ˈɡʌv·ərn/ **verb** to officially control a country or state: *The state is now governed by a Democrat.*

government /ˈɡʌv·ərn·mənt, ˈɡʌv·ər·mənt/ **noun 1** **B1** the group of people who officially control a country: *The government has cut taxes.* **2** [no plural] the method or process of governing a country: *The country has returned to democratic government.*

governor /ˈɡʌv·ər·nər/ **noun** someone who controls a region or organization: *the governor of Texas*

gown /ɡaʊn/ **noun** a woman's long dress: *an evening gown*
→ See **Clothes** on page C5

GPS **noun** [no plural] abbreviation for global positioning system: a system that uses satellites (=devices that move around the Earth) to show the position of a person or thing anywhere in the world

grab /ɡræb/ **verb** (present participle **grabbing**, past tense and past participle **grabbed**) **1** **B1** to take hold of something or someone suddenly with your hand: *He grabbed my arm and pulled me away.* **2** informal to quickly take the opportunity to get, use, or enjoy something: *We'd better get there early, or someone else will grab the best seats.*

grace /greɪs/ **noun** [no plural] the quality of moving in a smooth and attractive way: *She moved* **with such grace**.

graceful /ˈgreɪsfəl/ **adj** moving in a smooth and attractive way: *graceful movements*

• **gracefully adv**

grade[1] /greɪd/ **noun** 1 **A2** a school class for students of the same age or ability: *My son is in fifth grade.* 2 **B1** a number or letter that shows how good your work is: *Did you get a good grade on the test?* 3 a level of quality, size, importance, etc.: *I applied for a position a grade higher than my current job.*

grade[2] /greɪd/ **verb** (present participle **grading**, past tense and past participle **graded**) to separate people or things into different levels of quality, size, importance, etc.: *The fruit is washed and then* **graded by** *size.*

grade school /ˈgreɪd ˌskul/ **noun** a school where children begin their education, usually for children between five and eleven years old

gradual /ˈgrædʒuəl/ **adj** happening slowly: *a gradual change*

gradually /ˈgrædʒuəli/ **adv** slowly over a period of time: *Gradually he got better.*

graduate[1] /ˈgrædʒuɪt/ **noun** **A2** someone who has completed his or her education successfully at a school, college, or university: *a high school graduate*

graduate[2] /ˈgrædʒuˌeɪt/ **verb** (present participle **graduating**, past tense and past participle **graduated**) to complete your education successfully at a school, college, or university: *He* **graduated from** *Duke University in 2006.*

graduation /ˌgrædʒuˈeɪʃən/ **noun** 1 **B1** a formal event at which students receive a certificate for successfully completing a course of study: *We all went out to lunch after the* **graduation ceremony.** 2 **B1** [no plural] the act of successfully completing your education or course of study: *What do you plan to do after graduation?*

graffiti /grəˈfiti/ **noun** [no plural] writing or pictures painted on walls and public places, usually illegally: *The walls are covered in graffiti.*

grain /greɪn/ **noun** 1 a seed or seeds from types of grass that are eaten as food: *grains of wheat/rice* 2 a very small piece of something: *a grain of sand/sugar*

gram /græm/ **noun** (written abbreviation **g**) **A2** a unit for measuring weight, equal to 0.001 kilograms

grammar /ˈgræmər/ **noun** [no plural] **A2** the way you combine words and change their form and position in a sentence, or the rules of this

grammatical /grəˈmætɪkəl/ **adj** obeying the rules of grammar: *a grammatical sentence*

grand /grænd/ **adj** very large and special: *a grand hotel*

grandchild /ˈgræntʃaɪld/ **noun** (plural **grandchildren**) **A2** the child of someone's son or daughter: *We have three children and seven grandchildren.*

granddad /ˈgrændæd/ **noun** informal **A2** another word for grandfather

granddaughter /ˈgrændɔtər/ **noun** **A2** the daughter of someone's son or daughter: *We're excited to see our new baby granddaughter.*

grandfather /ˈgrændfɑðər/ **noun** **A2** the father of someone's mother or father: *My grandfather lived to age 92.*

grandma /ˈgrænmɑ/ **noun** informal **A2** another word for grandmother

grandmother /ˈgrændmʌðər/ **noun** **A2** the mother of someone's mother or father: *His grandmother sent him some money for his birthday.*

grandpa /ˈgrænpɑ/ **noun** informal **A2** another word for grandfather

grandparent /ˈgrændpærənt/ **noun** **A2** the parent of someone's mother or father: *Her grandparents lived far away from her.*

grandson /ˈgrændsʌn/ **noun** **A2** the son of someone's son or daughter: *Our grandson is doing well in school.*

granny /ˈɡræn·i/ noun (plural **grannies**) informal **A2** another word for grandmother

grant[1] /ɡrænt/ verb formal **1 B2** to give or allow someone to have something, usually in an official way: *He was granted a visa.* **2 B2** take *something/someone* for granted to expect something and not understand that you are lucky to have it: *Most of us take our freedom for granted.*

grant[2] /ɡrænt/ noun **B1** an amount of money that an organization gives you for a special purpose: *They received a grant for the project.*

grape /ɡreɪp/ noun **A2** a small, round fruit that grows in large groups and is used to make wine: *a bunch of grapes*
→ See **Fruits and Vegetables** on page C8

grapefruit /ˈɡreɪpˌfrut/ noun (plural **grapefruit, grapefruits**) a large, round, yellow fruit with a sour taste

graph /ɡræf/ noun a picture that shows different amounts by using a line or many lines

graph

graphics /ˈɡræf·ɪks/ plural noun **B1** images shown on a computer screen: *computer graphics*

grapple /ˈɡræp·əl/ verb (present participle **grappling**, past tense and past participle **grappled**)
grapple with *something* phrasal verb to try to understand something difficult

grasp /ɡræsp/ verb **1** to take hold of something firmly with your hand: *He grasped my hand.* **2** to understand something: *I didn't grasp what she was saying.*

grass /ɡræs/ noun [no plural] **A1** a common plant with thin green leaves that grows close to the ground: *We like to lie on the grass in the sunshine.*

grasshopper /ˈɡræsˌhɑp·ər/ noun a green insect that jumps using its long back legs

grasshopper

grate /ɡreɪt/ verb (present participle **grating**, past tense and past participle **grated**) to break food such as cheese into small, thin pieces by rubbing it against a grater (=kitchen tool with holes): *grated cheese*

grateful /ˈɡreɪt·fəl/ adj **B1** wanting to say "thank you" to someone who has done something good for you: *I'm really grateful to you for all your help.*
→ Opposite **ungrateful** adj
• **gratefully** adv

grater /ˈɡreɪ·tər/ noun a kitchen tool with a surface full of holes, used to grate (=break into small pieces) food such as cheese
→ See **The Kitchen** on page C10

gratitude /ˈɡræt·ɪˌtud/ noun [no plural] a feeling of being grateful to someone who has done something good for you

grave[1] /ɡreɪv/ noun a place in the ground where a dead body is buried

grave[2] /ɡreɪv/ adj very serious: *grave doubts* ○ *a grave mistake*

gravel /ˈɡræv·əl/ noun [no plural] small pieces of stone used to make paths and roads

gravestone /ˈɡreɪvˌstoʊn/ noun a stone that shows the name of a dead person who is buried under it

graveyard /ˈɡreɪvˌjɑrd/ noun an area of land where dead bodies are buried, usually next to a church

gravity /ˈɡræv·ɪ·ti/ noun [no plural] **1** the force that makes objects fall to the ground: *the laws of gravity* **2** formal the seriousness of a problem

gravy /ˈɡreɪ·vi/ noun [no plural] a warm, brown sauce that you put on meat

gray[1] (also **grey**) /ɡreɪ/ adj **A1** being a color that is a mixture of black and white: *gray clouds* ○ *an old man with gray hair*
→ See **Hair** on page C9

gray[2] (also **grey**) /ɡreɪ/ noun **A2** a color that is a mixture of black and white
→ See **Colors** on page C6

graze /ɡreɪz/ verb (present participle **grazing**, past tense and past participle **grazed**) to eat grass

groceries

grease /gris/ **noun** [no plural]
a substance such as oil or fat

greasy /ˈgri·si/, /ˈgri·zi/ **adj** (comparative
greasier, superlative **greasiest**) containing or covered with fat or oil: *greasy food*

great /greɪt/ **adj** **1** **A1** very good: *We
had a great time.* **2** **A2** large: *A great
number of buildings were damaged in the
flood.* **3** **B1** extreme: *He has great difficulty walking.* **4** important or famous:
a great actor **5** **great big** very big: *He
has a great big house.*

great- /ˌgreɪt/ **prefix** **1** **great-grand-**
father/-grandmother the father or
mother of your grandfather or grandmother **2** **great-aunt/-uncle** the aunt
or uncle of your mother or father
3 **great-grandchild, -granddaughter,**
etc. the child, daughter, etc. of your
grandson or granddaughter **4** **great-**
niece/-nephew the daughter or son of
your niece or nephew

greatly /ˈgreɪt·li/ **adv** very much: *We
will miss her greatly.*

greed /grid/ **noun** [no plural] a desire for
a lot more food, money, or things than
you need

greedy /ˈgri·di/ **adj** (comparative **greedier**,
superlative **greediest**) wanting a lot more
food, money, etc. than you need:
greedy, selfish people

green¹ /grin/ **adj** **1** **A1** being the same
color as grass **2** **B1** covered with grass
or other plants: *green spaces* **3** relating
to nature and protecting the environment: *green issues*

green² /grin/ **noun** **A2** the color of grass
→ See **Colors** on page C6

greenhouse /ˈgrin.haʊs/ **noun** a building made of glass for growing plants in

greens /grinz/ **plural noun** green leafy
vegetables, especially ones that you
cook

greet /grit/ **verb** **B1** to say hello to
someone: *He greeted me at the door.*

greeting /ˈgri·tɪŋ/ **noun** **B1** something
friendly or polite that you say or do
when you see someone

grew /gru/ past tense of grow

grief /grif/ **noun** [no plural] the great sadness that you feel when someone dies

grieve /griv/ **verb** (present participle
grieving, past tense and past participle
grieved) to feel very sad because
someone has died: *He is still grieving
for his wife.*

grill¹ /grɪl/ **noun** (also **barbecue**) **B1** a
piece of equipment with a metal frame
for cooking food over a fire outdoors

grill² /grɪl/ **verb** (also **broil**) **B1** to cook
food over a fire: *Grill the fish for 2 to 3
minutes on each side.*

grilled /grɪld/ **adj** **A2** cooked on a grill:
grilled fish

grim /grɪm/ **adj** (comparative **grimmer**,
superlative **grimmest**) **1** worrying and
bad: *grim news* **2** sad and serious: *a
grim expression* **3** A grim place is ugly
and unpleasant.

grin /grɪn/ **verb** (present participle **grinning**,
past tense and past participle **grinned**) to
smile a big smile: *He grinned at me.*
• **grin noun** *She had a big grin on her
face.*

grind /graɪnd/ **verb** (past tense and past
participle **ground**) to make something
change into powder by rubbing it between two hard things: *to grind coffee*

grip¹ /grɪp/ **noun** an act of holding
something tightly: *She tightened her
grip on my arm.*

grip² /grɪp/ **verb** (present participle **gripping**,
past tense and past participle **gripped**) **1** to
hold something tightly: *She gripped his
arm.* **2** to keep someone's attention
completely: *This trial has gripped the
nation.*

groan /groʊn/ **verb** to make a long, low
sound because you are sad or in pain:
He collapsed, groaning with pain.
• **groan noun**

groceries /ˈgroʊ·sə·riz/ **plural noun**
B1 the food and other things for your
home that you buy in a food store: *a
bag of groceries*

grocery store /ˈɡroʊ·sə·ri ˌstɔr/ noun (also **grocery**) **A2** a store that sells food and other small items for the home

groom /ɡrum/ noun (also **bridegroom**) **B1** a man who is getting married

grope /ɡroʊp/ verb (present participle **groping**, past tense and past participle **groped**) to try to get hold of something with your hand, usually when you cannot see it: I **groped** in my bag **for** my keys.

ground[1] /ɡraʊnd/ past tense and past participle of grind

ground[2] /ɡraʊnd/ noun **1 the ground** **B1** the surface of the Earth: I sat down **on the ground**. **2** the soil in an area: The ground was soft after the rain.

ground floor /ˌɡraʊnd ˈflɔr/ noun (also **first floor**) **B1** the level of a building that is on the ground

grounds /ɡraʊndz/ plural noun the land around a building: Smoking is not allowed on school grounds.

group /ɡrup/ noun **1 A1** a number of people or things that are together in one place: She was with a **group of** friends. **2 A1** a few musicians or singers who perform together, usually playing popular music: a rock group

grow /ɡroʊ/ verb (past tense **grew**, past participle **grown**) **1 A2** to become bigger or taller as time passes: Children grow very quickly. **2 A2** If a plant grows, or you grow it, it develops from a seed to a full plant: These plants grow well in sandy soil. **3 B1** to increase: The problem grows every year. **4** to become: We've grown older. **5 B1** If your hair or nails grow, or if you grow them, they get longer.

grow up phrasal verb **A2** to become older or an adult: She grew up in Texas.

growing /ˈɡroʊ·ɪŋ/ adj increasing in size or quantity: A growing number of people are shopping on the Internet.

growl /ɡraʊl/ verb If a dog growls, it makes a deep, angry noise.
• **growl** noun

grown /ɡroʊn/ past participle of grow

grown-up[1] /ˈɡroʊn.ʌp/ noun an adult, used especially when talking to children: Ask a grown-up to help you.

grown-up[2] /ˈɡroʊn.ʌp/ adj adult: Anne has two grown-up sons.

growth /ɡroʊθ/ noun **1** the process of getting bigger or developing: population growth **2** something that grows on your skin or inside your body, that should not be there

grumble /ˈɡrʌm·bəl/ verb (present participle **grumbling**, past tense and past participle **grumbled**) to keep complaining about something: She's always **grumbling about** something.
• **grumble** noun

grumpy /ˈɡrʌm·pi/ adj (comparative **grumpier**, superlative **grumpiest**) easily annoyed and often complaining: a grumpy old man

grunt /ɡrʌnt/ verb If a pig grunts, it makes short, low sounds.

guarantee[1] /ˌɡær·ən'ti/ verb (present participle **guaranteeing**, past tense and past participle **guaranteed**) **1** to promise that something is true or will happen: We can't guarantee that it will arrive in time. **2** If a company guarantees a product, it promises to repair it or give you a new one if it has a fault: The TV is guaranteed for twelve months.

guarantee[2] /ˌɡær·ən'ti/ noun **1** a written promise made by a company to repair one of its products or give you a new one if it has a fault: a three-year guarantee **2** a promise that something will be done or will happen: There's no guarantee that it actually works.

guard[1] /ɡard/ noun **1 B1** someone whose job is to protect a person or make sure that a person does not escape: prison guards **2 be on your guard** to be ready to do something if a problem happens: Companies are warned to be on their guard for suspicious packages.

guard[2] /ɡard/ verb **1** to protect someone or something so that no one attacks the person or thing, or steals the thing: *Soldiers guarded the main doors of the embassy.* **2** to watch someone so that he or she does not escape from a place: *Five prison officers guarded the prisoners.*

guardian /ˈɡɑr·di·ən/ *noun* someone who is legally responsible for someone else's child

guerrilla /ɡəˈrɪl·ə/ *noun* a soldier who is not a member of a country's army and who fights to achieve political goals: *guerrilla warfare*

guess[1] /ɡes/ *verb* **1** **A2** to give an answer or opinion about something without knowing all the facts: *Guess how old he is.* **2** **A2** to say something that is right without knowing all the facts: *How did you guess I was pregnant?* **3 guess what?** *informal* **A2** used before telling someone something interesting or surprising: *Guess what? We're going to Hawaii!* **4 I guess** **B1** used when you think something is probably true: *I guess you're mad at me.* **5 I guess so/not** used when you agree or disagree but are not completely certain about something: *"It would be better to buy a new car than to try to fix this one." "Yeah, I guess so."*

guess[2] /ɡes/ *noun* **1** **B1** an attempt to give the right answer when you are not certain: *How old do you think John is? Go on, take a guess.* **2** an opinion that you have formed by guessing: *My guess is she probably won't come.*

guest /ɡest/ *noun* **1** **A2** someone who comes to visit you: *We have some guests coming this weekend.* **2** **A2** someone who is staying in a hotel: *The hotel has room for 200 guests.* **3** a famous person who has been invited to appear on a television or radio program, or at an event: *Our special guest on the show tonight is musician Wynton Marsalis.*

guidance /ˈɡɑr·dəns/ *noun* [no plural] help or advice: *I need some career guidance.*

guide[1] /ɡɑɪd/ *noun* **1** **A2** someone whose job is to show interesting places to visitors: *a tour guide* **2** **B1** a book

that gives information about something or tells you how to do something: *a hotel/restaurant guide* ∘ *a user's guide*

guide[2] /ɡɑɪd/ *verb* (present participle **guiding**, past tense and past participle **guided**) **B1** to help someone or something go somewhere: *He gently guided her back to her chair.*

guidebook /ˈɡɑɪd·bʊk/ *noun* **A2** a book that gives visitors information about a particular place

guided tour /ˈɡɑr·dɪd ˈtʊər/ *noun* a visit to a place such as a museum with a guide who explains facts about the place

guilt /ɡɪlt/ *noun* [no plural] **1** the bad feeling you get when you know you have done something wrong: *She had feelings of guilt about not staying on her diet.* **2** the fact that someone has done something illegal: *He was never convinced of her guilt.*

→ Opposite **innocence** *noun*

guilty /ˈɡɪl·ti/ *adj* (comparative **guiltier**, superlative **guiltiest**) **1** **B1** feeling bad because you have done something wrong: *I feel guilty about lying to her.* **2** having broken a law: *The jury found her guilty* (= decided that she was guilty of a crime). ∘ *They found him guilty of murder.*

→ Opposite **innocent** *adj*

guitar /ɡɪˈtɑr/ *noun* **A1** a musical instrument with strings that you play by pulling the strings: *an electric guitar*   guitar

guitarist /ɡɪˈtɑr·ɪst/ *noun* **B1** someone who plays the guitar

gulf /ɡʌlf/ *noun* a large area of ocean that has land almost all the way around it: *the Gulf of Mexico*

gulp[1] /ɡʌlp/ *verb* (also **gulp down**) to drink or eat something quickly: *I only had time to gulp down a cup of coffee.*

gulp[2] /ɡʌlp/ *noun* an amount of something that you swallow: *He took a gulp of water.*

gum /gʌm/ noun the hard pink part inside your mouth that your teeth grow out of

gun /gʌn/ noun **B1** a weapon that you fire bullets out of

gush /gʌʃ/ verb If liquid gushes from an opening, a lot of it comes out quickly: *Blood was gushing from the wound.*

gust[1] /gʌst/ verb If winds gust, they blow strongly.

gust[2] /gʌst/ noun a sudden, strong movement of wind: *a gust of air*

guts /gʌts/ plural noun informal the courage that you need to do something difficult or frightening: *It takes guts to admit that you were wrong.*

gutter /ˈgʌt̬ər/ noun the edge of a road where water flows away

guy /gaɪ/ noun informal **1 A2** a man: *What a nice guy!* **2 (you) guys** informal Used when speaking to or about two or more people: *What movie do you guys want to see?*

gym /dʒɪm/ noun **1 A2** a building with equipment for doing exercises: *Nick goes to the gym three times a week.* **2 A2** [no plural] exercises done inside, especially as a school subject: *gym class*

gymnast /ˈdʒɪm·næst/ noun someone who does gymnastics: *an Olympic gymnast*

gymnastics /dʒɪmˈnæs·tɪks/ noun [no plural] **B1** a sport in which you do physical exercises on the floor and on different pieces of equipment

gymnastics

H h

H, h /eɪtʃ/ the eighth letter of the alphabet

habit /ˈhæb·ɪt/ noun **B1** something that you often do, almost without thinking about it: *I got into the **habit of** drinking coffee every morning.*

hack /hæk/ verb to use a computer to illegally get into someone else's computer system

had /hæd/, /həd/ verb past tense and past participle of have

hadn't /ˈhæd·ənt/ short form of had not: *I hadn't seen Megan since college.*

hail[1] /heɪl/ noun [no plural] small, hard balls of ice that fall from the sky like rain

hail[2] /heɪl/ verb **it hails** If it hails, small, hard balls of ice fall from the sky like rain.

hailstone /ˈheɪlˌstoʊn/ noun a small, hard ball of ice that falls from the sky like rain

hair /heər/ noun **1 A1** [no plural] the thin threads that grow on the head and body of people and animals: *a girl with long, dark hair* → See **Hair** on page C9 **2** one of the thin threads that grow on a person's or animal's skin: *My skirt was covered with cat hairs.*

hairbrush /ˈheərˌbrʌʃ/ noun a brush that you use to make your hair look neat
→ See picture at **brush noun**

haircut /ˈheərˌkʌt/ noun **1 B1** an act of having your hair cut: *I really need a haircut.* **2** the style in which your hair has been cut: *I like your new haircut.*

hairdresser /ˈheərˌdres·ər/ noun **B1** someone whose job is to cut people's hair

hair dryer /ˈheərˌdraɪ·ər/ noun **B1** a piece of electrical equipment you use to dry your hair with hot air

hairstyle /ˈheərˌstaɪl/ *noun* the style in which someone's hair is cut and arranged: *Do you like my new hairstyle?*

hairy /ˈheər·i/ *adj* (comparative **hairier**, superlative **hairiest**) covered in hair: *a hairy chest*

half[1] /hæf/ *noun, determiner* (plural **halves**) **1** 🅰🄉 one of two equal parts of something; 1/2: *Cut the lemons into halves.* ○ *It'll take **half an hour** to get there.* ○ *Jenny lived in Beijing for a year and a half.* **2** break, cut, etc. *something* **in half** 🄱🄵 to divide something into two equal parts: *Fold the piece of paper in half.* **3** informal a lot: *I don't even know where she is **half the time**.*

half[2] /hæf/ *adv* 🄱🄵 partly, but not completely: *The room was half empty.* ○ *Sophia is half Greek and half Spanish (= she has one Greek parent and one Spanish parent).*

half-price[1] /ˈhæf ˈpraɪs/ *adj* 🅰🄉 costing half the usual price: *I got some half-price pizzas at the supermarket.*

half-price[2] /ˈhæf praɪs/ *adv* 🅰🄉 for half the usual price: *I got this dress half price.*

half price /ˈhæf ˈpraɪs/ *noun* [no plural] 🅰🄉 half the usual price: *Kids under 12 can ride **for half price**.*

halftime /ˈhæf taɪm/ *noun* a time between the two main parts of some sports games when the players rest: *We were ahead by 10 points at halftime.*

halfway /ˈhæfˈweɪ/ *adj, adv* in the middle between two places, or in the middle of a period of time: *halfway between Chicago and St. Louis* ○ *We were already halfway through the week.*

hall /hɔl/ *noun* **1** 🅰🄉 a room that leads to other rooms: *Her office is at the end of the hall.* **2** 🅰🄉 a large room or building where meetings, concerts, etc. happen: *The concert was held in Carnegie Hall.* ○ *a college lecture hall (= that can hold a large number of students)* **3** **Town Hall/ City Hall** the building where a town or city government is based: *The mayor's office is in City Hall.* **4** used in the names of buildings where college students live: *I live in Ashton Hall.*

Halloween /ˌhæl·əˈwin/ *noun* [no plural] the night of October 31 when children dress in special clothes and visit houses to ask for candy, and people try to frighten each other

halt[1] /hɔlt/ *noun* the action of stopping something from moving or happening: *The car **came to a halt**.*

halt[2] /hɔlt/ *verb* formal to stop or make something stop: *Work on the project was halted immediately.*

halve /hæv/ *verb* (present participle **halving**, past tense and past participle **halved**) to divide something into two equal parts: *Peel and halve the potatoes.*

ham /hæm/ *noun* 🅰🄉 meat from a pig's leg: *a ham sandwich*

hamburger /ˈhæmˌbɜr·gər/ *noun* meat that is cooked in a round, flat shape and eaten between round pieces of bread: *a hamburger and fries*

hammer /ˈhæm·ər/ *noun*   **hammer**
a tool with a heavy metal part at the top that you use to hit nails into something

hamster /ˈhæm·stər/ *noun* a small animal with soft fur and no tail that is often kept as a pet

hand[1] /hænd/ *noun* **1** 🄰🄉 the part of your body on the end of your arm that has fingers: *I had my hands in my pockets.* → See **The Body** on page C2 **2** **hold hands** If two people hold hands, they hold each other's hand. **3** **by hand** 🄱🄵 done or made by a person and not a machine: *This sweater has to be washed by hand.* **4** one of the long, thin pieces that point to the numbers on a clock or watch **5** **give** *someone* **a hand** 🄱🄵 to help someone: *Could you give me a hand with these suitcases?* **6** **on the one hand… on the other hand** used when you are comparing two different ideas or opinions: *On the one hand, I'd like more money, but on the other hand, I don't want to work longer hours.*

hand[2] /hænd/ *verb* 🄱🄵 to give something to someone: *Could you hand me that book, please?*

a
b
c
d
e
f
g
h
i
j
k
l
m
n
o
p
q
r
s
t
u
v
w
x
y
z

hand *something* **in** phrasal verb **B1** to give your finished work to a teacher: *Have you handed your history essay in yet?*

hand *something* **out** phrasal verb **B1** to give something to all the people in a group: *The teacher handed out worksheets to the class.*

hand *someone/something* **over** phrasal verb to give someone or something to someone else: *We were ordered to hand over our passports.*

handbag /'hænd,bæg/ noun **A2** a bag carried by a woman with her money, keys, etc. inside

handcuffs /'hænd,kʌfs/ **plural noun** two metal rings joined by a chain that are used for holding a prisoner's hands together

handcuffs

handful /'hænd,fʊl/ noun **1** the amount of something that you can hold in one hand: *a handful of nuts* **2** a **handful of** *something* a small number of people or things: *Only a handful of people came to the meeting.*

handheld[1] /'hænd'held/ adj **B1** describes something that is designed to be held and used easily with one or two hands: *a handheld computer*

handheld[2] /'hænd'held/ noun a small computer or electronic device that is designed to be held and used easily with one or two hands

handicap /'hæn,di,kæp/ noun **1** something that is wrong with your mind or body permanently: *a mental/physical handicap* **2** something that makes it more difficult for you to do something: *Not having a car was a real handicap in the suburbs.*

handicapped /'hæn,di,kæpt/ adj not able to use part of your body or your mind because it has been damaged: *mentally/physically handicapped*

handkerchief /'hæŋ,kər,tʃif/ **B1** a small piece of cloth or soft paper that you use to dry your eyes or nose

handle[1] /'hæn,dəl/ verb (present participle **handling**, past tense and past participle

handled) 1 B1 to take action to improve a difficult situation: *He handled the situation very well.* **2** to touch, hold, or pick up something: *You must wash your hands before handling food.*

handles

handle

handle[2] /'hæn,dəl/ noun the part of something that you use to hold it or open it: *a door handle* ∘ *the handle on a suitcase*

handlebars /'hæn,dəl,barz/ **plural noun** the metal bars at the front of a bicycle or motorcycle that you hold on to

handlebars

hand luggage /'hænd ,lʌg,idʒ/ noun [no plural] small bags that you can carry onto a plane with you: *How many items of hand luggage can I take onto the plane?*

handout /'hænd,aʊt/ noun a copy of a document that is given to all the people in a class or meeting: *You will find the exercises on page two of your handout.*

handsome /'hæn,səm/ adj **B1** A handsome man is attractive: *He was tall, dark, and handsome.*

hands-on /'hændz,ɒn/, /'hændz,ɑn/ adj doing something instead of only studying it or watching someone else do it: *hands-on experience*

handwriting /'hænd,rai,tiŋ/ noun [no plural] **B1** the way that someone forms letters when he or she writes with a pen or pencil

handy /ˈhæn·di/ adj (comparative **handier**, superlative **handiest**) useful or easy to use: *a handy container/tool*

hang /hæŋ/ verb (present participle **hanging**, past tense and past participle **hung**) **1 B1** to fasten something so that the top part is fixed but the lower part is free to move: *He **hung** his coat on the hook behind the door.* **2** to kill someone by putting a rope around his or her neck and making the person drop

hang around phrasal verb informal **B1** to spend time somewhere, usually doing little: *A lot of teenagers hang around at the mall.*

hang on phrasal verb informal **B1** to wait for a short time: *Hang on – I'm coming.*

hang out phrasal verb informal **B1** to spend a lot of time in a place or with someone: *I was **hanging out with** my friends last night.*

hang up phrasal verb **B1** to finish talking on the telephone

hang something up phrasal verb **B1** to put something such as a coat in a place where it can hang: *You can hang up your jacket over there.*

hanger /ˈhæŋ·ər/ noun a wire, wooden, or plastic object for hanging clothes on

happen /ˈhæp·ən/ verb **1 A2** If an event or situation happens, it exists or starts to be done: *Accidents can happen to anyone.* ○ *We can't let a mistake like this happen again.* ○ *Did you hear what **happened to** Jamie last night?* **2 A2** to be the result of an action, situation, or event that someone or something experiences: *What happens if we miss the flight?*

happily /ˈhæp·ə·li/ adv **1 B1** in a happy way: *They are very happily married.* **2** in a way that is very willing: *I'd happily drive you to the airport.*

happiness /ˈhæp·i·nəs/ noun [no plural] **B1** the feeling of being happy

happy /ˈhæp·i/ adj (comparative **happier**, superlative **happiest**) **1 A1** having very good feelings, especially because something good has happened: *She looked really happy.*

→ Opposite **unhappy** adj **2** happy birthday, New Year, etc. **A1** something friendly that you say to someone on a special day or holiday **3 A2** satisfied and not worried: *Are you **happy with** your test scores?* **4** happy to do something **A2** to be willing to do something: *I'd be happy to help if you need a hand.*

harbor /ˈhɑr·bər/ noun **B1** an area of water near the coast where ships are kept

hard¹ /hɑrd/ adj **1 A2** firm and not easy to press or bend: *a hard surface* ○ *The seats were really hard.* → Opposite **soft** adj **2 A1** difficult to do or understand: *It must be hard to study with all this noise.* → Opposite **easy** adj **3 B1** needing or using a lot of physical or mental effort: *It was **hard work** on the farm, but satisfying.* **4** be hard on someone to criticize someone too much, or to treat someone unfairly: *Don't be too hard on him – he's only trying to help.*

hard² /hɑrd/ adv **1 A2** with a lot of effort: *He tried really hard.* ○ *You must work harder.* **2 B1** with a lot of force: *She kicked the ball hard.*

hard drive /ˈhɑrd ˈdraɪv/ noun (also **hard disk**) the part inside a computer that is not removed and keeps very large amounts of information

harden /ˈhɑr·dən/ verb to become hard and stiff, or to make something become hard and stiff

hardly /ˈhɑrd·li/ adv **1 B1** almost not, or only a very small amount: *I was so tired that I could hardly walk.* ○ *There's **hardly any** food left in the fridge.* **2** certainly not: *Don't get mad at me – it's hardly my fault you didn't win!*

⚠ Common mistake: hardly or hard?

When you mean "with a lot of effort or force," you should use the adverb **hard**, not "hardly."
We worked very hard.
~~We worked very hardly.~~

hardware /ˈhɑrd·wɛər/ noun [no plural] **B1** the machines or equipment that your computer system is made from, not the programs

hard-working /ˈhɑrdˌwɜrkɪŋ/ **adj** doing a job seriously and with a lot of effort: *She was a very hard-working student.*

harm[1] /hɑrm/ **noun** [no plural] hurt or damage: *Smoking can **cause** serious **harm to** the lungs.*

harm[2] /hɑrm/ **verb** to hurt someone or damage something: *Luckily, no one was harmed in the accident.*

harmful /ˈhɑrm·fəl/ **adj** causing damage or injury: *Eating too much fat is **harmful to** your health.*

harmless /ˈhɑrm·ləs/ **adj** not causing hurt or damage: *Taken in small doses, this drug is completely harmless.*

harsh /hɑrʃ/ **adj** **1** cruel or unkind: *harsh criticism* **2** too strong, bright, loud, etc.: *harsh chemicals* ○ *harsh lighting*
• **harshly adv** *She felt that she had been treated harshly.*

harvest[1] /ˈhɑr·vəst/ **noun** **1** the job of cutting and collecting crops from fields **2** the amount of crops that are collected

harvest[2] /ˈhɑr·vəst/ **verb** to cut and collect crops when they are ready

has /hæz,/,/həz/ present simple of have, used with "he," "she," and "it"

hasn't /ˈhæz·ənt/ short form of has not: *It hasn't rained for three weeks.*

hassle[1] /ˈhæs·əl/ **noun** a problem: *It's such a hassle finding a place to park.*

hassle[2] /ˈhæs·əl/ **verb** (present participle **hassling**, past tense and past participle **hassled**) to annoy someone, mainly by asking for something again and again: *He's always **hassling** me **for** money.*

haste /heɪst/ **noun** [no plural] speed in doing something, especially because you do not have much time: *In their haste to escape, they left behind all their belongings.*

hasty /ˈheɪ·sti/ **adj** (comparative **hastier**, superlative **hastiest**) done very quickly: *I don't want to make a hasty decision.*

hat /hæt/ **noun** **A1** something that you wear to cover your head that often has a

hard part around the edge and a soft top: *a cowboy hat*
→ See **Clothes** on page C5

hatch /hætʃ/ **verb** to come out of an egg: *When will the chicks hatch?*

hate /heɪt/ **verb** (present participle **hating**, past tense and past participle **hated**) **A2** to dislike someone or something very much: *I hate going to the dentist's.*

hatred /ˈheɪ·trɪd/ **noun** [no plural] a great dislike of someone or something: *He developed an intense **hatred of** all women.*

haul /hɔl/ **verb** to pull something somewhere slowly and with difficulty: *They hauled the piano into the living room.*

haunt /hɔnt/ **verb** **1** If a ghost haunts a place, it appears there often: *a haunted house* **2** If an unpleasant memory or feeling haunts you, you think about or feel it often: *His experiences in the war haunted him for the rest of his life.*

have[1] /hæv,/,/həv/ **auxiliary verb** (present participle **having**, past tense and past participle **had**) **A2** used with the past participle of another verb to make the present and past perfect tenses: *Have you seen Anna?* ○ *I've (= I have) forgotten his name.* ○ *He hadn't (= had not) thought about what could happen.*

have[2] /hæv,/,/həv/ **verb** (present participle **having**, past tense and past participle **had**) **1** (also **have got**) used for saying what or who is yours: *Laura has beautiful blue eyes.* ○ *We have two children.* ○ *I had a bike, but I sold it.* **2** (also **have got**) If you have a particular illness, you are suffering from it: *I have a bad cold.* **3** to eat or drink something: *Can I have a drink of water?* **4** (also **have got**) used to talk about the position of something in relation to a person or thing: *He had a pen in his hand.* ○ *She had a baby with her.* ○ *What have you gotten on your dress?* **5** to cause something to be in a particular state: *He had dinner ready by the time we got home.* **6 have (got) to do** *something* to need to do something: *I have to go to* work now. ○ *Do we have to finish this today?* **7 have difficulty, fun, problems, etc.** **A2** used with nouns to say that someone experiences something: *We had a great time at the beach.* **8 have a baby** **A2** to give birth to a baby **9 have something cleaned, cut, repaired, etc.** **B1** to arrange for someone to do something for you: *I'm having the house painted.* **10 have something stolen, taken, etc.** **B1** If you have something stolen, taken, etc., someone takes something that belongs to you: *She had her car stolen last week.*

hawk /hɔk/ noun a large bird that kills small animals for food

hay /heɪ/ noun [no plural] dried grass for animals to eat

hay fever /ˈheɪ ˌfiˑvər/ noun [no plural] an illness like a cold, caused by pollen (= a powder made by flowers): *She gets really bad hay fever.*

hazard /ˈhæzˑərd/ noun something that is dangerous: *a fire hazard* ○ *a health hazard*

hazardous /ˈhæzˑərˑdəs/ adj dangerous: *hazardous chemicals*

haze /heɪz/ noun [no plural] smoke or water in the air, making it difficult to see: *There was a haze over the horizon.*

hazy /ˈheɪˑzi/ adj (comparative **hazier**, superlative **haziest**) If the air is hazy, it is not clear: *a hazy day*

he /hi/ pronoun **A1** used when talking about a man or male animal who has already been talked about: *"When is Dan coming?" "He should be here soon."*

head[1] /hed/ noun **1 A1** the part of your body that contains your brain, eyes, ears, mouth, nose, etc.: *He fell and hit his head on the table.* → See **The Body** on page C2 **2 B1** your mind: *I keep hearing that song in my head.* **3 B1** the person who is in charge of an organization: *Her father is the head of an oil company.* **4** the front or top part of something: *Who is that at the head of the table?* **5 come to a head** If a problem comes to a head, it becomes very bad. **6 go**

over someone's head to be too difficult for someone to understand: *All this talk about philosophy went right over my head.*

head[2] /hed/ verb **1** to move in a particular direction: *I was **heading toward** the park.* ○ *I think we should **head home** now, before it gets too dark.* **2** to be in charge of a group, organization, etc.: *She heads the country's leading travel company.*

headache /ˈhedˌeɪk/ noun **A2** pain inside your head: *I've got a bad headache.*

heading /ˈhedˑɪŋ/ noun words at the top of a piece of writing that tell you its subject

headlight /ˈhedˌlaɪt/ noun one of the two large lights on the front of a car → See picture at **light noun**

headline /ˈhedˌlaɪn/ noun **1 B1** the title of a newspaper story that is printed in large letters above it: *a front-page headline* **2 the headlines** the main stories in newspapers, on television, etc.: *That story was in the headlines all weekend.*

headphones /ˈhedˌfoʊnz/ plural noun a piece of equipment that you wear over your ears so that you can listen to music: *a pair of headphones*

headphones
headphones
earphones

headquarters /ˈhedˌkwɔrˑtərz/ noun (plural **headquarters**) the place from where an organization is controlled: *police headquarters*

heal /hil/ verb (also **heal up**) If an injury heals, it becomes healthy again, and if something heals it, it makes it healthy again: *The wound on his head had begun to heal.*

health /helθ/ noun [no plural] **A2** the condition of your body: *She is in poor health.*

health care (also **healthcare**) /ˈhelθ ˌkeər/ noun [no plural] the set of services provided by a country or an organization for treating people who are ill

health club /'helθ ˌklʌb/ noun a private club where people can go to exercise to keep fit

healthy /'helθi/ adj (comparative **healthier**, superlative **healthiest**) **1** **A2** not sick: *Maria is a normal, healthy child.* **2** **A2** good for your health: *a healthy diet*

> **!** Common mistake: **healthy** or **health**?
>
> Remember not to use "healthy" as a noun. If you need a noun, use **health**.
> *She has some health problems.*
> ~~She has some healthy problems.~~

heap /hiːp/ noun a messy pile of things: *a heap of garbage*

hear /hɪər/ verb (past tense and past participle **heard**) **1** **A1** to be aware of a sound through your ears: *I could hear his voice in the distance.* **2** **A2** to listen to someone or something: *I heard a program about tigers on the radio this morning.* **3** **B1** to be told some information: *When did you first **hear about** this?* ∘ *Have you heard the news?*

have heard of *something* phrasal verb to know that someone or something exists: *It's a tiny country that most people have never heard of.*

hear from *someone* phrasal verb **B1** to get a letter, telephone call, or other message from someone: *Have you heard from Helena recently?*

hearing /'hɪər·ɪŋ/ noun [no plural] the ability to hear sounds: *He lost his hearing when he was a child.*

heart /hɑrt/ noun **1** **A2** the thing inside your chest that sends blood around your body: *My heart was beating fast.* **2** **B1** the center of something: *Her office is **in the heart of** Tokyo.* **3** **B1** someone's deepest feelings and true character: *She has a kind heart.* **4** a shape that is used to mean love → See picture at **shape** noun (1) **5 with all your heart** used to say that you feel something very strongly: *I thank you with all my heart.* **6 break** *someone's* **heart** to make someone very unhappy

heart attack /'hɑrt əˌtæk/ noun **B1** a serious medical condition in which the heart stops working correctly: *John **had a heart attack** three years ago.*

heartbeat /'hɑrtˌbit/ noun the regular movement of the heart as it moves blood around the body

hearth /hɑrθ/ noun the bottom of a fireplace and the hard, flat area in front of it
→ See **The Living Room** on page C11

heartless /'hɑrt·ləs/ adj cruel and not caring about other people

hearts /hɑrts/ plural noun one of the four suits (=groups) of playing cards: *the five of hearts*

heat¹ /hit/ noun **1** **A2** [no plural] the system that keeps a building warm: *Please turn up the heat.* **2** **B1** [no plural] the quality of being hot or warm: *the heat of summer* **3** **B1** the temperature of something: *Cook over low heat.* **4** a competition, especially in a race, that decides who will be in the final event **5** the heat hot weather or hot conditions: *I'd rather stay indoors – I don't like the heat.*

heat² /hit/ verb (also **heat up**) to make something become hot or warm: *I'll just heat up some soup.*

heater /'hi·t̬ər/ noun **B1** a machine that heats air or water

heaven /'hev·ən/ noun [no plural] **1** the place where some people think good people go when they die → Opposite **hell** noun **2** informal something very nice that gives you great pleasure: *I just lay in the sun and did nothing – it was heaven.*

heavily /'hev·ə·li/ adv **1** **B1** a lot or to a great degree: *She's heavily involved in politics.* **2 drink/smoke heavily** to drink or smoke a lot **3 rain/snow heavily** to rain or snow a lot

heavy /'hev·i/ adj (comparative **heavier**, superlative **heaviest**) **1** **A2** Heavy objects weigh a lot: *heavy bags* → Opposite **light** adj **2** **A2** used to say how much someone or something weighs: *How heavy are you?* **3** **B1** large in amount or degree: *heavy traffic* **4 a heavy drinker/**

smoker someone who drinks or smokes a lot **5 heavy snow/rain** a large amount of snow or rain

hectare /ˈhek·teər/ **noun** a unit for measuring area, equal to 10,000 square meters

hectic /ˈhek·tɪk/ **adj** very busy and full of activity: *I've had a very hectic day.*

he'd /hid/ **1** short form of he had: *We knew he'd taken the money.* **2** short form of he would: *I knew he'd get the job.*

hedge /hedʒ/ **noun** a row of bushes growing close together

heel /hil/ **noun 1** the back part of your foot → See **The Body** on page C2 **2** B1 the part of a shoe that is under your heel: *high heels*

height /haɪt/ **noun 1** B1 how tall or high something or someone is: *The tower is over 300 feet in height.* → See picture at **length noun** (1) **2** B1 how far above the ground something is: *The plane was flying at a height of about 6,000 meters.*

held /held/ past tense and past participle of hold

helicopter /ˈhel·ɪˌkɑp·tər/ **noun** A2 a plane that flies using long, thin parts on top of it that turn around very fast

helicopter

hell /hel/ **noun 1** [no plural] the place where some people think bad people go when they die → Opposite **heaven noun** **2** [no plural] informal an experience that is very bad: *It's been hell dealing with Dad's bad health.*

he'll /hil/ short form of he will: *He'll be home soon.*

hello /heˈloʊ/ **exclamation 1** A1 said when you meet someone or start talking with someone: *Hello, Sue. How are you?* **2** A1 used when you start speaking on the telephone: *Hello, this is Alex.*

helmet /ˈhel·mət/ **noun** a hard hat that protects your head: *a motorcycle helmet* → See **Sports 2** on page C16

helmet

help¹ /help/ **verb** **1** A1 to do something for someone: *Thank you for helping.* ○ *Dad always helps me with my homework.* **2** A2 to provide advice, money, support, etc. to make it possible or easier for someone to do something: *My mom said she would help with the costs of buying a house.* **3** to make something better or easier: *When you're nervous or frightened, it helps to breathe slowly.* **4 help yourself to something** B1 to take something, especially food or drink, without asking: *Please help yourself to some coffee.* **5 can't/couldn't help something** B1 to not be able to stop doing something: *I couldn't help laughing.*

help (someone) out phrasal verb to help someone, especially by giving him or her money or doing work for him or her: *Sophia has been helping out in the store this week.*

help² /help/ **noun 1** A2 [no plural] things you do to make it easier for another person to do something: *Do you want any help?* **2 with the help of something** B1 using something: *We managed to open the box with the help of a knife.* **3** something or someone that makes things easier for you: *Dave has been a great help to me.*

help³ /help/ **exclamation** A2 something that you shout when you are in danger: *Help! I'm drowning!*

helper /ˈhel·pər/ **noun** someone who helps another person to do something: *We need more helpers for the school play.*

a
b
c
d
e
f
g
h
i
j
k
l
m
n
o
p
q
r
s
t
u
v
w
x
y
z

|æ cat|ɑ hot|e get|ɪ sit|i see|c was|ʊ book|u too|ʌ cut|ə about|ɚ mother|ɝ turn|ɔr for|ɑr my|aʊ how|eɪ say|ɔɪ boy|

helpful /'help·fəl/ **adj** 1 **B1** useful: *helpful advice* 2 **B1** willing to help: *The staff here is very helpful.*

→ Opposite **unhelpful adj**

helping /'hel·pɪŋ/ **noun** an amount of food given to one person at one time: *She gave me a large helping of pasta.*

helpless /'help·ləs/ **adj** not able to do things for yourself or protect yourself: *a helpless animal*

hem /hem/ **noun** the edge of a piece of clothing or cloth that has been folded under and sewn

hen /hen/ **noun** a female bird, especially a chicken

her[1] /hɜr/, /hər/ **pronoun** **A1** used to mean a woman or girl who you have already talked about: *Where's Katie – have you seen her?*

her[2] /hɜr/, /hər/ **determiner** **A1** belonging or relating to a woman or girl whom you have already talked about: *That's her house on the corner. ○ It's not her fault.*

herb /ɜrb/, /hɜrb/ **noun** **B1** a plant that is used in cooking to add flavor to food

herd[1] /hɜrd/ **noun** a large group of animals such as cows that live and eat together: *a herd of cattle/deer*

herd[2] /hɜrd/ **verb** to move a group of people or animals somewhere: *The passengers were quickly herded onto a bus.*

here /hɪər/ **adv** 1 **A1** in the place where you are: *Does Lily live near here? ○ Come here!* 2 **here you are** **A2** used when you are giving someone something: *"Please pass me the bread." "Here you are."* 3 **here you are, here it is, etc.** **A2** used when you see someone or something you have been looking for or waiting for: *Here's our bus. ○ I can't find my keys – oh, here they are.* 4 at this point in a discussion or piece of writing: *I don't have time to examine the issue here.* 5 **here and there** in many different places: *Weeds were growing here and there in the garden.*

hero /'hɪər·oʊ/ **noun** (plural **heroes**) 1 **B1** a very brave person, often a man, whom a lot of people admire: *He became a national hero for his part in the revolution.* 2 **B1** the main man in a book or movie: *the hero of her new novel* 3 a type of long sandwich

→ See **Food** on page C7

heroic /hɪ'roʊ·ɪk/ **adj** very brave: *a heroic figure*

heroine /'her·oʊ·ɪn/ **noun** 1 a very brave woman whom a lot of people admire 2 **B1** the main woman in a book or movie: *the heroine of "Little Women"*

hers /hɜrz/ **pronoun** **A2** the thing or things that belong to or relate to a woman or girl: *That's Sara's coat over there – at least I think it's hers.*

herself /hər'self/ **pronoun** 1 **A2** used to show that the woman or girl who does the action is also the person who is affected by it: *She looked at herself in the mirror.* 2 **by herself** **A2** alone or without anyone else's help: *She shouldn't walk home by herself.* 3 used to show that a particular woman or girl did something: *She fixed the bike herself.*

he's /hiz/ 1 short form of he is: *He's my best friend.* 2 short form of he has: *Sam must be tired – he's been dancing all night!*

hesitate /'hez·ɪ,teɪt/ **verb** (present participle **hesitating**, past tense and past participle **hesitated**) 1 to stop before you do something, especially because you are nervous or not sure: *Richard hesitated before answering.* 2 **don't hesitate to do something** used to encourage someone to do something: *If you need any help, don't hesitate to call me.*

hesitation /,hez·ɪ'teɪ·ʃən/ **noun** a pause before you do something, especially because you are not sure: *After a moment's hesitation, he unlocked the door.*

hey /heɪ/ **exclamation** informal **A2** used to get someone's attention or to show that you are interested, excited, or angry: *Hey, Helen, look at this! ○ Hey, wait a minute!*

hi /haɪ/ **exclamation** informal **A1** hello: *Hi! How are you?*

hibernate /'haɪ·bər,neɪt/ **verb** (present participle **hibernating**, past tense and past partici-

ple hibernated) If an animal hibernates, it goes to sleep for the winter.

hiccups /ˈhɪk·ʌps/ **plural noun** sudden noises you make in your throat when a muscle in your chest moves: *I got the hiccups from drinking too quickly.*

hidden /ˈhɪd·ᵊn/ **adj 1** **B1** A hidden thing or place is not easy to find: *There were hidden microphones in the room.* **2** If something is hidden, most people do not know about it: *Beware of the hidden costs of joining a gym.*

hide /haɪd/ **verb** (present participle **hiding**, past tense **hid**, past participle **hidden**) **1** **B1** to put something in a place where no one can see it: *I hid the money in a drawer.* **2** **B1** to go to a place where no one can see you: *She ran off and hid behind a tree.* **3** **B1** to keep a feeling or information secret: *He couldn't hide his embarrassment.*

hide

hideous /ˈhɪd·i·əs/ **adj** very ugly: *a hideous monster*

high¹ /haɪ/ **adj 1** **A2** having a long distance from the bottom to the top: *a high building/mountain* → Opposite **low adj 2** **B1** a long distance above the ground or the level of the sea: *The village was high up in the mountains.* **3** used to say how long the distance is from the bottom to the top: *How high is it?* ○ *It's ten feet high.* **4** **B1** great in amount or level: *a high temperature* ○ *high prices* → Opposite **low adj 5** **B1** very good: *of high quality* ○ *She got a high score on the last test.* **6** A high sound or note is near the top of the set of sounds that people can hear. → Opposite **low adj 7** important, powerful, or at an upper level of something: *a high rank in the army*

high² /haɪ/ **adv 1** **B1** at or to a long distance above the ground: *He threw the ball high into the air.* ○ *We flew high above the city.* **2** **B1** at or to a large amount or level: *Temperatures rose as high as 90 degrees.*

higher education /ˈhaɪ·ər ˌedʒ·ʊ'keɪ·ʃən/ **noun** [no plural] education at a college or university

high heels /ˈhaɪ ˈhilz/ **plural noun** women's shoes that have heels that are raised high off the ground

high jump /ˈhaɪ ˌdʒʌmp/ **no plural** a sport in which competitors try to jump over a bar that is raised higher after each jump
→ See **Sports (1)** on page C15

highlight¹ /ˈhaɪˌlaɪt/ **noun** the best or most important part of something: *The boat trip was a highlight of our vacation.*

highlight² /ˈhaɪˌlaɪt/ **verb** to emphasize something or make people notice something: *The report highlights the problems with the project.*

highlighter /ˈhaɪˌlaɪ·t̬ər/ **noun** a pen containing brightly colored ink that is used to mark words in a text
→ See **The Office** on page C12

highly /ˈhaɪ·li/ **adv** very: *a highly intelligent child*

high school /ˈhaɪ ˌskuːl/ *noun* a school that children go to between the ages of 14 and 18

high-tech /ˈhaɪˈtek/ *adj* (also **hi-tech**) using the most recent and advanced electronic machines, computers, and methods: *a high-tech computer company*

highway /ˈhaɪˌweɪ/ *noun* **A2** a main road, especially between two cities

hijack /ˈhaɪˌdʒæk/ *verb* to take control of a plane during a flight, especially using violence: *The plane was hijacked by terrorists.*
• **hijacker** *noun*

hike[1] /haɪk/ *verb* to walk a long distance, especially in the country: *We're **going hiking** this weekend.*
• **hiker** *noun We met some other hikers on the trail.*

hike[2] /haɪk/ *noun* a long walk, especially in the country: *a ten-mile hike*

hill /hɪl/ *noun* **A2** a high area of land that is smaller than a mountain: *They climbed up the hill to get a better view.*

him /hɪm/ *pronoun* **A1** used to mean a man or boy whom you have already talked about: *I'm looking for Al – have you seen him?*

himself /hɪmˈself/ *pronoun* **1** **A2** used to show that the man or boy who does the action is also the person who is affected by it: *John always cuts himself when he's shaving.* **2 by himself** **A2** alone or without anyone else's help: *My three-year-old son can tie his shoelaces by himself.* **3** used to show that a particular man or boy did something: *He baked the cake himself.*

hinder /ˈhɪnˌdər/ *verb* to make it difficult to do something: *Our progress was hindered by bad weather.*

Hindu /ˈhɪnˌduː/ *noun* someone whose religion is Hinduism
• **Hindu** *adj*

Hinduism /ˈhɪnˌduːˌɪzˌəm/ *noun* [no plural] the main religion of India, based on belief in one or more gods, and the belief that when a person dies his or her spirit returns to life in another body

hinge /hɪndʒ/ *noun* a metal fastening that joins the edge of a door or window and allows you to open or close it

hint[1] /hɪnt/ *noun* **1** something you say that suggests what you think or want, but not in a direct way: *He **dropped** (=made) several **hints** that he wanted a computer for his birthday.* **2** a small piece of advice: *The magazine gives lots of useful hints on how to save money.*

hint[2] /hɪnt/ *verb* to suggest something, but not in a direct way: *He **hinted that** he wanted to leave the company.*

hip /hɪp/ *noun* one of the two parts of your body above your leg and below your waist
→ See **The Body** on page C2

hip-hop /ˈhɪpˌhɑːp/ *noun* [no plural] a type of popular music with words spoken rather than sung, originally performed by African Americans

hippopotamus /ˌhɪpˌəˈpɑːtˌəˌməs/ *noun* (plural **hippopotamuses**, **hippopotami**) a very large animal with thick skin that lives near water in parts of Africa

hire /haɪər/ *verb* (present participle **hiring**, past tense and past participle **hired**) to employ someone or pay him or her to do a particular job: *We hired a new secretary.*

his[1] /hɪz/ *determiner* **A1** belonging or relating to a man or boy whom you have already talked about: *Phillip is sitting over there with his daughter.* ∘ *It's not his fault.*

his[2] /hɪz/ *pronoun* **A2** the thing or things that belong or relate to a man or boy: *That's Brian's coat – at least I think it's his.*

hiss /hɪs/ *verb* to make a long noise like the letter "s": *The gas hissed through the pipes.*

historic /hɪˈstɔːrˌɪk/ *adj* **B1** important in history: *historic buildings* ∘ *a historic day*

historical /hɪˈstɔːrˌɪˌkəl/ *adj* **B1** relating to the past: *historical documents*

history /ˈhɪsˌtəˌri/ *noun* [no plural] **1** **A2** events that happened in the past:

American history **2** **A2** the study of events in the past: *a history book*

> **! Common mistake: history or story?**
>
> **History** means "events that happened in the past."
>   *He's studying for a degree in history.*
> A **story** is a description of real or imaginary events, often told to entertain people.
>   *The story is about two friends traveling across India.*

hit¹ /hɪt/ **verb** (present participle **hitting**, past tense and past participle **hit**) **1** **A2** to touch something or someone quickly and with force, usually hurting or damaging something: *The ball hit him on the head.* ○ *She hit her head on the sidewalk when she fell.* **2** to affect something in a bad way: *The city has been **hit hard** by the budget cuts.* **3** **hit it off** informal If people hit it off, they like each other immediately.

hit

hit² /hɪt/ **noun** **1** **B1** a very successful song, movie, book, etc.: *The movie should be a **big hit**.* **2** **B1** an occasion when you touch something or when something touches you quickly and

with force **3** an occasion when someone visits a website on the Internet, which is then counted to find the number of people who look at the page

hitchhike /ˈhɪtʃˌhaɪk/ **verb** (present participle **hitchhiking**, past tense and past participle **hitchhiked**) **B1** to get free rides in other people's cars by waiting next to the road
• **hitchhiker** noun

hi-tech /ˈhaɪˈtek/ **adj** another spelling of high-tech

HIV /ˌeɪtʃˌaɪˈviː/ **noun** [no plural] a virus that causes AIDS (= a serious disease that destroys the body's ability to fight infection)

hive /haɪv/ **noun** (also **beehive**) a special container for keeping bees

hoard /hɔrd/ **verb** to collect a lot of something, often secretly: *He hoarded antique books in the attic.*

hoarse /hɔrs/ **adj** If you are hoarse, your voice sounds rough, often because you are ill: *I was hoarse from shouting.*

hobby /ˈhɑbi/ **noun** (plural **hobbies**) **A2** an activity that you like and often do when you are not working: *Do you have any hobbies?*

hockey /ˈhɑki/ **noun** [no plural] **A2** (also **ice hockey**) a game that two teams play on ice, in which players hit a flat, round object with long, curved sticks

hold¹ /hoʊld/ **verb** (past tense and past participle **held**) **1** **A2** to have something in your hand or arms: *He was holding a glass of wine.* ○ *She held the baby in her arms.* **2** **B1** to keep something in a particular position: *Can you hold the door open, please?* ○ *Hold your hand up if you know the answer.* **3** **B1** to organize an event: *The meeting will be held on Tuesday morning.* **4** **B1** to contain something: *The bucket holds about 2 gallons.* **5** to keep someone in a place so that the person cannot leave: *I was **held prisoner** in a tiny room.* **6 Hold it!** informal used to tell someone to wait: *Hold it! I forgot my coat.* **7 hold your breath** to stop breathing for a time

| æ cat | ɑ hot | e get | ɪ sit | i see | ɔ saw | ʊ book | u too | ʌ cut | ə about | ɑr mother | ɜr turn | ɔr for | aɪ my | aʊ how | eɪ say | ɔɪ boy |

hold on phrasal verb informal **B1** to wait: *Hold on! Let me check my calendar.*

hold *something/someone* **up** phrasal verb **B1** to make something or someone slow or late: *Sorry I'm late. I got held up in traffic.*

hold² /hould/ noun **1** the act of holding something in your hand: *Keep a tight hold on your tickets.* **2 catch, grab, etc. hold of** *something/someone* to start holding something or someone: *He tried to escape, but I grabbed hold of his jacket.* **3 get hold of** *something/someone* to get something: *I got hold of the book at the local library.* **4** an area on a plane or ship for storing things: *a cargo hold*

holdup /ˈhould.ʌp/ noun **1** something that makes you move slowly or makes you late: *Everyone agrees what needs to be done, so what's the holdup?* **2** an act of stealing money from a bank or store using a gun

hole /houl/ noun **B1** a hollow space in something, or an opening in something: *There's a **hole** in the roof.* ○ *We dug a hole to plant the tree.*

holiday /ˈhɑl·ɪˌdeɪ/ noun **A1** a day for celebrating or remembering a special event, especially one on which many people are allowed not to go to work or school: *the Fourth of July holiday* ○ *There are several holidays in December.*

hollow /ˈhɑl·oʊ/ adj having a hole or empty space inside: *a hollow shell/tube*
→ See picture at **flat adj (1)**
→ Opposite **solid adj**

holy /ˈhoʊ·li/ adj (comparative **holier**, superlative **holiest**) **1** relating to a religion or a god: *the holy city of Jerusalem* **2** very religious or pure: *a holy man*

home¹ /houm/ noun **1 A1** the place where you live: *He wasn't **at home**.* **2** a place where people who need special care live: *an old people's home* **3 feel at home B1** to feel happy and confident in a place or situation: *After a month she felt at home in her new job.*

home² /houm/ adv **A2** to the place where you live: *He didn't **come home** until midnight.* ○ *I **went home** to visit my parents.*

> **! Common mistake: home**
>
> When you use verbs of movement with **home**, for example "go" or "come," you do not use a preposition.
>
> *What time did you go home?*
> *Come home right after school.*
>
> You also do not need to use a preposition with the verbs **stay** or **be**, but you may use the preposition **at**.
>
> *I'm going to stay (at) home tonight and watch TV.*
> *I was (at) home all afternoon.*

home³ /houm/ adj **1 home address/ phone number** an address or telephone number for the place where someone lives **2** made or used in the place where someone lives: *home cooking* ○ *a home computer*

home improvement /ˈhoʊm ɪmˈpruv·mənt/ noun [no plural] the activity of making your home better by fixing things, painting, building new rooms, adding new plants, etc.: *a home improvement center (= where you can buy equipment, tools, plants, etc.)*

homeless /ˈhoʊm·ləs/ adj without a place to live: *10,000 people were made homeless by the floods.*

homemade /ˈhoʊmˈmeɪd/ adj made at home and not bought from a store: *homemade bread*

home page /ˈhoʊm ˌpeɪdʒ/ noun the first page that you see when you look at a website on the Internet

homesick /ˈhoʊmˌsɪk/ adj feeling sad because you are away from your home

homework /ˈhoʊmˌwɜrk/ noun [no plural] **A1** work that teachers give students to do at home: *Have you **done** your **homework** yet?*

Common mistake: homework

Remember that you cannot make **homework** plural. Do not say "homeworks." Say **homework, some homework,** or **pieces of homework.**

~~Our new teacher gives us lots of homeworks.~~

Our new teacher gives us lots of homework.

honest /ˈɒn·əst/ adj **1** 🔵 sincere and truthful: *What is your honest opinion?* **2** 🔵 not likely to lie, cheat, or steal: *I'm just an honest man, trying to live my life.* **3 to be honest** informal 🔵 used to say your real opinion: *To be honest, I didn't really enjoy the party.*

honestly /ˈɒn·əst·li/ adv **1** 🔵 used to say that you are telling the truth: *I honestly couldn't eat any more cake.* **2** without lying or stealing: *We will always deal honestly with our customers.*

honesty /ˈɒn·ə·sti/ noun [no plural] the quality of being honest: *I appreciate your honesty.*

honey /ˈhʌn·i/ noun **1** 🔵 [no plural] a sweet, sticky food that is made by bees → See **Food** on page C7 **2** a name that you call someone love or like very much

honeymoon /ˈhʌn·i·mun/ noun 🔵 a vacation for two people who have just gotten married: *We went to Paris on our honeymoon.*

honor /ˈɒn·ər/ noun **1** [no plural] qualities such as goodness, honesty, and bravery that make people respect you: *a man of honor* **2 in honor of someone/something** in order to show great respect for someone or something: *a banquet in honor of the award winners* **3** something that makes you feel proud and happy: *I had the great honor of meeting the President.*

hood /hʊd/ noun **1** a part of a coat or jacket that covers your head and neck: *a raincoat with a hood* **2** the metal part that covers a car engine → See **Car** on

page C3 **3** a metal structure over a stove that carries away smoke and steam → See **The Kitchen** on page C10

hoof /huf/ noun (plural **hooves, hoofs**) the hard part on the foot of a horse and some other large animals

hook /hʊk/ noun a curved piece of metal or plastic used for hanging something on, or a similar object used for catching fish: *His coat was hanging from a hook on the door.*

hoop /hup/ noun a ring of wood, metal, or plastic: *a basketball hoop* (=that the net is tied to)

hooray /hʊˈreɪ/ exclamation something that you shout when you are happy because of something that has just happened: *We won – hooray!*

hoot /hut/ noun a short sound made by an owl (=bird)

hooves /huvz/ plural of hoof

hop[1] /hɒp/ verb (present participle **hopping**, past tense and past participle **hopped**) **1** to jump on one foot **2** If an animal hops, it moves by jumping on two or four feet at the same time: *Rabbits were hopping across the field.*

hop[2] /hɒp/ noun a short jump, especially on one leg

hope[1] /hoʊp/ verb (present participle **hoping**, past tense and past participle **hoped**) **1** 🔵 to want something to happen or be true: *I hope that the bus won't be late.* ○ *We had hoped for better weather than this.* ○ *"Is he coming?" "I hope so."* **2 hope to do something** 🔵 to want to do something: *Dad hopes to retire soon.*

hope[2] /hoʊp/ noun **1** 🔵 a good feeling about the future, or something that you want to happen: *a message full of hope* ○ *What are your hopes for the future?* **2** a person or thing that could help you and make you succeed: *Doctors say his only hope is an operation.* **3 in the hope of/that** because you want something good to happen: *She went to Paris in the hope of improving her French.*

hopeful /ˈhoʊp·fəl/ adj 🔵 feeling good or confident about something in the future: *Many teenagers do not feel* **hopeful about** *the future.* ○ *Police are still* **hopeful that** *they will find the missing girl.*

hopefully /'houp·fə·li/ *adv* **1** 🅱1 used when you are saying what you would like to happen: *Hopefully it won't rain.* **2** in a hopeful way: *"Are there any tickets left?" she asked hopefully.*

hopeless /'houp·ləs/ *adj* **1** 🅱1 very bad and probably not going to improve: *a hopeless situation* **2** very bad at a particular activity: *I'm* **hopeless at** *sports.*

horizon /həˈrɑɪ·zən/ *noun* the line in the distance where the sky and the land or sea seem to meet

horizontal /ˌhɔr·əˈzɑn·t̬ᵊl/,/ˌhɑr·əˈzɑn·t̬ᵊl/ *adj* level and flat, or parallel to the ground: *a horizontal line*

horizontal/vertical

horizontal
stripes

vertical stripes

hormone /'hɔr·moun/ *noun* one of many chemicals made in your body that make the body grow and develop

horn /hɔrn/ *noun* **1** one of the two long, hard things on the heads of cows, goats, and some other animals **2** a piece of equipment used to make a loud sound as a warning: *a car horn* **3** a musical instrument that you blow into to make a sound

horoscope /'hɔr·əˌskoup/,/'hɑr·əˌskoup/ *noun* a description of what might happen to someone in the future, based on the position of the stars and planets: *What does your horoscope say?*

horrible /'hɔr·ə·bəl/,/'hɑr·ə·bəl/ *adj* 🅰2 very unpleasant or bad: *What's that horrible smell?*

horrific /həˈrɪf·ɪk/ *adj* very bad and shocking: *a horrific crime* ○ *horrific injuries*

horrify /'hɔr·əˌfɑɪ/,/'hɑr·əˌfɑɪ/ *verb* (present participle **horrifying**, past tense and past participle **horrified**) to make someone feel very shocked: *I was horrified to hear about her accident.*

horror /'hɔr·ər/,/'hɑr·ər/ *noun* **1** a strong feeling of shock or fear: *She watched* **in horror** *as the car skidded across the road.* **2** a **horror film/movie/ story** 🅱1 a movie or story that entertains people by shocking or frightening them: *I love reading horror stories.*

horse /hɔrs/ *noun* 🅰1 a large animal with four legs that people ride or use to pull heavy things

horseback /'hɔrs·bæk/ *noun* **on horseback** riding a horse: *police on horseback*

horseshoe /'hɔrs·ʃu/ *noun* a U-shaped piece of metal on a horse's foot

hose /houz/ *noun* a long pipe made of plastic and used for putting water somewhere, usually onto a garden or fire

hospitable /'hɑs·pɪˌt̬ə·bəl/ *adj* A hospitable person or place is friendly and pleasant for people who visit.

hospital /'hɑs·pɪˌt̬ᵊl/ *noun* 🅰1 a place where ill or injured people go to be treated by doctors and nurses: *He was in the hospital for two weeks.*

host /houst/ *noun* **1** someone who is having a party **2** someone who presents a television program
• **host** *verb*

hostage /'hɑs·tɪdʒ/ *noun* someone who is kept as a prisoner and may be hurt or killed in order to make other people do something

hostel /'hɑs·t̬ᵊl/ *noun* 🅱1 a cheap hotel where you can live when you are away from home: *a youth hostel*

hostess /'hous·təs/ *noun* a woman who is having a party

hostile /'hɑs·t̬ᵊl/ *adj* not friendly and not liking or agreeing with something: *Some politicians were* **hostile to** *the idea.*

hot /hɑt/ **adj** (comparative **hotter**, superlative **hottest**) **1** 🔵 very warm: *a hot summer's day* ○ *a hot drink* ○ *I'm too hot in this jacket.* → Opposite **cold adj** **2** 🔵 Hot food contains strong spices that cause a burning feeling in your mouth: *Careful! The sauce is very hot.* → Opposite **mild adj**

hot chocolate /ˈhɑt ˈtʃɔk·lət/, /ˈhɑt ˈtʃɔ·kə·lət/ **noun** [no plural] (also **cocoa**) 🔵 a sweet drink made with chocolate and hot milk: *a mug of hot chocolate*

hot dog /ˈhɑt ˌdɔg/ **noun** a cooked sausage (=tube of meat and spices) that you usually eat inside bread

hotel /houˈtel/ **noun** 🔵 a place where you pay to stay when you are traveling

hour /aʊər/ **noun** **1** 🔵 a period of time equal to 60 minutes: *It's a six-hour flight.* **2** the period of time when a particular activity happens or when a store, business, etc. is open: *working hours* ○ *Our opening hours are from 8 to 6.* **3** **hours** informal 🔵 a long time: *I spent hours doing my homework.*

> **⚠ Common mistake: hour or time?**
>
> An **hour** is a period of 60 minutes.
>   *The trip takes about three hours.*
>   *We went for a two-hour walk.*
>
> **Time** is measured in hours and minutes. We use **time** to refer to a particular point during the day or night, or to say when something happens.
>   *What time do you get up in the morning?*
>   *There's only one bus at that time of night.*
>
> Remember to use **time**, not "hour," when you are talking about what time it is.
>   *"What time is it?" "Two o'clock."*
>   ~~*"What hour is it?" "Two o'clock."*~~

hourly /ˈaʊər·li/ **adj, adv** **1** happening every hour: *an hourly bus service* **2** for each hour: *an hourly rate/wage*

house /haʊs/ **noun** (plural **houses**) 🔵 a building where people live, usually one family or group: *We went to my aunt's house for dinner.*

household /ˈhaʊs·hoʊld/ **noun** a family or group of people who live together in a house

housewife /ˈhaʊs·waɪf/ **noun** (plural **housewives**) 🔵 a woman who stays at home to cook, clean, and take care of her family

housework /ˈhaʊs·wɜrk/ **noun** [no plural] 🔵 the work that you do to keep your house clean: *I hate **doing housework**.*

the House of Representatives /ˈhaʊs əv ˌrep·rɪˈzen·tə·tɪvz/ **noun** one of the two parts of the government in the U.S. that make laws

housing /ˈhaʊ·zɪŋ/ **noun** [no plural] used to talk in general about places to live in such as apartments or houses: *student housing* ○ *Housing is expensive in the city.*

hover /ˈhʌv·ər/ **verb** to stay up in the air but without moving anywhere: *A helicopter hovered over us.*

> **⚠ Common mistake: how or what?**
>
> In these expressions we use **what**. Be careful not to use "how."
> **what something is called**
>   *I don't know what it's called in English.*
>   ~~*I don't know how it's called in English.*~~
> **what something/someone looks like**
>   *I'd like to see what it looks like before I buy it.*
>   *What does your brother look like?*

how /haʊ/ **adv** **1** 🔵 used to ask about quantity, size, or age: *How big is the house?* ○ *How old are they?* ○ *How much* (= what price) *was that dress?* **2** **how are you?** 🔵 used to ask someone if he or she is well and happy: *"How are you, Ellie?" "Oh, not bad, thanks."* **3** 🔵 used to ask about the way something happens or is done: *How did he die?* ○ *How*

| æ cat | ɑ hot | e get | ɪ sit | i see | ɔ saw | ʊ book | u too | ʌ cut | ə about | ɑr mother | ɜr turn | ɔr for | aɪ my | aʊ how | eɪ say | ɪ boy |

a
b
c
d
e
f
g
h
i
j
k
l
m
n
o
p
q
r
s
t
u
v
w
x
y
z

do you keep the house so clean? **4 how about...?** **A2** used to make a suggestion: *How about going to the movies?* **5 how do you do?** **A2** a polite thing to say to someone you are meeting for the first time **6** **B1** used to ask about what an experience or event was like: *How was your flight?* **7** **B1** used for emphasis: *How nice to see you!* ○ *I was amazed at how quickly she finished.*

however /haʊˈev·ər/ adv **1** **A2** but: *This is one solution to the problem. However, there are others.* **2 however cold, difficult, slowly, etc.** used to say that it does not make any difference how cold, difficult, slowly, etc.: *We're not going to get there in time, however fast we drive.*

howl /haʊl/ verb to make a long, high sound: *He howled in pain.*
• **howl** noun

huddle /ˈhʌd·ᵊl/ verb (present participle **huddling**, past tense and past participle **huddled**) to move closer to other people because you are cold or frightened: *They huddled around the fire to keep warm.*

hug[1] /hʌɡ/ verb (present participle **hugging**, past tense and past participle **hugged**) **B1** to put your arms around someone and hold the person, usually because you love him or her: *They hugged and kissed each other.*

hug[2] /hʌɡ/ noun **B1** the action of putting your arms around someone and holding him or her: *She gave me a big hug before she left.*

huge /hjuːdʒ/ adj **B1** very large: *a huge house*

hum[1] /hʌm/ verb (present participle **humming**, past tense and past participle **hummed**) **1** to sing without opening your mouth: *He was humming a tune.* **2** to make a continuous, low sound: *The computers were humming in the background.*

hum[2] /hʌm/ noun a low, continuous sound: *the hum of traffic*

human[1] /ˈhjuː·mən/ adj **B1** relating to people: *the human body* ○ *human behavior*

human[2] /ˈhjuː·mən/ noun (also **human being**) **B1** a man, woman, or child: *The disease affects both humans and animals.*

humankind /ˈhjuː·mənˌkaɪnd/ noun [no plural] all the people in the world

human rights /ˈhjuː·mən ˈraɪts/ plural noun the basic rights that every person should have, such as justice and freedom to say what you think: *international laws protecting human rights*

humble /ˈhʌm·bəl/ adj not believing that you are important: *He's very humble about his success.*

humid /ˈhjuː·mɪd/ adj **B1** Humid air or weather is hot and slightly wet: *It's very humid today.*

humor /ˈhjuː·mər/ noun [no plural] **1** **B1** the ability to laugh and know that something is funny: *He's got a great sense of humor.* **2** things that are funny: *His speech was full of humor.*

humorous /ˈhjuː·mər·əs/ adj funny, or making you laugh: *a humorous book*

hump /hʌmp/ noun a round, hard part on an animal's or a person's back: *a camel's hump*

hundred /ˈhʌn·drəd/ **1** **A2** the number 100: *There were over a hundred people at the party.* ○ *Water boils at one hundred degrees Celsius.* **2 hundreds** informal a lot: *Hundreds of people wrote in to complain.*

hundredth /ˈhʌn·drədθ/ one of a hundred equal parts of something

hung /hʌŋ/ past tense and past participle of hang

hunger /ˈhʌŋ·ɡər/ noun [no plural] **1** **B1** the feeling that you want to eat **2** the state of not having enough food: *Many of the refugees died of hunger.*

hungry /ˈhʌŋ·ɡri/ adj (comparative **hungrier**, superlative **hungriest**) **A1** wanting or needing food: *I'm hungry. What's for dinner?*
• **hungrily** adv

hunt /hʌnt/ verb **1** 🔵 to chase and kill wild animals: *They are hunting rabbits.* **2** to search for something: *The children hunted for sea shells on the beach.*
• **hunting** noun *deer hunting*

hunter /ˈhʌn·tər/ noun a person who hunts wild animals

hurricane /ˈhɜr·əˌkein/, /ˈhʌr·əˌkein/ noun a violent storm with very strong winds

hurry¹ /ˈhɜr·i/, /ˈhʌr·i/ verb (present participle **hurrying**, past tense and past participle **hurried**) 🔵 to move or to do things quickly: *Please hurry – the train is about to leave.*
hurry up phrasal verb 🔵 to start moving or doing something more quickly: *Hurry up! We're going to be late.*

hurry² /ˈhɜr·i/, /ˈhʌr·i/ noun **be in a hurry** 🔵 If you are in a hurry, you need to do something quickly: *I was in a hurry so I took a taxi.*

hurt¹ /hɜrt/ verb (past tense and past participle **hurt**) **1** 🔵 to cause someone pain or to injure someone: *Mark hurt his knee playing football.* **2** 🔵 If a part of your body hurts, it is painful: *My eyes really hurt.* **3** 🔵 to upset someone: *I hope that what I said didn't hurt him.*

hurt² /hɜrt/ adj **1** 🔵 injured or in pain: *Several people were seriously hurt in the accident.* **2** 🔵 upset or unhappy: *She was deeply hurt by what he said.*

husband /ˈhʌz·bənd/ noun 🔵 the man that someone is married to

hush /hʌʃ/ noun [no plural] a period of silence: *A hush fell over the room.*

hut /hʌt/ noun 🔵 a small, simple building, often made of wood: *a mountain hut*

hydrogen /ˈhai·drə·dʒən/ noun [no plural] a gas that combines with oxygen to form water

hymn /hɪm/ noun a song sung by Christians in church

hype /haip/ noun [no plural] discussion that makes something seem more important or exciting than it actually is: *media hype* ○ *There's been a lot of **hype** surrounding his latest movie.*

hyphen /ˈhai·fən/ noun a mark [-] used to join two words together, or to show that a word continues on the next line

hypnotize /ˈhɪp·nəˌtaiz/ verb (present participle **hypnotizing**, past tense and past participle **hypnotized**) to place someone in a mental state in which you can influence what he or she thinks and does

hysterical /hɪˈster·ɪ·kəl/ adj not able to control your behavior because you are very frightened, angry, excited, etc.: *hysterical laughter* ○ *As soon as Wendy saw the blood, she became hysterical.*

I i

I, i /ai/ the ninth letter of the alphabet

I /ai/ pronoun 🔵 used when the person speaking or writing is the subject of the verb: *I bought some chocolate.* ○ *I'll see you later.*

> ⚠ **Common mistake: I**
> Remember that **I** is always written with a capital letter.

ice /ais/ noun [no plural] **1** 🔵 water that is so cold it has become solid: *Could I have more ice in my drink?* **2 break the ice** to make people who have not met before feel more relaxed with each other: *I told everyone a joke, which helped to break the ice.*

iceberg /ˈaisˌbɜrg/ noun a very large piece of ice that floats in the sea

ice cream /ˈais ˌkrim/ noun 🔵 a sweet, cold food made from frozen milk: *vanilla ice cream*

ice cream cone

ice cube /ˈais ˌkjub/ noun a small piece of ice that you put into a drink to make it cold

ice hockey /'aɪs ˌhɑ·ki/ **noun** [no plural]
B1 the full form of hockey
→ See **Sports 1** on page C15

ice skate /'aɪs ˌskeɪt/ **noun** a boot with a metal part on the bottom, used for moving across ice
• **ice skating noun** [no plural]
→ See **Sports 1** on page C15

icicle /'aɪˌsɪ·kəl/ **noun** **icicles** a long, thin piece of ice that hangs down from something

icing /'aɪ·sɪŋ/ **noun** [no plural] a sweet mixture used to cover or fill cakes

icon /'aɪ·kɑn/ **noun** **1** a small picture on a computer screen that you choose in order to make the computer do something: *Click on the print icon.* **2** a person or thing that is famous because he, she, or it represents a particular idea or way of life: *a fashion icon*

icy /'aɪ·si/ **adj** **1** **B1** covered in ice: *icy roads* **2** **B1** very cold: *an icy wind*

ID /'aɪ'di/ **noun** **A2** an official document that shows or proves who you are: *Make sure you carry some ID with you.* ○ *You will need a passport or an ID card.*

I'd /aɪd/ **1** short form of I had: *Everyone thought I'd gone.* **2** short form of I would: *I'd like to buy some stamps, please.*

idea /aɪ'di·ə/ **noun** **A2** **1** a suggestion or plan: *What a good idea! ○ It was Kate's idea to rent a car.* **2** **B1** an opinion or belief: *We have very different ideas about politics.* **3** **have no idea** **B1** to not know: *"Where's Matt?" "I have no idea."* **4** an understanding, thought, or picture in your mind: *I think you've got the wrong idea about this.*

ideal /aɪ'dil/ **adj** perfect, or the best possible: *She's the ideal person for the job.*

ideally /aɪ'di·ə·li/ **adv** **1** in a perfect way: *They're ideally suited to each other.* **2** used to talk about how something would be in a perfect situation: *Ideally, I'd like to work at home.*

identical /aɪ'den·tɪ·kəl/ **adj** exactly the same: *She found a dress identical to the one in the picture.*

identification /aɪˌden·tə·fɪ'keɪ·ʃən/ **noun** [no plural] **1** **A2** an official document that shows or proves who you are: *Do you have any identification on you?* **2** the act of recognizing and naming someone or something: *Most of the bodies were badly burned, making identification almost impossible.*

identify /aɪ'den·tə·faɪ/ **verb** (present participle **identifying**, past tense and past participle **identified**) to say what the name of someone or something is: *The victim has not yet been identified.*

identify with *someone/something* **phrasal verb** to feel that you are similar to someone and can understand them or their situation: *Readers can identify with the hero of the novel.*

identity /aɪ'den·tɪ·t̬i/ **noun** (plural **identities**) **1** who someone is: *They kept her identity secret.* **2** the things that make one person or group of people different from others: *a sense of national identity*

identity card /aɪ'den·tɪ·t̬i ˌkɑrd/ **noun** **B1** a card that shows your name, photograph, and information to prove who you are: *Her identity card was stolen.*

idiom /'ɪd·i·əm/ **noun** a group of words used together with a meaning that you cannot guess

idiot /'ɪd·i·ət/ **noun** a stupid person: *This idiot ran in front of my car.*

idiotic /ˌɪd·i'ɑt·ɪk/ **adj** stupid: *an idiotic idea*

idol /'aɪ·dᵊl/ **noun** **1** someone you admire and respect very much: *He met his childhood idol.* **2** a picture or object that people pray to as part of their religion

i.e. used to explain exactly what you mean: *The price must be more realistic, i.e., lower.*

if /ɪf/ **conjunction** **1** **A2** used to say that something will happen only after something else happens or is true: *We'll have* *the party in the garden if the weather's good.* **2 B1** used to talk about something that might happen or be true: *What will we do if this doesn't work?* **3 B1** whether: *I wonder if he'll get the job.* **4 B1** used to mean "always" or "every time": *If you mention his mother, he always cries.* **5 if not A2** used to say what the situation will be if something does not happen: *I hope to see you there but, if not, I'll call you.* **6 if you like A2** used when you offer someone something: *If you like, I could drive you there.* **7 if I were you B1** used when you give someone advice: *I think I'd take the money if I were you.* **8 if only B1** used to express a wish for something that is impossible or unlikely to happen: *If only I knew the answer!* **9 if so** if this is the case: *It might rain this afternoon. If so, we'll have the party indoors.*

ignition /ɪgˈnɪʃ·ən/ **noun** the electrical system that starts a vehicle's engine
→ See **Car** on page C3

ignorance /ˈɪg·nər·əns/ **noun** [no plural] a lack of knowledge about something: *I was shocked by her ignorance of the subject.*

ignorant /ˈɪg·nər·ənt/ **adj** not knowing enough about something: *She's completely **ignorant about** computers. ∘ The young people were **ignorant of** the election process.*

ignore /ɪgˈnɔr/ **verb** (present participle **ignoring**, past tense and past participle **ignored**) to not give attention to something or someone: *I said hello but she ignored me.*

ill /ɪl/ **adj** **A2** not feeling well, or suffering from a disease: *He was in bed, ill.*

I'll /aɪl/ short form of I will: *I'll see you tomorrow.*

illegal /ɪˈli·gəl/ **adj** not allowed by law: *illegal drugs ∘ It is **illegal** to sell cigarettes to anyone under 18.*
→ Opposite **legal adj**
• **illegally adv** *an illegally parked car*

illegible /ɪˈledʒ·ə·bəl/ **adj** Illegible writing is impossible to read.
→ Opposite **legible adj**

illiterate /ɪˈlɪt̬·ər·ət/ **adj** not able to read or write

illness /ˈɪl·nəs/ **noun** **1 B1** a disease: *He has a serious illness.* **2** [no plural] being ill: *Unfortunately I couldn't go because of illness.*

illusion /ɪˈlu·ʒən/ **noun** something that is not really what it seems to be: *There is a large mirror at one end to create the illusion of space.*

illustrate /ˈɪl·əˌstreɪt/ **verb** (present participle **illustrating**, past tense and past participle **illustrated**) to draw pictures for a book

illustration /ˌɪl·əˈstreɪ·ʃən/ **noun** a picture in a book

I'm /aɪm/ short form of I am: *I'm Amy. ∘ I'm too hot.*

> **⚠ Common mistake: I'm**
>
> Remember that **I'm** is always written with an apostrophe.
>
> *I'm glad you could come.*
> ~~I'm too hot.~~

image /ˈɪm·ɪdʒ/ **noun** **1** the way that other people think someone or something is: *They want to improve the **public image** of the police.* **2** a picture, especially in movies or television or in a mirror: *television images of starving children* **3** a picture in your mind: *I have an **image** of the way I want the garden to look.*

imaginary /ɪˈmædʒ·əˌner·i/ **adj** not real but imagined in your mind: *The story takes place in an imaginary world.*

imagination /ɪˌmædʒ·əˈneɪ·ʃən/ **noun** **1 B1** [no plural] the ability to have ideas or pictures in your mind: *The job needs someone with some imagination.* **2 B1** the part of your mind that creates ideas or pictures of things that are not real or that you have not seen: *My son has a very vivid (= active) imagination.*

imagine /ɪˈmædʒ·ən/ **verb** (present participle **imagining**, past tense and past participle **imagined**) **1 B1** to make an idea or picture of something in your mind: *Imagine being able to do all your shop-*

ping from home. **2** to believe that something is probably true: *I imagine he is quite difficult to live with.* **3 B1** to have an idea of what something is like or might be like: *Can you imagine how it feels to be blind?* **4 B1** to think that you hear or see something that does not really exist: *"Did you hear a noise?" "No, you're imagining things."*

imitate /ˈɪmɪˌteɪt/ verb (present participle **imitating**, past tense and past participle **imitated**) to copy someone: *He was imitating the president.*

imitation /ˌɪmɪˈteɪʃən/ noun a copy of something that looks like the real thing: *It wasn't a genuine Gucci handbag, just a cheap imitation.*

immature /ˌɪməˈtʃʊər/, /ˌɪməˈtʊər/ adj behaving like a younger person: *Some of the boys are quite immature for their age.*

immediate /ɪˈmiːdiət/ adj **1** happening now or very soon after something else: *The drugs had an immediate effect.* **2** important now and needing attention: *Our immediate concern is getting food to the refugees.*

immediately /ɪˈmiːdiətli/ adv **A2** now, without waiting: *She asked him to come home immediately.*

immense /ɪˈmens/ adj very big: *He won an immense amount of money.*

immigrant /ˈɪmɪɡrənt/ noun someone who comes to live in a different country

immigration /ˌɪmɪˈɡreɪʃən/ noun [no plural] **1 B1** the place where people's official documents are checked when they enter a country, for example, at an airport: *After you've been through immigration, you can go and get your luggage.* **2** the process of coming to live in a different country: *immigration policy*

immoral /ɪˈmɒrəl/, /ɪˈmɑːrəl/ adj not correct, honest, or good: *immoral behavior*

immune /ɪˈmjuːn/ adj If you are immune to a disease, you will not get it: *Once you've had the virus, you are immune to it.*

immunize /ˈɪmjənaɪz/ verb (present participle **immunizing**, past tense and past participle **immunized**) to stop someone from getting a disease by giving them medicine: *He was immunized against the disease as a child.*

impact /ˈɪmpækt/ noun [no plural] the effect that a person, event, or situation has on someone or something: *She has had a major impact on pop music.*

impatient /ɪmˈpeɪʃənt/ adj **1** If you are impatient, you get angry with people who make mistakes or you hate waiting for things: *I get very impatient with the children when they won't do their homework.* → Opposite **patient** adj **2** wanting something to happen as soon as possible: *People are impatient for change in this country.*

• **impatiently** adv *We waited impatiently for the show to begin.*

imperative /ɪmˈperətɪv/ noun in grammar, the form of a verb that is used to say an order. In the sentence "Stop the machine!," the verb "stop" is in the imperative.

imply /ɪmˈplaɪ/ verb (present participle **implying**, past tense and past participle **implied**) to suggest or show something, without saying it directly: *She implied that she wasn't happy at work.*

impolite /ˌɪmpəˈlaɪt/ adj formal rude

import[1] /ˈɪmpɔːrt/ noun a product that one country brings in from another country to be sold: *imports from Korea* → Opposite **export**

import[2] /ɪmˈpɔːrt/ verb to bring something that is made in another country into your country for people to buy: *We import about 20 percent of our food.* → Opposite **export**

importance /ɪmˈpɔːrtəns/ noun [no plural] **B1** how important someone or something is: *I'm not sure you understand the importance of what I'm saying.*

important /ɪmˈpɔːrtənt/ adj **1 A1** valuable, useful, or necessary: *My family is very important to me.* **2 B1** having a lot of power: *an important person*

importantly /ɪmˈpɔr·t⁰nt·li/ *adv*
in a way that is important: *They provided showers and, more importantly,
clean clothes.*

impossible /ɪmˈpɑs·ə·bəl/ *adj* **B1** not
able to happen: *It is impossible to work
with all this noise.*
→ Opposite **possible** *adj*

impress /ɪmˈpres/ *verb* to make someone admire or respect you: *I was hoping
to impress him with my knowledge.*

impression /ɪmˈpreʃ·ən/ *noun* **1** an
idea, feeling, or opinion about something or someone: *What was your impression of Carla's husband? ○ I got the
impression that he was bored.* **2** [no
plural] the way that something seems,
looks, or feels to a particular person: *It
makes a very bad impression if you're
late for an interview. ○ Monica gives the
impression of being shy.* **3 be under
the impression** to think or understand
something: *I was under the impression
that you didn't like him.*

impressive /ɪmˈpres·ɪv/ *adj* Someone
or something that is impressive makes
you admire and respect them: *an impressive performance*

imprison /ɪmˈprɪz·ən/ *verb* to put
someone in prison: *Taylor was impris-
oned in 1969 for burglary.*

improve /ɪmˈpruv/ *verb* (present participle
improving, past tense and past participle
improved) **A2** to get better or to make
something better: *Scott's behavior has
improved a lot lately.*

improvement /ɪmˈpruv·mənt/ *noun*
1 **B1** the process or result of something
getting better: *There's been a big improvement in her work this semester.*
2 **B1** a change to something that makes
it better: *home improvements*

impulse /ˈɪm·pʌls/ *noun* a sudden feeling that you must do something: *Her
first impulse was to run away.*

impulsive /ɪmˈpʌl·sɪv/ *adj* doing
things suddenly, without planning or
thinking carefully: *It was an impulsive
response.*

in[1] /ɪn/ *preposition* **1** **A1** inside a container or place: *He put his hand in his
pocket. ○ a store in Manhattan* **2** **A1** during a period of time: *We're going to Italy
in April.* **3** **A2** needing or using no
more time than a particular amount of
time: *I finished the job in two weeks.*
4 **A2** after a particular amount of time
in the future: *Dinner will be ready in ten
minutes.* **5** **A2** forming a part of something: *I've been waiting in this line for a
long time.* **6** **B1** connected with a particular subject: *advances in medical science* **7** **B1** wearing: *Do you know that
man in the gray suit?* **8** **B1** experiencing an emotion or condition: *She's in a
good mood this morning. ○ They are in
danger.* **9** **B1** arranged in a particular
way: *Is this list in alphabetical order? ○ We
all sat down in a circle.* **10** **B1** expressed or written in a particular way: *They
spoke in Russian the whole time.*
11 involved in a particular type of job:
He wants a career in politics.

in[2] /ɪn/ *adv* **1** **A2** into an area or space
from the outside of it: *She took off her
shoes and socks and jumped in.* **2** **B1** at
the place where a person usually lives
or works: *I called, but she wasn't in.*
3 **B1** If a train, plane, etc. is in, it has arrived at the place it was going to: *My
train gets in at 9:54 a.m.*

in. written abbreviation for inch: a unit for
measuring length

inability /ˌɪn·əˈbɪl·ɪ·ti/ *noun* [no plural]
the state of not being able to do something: *her inability to answer the question
○ They are worried about their son's inability to speak.*

inaccurate /ɪnˈæk·jər·ət/ *adj* not correct
or exact: *inaccurate information*
→ Opposite **accurate** *adj*

inadequate /ɪnˈæd·ɪ·kwət/ *adj* not
enough or not good enough: *Her skills
were inadequate for the job.*
→ Opposite **adequate** *adj*

inappropriate /ˌɪn·əˈprou·pri·ət/ *adj*
not suitable: *inappropriate behavior*
→ Opposite **appropriate** *adj*

in box /'ɪn ˌbɑks/ noun a container on your desk where you keep letters and documents that need to be dealt with
→ See **The Office** on page C12

incapable /ɪn'keɪ·pə·bəl/ adj not able to do something: *He is incapable of listening.*
→ Opposite **capable** adj

inch /ɪntʃ/ noun (plural **inches**) (written abbreviation **in.**) **B1** a unit for measuring length. 12 inches equal one foot.

incident /'ɪn·sɪ·dənt/ noun formal something that happens, especially something bad: *Police are investigating the incident.*

incidentally /ˌɪn·sɪ'dent·li/ adv used when you say something that is not as important as the main thing that you are talking about but is connected to it: *Incidentally, speaking of Stephen, have you met his girlfriend?*

inclined /ɪn'klaɪnd/ adj **inclined to do something** often behaving in a particular way: *Tom is inclined to be forgetful.*

include /ɪn'klud/ verb (present participle **including**, past tense and past participle **included**) **1 A2** to have something or someone as part of something larger: *The price includes flights and three nights' accommodation.* **2** to allow someone to take part in an activity: *Local residents were included in the planning discussions.*
→ Opposite **exclude** verb

including /ɪn'klu·dɪŋ/ preposition **A2** used to show that someone or something is part of something larger: *It's $24.99, including shipping and handling.*
→ Opposite **excluding** preposition

income /'ɪn·kʌm/ noun the money that you regularly get, for example from your job: *Many families are on low incomes.*

income tax /'ɪn·kʌm ˌtæks/ noun money that the government takes from the money that you earn

incomplete /ˌɪn·kəm'plit/ adj not finished, or with parts missing: *The building is still incomplete.*
→ Opposite **complete** adj

inconsiderate /ˌɪn·kən'sɪd·ər·ət/ adj not caring when you make problems for other people: *He shouldn't keep us waiting like this – it's very inconsiderate.*

inconvenience /ˌɪn·kən'vin·jəns/ noun problems: *We apologize for any inconvenience caused.*

inconvenient /ˌɪn·kən'vin·jənt/ adj causing problems: *It's very inconvenient living so far away from the shopping center.*
→ Opposite **convenient** adj

incorrect /ˌɪn·kə'rekt/ adj **B1** wrong: *His answers were incorrect.*
→ Opposite **correct** adj
• **incorrectly** adv *My name was spelled incorrectly.*

increase[1] /ɪn'kris/ verb (present participle **increasing**, past tense and past participle **increased**) **B1** to get bigger or to make something bigger: *Smoking increases the risk of serious illnesses.* ○ *Sales of computers have increased by 15% since January.*
→ Opposite **decrease** verb

increase[2] /'ɪn·kris/ noun a rise in the amount or size of something: *a price increase* ○ *We are seeing an increase in standards of living.*
→ Opposite **decrease**

> **⚠ Common mistake: increase in or increase of?**
>
> Use **increase in** before the thing that is increasing.
>
> *an increase in profits/sales*
> *an increase in the number of flu cases*
>
> Use **increase of** before the size of the increase.
>
> *an increase of 30%*

increasingly /ɪn'kri·sɪŋ·li/ adv more and more: *The sport is becoming increasingly popular.*

incredible /ɪn'kred·ə·bəl/ adj **1 B1** informal very good and exciting: *The city itself is incredible.* **2** very large in amount or high in level: *She earned an incredible amount of money.* ○ *The planes make an incredible noise.* **3** If a fact is incredible, it is so strange that

you cannot believe it: *It seems incredible that she didn't know what was happening.*
• **incredibly** *adv The team played incredibly well.*

indeed /ɪnˈdiːd/ *adv* **1** 🄱 used to make the word "very" stronger: *Many people are very poor indeed.* **2** 🄱 used when saying that something is correct: *"Is this your dog?" "It is indeed."*

indefinite /ɪnˈdef·ə·nət/ *adj* with no definite end: *He will be staying here for an indefinite period.*

indefinite article /ɪnˈdef·ɪ·nət ˈɑr·tɪ·kəl/ *noun* in grammar, used to mean the words "a" or "an"

independence /ˌɪn·dɪˈpen·dəns/ *noun* [no plural] **1** a situation in which individuals take care of themselves and do not need help from other people: *Teenagers need a certain amount of independence.* **2** a situation in which a country has its own government and is not ruled by another country: *Mexico gained its independence from Spain in 1821.*

Independence Day /ˌɪn·dɪˈpen·dəns ˌdeɪ/ *noun* the Fourth of July

independent /ˌɪn·dɪˈpen·dənt/ *adj* **1** 🄱 not wanting or needing anyone else to help you: *She's a very independent four-year-old.* ◦ *Grandma's very independent and does all her own cooking.*
→ Opposite **dependent** *adj* **2** not controlled or ruled by anyone else: *an independent state* **3** not influenced or controlled in any way by other people, events, or things: *an independent organization* ◦ *The group is independent of any political party.*
• **independently** *adv Both scientists made the same discovery independently.*

index /ˈɪn·deks/ *noun* (plural **indexes**) a list of subjects or names at the end of a book, showing on what page in the book you can find them

indicate /ˈɪn·dɪ·keɪt/ *verb* (present participle **indicating**, past tense and past participle **indicated**) **1** to show that something exists or is true: *Evidence indicates that the skeleton is about 3 million years old.*

2 to point to someone or something: *He indicated a man in a dark coat.*

indication /ˌɪn·dɪˈkeɪ·ʃən/ *noun* a sign showing that something exists or is true: *She gave no indication that she was unhappy.*

indigestion /ˌɪn·dɪˈdʒes·tʃən/ *noun* [no plural] a painful or uncomfortable feeling in your stomach after you have eaten something

indignant /ɪnˈdɪg·nənt/ *adj* angry because of something that is wrong or not fair: *He was very indignant when I suggested that he had made a mistake.*

indirect /ˌɪn·dəˈrekt/ *adj* connected with something, but not directly: *Her health problems are an indirect result of her stressful job.*
→ Opposite **direct** *adj*

individual[1] /ˌɪn·dəˈvɪdʒ·u·əl/ *adj* **1** 🄱 considered separately from other things in a group: *Read up the individual letters of each word.* **2** 🄱 relating to one particular person or thing: *He gets more individual attention from his teacher.*

individual[2] /ˌɪn·dəˈvɪdʒ·u·əl/ *noun* a person, especially when considered separately and not as part of a group: *We try to treat our students as individuals.*

individually /ˌɪn·dəˈvɪdʒ·u·ə·li/ *adv* separately and not as a group: *Ask the students to work individually.*

indoor /ˈɪn·dɔr/ *adj* 🄰 in a building: *an indoor swimming pool*
→ Opposite **outdoor** *adj*

indoors /ˈɪn·dɔrz/ *adv* 🄱 into or inside a building: *If you're feeling cold, we can go indoors.*
→ Opposite **outdoors** *adv*

industrial /ɪnˈdʌs·tri·əl/ *adj* connected with industry: *an industrial city*

industry /ˈɪn·də·stri/ *noun* **1** 🄱 (plural **industries**) all the companies involved in a particular type of business: *the entertainment industry* **2** [no plural] the making of things in factories

inefficient /ˌɪn·ɪˈfɪʃ·ənt/ **adj** inefficient people or things waste time, money, or effort, and do not achieve as much as they should: *an inefficient heating system*
→ Opposite **efficient adj**

inevitable /ɪˈnev·ɪ·t̬ə·bəl/ **adj** If something is inevitable, you cannot avoid or stop it: *It was **inevitable** that his crime would be discovered.*
• **inevitably adv** *Inevitably, there was some fighting between the groups.*

inexpensive /ˌɪn·ɪkˈspen·sɪv/ **adj**
B1 cheap but of good quality: *inexpensive children's clothes*

inexperienced /ˌɪn·ɪkˈspɪər·i·ənst/ **adj** not having done something often: *Kennedy was young and inexperienced.*
→ Opposite **experienced adj**

infant /ˈɪn·fənt/ **noun** formal a baby or very young child

infect /ɪnˈfekt/ **verb** to give someone a disease: *Thousands of people were infected with the virus.*

infection /ɪnˈfek·ʃən/ **noun** a disease that is caused by bacteria or a virus: *a throat infection*
• **infectious adj** *an infectious disease*

inferior /ɪnˈfɪər·i·ər/ **adj** not as good as someone or something else: *These are inferior products.*
→ Opposite **superior adj**

infinite /ˈɪn·fə·nɪt/ **adj** without any end or without limits: *infinite possibilities*

infinitely /ˈɪn·fə·nɪt·li/ **adv** very or very much: *The book was infinitely better than the movie.*

infinitive /ɪnˈfɪn·ə·t̬ɪv/ **noun**
B1 in grammar, the basic form of a verb that usually follows "to." In the sentence "She decided to leave," "to leave" is an infinitive.

inflammable /ɪnˈflæm·ə·bəl/ **adj** Something that is inflammable burns very easily.

inflate /ɪnˈfleɪt/ **verb** (present participle **inflating**, past tense and past participle **inflated**) to fill something with air or gas: *The tires aren't inflated enough.*

inflation /ɪnˈfleɪ·ʃən/ **noun** [no plural] the rate at which prices increase, or an increase in prices: *rising inflation*

influence[1] /ˈɪn·flu·əns/ **noun** **1** the power to change people or things: *The drug companies have a lot of **influence on** doctors.* **2** someone or something that changes another person or thing: *Her father was a big **influence on** her.*

influence[2] /ˈɪn·flu·əns/ **verb** (present participle **influencing**, past tense and past participle **influenced**) to change the way that someone thinks or the way that something develops: *Were you influenced by anybody when you were starting your career?*

influential /ˌɪn·fluˈen·ʃəl/ **adj** having the power to change people or things: *an influential figure in modern jazz*

inform /ɪnˈfɔrm/ **verb** **B1** to tell someone about something: *He **informed us that** we would have to leave.* ○ *Patients should be **informed about** the risks.*

informal /ɪnˈfɔr·məl/ **adj** **1** relaxed and friendly: *an informal meeting* **2** suitable for normal situations: *informal clothes* ○ *informal language* → Opposite **formal adj**
• **informally adv** *We chatted informally (= in a relaxed, friendly way) before the interview.*

information /ˌɪn·fərˈmeɪ·ʃən/ **noun** [no plural] **A2** facts about a situation, person, event, etc.: *Do you have any **information** about local schools?* ○ *This was an important **piece of information**.*

> **❗ Common mistake: information**
>
> Remember that you cannot make **information** plural. Do not say "informations."
> *Could you send me some information about your courses?*

informative /ɪnˈfɔr·mə·t̬ɪv/ **adj** having a lot of useful facts: *an informative book*

ingredient /ɪnˈɡri·di·ənt/ **noun** **B1** one of the different foods that a particular type of food is made from: *I don't have the ingredients for a cake.*

inhabit /ɪnˈhæb·ɪt/ **verb** formal   to live in a place: *The islands are inhabited by birds and small animals.*

inhabitant /ɪnˈhæb·ɪ·tənt/ **noun** someone who lives somewhere: *a city with ten million inhabitants*

inherit /ɪnˈher·ət/ **verb**   to get money or things from someone after he or she dies: *He inherited money from his uncle.*
• **inheritance noun**

initial[1] /ɪˈnɪʃ·əl/ **adj**   first, or happening at the start: *My initial reaction was one of anger.*

initial[2] /ɪˈnɪʃ·əl/ **noun**   **B1** the first letter of a name, especially when used to represent a name: *He wrote his initials, P. M. R., at the bottom of the page.*

initially /ɪˈnɪʃ·ə·li/ **adv**   at the start: *Initially we thought it would cost six thousand dollars.*

inject /ɪnˈdʒekt/ **verb**   to put a drug into someone's body using a needle
• **injection noun** *I had an **injection**.*

injure /ˈɪn·dʒər/ **verb** (present participle **injuring**, past tense and past participle **injured**)   **B1** to hurt a person or animal: *She injured her ankle when she fell.*
○ *No one was injured in the accident.*
• **injured adj** **B1** *an injured arm*

injury /ˈɪn·dʒə·ri/ **noun** (plural **injuries**) damage to someone's body: *head injuries* ○ *The passenger in the car escaped with minor injuries.*

injustice /ɪnˈdʒʌs·tɪs/ **noun**   a situation or action in which people are not treated fairly: *the fight against racial injustice*

ink /ɪŋk/ **noun** [no plural]   **B1** a colored liquid that you use for writing, printing, or drawing

inland /ˈɪnˌlænd/ **adj, adv**   away from the sea: *The landscape changed as we drove further inland.*

inn /ɪn/ **noun**   a small hotel, especially one in the countryside

inner /ˈɪn·ər/ **adj**   **1** on the inside, or near the middle of something: *Leading off the main hall is a series of inner rooms.*
→ Opposite **outer adj**   **2** Inner feelings or thoughts are ones that you do not show or tell other people: *Karen seemed to have a deep sense of inner peace.*

innocence /ˈɪn·ə·səns/ **noun** [no plural]   the fact of not having done a crime: *She fought to prove her innocence.*
→ Opposite **guilt noun**

innocent /ˈɪn·ə·sənt/ **adj**   **1** If someone is innocent, he or she has not done a crime: *The jury decided he was innocent.*
→ Opposite **guilty adj**   **2** not having much experience of life and not knowing about the bad things that can happen: *an innocent young woman*

input /ˈɪnˌpʊt/ **noun** [no plural]   ideas, money, effort, etc. that you put into a process or activity in order to help it succeed: *We welcome your input.*

inquire /ɪnˈkwaɪər/ **verb** (present participle **inquiring**, past tense and past participle **inquired**) formal   to ask someone for information about something: *I am inquiring about French classes in the area.*

insane /ɪnˈseɪn/ **adj**   crazy or very silly: *She must be insane going out in this weather!*

insect /ˈɪnˌsekt/ **noun**   **A2** a small creature with six legs, for example a bee or a fly

insects

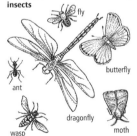

fly

butterfly

ant

dragonfly

wasp

moth

insensitive /ɪnˈsen·sə·t̬ɪv/ **adj**   not noticing when other people are upset, or showing this attitude: *an insensitive remark*

insert /ɪnˈsɜrt/ *verb formal* to put something into something else: *Insert the coin in the slot.*

inside[1] /ɪnˈsaɪd/, /ˈɪnˌsaɪd/ *adv, preposition* **1** **A1** in or into a room, building, or container: *There were some keys inside the box.* ○ *I'm cold – let's go back inside.* **2** If you have a feeling inside, people do not know about it if you do not tell them: *She looked calm but was feeling nervous inside.*

inside[2] /ɪnˈsaɪd/, /ˈɪnˌsaɪd/ *adj* in or on the part of something under its surface: *This jacket has an inside pocket.*

inside[3] /ɪnˈsaɪd/, /ˈɪnˌsaɪd/ *noun* **1** the inside the part of something that is under its surface: *The inside of her house is nice.* **2** inside out If a piece of clothing is inside out, the part that is usually outside is on the inside: *You have your sweater on inside out.*

insist /ɪnˈsɪst/ *verb* **1** **B1** to say that something is certainly true, especially when other people do not believe you: *Mia insisted that she was not lying.* **2** to say that something must be done: *She insisted on seeing her lawyer.*

inspect /ɪnˈspekt/ *verb* to look carefully at something to see if there is anything wrong: *Clara inspected her makeup in the mirror.*
• **inspection** *noun*

inspiration /ˌɪn·spəˈreɪ·ʃən/ *noun* someone or something that gives you ideas for doing something: *Africa is a source of inspiration for his painting.*

inspire /ɪnˈspaɪr/ *verb* (present participle **inspiring**, past tense and past participle **inspired**) **1** to make someone feel that he or she wants to do something: *A teacher has inspired Sam to become an actor.* **2** to give someone an idea for a book, play, painting, etc.: *This television drama was inspired by a true story.*
• **inspiring** *adj an inspiring book*

install /ɪnˈstɔl/ *verb* **1** **B1** to put a piece of equipment somewhere and make it

ready to use: *The school has installed a burglar alarm.* **2** **B1** to put software onto a computer

installment /ɪnˈstɔl·mənt/ *noun* **1** a regular payment: *You can pay for your computer in six monthly installments.* **2** one part of a story that you can read or see every day or week in a magazine or on television

instance /ˈɪn·stəns/ *noun* **for instance** **B1** for example: *Many teenagers earn money, for instance by babysitting or cleaning cars.*

instant /ˈɪn·stənt/ *adj* **1** happening immediately: *The book was an instant success in the U.S.* **2** Instant food or drink can be made quickly: *instant coffee*
• **instantly** *adv A car hit them, killing them both instantly.*

instead /ɪnˈsted/ *adv* **A2** in the place of someone or something else: *Why don't you help instead of complaining?*

instinct /ˈɪn·stɪŋkt/ *noun* the force that makes people and animals do things without first thinking: *It's the mother's instinct to protect her children.*

institute /ˈɪn·stɪˌtut/ *noun* a place where people do scientific or teaching work: *the Massachusetts Institute of Technology*

institution /ˌɪn·stɪˈtu·ʃən/ *noun* a large and important organization, such as a university or bank: *It is one of the country's top medical institutions.*

instruct /ɪnˈstrʌkt/ *verb* **1** to officially tell someone to do something: *Staff members are instructed not to use the telephones for personal calls.* **2** *formal* to teach someone about something

instructions /ɪnˈstrʌk·ʃənz/ *plural noun* **A2** information that explains how to do or use something: *I just followed the instructions.*

instructor /ɪnˈstrʌk·tər/ *noun* someone who teaches a particular sport or activity: *a driving instructor*

instrument /ˈɪn·strə·mənt/ *noun* **1** **A2** an object that is used for playing music, for example a piano   **2** a tool that is used for doing something: *scientific instruments*

insult[1] /ɪnˈsʌlt/ verb   to say or do something rude to someone and upset him or her: *He annoyed me by insulting one of my friends.*
• **insulting** adj *an insulting remark*

insult[2] /ˈɪnsʌlt/ noun   something rude that you say or do to someone: *They were shouting insults at each other.*

insurance /ɪnˈʃʊər·əns/ noun [no plural]   an agreement in which you pay a company money and it gives you money in the future if you have an accident, are hurt, etc.: *We need car insurance.*

insure /ɪnˈʃʊər/ verb (present participle **insuring**, past tense and past participle **insured**)   to buy insurance from a company: *I need to get my car insured.*

intellectual /ˌɪn·tɪˈlek·tʃu·əl/ adj   relating to your ability to think and to understand things, especially complicated ideas: *I like detective stories and romances – nothing too intellectual.*

intelligence /ɪnˈtel·ɪ·dʒəns/ noun [no plural]   the ability to learn and understand things: *a child of low intelligence*

intelligent /ɪnˈtel·ɪ·dʒənt/ adj **B1** able to learn and understand things easily: *She is a highly intelligent young woman.*
• **intelligently** adv

intend /ɪnˈtend/ verb   **1 B1** to want and plan to do something: *How long do you intend to stay in Paris?*   **2 be intended for someone; be intended as something** to be made for a particular person or reason: *The books are intended for young children.*

intense /ɪnˈtens/ adj   extreme or very strong: *intense heat*
• **intensely** adv *I dislike him intensely.*

intensive /ɪnˈten·sɪv/ adj   involving a lot of work in a little time: *ten weeks of intensive training*

intention /ɪnˈten·ʃən/ noun   something that you want and plan to do: *I have no intention of seeing him again.*

intentional /ɪnˈten·ʃə·nᵊl/ adj   planned: *I'm sorry I didn't let you know – it wasn't intentional.*
• **intentionally** adv *I didn't ignore her intentionally – I just didn't recognize her.*

interact /ˌɪn·tərˈækt/ verb   to talk and do things with other people: *At school, teachers said he interacted well with other students.*

interactive /ˌɪn·tərˈæk·tɪv/ adj   Interactive computer programs react to the person using them.

interest[1] /ˈɪn·trəst/ noun   **1 B1** the feeling of wanting to know more about something: *I have always had an interest in science.* ○ *After a while he simply lost interest in* (=stopped being interested in) *his studies.*   **2 B1** something you enjoy doing: *We share a lot of the same interests, particularly music and football.*   **3 B1** [no plural] the quality that makes you think that something is interesting: *Would this book be of any interest to you* (=are you interested in reading it)?   **4** [no plural] the extra money that you must pay to a bank if you borrow money, or that you receive from the bank if you keep your money there: *low interest rates*

interest[2] /ˈɪn·trəst/ verb   **B1** If someone or something interests you, you want to give them your attention and know more about them: *History doesn't really interest me.*

interested /ˈɪn·trə·stɪd/ adj   **A2** wanting to do something or know more about something: *Sarah's only interested in boys, CDs, and clothes.*

> ⚠ **Common mistake: interested and interesting**
>
> People often spell **interesting** and **interested** wrong. Remember that they begin with **inter**.

interesting /ˈɪn·trə·stɪŋ/ adj   **A1** keeping your attention: *an interesting person*
→ Opposite **boring** adj

a
b
c
d
e
f
g
h
i
j
k
l
m
n
o
p
q
r
s
t
u
v
w
x
y
z

⚠ Common mistake: interesting or interested?

Interested is used to describe how someone feels about a person or thing.

I'm interested in theater.
~~I'm interesting in theater.~~

If a person or thing is **interesting**, he, she, or it makes you feel interested.

It was an interesting movie.

---

interfere /ˌɪn·tərˈfɪər/ verb (present participle **interfering**, past tense and past participle **interfered**)   to try to become involved in a situation that you should not be involved in: *You shouldn't **interfere in** other people's business.*

interfere with something phrasal verb to spoil something: *I try not to let my dancing classes interfere with my studies.*
• **interference** noun [no plural]

interior /ɪnˈtɪər·i·ər/ noun the inside part of something: *I have never seen the interior of the hotel.*
→ Opposite **exterior** noun

intermediate /ˌɪn·tərˈmi·di·ət/ adj **B1** between the highest and lowest levels of knowledge or skill: *intermediate students*

internal /ɪnˈtɜr·nəl/ adj inside a place, or inside your body: *internal injuries*
→ Opposite **external** adj

international /ˌɪn·tərˈnæʃ·ə·nəl/ adj **A2** relating to or involving two or more countries: *an international team of scientists ∘ international politics*
• **internationally** adv

the Internet /ˈɪn·tərˌnet/ noun [no plural] (also **the Net**) **A1** a system that connects computers around the world so you can share information with other people: *Cambridge dictionaries are available on the Internet.*

interpret /ɪnˈtɜr·prɪt/ verb to change what someone has said into another

language: *We had to ask the guide to interpret for us.*

interpretation /ɪnˌtɜr·prɪˈteɪ·ʃən/ noun an explanation or opinion of what something means: *These are traditional **interpretations of** the Bible.*

interpreter /ɪnˈtɜr·prɪ·tər/ noun someone whose job is to change what someone else is saying into another language

interrupt /ˌɪn·təˈrʌpt/ verb **B1** to stop someone while he or she is talking or doing something, by saying or doing something yourself: *Sorry to interrupt, but what time is it?*

interruption /ˌɪn·təˈrʌp·ʃən/ noun something that causes someone to stop talking or doing something: *Due to interruptions, the meeting finished late.*

intersection /ˌɪn·tərˈsek·ʃən/ noun a place where two roads meet and cross

interval /ˈɪn·tər·vəl/ noun **B1** a period of time between two things: *After an interval of three days the peace talks started again.*

interview[1] /ˈɪn·tərˌvju/ noun **1 B1** a meeting in which someone asks you questions to see whether you are right for a job or can attend a school: *I had an interview last week for a job in Los Angeles.* **2 B1** a meeting in which someone asks a famous person questions for a newspaper, television, etc., which is then written about or broadcast: *Did you see the interview with the governor in today's paper?*

interview[2] /ˈɪn·tərˌvju/ verb **1 B1** to ask someone questions to see whether he or she is right for a job or can attend a school: *They interviewed several candidates for the job.* **2 B1** to ask someone questions for a newspaper, television, etc.: *She always refuses to be interviewed.*
• **interviewer** noun *The interviewer asked me some difficult questions.*

into /ˈɪn·tu/ preposition **1 A1** toward the inside or middle of something: *Get into bed! ∘ I went into the hotel.* **2 A2** used

---

to show a change from one condition to another or from one kind of thing to another: *Chop the apple into small pieces.* ○ *We turned the smallest bedroom into an office.* **3** ●B1● in the direction of something or someone: *She looked into his eyes.* **4** ●B1● moving toward something or someone and hitting it, him, or her: *I lost control of the car and crashed into a fence.* **5** involving or about something: *There was an investigation into the cause of the fire.* **6** be into something ●B1● informal to be very interested in something: *Will's really into jazz.*

intranet /ˈɪn·trəˌnet/ noun a system that connects the computers in an organization so that people can share information

intransitive /ɪnˈtræn·sɪtɪv/ adj ●B2● An intransitive verb does not have an object. In the sentence "John arrived first," "arrived" is an intransitive verb.

introduce /ˌɪn·trəˈdus/ verb (present participle **introducing**, past tense and past participle **introduced**) **1** ●B1● to tell someone another person's name the first time that they meet: *He took me around the room and introduced me to everyone.* **2** to make something exist or happen for the first time: *We have introduced a new training plan for employees.*

introduction /ˌɪn·trəˈdʌk·ʃən/ noun **1** [no plural] the first time something has happened or existed: *the introduction of a new policy* **2** the first part of a book, which tells you what the book is about **3** a book or course that gives basic knowledge about a subject: *an introduction to statistics*

invade /ɪnˈveɪd/ verb (present participle **invading**, past tense and past participle **invaded**) to enter a country by force in order to take control of it

invalid /ɪnˈvæl·ɪd/ adj An invalid document or ticket is not legally acceptable.

invasion /ɪnˈveɪ·ʒən/ noun an occasion when an army enters a country by force in order to take control of it

invent /ɪnˈvent/ verb **1** ●B1● to design or make something new: *Who invented the*

television? **2** to think of a story or explanation that is not true: *I didn't invent the story – everything I told you is true.*

invention /ɪnˈven·ʃən/ noun **1** ●B1● something that has been designed or made for the first time: *A lot of great inventions have come from America.* **2** ●B1● [no plural] the creation or design of something that has not existed before: *the invention of printing*

inventor /ɪnˈven·tər/ noun someone who designs and makes new things

invest /ɪnˈvest/ verb **1** to give money to a bank or business, or to buy something, because you hope to get a profit: *He's invested a million dollars in the project.* **2** to use a lot of time, effort, or emotions because you want to succeed: *She has invested a lot of energy in her job.*

investigate /ɪnˈves·tɪˌgeɪt/ verb (present participle **investigating**, past tense and past participle **investigated**) to try to get all the facts about something, especially a crime or accident: *The police are investigating the murder.*

• **investigation** noun *They have begun an investigation into his finances.*

investment /ɪnˈvest·mənt/ noun the money that you put in a bank, business, etc. in order to make a profit, or the act of doing this: *This bank account requires a minimum investment of $1,000.*

investor /ɪnˈves·tər/ noun someone who puts money into a bank, business, etc. in order to make a profit

invisible /ɪnˈvɪz·ə·bəl/ adj Something that is invisible cannot be seen.
→ Opposite **visible** adj

invitation /ˌɪn·vɪˈteɪ·ʃən/ noun ●A2● If someone gives you an invitation, he or she is asking whether you would like to do a particular thing or go to a particular event or place: *I got an invitation to Celia's party.*

invite /ɪnˈvaɪt/ verb (present participle **inviting**, past tense and past participle **invited**) ●A1● to ask someone to come to your house, to a party, etc.: *They've invited us to the wedding.*

! Common mistake: invite
someone **to** something

If you are talking about a social event, use the preposition **to**.
She invited me to the party.
~~She invited me for the party.~~
~~She invited me at the party.~~
If you are talking about a meal, you can use **to** or **for**.
He invited me for dinner/to dinner.
If you are talking about a particular type of food, or inviting someone for a particular activity, use **for**.
I was invited for an interview.
They invited her for a pizza.

invoice /'ɪn·vɔɪs/ **noun** a list that shows you how much you have to pay for work someone has done or for things someone has given you

involve /ɪn'vɑlv/ **verb** (present participle **involving**, past tense and past participle **involved**) **1 B1** If a situation or activity involves something, that thing is a part of it: *The trips often involve a lot of walking.* ○ *There are a lot of risks involved.* **2 B1** to affect or include someone or something in an activity: *The event involves hundreds of people.*

involved /ɪn'vɑlvd/ **adj** be/get involved in *something* to do things and be part of an activity or event: *How did you get involved in acting?*

involvement /ɪn'vɑlv·mənt/ **noun** [no plural] the fact of being part of an activity or event

inward[1] /'ɪn·wərd/ **adj** toward the center or the inside of something
→ Opposite **outward** adj

inward[2] /'ɪn·wərd·li/ **adv** toward the inside or the center: *The door slowly opened inward.*

IPA noun [no plural] a system of symbols for showing how words are spoken

IQ noun a person's intelligence when measured by a special test: *a high/low IQ*

iron[1] /'aɪ·ərn/ **noun 1 B1** [no plural] a dark gray metal **2 B1** a piece of electrical equipment that you use for making clothes smooth

iron[2] /'aɪ·ərn/ **verb 1 B1** to make clothes smooth using an iron

ironing /'aɪ·ər·nɪŋ/ **noun** [no plural] **B1** the activity of making clothes smooth using an iron (=a piece of electrical equipment): *John was doing the ironing.*

ironing board /'aɪ·ər·nɪŋ ˌbɔrd/ **noun** a thin table that you use for ironing

irregular /ɪ'reg·jə·lər/ **adj 1 B1** not following the general rules in grammar: *irregular verbs* → Opposite **regular** adj **2** Irregular actions or events happen with a different amount of time between each one: *an irregular heartbeat* **3** not smooth or straight, or having parts that are different sizes: *irregular teeth*

irrelevant /ɪ'rel·ə·vənt/ **adj** not important in a particular situation: *irrelevant information*
→ Opposite **relevant** adj

irresponsible /ˌɪr·ɪ'spɑn·sə·bəl/ **adj** not thinking about the possible bad results of what you are doing: *an irresponsible attitude*

irritate /'ɪr·ɪˌteɪt/ **verb** (present participle **irritating**, past tense and past participle **irritated**) **1** to make someone slightly angry: *His comments really irritated me.* **2** to make a part of your body hurt: *The smoke irritated her eyes.*

irritated /'ɪr·ɪˌteɪ·tɪd/ **adj** slightly angry: *I was irritated that he didn't thank me.*

irritating /'ɪr·ɪˌteɪ·tɪŋ/ **adj** making you feel slightly angry: *an irritating habit*

is /ɪz/ present simple of be, used with "he," "she," and "it"

Islam /ɪs'lɑm/ **noun** [no plural] a religion based on belief in one God and shown to people through Muhammad
• **Islamic adj**

island /'aɪ·lənd/ **noun A2** an area of land that has water around it: *the Hawaiian Islands*

isn't /'ɪz·ənt/ short form of is not: *Mike isn't coming with us.*

isolated /'aɪ·sə‚leɪ·tɪd/ **adj** a long way from other places: *He lives in an isolated village in the mountains.*

issue¹ /'ɪʃ·u/ **noun 1** **B1** an important subject or problem that people are talking about: *environmental issues* **2** the newspaper, magazine, etc. from a particular day

issue² /'ɪʃ·u/ **verb** (present participle **issuing**, past tense and past participle **issued**) to officially give something to someone: *All members will be **issued with** a membership card.*

it /ɪt/ **pronoun 1** **A1** used to mean the thing, situation, or idea that has already been talked about: *"Have you seen my bag?" "It's in the hall."* ○ *It was a bad experience and I don't want to talk about it.* **2** **A1** used before some adjectives, nouns, or verbs to introduce an opinion or description of a situation: *It's unlikely that she'll arrive on time.* ○ *It's a shame you can't come with us.* **3** **A2** used with a verb in sentences giving the time, date, weather, or distances: *It rained all day.* ○ *What time is it?* **4** used to say the name of a person or thing when the person you are speaking to does not know it: *It's your dad on the phone.*

IT /'aɪ·ti/ **noun** [no plural] **A2** the use of computers and other electronic equipment to keep and send information

itch /ɪtʃ/ **verb** If a part of your body itches, you want to rub it with your nails: *Wool sweaters make my arms itch.*
• **itch noun** *I **have an itch** in the middle of my back.*

itchy /'ɪtʃ·i/ **adj** If a part of your body is itchy, you want to rub it: *an itchy nose*

it'd /'ɪt·əd/ **1** short form of it would: *It'd be great if we could meet next week.* **2** short form of it had: *It'd taken us an hour to find Bruce's house.*

item /'aɪ·t̬əm/ **noun 1** **B1** a single thing in a set or on a list: *This is the last item on the list.* ○ *Various stolen items were*

found. **2** a piece of news on television or radio, or in a newspaper: *a small item on the back page of the newspaper*

it'll /'ɪt·əl/ short form of it will: *It'll take about twenty minutes to get there.*

its /ɪts/ **determiner A1** belonging to or relating to the thing that has already been talked about: *The house has its own swimming pool.*

> ⚠ **Common mistake: its or it's?**
>
> **It's** is short for "it is," and is always written with an apostrophe.
>   *It's cold today.*
> **Its** means "of it."
>   *The snake put out its tongue.*

---

it's /ɪts/ **1** short form of it is: *"What time is it?" "It's one o'clock."* **2** short form of it has: *It's been hard work.*

itself /ɪt'self/ **pronoun 1** **A2** used to show that the thing or animal that does the action is also the thing or animal that is affected by it: *The cat licked itself clean.* **2** **B1** the thing that you are talking about: *The garden is enormous but the house itself is very small.* **3** **(by) it-self** **B1** alone or without help: *The dog was in the house by itself for several days.*

I've /aɪv/ short form of I have: *I've decided not to go.*

ivy /'aɪ·vi/ **noun** [no plural] a dark green plant that grows up walls

Jj

J, j /dʒeɪ/ the tenth letter of the alphabet

jab /dʒæb/ **verb** (present participle **jabbing**, past tense and past participle **jabbed**) to push something quickly into another thing or toward another thing: *He was yelling and **jabbing** a finger **in** her face.*

jack /dʒæk/ **noun 1** a playing card that has a picture of a young man on it: *the*

a b c d e f g h i j k l m n o p q r s t u v w x y z

jack of diamonds **2** a hole into which a wire connectd to a piece of electrical equipment can be plugged so that the equipment can operate: *a phone jack*

jacket /ˈdʒæk·ɪt/ *noun* **A2** a short coat: *a leather jacket*

jacket

collar

sleeve

cuff

jagged /ˈdʒæg·ɪd/ *adj* very rough and sharp: *jagged rocks*

jaguar /ˈdʒæg·wɑr/ *noun* a large, wild cat that lives in Central and South America

jail /dʒeɪl/ *noun* **B1** a place where criminals are kept as a punishment: *He is in jail.*

jam[1] /dʒæm/ *noun* **1** **A2** [no plural] a sweet food made from fruit, which you put on bread: *a jar of strawberry jam* → See **Food** on page C7 **2** (also **traffic jam**) a line of cars, trucks, etc. that are moving slowly or not moving: *We were stuck in a jam for hours.*

jam[2] /dʒæm/ *verb* (present participle **jamming**, past tense and past participle **jammed**) **1** to push something somewhere firmly and tightly: *She jammed her hands into her pockets.* **2** If a machine or something that moves jams, or you jam it, it stops moving or working: *The paper keeps jamming in the machine.* **3** to fill a place completely: *The streets were jammed with cars.*

jangle /ˈdʒæŋ·gəl/ *verb* (present participle **jangling**, past tense and past participle **jangled**) If small metal objects jangle,

they hit together making a ringing noise: *jangling bracelets*

janitor /ˈdʒæn·ɪ·tər/ *noun* a person whose job is to clean and take care of a building

January /ˈdʒæn·juˌer·i/ *noun* **A1** the first month of the year

jar /dʒɑr/ *noun* **B1** a glass container used for keeping food: *a jar of jam* → See picture at **container**

javelin /ˈdʒæv·ə·lɪn/ *noun* a long, pointed stick that you throw as a sport → See **Sports 1** on page C15

jaw /dʒɔ/ *noun* either of the two bones in your mouth that contain your teeth → See **The Body** on page C2

jazz /dʒæz/ *noun* [no plural] **A2** music with a strong beat that people often play without looking at written music: *a jazz band*

jealous /ˈdʒel·əs/ *adj* **1** **B1** upset and angry because someone you love seems to like another person: *a jealous husband* **2** not happy because you want something that someone else has: *Dan's new bike was making his friends jealous.* ○ *I'm jealous of your new car.*
• **jealously** *adv She looked jealously at Gwen's ring.*

jealousy /ˈdʒel·ə·si/ *noun* [no plural] jealous feelings

jeans /dʒinz/ *plural noun* **A1** pants made from denim (= a strong, usually blue, material): *a pair of jeans* → See **Clothes** on page C5

> **⚠ Common mistake: jeans**
>
> Jeans is a plural word.
> *These jeans are too big for me.*

Jell-O /ˈdʒel·oʊ/ *noun* trademark a soft, sweet food that shakes when you move it: *a bowl of Jell-O*

jelly /ˈdʒel·i/ *noun* [no plural] a soft, sweet food made from fruit: *a peanut butter and jelly sandwich*

195   **joint**

jellyfish /ˈdʒel·iˌfɪʃ/
noun (plural **jellyfish**)
a sea creature with a
clear body that can
sting you (=put poi-
son into your skin)

jellyfish

jerk[1] /dʒɜrk/ verb
to move very quickly
and suddenly, or to make something
move like this: *The truck jerked forward.*

jerk[2] /dʒɜrk/ noun   a mean or annoying
person: *That guy is a real jerk.*

Jesus Christ /ˈdʒi·zəs ˈkraɪst/ noun
the holy man that Christians believe is
the Son of God

jet /dʒet/ noun   **1** 🔵**B1** a plane that flies
very fast   **2** water or gas that is forced
out of something in a thin, strong line

Jew /dʒu/ noun   someone whose religion is Judaism, or who is related to the
ancient people of Israel

jewel /ˈdʒu·əl/ noun   a valuable stone
that is used to make jewelry

jewelry /ˈdʒu·əl·ri/ noun [no plural]
🔵**A2** objects made from gold, silver, and
valuable stones that you wear for
decoration

jewelry

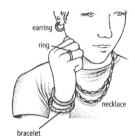

earring

ring

necklace

bracelet

Jewish /ˈdʒu·ɪʃ/ adj   relating to the religion of Judaism or
to Jews

jigsaw /ˈdʒɪɡˌsɔ/
noun (also **jigsaw
puzzle**)   a picture in
many small pieces
that you put to-
gether as a game

jigsaw

jingle /ˈdʒɪŋ·ɡəl/ verb (present participle
jingling, past tense and past participle
jingled)   to make repeated, gentle ringing sounds, or to cause small objects to
make these sounds: *He jingled the coins
in his pocket.*

job /dʒɑb/ noun   **1** 🔵**A1** the work that
you do in order to get money: *He got a
job as a waiter.*   **2** 🔵**A2** a piece of work: *I
did a few jobs around the house.*
3 something that you have to do: *It's
my job to water the plants.*   **4 do a bad,
good, etc. job of** *something* to do
something badly, well, etc.: *She did an
excellent job planning the party.*

jog[1] /dʒɑɡ/ verb (present participle **jogging**,
past tense and past participle **jogged**)   🔵**B1** to
run slowly for exercise: *I jog through the
park every morning.*
• **jogging** noun [no plural]   🔵**B1** *I go jogging
every morning.*

jog[2] /dʒɑɡ/ noun   a slow run that you
do for exercise: *We could go for a jog.*

join /dʒɔɪn/ verb   **1** 🔵**A2** to become a
member of an organization: *He joined
the army when he was 18.*   **2** 🔵**A2** to do
something or go somewhere with someone: *Would you like to join us for dinner?*
3 🔵**B1** to fasten or connect things together: *Join the ends together with glue.*
4 🔵**B1** to meet at a particular point: *This
is the point where the two rivers join.*

join in (*something*) phrasal verb   🔵**B1** to
do an activity with other people: *We're
playing cards. Would you like to join in?*

> ❗ **Common mistake: join**
>
> **Join** is not followed by a preposition
> when it is used in expressions such as
> "join a company."
> *He joined the team in 2008.*
> ~~He joined to the team in 2008.~~

joint[1] /dʒɔɪnt/ adj   belonging to or done
by two or more people: *The project was a
joint effort by all the children in the class.*
• **jointly** adv   *The house is jointly owned
by the couple.*

| æ cat | ɑ hot | e get | ɪ sit | i see | ɔ saw | ʊ book | u too | ʌ cut | ə about | ɑr mother | ɜr turn | ɔr for | ɑɪ my | ɑʊ how | eɪ say | ɔɪ boy |

joint² /dʒɔɪnt/ *noun*

joint

1 a place in your body where two bones meet: *the knee joint* **2** a place where parts of something are connected

joke¹ /dʒoʊk/ *noun* **B1** a short, funny story that someone tells to make people laugh: *Ben was **telling jokes** at the other end of the table.*

joke² /dʒoʊk/ *verb* (present participle **joking**, past tense and past participle **joked**) **1** **B1** to say funny things, or not be serious: *She always **jokes about** her husband's cooking.* **2 You must be joking!** informal **B1** used to say that something is certainly not true: *"Does Rick go to the gym?" "You must be joking – he never exercises!"*

jolt¹ /dʒoʊlt/ *noun* a sudden, violent movement: *With a sudden jolt the train started moving.*

jolt² /dʒoʊlt/ *verb* to make someone or something suddenly move forward: *We were jolted forward when the bus stopped suddenly.*

jot /dʒɑt/ *verb* (present participle **jotting**, past tense and past participle **jotted**)

jot *something* **down** *phrasal verb* to write something quickly: *I jotted down some notes during his speech.*

journalism /ˈdʒɜr·nᵊl·ɪz·əm/ *noun* [no plural] the work of writing for newspapers, magazines, television, or radio

journalist /ˈdʒɜr·nᵊl·ɪst/ *noun* **B1** someone whose job is writing for newspapers, magazines, television, or radio

journey /ˈdʒɜr·ni/ *noun* a trip from one place to another, especially for a long distance or a long period of time: *a three-week journey through China*

joy /dʒɔɪ/ *noun* **1** [no plural] a feeling of strong happiness: *The children have brought her so much joy.* **2** something or someone that makes you feel very happy: *She's a joy to work with.*

joyful /ˈdʒɔɪ·fəl/ *adj* very happy, or making people feel very happy: *joyful news*

Jr. /ˈdʒʊn·jər/ *adj* abbreviation for junior: the younger of two men in a family with the same name: *John F. Kennedy, Jr.*

Judaism /ˈdʒu·di͵ɪz·əm/ *noun* [no plural] a religion based on belief in one God and on the Talmud and Torah

judge¹ /dʒʌdʒ/ *noun* **1** **B1** someone who controls a court and decides how criminals should be punished: *The judge ruled that he was not guilty of murder.* **2** **B1** someone who decides which person or thing wins a competition: *the Olympic judges*

judge² /dʒʌdʒ/ *verb* (present participle **judging**, past tense and past participle **judged**) **1** **B1** to have or develop an opinion about something or someone, usually after thinking carefully: *The meeting was judged to be a great success.* ○ *You shouldn't **judge** people **on** their appearance.* ○ *He was judged guilty/insane.* **2** **B1** to decide the winner or results of a competition: *I was asked to judge the art contest.* **3 judging by/from** used for saying the reasons why you have a particular opinion: *She must be popular, judging by the number of letters that she receives.*

judgment /ˈdʒʌdʒ·mənt/ *noun* **1** an opinion about someone or something after thinking carefully: *He has to **make** a **judgment** about who will win the contest.* **2** [no plural] the ability to make good decisions or to be right in your opinions: *I trust her judgment.* **3** an official decision made by a judge

jug /dʒʌɡ/ *noun* a container for liquids that has a small opening and a handle: *a jug of cider*

juggle /ˈdʒʌɡ·əl/ *verb* (present participle **juggling**, past tense and past participle **juggled**) **1** to try to do many things at the same time: *Many women have to juggle work and family.* **2** to throw two or more things, such as balls, into the air and catch them continuously

juice /dʒus/ *noun* [no plural] **A1** the liquid that comes from fruit or vegetables

juicy /ˈdʒu·si/ *adj* (comparative **juicier**,

superlative **juiciest**) **B1** full of juice: *juicy apples*

July /dʒʊˈlaɪ/ **noun** **A1** the seventh month of the year

jumble /ˈdʒʌm·bəl/ **noun** a lot of things together in a messy group: *He looked at the jumble of papers on his desk.*

jump[1] /dʒʌmp/ **verb** **1** **A2** to push your body up and away from the ground using your feet and legs: *The children were jumping up and down with excitement.* ○ *They jumped into the water.* **2** **A2** to go over something by moving up into the air: *Can you **jump across** this puddle?* **3** **B1** to move somewhere suddenly and quickly: *She jumped into a taxi and rushed to the station.* **4** to make a sudden movement because you are frightened or surprised: *Her scream **made me jump**.*

jump[2] /dʒʌmp/ **noun** **B1** the act of pushing your body up into the air using your feet and legs: *He won with a jump of 8.5 meters.*

jumper /ˈdʒʌm·pər/ **noun** a dress with no sleeves that is worn over a shirt

June /dʒun/ **noun** **A1** the sixth month of the year

jungle /ˈdʒʌŋ·gəl/ **noun** **B1** an area of land in a hot country where trees and plants grow close together

junior[1] /ˈdʒun·jər/ **adj** **1** less important than other people doing the same job: *a junior officer* → Opposite **senior** adj **2** for or relating to young people: *a junior tennis tournament* **3** relating to a student's third year of high school or college: *my junior year*

junior[2] /ˈdʒun·jər/ **noun** a student in his or her third year of high school or college: *Many team members are juniors who will play again next year.*

junk /dʒʌŋk/ **noun** [no plural] informal old or useless things that no one wants

junk food /ˈdʒʌŋk ˌfud/ **noun** [no plural] food that is bad for your body but quick to prepare and eat

jury /ˈdʒʊr·i/ **noun** (plural **juries**) a group of people in a court of law who decide whether someone has done a crime

just[1] /dʒʌst/ **adv** **1** **A2** a very short time ago: *I just saw him.* ○ *We've only just begun.* **2** **A2** now or very soon: *The game is just beginning.* **3** **B1** only: *I'll just have a small piece.* ○ *He just wants to win.* ○ *The movie is not just about love.* **4** **B1** used to make something you are saying strong: *I just hate it!* **5** **B1** almost not: *This dress **only just** fits.* **6** **B1** exactly: *Tim looks just like his father.* **7** just about **B1** almost: *I think I remembered just about everything.* **8** be just about to do *something* to be going to do something very soon: *I was just about to call you.* **9** just as bad, good, important, etc. (as *someone/something*) **B1** equally bad, good, important, etc.: *He's just as smart as his brother.* ○ *Your attitude is just as important as your skill.* **10** just before, over, under, etc. **B1** a little before, over, under, etc. something else: *It costs just under $10.* **11** it's just as well used to say that it is lucky that something happened: *It's just as well that we brought an umbrella.*

just[2] /dʒʌst/ **adj** fair or morally right: *a just society*

justice /ˈdʒʌs·tɪs/ **noun** [no plural] **1** treatment of people that is fair: *She worked hard for economic justice for all.* → Opposite **injustice** noun **2** the system of laws that judges or punishes people: *the criminal justice system*

K k

K, k /keɪ/ the eleventh letter of the alphabet

kangaroo /ˌkæŋ·gəˈru/ **noun** a large Australian animal that moves by jumping on its back legs

kangaroo

a
b
c
d
e
f
g
h
i
j
k
l
m
n
o
p
q
r
s
t
u
v
w
x
y
z

karaoke /ˌkær·i·ˈou·ki/ *noun* [no plural]
a type of entertainment in which people sing songs with recorded music that is played by a machine: *We're having a karaoke night tonight.*

karate /kəˈrɑ·t̬i/ *noun* [no plural]   a sport from Japan in which people fight with the hands or feet

keen /kin/ *adj*   very good: *a keen sense of smell* ○ *a keen observation*

keep /kip/ *verb* (past tense and past participle **kept**)   **1** ⓐ to have something always, as your own: *You can keep that dress if you like it.* ○ *I kept every letter he ever sent to me.* **2** *keep something* **in, on,** etc. to always put something in a particular place: *I keep the keys in the drawer.* **3** *keep (someone/something)* **awake, clean, safe,** etc. ⓐ to make someone or something stay in a particular state: *This coat should keep you warm.* ○ *He keeps his car very clean.* **4** *keep doing something* ⓑ to continue to do something, or to often do something: *I keep telling her not to do it.* ○ *He keeps hitting me.* **5** *keep in touch* ⓑ to communicate or continue to communicate with someone by e-mail or telephone: *Do you still keep in touch with your friends from college?* **6** ⓑ to delay someone or prevent someone from doing something: *He's very late – what's keeping him?* ○ *I'm so sorry to keep you waiting.* **7** *keep a secret* ⓑ to not tell anyone a secret **8** to write something down in order to remember it: *Remember to keep a record of how much money you spend.* ○ *Keep a list of the missing items.* **9** If food or drink keeps, it stays fresh: *The fish will keep for only two days.* **10** to have and take care of animals: *Our neighbors keep chickens.*

keep at *something* **phrasal verb** to continue working hard at something difficult: *Learning a language is hard, but you just have to keep at it.*

keep *something* **down phrasal verb** to stop the number, level, or size of something from increasing: *I have to exercise to keep my weight down.*

keep (*someone/something***) off** *something* **phrasal verb** ⓑ to not go onto an area, or to stop someone or something from going onto an area: *Keep off the grass.*

keep on doing *something* **phrasal verb** ⓑ to continue to do something, or to do something again and again: *She kept on asking me questions.*

keep (*someone/something***) out phrasal verb** ⓑ to not go into a place, or to stop someone or something from going into a place: *Keep out of the kitchen until lunch is ready.*

keep up phrasal verb **1** to stay with someone who is moving forward by moving as quickly as that person: *She was walking so fast I couldn't **keep up** with her.* **2** to be able to understand or deal with something that is happening or changing very fast: *It's important to **keep up with** international news.* **3** to increase as quickly as something or someone else: *Prices are rising fast and wages aren't keeping up.*

keep *something* **up phrasal verb** ⓑ to not allow something that is good, strong, etc. to become less good, strong, etc.: *Keep up the good work!*

kept /kept/   past tense and past participle of keep

ketchup /ˈketʃ·əp/ *noun* [no plural]   a cold, red sauce made from tomatoes

kettle /ˈket̬·ᵊl/ *noun* ⓑ a metal container with a lid, used for boiling water: *Is the kettle boiling yet?*

key[1] /ki/ *noun*

keys

1 ⓐ a piece of metal that you use for locking a door or starting an engine: *I lost my car keys.* **2** ⓐ a list of answers to an exercise or game: *The answer key is on page 134.* **3** ⓑ one of the parts you press on a keyboard or musical instrument to produce letters and numbers, or to make a sound **4** a set of musical notes based on one particular scale: *the key of D major* **5** the **key to** *something* the thing that you must do in order to achieve something: *Hard work is the key to success.*

key[2] /ki/ adj   very important in influencing or achieving something: *a key factor in solving the problem*

key[3] /ki/ verb

key *something* **in** phrasal verb **B1** to put information into a computer using a keyboard: *Key in your name and password.*

keyboard /'ki,bɔrd/ noun   **1** **A2** a set of keys on a computer that you press to make it work, or the rows of keys on a piano → See **The Office** on page C12   **2** an electronic musical instrument similar to a piano: *Laurie plays keyboards in the band.*

keyhole /'ki,houl/ noun   a hole in a lock where you put a key

kg   written abbreviation for kilogram: a unit for measuring weight

khaki /'kæk·i/ noun [no plural]   **1** a yellow-brown color, originally worn by soldiers → See **Colors** on page C6   **2** khakis pants made from yellow-brown cloth: *He was wearing khakis and a blue shirt.*
 • **khaki** adj

kick[1] /kɪk/ verb   **1** **A1** to hit or move something or someone with your foot: *The boys were kicking a ball around.*
2 to move your feet and legs forward or backward quickly: *The baby lay kicking on the mat.*

kick *someone* **out** phrasal verb informal to make someone leave a place or an organization: *His wife kicked him out of the house.*

kick[2] /kɪk/ noun   **1** **A2** the act of hitting something with your foot: *He gave her a kick in the ribs.*   **2** informal a feeling of excitement and energy: *She gets a kick out of performing live.*

kid /kɪd/ noun   **1** **B1** informal a child: *school kids*   **2** a young goat

kidnap /'kɪd·næp/ verb (present participle **kidnapping**, past tense and past participle **kidnapped**)   to take someone away using force, saying that you will only bring the person back if someone gives you money
 • **kidnapper** noun

kidney /'kɪd·ni/ noun   one of the two parts in your body that remove bad things from the blood

kill /kɪl/ verb   **1** **A2** to make someone or something die: *Their son was killed in a car accident.*   **2** informal to hurt a lot: *My feet are killing me.*

killer /'kɪl·ər/ noun   **B1** someone who kills, or a disease or animal that kills: *Heart disease is the biggest killer in the United States.*

killing /'kɪl·ɪŋ/ noun   **B1** an act of killing someone: *a series of brutal killings*

kilo /'kiː·loʊ/ noun   **A2** short form of kilogram

kilobyte /'kɪl·ə,baɪt/ noun   a unit for measuring the amount of information you can put on a computer

kilogram /'kɪl·ə,ɡræm/ noun (written abbreviation **kg**)   **A2** a unit for measuring weight, equal to 1,000 grams

kilometer /kɪ'lɑm·ɪ·t̬ər/ noun (written abbreviation **km**)   a unit for measuring distance, equal to 1,000 meters

kin /kɪn/ noun formal   the people in your family

kind[1] /kaɪnd/ noun   **1** **A1** a type of thing or person: *What kind of music do you like?*   **2** all kinds of something **A2** many different types of something: *All kinds of people come to our church.*   **3** some kind of used to talk about something when you are not sure of its exact type: *She has some kind of medical problem.*   **4** that kind of thing **B1** used to show that what you have just said is only an example from a larger group of things: *I like pasta, pizza – that kind of thing.*   **5** kind of informal used when you are trying to explain or describe something, but you cannot be exact: *It's kind of unusual.*

kind[2] /kaɪnd/ adj   **A2** Kind people do things to help others and show that they care about them: *Your mother was very kind to us.* ○ *It was very kind of you to come and see me.*
 → Opposite **unkind** adj

kindergarten /'kɪn·dər,ɡɑr·t³n/ noun   a class in school for children aged five or six

kindly /'kaɪnd·li/ *adv* **B1** in a kind way: *She kindly offered to cook me lunch.*

kindness /'kaɪnd·nəs/ *noun* [no plural] behavior that is kind: *I wanted to thank her for her kindness.*

king /kɪŋ/ *noun* **1** **A2** a man who rules a country and is part of the royal family: *the kings and queens of England* **2** a playing card that has a picture of a king on it: *the king of hearts*

kingdom /'kɪŋ·dəm/ *noun* **1** a country with a king or queen: *the Kingdom of Belgium* **2 the animal kingdom** all animals considered together

kiosk /'ki·ɑsk/ *noun* a small building where things like tickets or newspapers are sold through an open window

kiss[1] /kɪs/ *verb* **A2** to put your lips against another person's lips or skin because you love or like that person: *He kissed her cheek.* ∘ *I kissed her goodbye.*

kiss

kiss[2] /kɪs/ *noun* **A2** the action of kissing someone: *She ran up and gave me a kiss.*

kit /kɪt/ *noun* **1** **B1** things that you keep in a container ready for a particular use: *a tool kit* **2** a set of parts that you put together to make something: *He's making a model airplane from a kit.*

kitchen /'kɪtʃ·ən/ *noun* **A1** a room used to prepare and cook food in
→ See **The Kitchen** on page C10

kite /kaɪt/ *noun* **A2** a toy made of paper or cloth that flies in the air on the end of a long string

kite

kitten /'kɪt·ən/ *noun* **B1** a young cat

kiwi /'ki·wi/ *noun* (also **kiwi fruit**) a small fruit that is green inside and has black seeds and brown, hairy skin

km written abbreviation for kilometer: a unit for measuring distance

knead /nid/ *verb* to press the mixture for making bread with your hands before you cook it

knee /ni/ *noun* **B1** the middle part of your leg where it bends: *a knee injury*
→ See **The Body** on page C2

kneel /nil/ *verb* (past tense and past participle **knelt**) to bend your legs and put one knee or both knees on the floor: *She knelt down beside the child.*

kneel

knew /nu/ past tense of know

knife /naɪf/ *noun* (plural **knives** /naɪvz/) **A1** a sharp metal tool used for cutting: *a knife and fork*
→ See **The Kitchen** on page C10

knit /nɪt/ *verb* (present participle **knitting**, past tense **knitted**, past participle **knitted**) **B1** to make clothes using thick thread and two long needles to join the thread together: *She was knitting him a sweater.*
• **knitting** noun [no plural] **B1** *She sat doing her knitting.*

knit

knob /nɑb/ *noun* a round handle, or a round button on a machine: *a door knob* ∘ *Turn the black knob to the left.*

knock[1] /nɑk/ *verb* **1** **B1** to hit a door with your closed hand so that people know you are there: *There's someone knocking at/on the door.* **2** **B1** to hit something or someone and make the person or thing move or fall down: *He* *accidentally knocked the plate off the table.* ○ *I knocked my glass over.*

> **! Common mistake: knock**
>
> Be careful to use the correct prepositions. You do not always need one.
>
> The policeman **knocked on/knocked at** the door.
>
> ~~Listen! There is someone knocking to the door.~~
>
> Knock before you come in.

knock someone down phrasal verb **B1** to hit or push someone, especially accidentally, so that he or she falls to the ground: *I saw that bike rider knock a lady down.*

knock someone out phrasal verb **1** to make someone become unconscious, usually by hitting him or her on the head: *He was knocked out halfway through the fight.* **2** to defeat a person or team in a competition so that the person or team cannot take part any more: *Our team was knocked out in the semifinals.*

knock something over phrasal verb to hit or push something, especially accidentally, so that the thing falls to the ground or onto one side: *I knocked a bottle of wine over when I reached across the table.*

knock² /nɑk/ noun a sudden short noise made when something hits a surface: *There was a **knock** at the door.*

knot /nɑt/ noun a place where pieces of string, rope, etc. have been tied together

knot

know /noʊ/ verb (past tense **knew**, past participle **known**) **1** **A1** to have information about something in your mind: *Andrew **knows** a lot **about** cars.* ○ *"How old is she?" "I don't know."* ○ *He **knew that** she was lying.* **2** **A1** used to ask someone to tell you a piece of information: *Do you know where the post office is?* **3** **A2** to be certain: *I know she'll be really pleased to hear the news.* **4** **A2** to be able to do

something: *Do you **know how to** ski?* **5** **B1** to have spent time with someone or in a place so that the person or place is not new to you: *I've known Al since we were children.* ○ *I grew up in Boston, so I know it well.* **6 let someone know** **A2** to tell someone something: *Let me know if you're going to the party.* **7** I know used when you agree with something someone has just said: *"It's a beautiful day, isn't it?" "I know – let's hope it lasts."* **8 you know** **B1** used to make sure someone understands which person or thing you are talking about: *I had lunch with Rachel – you know, my friend from work?* **9** **B1** (also **know about**) If you know a subject, you are familiar with it and understand it: *Ask Andy to fix it – he knows about computers.* **10 be known as something** **B1** to be called: *California is also known as the Sunshine State.* **11 get to know someone/something** **B1** to gradually learn more about someone or something: *I got to know Frank at work.* **12 as far as I know** used to say that you think something is true, but cannot be sure: *As far as I know, he isn't married.*

> **! Common mistake: know or find out?**
>
> To **know** something means to already have information about something.
>
> Kelly knows what time the train leaves.
>
> His parents already know what he did.
>
> To **find out** something means to learn new information for the first time.
>
> Can you find out what time the train leaves?
>
> His parents were angry when they found out what he did.

knowledge /ˈnɑl·ɪdʒ/ noun [no plural] **B1** information and understanding that you have in your mind: *His **knowledge of** history is amazing.*

> ⚠ **Common mistake: knowledge**
>
> Remember you cannot make **knowledge** plural. Do not say "knowledges."
> *I have some **knowledge of** Spanish and German.*

knowledgeable /ˈnɑl·ɪdʒ·ə·bəl/ **adj** knowing a lot: *He's very **knowledgeable about** art.*

known /noʊn/ past participle of know

knuckle /ˈnʌk·əl/ **noun** one of the parts of a finger that bends

koala /koʊˈɑ·lə/ **noun** an Australian animal like a small bear with grayfur that lives in trees

koala

the Koran /kəˈrɑn/ **noun** the holy book of Islam

Ll

L, l /el/ the twelfth letter of the alphabet

l written abbreviation for liter: a unit for measuring liquid

lab /læb/ **noun** 🔵 short form of laboratory: a room used for scientific work

label[1] /ˈleɪ·bəl/ **noun** **1** 🔵 a piece of paper or material that is attached to something and gives you information about it: *There are washing instructions on the label.* **2** 🔵 a company that makes things for sale, mainly clothes: *Her favorite **designer label** (=company that makes expensive clothes) is Armani.*

label[2] /ˈleɪ·bəl/ **verb** (present participle **labeling**, past tense and past participle **labeled**) 🔵 to attach a small piece of paper or material to something that gives information about it: *Was the package clearly labeled?*

labor /ˈleɪ·bər/ **noun** [no plural] **1** work that you do with your hands and body: *Does that price include the cost of labor?* **2** people who work: *cheap labor* **3** the process of giving birth to a baby

laboratory /ˈlæb·rəˌtɔr·i/ **noun** (plural **laboratories**) 🔵 a room used for scientific work: *research laboratories*

laborer /ˈleɪ·bər·ər/ **noun** a worker who does hard work with this or her hands and body: *a farm laborer*

lace /leɪs/ **noun** **1** [no plural] a thin, white cloth with a pattern of holes in it: *a lace curtain* **2** a string used to tie shoes

lack[1] /læk/ **noun** [no plural] **lack of** *something* 🔵 not having something, or not having enough of something: *My only problem is lack of money.*

lack[2] /læk/ **verb** to not have something, or to not have enough of something: *She really lacks confidence.*

ladder /ˈlæd·ər/ **noun** 🔵 a thing that you climb up when you want to reach a high place, which has two long pieces joined together by shorter pieces

ladder

lady /ˈleɪ·di/ **noun** (plural **ladies**) 🔵 a polite way of saying "woman": ***Ladies and gentlemen**, can I have your attention please?*

laid /leɪd/ past tense and past participle of lay

lain /leɪn/ past participle of lie

lake /leɪk/ **noun** 🔵 a large area of water that has land all around it: *Lake Erie*

lamb /læm/ **noun** **1** 🔵 a young sheep **2** 🔵 [no plural] meat from a young sheep

lame /leɪm/ **adj** A lame animal or person cannot walk because his, her, or its foot or leg is hurt: *a lame horse*

lamp /læmp/ **noun** 🔵 an object that makes light: *I have a lamp next to my bed.*
→ See **The Living Room** on page C11

lamppost /ˈlæmpˌpoʊst/ **noun** a tall post with a light at the top

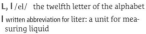

lampshade /'læmp.ʃeɪd/ noun a cover for an electric light

land¹ /lænd/ noun 1 **B1** [no plural] an area of ground: *agricultural land* 2 [no plural] the surface of the Earth that is not ocean: *We traveled over land and sea.* 3 literary a country: *a land of ice and snow*

> ⚠ **Common mistake: land or country?**
>
> Land is only used to mean "country" in literary writing or poems. In ordinary speech or writing, it is better to use country.
>
> *I enjoyed visiting their country.*
> ~~I enjoyed visiting their land.~~

land² /lænd/ verb 1 **B1** The action of a plane arriving on the ground after flying: *We should land in Madrid at 7 a.m.* 2 land in, on, etc. If an object or person lands somewhere, he or she falls to the ground there: *She landed flat on her back.*

landing /'læn.dɪŋ/ noun 1 the act of bringing a plane to the ground: *The plane had to make an emergency landing in Chicago.* 2 the area of floor at the top of a set of stairs

landlady /'lænd.leɪ.di/ noun (plural **landladies**) a woman who owns the house that you live in and whom you pay rent to

landlord /'lænd.lɔrd/ noun a man who owns the house that you live in and whom you pay rent to

landmark /'lænd.mɑrk/ noun 1 a building or place that is easy to recognize, especially one that helps you judge where you are: *a familiar landmark* 2 a structure that is famous or that is a particularly important example of its type

landscape /'lænd.skeɪp/ noun [no plural] **B1** the appearance of an area of land, especially in the country: *The landscape is very beautiful.*

lane /leɪn/ noun one of the parts of a big road that is shown by a painted line: *He was driving in the fast lane.*

language /'læŋ.gwɪdʒ/ noun 1 **A1** the words used by the people of a country: *How many languages do you speak?* 2 **B1** [no plural] words that people use to speak or write: *The way that children's language develops is fascinating.*

lap /læp/ noun 1 the top part of your legs when you are sitting down: *His little daughter was sitting on his lap.* 2 one journey around a race track: *He's two laps behind the leaders.*

laptop /'læp.tɑp/ noun **A2** a small computer that you can carry around with you

laptop

large /lɑrdʒ/ adj **A2** big: *a large number of people* ○ *He won a large amount of money.* ○ *She comes from quite a large family.*
→ Opposite **small adj, little adj**

laser /'leɪ.zər/ noun a very strong line of light that is used in machines and used for repairing parts of the body: *a laser beam* ○ *a laser printer*

lashes /'læʃ.ɪz/ noun the small hairs on the edges of your eye: *She's got lovely, long lashes.*

last¹ /læst/ adj, determiner 1 last week, year, Monday, etc. **A1** the week, year, Monday, etc. before the present one: *I went to Barcelona last month.* 2 **A2** the most recent: *What was the last movie you saw?* ○ *It's rained for the last three days.* 3 **A2** Your last book, house, job, etc. is the one before the one that you have now: *My last house was half this size.* 4 **A2** happening or coming at the end: *It's the last room on the left.* ○ *That's the last program of the season.* ○ *I was the last person to arrive.* → Opposite **first adj** 5 **B1** only remaining: *Who wants the last piece of cake?* 6 the last person, thing, etc. a person or thing that you do not want or expect: *Three extra people to feed – that's the last thing I need!*

last² /læst/ adv 1 **B1** used to talk about the most recent time you did something:

When did you last see her? ∘ *I think it was July when I last spoke to him.* **2** after everything or everyone else: *I came in last in the race.* ∘ *We've still got to check the figures but we'll do that last.* → Opposite **first adv 3 last but not least** something you say before you say the last person or thing on a list: *This is Jeremy, this is Olivia, and, last but not least, this is Eva.*

last³ /læst/ **noun, pronoun 1 at last** **B1** finally: *At last, I've found a jacket I like.* **2 the last** a person or thing that comes after all the others: *We were the last to get there.* **3 the last of** *something* the only part of something that remains: *We finished the last of the wine.*

last⁴ /læst/ **verb 1 B1** to continue to happen or exist: *How long will the meeting last?* ∘ *The batteries last about ten hours.* ∘ *Enjoy the sun while it lasts!* **2** to be enough for a period of time: *We have enough food to last another week.*

lasting /ˈlæs·tɪŋ/ **adj** continuing to exist for a long time: *lasting peace*

lastly /ˈlæst·li/ **adv** finally: *And lastly, I'd like to thank everyone who took part in the event.*

last-minute /ˈlæstˈmɪn·ɪt/ **adj** done at the latest possible time: *I was just doing some last-minute preparation.*

the last minute /ˈlæstˈmɪn·ɪt/ **noun** [no plural] the latest possible time of doing something: *They only told me **at the last minute** that they couldn't come.*

last name /ˈlæst ˈneɪm/ **noun** **A2** the name that you and your family all have

late /leɪt/ **adj, adv 1 A1** after the usual time or the time that was arranged: *I was **late for** work this morning.* ∘ *We got there too late and all the food was gone.* ∘ *We had a late lunch.* **2 A1** near the end of a period of time: *It was built in the late 19th century.* ∘ *It was late at night.* **3 it's late A1** something that you say when it is near the end of a day: *It's late – I really should be going.*

lately /ˈleɪt·li/ **adv** **B1** recently: *Lately, I've been walking to work.*

later¹ /ˈleɪ·tər/ **adj 1** after some time: *I arranged it for a later date.* **2** more recent: *I'm not familiar with his later work.*

later² /ˈleɪ·tər/ **adv 1** after some time: *He arrived later that night.* ∘ *I'll be joining them later.* **2 later on** at a time in the future: *What are you doing later on this evening?* **3 see you later** **A1** used for saying goodbye to someone you are going to meet again soon: *I'm off now – see you later!*

latest¹ /ˈleɪ·tɪst/ **adj** **A2** most recent: *She wears all the latest fashions.*

latest² /ˈleɪ·tɪst/ **noun** **at the latest** If you tell someone to do something by a particular time at the latest, you mean he or she must do it before that time: *You need to be there by eight o'clock at the latest.*

Latin /ˈlæt·ən/ **noun** [no plural] the language used by ancient Romans

latitude /ˈlæt·ɪˌtud/ **noun** the distance of a place north or south of the Equator (=imaginary line around the Earth's middle): *The latitude of Helsinki is approximately 60 degrees north.*

the latter /ˈlæt·ər/ **noun** [no plural] the second of two people or things that you have just talked about: *She offered me money or a car, and I chose the latter.*

laugh¹ /læf/ **verb** **A2** to smile and make sounds with your voice because something is funny: *You never **laugh at** my jokes.* ∘ *She really **makes** me **laugh**.* **laugh at** *someone/something* **phrasal verb** **B1** to show that you think someone or something is stupid: *The other children laughed at him because of his strange clothes.*

laugh² /læf/ **noun 1 B1** the action of smiling and making sounds with your voice because something is funny: *He gave a nervous laugh.* ∘ *At the time I was embarrassed, but I **had a good laugh** (= laughed a lot) about it later.* **2 for a laugh** informal If you do something for a laugh, you do it because it will be funny: *Just for a laugh, I pretended that I'd forgotten his birthday.*

lead

laughter /ˈlæf·tər/ *noun* [no plural]
the sound or act of laughing: *I heard the sound of laughter in the room next door.*

launch /lɔntʃ/ *verb* **1** to send a spacecraft or bomb into the sky, or to send a ship into the water **2** to begin an important activity: *They have launched an inquiry into his death.* **3** to start selling a product: *The book was launched last February.*

laundromat /ˈlɔn·drəˌmæt/ *noun*
a place where you pay to wash and dry your clothes

laundry /ˈlɔn·dri/ *noun* [no plural]
clothes, sheets, etc. that need to be washed: *a laundry basket*

lava /ˈlɑ·və/ *noun* [no plural] hot melted rock that comes out of a volcano

law /lɔ/ *noun* **1** 🔵 the subject or job of understanding and dealing with the laws of a country: *I studied law at college.* **2** an official rule in a country: *There are **laws against** drinking in the street.* **3 by law** If you have to do something by law, it is illegal not to do it: *Children have to go to school by law.* **4 the law** the system of official rules in a country: *You're **breaking the law.*** ○ *It's **against the law** (=illegal) not to wear seat belts.*

lawn /lɔn/ *noun* an area of grass that is often cut

lawn mower /ˈlɔn ˌmoʊ·ər/ *noun*
a machine that you use to cut grass

lawyer /ˈlɔɪ·ər/ *noun* 🔵 someone whose job is to explain the law to people and give advice

lay¹ /leɪ/ past tense of **lie**¹

lay² /leɪ/ *verb* (present participle **laying**, past tense and past participle **laid**) **1** to put something down somewhere: *She laid the baby on the bed.* ○ *He laid the plate on the table.* **2 lay eggs** If an animal lays eggs, eggs come out of its body.

lay off *someone phrasal verb* to tell someone that there is not enough work for him or her to continue working at a job: *The factory laid off more than a thousand employees.*

⚠ Common mistake: lay and lie

Be careful not to confuse these verbs. **Lay** means "put down carefully" or "put down flat." This verb is always followed by an object. **Laying** is the present participle. **Laid** is the past simple and the past participle.

She laid the papers on the desk.

Lie means "be in a horizontal position" or "be in a particular place." This verb is irregular and is never followed by an object. **Lying** is the present participle. **Lay** is the past simple and **lain** is the past participle.

The papers were lying on the desk.
~~The papers were laying on the desk.~~
I lay down and went to sleep.
~~I laid down and went to sleep.~~

The regular verb **lie** means "not say the truth."

He lied to me about his age.

---

layer /ˈleɪ·ər/ *noun* something that covers a surface, or something that is between two things: *The shelf was covered in a thick layer of dust.*
→ See picture at **cake**

lazy /ˈleɪ·zi/ *adj* (comparative **lazier**, superlative **laziest**) 🔵 Someone who is lazy does not like working: *He's too lazy to make his bed in the morning.*
• **laziness** *noun* [no plural]

lb. written abbreviation for pound: a unit for measuring weight

lead¹ /lid/ *verb* (past tense and past participle **led**) **1** 🔵 to show someone where to go, usually by taking him or her to a place: *You lead and we'll follow.* ○ *She led them down the hall.* **2** If a path or road leads somewhere, it goes there: *That path leads to the beach.* **3** to be winning a game: *They were **leading by** 11 points at halftime.* **4** to live in a particular way: *He led a normal life despite his illness* **5** to be in control of a group, country, or situation: *Amy was leading the discussion.*

lead to *something phrasal verb* to make something happen: *A bad diet can lead to health problems.*

|æ cat|ɒ hot|e get|ɪ sit|i see|ɔ saw|ʊ book|u too|ʌ cut|ə about|ər mother|ɜr turn|ɔr for|aɪ my|aʊ how|eɪ say|ɔɪ boy|

lead² /lid/ *noun* **1** the state of winning a competition: *She's **in the lead** (= winning).* ○ *Houston has a six-point lead.* **2** the main person in a movie or play: *She **plays the lead** in both movies.*

lead³ /led/ *noun* **1** [no plural] a soft, heavy, gray metal **2** the black part inside a pencil

leader /ˈliːdər/ *noun* **B1** a person in control of a group, country, or situation: *a religious leader* ○ *He is the new **leader of** the Democratic Party.*

leadership /ˈliːdərˌʃɪp/ *noun* [no plural] the job of being in control of a group, country, or situation: *the **leadership of** the Republican party* ○ *leadership skills*

leading /ˈliːdɪŋ/ *adj* very important: *He's a leading Hollywood producer.*

leaf /lif/ *noun* (plural **leaves**) **B1** a flat, green part of a plant that grows from a stem or branch: *an oak leaf* ○ *the falling leaves*

leaf

leafy /ˈliːfi/ *adj* **1** full of trees: *a leafy suburb* **2** Leafy vegetables consist of green leaves.

league /liɡ/ *noun* **B1** a group of teams that compete against each other in a sport: *the National Football league*

leak¹ /lik/ *verb* **1** If a container leaks, it allows liquid or gas to come out when it should not: *The bottle had leaked and the bag was all wet.* **2** to tell people information that is secret: *Details of the report had been **leaked** to the press.*

leak² /lik/ *noun* **1** a hole in something that a liquid or gas comes out of: *There is a **leak** in the roof.* **2** an act of telling people secret information

leaky /ˈliːki/ *adj* (comparative **leakier**, superlative **leakiest**) *informal* Something that is leaky has a hole in it and liquid or gas can get through: *a leaky roof*

lean¹ /lin/ *verb* to move the top part of your body in a particular direction: *She leaned forward so she could hear better.* ○ *Don't lean out of the window.*

lean (*something*) **against/on** *something* *phrasal verb* to sit or stand with part of your body against something: *He leaned against the door.*

lean *something* **against/on** *something* *phrasal verb* to put something against a wall or other surface: *Lean the ladder against the wall.*

lean² /lin/ *adj* **1** thin and healthy: *He is lean and fit.* **2** Lean meat has very little fat on it.

leap /lip/ *verb* **1** to suddenly move somewhere: *I leaped up to answer the phone.* **2** to jump somewhere: *A big deer leaped over our fence.*

leap year /ˈlip ˌjɪər/ *noun* a year that happens every four years, in which February has 29 days and not 28

learn /lɜrn/ *verb* **1** **A1** to get knowledge or a new skill: *I learned a lot about computers.* ○ *I'm **learning** to drive.* **2** **B1** to make yourself remember some writing: *How do actors learn all those lines?* **3** **B1** to be told facts or information that you did not know: *We were all shocked to **learn of** his death.* ○ *I only **learned about** the accident later.* **4** to start to understand that you must change the way you behave: *She'll soon **learn that** she can't treat people so badly.* ○ *You **learn from** your mistakes.*

> **⚠ Common mistake: learn, teach,** or **study?**
>
> To **learn** is to get new knowledge or skills.
>
> *I want to learn how to drive.*
>
> When you **teach** someone, you give him or her new knowledge or skills.
>
> *My dad taught me how to drive.*
>
> ~~My dad learned me how to drive.~~
>
> When you **study**, you go to classes, read books, etc. to try to understand new ideas and facts.
>
> *He is studying biology in college.*

learner /ˈlɜrnər/ *noun* someone who is getting knowledge or a new skill: *learners of English*

least[1] /list/ *adv* **1** 🄱 less than anyone or anything else: *Which car costs least?* ○ *I chose the least expensive restaurant.* **2 at least** 🄰 as much as, or more than, a number or amount: *You'll have to wait at least an hour.* **3 at least** 🄱 something that you say when you are telling someone about a good thing in a bad situation: *It's a small house but at least there's a garden.* **4 at least** 🄱 even if nothing else happens or is true: *If you can't manage to clean the whole house, at least make sure the kitchen is clean.* **5 at least** used to reduce the effect of a statement: *I've met the President – at least, he shook my hand once.* **6 not in the least** not at all: *I don't mind staying at home, not in the least.*

least[2] /list/ *quantifier* the smallest amount: *She earns the least money of all of us.*

leather /ˈleð·ər/ *noun* [no plural] 🄰 the skin of animals that is used to make shoes and bags: *a leather jacket*

leave[1] /liv/ *verb* (present participle **leaving**, past tense and past participle **left**) **1** 🄰 to go away from a place: *I leave work at five o'clock.* ○ *They left for Paris last night.* ○ *She left school at 16.* **2** 🄰 to not take something with you when you go away from a place: *I left my jacket in the car.* ○ *She left a letter for me in the kitchen.* **3** 🄰 to not use all of something: *They drank all the wine but they left some food.* **4** 🄰 to put something in a place where it will stay: *You can leave your bags at the station.* **5** 🄰 to put something somewhere for another person to have later: *I left some sandwiches for them.* **6** 🄱 to end a relationship with a husband, wife, or partner and stop living with him or her: *I'll never leave you.* ○ *She left him for a younger man.* **7** to give something to someone after you die: *His aunt left him a lot of money.* ○ *He left the house to Julia.* **8 leave someone alone** to stop speaking to someone: *Leave me alone! I'm trying to work.* **9 leave something open, on, off, etc.** to make something stay open, on, off, etc.: *Who left the window open?*

be left out *phrasal verb* to be sad because other people are doing something without you: *The older children had gone upstairs to play and she felt left out.*

leave someone/something behind *phrasal verb* 🄰 to leave a place without taking someone or something with you: *We were in a hurry and I left my keys behind.*

leave someone/something out *phrasal verb* to not include someone or something: *Have I left anyone out of that list?*

leave[2] /liv/ *noun* [no plural] time when you do not go to work: *She's on sick leave.*

leaves /livz/ plural of leaf

lecture /ˈlek·tʃər/ *noun* 🄱 a talk to a group of people about a subject: *We went to a lecture on Italian art.*

led /led/ past tense and past participle of lead

ledge /ledʒ/ *noun* a long, flat surface that comes out under a window

leek /lik/ *noun* a long, white and green vegetable that is similar to an onion

left[1] /left/ past tense and past participle of leave

left[2] /left/ *adj, adv* 🄰 on or toward the side of your body where your heart is: *She had a beautiful ring on her left hand.* ○ *Turn left at the end of the hall.* → Opposite **right adj**

left[3] /left/ *noun* [no plural] 🄰 the left of your body, or the direction toward this side: *Ted was sitting on my left.* → Opposite **right noun**

left-hand /ˈleftˌhænd/ *adj* 🄰 on the left: *The swimming pool is on the left-hand side of the road.*

left-handed /ˈleftˈhæn·dɪd/ *adj* using your left hand to do most things → Opposite **right-handed adj**

leg /leg/ *noun* **1** 🄰 one of the parts of the body that is used for walking: *My legs are tired after so much walking.* ○ *He broke his leg in the accident.* → See **The Body** on page C2 **2** one of the parts of a chair, table, etc. that it stands on: *a table leg*

legal /'li·gəl/ **adj** **1** relating to the law: *legal advice* **2** allowed by law: *Is it legal to carry a gun?* → Opposite **illegal adj**
• **legally adv** *Children under eighteen are not legally allowed to buy cigarettes.*

legend /'ledʒ·ənd/ **noun** **1** a story from a time in the past that was very long ago: *the legend of King Arthur* **2** a famous person: *Jazz legend Ella Fitzgerald once sang in this bar.*

leggings /'leg·ɪŋz/ **plural noun** tight pants that are made of soft material that stretches and are worn mainly by women: *a pair of leggings*

legible /'ledʒ·ə·bəl/ **adj** If writing is legible, you can read it.
→ Opposite **illegible adj**

leisure /'li·ʒər/ **noun** [no plural]
B1 the time when you are not working: *Do you have a lot of leisure time?*

lemon /'lem·ən/ **noun** **A2** an oval, yellow fruit that has sour juice: *lemon juice*
→ See **Fruits and Vegetables** on page C8

lemonade /ˌlem·ə'neɪd/ **noun**
A2 a drink made from lemon juice, water, and sugar

lend /lend/ **verb** (past tense and past participle **lent**) **1** **A2** to give something to someone for a period of time: *I lent my bike to Sara.* ○ *She lent me her car for the weekend.* **2** If a bank lends money, it gives money to someone who then pays the money back in small amounts over a period.

> ⚠️ **Common mistake: lend and borrow**
>
> Be careful not to confuse these two verbs. **Lend** means to give something to someone for a period of time.
> *It was raining so she lent me her umbrella.*
> **Borrow** means to use something that belongs to someone else and give it back later.
> *Can I borrow your umbrella? It's raining.*
> ~~Can I lend your umbrella? It's raining.~~

length /leŋkθ/ **noun**

length

width, height, length

1 **B1** how long something is from one end to the other: *The room is over 20 feet in length.* ○ *What length are the curtains?* **2** **B1** the amount of time that something lasts: *the length of a movie*

lengthen /'leŋk·θən/ **verb** to become longer or to make something longer: *They have lengthened the school day.*

lens /lenz/ **noun** a curved piece of glass in cameras, glasses, and scientific equipment used for looking at things

lent /lent/ past tense and past participle of **lend**

lentil /'len·t̬əl/ **noun** a very small, round, dried bean that you cook and eat

leopard /'lep·ərd/ **noun** a large wild animal of the cat family, with yellow fur and dark spots

leopard

less[1] /les/ **adv** **A2** not as much: *You should eat less.*

less[2] /les/ **quantifier** **A2** a smaller amount: *She gets about $50 a week or less.* ○ *I prefer my coffee with a little less sugar.*

> ⚠️ **Common mistake: less or fewer?**
>
> **Less** is used before uncountable nouns.
> *I should eat less candy.*
> **Fewer** is used before countable nouns.
> *I should make fewer mistakes.*

lessen /'les·ən/ **verb** to become less or to make something less: *Exercise lessens the chance of heart disease.*

lesson /ˈles·ən/ *noun* **1** A1 a period of time when a teacher teaches people: *I am **taking** guitar **lessons**.* ○ *Lessons start at 9 a.m.* **2 teach someone a lesson** to punish someone so that he or she will not behave badly again

let /let/ *verb* (present participle **letting**, past tense and past participle **let**) **1 let's** A2 something that you say to ask someone if he or she wants to do something with you: *Let's go shopping.* **2 let someone know** A2 to tell someone something: *I'll let you know where we are meeting when I know my schedule.* **3** B1 to allow someone to do something or to allow someone to have something: *She let me use her camera.* ○ *I let her have some money.* **4 let someone/something in, past, through, etc.** to allow someone or something to move to a particular place: *They won't let us past the gate.* **5 let (something) go** to stop holding something: *I **let go** of the rope.*

let someone down *phrasal verb* to not do something that you promised to do: *I promised Sophie I would meet her and I can't let her down.*

let someone in *phrasal verb* to allow someone to enter a room or building, often by opening the door: *Could you go down and let Rosa in?*

let someone off *phrasal verb* to not punish someone who has done something wrong: *I'll let you off this time, but don't ever lie to me again.*

let someone/something out *phrasal verb* to allow a person or animal to leave somewhere, especially by opening a door

lethal /ˈli·θəl/ *adj* able to kill someone: *a lethal weapon*

letter /ˈleɾ·ər/ *noun* **1** A1 some writing that you send to someone, usually in the mail: *I got a letter from Bob this morning.* **2** A2 one of the symbols (for example, a, j, p) that we use to write words: *the letter K*

lettuce /ˈleɾ·əs/ *noun* B1 a plant with green leaves, which you eat in salads
→ See **Fruits and Vegetables** on page C8

level¹ /ˈlev·əl/ *noun* **1** A2 how good someone is at doing something

compared to other people: *Students at this level need a lot of help.* **2** how high something is: *the water level* **3** the amount or number of something: *The level of iron in her blood was too low.* **4** a floor in a building: *The store had three levels.*

level² /ˈlev·əl/ *adj* **1** flat or horizontal: *Make sure the camera is level before you take the picture.* **2** at the same height: *I got down till my face was **level with** his.*

lever /ˈlev·ər/, /ˈli·vər/ *noun* **1** a handle that you push or pull to make a machine work **2** a long bar that you use to lift or move something by pushing or pulling on one end

liable /ˈlaɪ·ə·bəl/ *adj* **be liable to do something** to be likely to do something: *The dog's liable to bite if you scare him.*

liar /ˈlaɪ·ər/ *noun* someone who tells lies

liberal /ˈlɪb·ər·əl/ *adj* accepting beliefs and behavior that are new or different from your own: *Her parents were very liberal.*

liberty /ˈlɪb·ər· t̬i/ *noun* [no plural] the freedom to live, work, and travel as you want to: *Many people fight to preserve their liberty.*

library /ˈlaɪ·brer·i/ *noun* (plural **libraries**) A2 a place with a lot of books that you can read or borrow

lice /laɪs/ plural of louse

license¹ /ˈlaɪ·səns/ *noun* A2 a piece of paper that allows you to do or have something: *The photo on my driver's license is terrible.*

license² /ˈlaɪ·səns/ *verb* (present participle **licensing**, past tense and past participle **licensed**) to allow someone officially to do or have something: *Are they licensed to carry guns?*

license plate /ˈlaɪ·səns ˌpleɪt/ *noun* a sign with numbers and letters on the front and back of a car
→ See **Car** on page C3

lick /lɪk/ *verb* to move your tongue across something: *She licked her lips* ○ *We licked the chocolate off our fingers.*

a b c d e f g h i j k l m n o p q r s t u v w x y z

| æ cat | ɑ hot | e get | ɪ sit | i see | ɔ saw | ʊ book | u too | ʌ cut | ə about | ɚ mother | ɝ turn | ɔr for | aɪ my | aʊ how | eɪ say | ɔɪ boy |

lid /lɪd/ **noun** the top part of a container that you can take off: *Can you get the lid off this jar?*

lie¹ /laɪ/ **verb** (present participle **lying**, past tense and past participle **lay**, past participle **lain**) **1 A2** to put your body flat on something, or to be in this position: *He lay on the bed.* ○ *She was lying on her side.* **2 B1** to be in a place: *The river lies 30 miles to the south of the city.* **3 B1** to be on a particular surface: *A pen lay on the desk.*

lie down *phrasal verb* **A2** to move into a position in which your body is flat, usually in order to sleep or rest: *I'm not feeling well – I'm going to lie down.*
→ See **Phrasal Verbs** on page C13

lie² /laɪ/ **verb** (present participle **lying**, past tense and past participle **lied**) **B1** to say or write something that you know is not true: *Are you lying to me?* ○ *He lied about his qualifications for the job.*

lie³ /laɪ/ **noun** **B1** something that you say or write that you know is not true: *I told a lie when I said I liked her haircut.*

lieutenant /luˈten·ənt/ **noun** an officer of middle rank in the army, navy, or air force: *first lieutenant*

life /laɪf/ **noun** (plural **lives**) **1 A1** the time between a person's birth and his or her death: *He had a happy life.* ○ *Do you want to spend the rest of your life with him?* **2 B1** [no plural] living things, such as animals and plants: *human life* ○ *Is there life in outer space?* **3 B1** a way of living: *You lead an exciting life.* **4** the state of being alive: *She was badly injured, but the doctor saved her life.* **5** [no plural] energy and activity: *Like all small children, she was always so full of life.* **6 that's life** something you say that means bad things happen and you cannot stop them: *You don't get everything you want, but that's life, isn't it?*

lifeboat /ˈlaɪfˌboʊt/ **noun** a small boat that is used to help people who are in danger at sea

lifestyle /ˈlaɪfˌstaɪl/ **noun** the way that you live: *She has an unhealthy lifestyle.*

lifetime /ˈlaɪfˌtaɪm/ **noun** the period of time that someone is alive: *She saw such huge changes in her lifetime.*

lift /lɪft/ **verb** **B1** to put something or someone in a higher position: *She lifted the baby up and put him in his chair.* ○ *He lifted his glass to his lips.*

light¹ /laɪt/ **noun** **1 A2** an object that produces light: *car lights* ○ *Could you turn the kitchen light off?* **2 B1** [no plural] the brightness that shines from the sun, from fire, or from an object, allowing you to see things: *bright light* ○ *This room gets a lot of light in the morning.*

lights

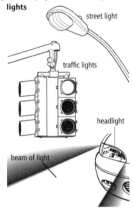

street light

traffic lights

headlight

beam of light

light² /laɪt/ **adj 1 A1** nearer to white than black in color: *a light blue shirt*
→ Opposite **dark adj 2 A2** not heavy: *My bag is very light.* **3 B1** small in amount: *light rain* ○ *I only had a light lunch.* **4 it is light B1** bright from the sun: *Let's go now while it's still light.* **5** not strong: *a light breeze*

• **lightness noun** [no plural]

light³ /laɪt/ **verb** (past tense and past participle **lit**) **1 B1** to start to burn, or to make something start to burn: *She lit a cigarette.* ○ *The wood won't light.* **2** to make light somewhere so that you can see things: *The room was lit by a single lamp.*

light bulb /ˈlaɪt ˌbʌlb/ **noun** a glass object containing a wire that produces light from electricity

light bulb

lighten /ˈlaɪ·tᵊn/ **verb** to become less dark, or to make something less dark: *The sun had lightened her hair.*

lighter /ˈlaɪ·t̬ər/ **noun** B1 a small object that makes fire and is used to make cigarettes start burning

lighthouse

lighthouse /ˈlaɪtˌhaʊs/ **noun** a tall building with a large light that shows ships where there are rocks

lighting /ˈlaɪ·t̬ɪŋ/ **noun** [no plural] the light that is used in a room or building

lightly /ˈlaɪt·li/ **adv** **1** B1 gently, without force: *He kissed her lightly on the cheek.* **2** not much: *I like lightly cooked vegetables.*

lightning /ˈlaɪt·nɪŋ/ **noun** [no plural] B1 sudden, bright light in the sky during a storm: *thunder and lightning*

like¹ /laɪk/ **preposition** **1** A2 similar to someone or something: *He looks like his father.* ○ *They were acting like children.* ○ *It sounded like Michelle.* **2 what is *someone/something* like?** A2 something you say when you want someone to describe someone or something: *I haven't met him – what's he like?* ○ *What's your new dress like?* **3** B1 for example: *She looks best in bright colors like red and pink.* **4** typical or characteristic of: *It's not like you to be so quiet – are you all right?*

like² /laɪk/ **verb** (present participle **liking**, past tense and past participle **liked**) **1** A1 to enjoy something or think that someone or something is nice: *I like to paint in my spare time.* ○ *He really likes her.* ○ *What do you **like about** him?* → Opposite **dislike verb** **2 would like *something*** A1 to want something: *I'd **like to** meet him.* ○ *I'd like some bread, please.* **3 would you like...?** A1 used to offer someone something: *Would you like a drink?* ○ *Would you like to eat now?* **4 if you like** A2 used when you offer someone something: *If you like, I can drive you there.*

like³ /laɪk/ **conjunction** informal B1 in the same way as: *Do it exactly like I told you to.*

likeable /ˈlaɪ·kə·bəl/ **adj** If you are likeable, you are nice and people like you.

likely /ˈlaɪk·li/ **adj** **1** B1 expected: *I'm **likely to** forget if you don't remind me.* ○ *It's **likely that** he'll say no.* **2** probably true: *This is the most likely explanation.* → Opposite **unlikely adj**

likes /laɪks/ **plural noun** **likes and dislikes** B1 things that you like and things that you do not like

likewise /ˈlaɪkˌwaɪz/ **adv** formal in the same way: *Water these plants every day and likewise the ones in the bedroom.*

limb /lɪm/ **noun** a leg or an arm of a person

lime /laɪm/ **noun** a small, green fruit that is sour like a lemon

limit¹ /ˈlɪm·ɪt/ **noun** B1 the largest amount of something that is possible or allowed: *a time limit* ○ *There's a **limit to** how much time we can spend on this.*

limit² /ˈlɪm·ɪt/ **verb** to control something so that it is less than a particular amount or number: *We'll have to limit the number of guests.*

limited /ˈlɪm·ɪ·t̬ɪd/ **adj** B1 small in amount or number: *There is a **limited choice** of drinks.*

limp¹ /lɪmp/ **adj** soft and weak: *Her arms were limp, hanging by her side.*

limp² /lɪmp/ **verb** to walk with difficulty because one of your legs or feet is hurt • **limp noun** *She walks **with a limp**.*

line¹ /laɪn/ **noun** **1** A2 a long, thin mark: *Sign your name on the line at the bottom.* ○ *Draw a line around your hand.* **2** B1 a row of words on a page, for example in a song or poem: *The same line is repeated throughout the poem.* **3** B1 a track that a train travels along: *Which train line do you take to work?* **4** a connection between two telephones **5** a row of people or things: *a line of trees* ○ *There was a long line of people outside the shop.* **6** a piece of rope or wire with a special purpose: *a fishing line*

line

line² /laɪn/ **verb** (present participle **lining**, past tense and past participle **lined**) **1** to form a row along the side of something: *Trees and cafes lined the street.* **2** be lined with *something* to cover the inside of a piece of clothing with a material: *a jacket lined with fur*

line up phrasal verb to wait in a row of people, often to buy something: *We lined up outside the theater before the show.*

line *something* **up phrasal verb** to move items in a row: *She lined up her shoes in the closet.*

linen /ˈlɪn·ən/ **noun** [no plural] **1** a lightweight cloth that is like rough cotton: *a linen jacket* **2** pieces of cloth that you use to cover tables and beds: *bed linen*

linger /ˈlɪŋ·gər/ **verb** to stay somewhere for a long time: *The smell of onions lingers.*

lining /ˈlaɪ·nɪŋ/ **noun** a material that covers the inside of something: *a jacket lining*

link¹ /lɪŋk/ **noun** **1** a connection between two people, things, or ideas: *There's a direct link between smoking and cancer.* ○ *Their links with Britain are still strong.* **2** one ring of a chain **3** **B1** (also **hyperlink**) a connection between documents or areas on the Internet: *Click on this link to visit our online bookstore.*

link² /lɪŋk/ **verb** to make a connection between two or more people, things, or ideas: *The drug has been linked to the deaths of several athletes.* ○ *The two offices will be linked by computer.*

lion /ˈlaɪ·ən/ **noun** **A2** a large wild animal of the cat family, with light brown fur

lion

lip /lɪp/ **noun** **B1** one of the two soft, red edges of the mouth: *He licked his lips.*
→ See **The Body** on page C2

lipstick /ˈlɪpˌstɪk/ **noun** makeup that people put on their lips

liquid /ˈlɪk·wɪd/ **noun** **B1** a substance, for example water, that is not solid and that you can pour easily
• **liquid adj** *liquid fuel*

liquor store /ˈlɪk·ər ˌstɔr/ **noun** a store that sells bottles of alcoholic drinks

list¹ /lɪst/ **noun** **A2** a lot of words that are written one under the other: *a shopping list* ○ *Is your name on the list?*
• **Make a list** *of everything you need.*

list² /lɪst/ **verb** to make a list: *All names are listed alphabetically.*

⚠ Common mistake: listen, listen to, or hear?

Use **hear** when you want to say that sounds, music, etc. come to your ears. You can **hear** something without wanting to.

I can hear my neighbor's music through the wall.

Use **listen** to say that you pay attention to sounds or try to hear something.

The audience listened carefully.
Ssh! I'm listening!

Use **listen to** when you want to say what it is that you are trying to hear.

The audience listened to the speaker.
Ssh! I'm listening to the radio!

---

listen /ˈlɪs·ən/ verb **1** Ⓐ1 to give attention to someone or something in order to hear him or her: *I listen to the radio while I have breakfast.* ◦ *She does all the talking – I just sit and listen.* ◦ *Listen, if you need money, I can give you some.* **2** Ⓑ1 to pay attention to what someone tells you and accept what he or she says: *Why didn't you listen to me when I told you to be careful?*

listener /ˈlɪs·ə·nər/ noun someone who listens, especially to the radio: *The new radio station already has twelve million listeners.*

lit /lɪt/ past tense and past participle of light

liter /ˈliː·t̬ər/ noun (written abbreviation l) a unit for measuring liquid

literally /ˈlɪt̬·ər·ə·li/ adv **1** having the original meaning of a word or phrase: *There are literally hundreds of people here.* **2** used to emphasize what you are saying: *My computer is literally an antique (= it is very old).*

literature /ˈlɪt̬·ər·ə·tʃər/ noun [no plural] Ⓑ1 books, poems, etc. that are considered to be art: *classical literature*

litter /ˈlɪt̬·ər/ noun [no plural] pieces of paper and other waste that are left in public places: *Please pick up any litter you see in the park.*

little¹ /ˈlɪt̬·əl/ adj **1** Ⓐ1 small in size or amount: *I have a little bag.* ◦ *Your kitten is so little!* ◦ *I had a little bit of cake.* → Opposite **big adj (1), large adj 2** Ⓐ1 young: *When I was little, my hair was curly.* **3** Ⓑ1 not important: *It's only a little problem.* **4** short in time or distance: *Sit down for a little while.* ◦ *Let's have a little break.* **5** used to show affection or dislike for someone or something: *Oh, what a sweet little house!* ◦ *He's a nasty little man.*

! Common mistake: **little**

When **little** is used as a quantifier, it can only be used with uncountable nouns.
We have little time.
We have little resources.

little² /ˈlɪt̬·əl/ quantifier Ⓑ1 not much or not enough: *There's so little time.*

little³ /ˈlɪt̬·əl/ pronoun **1** Ⓑ1 not much, or not enough: *We did very little on Sunday.* **2 a little** Ⓑ1 a small amount: *"More wine?" "Just a little, please."*

little⁴ /ˈlɪt̬·əl/ adv **1** a little Ⓐ2 slightly: *There's only a little further to go.* **2** not much or not enough: *She ate very little at dinner.*

live¹ /lɪv/ verb (present participle **living**, past tense and past participle **lived**) **1** Ⓐ1 to have your home somewhere: *They live in New York.* ◦ *Where do you live?* **2** to be alive: *I hope I live to see my grandchildren.* **3** Ⓑ1 to spend your life in a particular way: *My grandmother lives alone.*

live together phrasal verb If two people live together, they share a house and have a sexual relationship but are not married: *Now many young people live together before they get married.*

live with *someone* phrasal verb to share a home with someone and have a sexual relationship with him or her although you are not married: *She's living with her boyfriend.*

! Common mistake: **live** or **life**?

Live cannot be used as a noun. The correct noun to use is **life**.
It was the best day of my life.

live² /laɪv/ adj **1** Ⓑ1 A **live** performance is done with people watching or listening: *a live concert* ◦ *live music* **2** having life: *Millions of live animals are moved around the world each year.*

lively /ˈlaɪv·li/ adj (comparative **livelier**, superlative **liveliest**) Ⓑ1 full of energy and interest: *a lively debate* ◦ *a lively child*

liver /ˈlɪv·ər/ noun **1** a part in your body that cleans your blood **2** [no plural] the liver of an animal that is eaten by people

lives /laɪvz/ plural of life

living /ˈlɪv·ɪŋ/ noun [no plural] the money that you get from your job: *Like everyone else, I have to make a living.* ◦ *What* does he **do for a living** (= how does he get money)?

living room /ˈlɪv·ɪŋ ˌrum/, /ˈlɪv·ɪŋ ˌrʊm/ **noun** **A1** the room in a house where people sit to relax
→ See **The Living Room** on page C11

lizard /ˈlɪz·ərd/ **noun** a small animal with thick skin, a long tail, and four short legs

load[1] /loʊd/ **noun** things that are carried, often by a vehicle: We were behind a truck carrying a load of logs.

load[2] /loʊd/ **verb** **1** to put a lot of things into a vehicle or machine: I was just loading the washing machine. **2** to put film in a camera or bullets in a gun

loaf /loʊf/ **noun** (plural **loaves**) bread that has been made in one large piece: a loaf of bread

loan[1] /loʊn/ **noun** **B1** money that someone borrows: a bank loan ○ a student loan

loan[2] /loʊn/ **verb** to give something to someone for a period of time: My dad loaned me the money.

loaves /loʊvz/ plural of loaf

lobby /ˈlɑb·i/ **noun** (plural **lobbies**) a room at the main entrance of a building: a hotel lobby

lobster /ˈlɑb·stər/ **noun** a sea animal that has two claws (= sharp, curved parts) and eight legs, or the meat of this animal

local /ˈloʊ·kəl/ **adj** **B1** relating to an area near you: She goes to the local school.
• **locally** adv locally grown vegetables

locate /ˈloʊ·keɪt/ **verb** (present participle **locating**, past tense and past participle **located**) formal **1** **be located** **B1** to be in a particular place: Both schools are located nearby. **2** to find the exact position of someone or something: Police are still trying to locate the criminal.

location /loʊˈkeɪ·ʃən/ **noun** **B1** a place or position: Have they decided on **the location** of the factory?

lock[1] /lɑk/ **verb** **1** **B1** to fasten something with a key: Did you lock the door?

→ Opposite **unlock** verb **2** to put something or someone in a place or container that is fastened with a key: She locked herself in her bedroom.

lock[2] /lɑk/ **noun** **B1** the thing that you use to close a door, window, etc. that needs a key to open it: I heard someone turn a key in the lock. ○ safety locks

locker /ˈlɑk·ər/ **noun** a small cupboard in a public area where you can keep things: a luggage locker ○ a gym locker

locker room /ˈlɑk·ər ˌrum/, /ˈlɑk·ər ˌrʊm/ [noun] a room where people can change their clothes before playing sports

lodge /lɑdʒ/ **verb** (present participle **lodging**, past tense and past participle **lodged**) to become stuck somewhere: The bullet had lodged near his heart.

loft /lɔft/ **noun** the space under the roof of a house or other building

log[1] /lɔg/, /lɑg/ **noun** a thick piece of wood that has been cut from a tree: We need more logs for the fire.
→ See picture at **fireplace**

log[2] /lɔg/, /lɑg/ **verb** (present participle **logging**, past tense and past participle **logged**)
log in/on phrasal verb to connect a computer to a system of computers by typing your name and a password
log off/out phrasal verb to stop a computer being connected to a computer system, usually to stop working

logical /ˈlɑdʒ·ɪ·kəl/ **adj** using reason and good judgment: a logical choice

logo /ˈloʊ·goʊ/ **noun** **B1** a special design that a company uses to sell its products: the company's logo

lollipop /ˈlɑl·iˌpɑp/ **noun** a large, hard candy on a stick

lonely /ˈloʊn·li/ **adj** (comparative **lonelier**, superlative **loneliest**) **B1** sad because you are not with other people: She gets lonely now that the kids have left home.

long[1] /lɔŋ/ **adj** **1** **A1** having a large distance from one end to another: long hair ○ long legs ○ a long dress → Opposite **short** adj **2** **A1** continuing for a large

amount of time: *a long movie* ○ *I waited a long time.* → Opposite **short adj**
3 describes a piece of writing that has a lot of pages or words: *a long book*
4 used when asking for or giving information about the distance or time of something: *It's about four feet long.* ○ *The concert was three hours long.* ○ *How long was the skirt?* ○ *How long is the movie?*

long² /lɒŋ/ *adv* **1** **A2** for a long time: *Did you have to wait long for the train?*
2 **as long as** **B1** used when you are talking about something that must happen before something else can happen: *You can play outside as long as you do your homework first.* **3** **no longer** **B1** in the past but not now: *The old barn is no longer used.* **4** **before (very/too) long** soon: *They'll be home before very long.*

long³ /lɒŋ/ *noun* [no plural]   a large amount of time: *She won't be away for long.*

long⁴ /lɒŋ/ *verb formal*   to want something very much: *She* ***longed*** *to see him again.* ○ *I'm* ***longing*** *for some sun.*

long-haul /ˈlɒŋˌhɔl/ *adj*   traveling a long distance: *a long-haul truck*

long haul /ˈlɒŋ ˈhɔl/ *noun*   a long period, from its beginning all the way to its end: *We want people who will be in this job* ***for the long haul****.*

longing /ˈlɒŋ·ɪŋ/ *noun*   a feeling of wanting something or someone very much: *He gazed at her, his eyes full of longing.*

longitude /ˈlɑn·dʒɪˌtud/ *noun* [no plural]   the distance of a place east or west of an imaginary line from the top to the bottom of the Earth

long-term /ˈlɒŋˌtɜrm/ *adj*   continuing a long time into the future: *Seriously ill people need long-term care.*

look¹ /lʊk/ *verb*   **verb 1** **A1** to turn your eyes in the direction of something or someone so that you can see him, her, or it: ***Look at*** *the picture on page two.* ○ *He was looking out of the window.* **2** **A1** to try to find someone or something: *I'm* ***looking for*** *my keys.* ○ *I've looked*

everywhere but I can't find my bag.
3 **look nice, strange, etc.** **A2** used to describe the appearance of a person or thing: *Her dress looks really nice.* ○ *You look tired.* **4** **look like** **B1** used to describe the appearance of a person or thing: *He looks like a friendly person.*
5 **it looks like; it looks as if** **B1** used to say that something will probably happen: *It looks as if he isn't coming.* **6** **look as if/as though** used to describe the appearance of a person or thing: *She looked as if she was going to cry.* **7** **Look!** something you say when you are annoyed and you want people to listen to you: *Look! That's enough complaining.*

> ⚠ **Common mistake: look, see, or watch?**
>
> **See** means to notice people and things with your eyes.
>
> *Oh! I just saw a big spider!*
> *Did you see anyone you knew at the party?*
>
> **Look (at)** is used when you are trying to see something or someone. **Look** cannot be followed by an object.
>
> *I've looked everywhere, but I can't find my keys.*
> *He looked at the map to find the road.*
> ~~He looked the photographs.~~
>
> **Watch** means to look at something for a period of time, usually something that moves or changes.
>
> *He watched television all evening.*
> *I watched them playing football.*

look around (*something*) *phrasal verb* **B1** to visit a place and look at the things in it: *She spent the afternoon looking around the neighborhood.*

look at *something* *phrasal verb* **1** to think about a subject carefully so that you can make a decision about it: *Our manager is looking at ways of reducing costs.* **2** to read something in order to check it or see how good it is: *Can you look at my essay?* **3** to examine something: *Did the doctor look at your knee?*

a
b
c
d
e
f
g
h
i
j
k
l
m
n
o
p
q
r
s
t
u
v
w
x
y
z

|æ cat|ɑ hot|e get|ɪ sit|i see|ɔ saw|ʊ book|u too|ʌ cut|ə about|ər mother|ɜr turn|ɔr for|aɪ my|aʊ how|eɪ say|ɔɪ boy|

look forward to *something* phrasal verb
1 🔵 to feel happy and excited about something that is going to happen: *I'm really looking forward to seeing him.*
2 formal used at the end of a formal letter to say you hope to hear from or see someone soon, or that you expect something from him or her: *I **look forward to hearing from you**.*

look into *something* phrasal verb to examine the facts about a situation: *They are investigating the causes of the accident.*

Look out! phrasal verb 🔵 something you say when someone is in danger: *Look out – there's a car coming!*

look *something* **up** phrasal verb 🔵 to look at a book or computer in order to find information: *I looked it up on the Internet.*

look² /lʊk/ noun **1** 🔵 an act of looking at someone or something: *Take a look at this website.* ○ *You took some new pictures – can I **have a look**?* **2** 🔵 the act of looking for someone or something: *I **took another look for** the watch, but couldn't find it.* **3** an expression on someone's face: *She had a worried look on her face.* **4** *someone's* **looks** a person's appearance, especially how attractive he or she is: *I liked his looks.* **5 the look of** *someone/something* the appearance of someone or something: *They liked the look of the hotel, but it was too expensive.*

loop /luːp/ noun a circle of something long and thin, such as a piece of string or wire

> ### ❗ Common mistake: **loose** or **lose**?
>
> Be careful! These two words look and sound similar but have completely different meanings.
> **Loose** is an adjective, meaning "not fixed or not tight."
> *These shorts are a little loose.*
> Be careful not to use **loose** when you really mean the verb **lose**.
> *I hope he doesn't lose his job.*
> ~~I hope he doesn't loose his job.~~

loose /luːs/ adj **1** 🔵 Loose clothes are large and not tight: *a loose dress* **2** not firmly attached: *One of my buttons is loose.* **3** An animal that is loose is free to move around: *Two lions escaped and are still loose.*

loosen /ˈluːsən/ verb to become loose or make something loose: *He loosened his tie.*

Lord /lɔːrd/ noun **the Lord** a name for God or Jesus

lose /luːz/ verb (present participle **losing**, past tense and past participle **lost**) **1** 🅰🔵 to not be able to find someone or something: *I lost my passport.* ○ *She's always losing her keys.* **2** 🔵 to stop having something that you had before: *She lost a leg in a car accident.* ○ *He lost his job.* **3** 🔵 to have less of something than you had before: *She's lost a lot of weight.* ○ *He's losing his hair.* **4** 🔵 If you lose a game, the team or person that you are playing against wins: *The Jets lost by three points.* ○ *They're losing 3-1.* **5 lose interest, patience, etc.** to stop feeling something: *I've lost interest in the subject.* ○ *He kept on crying, and I lost my patience.* **6** to waste something such as time or an opportunity: *Because of illness, she lost the chance of a place in the team.*

> ### ❗ Common mistake: **lose** or **miss**?
>
> Usually you **miss** something that happens, such as an event, a train leaving, or an opportunity.
> *I don't want to miss my class.*
> ~~I don't want to lose my class.~~
> Usually you **lose** a thing.
> *I lost my sunglasses.*

loser /ˈluːzər/ noun **1** someone who does not win a game or competition **2** informal someone who is not successful in anything he or she does

loss /lɔːs/ noun **1** a state of not having something that you had before: *loss of memory* ○ *job losses* **2** a situation in which a company spends more money than it earns: *Both companies **suffered***

losses this year. **3** the death of a person: *They never got over the loss of their son.*

lost[1] /lɔst/ past tense and past participle of lose

lost[2] /lɔst/ adj **1** **A2** not knowing where you are: *I got lost on the way.* **2** **B1** If something is lost, no one knows where it is: *The letter got lost in the mail.*

lost and found /ˌlɔst ən ˈfaʊnd/ noun [no plural] a place where things that people have lost in a public place are kept: *Have you tried checking in the lost and found?*

lot /lɑt/ noun **1 a lot; lots** **A1** a large number or amount of people or things: *There were **a lot of** people outside the building.* ∘ *He earns **lots of** money.* ∘ *I've got a lot to do this morning.* **2 a lot** **A1** a large amount or very often: *We used to go there a lot.* **3 a lot better, older, quicker, etc.** much better, older, quicker, etc.: *He looks a lot older than his wife.* ∘ *It's a lot quicker by car.*

> **!** **Common mistake: a lot of something**
>
> Remember to use the preposition *of* before the thing that there is a large number of.
>
> *A lot of people enjoy traveling to other countries.*
>
> ~~A lot people enjoy traveling to other countries.~~

lotion /ˈloʊ·ʃən/ noun a liquid that you put on your skin to make it soft or healthy: *suntan lotion*

lottery /ˈlɑt̬·ər·i/ noun (plural **lotteries**) **B1** a competition in which people buy tickets with numbers on them and then win money if their ticket has a particular number

loud[1] /laʊd/ adj **A2** making a lot of noise: *a loud noise* ∘ *a loud voice*
• **loudly** adv **B1** *They were all talking loudly.*

loud[2] /laʊd/ adv **1** **B1** in a way that makes a lot of noise: *Could you speak a little louder, please?* **2 out loud** **B1** If you say or read something out loud,

you say or read it so that other people can hear you: *I had to read the poem out loud in front of the whole class.*

loudspeaker /ˈlaʊdˌspi·kər/ noun something that is used for making voices or sounds louder

lounge /laʊndʒ/ noun a room with chairs where you can sit and relax

louse /laʊs/ noun (plural **lice**) a small insect that lives on the bodies or in the hair of people or animals

lousy /ˈlaʊ·zi/ adj (comparative **lousier**, superlative **lousiest**) informal very bad: *The food in the hotel was lousy.*

lovable /ˈlʌv·ə·bəl/ adj (also **loveable**) very nice and easy to love: *a lovable child*

love[1] /lʌv/ verb (present participle **loving**, past tense and past participle **loved**) **1** **A1** to like someone very much and have sexual feelings for him or her: *Last night he told me he loved me.* **2** **A1** to like a friend or a person in your family very much: *I'm sure he loves his kids.* **3** **A1** to like something very much: *He loves his music.* ∘ *She loves animals.* **4 I'd love to** **A2** used to say that you would very much like to do something that someone is offering: *"Would you like to meet up sometime?" "I'd love to."* **5 would love something/to do something** **A2** used to say that you want something very much: *I'd love some chocolate right now!* ∘ *I'd love to be an actor.*

love[2] /lʌv/ noun **1 love; all my love** **A2** something you write at the end of a letter to a friend or someone in your family: *Love, Mom* **2** **B1** [no plural] the feeling of liking someone very much and having sexual feelings for him or her: *a love song* **3 in love** **B1** having a strong feeling that you love someone: *I'm **in love with** him.* ∘ *I was 20 when I first **fell in love** (= started to love someone).* **4** **B1** [no plural] the feeling of liking a friend or person in your family very much: *Nothing is as strong as the **love** you have **for** your kids.* **5** **B1** a person that you love and feel attracted to:

a
b
c
d
e
f
g
h
i
j
k
l
m
n
o
p
q
r
s
t
u
v
w
x
y
z

She was my first love. **6** something that interests you a lot: *his love of books*
7 make love to have sex

lovely /ˈlʌv·li/ adj (comparative **lovelier**, superlative **loveliest**) **1** A2 very nice or enjoyable: *We had a lovely day together.* ○ *What lovely weather!* **2** A2 very attractive: *a lovely dress* ○ *You look lovely!*

lover /ˈlʌv·ər/ noun **1** B1 If two people are lovers, they have a sexual relationship but they are not married. **2** B1 someone who likes something very much: *She's a cat lover.*

loving /ˈlʌv·ɪŋ/ adj showing that you love someone: *a loving father*

low /loʊ/ adj **1** A2 under the usual level: *Their prices are very low.* ○ *a low number* **2** B1 near the ground, not high: *low aircraft* ○ *low ceilings* **3** A low sound is deep or quiet: *a low voice* ○ *a low note*

lower[1] /ˈloʊ·ər/ verb **1** to make something less in amount or degree: *They've lowered the prices on their summer clothes.* ○ *ways to lower your risk of cancer* **2** to move something into a low position: *Please lower the blind on the kitchen window.*

lower[2] /ˈloʊ·ər/ adj being the bottom part of something: *My lower back hurts.*

lowercase /ˈloʊ·ərˌkeɪs/ noun [no plural] letters of the alphabet that are not written as capital letters, for example a, b, c
• **lowercase** adjective

loyal /ˈlɔɪ·əl/ adj always liking and supporting someone or something: *a loyal supporter* ○ *She's very loyal to her friends.*

loyalty /ˈlɔɪ·əl·ti/ noun [no plural] the quality of always liking and supporting someone or something: *Your loyalty to the company is impressive.*

lozenge /ˈlɑz·əndʒ/ noun an oval or round candy with medicine in it, that dissolves when you suck it

Ltd. written abbreviation for limited company: used after the name of some companies: *Pinewood Supplies Ltd.*

luck /lʌk/ noun [no plural] **1** A2 good and bad things caused by chance and not by

your own actions: *It was just luck that we got on the same train.* ○ *He has had a lot of bad luck in his life.* **2** success: *He's been trying to find work but with no luck so far.* **3** good luck! something you say to someone when you hope he or she will do well: *Good luck with your test!*

luckily /ˈlʌk·ə·li/ adv B1 happening because of good luck: *Luckily I had some money with me.*

lucky /ˈlʌk·i/ adj (comparative **luckier**, superlative **luckiest**) A2 having good things happen to you: *"I'm going on a vacation." "Lucky you!"* ○ *And the lucky winner is ticket number 38!* ○ *You're lucky to live in such a beautiful city.*
→ Opposite **unlucky** adj

luggage /ˈlʌg·ɪdʒ/ noun [no plural] A2 bags that you carry with you when you travel

luggage

suitcase

briefcase

carryall

lukewarm /ˈlukˈwɔrm/ adj A liquid that is lukewarm is only slightly warm.

lump /lʌmp/ noun a bit of something solid with no particular shape: *a lump of coal* ○ *She found a lump in her breast.*

lunatic /ˈlu·nəˌtɪk/ noun someone who behaves in a crazy way: *He drives like a lunatic.*

lunch /lʌntʃ/ noun A1 the food that you eat in the middle of the day: *Should we have lunch?*

lunchtime /ˈlʌntʃˌtaɪm/ *noun* **A2** the time when you eat lunch

lung /lʌŋ/ *noun* one of the two parts inside your chest that is used for breathing: *lung cancer*

luxurious /ləɡˈʒʊr·i·əs/, /ləɡˈʃʊr·i·əs/ *adj* very comfortable and expensive: *a luxurious hotel*

luxury /ˈlʌk·ʃər·i/, /ˈlʌɡ·ʒər·i/ *noun* **1** **B1** [no plural] very expensive and beautiful things: *They live **in luxury** in a fabulous apartment in Paris.* **2** (plural **luxuries**) something that you like having but do not need: *Having a car each is a luxury really.* **3** [no plural] something that gives you a lot of pleasure, but which you cannot often do: *A day off work is a luxury.*

lying /ˈlaɪ·ɪŋ/ present participle of lie[1,2]

lyrics /ˈlɪr·ɪks/ *plural noun* the words of a song

M m

M, m /em/ the thirteenth letter of the alphabet

m written abbreviation for meter: a unit for measuring length

m. written abbreviation for mile: a unit for measuring distance

ma'am /mæm/ *noun* (also **Ma'am**) formal **B1** You call a woman "ma'am" when you are speaking to her politely: *Thank you, ma'am.*

machine /məˈʃin/ *noun* **1** **A2** a piece of equipment with moving parts that uses power to do a particular job: *a fax machine* ○ *a coffee machine* **2** a computer

machine gun /məˈʃin ˌɡʌn/ *noun* a gun that fires a lot of bullets very quickly

machinery /məˈʃi·nər·i/ *noun* [no plural] machines, often large machines: *farm machinery*

mad /mæd/ *adj* (comparative **madder**, superlative **maddest**) **1** **A2** angry: *Were your parents **mad at** you when you got home late?* **2** **B1** (usually **crazy**) mentally ill: *I think I'm **going mad**.* **3** be mad about *someone/something* **B1** to love something or someone: *Ali is mad about skiing.* **4** like mad informal If you run, work, etc. like mad, you do it very quickly.

madam /ˈmæd·əm/ *noun* formal **Dear Madam** a way of beginning a formal letter to a woman whose name you do not know

made /meɪd/ past tense and past participle of make

madly /ˈmæd·li/ *adv* **1** with a lot of energy and enthusiasm: *We cheered madly as the team came out onto the field.* **2** be madly in love to love someone very much: *He's madly in love with Denise.*

magazine /ˌmæɡ·əˈzin/ *noun* **A2** a big, thin book that you can buy every week or month, that has pictures and writing: *a fashion magazine*

magazine

magic[1] /ˈmædʒ·ɪk/ *noun* [no plural] **1** **A2** special powers that can make things happen that seem impossible: *Do you believe in magic?* **2** **A2** tricks that a person performs while other people watch, such as making things disappear: *My daughter loves doing magic.* **3** a quality that makes something or someone seem special or exciting: *Everyone enjoys the magic of this wonderful city.*

magic[2] /ˈmædʒ·ɪk/ *adj* **1** **A2** relating to magic: *a magic show* **2** **B1** with special powers that make impossible things happen: *a magic spell*

magical /ˈmædʒ·ɪ·kəl/ *adj* **1** with special powers: *Diamonds were once thought to have **magical powers**.* **2** special or exciting: *It was a magical night.*

magician /məˈdʒɪʃ·ən/ *noun* someone who performs tricks as entertainment, such as making things disappear

a
b
c
d
e
f
g
h
i
j
k
l
m
n
o
p
q
r
s
t
u
v
w
x
y
z

magnet /'mæg·nət/
noun an iron object that makes other pieces of iron move toward it

magnet

magnetic
/mæg'nɛt·ɪk/ adj
with the power of a magnet: *a magnetic field*

magnificent
/mæg'nɪf·ə·sənt/ adj
B1 very good or very beautiful: *The view from our room was magnificent.*

magnify /'mæg·nə,faɪ/ verb (present participle **magnifying**, past tense and past participle **magnified**) to make an object look bigger than it is: *The cells are first magnified under a microscope.*

magnifying glass
/'mæg·nɪ,faɪ·ɪŋ ˌglæs/
noun a piece of curved glass that makes objects look bigger than they are

magnifying glass

maid /meɪd/ noun
a woman who cleans or cooks in a hotel or in someone's home

maiden name /'meɪ·dᵊn ˌneɪm/ noun
the family name that a woman has before she gets married

mail¹ /meɪl/ noun [no plural] **1** **A2** letters and packages that you get or send: *We got lots of mail this morning.* **2** **A2** the system by which letters and packages are taken and brought: *The book came in yesterday's mail.* **3** **A2** email: *You've got mail.*

mail² /meɪl/ verb **B1** to send a letter or package or email something: *Could you mail it to me?*

mailbox /'meɪl,bɑks/ noun **1** a small box outside your home where letters are put **2** a large, metal container in a public place where you can mail letters

mail carrier /'meɪl ˌkær·i·ər/ noun
someone who takes and brings letters and packages as a job

mailman /'meɪl,mæn/ noun (plural **mailmen**) a man who takes and brings letters and packages as a job

main /meɪn/ adj **1** **B1** most important or largest: *Our main problem is lack of money.* ○ *The main airport is 15 miles from the capital.* **2** **the main thing** the most important fact in a situation: *You're happy, and that's the main thing.*

main course /'meɪn ˌkɔrs/ noun
A2 the largest or most important part of a meal: *I had fish **for** my **main course**.*

mainly /'meɪn·li/ adv **B1** mostly: *The trees here are mainly oaks.*

main road /meɪn ˈroʊd/ noun a large road that goes from one town to another: *They live on the main road out of town.*

main street /'meɪn ˌstrit/ noun the main road in the middle of a town where there are stores and other businesses

maintain /meɪnˈteɪn/ verb **1** to make a situation or activity continue in the same way: *The army has been brought in to maintain order in the region.* **2** to keep a building or area in good condition: *A large house is very expensive to maintain.*

maintenance /'meɪn·tᵊn·əns/ noun
[no plural] the work that you do to keep something in good condition: *car maintenance*

majestic /məˈdʒes·tɪk/ adj very beautiful and big: *majestic scenery*

major¹ /'meɪ·dʒər/ adj important or big: *a major problem* ○ *a major city*
→ Opposite **minor adj**

major² /'meɪ·dʒər/ noun an officer of middle rank in the army or air force

majority /məˈdʒɔr·ɪ·ţi/, /məˈdʒɑr·ɪ·ţi/ noun [no plural] more than half of a group of people or things: *The majority of people in this country own their houses.*
→ Opposite **minority noun**

make /meɪk/ verb (present participle **making**, past tense and past participle **made**) **1** **A1** to create something: *I'll make* *some coffee.* ○ *They've made a movie about her life.* ○ *Butter is **made from** milk.* **2 be made of** *something* to consist of a particular material: *The ring is made of gold.* **3** Ⓐ② to perform an action: *I must make a telephone call.* ○ *Someone's made a mistake.* **4** Ⓑ① to cause something to happen or cause a particular state: *He really makes me laugh.* ○ *This heat makes me very tired.* **5 make** *someone* **do** *something* Ⓑ① to force someone to do something: *You can't make me go.* **6 make** *someone/something* **happy, sad, difficult, etc.** to cause someone or something to become happy, sad, difficult, etc.: *You've made me very happy.* **7** If you make an amount of money, you earn it: *He makes $60,000 a year.* **8** If two or more numbers make a particular amount, that is the amount when they are added together: *That makes $40 altogether.* **9 make the bed** to make the sheets and covers on a bed neat **10 make it** informal Ⓑ① to arrive at a place at the right time: *Will we make it in time for the movie?* **11 make it** informal to be successful: *Very few actors actually make it.*

make *something* **into** *something* phrasal verb to change something into something else: *They've made the spare room into an office.*

make *something/someone* **out** phrasal verb to be able to see, hear, or understand something or someone: *We could just make out a building through the trees.*

make *something* **up** phrasal verb to say or write something that is not true: *I made up an excuse because I didn't want to go.*

makeup /ˈmeɪkˌʌp/ noun [no plural] colored substances that a woman puts on her face in order to make herself more attractive: *She doesn't **wear** much **makeup**.*

male[1] /meɪl/ adj Ⓑ① belonging to or relating to the sex that cannot have babies: *a male colleague*
→ Opposite **female adj**

male[2] /meɪl/ noun a male person or animal

mall /mɔl/ noun (also **shopping mall**) Ⓑ① a large, covered shopping area

mammal /ˈmæm·əl/ noun an animal that drinks milk from its mother's body when it is young

man /mæn/ noun (plural **men**) **1** Ⓐ① an adult male human: *a young man* ○ *men and women* **2** [no plural] used to refer to both men and women: *Man is still more intelligent than the smartest robot.*

manage /ˈmæn·ɪdʒ/ verb (present participle **managing**, past tense and past participle **managed**) **1** Ⓑ① to do something that you have been trying to do: *I managed to persuade him to come.* **2** Ⓑ① to be in control of an office, shop, team, etc.: *He used to manage the bookstore on King Street.*

management /ˈmæn·ɪdʒ·mənt/ noun **1** [no plural] being in control of an office, store, team, etc.: *management skills* **2** the people who are in control of an office, store, team, etc.: *The management has accepted the proposal.*

manager /ˈmæn·ɪ·dʒər/ noun Ⓐ② someone in control of an office, store, team, etc.: *She's the manager of the hotel.* ○ *a sales manager*

mane /meɪn/ noun the long hair on the necks of animals such as horses or lions

mango /ˈmæŋ·ɡoʊ/ noun (plural **mangoes, mangos**) Ⓐ② a sweet orange fruit with a green skin and one big seed

manipulate /məˈnɪp·jəˌleɪt/ verb (present participle **manipulating**, past tense and past participle **manipulated**) to control someone or something in a skillful way: *She knows how to manipulate the press.*

mankind /ˈmænˈkaɪnd/ noun [no plural] all people, considered as a group: *the history of mankind*

man-made /ˈmænˈmeɪd/ adj not natural, but made by people: *man-made fibers*

manner /ˈmæn·ər/ noun [no plural] **1** the way in which a person talks and behaves with other people: *She has a very friendly manner.* **2** the way something happens or something is done: *They dealt with the problem **in a** very efficient **manner**.*

manners /ˈmæn·ərz/ plural noun
ways of behaving with other people: *It is bad manners to be late.*

mansion /ˈmæn·ʃən/ noun a very large house

mantelpiece /ˈmæn·t³l‚pis/ noun (also **mantel**) a shelf above a fireplace, usually part of a frame around the fireplace
→ See **The Living Room** on page C11

manual[1] /ˈmæn·ju·əl/ adj using your hands: *manual work*
• **manually** adv

manual[2] /ˈmæn·ju·əl/ noun a book that tells you how to use something or do something: *an online training manual*

manufacture /‚mæn·jəˈfæk·tʃər/ verb (present participle **manufacturing**, past tense and past participle **manufactured**) to make something, usually in large numbers in a factory: *He works for a company that manufactures plastic products.*
• **manufacture** noun [no plural] *the manufacture of computers*

manufacturer /‚mæn·jəˈfæk·tʃər·ər/ noun a company that makes something: *a shoe manufacturer*

manufacturing /‚mæn·jəˈfæk·tʃə·rɪŋ/ noun [no plural] the business of producing goods in large numbers in a factory: *car manufacturing*

> **⚠ Common mistake: many, much, or a lot of?**
>
> **Many** is used with countable nouns in negative sentences and questions. **Much** is used with uncountable nouns in negative sentences and questions.
>
> *Do you have many friends?*
> *I don't earn much money.*
>
> A lot of can be used to mean **much** or **many**. In positive sentences it sounds formal to use **much** or **many**. You can use a lot of instead.
>
> ~~There was much enthusiasm for the project.~~
> *There was a lot of enthusiasm for the project.*

many /ˈmen·i/ pronoun, quantifier
1 🅐🅵 a large number of: *I don't have many clothes.* ∘ *Were there many cars on the road?* ∘ *I've got **so many** things to do this morning.* **2 how many?** 🅐🅵 used in questions to ask about the number of something: *How many hours a week do you work?*

map /mæp/ noun 🅐🅵 a picture that shows where countries, towns, roads, etc. are: *a road map* ∘ *a map of Europe*

marathon /ˈmær·ə‚θɑn/ noun a race in which people run for 26.2 miles

marble /ˈmɑr·bəl/ noun [no plural] hard, smooth stone that is often used for buildings and decoration

march /mɑrtʃ/ verb **1** to walk somewhere as a group to show that you agree or disagree strongly with something: *They marched to City Hall to protest the tax increases.* **2** When soldiers march, they walk together with regular steps. **3** to walk somewhere fast: *She marched off angrily.*

March /mɑrtʃ/ noun 🅐🅵 the third month of the year

margarine /ˈmɑr·dʒə·rɪn/ noun [no plural] a soft food that you put on bread and use in cooking

margin /ˈmɑr·dʒɪn/ noun an empty space down the side of a page of writing: *You can make notes **in the margin**.*

mark[1] /mɑrk/ noun a dirty area on something: *He left dirty marks all over the carpet.*

mark[2] /mɑrk/ verb to show where something is by drawing or putting something somewhere: *I marked my street on the map for you.*

marker /ˈmɑr·kər/ noun a thick pen used especially for writing on boards
→ See **The Classroom** on page C4

market[1] /ˈmɑr·kɪt/ noun **1** 🅐🅶 a place where people go to buy or sell things, often outside: *a flower market* ∘ *a market stall* **2** all the people who want to buy a particular thing, or the area where they

live: *South America is our largest market.*
3 on the market ready to buy: *His house is on the market.*

market

market² /ˈmɑr·kɪt/ **verb** to try to sell things using advertising: *They market their products very cleverly.*
• **marketing noun** [no plural] *a marketing campaign*

maroon¹ /məˈrun/ **adjective** being a dark brown-red color

maroon² /məˈrun/ **noun** the color maroon
→ See **Colors** on page C6

marriage /ˈmær·ɪdʒ/ **noun** **1** 🔒 the legal relationship of two people who are married: *It was a very happy marriage.* **2** the ceremony at which two people marry

married /ˈmær·id/ **adj** **1** If someone is married, he or she is in a legal relationship with someone else as his or her husband or wife: *a married couple* ○ *She's been married to David for nearly ten years.* **2 get married** to begin a legal relationship with someone as that person's husband or wife: *We got married last year.*

marry /ˈmær·i/ **verb** (present participle **marrying**, past tense and past participle **married**) 🔒 to begin a legal relationship with someone as his or her husband or wife: *Will you marry me?* ○ *He never married.*

marsh /mɑrʃ/ **noun** an area of soft, wet land

martial art /ˈmɑr·ʃəl ˈɑrt/ **noun** a sport that is based on traditional forms of

fighting from Asia: *Kung fu and karate are martial arts.*

marvelous /ˈmɑr·və·ləs/ **adj** very good: *What a marvelous idea!*

masculine /ˈmæs·kjə·lɪn/ **adj** having qualities that are like a man: *a masculine voice*

mash /mæʃ/ **verb** to crush food until it is soft: *mashed potatoes*

mask /mæsk/ **noun** a cover for the face: *a surgeon's mask*

mask

mass¹ /mæs/ **noun** a lot of something together, with no clear shape: *Her hair was a mass of blond curls.*

mass² /mæs/ **adj** affecting a lot of people: *mass destruction* ○ *a mass murderer*

massacre /ˈmæs·ə·kər/ **verb** (present participle **massacring**, past tense and past participle **massacred**) to kill a lot of people
• **massacre noun**

massage /məˈsɑʒ/ **noun** the action of pressing and rubbing parts of someone's body in order to make them relax: *She gave me a foot massage.*
• **massage verb** (present participle **massaging**, past tense and past participle **massaged**)

massive /ˈmæs·ɪv/ **adj** very big: *a massive building*

mast /mæst/ **noun** a tall pole on a boat that supports its sails

master¹ /ˈmæs·tər/ **noun** someone who does something very well: *He was a master of disguise.*

master² /ˈmæs·tər/ **verb** to learn how to do something well: *I lived in Italy for a year but didn't master the language.*

master's degree /ˈmæs·tərz dɪ‚gri/ **noun** (also **master's**) a college or university degree that is higher than a bachelor's degree and that typically takes one or two years to complete: *She has a master's in psychology.*

mat /mæt/ **noun** a piece of material that you put on the floor, in order to protect it

→ See **The Bathroom** on page C1

match[1] /mætʃ/ **noun** **1** A2 a sports competition in which two people or teams compete against each other: *a tennis match* **2** a thin wooden stick that makes fire when you rub one end of it against a rough surface: *a box of matches*

match[2] /mætʃ/ **verb** **1** B1 If two things match, they are the same color or type: *I can't find anything to match my green shirt.* ○ *Your socks don't match.* **2** B1 to choose someone or something that is right for a particular person, activity, or purpose: *In this exercise you have to match each capital city to its country.*

mate[1] /meɪt/ **noun** an animal's sexual partner

mate[2] /meɪt/ **verb** (present participle **mating**, past tense and past participle **mated**) When animals mate, they have sex in order to produce babies.

material /məˈtɪr·i·əl/ **noun** **1** B1 cloth for making clothes, curtains, etc.: *Her dress was made of a soft, silky material.* **2** B1 documents, recorded information, etc. that are used for a particular activity: *She writes all her own teaching materials.* **3** a solid substance from which things can be made: *building materials*

maternal /məˈtɜːr·nᵊl/ **adj** **1** like a mother **2** A maternal relation is part of your mother's family: *my maternal grandfather*

math /mæθ/ **noun** [no plural] the study or science of numbers and shapes: *Are you good at math?*

mathematical /ˌmæθ·əˈmæt·ɪ·kəl/ **adj** relating to mathematics

mathematics /ˌmæθ·əˈmæt·ɪks/ **noun** [no plural] formal for math

matter[1] /ˈmæt·ər/ **noun** **1** a subject or situation that you need to think about

or do something about: *Could I talk to you about a personal matter?* ○ *This is a matter of some importance.* **2** [no plural] In science, matter is the physical substances that exist in the universe. **3 what's the matter?** A2 used to ask about the reason for a problem: *What's the matter with your leg?* **4 no matter how, what, when, etc.** used to say that something cannot be changed: *I never manage to lose any weight, no matter how hard I try.* **5 as a matter of fact** used to say that something is true, especially when it is surprising: *As a matter of fact, I used to live near him.*

matter[2] /ˈmæt·ər/ **verb** B1 to be important: *We were late, but it didn't seem to matter.* ○ *It doesn't **matter to** me whether he comes or not.*

mattress /ˈmæ·trɪs/ **noun** the soft part of a bed that you lie on

mature[1] /məˈtʃʊər/ **adj** **1** completely grown or developed: *mature trees* **2** behaving well, like an adult: *She seems very mature for 13.*

→ Opposite **immature adj**

mature[2] /məˈtʃʊər/ **verb** (present participle **maturing**, past tense and past participle **matured**) **1** to become completely grown or developed **2** to start to behave well, like an adult: *Girls mature sooner than boys.*

maximum[1] /ˈmæk·sə·məm/ **adj** B1 The maximum amount of something is the largest amount that is allowed or possible: *the maximum temperature*

→ Opposite **minimum adj**

maximum[2] /ˈmæk·sə·məm/ **noun** B1 the largest amount that is allowed or possible: *The school has **a maximum of** 30 students per class.*

may /meɪ/ **verb** **1** A2 used to talk about what is possibly true or will possibly happen: *There may be other problems that we don't know about.* ○ *I think I may have a cold.* **2** B1 formal used when you ask if you can do something or say that someone can do something: *May I be excused, please?* ○ *You may begin.*

May /meɪ/ **noun** **A1** the fifth month of the year

maybe /ˈmeɪ.bi/ **adv** **1** **A2** possibly: *Maybe we're too early.* ○ *It could take a month, or maybe more, to complete.* **2** **A2** used to suggest something politely: *Maybe we should start again.*

> ### ⚠ Common mistake: **may be** or **maybe**?
>
> **May be** is written as two separate words when **be** is used as a verb.
> *I may be late this evening.*
> ~~I maybe late this evening.~~
> **Maybe** is an adverb, and is written as one word.
> *Maybe we should do it tomorrow.*
> ~~May be we should do it tomorrow.~~

mayonnaise /ˈmeɪ.ə.neɪz/ **noun** [no plural] a thick, white, cold sauce that is made from eggs and oil

mayor /ˈmeɪ.ər/ **noun** the leader of a town or city

me /mi/ **pronoun** **A1** the person who is speaking or writing: *She gave me some money.* ○ *She never gave it to me.* ○ *Lydia is three years younger than me.*

meal /mil/ **noun** **A1** an occasion when you sit down to eat food, or the food that you eat at that time: *a three-course meal* ○ *We **had** a nice **meal** together.*

mean[1] /min/ **verb** (past tense and past participle **meant**) **1** **A2** to have a particular meaning: *What does this word mean?* ○ *The green light means go.* **2 I mean** **A2** something that you say in order to correct yourself: *We went there in May – I mean June.* **3 mean to do something** **B1** to want to do something: *I didn't mean to hurt her.* **4 be meaning to do something** **B1** to be planning to do something: *I've been meaning to call you for weeks.* **5** **B1** to have a particular result: *These changes will mean better health care for everyone.* **6** **B1** to intend to express a fact or opinion: *I didn't **mean** that **as** a criticism.* ○ *What exactly do you **mean** by "old-fashioned"?* **7** **B1** to have an important emotional effect on someone: *It wasn't a valuable picture but it **meant** a lot to me.*

> ### ⚠ Common mistake: **mean**
>
> When you want to ask the meaning of something, remember to use **does** or **do**.
> *What does this word mean?*
> ~~What means this word?~~

mean[2] /min/ **adj** not kind: *I thought my sister was being **mean** to me.*

meaning /ˈmi.nɪŋ/ **noun** **1** **B1** The meaning of words, signs, or actions is what they represent or show: *The word "squash" has several meanings.* **2** purpose: *She felt that her life had no meaning.*

means /minz/ **noun** **1** (plural **means**) a way of doing something: *We had no **means of** communication.* **2** money: *We don't have **the means to** buy the house.* **3 by no means** not at all: *I am by no means an expert.*

meant /ment/ past tense and past participle of mean

meantime /ˈmin.taɪm/ **noun** **in the meantime** in the time between two things happening, or while something else is happening: *My car's being fixed, so I'm renting one in the meantime.*

meanwhile /ˈmin.hwaɪl/ **adv** **B1** in the time between two things happening, or while something else is happening: *The mother is ill. The child, meanwhile, is living with her grandparents.*

the measles /ˈmi.zəlz/ **noun** [no plural] a dangerous illness that children get that causes red spots and a high fever

measure[1] /ˈmeʒ.ər/ **verb** (present participle **measuring**, past tense and past participle **measured**) **1** to find the size, weight, amount, or speed of something: *I've measured all the windows.* **2** to be a certain size: *The whale measured around 60 feet in length.*

measure[2] /ˈmeʒ.ər/ **noun** something that is done so that a bad situation is stopped: *We must **take measures** to stop the spread of the disease.* ○ *security measures*

a b c d e f g h i j k l **m** n o p q r s t u v w x y z

measurement /'meʒ·ər·mənt/ noun
the size and shape of something: *I've* **taken measurements** *of all the rooms.*

meat /miːt/ noun **A1** the soft parts of animals, used as food: *I don't eat meat.* ○ *red/white meat* ○ *cold sandwich meats*
→ See **Food** on page C7

mechanic /mə'kæn·ɪk/ noun **A2** someone whose job is to repair machines: *a car mechanic*

mechanical /mə'kæn·ɪ·kəl/ adj relating to or operated by machines: *a mechanical engineer*
• **mechanically** adv

medal /'med·əl/ noun a piece of metal given as a prize in a competition or given to someone who has been very brave: *a bronze medal* ○ *an Olympic medal*

the media /'miː·di·ə/ plural noun television, newspapers, magazines, and radio considered as a group: *The issue has been much discussed* **in the media**.

medical /'med·ɪ·kəl/ adj relating to medicine and different ways of curing illness: *medical treatment* ○ *a medical student*
• **medically** adv

medicine

a bottle of pills   a tube of ointment

a bottle of medicine   a box of lozenges

medicine /'med·ə·sɪn/ noun
1 **A2** something that you drink or eat when you are ill, to stop you being ill: *cough medicine* ○ *Have you* **taken** *your* **medicine** *today?* **2** **B1** [no plural] the science of treating and preventing illness

medicine cabinet /'med·ə·sɪn ˌkæb·ə·nət/ noun a shelf with a door on it, often with a mirror on its front, used to hold medicine in a bathroom
→ See **The Bathroom** on page C1

medieval /ˌmiː·di'iː·vəl/ adj relating to the period in Europe between about 500 A.D. and 1500 A.D.: *a medieval building*

medium /'miː·di·əm/ adj **B1** in the middle of a group of different amounts or sizes: *people of medium weight* ○ *The shirt comes in small, medium, and large.*

meet /miːt/ verb (past tense and past participle **met**) **1** **A1** to come to the same place as someone else: *We met for coffee last Sunday.* ○ *I met an old friend at a party last Saturday.* **2** **A1** to see and speak to someone for the first time: *"This is Helen." "Pleased to meet you."* **3** **B1** to wait at a place for someone or something to arrive: *They met me at the airport.* **4** **B1** If a group of people meet, they come to a place in order to do something: *The group meets every Thursday.*

> **⚠ Common mistake: meet** or **visit?**
>
> You **meet** a person, but not a place or thing.
> *I met John's parents for the first time last week.*
> You **visit** a person, place, or thing.
> *I visited my aunt today.*
> *We visited Paris and the Eiffel Tower.*

meet up phrasal verb to meet another person in order to do something together: *I* **met up with** *a few friends yesterday.*

meeting /'miː·t̬ɪŋ/ noun **A2** an occasion when people come together for a reason, usually to talk about something: *We're having a meeting on Thursday to discuss the problem.* ○ *He's* **in a meeting**.

melody /'mel·ə·di/ noun (plural **melodies**)
a song or tune

melon /'mel·ən/ noun **A2** a large,
round, sweet fruit with a thick, green or
yellow skin

melt /melt/ verb to change from a solid
into a liquid because of heat: *The sun
soon melted the ice on the pond.* ○ *The
chocolate had melted in my pocket.*

member /'mem·bər/ noun **A2** a person
who belongs to a group or an organization: *family members* ○ *He was a **member of** the university rowing club.*

membership /'mem·bər,ʃɪp/ noun [no
plural] the fact of belonging to a group
or an organization: *I've applied for membership in the union.* ○ *a membership
card*

memorable /'mem·ər·ə·bəl/ adj If an
occasion is memorable, you will remember it for a long time because it is so
good: *a memorable performance*

memorize /'mem·ə,raɪz/ verb (present participle **memorizing**, past tense and past participle **memorized**) to learn something
so that you remember it exactly: *I've
memorized all my friends' birthdays.*

memory /'mem·ər·i/ noun (plural
memories) **1** **B1** your ability to remember things: *I have a good **memory
for** names.* **2** **B1** something that you
remember: *I have nice **memories** of my
childhood.* **3** **A2** the part of a computer
where information is stored, or the
amount of information that can be
stored there: *This computer is more expensive because it has a bigger memory.*

Memory Stick /'mem·ər·i ,stɪk/ noun
trademark a small piece of equipment
that stores information and that can be
put into a computer, cell phone, etc.

men /men/ plural of man

mend /mend/ verb **B1** to repair cloth
that is torn or something that is damaged: *Could you mend the hole in my
jeans?*

mental /'men·t̬ᵊl/ adj relating to the
mind: *mental illness*
• **mentally** adv *a mentally ill person*

mention /'men·tʃən/ verb **1** **B1** to
speak or write a few words about something or someone: *She didn't mention
her daughter.* ○ *He **mentioned that** he
liked skiing.* **2** **not to mention** used to
emphasize the importance of some-
thing that you are adding to a list: *The
resort has a great hotel, not to mention
some of the best skiing in the region.*

> ⚠ **Common mistake: mention**
>
> Do not use a preposition after the
> verb **mention**.
> *He didn't mention the price.*
> ~~He didn't mention about the price.~~

menu /'men·ju/ noun **1** **A2** a list of food
and drinks that you can get in a restaurant: *a dinner menu* **2** **A2** a list of choices
on a computer screen

meow /mi'aʊ/ noun the sound that a
cat makes

mercy /'mɜr·si/ noun [no plural] kindness
that makes you forgive someone and
not punish them: *The prisoners pleaded
for mercy.*

merely /'mɪər·li/ adv only: *I'm not arguing with you – I'm merely explaining the
problem.*

merge /mɜrdʒ/ verb to join together:
*The city's smaller libraries will **merge
into** a large one.*

merry /'mer·i/ adj (comparative **merrier**,
superlative **merriest**) happy: *Merry Christmas!*

mess¹ /mes/ noun **1** **B1** a place or
thing that is dirty or not neat: *Your bedroom is a mess.* ○ *He **makes** such **a mess**
in the kitchen.* ○ *Don't leave things **in a
mess**.* **2** a situation in which there are
a lot of problems: *My life's a mess.*

mess² /mes/ verb
mess around phrasal verb informal to do
silly things that are not important: *Stop
messing around and do your homework!*
mess something up phrasal verb informal
to spoil something, or to do something
badly: *Susan messed up the arrangements
for the trip.*

a
b
c
d
e
f
g
h
i
j
k
l
m
n
o
p
q
r
s
t
u
v
w
x
y
z

message /ˈmes·ɪdʒ/ *noun* **A1** a piece of written or spoken information that one person gives to another: *Did you **get** my **message**?* ∘ *I called her and left a message.*

messenger /ˈmes·ən·dʒər/ *noun* someone who takes a message between two people

messy /ˈmes·i/ *adj* (comparative **messier**, superlative **messiest**) **B1** dirty or not neat: *messy hair* ∘ *a messy house/car*

met /met/ past tense and past participle of meet

metal /ˈmet·ᵊl/ *noun* **B1** a hard, shiny material such as iron, gold, or silver

meter /ˈmi·t̬ər/ *noun* **1 A2** (written abbreviation **m**) a unit for measuring length, equal to 100 centimeters **2** a piece of equipment for measuring the amount of something such as electricity, time, or light: *a gas meter* ∘ *a parking meter*

method /ˈmeθ·əd/ *noun* **B1** a way of doing something, often one that involves a system or plan: *What's the best **method of** solving this problem?* ∘ *traditional teaching methods*

metric /ˈme·trɪk/ *adj* The metric system of measurement uses units based on the gram, meter, and liter.

metro /ˈme·troʊ/ *adjective* short for metropolitan: relating to a large city and the people around it: *About two million people live in the metro area.*

mice /maɪs/ plural of mouse

microphone
/ˈmaɪ·krə·foʊn/ *noun* a piece of electrical equipment for recording sounds, or for making sounds louder

microscope
/ˈmaɪ·krə·skoʊp/ *noun* a piece of scientific equipment that uses lenses (= pieces of curved glass) to make very small objects look bigger

microphone

microscope

microwave /ˈmaɪ·krə·weɪv/ *noun* an electric oven that uses waves of energy to quickly cook food or make it warmer
→ See **The Kitchen** on page C10

midday /ˈmɪd·deɪ/ *noun* [no plural] **A2** twelve o'clock in the middle of the day: *Beware the heat of the midday sun.*

middle¹ /ˈmɪd·ᵊl/ *noun* **1 A2** the center of something: *We live right **in the middle** of the town.* **2 B1** not the beginning or the end but the time in between: *The letter should arrive by **the middle of** next week.* **3 be in the middle of doing something B1** to be busy: *I can't talk now – I'm in the middle of cooking.*

middle² /ˈmɪd·ᵊl/ *adj* in a central position: *The middle layer is made of plastic.*

middle-aged /ˈmɪd·ᵊl ˈeɪdʒd/ *adj* **B1** in the middle of your life before you are old: *a middle-aged couple*

midnight /ˈmɪd·naɪt/ *noun* [no plural] **A2** twelve o'clock at night

the Midwest /ˈmɪdˈwest/ *n* [no plural] the north central part of the United States
• **midwestern, Midwestern** *adj* a midwestern state

might /maɪt/ *verb* **1 A2** used to talk about what will possibly happen: *I might come.* ∘ *It might be finished by Thursday.* **2 B1** used to talk about what is possibly true: *I think Isabel might be pregnant.*

mighty /ˈmaɪ·t̬i/ *adj* very powerful or successful: *a mighty wind*

migraine /ˈmaɪ·greɪn/ *noun* a very bad pain in the head, often one that makes you feel sick: *I have a migraine.*

migrate /ˈmaɪ·greɪt/ *verb* (present participle **migrating**, past tense and past participle **migrated**) When birds or animals migrate, they travel from one place to another at the same time each year: *Many birds migrate from Europe to Africa for the winter.*

migration /maɪˈgreɪ·ʃən/ *noun* [no plural] the travel of birds or animals from one place to another at the same time each year.

mild /maɪld/ adj **1** 🄱 If the weather in winter is mild, it is not cold. **2** Mild food does not have a strong taste: *a mild curry*
→ Opposite **hot adj**

mile /maɪl/ noun (written abbreviation **m.**) 🄱 a unit for measuring distance, equal to 1,760 yards: *The nearest gas station is two miles from here.*

military[1] /ˈmɪl·ɪˌter·i/ noun [no plural] the armed forces of a country: *My dad was in the military.*

military[2] /ˈmɪl·ɪˌter·i/ adj relating to a country's army, navy, air force, or other armed forces: *military service*

milk[1] /mɪlk/ noun [no plural] 🄰 a white liquid that babies and baby animals drink that comes from their mothers' bodies: *a carton of milk* ○ *breast milk*

milk[2] /mɪlk/ verb to take milk from a cow using your hands or a machine

milkshake /ˈmɪlkˌʃeɪk/ noun a sweet drink made of milk and ice cream, usually with chocolate or fruit flavor: *a chocolate milkshake*

mill /mɪl/ noun **1** a place where grain is pressed and made into flour: *a flour mill* **2** a factory where one material is made: *a cotton mill* ○ *a paper mill*

millennium /məˈlen·i·əm/ noun (plural **millennia**) a period of 1000 years

milliliter /ˈmɪl·əˌli·tər/ noun (written abbreviation **ml**) 🄰 a unit for measuring liquid, equal to 0.001 liters

millimeter /ˈmɪl·əˌmi·tər/ noun (written abbreviation **mm**) a unit for measuring length, equal to 0.001 meters (0.39 inches)

million /ˈmɪl·jən/ **1** 🄰 the number 1,000,000 **2** millions informal a lot: *I've seen that movie millions of times.*

millionaire /ˌmɪl·jəˈneər/ noun a very rich person

mime /maɪm/ verb (present participle **miming**, past tense and past participle **mimed**) to act or tell a story without speaking, using movements of your hands, body, and face
• **mime** noun *a mime artist*

mimic /ˈmɪm·ɪk/ verb (present participle **mimicking**, past tense and past participle **mimicked**) to copy the way someone talks and behaves, usually to make people laugh: *He's always getting into trouble for mimicking his teachers.*

mince /mɪns/ verb (present participle **mincing**, past tense and past participle **minced**) to cut food into very small pieces: *Mince the garlic and add it to the pan.* ○ *minced onions*

mind[1] /maɪnd/ noun **1** 🄱 someone's memory, or his or her ability to think and feel emotions: *She has a very logical mind.* **2** change your mind 🄱 to change a decision or opinion: *We changed our minds about selling the house.* **3** make your mind up 🄱 to make a decision: *I haven't made up my mind whether to go yet.* **4** bear/keep *someone/something* in mind to remember someone or something that may be useful in the future: *I'll keep you in mind if another job comes up.* **5** cross *someone*'s mind If an idea crosses your mind, you think about it for a short time: *It crossed my mind that she might not want to go.* **6** have/keep an open mind to wait until you know all the facts before you form an opinion about something or judge someone: *We're keeping an open mind about the causes of the fire.* **7** have *something* on your mind to worry about something: *Jim has a lot on his mind right now.* **8** be out of your mind informal to be crazy or very stupid: *You must be out of your mind going jogging in this weather.* **9** put/set *someone*'s mind at rest to say something to someone to stop him or her from worrying: *Talking to the doctor put my mind at rest.*

mind[2] /maɪnd/ verb **1** do you mind?/ would you mind? 🄰 something you say when politely asking someone to do something: *Do you mind not smoking in here, please?* **2** I don't mind 🄰 used to say that a choice is not important: *I don't mind which movie we see as long as it's a funny one.* **3** never mind 🄰 used to tell someone not to worry about something he or she has done: *"I didn't bring enough cash." "Never mind, you can pay me next week."*   **4** 🅱1 to be angry or worried about something: *Would he mind if I borrowed his book? ∘ I don't mind driving.*

mine¹ /maɪn/ **pronoun** 🅰2 the thing or things belonging to or relating to the person who is speaking or writing: *"Whose book is this?" "It's mine." ∘ Can I use your pen? Mine's not working.*

mine² /maɪn/ **noun** **1** a hole in the ground where people dig out coal, gold, etc. **2** a bomb hidden in the ground or water that explodes when it is touched: *He was killed when he drove over a mine.*

miner /ˈmaɪ·nər/ **noun** someone who works in a hole in the ground, digging out coal, gold, etc.: *a coal miner*

mineral /ˈmɪn·ər·əl/ **noun** **1** a valuable or useful substance that is dug out of the ground: *The region's rich mineral deposits include oil, gold, and aluminum.* **2** a chemical that your body needs to stay healthy

mineral water /ˈmɪn·ər·əl ˌwɔ·tər/ **noun** 🅰2 water that is taken from the ground

mingle /ˈmɪŋ·ɡəl/ **verb** (present participle **mingling**, past tense and past participle **mingled**) to mix, or be mixed: *The smell of coffee mingled with freshly baked cookies.*

miniature /ˈmɪn·i·ə·tʃər/ **adj** very small: *a miniature camera*

minimum¹ /ˈmɪn·ə·məm/ **adj** 🅱1 The minimum amount of something is the smallest amount that is allowed or possible: *There is a minimum charge of $5 for postage.*
→ Opposite **maximum adj**

minimum² /ˈmɪn·ə·məm/ **noun** 🅱1 the smallest amount that is allowed or possible: *Please keep noise to an absolute minimum.*
→ Opposite **maximum noun**

mining /ˈmaɪ·nɪŋ/ **noun** [no plural] the process of digging coal, gold, etc. out of the ground

miniskirt /ˈmɪn·iˌskɜrt/ **noun** a very short skirt
→ See **Clothes** on page C5

minister /ˈmɪn·ə·stər/ **noun** a religious leader in some Christian churches

ministry /ˈmɪn·ə·stri/ **noun** the work that a religious leader or group does: *the church's ministry to the homeless*

minor /ˈmaɪ·nər/ **adj** not important or serious: *There are a few minor problems. ∘ He suffered only minor injuries.*
→ Opposite **major adj**

minority /məˈnɔr·ɪ·ti/, /məˈnɑr·ɪ·ti/ **noun** (plural **minorities**) less than half of a group of people or things: *The violence was caused by a small minority of soccer fans. ∘ I agreed to the suggestion, but I was in the minority.*
→ Opposite **majority noun**

mint /mɪnt/ **noun** **1** a candy with a fresh, strong taste **2** [no plural] a plant whose leaves are used to add flavor to food and drinks

minus¹ /ˈmaɪ·nəs/ **preposition** **1** 🅰2 used when the second of two numbers should be taken away from the first: *Five minus three is two.* **2** without something: *She arrived at the meeting minus her briefcase.*

minus² /ˈmaɪ·nəs/ **adj** A minus number is less than zero: *The temperature last night was minus ten.*

minute¹ /ˈmɪn·ət/ **noun** **1** 🅰1 a period of time equal to 60 seconds: *It'll take you thirty minutes to get to the airport. ∘ She was ten minutes late for her interview.* **2** 🅰2 a very short period of time: *I'll be with you in a minute.* **3** wait/ just a minute 🅱1 used when asking someone to wait for a short time: *Just a minute – I left my coat in the restaurant.* **4** at the last minute at the latest time possible: *The concert was canceled at the last minute.* **5** (at) any minute very soon: *Her train will be arriving any minute.*

minute² /maɪˈnut/ **adj** very small: *Her hands are minute.*

miracle /ˈmɪr·ə·kəl/ **noun** **1** something that is very surprising or difficult to be-

lieve: *It's a **miracle that** he's still alive.*
2 something very strange that happens
which you cannot explain: *One of Christ's
miracles are turning water into wine.*

miraculous /məˈræk·jə·ləs/ *adj* very
surprising or difficult to believe: *He made
a miraculous recovery from his illness.*

• **miraculously** *adv One person miraculously survived the crash.*

mirror /ˈmɪr·ər/ *noun* **A2** a piece of
special glass in which you can see yourself: *a bathroom mirror* ∘ *He looked at
himself **in the mirror**.*
→ See **The Living Room** on page C11

misbehave /ˌmɪs·bɪˈheɪv/ *verb* (present
participle **misbehaving**, past tense and past
participle **misbehaved**) to behave badly

mischief /ˈmɪs·tʃəf/ *noun* [no plural]
behavior, usually of a child, that is
slightly bad

mischievous /ˈmɪs·tʃə·vəs/ *adj*
behaving in a way that is slightly bad but
not serious: *a mischievous five-year-old*

miserable /ˈmɪz·ər·ə·bəl/ *adj* **1** **B1** sad:
I just woke up feeling miserable. **2** bad
and making you sad: *People are living in
miserable conditions.*

misery /ˈmɪz·ər·i/ *noun* [no plural]
sadness and suffering: *The war brought
misery to millions of people.*

misfortune /mɪsˈfɔr·tʃən/ *noun*
something bad that happens to you: *He
had the misfortune to fall in love with a
married woman.*

misleading /mɪsˈli·dɪŋ/ *adj* making
someone believe something that is not
true: *misleading information*

miss /mɪs/ *verb* **1** **A2** to feel sad about
someone or something that you have
stopped seeing or having: *I'll miss you
when you go.* ∘ *He misses having a room
of his own.* **2** **A2** to not go to something: *I missed my class this morning.*
3 **A2** to arrive too late to get on a bus,
train, or plane: *If I don't leave now, I'll
miss my train.* **4** **B1** to not see or hear
something: *Sorry, I missed that, could
you repeat it please?* **5** **B1** to avoid

doing or experiencing something: *You
should leave early if you want to miss the
traffic.* **6** **miss a chance/opportunity**
B1 to not use an opportunity to do
something: *She missed the chance to
speak to him.* **7** to fail to hit or catch
something, or to fail to make a score
with a ball: *The bomb missed its target.*
∘ *It should have been an easy shot, but he
missed.*

Miss /mɪs/ *noun* **A1** a title for a girl or
woman who is not married: *Miss Olivia
Allenby* ∘ *Tell Miss Russell I'm here.*

missile /ˈmɪs·əl/ *noun* an explosive
weapon that can travel long distances
through the air: *nuclear missiles*

missing /ˈmɪs·ɪŋ/ *adj* **1** lost, not in
the usual place: *My favorite earrings
have **gone missing**.* **2** **B1** not included
in something: *There are a couple of
things **missing from** the list.*

mission /ˈmɪʃ·ən/ *noun* an important
job, usually traveling somewhere: *The
soldiers' mission is to destroy the bridge.*

mist /mɪst/ *noun* small drops of water
in the air that make it difficult to see objects that are not close: *Gradually the
mist cleared and the sun began to shine.*

mistake[1] /mɪˈsteɪk/ *noun* **1** **A2** something that you do or think that is wrong:
a spelling mistake ∘ *He **made** a lot of **mistakes** in his written test.* **2** **by mistake**
B1 If you do something wrong by
mistake, you do it without wanting to: *I
picked up someone else's book by mistake.*

! Common mistake: **mistake**

Remember to use the correct verb
with this word.

*I always **make mistakes** in my essays.*

~~I always do mistakes in my essays.~~

---

mistake[2] /mɪˈsteɪk/ *verb* (present participle
mistaking, past tense **mistook**, past participle **mistaken**) to not understand something correctly: *I think you mistook what
I said.*

mistake someone for someone *phrasal
verb* to think that someone is a different

person: *People sometimes mistake him for a girl.*

misty /ˈmɪs·ti/ **adj** (comparative **mistier**, superlative **mistiest**) If the weather is misty, there is a cloud of small drops of water in the air: *a cold and misty morning*

misunderstand /ˌmɪs·ˌʌn·dərˈstænd/ **verb** (past tense and past participle **misunderstood**) to not understand someone or something correctly: *He misunderstood the question completely.*

misunderstanding /ˌmɪs·ˌʌn·dərˈstæn·dɪŋ/ **noun** a situation in which someone does not understand something correctly: *I think there's been a misunderstanding. I never asked for these chairs to be delivered.*

mitt /mɪt/ **noun** a large glove used to protect your hand: *a baseball catcher's mitt* ○ *an oven mitt*
→ See **The Kitchen** on page C10

mix[1] /mɪks/ **verb** **1** A2 to put different things together in order to make something new: *Mix the powder **with** water to form a paste.* ○ *Put the chocolate, butter, and egg in a bowl and **mix** them all **together**.* **2** B1 to have two or more qualities, or to do two or more activities, etc. at the same time: *a feeling of anger mixed with sadness* **3** to meet and talk to people: *She enjoys going to parties and **mixing with** people.*

mix something up phrasal verb to make a group of things untidy: *The books were all mixed up in a box.*

mix[2] /mɪks/ **noun** [no plural] B1 a combination of things or people, often in a group: *There's a good **mix of** nationalities in the class.*

mixed /mɪkst/ **adj** **1** combining different things, especially ones that are good or useful ones with ones that are bad or not useful: *The study produced mixed results.* **2** combining people of different races, sexes, or religions

mixture /ˈmɪks·tʃər/ **noun** **1** two or more different things or people that have been put together: *Add milk to the mixture and stir until smooth.* ○ *The class is*

an odd mixture of people. **2** [no plural] a combination of two or more ideas, qualities, styles, etc.: *Their house is decorated in a mixture of styles.*

ml written abbreviation for milliliter: a unit for measuring liquid

mm written abbreviation for millimeter: a unit for measuring length

moan /moʊn/ **verb** to make a low sound, especially because part of your body hurts: *He lay on the floor moaning.*
• **moan** noun

mobile home /ˈmoʊ·bəl ˈhoʊm/ **noun** a small house with metal walls that can be pulled by a vehicle to another location

mobile phone /ˈmoʊ·bəl ˈfoʊn/ (usually **cell phone**) a telephone that you can carry everywhere with you

mock /mɑk/ **verb** to laugh at someone in a way that is not kind: *The other children mocked him whenever he spoke.*

modal verb /ˈmoʊ·dəl ˈvɜrb/ **noun** (also **modal**) B1 a verb, for example "can," "might," or "must," that is used before another verb to show that something is possible, necessary, etc.

model[1] /ˈmɑd·əl/ **noun** **1** A2 a smaller copy of a real object: *He makes models as a hobby.* **2** A2 a particular type of machine or car that a company makes: *I think her car is a slightly older model.* **3** B1 someone whose job is wearing clothes for photographs or fashion shows: *a top fashion model*

model[2] /ˈmɑd·əl/ **verb** to wear clothes in fashion shows and photographs as a model: *She's been modeling for the same designer for years.*

modem /ˈmoʊ·dəm/ **noun** a piece of equipment that is used to send information from a computer through a telephone system

moderate /ˈmɑd·ə·rɪt/ **adj** average in size or amount and not too much: *Eating a moderate amount of fat is healthy.*
• **moderately** adv

modern /ˈmɑd·ərn/ **adj** **1** A2 designed and made using the most recent ideas

and methods: *modern art/architecture*
2 🄱 relating to the present time and
not to the past: *modern society* ○ *the
stresses of modern life*

modest /'mɑd·ɪst/ adj A modest person
does not talk about how good he or she
is: *He's modest about his achievements.*
• **modestly** adv *She spoke modestly about
her work.*

moist /mɔɪst/ adj slightly wet: *Keep the
soil moist but not wet.*

moisture /'mɔɪs·tʃər/ noun [no plural]
very small drops of water in the air or on
a surface

mold[1] /moʊld/ noun **1** [no plural] a green
or black substance that grows in wet
places or on old food **2** a container that
is used to make something in a particular shape: *a chocolate mold*

mold[2] /moʊld/ verb to make a soft substance a particular shape: *You mold the
clay while it is wet.*

moldy /'moʊl·di/ adj (comparative **moldier**,
superlative **moldiest**) covered with mold:
moldy cheese

mole /moʊl/ noun **1** a small, dark mark
on the skin **2** a small animal with black
fur that lives under the ground

molecule /'mɑl·ə,kjul/ noun
the smallest unit of a substance, with
one or more atoms

mom /mɑm/ noun 🄰 mother: *My mom
works at a bank.*

moment /'moʊ·mənt/ noun **1** 🄰 a very
short period of time: *I'll be back in a moment.* ○ *For a moment, I thought it was
Anna.* ○ *Could you wait a moment?* **2 at
the moment** 🄰 now: *She's not here at
the moment.* **3** 🄱 a point in time: *Just
at that moment, the phone rang.*

mommy /'mɑm·i/ noun a word for
"mother," used mainly by children

monarch /'mɑn·ərk/ noun a king or
queen

monarchy /'mɑn·ər·ki/ noun (plural
monarchies) a system of government
in which a country is ruled by a king or
queen

monastery /'mɑn·ə,ster·i/ noun (plural
monasteries) a building where men
live as a religious group

Monday /'mʌn·deɪ/ noun 🄰 the day of
the week after Sunday and before Tuesday

money /'mʌn·i/ noun [no plural] 🄰 the
coins or pieces of paper that are used for
buying things: *How much money do you
have?* ○ *He spends all his money on
clothes and CDs.* ○ *The company's not
making (=earning) any money right now.*

monitor /'mɑn·ɪ,tər/ noun a screen that
shows information or pictures, usually
connected to a computer: *a color monitor*
→ See **The Office** on page C12

monk /mʌŋk/ noun a member of a
group of religious men living away from
other people

monkey /'mʌŋ·ki/ noun 🄰 a hairy
animal with a long tail that lives in hot
countries and climbs trees

monolingual /,mɑn·ə'lɪŋ·gwəl/ adj
speaking or using only one language:
This is a monolingual dictionary.

monotonous /mə'nɑt·ᵊn·əs/ adj
always the same and boring: *The work is
very monotonous.*

monsoon /mɑn'sun/ noun the season
when there is a lot of rain in Southern
Asia

monster /'mɑn·stər/ noun 🄱 an imaginary creature that is large, ugly, and
frightening

month /mʌnθ/ noun **1** 🄰 one of the
twelve periods of time that a year is divided into: *Next month will be very busy.*
2 🄰 a period of approximately four
weeks: *She'll be working here for six
months.*

monthly /'mʌnθ·li/ adj, adv
🄱 happening or made once a month: *a
monthly magazine*

monument /'mɑn·jə·mənt/ noun
1 something that is built to make
people remember a famous person or
something important that happened:

a national monument **2** **B1** an old building or place that is important in history: *an ancient monument*

moo /muː/ *noun* the sound that a cow makes

• **moo** *verb*

mood /muːd/ *noun* **1** **B1** the way someone feels at a particular time: *You're **in a good mood**! ○ Ignore him – he's **in a bad mood**.* **2** **be in the mood for** *something* to want to do something: *I'm not really in the mood for shopping.*

moon /muːn/ *noun* **A2** the round object that shines in the sky at night and moves around the Earth

moonlight /ˈmuːn.laɪt/ *noun* [no plural] light that comes from the moon: *In the moonlight she looked even more beautiful.*

mop[1] /mɒp/ *noun* a thing for cleaning floors that has a long handle and thick strings at one end

mop[2] /mɒp/ *verb* (present participle **mopping**, past tense and past participle **mopped**) to use a mop: *I mopped the floor.*

moral[1] /ˈmɒr.əl/, /ˈmɑːr.əl/ *adj* relating to beliefs about what behavior is good and what behavior is bad: *He has very high moral standards.*

• **morally** *adv* *morally wrong*

moral[2] /ˈmɒr.əl/, /ˈmɑːr.əl/ *noun* something that teaches you how to behave better: *The moral of the story is: never lie.*

morals /ˈmɒr.əlz/, /ˈmɑːr.əlz/ *plural noun* beliefs that you should behave well and treat other people well: *He doesn't care what he does – he has no morals at all.*

more[1] /mɔːr/ *quantifier* **1** **A1** something extra that you have now: *Is there any more soup? ○ Would anyone like some more food?* **2** **A1** a greater number or amount of people or things: *There are **a lot more** people here today than there were yesterday. ○ He knows more about computers than I do.* **3** **more and more** an increasing number: *More and more people are choosing not to get married.*

more[2] /mɔːr/ *adv* **1** **more beautiful, difficult, interesting, etc.** **A1** used to show that someone or something has a greater amount of a quality than someone or something else: *It's **more** expensive **than** the others. ○ She's **far more** intelligent than her sister.* **2** **B1** used to show that something happens a greater number of times than before: *We eat out a lot **more than** we used to.* **3** **more and more** more as time passes: *It's becoming more and more difficult to pass the exam.* **4** **more or less** almost: *We've more or less finished work on the house.*

moreover /mɔːrˈoʊ.vər/ *adv formal* also and more importantly: *It is a cheap and, moreover, effective way of dealing with the problem.*

morning /ˈmɔːr.nɪŋ/ *noun* **1** **A1** the first half of the day, from the time when the sun rises until the middle of the day: *Friday morning ○ tomorrow morning ○ I got up late this morning. ○ I listen to the radio **in the morning**. ○ I'll pack my bags **in the morning** (=tomorrow morning).* **2** **(good) morning** **A1** used to say hello to someone in the morning: *Good morning, Sarah!* **3** **two, three, etc.**

THE BATHROOM

shower head

medicine cabinet

shower curtain

towel

faucet

soap

toilet paper

sink

bathtub

toilet

scale

bath mat

toothbrush

nail brush

cotton balls

shaver

toothpaste

razor

THE BODY

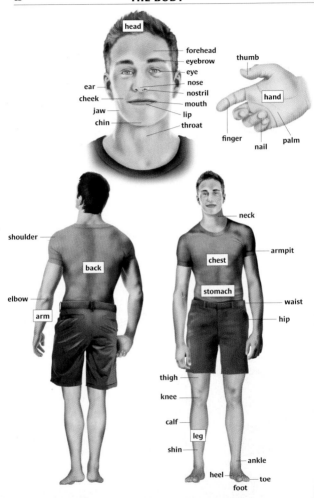

antenna · rear window · license plate · hood · trunk · turn signal · tire · tail light · tailpipe

side mirror · windshield · rearview mirror · windshield wiper · speedometer · dashboard · steering wheel · ignition · brake pedal · accelerator · seatbelt · gearshift · emergency brake

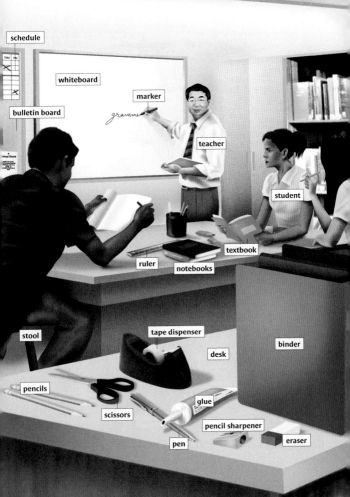

shirt

t-shirt

overcoat

dress

evening gown

miniskirt

sweatshirt

pullover

sweater

skirt

windbreaker

belt

vest

tie

scarves

jacket

buckle

sandals

shorts

shoes

boots

tennis shoes

dress pants

jeans

bike shorts

leggings

stockings

socks

pantyhose

bra

panties

boxers

briefs

hat

bikini

sunglasses

swimming trunks

tank top

baseball cap

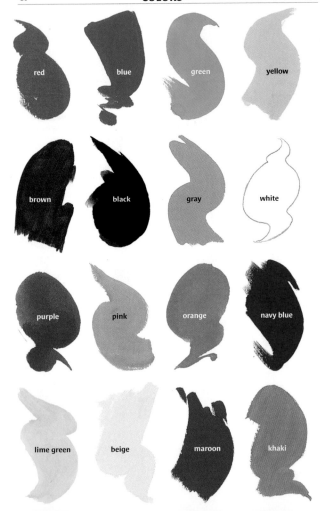

red

blue

green

yellow

brown

black

gray

white

purple

pink

orange

navy blue

lime green

beige

maroon

khaki

FOOD

sub/hero

sandwich

soup

cookies

cake

salad

pizza

rice

French fries

cereal

pasta

potato chips

peanuts

honey

jam

butter

seafood

eggs

yogurt

cheese

meat

FRUITS AND VEGETABLES

apples

bananas

grapes

pears

oranges

pineapples

lemons

watermelon

ears of corn

carrots

tomatoes

potatoes

celery

lettuce

cucumbers

garlic

onions

cauliflower

mushrooms

eggplants

peppers

blonde/fair   brown/dark   black   red   gray

straight   curly   wavy   spiky

moustache   stubble   braid   bangs   ponytail

beard

shoulder-length   long   short   bald

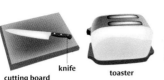

knife

cutting board   toaster   grater   oven mitt   utensils

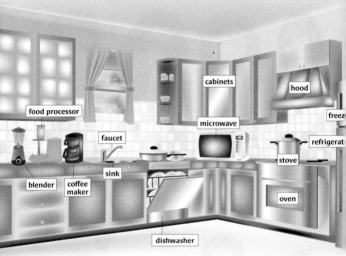

cabinets

hood

food processor

freez

microwave

faucet

refrigerat

blender

coffee
maker

sink

stove

oven

dishwasher

can opener

rolling pin

teapot

cake pan

strainer

pot/saucepan

measuring
spoons

roasting pan

frying pan

THE LIVING ROOM

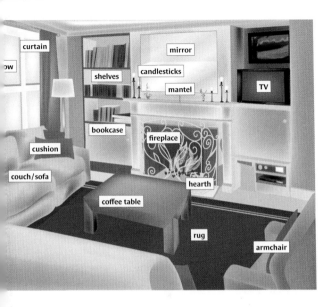

curtain

ow

mirror

shelves

candlesticks

mantel

TV

bookcase

cushion

fireplace

couch / sofa

hearth

coffee table

rug

armchair

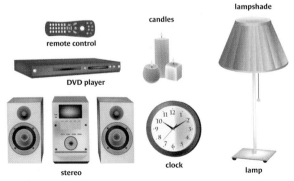

remote control

candles

lampshade

DVD player

stereo

clock

lamp

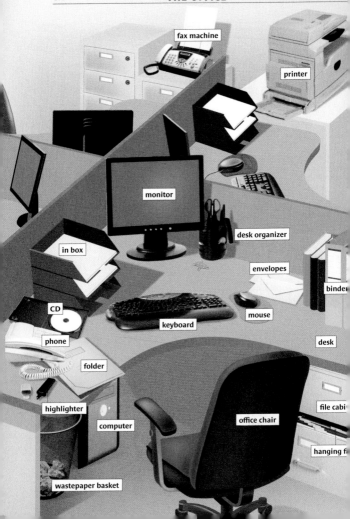

fax machine

printer

monitor

desk organizer

in box

envelopes

binder

CD

mouse

phone

keyboard

desk

folder

highlighter

file cabi

computer

office chair

hanging f

wastepaper basket

wake up

get up

put on

take off

lie down

sit up

stand up

put down

pick up

throw away

put away

tell off

eat out

turn on

turn off

get on

get off

fall down

work out

a slice of...

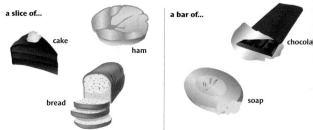

cake

ham

bread

a bar of...

chocola

soap

a bunch of...

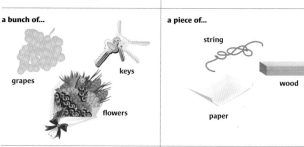

grapes

keys

flowers

a piece of...

string

wood

paper

a chunk of...

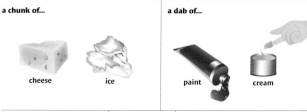

cheese

ice

a dab of...

paint

cream

crumb

cake crumbs   breadcrumbs

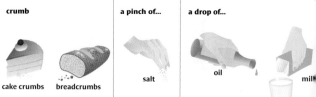

a pinch of...

salt

a drop of...

oil

mil

SPORTS (1)

track and field

boxing

skiing

javelin

running

high jump

boxing gloves

snowboarding

ice hockey

ice skating

puck

Rollerblading

skateboarding

swimming

horse racing

SPORTS (2)

football

soccer **goal**

goalposts **helmet**

basketball

golf

tennis

baseball

racket

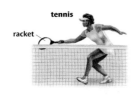

cycling/biking

volleyball

o'clock in the morning **B1** two, three, etc. o'clock at night: *My car alarm went off at three o'clock in the morning.*

Moslem /ˈmɒz·ləm/ another spelling of Muslim

mosque /mɒsk/ noun **A2** a building where Muslims say their prayers

mosquito /məˈski·toʊ/ noun (plural **mosquitoes**) **B1** a small flying insect that drinks your blood, sometimes causing a disease

moss /mɒs/ noun a very small, green plant that grows on the surface of rocks, trees, etc.

most[1] /moʊst/ adv **1 the most important, popular, etc.** **A2** used to show that someone or something has the greatest amount of a quality: *She's the most beautiful girl I've ever seen.* ○ *There are various reasons but this is the most important.* **2** **A2** more than anyone or anything else: *Which subject do you like most?* ○ *I liked all the cities but I liked Venice most of all.*

! **Common mistake: most**

The adverb **most** is used to form the superlative of many adjectives and adverbs.

the most beautiful actress in the world

---

most[2] /moʊst/ quantifier **1** **A2** almost all of a group of people or things: *Most people like her.* ○ *She wears jeans most of the time.* **2** a larger amount than anyone or anything else: *This one costs the most.* ○ *Which of you earns most?* **3 make the most of something** to enjoy something as much as you can because it will end soon: *We should make the most of this good weather.* **4 at the most** not more than a particular amount or number: *The journey will take an hour at the most.*

most[3] /moʊst/ determiner **1** **A2** almost all: *I don't eat meat, but I like most types of fish.* **2** **B1** the largest amount: *Mike earns the most money of all of us.*

mostly /ˈmoʊst·li/ adv **B1** mainly or most of the time: *The students are mostly Spanish.* ○ *It's mostly quiet at night.*

moth /mɔθ/ noun an insect with large wings that often flies at night
→ See picture at **insect**

mother /ˈmʌð·ər/ noun **1** **A1** someone's female parent: *My mother and father are divorced.* **2** a name used by a woman's child. Saying "mother" is more formal than saying "mom": *Mother, may I take dance lessons?*

motherhood /ˈmʌð·ərˌhʊd/ noun [no plural] being a mother

mother-in-law /ˈmʌð·ər·ɪnˌlɔ/ noun (plural **mothers-in-law**) the mother of someone's husband or wife: *My mother-in-law gave me a nice birthday card.*

motion /ˈmoʊ·ʃən/ noun [no plural] the action of something moving: *The motion of the boat made him feel sick.*

motivate /ˈmoʊ·təˌveɪt/ verb (present participle **motivating**, past tense and past participle **motivated**) to make someone want to do something: *Teaching is all about motivating people to learn.*

motivated /ˈmoʊ·təˌveɪ·tɪd/ adj working hard and wanting to succeed: *She is a very motivated student.*

motive /ˈmoʊ·tɪv/ noun a reason for doing something: *The police don't yet know the motive for the killing.*

motor /ˈmoʊ·tər/ noun the part of a machine, car, etc. that makes it work: *an electric motor*

motorcycle /ˈmoʊ·tərˌsaɪ·kəl/ noun (also **motorbike**) **A2** a vehicle with two wheels and an engine

mound /maʊnd/ noun **1** a large pile of something: *There was a mound of clothes on the floor.* **2** a higher area of soil, like a small hill: *an ancient burial mound*

mount /maʊnt/ verb to increase in amount or level: *Concern is mounting over fighting in the region.* ○ *mounting problems*

mount up phrasal verb to become a large amount: *My homework is really mounting up this week.*

Mount /maʊnt/ noun used in the names of mountains: *Mount Everest*

mountain
/ˈmaʊn·t̬ᵊn/ *noun*
A2 a very high hill:
to climb a mountain

mountain

mountain bike
/ˈmaʊn·t̬ᵊn ˌbaɪk/
noun a bicycle
with thick tires that you can use to ride
on hills and rough ground

mourn /mɔrn/ *verb* to feel very sad because someone has died: *He mourned
for his son every day.*

mourning /ˈmɔr·nɪŋ/ *noun* [no plural]
a feeling of sadness because someone has
died: *The whole nation was in mourning.*

mouse /maʊs/ *noun*
(plural **mice**) **1 A2** a
thing that you move
with your hand to
control what a com-
puter does **2 A2** a
small animal with fur
and a long, thin tail

mouse

mouth /maʊθ/ *noun* **1 A1** the part of
the face that is used for eating and
speaking → See **The Body** on page C2
2 mouth of a cave, tunnel, etc. the
opening or entrance of a cave, tunnel,
etc. **3 mouth of a river** where a river
goes into the sea

mouthful /ˈmaʊθ·fʊl/ *noun*
the amount of food or drink that you
can put into your mouth at one time

move /muv/ *verb* (present participle
moving, past tense and past participle
moved) **1 A2** to change place or position, or to make something change
place or position: *We moved the chairs
to another room.* ∘ *Someone was moving
around upstairs.* **2 B1** to go to a different place: *Eventually, she moved to Germany.* ∘ *She's moving into a new
apartment.* **3** to make someone feel
sad: *I was deeply moved by his speech.*

move in phrasal verb **B1** to begin living
in a new home: *We're moving in next
week.* ∘ *She just moved in with her boyfriend.* ∘ *They want to move in together.*

move out phrasal verb **B1** to stop living
in a particular home: *He moved out
when he was only 18.*

movement /ˈmuv·mənt/ *noun*
1 a group of people with the same
beliefs who work together to do something: *the women's movement* **2** a
change of position or place: *His movements were clumsy.*

movie /ˈmu·vi/ *noun* **A1** a story that is
shown in moving pictures on a screen,
usually at a theater or on television: *a
Hollywood movie*

movie theater /ˈmu·vi ˌθi·ə·t̬ər/ *noun*
a building where you go to watch movies

moving /ˈmu·vɪŋ/ *adj* causing strong
feelings of sadness or sympathy: *It's a
very moving story.*

mow /moʊ/ *verb* (past tense **mowed**, past
participle **mown**) to cut grass using a
machine: *He was mowing the lawn.*

MP3 player /ˌem·piˈθri ˌpleɪ·ər/ *noun*
A2 a piece of electronic equipment that
holds and plays music as computer files:
I listened to the song on my MP3 player.

mph written abbreviation for miles per hour:
a unit for measuring speed: *a 30 mph
speed limit*

Mr. /ˈmɪs·t̬ər/ *noun* a title for a man,
used before his last name or full name:
Good morning, Mr. Smith.

> **❗ Common mistake: Mr., Mrs.,
> Ms., Miss**
>
> All of these titles are used before
> someone's name.
> **Mr.** is used for men. **Mrs.** is used for
> women who are married. **Miss** is
> used for girls or for women who are
> not married. **Ms.** is used for women
> and does not show if a woman is
> married. Many women prefer to use
> this title to **Miss** or **Mrs.**
> We do not use these titles on their
> own as a way of speaking to some-
> one. Usually, we use no name.
> *Can I help you?*
> ~~Can I help you, Mrs.?~~

Mrs. /ˈmɪs·ɪz/ noun   a title for a married woman, used before her last name or full name: *Hello, Mrs. Jones.*

Ms. /mɪz/ noun   a title for a woman, used before her last name or full name: *Ms. Holly Fox*

much¹ /mʌtʃ/ quantifier   **1** A1 In questions, "much" is used to ask about the amount of something: *How much money will I need?* **2** A2 In negative sentences, "much" is used to say that there is not a large amount of something: *She doesn't earn much money.* ∘ *Pete didn't say much at dinner.* ∘ *"Is there any coffee left?" "Not much."* **3** too much/so much A2 a large amount of something, often more than you want: *I'd love to come, but I've got too much work.* ∘ *They have so much money.*

much² /mʌtʃ/ adv   **1** very much A1 a large amount or degree: *I like her very much.* **2** B1 often or a lot: *I don't like curry very much.* **3** much better, bigger, smaller, etc. B1 a lot better, bigger, smaller, etc.: *Their old house was much bigger.*

mud /mʌd/ noun [no plural]   wet dirt: *The kids came home covered in mud.*

muddy /ˈmʌd·i/ adj (comparative **muddier**, superlative **muddiest**)   covered with wet dirt: *muddy boots*

mug¹ /mʌɡ/ noun   A2 a large cup with straight sides, used for hot drinks: *a coffee mug*

mug² /mʌɡ/ verb (present participle **mugging**, past tense and past participle **mugged**)   to attack someone and take something from him or her in a public place: *He was mugged as he walked across the park.*

mugger /mʌɡ·ər/ noun   a person who attacks people in order to steal their money

multiply /ˈmʌl·tə.plaɪ/ verb (present participle **multiplying**, past tense and past participle **multiplied**)   to add one number to itself a particular number of times: *Six multiplied by two is twelve.*

mumble /ˈmʌm·bəl/ verb (present participle **mumbling**, past tense and past participle **mumbled**)   to speak too quietly and not clearly: *He mumbled something about it being a waste of time.*

the mumps /mʌmps/ noun [no plural]   an illness that children get that makes the neck swell

murder¹ /ˈmɜr·dər/ noun   B1 the crime of killing someone purposely

murder² /ˈmɜr·dər/ verb   B1 to kill someone purposely

murderer /ˈmɜr·dər·ər/ noun   B1 someone who has killed someone purposely

murmur¹ /ˈmɜr·mər/ verb   to speak very quietly: *"Go to sleep now," she murmured.*

murmur² /ˈmɜr·mər/ noun   the sound of someone saying something very quietly: *I could hear the low murmur of voices.*

muscle /ˈmʌs·əl/ noun   one of many parts in the body that are connected to your bones and help you to move: *stomach muscles*

museum /mjuˈzi·əm/ noun   A1 a building where you can look at important objects connected with art, history, or science: *a museum of modern art*

mushroom /ˈmʌʃ.rum/, /ˈmʌʃ.rʊm/ noun   A2 a type of fungus (=organism like a plant) with a short stem and a round top, some types of which can be eaten → See **Fruits and Vegetables** on page C8

music /ˈmju·zɪk/ noun [no plural]   **1** A1 a pattern of sounds that is made by playing instruments or singing, or a recording of this: *pop/dance music* ∘ *classical music* ∘ *He likes listening to music.* ∘ *a music lesson/teacher* **2** written signs that represent sounds that can be sung or played with instruments: *I never learned to read music* (=understand written music).

musical /ˈmju·zɪ·kəl/ adj   **1** A2 relating to music: *a musical instrument* **2** good at playing music: *She comes from a very musical family.*

musical[2] /ˈmju·zɪ·kəl/ *noun*   a play or movie with singing and dancing: *a Broadway musical*

musician /mjuˈzɪʃ·ən/ *noun* **B1** someone who plays a musical instrument, often as a job: *a jazz musician*

Muslim /ˈmʌz·lɪm/ (also **Moslem**) *noun* someone whose religion is Islam
• **Muslim** *adj*

must /mʌst/ *verb*   **1** **A2** used to say that it is necessary that something happens or is done: *The meat must be cooked thoroughly.*   **2** **B1** used to show that you think it is a good idea for someone to do something: *We must meet for lunch.*   **3** used to show that you are certain something is true: *You must be tired!* ○ *She must be very wealthy.*

mustache /ˈmʌs·tæʃ/ *noun* **B1** a line of hair that some men grow above their mouths
→ See **Hair** on page C9

mustard /ˈmʌs·tərd/ *noun* [no plural] a spicy yellow or brown sauce often eaten in small amounts with meat

mustn't /ˈmʌs·ənt/   short form of must not: *You mustn't let her know I'm coming.*

mutter /ˈmʌt·ər/ *verb*   to speak quietly, often when complaining about something: *She walked past me, muttering to herself.*

my /maɪ/ *determiner* **A1** belonging to or relating to the person who is speaking or writing: *Tom's my older son.* ○ *It's not my fault.*

myself /maɪˈself/ *pronoun*   **1** **A2** used to show that it is the person who is speaking who is affected by an action: *I bought myself a new coat.* ○ *I looked at myself in the mirror.*   **2** **(all) by myself** **A2** alone or without anyone else's help: *I live by myself in a small apartment.* ○ *Mommy, I got dressed all by myself!*   **3** used to give more attention to the word "I": *I'll tell her myself.* ○ *Jack likes vanilla ice cream but I prefer chocolate, myself.*

mysterious /mɪˈstɪər·i·əs/ *adj*   strange and not explained or understood: *the mysterious death of her son*

• **mysteriously** *adv* *The car was mysteriously in a different place from where we left it.*

mystery /ˈmɪs·tər·i/ *noun* (plural **mysteries**) **B1** something strange that cannot be explained or understood: *They never did solve the mystery of his disappearance.*

myth /mɪθ/ *noun*   **1** an ancient story about gods and brave people, often one that explains an event in history or the natural world: *a Greek myth*   **2** an idea that is not true but is believed by many people: *It's a myth that men are better drivers than women.*

N n

N, n /en/   the fourteenth letter of the alphabet

nag /næg/ *verb* (present participle **nagging**, past tense and past participle **nagged**)   to keep asking someone to do something: *She keeps nagging me to clean my room.*

nail /neɪl/ *noun*   **1** a thin piece of metal with a sharp end, used to join pieces of wood together: *a hammer and nails*   **2** the hard part at the end of your fingers and toes: *She bites her nails.*

nails

nail

nail polish /ˈneɪl ˌpɑl·ɪʃ/ *noun* [no plural] colored liquid that you put on your nails

naked /ˈneɪ·kɪd/ *adj*   without clothes: *naked shoulders*

name[1] /neɪm/ *noun* **A1** the word or group of words that is used to refer to a person, thing, or place: *What's your name?* ○ *My name is Alexis.* ○ *I can't remember the name of the street.*

name² /neɪm/ **verb** (present participle **naming**, past tense and past participle **named**) **1** 🔵B1 to give someone or something a name: *We named our first son Edward.* **2** 🔵B1 to say what the name of someone or something is: *Can you name three types of monkey?*

nanny /ˈnæn·i/ **noun** (plural **nannies**) someone whose job is to take care of a family's children

nap /næp/ **noun** a short sleep, especially during the day: *He likes to **take a nap** after lunch.*

napkin /ˈnæp·kɪn/ **noun** a piece of cloth or paper that you use when you eat to clean your mouth and hands, and keep your clothes clean

narrow /ˈnær·oʊ/ **adj** 🔵B1 not wide; being only a small distance from one side to the other: *a narrow street* ○ *narrow shoulders*

narrowly /ˈnær·oʊ·li/ **adv** only by a small amount: *An apple fell from the tree, **narrowly missing** my head.*

nasty /ˈnæs·ti/ **adj** (comparative **nastier**, superlative **nastiest**) **1** 🔵B1 very bad: *He had a nasty cut above his eye.* ○ *There's a nasty smell in here.* **2** not kind: *She's always being nasty to her little brother.*

nation /ˈneɪ·ʃən/ **noun** a country or the people living in a country: *the Asian nations* ○ *The entire nation mourned her death.*

national /ˈnæʃ·ə·nªl/ **adj** 🔴A2 relating to or shared by all parts of a country: *a national newspaper*

national anthem /ˈnæʃ·ə·nªl ˈæn·θəm/ **noun** the official song of a country

national holiday /ˈnæʃ·ə·nªl ˈhɑl·ɪ·deɪ/ **noun** a day when most people in a particular country do not have to go to work or school: *New Year's Day is a national holiday in many countries.*

nationality /ˌnæʃ·əˈnæl·ɪ·ti/ **noun** (plural **nationalities**) 🔴A1 If you have American, British, Swiss, etc. nationality, you are legally a member of that country: *What nationality is she?*

nationwide¹ /ˈneɪ·ʃənˌwaɪd/ **adj** existing or happening in all parts of a country: *a nationwide search*

nationwide² /ˈneɪ·ʃənˌwaɪd/ **adv** in all parts of a country: *Schools nationwide don't have enough teachers.*

native¹ /ˈneɪ·tɪv/ **adj** **1** Your native town or country is the place where you were born: *He returned to his native Algeria.* **2** Your native language is the first language you learn as a child: *native speakers of English*

native² /ˈneɪ·tɪv/ **noun** someone who was born in a particular place: *He's **a native of** Texas.*

native speaker /ˈneɪ·tɪv ˈspi·kər/ **noun** someone who has spoken a particular language since he or she was a baby, and not learned it later: *Our students are native speakers of other languages.*

natural /ˈnætʃ·ər·əl/ **adj** **1** 🔵B1 made or caused by nature and not by people or machines: *natural gas* ○ *This product contains only natural ingredients.* **2** normal or expected: *It's natural to feel sad when you leave home.*

→ Opposite **unnatural** adj

naturally /ˈnætʃ·ər·ə·li/ **adv** **1** as you would expect: *Naturally, he was really disappointed by his low scores.* **2** in a normal way: *Relax and try to act naturally.* **3** existing or happening as part of nature and not made or done by people: *Most fruit is naturally sweet.*

❗ Common mistake: nature, the environment, and the country

Nature means all the things in the world that exist naturally and are not created by people.
He's interested in wildlife and anything having to do with nature.

The environment means the land, water, and air that animals and plants live in. It is usually used when talking about the way people use or damage the natural world.
The government has introduced new policies to protect the environment.

The country means land where there are no towns or cities.
I love walking in the country.

---

nature /ˈneɪ.tʃər/ **noun** **1** A2 [no plural]
all the plants, creatures, and things that
exist in the world that are not made by
people: *I like to get out and enjoy nature.*
2 someone's character: *It is not in his
nature to be rude.*

nature reserve /ˈneɪ.tʃər rɪˌzɜːrv/ **noun**
an area of land where animals and
plants live and are protected

naughty /ˈnɔː.ti/ **adj** (comparative
naughtier, superlative **naughtiest**)
If a child is naughty, he or she behaves
badly: *What a naughty little girl!*

naval /ˈneɪ.vəl/ **adj** relating to the ships
that are used for fighting wars at sea: *a
naval officer*

navigate /ˈnæv.ɪˌɡeɪt/ **verb** (present participle **navigating**, past tense and past participle
navigated) to find the right direction
to travel by using maps or other equipment: *He navigated the ship back to
Plymouth.*

navigation /ˌnæv.ɪˈɡeɪ.ʃən/ **noun** [no
plural] the act of finding the right direction to travel by using maps or other
equipment

navy /ˈneɪ.vi/ **noun** **1** the Navy ships
and soldiers used for fighting wars at
sea: *He joined the navy.* **2** navy blue

navy blue /ˌneɪ.vi ˈbluː/ **adj** (also **navy**)
B1 very dark blue: *a navy blue sweater*
• **navy blue noun**

near¹ /nɪər/ **adv, preposition** **1** A1 not
far away in distance: *Could you park
near the entrance, please?* ○ *I stood near
the window.* **2** not far away in time: *We
can decide nearer to the time.*

near² /nɪər/ **adj** **1** B1 not far away in
distance or time: *The library is near to
the school.* ○ *The nearest garage is ten
miles away.* **2** in the near future at a
time that is not far away: *Space travel
may become common in the near future.*

nearby /ˈnɪərbaɪ/ **adj, adv** B1 not far
away: *a nearby town*

nearly /ˈnɪər.li/ **adv** A2 almost: *The
party is nearly over.* ○ *Nearly all the food
was gone when I arrived.*

neat /niːt/ **adj** **1** B1 well arranged and
clean: *Her house is always neat and
clean.* **2** informal good: *What a neat idea!*

neatly /ˈniːt.li/ **adv** in a well arranged
way: *He was neatly dressed.*

necessary /ˈnes.ə.ser.i/ **adj** B1 needed
in order to do something: *Is it really
necessary to spend so much?* ○ *The police
are prepared to use force, if necessary.*
→ Opposite **unnecessary adj**

necessity /nəˈses.ɪ.ti/ **noun** (plural
necessities) something that you need:
food, clothing, and other necessities

neck /nek/ **noun** A2 the part of the
body between your head and your
shoulders → See **The Body** on page C2

necklace /ˈnek.lɪs/ **noun** A2 a piece of
jewelry that you wear around your neck:
a pearl necklace → See picture at **jewelry**

need¹ /niːd/ **verb** **1** A1 If you need
something, you must have it, and if you
need to do something, you must do it: *I
need some new shoes.* ○ *I need to ask you
a few questions.* ○ *We need you to take
care of the children for us.* **2** don't need
to do something A2 used in order to
say that someone does not have to do
something or should not do something:
You don't need to go. **3** B1 If something
needs doing or needs to be done, it
should be done in order to be better: *Do
these clothes need washing?*

need² /niːd/ **noun** **1** something that is
necessary to have or do: *There's an
urgent need for fresh water.* ○ *Is there any
need to change the system?* **2** be in
need of something to need something:
My car is in need of repair. **3** no need If
there is no need to do something or no
need for something, it is not necessary
or it is wrong: *There's no need to go to the
store – there's plenty of food here.* ○ *I
understand why she was angry, but there
was no need to be so rude to him.*
4 needs the things you need in order to
have a good life: *A home and food are
basic needs.* ○ *her emotional needs*

needle /'ni·dᵊl/ noun   needle
1 a thin, pointed
metal object with a
small hole at one
end for thread,
used in sewing: *a
needle and thread*
2 the thin metal part of a piece of medical equipment used to take blood out of
the body, or to put drugs in

needless /'nid·ləs/ adj   **1** unnecessary:
a needless waste of time   **2 needless to
say** as you would expect: *Needless to say,
I did all the work.*
• **needlessly** adv

negative /'neg·ə·t̮ɪv/ adj   **1** 🄰🄰 with the
meaning "no" or "not": *We received a
negative response to our request.*   **2** 🄱🄰 not
hopeful or not interested: *She has a negative attitude about her work.*   **3** A negative sentence or phrase is one that
contains a word such as "not," "no,"
"never," or "nothing.": *"I've never seen
him in my life" is a negative sentence.*
○ *"Don't" and "do not" are negative forms
of "do."*   **4** A negative effect is bad and
causes damage to something: *Terrorism
has had a negative effect on tourism.*
5 A negative number is less than zero.

neglect¹ /nɪˈɡlekt/ verb   to not give
enough attention to something or
someone: *He neglects that poor dog.* ○ *I'm
afraid I have been neglecting the garden.*

neglect² /nɪˈɡlekt/ noun [no plural]   the
fact of not giving enough attention to
something or someone: *The children had
suffered years of neglect.*

negotiate /nɪˈɡoʊ·ʃiˌeɪt/ verb (present participle **negotiating**, past tense and past participle **negotiated**)   to try to make or
change an agreement by talking about
it: *We are negotiating for a new contract.*

neighbor /'neɪ·bər/ noun   **1** 🄰🄰 someone who lives very near you, especially
in the next house: *Our next-door neighbors are really noisy.*   **2** someone or
something that is near or next to someone or something else

neighborhood /'neɪ·bərˌhʊd/ noun
🄱🄰 an area of a town or city that people
live in: *Are there any good restaurants in
the neighborhood?*

neighboring /'neɪ·bə·rɪŋ/ adj   near
or next to somewhere: *neighboring
countries*

neither¹ /'ni·ðər/, /'naɪ·ðər/ adv   used to
say that a negative fact is also true of
someone or something else: *Jerry doesn't
like it, and neither do I.* ○ *She's not very
tall and neither is her husband.*

neither² /'ni·ðər/, /'naɪ·ðər/ pronoun,
determiner   not either of two people or
things: *Neither child was hurt in the accident.* ○ *Neither of us had ever been to
Houston before.*

neither³ /'ni·ðər/, /'naɪ·ðər/ conjunction
neither… nor used when a negative
fact is true of two people or things:
*Neither he nor his mother would talk to
the police.*

nephew /'nef·ju/ noun   🄱🄰 the son of
your brother or sister

nerve /nɜrv/ noun [no plural]   **1** one of
the very small parts in your body that
carry messages between your brain and
other parts of the body   **2** the act of doing something that you know someone
will not like: *I can't believe she had the
nerve to talk to me after what happened!*

nerve-racking (also **nerve-wracking**)
/'nɜrv ˌræk·ɪŋ/ adj   making you very
nervous: *It's nerve-racking to speak in
front of a lot of people.*

nerves /nɜrvz/ plural noun   **1** the state
of being nervous: *I took a deep breath to
calm my nerves.*   **2 get on someone's
nerves** to annoy someone: *My little sister
often gets on my nerves.*

nervous /'nɜr·vəs/ adj   **1** 🄱🄰 worried in
a way that affects your body, for example by making you shake: *He's very nervous about his driving test.*   **2** relating
to the nerves in the body: *the nervous
system*
• **nervously** adv *She waited nervously
for her turn to speak.*

nest /nest/ *noun* a home built by birds for their eggs

nest

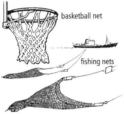

net /net/ *noun*
1 [no plural] material made of crossed threads with holes between them **2** 🔵 something made with a piece of net, for example for catching fish, or for sports: *a fishing net* ∘ *a basketball net*
→ See **Sports 2** on page C16 **3** the **Net** 🅰️ short form of the Internet

nets

basketball net

fishing nets

nettle /ˈnet̬·ˀl/ *noun* a wild plant whose leaves hurt you if you touch them

network /ˈnet̬ˌwɜrk/ *noun* **1** a system or group of connected parts: *a social network* ∘ *a network of tunnels* **2** a set of computers that are connected to each other: *Our offices are on the same network.*

neutral[1] /ˈnu·trəl/ *adj* **1** not supporting any side in an argument or fight: *He decided to remain neutral on the issue.* **2** Neutral colors are not strong or bright.

neutral[2] /ˈnu·trəl/ *noun* [no plural] in driving, the position of the gears (= parts of a vehicle that control how fast the wheels turn) when they are not connected: *The car was in neutral.*

⚠️ **Common mistake: never**

Never has a negative meaning, so you do not need "not" in the same sentence.
I'll never do that again.
~~I'll not never do that again.~~

never /ˈnev·ər/ *adv* 🅰️ not ever, not one time: *"Have you ever been to Australia?" "No, never."* ∘ *I've never thought about that before.*

nevertheless /ˌnev·ər·ðəˈles/ *adv* despite that: *I knew a lot about the subject already, but her talk was interesting nevertheless.*

new /nu/ *adj* **1** 🅰️ different from before: *I need some new shoes.* ∘ *He starts his new job on Monday.* **2** 🅰️ recently made: *We built a new house.* **3** 🅰️ found or learned about a short time ago: *They have a new way of treating this illness.* **4** 🔵 If you are new, you arrived recently or do not know something well yet: *I'm new to the area.* ∘ *I'm learning a new language.*

newcomer /ˈnuˌkʌm·ər/ *noun* someone who has only recently arrived or started doing something: *He's a newcomer to the area.*

newly /ˈnu·li/ *adv* only a short time ago: *a newly married couple*

news /nuz/ *noun* [no plural] **1** 🅰️ new information: *Have you heard any news about your job yet?* **2** the **news** 🔵 information about important things that have just happened on television, radio, and in newspapers: *the local/national news*

newspaper /ˈnuzˌpeɪ·pər/ *noun* **1** 🅰️ large, folded sheets of paper that are printed with the news and sold every day or every week: *I read about his death in the newspaper.* **2** 🅰️ [no plural] paper from a newspaper: *Wrap the cups in newspaper before you pack them.*

New Year /ˈnu ˈjɪər/ *noun* (also **new year**) the beginning of the year: *Happy New Year!*

New Year's Day /ˈnu ˌjɪərz ˈdeɪ/ *noun* January 1

New Year's Eve /ˈnu ˌjɪərz ˈiv/ *noun* [no plural] December 31, the last day of the year: *a New Year's Eve party*

next[1] /nekst/ *adj* **1** 🅰️ coming after this one: *I'm leaving next week.* ∘ *She'll* go to school next year. **2** A2 nearest to now: *What time is the next train to Boston?* **3** A2 The next place is the one nearest to this place: *Turn left at the next street.*

next[2] /nekst/ *adv* A2 immediately after: *Where should we go next?*

next[3] /nekst/ *preposition* **next to something/someone** A2 very close to something or someone, with nothing in between: *Come and sit next to me.*

next[4] /nekst/ *pronoun* **1** the person or thing that follows this person or thing: *What's next on the list?* **2 the weekend, week, etc. after next** the weekend, week, etc. that follows the next one: *We're seeing Paul the Saturday after next.*

next door /'nekst 'dɔr/ *adj, adv* B1 in the next room, house, building, or other place: *What are your next-door neighbors like?* ○ *He lives **next door to** the park.*

nibble /'nɪb·əl/ *verb* (present participle **nibbling**, past tense and past participle **nibbled**) to eat something by taking very small bites: *We nibbled on crackers and cheese before dinner.*

nice /naɪs/ *adj* **1** A1 pleasant: *They have a very nice house.* ○ *We'll go to the beach tomorrow if the weather's nice.* ○ *It was nice to meet you.* **2** A1 kind and friendly: *He's a really nice person.* ○ *She's always been very nice to me.*

nicely /'naɪs·li/ *adv* **1** well: *That table would fit nicely in the bedroom.* **2** in a pleasant way: *The room was nicely decorated.*

nickel /'nɪk·əl/ *noun* a coin with a value of five cents (= 5/100 of a dollar)

nickname /'nɪk,neɪm/ *noun* a name used informally instead of your real name: *After the race, his new nickname was "Speedy."*
• **nickname** *verb* (present participle **nicknaming**, past tense and past participle **nicknamed**) *They nicknamed her "The Cat Lady."*

nicotine /'nɪk·ə,tin/ *noun* [no plural] a poisonous chemical in tobacco

niece /nis/ *noun* B1 the daughter of your brother or sister

night /naɪt/ *noun* **1** A1 the time in every 24 hours when it is dark and people sleep: *I slept badly last night.* ○ *It gets really cold at night.* **2** A1 the period from the evening to the time when you go to sleep: *Are you doing anything on Friday night?*

nightclub /'naɪt,klʌb/ *noun* B1 a place where you can dance and drink at night

nightlife /'naɪt,laɪf/ *noun* [no plural] B1 things to do at night, such as dancing and visiting bars: *Is the nightlife good around here?*

nightmare /'naɪt,meər/ *noun* **1** B1 something very bad that happened to you: *The whole trip was a nightmare.* **2** B1 a frightening dream

night school /'naɪt ,skul/ *noun* [no plural] classes for adults that are taught in the evening

nine /naɪn/ A1 the number 9

nineteen /'naɪn'tin/ A1 the number 19

nineteenth /'naɪn'tinθ/ 19th written as a word

nineties /'naɪn·tiz/ *plural noun* **1** the nineties the years from 1990 to 1999: *I moved to Arizona in the nineties.* **2** be in your nineties to be aged between 90 and 99: *She was in her nineties when she died.*

ninety /'naɪn·ti/ A2 the number 90

ninth[1] /naɪnθ/ A2 9th written as a word

ninth[2] /naɪnθ/ *noun* one of nine equal parts of something; 1/9

nip /nɪp/ *verb* (present participle **nipping**, past tense and past participle **nipped**) to quickly bite someone

nipple /'nɪp·əl/ *noun* the small, round area of darker skin in the center of each breast in women, or on each side of the chest in men

no[1] /noʊ/ *exclamation* **1** A1 something that you say in order to disagree, refuse something, or say that something is not true: *"Have you seen Louise?" "No, I haven't."* ○ *"Can I come too?" "No, I'm sorry."* ○ *"He's horrible." "No he isn't!"* **2** A2 something that you say to agree with something that is negative: *"He's not very smart, is he?" "No, he isn't."* **3** oh no! A2 something that you say when you are shocked and upset: *Oh no! I lost my ring!*

no² /noʊ/ determiner **1** A1 not any: *We have no money.* **2** A2 a word used to say that something is not allowed: *No smoking.*

no. written abbreviation for number

nobody /ˈnoʊ·bʌd·i/, /ˈnoʊ·bad·i/ pronoun A2 no person: *There was nobody I could talk to.* ○ *Nobody was listening.*

nod /nɑd/ verb (present participle **nodding**, past tense and past participle **nodded**) to move your head up and down as a way of agreeing: *I asked Barbara if she liked him and she nodded.*
• **nod** noun *He gave a nod of approval.*
nod off phrasal verb informal to start sleeping: *I nodded off after lunch.*

noise /nɔɪz/ noun A1 a sound, especially a loud, bad sound: *Stop making so much noise!* ○ *I had to shout above the noise of the party.*

noisy /ˈnɔɪ·zi/ adj (comparative **noisier**, superlative **noisiest**) A2 Noisy people or things make a lot of noise: *We've had problems with noisy neighbors.*
→ Opposite **quiet** adj
• **noisily** adv

none /nʌn/ quantifier B1 not any: *None of us smokes.* ○ *He wanted some food but there was none left.*

nonsense /ˈnɑn·sens/ noun [no plural]
1 something silly and not true that someone has said or written: *The rumors about the mayor are nonsense.* ○ *It's nonsense to suggest they could have cheated.*
2 silly behavior: *Please stop this childish nonsense!*

non-smoking /ˈnɑnˈsmoʊ·kɪŋ/ adj describes a place where people are not

allowed to smoke: *Let's get a table in the non-smoking area.*

nonstop /ˌnɑnˈstɑp/ adj, adv without stopping: *nonstop flights from Chicago to Tokyo* ○ *We talked nonstop the whole trip.*

noodle /ˈnuː·dᵊl/ noun a thin piece of pasta (=food made from flour and water)

noon /nun/ noun [no plural] A2 twelve o'clock in the middle of the day: *The service will be held at noon.*

no one /ˈnoʊ ˌwʌn/ pronoun A2 no person: *No one knows where he is.* ○ *There was no one there.*

nor /nɔr/ adv, conjunction **neither... nor...** used after "neither" and before the second thing in a negative sentence: *Strangely, neither Jack nor Ella saw what happened.*

normal /ˈnɔr·məl/ adj A2 usual and ordinary: *It's normal for couples to argue now and then.*

normally /ˈnɔr·mə·li/ adv **1** B1 usually: *Normally, I start work around nine o'clock.* **2** in the ordinary way that you expect: *The car is working normally now.*

north, North /nɔrθ/ noun [no plural]
1 B1 the direction that is on your left when you face toward the rising sun: *Which way is north?* **2** the north A2 the part of an area that is farther toward the north than the rest: *She's from a town in the north of Oregon.*
• **north** adj A2 *the north bank of the river* ○ *North America*
• **north** adv A2 *We drove north.*

northeast, Northeast /ˌnɔrθˈist/ noun [no plural] **1** B1 the direction between north and east **2** the northeast B1 the northeast part of a country
• **northeast, Northeast** adj, adv

northeastern, Northeastern /ˌnɔrθˈis·tərn/ adj in or from the northeast

northern, Northern /ˈnɔr·ðərn/ adj B1 in or from the north part of an area: *Northern England* ○ *the northern states*

the North Pole /ˌnɔrθ ˈpoʊl/ *noun* [no plural] the point on the Earth's surface that is farthest north

northwest, Northwest /ˌnɔrθˈwest/ *noun* [no plural] **1** 🅑🄵 the direction between north and west **2 the northwest** 🅑🄵 the northwest part of a country

• **northwest, Northwest** *adj, adv*

northwestern, Northwestern /ˌnɔrθˈwesˈtərn/ *adj* in or from the northwest

nose /noʊz/ *noun* 🄰🄵 the part of your face that you breathe through and smell with

→ See **The Body** on page C2

nostril /ˈnɑs·trəl/ *noun* one of the two holes at the end of your nose

→ See **The Body** on page C2

not /nɑt/ *adv* **1** 🄰🄵 used to give something the opposite meaning: *I'm not interested.* ∘ *It's not mine.* ∘ *It's for you, not Daniel.* **2** 🄰🄵 used after verbs such as "be afraid," "hope," or "suspect" in short, negative replies: *"Is he coming with us?" "I hope not."* ∘ *"Are you done yet?" "I'm afraid not."* **3 or not** 🄰🄵 used to express the possibility that something might not happen: *Are you going to the party or not?* ∘ *I don't know if she's coming or not.*

> **⚠ Common mistake: not … either**
>
> The words **not … either** are used to add another piece of negative information.
>
> *I forgot my credit card and I don't have any cash either.*
> ~~I forgot my credit card and I don't have any cash neither.~~
> *Helen didn't enjoy it either.*
> ~~Helen didn't enjoy it too.~~

note[1] /noʊt/ *noun* **1** 🄰🄵 a short letter: *He left a note on her desk.* **2** 🄰🄵 (also **notes**) words that you write down to help you remember something: *She studied her notes before the test.* ∘ *Let me*

make a note of (= write) *your phone number.* **3** a single musical sound

note[2] /noʊt/ *verb* (present participle **noting**, past tense and past participle **noted**) 🅑🄵 to notice something: *I noted her absence.*
note down *something* phrasal verb to write something so that you do not forget it: *Did you note down her address?*

notebook /ˈnoʊtˌbʊk/ *noun* **1** 🄰🄷 a book with empty pages that you can write in → See **The Classroom** on page C4 **2** a small computer that can be carried around and used anywhere

notepad /ˈnoʊtˌpæd/ *noun* a set of pieces of paper that are joined together at one edge and used for writing on

nothing /ˈnʌθ·ɪŋ/ *pronoun* **1** 🄰🄷 not anything: *There was nothing in her suitcase.* ∘ *He said he did nothing wrong.* **2** 🅑🄵 something not important or valuable: *She was crying about nothing.* **3 have nothing to do with** *someone/something* to not involve or affect someone or something: *He made his own decision – I had nothing to do with it.* **4 for nothing** without a successful result: *I came all this way for nothing.*

notice[1] /ˈnoʊ·t̬ɪs/ *verb* (present participle **noticing**, past tense and past participle **noticed**) 🅑🄷 to see something and be aware of it: *I noticed that he was alone.* ∘ *No one noticed my new haircut.*

notice[2] /ˈnoʊ·t̬ɪs/ *noun* **1** 🄰🄷 a sign giving information about something: *The notice said that the pool was closed for repairs.* **2** 🅑🄷 [no plural] attention: *I didn't take any notice of* (= give attention to) *his advice.* **3** 🅑🄷 [no plural] a warning that something will happen: *The next time you visit, can you give me more notice?*

> **⚠ Common mistake: notice or news?**
>
> A **notice** is a sign giving information about something. If you want to talk about new information, you should use **news**.
>
> *I have some great news for you!*
> ~~I have a great notice for you!~~

noticeable /ˈnou·tɪ·sə·bəl/ **adj** easy to see or be aware of: *There has been a noticeable improvement in his work.*

• **noticeably** adv *As summer approaches, the days get noticeably longer.*

notorious /nəˈtɔr·i·əs/ **adj** famous for something bad: *a notorious criminal* ○ *She was notorious for her bad temper.*

• **notoriously** adv

noun /nɑun/ **noun** **A2** a word that refers to a person, place, object, event, substance, idea, feeling, or quality. For example the words "teacher," "book," and "beauty" are nouns.

novel /ˈnɑv·əl/ **noun** **B1** a book that tells a story about people and things that are not real: *Have you read any good novels lately?*

November /nouˈvem·bər/ **noun** **A1** the eleventh month of the year

now[1] /nɑu/ **adv** **1** **A1** at this time: *I'm going now.* ○ *What is Eva doing now?* ○ *I don't want to wait – I want it now!* **2** **A2** immediately: *We're going home now.* **3** used to show the length of time that something has been happening, from the time it began until the present: *I've lived in Seattle for two years now.* **4** now and then If something happens now and then, it happens sometimes but not very often: *I love chocolate, but I only eat it now and then.*

now[2] /nɑu/ **conjunction** now that as a result of a new situation: *Now that I have a car, I can visit here more often.*

nowadays /ˈnɑu·əˌdeɪz/ **adv** **B1** at the present time, especially when compared to the past: *Everything seems more expensive nowadays.*

nowhere /ˈnouˌhwear/ **adv** **B1** not anywhere: *There was nowhere to sit.* ○ *We had nowhere else to go.*

nuclear /ˈnu·kli·ər/ **adj** **1** relating to the energy that is made when the nucleus (= central part) of an atom is divided: *nuclear weapons* ○ *a nuclear power plant* **2** relating to the nucleus (= central part) of an atom: *nuclear physics*

nucleus /ˈnu·kli·əs/ **noun** (plural **nuclei**) the central part of an atom or cell

nude /nud/ **adj** not wearing any clothes

• **nude** noun *Both children were in the nude.*

nudge /nʌdʒ/ **verb** (present participle **nudging**, past tense and past participle **nudged**) to gently push someone or something: *She nudged me toward the door.*

• **nudge** noun *I gave him a nudge.*

nuisance /ˈnu·səns/ **noun** a person, thing, or situation that annoys you or causes problems for you: *Not being able to use my computer is a real nuisance.*

numb /nʌm/ **adj** If a part of your body is numb, you cannot feel it: *My fingers and toes were numb with cold.*

number[1] /ˈnʌm·bər/ **noun** **1** **A1** a symbol or word used in a counting system: *Think of a number between 1 and 100.* **2** **A1** a group of numbers that represents something: *What is your phone number?* **3** **B1** an amount: *We contacted a large number of people.* **4** a number of *something* many: *There have been a number of problems.*

> **⚠ Common mistake: number**
>
> We use the adjectives **large** and **small** with the word **number**, not "big" and "little".
>
> *A large number of people attended the concert.*
>
> ~~A big number of people attended the concert.~~

number[2] /ˈnʌm·bər/ **verb** to give something a number: *I numbered the pages.*

numerous /ˈnu·mər·əs/ **adj** formal many: *He has written numerous articles.*

nun /nʌn/ **noun** a member of a group of religious women who live away from other people

nurse[1] /nɜrs/ **noun** **A2** someone whose job is taking care of people who are sick and hurt

nurse² /nɜrs/ **verb** (present participle **nursing**, past tense and past participle **nursed**) to take care of a person or animal that is sick

nursery /ˈnɜr·sər·i/ **noun** (plural **nurseries**) **1** a room in a house where a baby sleeps **2** a place where plants are grown and sold

nursery rhyme /ˈnɜr·sər·i ˌraɪm/ **noun** a short poem or song for young children

nursery school /ˈnɜr·sər·i ˌskul/ **noun** a school for very young children

nut /nʌt/ **noun** **1** the dry fruit of some trees that grows in a hard shell, and can often be eaten: *a Brazil nut* **2** a piece of metal with a hole in it that you screw onto a bolt (=metal pin) to hold pieces of wood or metal together

nutritious /nuˈtrɪʃ·əs/ **adj** Nutritious food contains things that your body needs to stay healthy: *a nutritious meal*

nylon /ˈnaɪ·lɑn/ **noun** [no plural] a strong material that is not natural, which is used to make things like clothes and ropes: *nylon stockings*

Oo

O, o /oʊ/ the fifteenth letter of the alphabet

oak /oʊk/ **noun** a large tree found in northern countries, or the wood of this tree

oar /ɔr/ **noun** a long pole with a flat end that you use to move a boat through water

oasis /oʊˈeɪ·sɪs/ **noun** (plural **oases**) a place in the desert where there is water and where plants grow

oath /oʊθ/ **noun** a formal promise

oats /oʊts/ **plural noun** grain that people eat or feed to animals

obedience /oʊˈbi·di·əns/ **noun** [no plural] the condition of being willing to do what someone tells you to do: *He needs complete obedience from his soldiers.*

obedient /oʊˈbi·di·ənt/ **adj** willing to do what people tell you to do: *an obedient child*

→ Opposite **disobedient**

• **obediently adv** *The dog sat obediently by his owner.*

obese /oʊˈbis/ **adj** very fat: *Obese people are more likely to suffer heart attacks.*

obey /oʊˈbeɪ/ **verb** to do what someone tells you to do: *If you do not obey the law, you will be arrested.*

→ Opposite **disobey**

object¹ /ˈɑb·dʒɪkt/ **noun** **1** 🔒 a thing that you can see or touch but that is not alive: *I could see a bright, shiny object in the sky.* **2** the object of *something* the purpose of something: *The object of the game is to score more points than the other team.* **3** 🔒 in grammar, the person or thing that is affected by the action of a verb

object² /əbˈdʒɛkt/ **verb** to say that you do not agree with a plan: *Kim objected to the proposal.*

objection /əbˈdʒɛk·ʃən/ **noun** a reason why you do not like or agree with a plan: *Our main objection to the new factory is that it's noisy.*

objective¹ /əbˈdʒɛk·tɪv/ **noun** something that you are trying to do: *His main objective was to increase profits.*

objective² /əbˈdʒɛk·tɪv/ **adj** influenced only by facts and not by feelings: *I can't be objective when I judge my daughter's work.*

obligation /ˌɑb·ləˈɡeɪ·ʃən/ **noun** something that you have to do because it is your duty: *Parents have an obligation to make sure their children receive a good education.*

oblivious /əˈblɪv·i·əs/ **adj** not knowing anything about something that is happening: *She seemed completely oblivious to what was happening around her.*

obnoxious /əbˈnɑk·ʃəs/ **adj** very unpleasant or rude: *He was loud and obnoxious.*

observant /əbˈzɜr·vənt/ *adj* good or quick at noticing things: *Observant hikers might see eagles in the mountains.*

observation /ˌɑb·zɜrˈveɪ·ʃən/ *noun* [no plural] the act of watching someone or something carefully: *The doctor wants to keep him **under observation** for a week.*

observe /əbˈzɜrv/ *verb* (present participle **observing**, past tense and past participle **observed**) to watch someone or something carefully: *Children learn by observing adults.*

obsessed /əbˈsest/ *adj* **be obsessed with** *someone/something* to think about someone or something all the time: *He is obsessed with money.*

obsession /əbˈseʃ·ən/ *noun* someone or something that you think about all the time: *They have an **obsession with** making money.*

obstacle /ˈɑb·stə·kəl/ *noun* something that makes it difficult for you to go somewhere or do something: *There are many **obstacles to** success in the peace talks.*

obstruct /əbˈstrʌkt/ *verb* **1** to be in a place that stops someone or something from moving: *The car had stopped and was obstructing traffic.* **2** to try to stop something from happening: *He was accused of obstructing a police investigation.*

obstruction /əbˈstrʌk·ʃən/ *noun* something that stops someone or something from moving: *The accident caused an obstruction on the highway.*

obtain /əbˈteɪn/ *verb* formal to get something: *He obtained a law degree from Brown University.*

obvious /ˈɑb·vi·əs/ *adj* **B1** easy to understand or see: *It's obvious that he doesn't like her.*

obviously /ˈɑb·vi·əs·li/ *adv* **B1** in a way that is easy to understand or see: *They're obviously in love.* ○ *Obviously, we want to start as soon as possible.*

occasion /əˈkeɪ·ʒən/ *noun* **1** **B1** an important event: *a special occasion* ○ *She bought a new dress for the occasion.* **2** a time when something happens: *We met on several occasions to discuss the issue.*

occasional /əˈkeɪ·ʒə·nəl/ *adj* not happening often: *He still plays the occasional game of tennis.*
• **occasionally** *adv*

occupation /ˌɑk·jəˈpeɪ·ʃən/ *noun* **A2** formal your job: *Put your name, address, and occupation on the form.*

occupy /ˈɑk·jə·paɪ/ *verb* (present participle **occupying**, past tense and past participle **occupied**) **1** to fill a place or period of time: *His book collection occupies most of the room.* ○ *The baby seems to occupy all our time.* **2** to live or work in a room or building: *They occupy the second floor of the building.* **3** to keep someone busy or interested: *The games **kept** the kids **occupied** for hours.*

occur /əˈkɜr/ *verb* (present participle **occurring**, past tense and past participle **occurred**) **1** formal to happen, often without being planned: *According to the police, the shooting occurred at about 12:30 a.m.* **2** to exist or be present: *The disease mainly **occurs in** women over 40.*
occur to *someone phrasal verb* to suddenly think of something: ***It occurred to** me that he might be lying.*

ocean /ˈoʊ·ʃən/ *noun* **1** **A2** one of the five main areas of sea: *the Pacific Ocean* **2** a large area of salt water: *We went swimming **in the ocean.***

o'clock /əˈklɑk/ *adv* **one, two, three, etc. o'clock** **A1** used after the numbers one to twelve to mean exactly that hour when you tell the time: *We got home at ten o'clock.*

October /ɑkˈtoʊ·bər/ *noun* **A1** the tenth month of the year

octopus /ˈɑk·tə·pəs/ *noun* a sea creature with eight long arms

octopus

odd /ɑd/ *adj* **1** strange or unusual: *There is something odd about her.* ○ *It's a little odd that he didn't come.* **2** not happening often or regularly: *He does **odd jobs** for extra cash.*

odd number /ˈɑd ˈnʌm·bər/ *noun*
a number that does not produce a
whole number when it is divided by two
→ Opposite **even number noun**

odds /ɑdz/ *plural noun* **1** the chance of
something happening: *What are the odds
of winning the grand prize?* **2 odds and
ends** informal a group of different objects
that have little value

of /ʌv/ *preposition* **1** Ⓐ belonging or
relating to someone or something: *She
is a friend of my cousin.* ○ *I like the color
of her hair.* **2** Ⓐ used after words that
show an amount: *a bag of apples* ○ *both
of us* **3** Ⓐ used with numbers, ages,
and dates: *a boy of six* ○ *the 14th of February 1995* **4** Ⓐ containing: *a glass of
milk* **5** Ⓐ showing position or direction: *the front of the line* ○ *a small town
north of Pittsburgh* **6** Ⓐ showing
someone or something: *a map of the city*
○ *a photo of my boyfriend* **7** Ⓐ used
when comparing related things: *He's the
best-looking of the three brothers.* **8** Ⓑ
showing a reason or cause: *He died of
cancer.* **9** used after an adjective when
judging someone's behavior: *It was very
nice of you to think of us.*

off¹ /ɔf/ *adv, preposition* **1** Ⓐ not touching or connected to something: *Keep off
the grass!* ○ *A button came off my coat.*
2 Ⓐ not operating or being used: *Make
sure you turn your computer off.* **3** Ⓐ not
at work: *I had three months off after my
son was born.* **4** Ⓑ away from a place
or position: *He ran off to find his friend.*
5 Ⓑ If a price has a certain amount of
money off, it costs that much less than
the usual price: *There's 40% off this week
on all winter coats.* **6** near to a building
or place: *an island off the coast of Maine*

off² /ɔf/ *adj* not at work: *He's off this
week – I think he's on vacation.*

offend /əˈfend/ *verb* to make someone
upset or angry: *I was deeply offended by
her comments.*

offender /əˈfen·dər/ *noun* someone
who has committed a crime: *a frequent
offender*

offense¹ /əˈfens/ *noun* **1** [no plural] an
act of upsetting or insulting someone
by doing or saying something rude: *I
didn't intend to cause offense.* **2** a crime:
He committed several serious offenses.

offense² /ˈɔfens/ *noun* the part of a
sports team that tries to score points:
They have a strong offense this year.

offensive /əˈfen·sɪv/ *adj* likely to make
people angry or upset: *an offensive
remark*

offer¹ /ˈɔ·fər/ *verb* **1** Ⓐ to say that you
will do something for someone: *He
offered to get me a cab.* **2** Ⓑ to ask
someone if he or she would like something: *They offered me a job.* **3** Ⓑ to
give or provide something: *to offer advice* ○ *Did he offer any explanation for his
behavior?* **4** to say that you will pay a
particular amount of money: *I offered
him $2,500 for the car.*

offer² /ˈɔ·fər/ *noun* **1** Ⓐ an act of asking someone if he or she would like
something: *an offer of help* ○ *a job offer*
2 Ⓑ a reduction in the price of something for a short time: *This special offer
is good through Saturday.* **3** an amount
of money that you say you will pay for
something: *They made an offer on the
house.*

office /ˈɔ·fɪs/ *noun* **1** Ⓐ a room or
building where people work: *an office
worker* ○ *I get to the office around nine.*
→ See **The Office** on page C12 **2** Ⓐ a
room or building where you can get
information, tickets, or a particular
service: *a ticket office* ○ *a post office*
○ *a doctor's office*

officer /ˈɔ·fə·sər/ *noun* **1** Ⓑ someone
who works for a government department: *a customs officer* **2** Ⓑ someone
who is a member of the police: *a police
officer* **3** someone with an important
job in the military: *an army officer*

official¹ /əˈfɪʃ·əl/ *adj* approved by the
government or someone in power: *the
official language of Singapore* ○ *an official
document*
• **officially** *adv*

official[2] /ə'fɪʃ·əl/ *noun* someone who has an important position in an organization, such as the government: *a senior official*

often /'ɔ·fən/ *adv* **1** ⒶⒷ many times or regularly: *I often see her there.* ○ **How often** (= How many times) *do you go to the gym?* **2** If something often happens or is often true, it is normal for it to happen or it is usually true: *Brothers and sisters often argue.* ○ *Headaches are often caused by stress.*

oh /oʊ/ *exclamation* **1** ⒶⒷ said when you are surprised, pleased, disappointed, etc.: *Oh, no! I don't believe it!* ○ *"I don't think I can come." "Oh, that's a shame."* **2** ⒶⒷ used to introduce an idea that you have just thought of, or something that you have just remembered: *Oh, and don't forget to lock the door.* **3** used before you say something, often before replying to what someone has said: *"Ian is leaving now." "Oh, I didn't realize that."*

oil /ɔɪl/ *noun* [no plural] **1** ⒶⒷ a thick liquid made from plants or animals that is used in cooking: *vegetable oil* **2** ⒷⒷ a thick liquid that comes from under the Earth's surface and is used as a fuel: *an oil company* ○ *an oil well*

ointment /'ɔɪnt·mənt/ *noun* a smooth, thick substance that is put on painful skin

OK /ˌoʊ'keɪ/, /'oʊ·keɪ/ *exclamation, adj, adv informal* short form of okay

okay[1] /ˌoʊ'keɪ/, /'oʊ·keɪ/ *exclamation informal* (also **OK**) **1** ⒶⒷ used when agreeing to do something or when allowing someone to do something: *"Let's meet this afternoon." "Okay." ○ "Can I use the car?" "Okay."* **2** ⒶⒷ used to check that someone understands or agrees to something: *I'll see you at six o'clock, okay?* **3** ⒶⒷ used as a way of showing that you are going to take action, start speaking, or start something new: *OK, if you're ready we'll start.* ○ *Okay, let's go.*

okay[2] /ˌoʊ'keɪ/, /'oʊ·keɪ/ *adj* (also **OK**) **1** ⒶⒷ safe or healthy: *Is your*

grandmother okay now? **2** ⒶⒷ good enough: *Is your food okay?* **3** ⒶⒷ allowed: *Is it okay if I leave early today?* **4** ⒶⒷ in a satisfactory way: *Did you sleep okay?*

old /oʊld/ *adj* **1** ⒶⒷ having lived or existed for a long time: *an old man* ○ *an old house* ○ *We're all **getting older**.* **2** having been used or owned for a long time: *You might get dirty, so wear some old clothes.* **3** ⒶⒷ used to describe or ask about someone's age: *How old are you?* ○ *She'll be four **years old** in March.* **4** ⒶⒷ used before or in the past: *I think the old system was better in many ways.* **5** ⒶⒷ an old friend is one you have known and liked for a long time: *She's one of my oldest friends.*

old-fashioned /ˌoʊld'fæʃ·ənd/ *adj* ⒷⒷ not modern: *old-fashioned clothes*

olive /'ɑl·ɪv/ *noun* ⒷⒷ a small green or black fruit that is eaten or used to produce oil

olive oil /ˈɑl·ɪv ˈɔɪl/ *noun* [no plural] oil made from olives, used for cooking or on salads

the Olympic Games /ə'lɪm·pɪk 'ɡeɪmz/ *plural noun* (also **the Olympics**) two international sports competitions, one for summer and one for winter sports, each of which happens every four years

omelet /'ɑm·lət/, /'ɑm·ə·lət/ *noun* (also **omelette**) ⒶⒷ a food made with eggs that have been mixed and fried: *a cheese omelet*

omit /oʊ'mɪt/ *verb* (present participle **omitting**, past tense and past participle **omitted**) to not include someone or something: *The information was **omitted from** the document.*

on[1] /ɑn/, /ɑn/ *preposition* **1** ⒶⒷ on a surface of something: *I put the book on that shelf.* ○ *He stepped on my foot.* **2** ⒶⒷ covering, touching, attached to, or hanging from something: *You have ketchup on your shirt.* ○ *Which finger do you wear your ring on?* **3** ⒶⒷ used to show the date or day when something happens: *He will arrive on February 14.* ○ *I have to*

| oʊ go | ɑɪər fire | aʊər hour | eər hair | ɪər ear | ʊər poor | j yet | ʒ measure | ʃ ship | dʒ judge | tʃ chin | ð that | θ thin | ŋ hang |

work on Saturday. **4** A2 used to refer to a place when giving directions: *Make the first turn on the right.* ○ *Our house is the second on the left after the stop sign.* **5** A2 in a particular place: *See the diagram on page 22.* ○ *I met her on a ship.* **6** A2 being broadcast or presented: *What's on TV tonight?* ○ *a musical playing on Broadway* **7** A2 used to show what money or time is used for: *She refuses to spend more than $40 on a pair of shoes.* ○ *We have wasted too much time on this already.* **8** A2 used to show some methods of traveling: *Sam loves riding on buses.* ○ *Did you go over on the ferry?* **9 on sale** A2 available at a reduced price: *I got this dress on sale.* **10** B1 about: *a book on pregnancy* **11** B1 next to or along the side of: *The bank is on Maple Street.* ○ *Cincinnati is on the Ohio River.* **12** B1 using something: *I spoke to Dad on the phone.* ○ *I was working on my computer.* **13 on purpose** B1 intentionally: *She didn't do it on purpose - it was an accident.* **14 on time** B1 not early or late: *Please be on time for the meeting.*

on² /ɔn/, /ɑn/ *adv* **1** B1 working or being used: *He left the computer on all day.* ○ *Is this microphone on?* **2 have/put something on** A2 If you have or put something on, you are wearing it: *She has on a black coat.* ○ *Why don't you put your new dress on?* **3** B1 into a bus, train, plane, etc.: *Amy got on at Grand Central Station.* **4** happening or planned: *Is the party still on?* **5** being broadcast or presented: *What's on TV tonight?* ○ *My favorite show is on tomorrow.* **6** used to show that an action or event continues: *Our old traditions live on.* **7 on and off** If something happens on and off during a period of time, it happens sometimes: *They've been seeing each other on and off since Christmas.*

once¹ /wʌns/ *adv* **1** A2 one time: *It only snowed once or twice this year.* ○ *I go swimming once a week* (=one time every week). **2** B1 in the past, but not now: *This house once belonged to my grandfather.* **3 at once** immediately: *I knew at once that I would like it here.* **4 at once** B1 at the same time: *They all started talking at once.* **5 once more** one more time: *If you say that once more, I'm going to leave.* **6 once upon a time** B1 used at the beginning of a children's story to mean that something happened a long time ago **7 once again** B1 again: *I'll explain it once again.* **8 for once** used to mean that something is happening that does not usually happen: *For once, I think I have good news for him.*

once² /wʌns/ *conjunction* as soon as: *Once I find somewhere to live, I'll send you my address.*

one¹ /wʌn/ A1 the number 1

one² /wʌn/ *pronoun* **1** A2 one person or thing in a group that has already been talked about: *I just made some cookies. Do you want one?* ○ *Chris is the one with glasses.* **2 one by one** separately, one after the other: *They entered the room one by one.* **3 one after another** (also **one after the other**) first one, then another, then another, and so on: *One after another, they left the room.* ○ *She ate the chocolates one after the other until the box was finished.* **4** formal any person in general: *One should respect one's parents.*

one³ /wʌn/ *determiner* **1** A2 one person or thing in a group: *One of their daughters just got married.* **2** A2 at a particular time in the past: *I first met him one day in the park.* **3 one or two** B1 a few: *I'd like to make one or two suggestions.* **4** used to refer to a time in the future that is not yet decided: *We should plan to go out one evening.* **5** used when saying there is no other person or thing: *He's the one person who never forgets my birthday.* **6** a single thing: *I think we should paint the bedroom all one color.*

one⁴ /wʌn/ *noun* a dollar bill: *Could I get a five and five ones for a ten?*

one another /ˈwʌn əˈnʌð·ɚ/ *pronoun* B1 used to show that each person in a group of three or more people does something to or with the others: *You all need to cooperate with one another.*

one-way /ˈwʌnˈweɪ/ **adj** If a road is one-way, you can only drive on it in one direction: *a one-way street*

onion /ˈʌn·jən/ **noun** A2 a round vegetable with layers that has a strong taste and smell

→ See **Fruits and Vegetables** on page C8

online /ˈɒnˈlaɪn/, /ˈɑnˈlaɪn/ **adj, adv** A2 connected to and shared by a system of computers, especially the Internet: *online services* ○ *to go online (= start using the Internet)* ○ *Most newspapers are now available online.*

only[1] /ˈoʊn·li/ **adv** **1** A1 not more than a particular size or amount: *It'll only take a few minutes.* ○ *She's only fifteen.* **2** A2 not anyone or anything else: *The offer is available to New York residents only.* **3** B1 used to mean that something happened a very short time ago: *She only just got here.* **4** B1 used to say that something is not important, or that you did not mean to upset someone: *Don't worry – it's only a scratch.* ○ *I was only joking.* **5** B1 not in any other place: *These birds are only found in New Zealand.* **6 if only** B1 used to express a wish for something that is impossible or unlikely to happen: *If only I knew the answer!* **7 I only hope/wish** used to emphasize that you are hoping or wishing for: *I only hope you know what you're doing.* ○ *I only wish that I had more time.* **8 not only… (but) also** used to say that more than one thing is true: *Not only did he show up late, he also forgot his books.*

only[2] /ˈoʊn·li/ **adj** A1 used to mean that there are no others: *This could be our only chance.* ○ *You're the only lawyer I know.*

only[3] /ˈoʊn·li/ **conjunction** but: *I would pay for it myself, only I don't have the money.*

onto /ˈɒn·tu/, /ˈɑn·tu/ (also **on to**) **preposition** **1** B1 used to show movement into or on a particular place: *I stepped onto the platform.* ○ *Can you get back onto the path?* **2** used to show that you are starting to talk about a different subject: *How did we get onto this subject?*

onward /ˈɒn·wərd/, /ˈɑn·wərd/ **adv** (also **onwards**) **1** beginning at a time and continuing after it: *I'll be at home from nine o'clock onwards.* **2** If you move onward, you continue to go forward.

oops /ʊps/, /ups/ **exclamation** something you say when you do something slightly wrong: *Oops! I spilled my coffee.*

ooze /uz/ **verb** (present participle **oozing**, past tense and past participle **oozed**) **1** If a liquid oozes from something, it comes out slowly: *Blood was oozing out of the wound.* **2** informal to show a lot of a quality: *He oozes charm.*

open[1] /ˈoʊ·pən/ **adj** **1** A2 not closed or fastened: *an open door* ○ *Is there an open bottle of wine?* **2** A1 An open store or business is open during the time it can do business: *Most stores are open on Sundays.* **3** B1 An open area of land has no buildings on it or near it: *large open spaces*

open

The windows are open.

The book is open.

open[2] /ˈoʊ·pən/ **verb** **1** A1 If you open something, you make it change to a position that is not closed: *Could you open the window?* ○ *Open your eyes.* **2** A1 If something opens, it changes to a position that is not closed: *The gate won't open, so we can't get in.* **3** A2 to remove part of a container or package so that you can see or use what it contains: *Come on, open your present!* ○ *I can't open this bottle.* **4** A2 If a store or office opens at a particular time of day, it starts to do business at that time: *What time does the bank open?* **5** B1 to make a computer document or program ready to be read or used: *First, open the file called Statistics.* **6** If a business or activity opens, or if you open it, it starts officially for the first time: *That restaurant's new – it only opened last month.* ○ *The new hospital will be officially opened by the mayor.*

open (something) up phrasal verb to start a new store or business: *Fast food restaurants are opening up everywhere.*

opener /ˈoʊ·pə·nər/ noun **bottle, can, etc. opener** a piece of kitchen equipment used to open bottles, cans, etc.

opening /ˈoʊ·pə·nɪŋ/ noun **1** a hole or space that something or someone can pass through: *We found an opening in the fence and climbed through.* **2** a ceremony at the beginning of an event or activity: *The official opening of the new school will take place next month.* **3** the beginning of something: *The opening of the novel is amazing.*

openly /ˈoʊ·pən·li/ adv without hiding any of your thoughts or feelings: *He talks openly about his feelings.*

opera /ˈɑp·ə·rə/ noun **A2** a musical play in which most of the words are sung

operate /ˈɑp·ə·reɪt/ verb (present participle **operating**, past tense and past participle **operated**) **1 B1** to cut someone's body and remove or repair part of it: *Did they have to operate on him?* **2** If an organization or business operates, it works: *Our company is operating under very difficult conditions.* **3** If a machine operates, it works, and if you operate it, you make it work: *You have to be trained to operate the machinery.*

operation /ˌɑp·əˈreɪ·ʃən/ noun **1 B1** the process of cutting someone's body to remove or repair part of it: *a heart operation.* ○ *My son is going to have an operation.* **2** an organization or business: *a large commercial operation*

operator /ˈɑp·ə·reɪ·tər/ noun **1** someone who helps to connect people on a telephone system **2** someone whose job is to control a machine or vehicle:

a computer operator **3** a company that does a particular type of business: *a tour operator*

opinion /əˈpɪn·jən/ noun **1 B1** a thought or belief about something or someone: *What's your opinion on the matter?* ○ *In my opinion* (=I think) he's the best football player in the country. **2** [no plural] the thoughts or beliefs that a group of people have: *The government will have to listen to public opinion.*

opponent /əˈpoʊ·nənt/ noun someone whom you compete against in a game or competition: *He beat his opponent six games to two.*

opportunity /ˌɑp·ərˈtu·nɪ·ti/ noun (plural **opportunities**) **1 B1** a chance to do something good: *If you get the opportunity to go there, it is a wonderful city.* **2 take the/this opportunity to do something** to use an occasion to do or say something: *I'd like to take this opportunity to thank all of you.*

oppose /əˈpoʊz/ verb (present participle **opposing**, past tense and past participle **opposed**) to disagree with a plan or activity and to try to stop it: *The committee opposed a proposal to allow women to join the club.*

opposed /əˈpoʊzd/ adj **be opposed to something** to disagree with a plan or activity: *We're not opposed to tax increases.*

opposite¹ /ˈɑp·ə·zɪt/, /ˈɑp·əˈsɪt/ adj **1 B1** in a position facing someone or something but on the other side: *We live on opposite sides of the city.* **2** completely different: *My attempt to calm him down had the opposite effect.*

opposite² /ˈɑp·ə·zɪt/, /ˈɑp·əˈsɪt/ adv, preposition **A2** in a position facing something or someone but on the other side: *The couple sat down opposite her.* ○ *Is there a bakery opposite your house?*

opposite³ /ˈɑp·ə·zɪt/, /ˈɑp·əˈsɪt/ noun **B1** someone or something that is completely different from another person or thing: *He's the exact opposite of my dad.*

opposition /ˌɑp·əˈzɪʃ·ən/ noun [no plural] strong disagreement: *There is a lot of*

a b c d e f g h i j k l m n **o** p q r s t u v w x y z

opposition to the new taxes.

opt /ɑpt/ verb **opt for** *something*; **opt to do** *something* to choose something or to decide to do something: *Most people opt to have the operation.*

optician /ɑpˈtɪʃ·ən/ noun someone whose job is to make glasses

optimist /ˈɑp·təˌmɪst/ noun someone who always thinks that good things will happen
→ Opposite **pessimist**

optimistic /ˌɑp·təˈmɪs·tɪk/ adj always thinking that good things will happen: *We're **optimistic about** our chances for success.*
→ Opposite **pessimistic** adj

option /ˈɑp·ʃən/ noun **B1** a choice: *The menu doesn't **have** many **options**.* ○ *You always have the **option of** not attending.*

optional /ˈɑp·ʃə·nᵊl/ adj If something is optional, you can decide to have or do it but it is not necessary: *You must take English and science, but art is optional.*

or /ɔr/ conjunction **1** **A1** used between possibilities, or before the last of many possibilities: *Is the baby a boy or a girl?* ○ *You can have beer or wine.* **2** **A2** used after a negative verb to mean not one thing and also not another: *Tim doesn't eat meat or fish.* **3** **B1** used to give someone a warning or advice: *Be careful, or you'll have an accident.* **4** used to change or correct something you have said: *He finished the work, or most of it, anyway.*

oral /ˈɔr·əl/ adj **1** spoken: *an oral examination* **2** relating to the mouth: *oral medicine*

orange[1] /ˈɔr·ɪndʒ/, /ˈɑr·ɪndʒ/ adj **A1** being a color that is a mixture of red and yellow: *a deep orange sunset*

orange[2] /ˈɔr·ɪndʒ/, /ˈɑr·ɪndʒ/ noun **1** **A1** a round, sweet fruit with a thick skin and a center that has many parts: *orange juice* → See **Fruits and Vegetables** on page C8 **2** **A2** a color that is a mixture of red and yellow → See **Colors** on page C6

orbit /ˈɔr·bɪt/ noun the journey that a spacecraft or planet makes around the sun, the moon, or another planet: *the Earth's orbit*
• **orbit** verb *The moon orbits the Earth.*

orchard /ˈɔr·tʃərd/ noun a piece of land where there are fruit trees

orchestra /ˈɔr·kə·strə/ noun **B1** a large group of musicians who play different instruments together

order[1] /ˈɔr·dər/ noun **1** **A2** a request for food and drinks in a restaurant: *Has the waiter **taken your order**?* **2** **B1** the arrangement of a group of people or things in a list from first to last: *The names are in alphabetical order.* ○ *We put the tasks **in order of** importance.* ○ *Don't get the pages **out of order** (= not arranged correctly).* ○ *Please keep the books **in order** (= arranged correctly) on the shelf.* **3** something that someone tells you that you must do: *You must **obey orders** at all times.* **4** [no plural] the state of everything being neat and in its correct place: *I like to have my desk **in order**.* **5 out of order** **B1** If a machine is out of order, it is not working: *The coffee machine is out of order.* **6 in order to do** *something* **B1** so that you can do something: *She worked all summer in order to save some money.*

order[2] /ˈɔr·dər/ verb **1** **A2** to ask for food or other things: *Did you order any drinks?* ○ *We ordered new lights for the kitchen.* **2** to tell someone that he or she must do something: *He **ordered** them to leave.* **3** to arrange a group of people or things in a list from first to last: *Did you order the pages correctly?*

ordinary /ˈɔr·dᵊnˌer·i/ adj **1** not special or different in any way: *an ordinary life* ○ *ordinary people* ○ *I had a very ordinary childhood.* **2 out of the ordinary** different from usual: *Their relationship was a little out of the ordinary.*

ore /ɔr/ noun [no plural] rock or soil from which metal is made: *iron ore*

organ /ˈɔr·gən/ noun **1** a part of an animal or plant that has a special purpose: *internal organs* **2** a large musical instrument like a piano that is played in churches: *a church organ*

organic /ɔrˈɡæn·ɪk/ **adj**   not using chemicals when keeping animals or growing plants for food: *organic vege tables*

organism /ˈɔr·ɡəˌnɪz·əm/ **noun**   a living thing, often a very small one

organization /ˌɔr·ɡə·nəˈzeɪ·ʃən/ **noun**   **1** **B1** a group of people who work to-gether for the same purpose: *a volun-teer organization*   **2** **B1** [no plural] the way that something is planned: *Who is responsible for the organization of the conference?*

organize /ˈɔr·ɡəˌnaɪz/ **verb** (present partici-ple **organizing**, past tense and past participle **organized**)   **B1** to plan or arrange something: *I need to organize my files better.*

organized /ˈɔr·ɡəˌnaɪzd/ **adj**   **1** An orga-nized person plans things well. → Opposite **disorganized adj**   **2** involving a group of people who plan to do something together: *organized crime*   **3** planned or arranged: *We're going on an organized tour.*

organizer /ˈɔr·ɡəˌnaɪ·zər/ **noun**   **1** someone who plans an event or activ-ity: *There aren't enough seats for all the guests – I need to tell the organizers.*   **2** an object that you use to keep things neat or in order: *a desk organizer*   → See **The Office** on page C12

origin /ˈɔr·ə·dʒɪn/ **noun**   **1** the cause of something, or where something comes from: *the origin of the universe*   **2** the country, race, or social class of a per-son's family: *She's of Irish origin.*

original /əˈrɪdʒ·ə·nªl/ **adj**   **1** **B1** inter-esting and different from others: *Her essay was full of original ideas.*   **2** **B1** being the first or existing at the begin-ning: *Do you still have the original docu-ment?*   **3** produced by the artist and not a copy: *an original drawing*

originally /əˈrɪdʒ·ə·nªl·i/ **adv**   at the beginning: *I originally planned to stay for a week, but ended up staying for a month.*

ornament /ˈɔr·nə·mənt/ **noun**   an object that is used as a decoration in a home or yard

orphan /ˈɔr·fən/ **noun**   a child whose parents are dead

ostrich /ˈɔ·strɪtʃ/ **noun**   a very large bird from Africa that cannot fly but can run very fast

ostrich

other[1] /ˈʌð·ər/ **adj, determiner**   **1** different from a thing or person that you have talked about: *Ask me some other time, when I'm not so busy.*   **2** **A2** used to talk about the remaining members of a group or items in a set: *I found one earring – where is the other one?* ○ *Mario and Anna sat down to watch the other danc-ers.*   **3** **B1** more, not this or these: *I don't like pie – do you have any other desserts?* ○ *I don't think he's funny, but other people do.*   **4** the other day, week, etc. **B1** a day or week in the recent past: *I asked Carlos about it just the other day.*   **5** the other side/end (of *something*) **B1** the opposite side or end of some-thing: *Put the chair at the other end of the desk.*   **6** the other way around happen-ing in the opposite way: *I thought the adults would be slower than the children, but it was the other way around.*

other[2] /ˈʌð·ər/ **pronoun**   **1** **A2** a thing or person that is part of this set: *Some of the pieces were damaged, others were missing.*   **2** others **B1** more things of the same type: *This bowl is broken – do you have any others?*

> **❗ Common mistake: other**
>
> Remember that **other** is used before a plural noun.
>
> *The other students were already there.*
>
> **Others** is used on its own.
>
> *Where are the others?*

others /ˈʌð·ərz/ **pronoun**   **B1** other peo-ple: *Don't expect others to do your work for you.*

otherwise[1] /ˈʌð·ərˌwaɪz/ **adv**   **1** except for what you have just said: *She hurt her*

a
b
c
d
e
f
g
h
i
j
k
l
m
n
o
p
q
r
s
t
u
v
w
x
y
z

arm in the accident, but otherwise she was fine. **2** different from what has just been said: *I'll meet you there at six o'clock unless I hear otherwise.*

otherwise² /ˈʌð·ərˌwaɪz/ **conjunction**
B1 used when saying what will happen if someone does not do something: *You'd better phone home, otherwise your parents will start to worry.*

ouch /aʊtʃ/ **exclamation** something you say when you have a sudden pain: *Ouch! That hurt!*

ought /ɔt/ **verb** **1 ought to do something** **B1** used to say or ask what someone should do: *You ought to see a doctor.* **2 ought to be/do something** used to say that you expect something to be true or that you expect something to happen: *She ought to be home by now.*

ounce /aʊns/ **noun** (written abbreviation **oz.**) **1** (also **fluid ounce**) a unit for measuring liquid. 16 ounces equal one pint. **2** a unit for measuring weight. 16 ounces equal one pound.

our /aʊər/ **determiner** **A1** belonging to us: *Alice is our youngest daughter.*

ours /aʊərz/ **pronoun** **A2** the thing or things that belong to us: *That's their problem – not ours.*

ourselves /aʊərˈselvz/ **pronoun**
1 A2 used to show that the person who is speaking and other people are affected by an action: *We promised ourselves a vacation this year.* **2 by ourselves** **A2** alone or without anyone else's help: *We could invite some friends or we could go by ourselves.*

out /aʊt/ **adj, adv** **1 B1** used to show movement away from the inside of somewhere: *He dropped the bag and all the apples fell out.* **2 A2** used to refer to a period of time when someone goes away from home for a social activity: *He asked me out to the movies next week.* **3 A2** not in the place where you usually live or work: *I went by to see her but she was out.* **4 B1** ready to buy or see: *When is the new Spielberg movie out?* **5 B1** able to be seen: *The stars are out*

tonight. **6 B1** to the point where something is removed or disappears: *The stain won't come out.* **7** A fire or light that is out is not burning or shining: *Bring some more wood, the fire went out.*

outbreak /ˈaʊtˌbreɪk/ **noun** a time when something unpleasant suddenly starts, such as a war or disease: *an outbreak of the flu*

outdoor /ˈaʊtˌdɔr/ **adj** **B1** happening or used outside and not in a building: *an outdoor pool* ○ *outdoor activities*
→ Opposite **indoor** adj

outdoors /ˌaʊtˈdɔrz/ **adv** **B1** not inside a building: *If it's warm this evening, we could eat outdoors.*
→ Opposite **indoors** adv

outer /ˈaʊ·tər/ **adj** on the edge or surface of something: *Remove the outer layers of the onion.*
→ Opposite **inner** adj

outfit /ˈaʊtˌfɪt/ **noun** all the clothes you wear at the same time, usually special clothes: *a cowboy outfit*

outgoing /ˈaʊtˌɡoʊ·ɪŋ/ **adj** Someone who is outgoing is friendly, talks a lot, and enjoys meeting people: *Ana is very outgoing, but her sister is shy.*

outgrow /aʊtˈɡroʊ/ **verb** (past tense **outgrew**, past participle **outgrown**) to grow too big for something: *He already outgrew these shoes.*

outlet /ˈaʊt·lɪt/ **noun** a device connected to an electricity system that a plug fits into in order to supply electricity to something: *a wall outlet*
→ See picture at **plug**

outline /ˈaʊtˌlaɪn/ **noun** the shape made by the outside edge of something

out of /ˈaʊt əv/ **preposition** **1 A2** no longer in a particular place or area: *He's out of the country until next month.* **2 B1** used to show movement away from the inside of a place or container: *A pen fell out of her bag.* ○ *She stepped out of the car and walked toward me.* **3 B1** used to show what something is made from: *The dress is made out of silk.*

○ *The statue was carved out of a single block of stone.* **4** (B1) from among an amount or number: *Nine out of ten people said they liked the product.* ○ *No one got 20 out of 20 on the test.* **5 out of order** (B1) If a machine or system is out of order, it is not working: *The coffee machine is out of order.* **6 out of work** (B1) not having a job: *I've been out of work for the last six months.* **7 be out of something** to have no more of something left: *We're almost out of milk.*

out-of-date /ˌaʊt·əvˈdeɪt/ adj (B1) old and no longer useful or correct: *an out-of-date road map*
→ Opposite **up-to-date adj**

outrageous /aʊtˈreɪ·dʒəs/ adj shocking or very unusual: *That's an outrageous thing to say!* ○ *outrageous behavior*

outside¹ /aʊtˈsaɪd/ preposition
1 (A2) near a building or room but not in it: *She waited outside the room for almost two hours.* → Opposite **inside preposition**
2 (A2) not in: *an apartment just outside Boston*

outside² /aʊtˈsaɪd/ adv (A1) not inside a building: *It's cold outside today.*

outside³ /aʊtˈsaɪd/ noun **the outside** the outer part or surface of something: *The outside of the house is very attractive.*
→ Opposite **inside noun**

outside⁴ /aʊtˈsaɪd/ adj not in a building: *an outside light*

the outskirts /ˈaʊtˌskɜrts/ plural noun the outer area of a city or town

outstanding /aʊtˈstæn·dɪŋ/ adj excellent and much better than most: *He was an outstanding football player.*

outward /ˈaʊt·wərd/ adj that you can see: *He was very sick, but there were no outward signs of it.*
→ Opposite **inward adj**

oval /ˈoʊ·vəl/ adj in the shape of an egg
→ See picture at **shape noun**
• **oval noun** an oval shape

oven /ˈʌv·ən/ noun (B1) a piece of kitchen equipment that is used for cooking food: *an electric oven*
→ See **The Kitchen** on page C10

over¹ /ˈoʊ·vər/ adv, preposition
1 (A2) covering someone or something: *I put the blanket over her.* **2** (A2) more than an amount, number, or age: *vitamins for women aged 50 and over* **3** (B1) above or higher than something: *A huge plane flew over our heads.* **4** (B1) from one side of something to the other side: *I climbed over the wall.* **5** (B1) during a particular period of time: *I was in Seattle over the summer.* **6** (B1) on the other side of: *The post office is over the bridge.* **7 over here/there** (B1) in this or that place: *Put your bags down over there.* **8 over and over (again)** happening or done many times: *I read the article over and over until it made sense.* **9** describes the way an object moves or is moved so that a different part of it is facing up: *Flip over the pancakes and cook for one minute.* **10** down from a higher to a lower position: *The little boy fell over and started to cry.*

over² /ˈoʊ·vər/ adj (B1) finished: *Spring semester will be over next week.*

over- /ˈoʊ·vər/ prefix too much: *The children were overexcited (=too excited).*

overall /ˈoʊ·vərˈɔl/ adj considering everything or everyone: *The overall cost of the trip was $1,900.*
• **overall adv** *We lost the first game, but won overall.* ○ *Overall it was a good year.*

overalls /ˈoʊ·vərˌɔlz/ plural noun pants with a part that covers your chest and straps that go over your shoulders

overcoat /ˈoʊ·vərˌkoʊt/ noun a heavy, long coat
→ See **Clothes** on page C5

overcome /ˌoʊ·vərˈkʌm/ verb (present participle **overcoming**, past tense and past participle **overcame**) to deal with and control a problem or feeling: *Eventually she overcame her fear of dogs.*

overflow /ˌoʊ·vərˈfloʊ/ verb If a container or a place overflows, the thing that is inside it starts coming out because it is too full: *I left the faucet on and the bathtub overflowed.*

| æ cat | ɑ hot | e get | ɪ sit | i see | ɔ saw | ʊ book | u too | ʌ cut | ə about | ər mother | ɜr turn | ɔr for | aɪ my | oʊ how | eɪ say | ɔɪ boy |

overhead /ˌoʊ·vərˈhed/ **adj, adv** above your head, usually in the sky: *A bird flew overhead.* ∘ *overhead lights*

overhear /ˌoʊ·vərˈhɪər/ **verb** (past tense and past participle **overheard**) to hear what someone is saying to someone else: *I overheard him telling her he was leaving.*

overlook /ˌoʊ·vərˈlʊk/ **verb** **1** to have a view of something from above: *Our hotel room had a balcony overlooking the sea.* **2** to not notice or consider something: *Two important facts have been overlooked in this case.*

overnight /ˌoʊ·vərˈnaɪt/ **adv** **1** 🅱1 during the night: *We stayed overnight at my grandmother's house.* **2** very quickly or suddenly: *Change does not happen overnight.*

overseas /ˈoʊ·vərˈsiz/ **adj** from another country: *an overseas adoption*
• **overseas adv** *He worked overseas.*

oversleep /ˌoʊ·vərˈslip/ **verb** (past tense and past participle **overslept**) to sleep longer than you wanted to: *Sorry I'm late – I overslept.*

overtime /ˈoʊ·vərˌtaɪm/ **noun** [no plural] extra time that you work after your usual working hours: *I **worked** a lot of **overtime** this week.*

overweight /ˈoʊ·vərˈweɪt/ **adj** weighing more than you should: *He's still a few pounds overweight.*

owe /oʊ/ **verb** (present participle **owing**, past tense and past participle **owed**) **1** 🅱1 to have to pay money back to someone who gave you money in the past: *You still owe me money.* ∘ *He **owes** about $5,000 **to** the bank.* **2** owe someone an apology, explanation, favor, etc. to have to give something to someone because he or she deserves it: *I think I owe you an apology.*

owl[1] /aʊl/ **noun**
a bird that has large eyes and hunts small animals at night

own[1] /oʊn/ **adj, pronoun, determiner**
1 🅰2 belonging to

a particular person: *Each student has his or her own dictionary.* ∘ *Petra makes all her own clothes.* **2** (all) on your own 🅱1 alone: *Jessica lives on her own.* **3** (all) on your own 🅱1 without any help: *I cooked dinner all on my own.*

own[2] /oʊn/ **verb** 🅱1 to have something that belongs to you: *He owns a lot of land.*

owner /ˈoʊ·nər/ **noun** 🅱1 someone who owns something: *car owners*

oxygen /ˈɑk·sɪ·dʒən/ **noun** [no plural] a gas in the air that people and animals need to breathe

oz. written abbreviation for ounce: a unit for measuring weight

the ozone layer /ˈoʊ·zoʊn ˌleɪ·ər/ **noun** the layer of ozone high above the Earth's surface

P p

P, p /pi/ the sixteenth letter of the alphabet

p. written abbreviation for page: *See p. 27.*

pace /peɪs/ **noun** [no plural] how fast someone walks or runs: *We started to walk at a much faster pace.*

pacifier /ˈpæs·əˌfɑɪ·ər/ **noun** a small rubber object that you put in a baby's mouth to stop him or her from crying

pack[1] /pæk/ **verb** **1** 🅰2 to put your things into bags or boxes when you are going on vacation or leaving the place where you live: *I have to go home and pack.* ∘ *She was **packing her bags**.*
→ Opposite **unpack verb** **2** If people pack a place, a lot of them go there: *Thousands of fans packed the stadium.*

pack (something) up phrasal verb to put all your things together when you have finished doing something: *I'm going to pack my stuff up and go home.*

owl

|oʊ go|aɪər fire|aʊər hour|eər hair|ɪər ear|ʊər poor|j yet|ʒ measure|ʃ ship |dʒ judge|tʃ chin|ð that|θ thin|ŋ hang|

pack² /pæk/ **noun** **1** a small box or paper container with a lot of things of the same kind in it: *a **pack of** gum* ◦ *a **pack of** cigarettes* **2** a bag that you carry on your back **3** a group of animals that live together, especially dogs

package /'pæk·ɪdʒ/ **noun** **1** something that is covered in paper so that it can be sent in the mail: *He was carrying a package under his arm.* **2** a related group of things that are offered together as a single unit: *This ski package includes hotel, flights, and four days of skiing.*

packages and packs

package

American Cheese Slices

GUM

packs

a package of cheese

Tissues

packaging /'pæk·ɪ·dʒɪŋ/ **noun** [no plural] the paper, box, plastic, etc., that something is put in so that it can be sold or sent somewhere

packed /pækt/ **adj** A packed place is full of people: *The hall was packed.*

packing /'pæk·ɪŋ/ **noun** [no plural] the act of putting things into bags or boxes so that you can take them somewhere: *I've got to **do** my **packing** because I'm leaving tomorrow.*

pad /pæd/ **noun** **1** pieces of paper that have been attached together at one edge: *There's a pad and pencil by the phone.* **2** a small piece of something soft that is used to protect something: *I wear knee pads when I go skating.*

padded /'pæd·ɪd/ **adj** Padded clothes are covered or filled with something soft, often so that they are warm: *a padded jacket*

paddle¹ /'pæd·ᵊl/ **noun** a short pole with one flat end that you use to make a small boat move through the water

paddle² /'pæd·ᵊl/ **verb** (present participle **paddling**, past tense and past participle **paddled**) to move a small boat through water with a paddle

padlock /'pæd,lɑk/ **noun** a metal lock with a U-shaped part that you use for fastening bicycles, doors, etc.
• **padlock verb**

padlock

page /peɪdʒ/ **noun** **1** **A1** a piece of paper in a book, magazine, etc., or one side of a piece of paper: *The article is on page 36.* ◦ *I've only read 50 pages so far.* **2** **A2** (also **web page**) one part of a website (=area of information on the Internet) that you can see or print separately

paid /peɪd/ past tense and past participle of pay

pail /peɪl/ **noun** a container with an open top and a handle used for carrying liquids

pain /peɪn/ **noun** **1** **A2** a bad feeling in a part of your body when you are sick or hurt: *stomach pains* ◦ *Are you **in pain?*** ◦ *I felt a sharp pain in my foot.* **2** [no plural] sadness: *I can't describe the pain I suffered when he died.* **3** **be a pain (in the neck)** informal to be annoying: *My brother can be a real pain in the neck sometimes.*

painful /'peɪn·fᵊl/ **adj** **1** **B1** causing pain: *a painful injury* ◦ *Oh, that bruise looks painful.* **2** making you feel sad or upset: *a painful memory*

painkiller /'peɪn,kɪl·ᵊr/ **noun** a drug that stops pain

paint¹ /peɪnt/ **noun** **A1** a colored liquid that you put on a surface to decorate it: *Have you chosen the paint for your bedroom?*

paint² /peɪnt/ **verb** **1** **A1** to make a picture of something or someone using paint: *These pictures were all painted by local artists.* **2** **A2** to cover a surface with paint: *We've painted the kitchen yellow.*

paintbrush /ˈpeɪntˌbrʌʃ/ noun
a brush that is used for painting
→ See picture at **brush noun**

painter /ˈpeɪn·tər/ noun **1** A2 someone who paints pictures **2** someone whose job is to paint walls and doors, etc.

painting /ˈpeɪn·t̬ɪŋ/ noun **1** A2 a picture that someone has painted **2** A2 [no plural] the activity of painting pictures or painting surfaces

pair /peər/ noun **1** A1 two people who are doing something together: *For the next exercise, you'll need to work in pairs.* **2** A2 two things that look the same and that are used together: *a pair of socks/shoes* **3** A2 something that is made of two parts that are joined together: *a pair of scissors* ○ *a pair of jeans*

pair

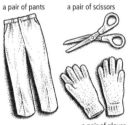

a pair of pants

a pair of scissors

a pair of gloves

pajamas /pəˈdʒɑ·məz/ plural noun
A1 soft clothing that you wear to bed, often a shirt and pants

pal /pæl/ noun infor-
mal a friend: *He's an old pal of mine.*

palace /ˈpæl·əs/ noun B1 a large house where a king or queen lives: *Buckingham Palace*

pale /peɪl/ adj **1** pale blue, green, red, etc. light blue, green, red, etc.: *a pale yellow dress* **2** If your face is pale, it has less color than usual because you are sick: *You look kind of pale – are you all right?*

palm /pɑm/ noun **1** the inside surface of your hand → See **The Body** on page C2 **2** a palm tree

palm tree /ˈpɑm ˌtri/ noun a tall tree with long leaves at the top that grows in hot countries

pan /pæn/ noun B1 a metal container with a handle that is used for cooking food in

pancake /ˈpæn̩keɪk/ noun a thin, flat cake that you cook in a pan

panda /ˈpæn·də/
noun a large, black and white animal that lives in forests in China

panda

pane /peɪn/ noun
a flat piece of glass in a window or door

panel /ˈpæn·ᵊl/ noun **1** a flat piece of wood, metal, etc. that is the surface of a door, wall, etc. **2** a group of people who are chosen to talk about something or make a decision about something: *a panel of experts*

pang /pæŋ/ noun a sudden, strong feeling: *hunger pangs*

panic¹ /ˈpæn·ɪk/ noun a sudden, strong feeling of fear that makes you stop thinking clearly and do silly things: *He was in a panic about his final exams.*

panic² /ˈpæn·ɪk/ verb (present participle **panicking**, past tense and past participle **panicked**) to suddenly feel very afraid so that you stop thinking clearly and do silly things: *Don't panic – we've got plenty of time.*

pant /pænt/ verb to breathe quickly and loudly because you have been exercising

panties /ˈpæn·tiz/ plural noun underwear worn by women and girls
→ See **Clothes** on page C5

pants /pænts/ plural noun A1 a piece of clothing that covers the legs and has a separate part for each leg
→ See picture at **pair noun**
→ See **Clothes** on page C5

⚠ Common mistake: pants

Pants is a plural word.
These pants are too big for me.

---

pantyhose /'pæn·ti·houz/ **plural noun**
a piece of women's clothing made of
very thin material that covers the legs
and bottom
→ See **Clothes** on page C5

paper /'peɪ·pər/ **noun** **1** **A1** [no plural]
thin, flat material used for writing on:
Have you got a piece of paper? **2** **B1** a
newspaper: *I buy a paper every morning.*
3 **B1** a written assignment: *Have you
finished writing your history paper yet?*

paperback /'peɪ·pər,bæk/ **noun** a book
that has a soft paper cover

paper clip /'peɪ·pər ˌklɪp/
noun a small piece of
metal used to hold pieces
of paper together

paper clips

parachute
/'pær·əˌʃut/ **noun** a
large piece of cloth
that is attached to
your body with
strings and helps
you to drop safely
from a plane

parachute

parade /pə'reɪd/
noun an event
where lines of peo-
ple walk through a
public place to celebrate
a special day: *a victory parade*

paradise /'pær·əˌdaɪs/ **noun** [no plural]
1 in some religions, a place where good
people go after they die **2** a perfect
place or situation: *a tropical paradise*

paragraph /'pær·əˌgræf/ **noun**
B1 a group of sentences that are
together and start on a new line

parallel /'pær·əˌlel/ **adj** If two or more
lines are parallel, the distance between
them is the same along all their length:
The streets are parallel.

paralyze /'pær·əˌlaɪz/ **verb** (present participle **paralyzing**, past tense and past participle
paralyzed) to make someone unable
to move all or part of his or her body:
*He was paralyzed from the waist down in
the accident.*

paramedic /ˌpær·ə'med·ɪk/ **noun**
someone who is not a doctor or nurse
but who is trained to help people who
are injured or very sick, until they get
to a hospital

pardon /'pɑr·dən/ **exclamation**
1 pardon (me)? a polite way of asking
someone to say again what he or she
has just said: *"You'll need an umbrella."
"Pardon me?" "I said you'll need an umbrella."* **2 pardon me** used to say
"sorry" after you have done something
rude, for example after burping (=let-
ting air from your stomach out of your
mouth)

parent /'peər·ənt/ **noun** **A1** someone's
mother or father: *Her parents live in Ohio.*

> **!** Common mistake: **parents** or
> **relations/relatives**?
>
> Your **parents** are only your mother
> and father. The other people in your
> family are **relations** or **relatives**.
> *We spent the holidays visiting all our
> relatives.*
> *We spent the holidays visiting all our
> parents.*

parentheses /pə'ren·θə·siz/ **plural noun**
two curved lines ( ) used around extra
information in a sentence: *The age of
each student is listed **in parentheses**.*

parenthood /'peər·ənt,hʊd/ **noun** [no
plural] the state of being a parent: *I am
not ready for parenthood.*

park[1] /pɑrk/ **noun** **A1** a large area of
grass, often in a town, where people can
walk and enjoy themselves: *We went for
a walk in the park.*

park[2] /pɑrk/ **verb** **A2** to leave a car in a
place for a period of time: *You can park
outside the school.*

parking /'pɑr·kɪŋ/ **noun** [no plural]
B1 leaving a car in a place for a period
of time: *free parking*

parking garage /'pɑr·kɪŋ gə'rɑʒ/ **noun**
a building or an underground structure
where you can leave your car for a short
time

parking lot /ˈpɑr·kɪŋ ˌlɑt/ *noun*
A2 an area of ground where you can leave your car for a short time

parking meter /ˈpɑr·kɪŋ ˌmi·tər/ *noun*
a machine at the side of the road that you put money into so that you can leave your vehicle on that road

parliament /ˈpɑr·lə·mənt/ *noun*
in some countries, a group of people who make the laws for the country: *the Russian parliament*

parochial school /pəˈrou·ki·əl ˌskul/ *noun*   a school that is controlled by a church or religious organization

parrot /ˈpær·ət/ *noun*   **B1** a brightly colored bird that can copy what people say

parsley /ˈpɑr·sli/ *noun* [no plural]   a plant that you add to food to give it flavor

part[1] /pɑrt/ *noun*   **1** **A1** one of the things that, with other things, makes the whole of something: *Part of this form seems to be missing.* ○ *That's only part of the problem.* ○ *You're part of the family.*   **2** *part of something* **A2** some but not all of a thing: *Kate spent part of the day shopping.*   **3** **B1** a person in a movie or play: *He **plays** the **part** of the father.* **take part (in something)** **B1** to do an activity with other people: *She doesn't usually take part in any class activities.*   **5** a piece of a machine or vehicle: *car parts*   **6** *have/play a part in something* to be one of the people or things that are involved in an event or situation: *We can all play a part in making our city a better place to live.*   **7** a line on someone's head made by brushing the hair in two different directions

part[2] /pɑrt/ *verb*
part with something *phrasal verb* to give something to someone else, often when you do not want to: *It is so hard to get Shaun to part with his money.*

partial /ˈpɑr·ʃəl/ *adj*   not complete: *He made a partial recovery.*

partially /ˈpɑr·ʃə·li/ *adv*   not completely: *The ham was only partially cooked.*

participant /pɑrˈtɪs·ə·pənt/ *noun*
someone who does an activity with

other people: *All participants finishing the race will receive a medal.*

participate /pɑrˈtɪs·əˌpeɪt/ *verb* (present participle **participating**, past tense and past participle **participated**)   to do an activity with other people: *She rarely **participates in** any of the discussions.*

participation /pɑrˌtɪs·əˈpeɪ·ʃən/ *noun*
[no plural]   the act of doing an activity with other people: *Both shows encourage audience participation.*

participle /ˈpɑr·tə·sɪp·əl/ *noun*
in grammar, the form of a verb that usually ends with "-ed" or "-ing" and is used in some verb tenses

particle /ˈpɑr·tɪ·kəl/ *noun*   a very small piece of something: *particles of dust*

particular /pərˈtɪk·jə·lər/ *adj*   **1** used to talk about one thing or person and not others: *Is there any particular restaurant you'd like to go to?* ○ *"Why did you ask?" "No particular reason."*   **2** special: *"Was anything important said at the meeting?" "Nothing of particular interest."*   **3 in particular** **B1** especially: *Are you looking for anything in particular?*

particularly /pərˈtɪk·jə·lər·li/ *adv*
B1 especially: *She didn't seem particularly interested.* ○ *"Was the food good?" "Not particularly."*

partly /ˈpɑrt·li/ *adv*   **B1** to some degree but not completely: *The house is partly owned by her father.*

partner /ˈpɑrt·nər/ *noun*   **1** **A2** someone that you are dancing or playing a sport or game with   **2** **B1** someone that you are married to or having a sexual relationship with: *Are partners invited to the office dinner?*   **3** someone who owns a business with another person: *He's a **partner in** a law firm.*

partnership /ˈpɑrt·nərˌʃɪp/ *noun*
a situation in which two people or organizations work together to achieve something: *She has a **business partnership** with someone she used to work with.*

part of speech /ˈpɑrt əv ˌspitʃ/ *noun*
one of the grammatical groups into which words are divided, such as noun, verb, and adjective

part-time /ˈpɑrtˌtaɪm/ **adj, adv**

B1 working or studying only for part of the day or the week: *a part-time job*

party /ˈpɑr·t̬i/ **noun** (plural **parties**)

1 **A1** an event where people come together to enjoy themselves by talking, eating, drinking, and dancing: *a birthday party* ○ *We're **having** a **party** to celebrate the occasion.* **2** **B1** an organization that has the same political beliefs and tries to win elections: *a political party* **3** a group of people who are working or traveling together: *a party of tourists*

pass[1] /pæs/ **verb** **1** **A2** to succeed on a test or an exam, or in a class: *I passed my driving test the first time.* **2** **B1** to go past something or someone: *She passed me this morning on the street.* ○ *Cars kept passing us on the highway.* **3** **B1** to go in a particular direction: *Another plane **passed over** our heads.* ○ *We **pass through** your neighborhood on the way home.* **4** **B1** to give something to someone: *Could you pass the salt, please?* **5** **B1** If a period of time passes, it happens: *Four years have passed since that day.* **6** **pass (the) time** to spend time doing something: *We played a few games to pass the time.* **7** pass a law, measure, etc. to officially approve something and make it into a law or rule: *The government passed a law to restrict the sale of guns.* **8** in sports, to throw or kick a ball to someone else: *Edwards **passes to** Brinkworth.*

pass *something* **around** phrasal verb to offer something to each person in a group of people: *Could you pass these sandwiches around, please?*

pass away phrasal verb to die: *She passed away peacefully in her sleep.*

pass *something* **on** phrasal verb **1** **B1** to tell someone something that someone else has told you: *Did you pass on my message to him?* **2** **B1** to give something to someone else: *Will you pass the book on to Lara when you're done with it?*

pass out phrasal verb to become unconscious: *I don't remember any more because I passed out at that point.*

pass[2] /pæs/ **noun** **1** **B1** an official paper that allows you to do something: *You need a pass to get into the building.* **2** a successful result on a test or in a class: *A pass is above 60%.* **3** in sports, an occasion when you throw or kick a ball to someone else

passage /ˈpæs·ɪdʒ/ **noun** **1** a long, thin space that connects one place to another: *There's a passage to the side of the house, leading to the garden.* **2** a short part of a book or speech: *She read a passage from the novel.*

passenger /ˈpæs·ən·dʒər/ **noun**

A2 someone who is traveling in a car, plane, etc., but not controlling the car, plane, etc.: *a car's passenger side* ○ *The plane can carry 360 passengers.*

passion /ˈpæʃ·ən/ **noun** **1** [no plural] a strong, sexual feeling for someone: *She saw the passion in his eyes.* **2** a very strong feeling about a subject: *She spoke with passion about the injustice.*

passionate /ˈpæʃ·ə·nət/ **adj** **1** having a strong, sexual feeling for someone: *They had a passionate love affair.* **2** showing a strong feeling about a subject: *She was a passionate speaker.*

• **passionately** adv

passive /ˈpæs·ɪv/ **adj** **1** **B1** In grammar, a passive verb or sentence is one in which the subject does not do the action. For example "It was written by a child" is a passive sentence. **2** letting things happen to you and not taking action: *He's very passive in the relationship.*

the passive /ˈpæs·ɪv/ **noun** [no plural]

B1 in grammar, the passive form of a verb

passport /ˈpæsˌpɔrt/ **noun** **A2** a small book with your photograph that you need to enter a country: *a Mexican passport*

password /ˈpæsˌwɜrd/ **noun**

B1 a secret word that allows you to do something, especially to use your computer: *Type in your password.*

past[1] /pæst/ **adv, preposition**

1 **A2** farther than: *I live on Maple Street,*

a
b
c
d
e
f
g
h
i
j
k
l
m
n
o
p
q
r
s
t
u
v
w
x
y
z

just past the high school. **2** **A2** up to and farther than someone or something: *Three boys went past us on mountain bikes.* ○ *I just saw the bus go past.* **3** above a particular age or farther than a particular point: *She's past the age where she needs a babysitter.*

past² /pæst/ adj **1** **B1** having happened or existed before now: *past relationships* ○ *I know this from past experience.* **2** **B1** used to refer to a period of time in the past that lasts until the present: *It's been raining for the past three days.*

past³ /pæst/ noun **1 the past** **A2** the time before the present and all the things that happened then: *In the past people would bathe once a month.* **2 the past** (also **the past tense**) **B1** in grammar, the form of a verb that is used to show what happened in the past **3** *someone's* **past** **B1** all of the things that someone has done in his or her life: *I knew nothing about his past.*

pasta /ˈpɑːstə/ noun [no plural] **A2** a food that is made from flour and water, and is made in many different shapes: *Spaghetti is my favorite pasta.*
→ See **Food** on page C7

paste¹ /peɪst/ noun [no plural] a wet, sticky substance that is used to stick things together: *wallpaper paste*

paste² /peɪst/ verb (present participle **pasting**, past tense and past participle **pasted**) to stick a piece of paper to another piece of paper: *He had pasted the pictures into a book.*

past participle /ˌpæst ˈpɑːrtəˌsɪpəl/ noun in grammar, the form of a verb that usually ends with "-ed." For example, "walked" is the past participle of "walk."

the past perfect /ˌpæst ˈpɜːrfɪkt/ noun in grammar, the form of a verb that is used to show that an action was already finished when another action happened. The sentence "I had never been to Canada" is in the past perfect.

pastry /ˈpeɪstri/ noun **1** [no plural] a food made of flour, fat, and water that you cook and use for covering or containing

other food **2** (plural **pastries**) a type of baked food like a small cake

pat¹ /pæt/ verb (present participle **patting**, past tense and past participle **patted**) to touch a person or animal with a flat hand in a gentle, friendly way: *She stopped to pat the dog.*

pat² /pæt/ noun a gentle, friendly touch with a flat hand

patch /pætʃ/ noun **1** a small area that is different from the area around it: *There are icy patches on the road.* **2** a piece of material that you use to cover a hole in your clothes or in other material **3** a **bad/rough patch** a difficult time: *Their marriage is going through a bad patch.*

paternal /pəˈtɜːrnəl/ adj **1** like a father: *paternal affection* **2** A paternal relation is part of your father's family: *He was my paternal grandfather.*

path /pæθ/ noun **A2** a long, thin area of ground for people to walk on: *There's a path through the forest.* ○ *a garden path*

pathetic /pəˈθetɪk/ adj informal bad and showing that you have not tried or are not brave: *He made a pathetic attempt to apologize.*

patience /ˈpeɪʃəns/ noun [no plural] the ability to stay calm and not get upset, especially when something takes a long time: *It takes patience to learn an instrument.* ○ *Finally, I lost my patience and shouted at her.*

patient¹ /ˈpeɪʃənt/ adj **B1** able to stay calm and not get upset, especially when something takes a long time: *You need to be patient with children.*
• **patiently** adv
→ Opposite **impatient** adj

patient² /ˈpeɪʃənt/ noun **B1** someone who is being treated by a doctor, nurse, etc.: *a cancer patient*

patio /ˈpætiˌoʊ/ noun an area outside a house with a hard floor, where people can sit to eat and relax: *Let's have lunch on the patio.*

patriotic /ˌpeɪtriˈɑːtɪk/ adj showing that you love your country and think it is very good: *a patriotic song*

patrol¹ /pəˈtroʊl/ **noun**   the act of looking for trouble or danger around an area or building: *We passed a group of soldiers **on patrol**.*

patrol² /pəˈtroʊl/ **verb** (present participle **patrolling**, past tense and past participle **patrolled**)   to look for trouble or danger in an area or around a building: *Police patrol the streets night and day.*

pattern /ˈpæt̬·ərn/ **noun**   **1** 🅱1 a design of lines, shapes, colors, etc.: *The shirt has a pattern on it.*   **2** a particular way that something is often done or repeated: *behavior patterns*   **3** a drawing, shape, or set of instructions that helps you to make something: *a dress pattern*

pause¹ /pɔz/ **verb** (present participle **pausing**, past tense and past participle **paused**)   **1** 🅱1 to stop doing something for a short time: *She **paused for** a moment and looked around her.*   **2** to make a CD, DVD, etc. stop for a short time by pressing a button: *Can you pause the movie there, please?*

pause² /pɔz/ **noun**   a short time during which you stop doing something before starting again: *There was a short pause before he spoke.*

pavement /ˈpeɪv·mənt/ **noun**   the hard surface of a road

paw /pɔ/ **noun**   the foot of an animal, such as a cat or a dog

pay¹ /peɪ/ **verb** (present participle **paying**, past tense and past participle **paid**)   **1** 🅰1 to give money to someone because you are buying something from him or her: *Helen **paid for** the tickets.*   **2** 🅱1 to give someone money for the work that he or she does: *She **gets paid** twice a month.* ○ *We **paid** them $600 **for** the work.*   **3 pay attention** 🅱1 to look at or listen to someone or something carefully: *I missed what she was saying because I wasn't paying attention.*
pay someone/something back phrasal verb 🅱1 to pay someone the money that you owe him or her: *Has he paid you back the money he owes you?*

pay off phrasal verb   If something you have done pays off, it is successful: *All her hard work paid off and she passed the exam.*

pay something off phrasal verb   to pay all of the money that you owe: *I'm planning to pay off my bank loan in five years.*

> ⚠ **Common mistake: pay for something**
>
> Remember that when **pay** means "give money to buy something," it is usually followed by the preposition **for**.
>
> *Rachel paid for the meal.*
> ~~*Rachel paid the meal.*~~

pay² /peɪ/ **noun** [no plural]   🅱1 the money that you get for working: *a pay raise*

payment /ˈpeɪ·mənt/ **noun**   **1** [no plural] the act of paying: *They will accept payment by credit card.*   **2** the amount of money that is paid: *monthly payments*

pay phone /ˈpeɪ ˌfoʊn/ **noun**   a telephone in a public place that you pay to use

PC /ˌpiˈsi/ **noun**   🅰2 a personal computer (=a computer for one person to use)

P.E. **noun** [no plural]   abbreviation for physical education: classes at school where children do exercises and play sports

pea /pi/ **noun**   🅱1 a small, round, green seed that people eat as a vegetable

peace /pis/ **noun** [no plural]   **1** 🅱1 a situation in which there is quiet and calm: *After a busy day, all I want is **peace and quiet**.*   **2** a situation in which there is no war, violence, or arguing: *There seems little hope for world peace.*

peaceful /ˈpis·fəl/ **adj**   **1** 🅱1 quiet and calm: *The park was quiet and peaceful.*   **2** without violence: *a peaceful protest*   • **peacefully** adv *He died peacefully at home.*

peach /pitʃ/ **noun**   🅱1 a soft, sweet, round fruit with red and yellow skin

| æ cat | ɑ hot | e get | ɪ sit | i see | ɔ saw | ʊ book | u too | ʌ cut | ə about | ər mother | ɜr turn | ɔr for | aɪ my | aʊ how | eɪ say | ɔɪ boy |

a b c d e f g h i j k l m n o **p** q r s t u v w x y z

peacock /ˈpiːˌkɑk/ **noun** a large, male bird with long, brightly colored tail feathers

peak /piːk/ **noun** **1** **B1** the top of a mountain: *snow-covered peaks* **2** the highest level or value of something: *House prices have probably **reached** their **peak**.* ∘ *peak travel times*

peak

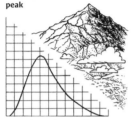

peanut /ˈpiˌnʌt/ **noun** **B1** an oval-shaped nut with a soft, brown shell
→ See **Food** on page C7

peanut butter /ˈpiˌnʌtˌbʌtˌər/ **noun** [no plural] a soft brown food made from peanuts that is often eaten on bread: *a peanut butter sandwich*

pear /peər/ **noun** **A2** an oval-shaped green or yellow fruit
→ See **Fruits and Vegetables** on page C8

pearl /pɜrl/ **noun** a hard, white, round object that is made inside the shell of a sea creature and that is used to make jewelry: *a string of pearls*

pebble /ˈpebˌəl/ **noun** a small stone

pecan /pɪˈkɑn/, /pɪˈkæn/ **noun** a sweet brown nut that is in two halves inside a smooth shell

peck /pek/ **verb** If a bird pecks something, it quickly bites it: *chickens **pecking at** grain*

peculiar /pɪˈkjuljər/ **adj** strange, often in a bad way: *a peculiar smell*

pedal /ˈpedˌəl/ **noun** a part of a machine that you press with your foot: *bicycle pedals*

pedestrian /pəˈdesˌtriˌən/ **noun** **B1** a person who is walking, not driving

peel[1] /piːl/ **verb** **B1** to take off the skin of fruit or vegetables: *Peel and chop the onions.*

peel[2] /piːl/ **noun** [no plural] the skin of fruit or vegetables: *orange peel*

peep[1] /piːp/ **verb** to quickly look at something, often when you do not want other people to see you: *She peeped at them through the fence.*

peep[2] /piːp/ **noun** [no plural] a quick look: *She **took a peep** at herself in the mirror.*

peer /pɪər/ **verb** to look carefully or with difficulty: *She peered at me over her glasses.*

peg /peg/ **noun** an object on a wall or door that you hang things on

pen /pen/ **noun** **A1** a long, thin object that you use to write or draw in ink
→ See **The Classroom** on page C4

penalty /ˈpenˌəlˌti/ **noun** (plural **penalties**) **1** a punishment for doing something that is against a law or rule: *There's a $50 penalty for late cancellation of tickets.* **2** in sports, an advantage given to a team when the other team has broken a rule: *They won a penalty in the first five minutes of the game.*

pencil /ˈpenˌsəl/ **noun** **A1** a long, thin wooden object with a black or colored point that you write or draw with
→ See **The Classroom** on page C4

pencil sharpener /ˈpenˌsəlˌʃɑrpəˌnər/ **noun** a tool that you use to make pencils sharp
→ See **The Classroom** on page C4

penguin /ˈpeŋˌgwɪn/ **noun** **B1** a large, black and white sea bird that swims and cannot fly

penicillin /ˌpenəˈsɪlˌən/ **noun** [no plural] a type of medicine that kills bacteria and is used to treat illness

penis /ˈpiˌnɪs/ **noun** the part of a man's or male animal's body that is used for having sex

penny /ˈpenˌi/ **noun** (**pennies**) **B1** a coin with a value of 1 cent (=1/100 of a dollar): *There are 100 pennies in a dollar.*

pension /'pen·ʃən/ noun   money that is
given to a person who has stopped
working because he or she is old or ill

people /'pi·pəl/ noun   **A1** more than
one person: *Our company employs over
400 people.*

pepper /'pep·ər/ noun   **1** [no plural] a
powder that is made from seeds, used to
give food a slightly spicy flavor: *salt and
pepper*   **2** a green, red, or yellow vegetable that can be eaten raw or cooked
→ See **Fruits and Vegetables** on page C8

peppermint /'pep·ər,mɪnt/ noun [no
plural]   oil from a plant that is added to
food to give it a strong, fresh taste

per /pər/ preposition   **A2** for each: *The
hotel room costs $60 per night.*

percent /pər'sent/ adj, adv   **B1** out of
every 100, shown by the symbol %: *a 40
percent increase in prices*

percentage /pər'sen·tɪdʒ/ noun
an amount of something, shown as a
number out of 100: *The percentage of
women who work has increased.*

perfect /'pɜr·fɪkt/ adj   **1** **A2** without
fault, or the best possible: *a perfect day*
◦ *He was **the perfect** father.*   **2** complete
and correct in every way: *She got a **perfect score** on the test.*   **3** exactly right
for someone or something: *You'd be **perfect** for the job.*

perfection /pər'fek·ʃən/ noun [no plural]
a state of having no mistakes, faults, or
damage: *We ask the children to do their
best but we don't expect perfection.*

perfectly /'pɜr·fɪkt·li/ adv   **1** **B1** in a
perfect way: *The jacket fits perfectly.*
2 very: *I made my feelings perfectly clear.*

perform /pər'fɔrm/ verb   **1** **A1** to act,
sing, dance, or play music for other people to enjoy: *The orchestra will perform
music by Mozart.*   **2** formal to do a job or
a piece of work: *Surgeons performed the
operation in less than two hours.*   **3** to
succeed or not succeed: *Neither company has performed well this year.*

performance /pər'fɔr·məns/ noun
1 **B1** acting, singing, dancing, or playing
music for other people to enjoy: *a performance of Shakespeare's "Hamlet"*   **2** [no
plural] how successful someone or something is: *The company's performance was
poor for the first two years.*

performer /pər'fɔr·mər/ noun
B1 someone who acts, sings, dances, or
plays music for other people to enjoy

perfume /'pɜr·fjum/ noun   **A2** a liquid
with a nice smell that women put on their
skin

perhaps /pər'hæps/ adv   **A2** possibly:
Perhaps I'll go to the gym after work.
◦ *Perhaps Ben will come.*

period /'pɪr·i·əd/ noun   **1** **B1** a length of
time: *a 24-hour period* ◦ *a period of four
months*   **2** **B1** in a school, one of the
parts of the day when a subject is taught:
We have six periods of science a week.
3 **B1** the punctuation mark [.] that is put
at the end of a sentence, or at the end of
a word that has been shortened

permanent /'pɜr·mə·nənt/ adj
B1 continuing always or for a long time:
She found a permanent job.
• **permanently** adv

permission /pər'mɪʃ·ən/ noun [no plural]
B1 the act of allowing someone to do
something: *I had to **get permission** to
use the car.* ◦ *He took the car **without
permission**.*

permit[1] /pər'mɪt/ verb (present participle
permitting, past tense and past participle
permitted) formal   **B1** to allow
something: *Photography is not permitted
inside the museum.*

permit[2] /'pɜr·mɪt/ noun   a paper that allows you to do something: *a work permit*

person /'pɜr·sən/ noun (plural **people**)
1 **A1** a human being: *You're the only
person I know here.*   **2 in person** If you
do something in person, you go somewhere to do it yourself: *You have to pick
up the document in person.*

personal /'pɜr·sə·nᵊl/ adj   **1** **B1** belonging to a particular person: *Please take all
personal belongings with you when you*

a
b
c
d
e
f
g
h
i
j
k
l
m
n
o
p
q
r
s
t
u
v
w
x
y
z

leave the train. **2** **B1** connected with relationships and feelings and the private parts of someone's life: *He is one of her personal problems right now.* **3** **B1** designed for or used by one person: *a personal computer*

personality /ˌpɜr·sə'næl·ɪ·t̬i/ **noun** (plural **personalities**) **1** the qualities that make one person different from another: *She has a lovely, warm personality.* **2** a famous person: *He is a well-known TV personality.*

personally /'pɜr·sə·nᵊl·i/ **adv** **1** done by you and not someone else: *I'd like to personally apologize for the delay.* **2** **B1** used when you are saying your opinion: *Personally, I don't like the man.*

personnel /ˌpɜr·sə'nel/ **plural noun** the people who work for an organization: *military personnel*

perspective /pər'spek·tɪv/ **noun** the way you think about something: *Being unemployed has made me see things from a different perspective.*

persuade /pər'sweɪd/ **verb** (present participle **persuading**, past tense and past participle **persuaded**) **1** **B1** to make someone agree to do something by talking to him or her a lot about it: *We managed to persuade him to come with us.* **2** to make someone believe that something is true: *You won't be able to persuade him that you're innocent.*

pessimist /'pes·ə·mɪst/ **noun** someone who always thinks that bad things will happen: *Don't be such a pessimist!*
→ Opposite **optimist** noun

pessimistic /ˌpes·ə'mɪs·tɪk/ **adj** always believing that bad things will happen: *He was feeling pessimistic about the future.*
→ Opposite **optimistic** adj

pest /pest/ **noun** **1** an animal that causes damage to plants, food, etc.: *garden pests* **2** informal an annoying person

pet /pet/ **noun** **A1** an animal that someone keeps in his or her home: *my pet rabbit*

petal /'pet̬·ᵊl/ **noun** one of the colored parts on the outside of a flower: *rose petals*

petition /pə'tɪʃ·ən/ **noun** a paper with a lot of people's names on it that asks someone in authority to do something: *Will you sign this petition against experiments on animals?*

pharmacist /'far·mə·sɪst/ **noun** someone who prepares or sells medicines

pharmacy /'far·mə·si/ **noun** (plural **pharmacies**) **B1** a store that prepares and sells medicines

phase /feɪz/ **noun** a stage or period that is part of a longer period: *The first phase of the project has been completed.*

Ph.D. noun abbreviation for doctor of philosophy: the highest degree that a college or university gives: *Maria Lopez, Ph.D.* ∘ *Maria has a Ph.D. in math.*

philosopher /fɪ'las·ə·fər/ **noun** someone who studies or writes about the meaning of life

philosophy /fɪ'las·ə·fi/ **noun** [no plural] the study or writing of ideas about the meaning of life

phone /foʊn/ **noun** (also **telephone**) **1** **A1** a piece of equipment that is used to talk to someone who is in another place: *Would you please answer the phone?* ∘ *I could hear the phone ringing.* **2** on **the phone** using the phone: *She's been on the phone all night.*

phone book /'foʊn ˌbʊk/ **noun** a book that has the telephone numbers of people who live in an area

phone call /'foʊn ˌkɔl/ **noun** an act of using the telephone: *I've got to make a phone call.*

phone number /'foʊn ˌnʌm·bər/ **noun** the number of a particular telephone

phonetic /fə'net̬·ɪk/ **adj** relating to the sounds you make when you speak: *the international phonetic alphabet*

photo /'foʊ·t̬oʊ/ **noun** **A1** a picture made with a camera: *I took a photo of Jack lying on the beach.*

photocopier /'fou·təˌkɑp·i·ər/ noun
a machine that makes copies of papers with writing on them by photographing them

photocopy /'fout·əˌkɑp·i/ noun (plural **photocopies**) **B1** a copy of a paper made with a photocopier: *I made a photocopy of my letter before sending it.*
• **photocopy** verb (present participle **photocopying**, past tense and past participle **photocopied**)

photograph¹ /'fou·təˌgræf/ noun **A2** a picture made with a camera: *He took a lovely photograph of the children.*

photograph² /'fou·təˌgræf/ verb to take a photograph of someone or something: *They were photographed leaving a nightclub together.*

photographer /fə'tɑg·rə·fər/ noun
A2 someone whose job is to take photographs

photography /fə'tɑg·rə·fi/ noun [no plural] **A2** the activity or job of taking photographs

phrasal verb /'frei·zəl 'vɜrb/ noun **B1** a verb that has two or three words. For example, "look up" and "come from" are phrasal verbs.
→ See **Phrasal Verbs** on page C13

phrase /freiz/ noun **B1** a group of words that are often used together and have a particular meaning

physical /'fiz·ɪ·kəl/ adj **1** relating to the body: *physical strength* **2** relating to real things that you can see and touch: *a physical object*

physical education /'fiz·ɪ·kəl ˌed·ʒ·u'kei·ʃən/ noun [no plural] classes at school where children exercise and play sports

physically /'fiz·ɪ·kli/ adv in a way that relates to the body: *He is physically fit.*

physicist /'fiz·ə·sɪst/ noun someone who studies physics

physics /'fiz·ɪks/ noun [no plural] **A2** the scientific study of natural forces, such as energy, heat, light, etc.

piano /pi'æn·ou/ noun **A2** a big, wooden musical instrument with black and white bars that make sounds when you press them

piano

pick¹ /pɪk/ verb **1** **B1** to choose something or someone: *He was picked for the school football team.* **2** **B1** If you pick flowers, fruit, etc., you take them off a tree or out of the ground: *I picked some apples this morning.*

pick on *someone* phrasal verb to treat one person badly in a group of people: *He started picking on me for no reason.*

pick *something/someone* **up** phrasal verb **1** to lift something or someone by using your hands: *He picked his coat up off the floor.* → See **Phrasal Verbs** on page C13 **2** **B1** to go somewhere in order to get someone or something: *Can you pick me up from the airport?*

pick *something* **up** phrasal verb **A2** to learn a new skill or language by practicing it, not by studying it: *When you live in a country you soon pick up the language.*

pick² /pɪk/ noun [no plural] **take your pick** to choose what you want: *We've got tea, coffee, or cocoa – take your pick.*

pickpocket /'pɪkˌpɑk·ɪt/ noun someone who steals things from people's pockets

picnic /'pɪk·nɪk/ noun **A1** food that you take from your home to eat outside: *We're going to have a picnic by the lake.*

picture¹ /'pɪk·tʃər/ noun **1** **A1** a drawing, painting, or photograph of something or someone: *She has pictures of pop*

a b c d e f g h i j k l m n o p q r s t u v w x y z

stars all over her bedroom. ○ *Did you **take
many pictures** (=photograph many things)
while you were at the Grand Canyon?*
2 🅱 a movie: *It won an Oscar for best
picture.* **3** an idea of what something is
like: *After watching the news, I have a
clearer **picture** of what is happening.*

picture² /ˈpɪk·tʃər/ *verb* (present participle
picturing, past tense and past participle
pictured) to imagine something in a
particular way: *The house was very different from how I pictured it.*

pie /paɪ/ *noun*
🅰 a type of food
made with meat,
vegetables, or fruit
that is covered in
pastry and baked:
an apple pie

pie

piece /piːs/ *noun* **1** 🅰 an amount of
something, or a part of something: *a
piece of paper* ○ *She cut the cake into
eight pieces.* → See **Quantities** on page C14
2 🅰 one of a particular type of thing: *a
piece of equipment* ○ *an old piece of furniture* **3** 🅱 a single amount of a particular type of thing: *I have an interesting
piece of information for you.* **4** something that has been created by an artist,
musician, or writer: *a beautiful **piece** of
music* **5 fall to pieces** to break into
smaller parts: *These shoes are falling to
pieces.*

pier /pɪər/ *noun* a long structure that is
built from the land out over water: *We
went for a walk along the pier.*

pierce /pɪərs/ *verb* (present participle
piercing, past tense and past participle
pierced) to make a hole in something
using a sharp point: *I got my ears
pierced.*

pig /pɪg/ *noun* **1** 🅰 a large, often pink
farm animal that is kept for its meat
2 *informal* someone who is very unpleasant, or someone who eats a lot

pigeon /ˈpɪdʒ·ən/ *noun* a gray bird that
often lives on buildings in towns

piglet /ˈpɪg·lət/ *noun* a baby pig

pile¹ /paɪl/ *noun* **1** 🅱 something in the
shape of a small hill, or a

number of things on top of each other:
*There was a big **pile** of dirt in the garden.*
○ *The clothes were arranged in piles on
the floor.* **2** a pile of/piles of *something*
informal a lot of something: *He has piles of
money.*

pile² /paɪl/ *verb* (present participle **piling**,
past tense and past participle **piled**)

pile up *phrasal verb* If something unpleasant piles up, you get more and
more of it.: *My work's really starting to
pile up.*

pile *something* **up** *phrasal verb* to make
a lot of things into a pile by putting
them on top of each other: *Just pile
those books up over there.*

pilgrim /ˈpɪl·grəm/ *noun* someone who
travels to a place that is important in
his or her religion

pill /pɪl/ *noun* 🅱 a small, round, hard
piece of medicine that you swallow

pillar /ˈpɪl·ər/ *noun* a tall structure
made of stone, wood, etc. that supports
something above it: *The new bridge will
be supported by 100 concrete pillars.*

pillow /ˈpɪl·oʊ/ *noun* 🅰 a soft object
that you put your head on in bed

pillow — pillow
cushion

pilot /ˈpaɪ·lət/ *noun* 🅰 someone who
flies a plane

pimple /ˈpɪm·pəl/ *noun* a small red
lump on your skin

pin¹ /pɪn/ *noun* **1** 🅱 a thin piece of
metal with a sharp point used to fasten
pieces of cloth together or to fasten an
object to cloth: *She pricked her finger on
a pin.* **2** a piece of jewelry or another
small object that is fastened to clothes
with a pin: *a gold butterfly pin*

pin² /pɪn/ *verb* (present participle **pinning**,
past tense and past participle **pinned**)

B1 to fasten something with a pin: *She had a ribbon **pinned to** her jacket.*

PIN /pɪn/ *noun* abbreviation for personal identification number: a number that no one else knows that allows you to use a plastic card to pay for things or get money from a bank

pinch[1] /pɪntʃ/ *verb* to press someone's skin between your thumb and finger, sometimes causing pain: *Her brother had pinched her and she was crying.*

pinch[2] /pɪntʃ/ *noun* a very small amount of something: *a pinch of salt*
→ See **Quantities** on page C14

pine /paɪn/ *noun* (also **pine tree**) a tall tree with long, thin leaves shaped like needles

pineapple /ˈpaɪˌnæp·əl/ *noun* **B1** a large fruit with leaves sticking out of the top that is sweet and yellow inside
→ See **Fruits and Vegetables** on page C8

Ping-Pong /ˈpɪŋ.pɑŋ/ *noun* [no plural] trademark a game in which two or four people hit a small ball over a low net on a large table

pink[1] /pɪŋk/ *adj* **A2** being a pale red color: *pretty, pink flowers*

pink[2] /pɪŋk/ *noun* **A2** the color pink
→ See **Colors** on page 6

pint /paɪnt/ *noun* (written abbreviation **pt.**) a unit for measuring liquid, equal to 16 ounces in the U.S. and 20 ounces in the U.K.

pioneer /ˌpaɪ·əˈnɪər/ *noun* **1** someone who is one of the first people to do something: *He was one of the pioneers of modern science.* **2** someone who goes to an area and establishes farms, houses, etc.: *We learned about the American pioneer and explorer, Daniel Boone.*

pipe /paɪp/ *noun* **1** **B1** a long tube that liquid or gas can move through: *a water pipe* **2** a tube with a bowl-shaped part at one end, used to smoke tobacco: *He smokes a pipe.*

pirate /ˈpaɪ·rət/ *noun* **B1** someone who attacks ships and steals from them

pit /pɪt/ *noun* **1** a large hole that has been dug in the ground **2** a large, hard seed that grows inside some types of fruits and vegetables **3** a place where coal is dug out from under the ground

pitch /pɪtʃ/ *noun* [no plural] how high or low a sound is

pitcher /ˈpɪtʃ·ər/ *noun*

pitcher

1 **B1** a container with a wide opening and a handle, used for holding and pouring out liquids: *a pitcher of water* **2** the person who throws the ball to the batter (=player who hits the ball) in the game of baseball

pity[1] /ˈpɪt̬·i/ *noun* **1** **it's a pity… A2** used to say that something is disappointing: *It's a pity you can't stay longer.* **2** [no plural] a feeling of sadness for someone who has problems: *She looked at me with pity in her eyes.* **3 take pity on** *someone* to help someone who is in a difficult situation because you feel sad for him or her: *I finally took pity on Ben and told him the truth.*

pity[2] /ˈpɪt̬·i/ *verb* (present participle **pitying**, past tense and past participle **pitied**) to feel sorry for someone: *I pity her because she is lonely.*

pizza /ˈpiːt·sə/ *noun* **A1** a flat, round piece of bread covered with tomato, cheese, etc. and cooked in an oven
→ See **Food** on page C7

place[1] /pleɪs/ *noun* **1** **A1** a position, building, town, area, etc.: *His leg was broken in two places.* ∘ *Seattle would be a nice place to live.* ∘ *What a stupid place to park!* **2** **A2** informal someone's home: *They just bought a place near the lake.* **3 take place B1** to happen: *The meeting will take place next week.* **4 in first, second, etc. place B1** If you are in first, second, etc. place in a race or competition, that is your position when you finish: *He got fifth place in race.* **5** **B1** your seat or position in a theater, train, line, etc.: *Do you want to **trade places** with* me (= move so that you are in my place and I am in yours)? **6 all over the place** in many different places: I knocked over my glass and wine spilled all over the place. **7 take** someone's **place** to do something instead of someone else: If I can't go to the show tonight, will you take my place? **8 in the first place** used to talk about whether something mentioned should have been done or not: Why did you invite her in the first place?

> **❗ Common mistake: place or room/space?**
>
> If you want to talk about whether an area is big enough for something, use **room** or **space**, not "place."
> The animals need enough space to run around.
> ~~The animals need enough place to run around.~~

place[2] /pleɪs/ verb (present participle **placing**, past tense and past participle **placed**) **1** Ⓑ to put something somewhere carefully: She placed a large dish in front of me. **2** to cause someone to be in a situation: He was placed in charge of the troops.

plain[1] /pleɪn/ adj **1** Ⓑ simple and not complicated: plain food ∘ Can you explain that in plain English? **2** Ⓑ not mixed with other colors: a plain blue coat

plain[2] /pleɪn/ noun (also **plains**) a large area of flat land

plainly /ˈpleɪn·li/ adv **1** in a simple way that is not complicated: She was plainly dressed. **2** in a clear and obvious way: This is plainly wrong.

plan[1] /plæn/ noun **1** ⒜ something that you are going to do: What are your **plans for** the weekend? ∘ The plan is to meet at the hotel. **2** a drawing that shows how something appears from above: a museum's floor plan

plan[2] /plæn/ verb (present participle **planning**, past tense and past participle **planned**) ⒜ to decide what you are going to do or how you are going to do

something: We're just planning our vacation. ∘ I **planned** the meeting **for** Friday. ∘ She **plans to** go to college next year.

plane /pleɪn/ noun ⒜ a vehicle that flies and has an engine and wings: What time does her plane get in (= arrive)?

plane

planet /ˈplæn·ɪt/ noun Ⓑ a large, round object in space that moves around the sun or another star

plank /plæŋk/ noun a long, flat piece of wood: wooden planks

planning /ˈplæn·ɪŋ/ noun [no plural] **1** the activity of thinking about and deciding how you are going to do something: The wedding took months of careful planning. **2** control over which buildings are built in an area: city planning

plant[1] /plænt/ noun ⒜ a living thing that grows in the soil or water and has leaves and roots: Did you **water the plants**? ∘ tomato plants

plant[2] /plænt/ verb Ⓑ to put seeds or plants in the ground so that they will grow: We planted some trees in the garden.

plaster /ˈplæs·tər/ noun [no plural] a substance that is spread on walls in order to make them smooth

plastic /ˈplæs·tɪk/ noun [no plural] ⒜ a light substance that can be made into different shapes when it is soft and has many uses: Most children's toys are made of plastic.
• **plastic** adj ⒜ plastic bags

plate /pleɪt/ noun ⒜ a flat, round object that is used for putting food on: a dinner plate ∘ a **plate of** cookies

platform /ˈplæt·fɔrm/ noun **1** ⒜ the area in a train station where you get on and off the train: The train to Washington, DC is leaving from platform 3. **2** a high part of a floor for a person to stand on: *The speakers stood on a platform.*

play[1] /pleɪ/ **verb 1** 🅰1 When you play a sport or game, you compete or are involved in it: *Sam plays tennis every weekend.* ○ *We often used to play cards.* **2** 🅰1 When children play, they enjoy themselves with toys and games: *She likes to play with her dolls.* **3** 🅰2 to make music with a musical instrument: *Tim was playing the piano.* **4** 🅰2 to make a CD, DVD, etc. produce sounds or pictures: *Can you play that song again?* **5** 🅱1 to be a character in a movie or play: *Who played Darth Vader in "Star Wars?"* **6** 🅱1 to compete against a person or team in a game: *Who is playing in the championship?* **7 play a joke/trick on *someone*** to make someone believe something that is not true as a joke: *The class played a trick on the teacher.*

play[2] /pleɪ/ **noun 1** 🅰2 a story that is written for actors to perform, usually in a theater: *We saw a play at the theater.* **2** [no plural] things that people, especially children, do to enjoy themselves: *children at play*

player /ˈpleɪ·ər/ **noun 1** 🅰1 someone who plays a sport or game: *tennis players* **2** 🅰2 someone who plays a musical instrument: *a trumpet player* **3** 🅰2 a machine that produces sound or pictures: *an MP3 player* ○ *a DVD player*

playful /ˈpleɪ·fəl/ **adj 1** showing that you are having fun and not being serious: *a playful remark* **2** showing that you want to play: *a playful puppy*

playground /ˈpleɪ·ɡraʊnd/ **noun** 🅰2 an area of land where children can play and that often has special equipment for playing on

playing card /ˈpleɪ·ɪŋ ˌkɑrd/ **noun** one of a set of 52 small pieces of stiff paper with numbers and pictures on them, used for playing games

playing field /ˈpleɪ·ɪŋ ˌfild/ **noun** an area of land used for sports such as soccer

plead /plid/ **verb** to say in a court of law if you have done a crime or not done a crime: *He pleaded not guilty to murder.*

pleasant /ˈplez·ənt/ **adj** 🅰2 good or enjoyable: *pleasant weather* ○ *We had a very pleasant evening.*
• **pleasantly adv** 🅱1 *I was pleasantly surprised by the election results.*

please[1] /pliz/ **exclamation 1** 🅰1 something that you say to be polite when you are asking for something: *Could I have some coffee, please?* ○ *Please may I use your telephone?* **2 yes, please** 🅰1 used to accept something politely: *"Would you like a drink?" "Oh yes, please."*

please[2] /pliz/ **verb** (present participle **pleasing**, past tense and past participle **pleased**) 🅱1 to make someone happy: *I only got married to please my parents.*

pleased /plizd/ **adj 1** 🅰2 happy about something: *I'm pleased to be back home.* ○ *I'm really pleased with her work.* ○ *I wasn't very pleased about having to pay for dinner.* **2 pleased to meet you** 🅰2 a polite thing to say to someone you are meeting for the first time

pleasure /ˈpleʒ·ər/ **noun 1** 🅱1 [no plural] a feeling of happiness or enjoyment: *The children give her a lot of pleasure.* **2** 🅱1 an enjoyable activity: *Food is one of life's great pleasures.*

plenty /ˈplen·ti/ **quantifier** 🅱1 a lot of something, more than you need: *Don't bring any food – we have plenty.* ○ *There's plenty of room here.*

pliers /ˈplaɪ·ərz/ **plural noun** a tool for holding or pulling small things like nails or for cutting wire: *a pair of pliers*

plot[1] /plɑt/ **noun 1** the things that happen in a story: *I don't like movies with complicated plots.* **2** a plan to do something bad: *There was a plot to blow up the embassy.* **3** a piece of land: *a building plot*

plot[2] /plɑt/ **verb** (present participle **plotting**, past tense and past participle **plotted**) to plan to do something bad: *They plotted to bring down the government.*

plow /plaʊ/ **noun** a large tool used by farmers to turn over the soil before planting crops

---

a
b
c
d
e
f
g
h
i
j
k
l
m
n
o
p
q
r
s
t
u
v
w
x
y
z

pluck /plʌk/ verb **1** to quickly pull something or someone from the place where he, she, or it is: *She plucked a business card from her pocket and handed it to him.* **2** If you pluck something, you pull hair or feathers from it: *plucking a chicken ∘ She plucked her eyebrows.*

plug[1] /plʌg/ noun **plug**
1 B1 an object with metal parts that stick out of its end, used to connect electrical equipment to an electricity supply: *This plug is for the computer and that one is for the printer.* **outlet**
2 B1 something you put in a hole to block it: *a sink plug*

plug[2] /plʌg/ verb (present participle **plugging**, past tense and past participle **plugged**) to block a hole
plug something in phrasal verb to connect a piece of electrical equipment to an electricity supply: *Could you plug the iron in for me?*

plum /plʌm/ noun a soft, round fruit with red or yellow skin and a pit (= large seed) in the middle

plumber /ˈplʌm·ər/ noun someone whose job is to repair or connect water pipes for kitchens, bathrooms, etc.

plumbing /ˈplʌm·ɪŋ/ noun [no plural] the water pipes in a building

plunge /plʌndʒ/ verb (present participle **plunging**, past tense and past participle **plunged**) to fall or move down very quickly and with force: *He plunged into the water.*

plural /ˈplʊr·əl/ noun A2 in grammar, a word or part of a word that shows you are talking about more than one person or thing. For example, "babies" is the plural of "baby."
• **plural** adj A2 *"Cattle" and "pants" are plural nouns.*

plus /plʌs/ preposition **1** A2 added to: *Five plus three is eight.* **2** B1 and also: *She won their latest CD plus two tickets to their concert.*

p.m. /ˈpiˈem/ A1 in the afternoon or evening: *Opening hours: 9 a.m. – 6 p.m.*

pneumonia /nʊˈmoʊn·jə/ noun [no plural] a serious illness in which your lungs fill with liquid and it is difficult to breathe

pocket /ˈpɑk·ɪt/ noun **pocket**
1 A2 a part of a piece of clothing that you can put things in: *My wallet was in my coat pocket.* **2** B1 a container or bag that is attached to something: *Faye put her keys in a pocket in her bag.*

pod /pɑd/ noun the long, flat part of some plants that has seeds in it: *a pea pod*

poem /ˈpoʊ·əm/ noun B1 a piece of writing, especially one that has short lines and uses words that sound the same: *love poems*

poet /ˈpoʊ·ɪt/ noun B1 someone who writes poems

poetic /poʊˈet·ɪk/ adj relating to poetry: *poetic language*

poetry /ˈpoʊ·ɪ·tri/ noun [no plural] B1 poems in general

point[1] /pɔɪnt/ noun **1** B1 an opinion, idea, or fact that someone says or writes: *He made some interesting points about the election. ∘ He explained his point by drawing a diagram.* **2** B1 a unit used for showing who is winning in a game: *The Knicks are ahead by 12 points.* **3** an opinion or fact that should be considered seriously: *"She's always complaining that the office is cold." "Well, she has a point (= that is true)." ∘ "How are we going to get there if there are no trains?" "That's a good point."* **4** a quality that someone has: *I know she's bossy, but she has lots of good points too.* **5** the thin, sharp end of something: *the point of a needle* **6** a particular place: *This is the point where the pipes enter the building.* **7** a particular time in an event or process: *At this point in the day, I'm too tired to think.* **8** the reason for or purpose of something: *What's the point of going to college if you can't get a job afterwards?* **9** the most important part of what has been said or written: *Come on, get to the point! ∘ The* *point is*, *if you don't claim the money now, you might never get it.* **10 up to a point** partly: *What he says is true up to a point.* **11** (also **decimal point**) the mark [.] that is used to separate the two parts of a decimal: *One mile equals one point six (=1.6) kilometers.* **12** one of the marks on a compass: *the points of the compass* **13 make a point of doing something** to be certain that you always do a particular thing: *He made a point of learning all the names of his staff.*

> ⚠ **Common mistake: point**
>
> A **point** [.] is used to separate a whole number from a fraction (=number less than 1).
>   *Normal body temperature is 98.6° Fahrenheit.*
> A **comma** [,] is used to divide large numbers into groups of three so that they are easier to read.
>   *28,071,973*
>   *1,378*

point² /pɔɪnt/ verb **1** 🅐🅑 to show where someone or something is by holding your finger or a thin object toward it: *She pointed to a bird in the tree.* **2** 🅑🅑 to hold something so that it faces toward someone or something: *She pointed her gun at them.* **3** 🅑🅑 to face toward a particular direction: *The road sign points left.*

point something out phrasal verb to tell someone a fact: *If he makes a mistake, I point it out immediately.*

pointed /ˈpɔɪn·tɪd/ adj A pointed object has a thin, sharp end: *He has a pointed chin.*

pointless /ˈpɔɪnt·ləs/ adj Something that is pointless has no purpose: *It would be pointless to argue with him.*
• **pointlessly** adv

point of view /ˈpɔɪnt əv ˈvju/ noun (plural **points of view**) **1** an opinion: *I can see (=understand) his point of view.* **2** a way of thinking about a situation: *From a medical point of view, it is an important discovery.*

poison¹ /ˈpɔɪ·zən/ noun a substance that makes you ill or kills you if you eat or drink it

poison² /ˈpɔɪ·zən/ verb **1** to try to kill someone by giving him or her a dangerous substance to drink or eat: *He tried to poison his wife.* **2** to put a dangerous substance in something: *Someone had poisoned his drink.*

poisonous /ˈpɔɪ·zə·nəs/ adj containing poison: *poisonous gas*

poke /poʊk/ verb (present participle **poking**, past tense and past participle **poked**) to quickly push your finger or other pointed object into someone or something: *Nell kept poking me in the arm.*

poker /ˈpoʊ·kər/ noun [no plural] a game played with cards in which people try to win money from each other

polar /ˈpoʊ·lər/ adj relating to the North or South Pole

polar bear /ˈpoʊ·lər ˌbeər/ noun a large, white bear that lives in the Arctic (=most northern part of the Earth)

pole /poʊl/ noun **1** a long, thin stick made of wood or metal, used to hold something up: *tent poles* **2 the North/South Pole** the part of the Earth that is farthest north or south

police /pəˈlis/ noun 🅐🅑 the government organization that makes people obey the law and that protects people against crime, or the people who work for this organization: *I heard a gun shot and decided to **call the police**.* ○ *A 30-year-old man is being questioned by **the police**.*

policeman /pəˈlis·mən/ noun (plural **policemen**) 🅐🅑 a man who is a member of the police

police officer /pəˈlis ˌɔ·fə·sər/ noun 🅐🅑 someone who is a member of the police

police station /pəˈlis ˌsteɪ·ʃən/ noun 🅐🅑 the office of the police

policewoman /pəˈlisˌwʊm·ən/ noun (plural **policewomen**) 🅐🅑 a woman who is a member of the police

a
b
c
d
e
f
g
h
i
j
k
l
m
n
o
p
q
r
s
t
u
v
w
x
y
z

policy /ˈpɒl·ɪ·si/ noun (plural **policies**)
a set of ideas or a plan that has been
agreed by a government, business, etc.:
the governor's economic policies ◦ *It is
company policy to help the members of
our staff progress in their careers.*

polish[1] /ˈpɒl·ɪʃ/ noun [no plural]
a substance that you rub on something
in order to make it shine

polish[2] /ˈpɒl·ɪʃ/ verb to rub something
with a cloth in order to make it shine: *I
polished my shoes.*

polite /pəˈlaɪt/ adj **A2** behaving in a
way that is not rude and shows that you
think about other people: *She was too
polite to point out my mistake.*
• **politely** adv **B1** *He thanked them politely.*
• **politeness** noun *We were impressed by
their politeness.*

political /pəˈlɪt·ɪ·kəl/ adj **B1** relating to
or involved in politics: *There are two
main political parties in my country.*

politician /ˌpɒl·əˈtɪʃ·ən/ noun
B1 someone who works in politics, es-
pecially a member of the government:
Kennedy was a distinguished politician.

politics /ˈpɒl·ɪ·tɪks/ noun [no plural]
1 **B1** ideas and activities relating to
how a country or area is governed: *He
has little interest in politics.* **2** **B1** a job
in politics: *She's planning to retire from
politics next year.*

poll /poʊl/ noun the process of asking
people questions to discover what they
think about a subject: *A recent poll indicated that 62 percent of Americans supported the president.*

pollen /ˈpɒl·ən/ noun [no plural]
a powder made by flowers, which is carried by insects and makes other flowers
produce seeds

pollute /pəˈlut/ verb (present participle
polluting, past tense and past participle
polluted) to make water, air, soil, etc.
dirty or harmful: *We need a fuel that
won't pollute the environment.*
• **polluted** adj *The beaches were polluted with oil.*

pollution /pəˈlu·ʃən/ noun [no plural]
B1 damage caused to water, air, etc. by
bad substances or waste

pond /pɒnd/ noun a small area of water

pony /ˈpoʊ·ni/ noun (plural **ponies**)
a small horse

ponytail /ˈpoʊ·niˌteɪl/ noun hair tied at
the back or sides of your head: *She looks
cute with her hair in a ponytail.*
→ See **Hair** on page C9

pool /pul/ noun **1** **A2** an area of water
that has been made for people to swim
in: *The hotel has an indoor pool.* **2** **B1** [no
plural] a game in which you use a long
stick to hit balls into holes around the
edge of a table: *We played pool all evening.* **3** a small area of water or other
liquid on a surface: *a pool of blood*

poor /pʊər/ adj **1** **A1** having little
money: *He comes from a very poor family.* ◦ *Modern fertilizers are too expensive
for poorer countries to afford.* ◦ *housing
for the poor* **2** **A2** used to show that
you are sad for someone: *That cold
sounds terrible, you poor thing!* **3** of bad
quality: *It was a poor performance.* ◦ *Last
year's test scores were poor.* ◦ *a poor harvest* ◦ *The meeting went smoothly, but attendance was poor (= not many people
came).* **4** not having much skill at a particular activity: *Sam is a poor swimmer.*

poorly /ˈpʊər·li/ adv badly: *They were
poorly educated.*

pop[1] /pɒp/ verb (present participle **popping**,
past tense and past participle **popped**) to
make a short sound like a small explosion: *The music played and champagne
corks popped.*

pop up phrasal verb informal to suddenly
appear or happen: *A message just
popped up on my screen.*

pop[2] /pɒp/ noun **1** **A2** [no plural] (also
pop music) modern music with a strong
beat that is popular with young people
2 a short sound like a small explosion

popcorn /ˈpɒpˌkɔrn/ noun [no plural]
hard seeds of corn that break open, get
bigger, and turn white when you cook
them

Pope /poʊp/ *noun* the leader of the Roman Catholic Church

popular /'pɑp·jə·lər/ *adj* **1** **A2** liked by many people: *a list of the most popular boys' names* → Opposite **unpopular** *adj* **2** for or involving ordinary people: *popular culture*

popularity /ˌpɑp·jə'lær·ɪ·t̬i/ *noun* [no plural] the quality of being liked by many people

population /ˌpɑp·jə'leɪ·ʃən/ *noun* **1** **B1** the number of people living in a particular area: *What's the **population** of Brazil?* **2** all the people living in a particular area, or all the people or animals of a particular type: *The deer population has increased in the northeast.*

porch /pɔrtʃ/ *noun* a structure built onto the front or back of a house, with a floor and a roof but no walls

pork /pɔrk/ *noun* [no plural] meat from a pig

port /pɔrt/ *noun* **B1** a town or an area of a town next to water where ships arrive and leave from: *the port of Boston*

portable /'pɔr·t̬ə·bəl/ *adj* able to be carried: *a portable computer*

portion /'pɔr·ʃən/ *noun* **1** the amount of food given to one person in a restaurant: *The portions in the restaurant were very small.* **2** a part of something: *A **portion** of their profits go to charity.*

portrait /'pɔr·trɪt/ *noun* a painting, drawing, or photograph of someone: *a portrait of the president*

position /pə'zɪʃ·ən/ *noun* **1** **B1** the way someone is sitting, standing, or lying: *I've been sitting in one **position** too long.* **2** **B1** the situation that someone is in: *She's in a very difficult **position**.* **3** **B1** the place where someone or something is: *I'm trying to find our position on the map.* **4** **B1** the part that someone plays in a game such as football: *I didn't know you played hockey – what **position** do you **play**?* **5** a job: *He applied for a senior position with the company.* **6** your level of importance in a company or society: *the position of women in society*

positive /'pɑz·ɪ·t̬ɪv/ *adj* **1** **B1** feeling happy and confident about life or a particular situation: *She has a very positive attitude.* **2** certain that something is true: *"Are you sure you saw him?" "Absolutely positive."*

positively /'pɑz·ə·t̬ɪv·li/ *adv* in a good way that makes you feel happier: *Most children respond positively to praise.*

possess /pə'zes/ *verb* formal to have or own something: *Does he possess the skills for the job?*

possession /pə'zeʃ·ən/ *noun* something that you own: *personal possessions*

possessive /pə'zes·ɪv/ *adj* **B1** In grammar, a possessive word or form of a word shows who or what something belongs to; for example, the words "my" and "mine" are possessive.

possibility /ˌpɑs·ə'bɪl·ɪ·t̬i/ *noun* (plural **possibilities**) **1** **B1** a chance that something may happen or be true: *Is there any **possibility** of changing this ticket?* ∘ *There's a **possibility** that Harvey might come.* **2** something that you can choose to do: *Have you considered the **possibility** of flying?*

possible /'pɑs·ə·bəl/ *adj* **1** **A1** If something is possible, it can happen or be done: *Is it **possible** to speak to the manager, please?* ∘ *I'll send it today, **if possible**.* → Opposite **impossible** *adj* **2** as much, quickly, soon, etc. as possible **A2** as much, quickly, soon, etc. as something can happen or be done: *Call me as soon as possible after you arrive.* **3** **B1** If something is possible, it might or might not exist or be true: *It's **possible that** the ring was stolen.* ∘ *That's one possible solution to the problem.*

possibly /'pɑs·ə·bli/ *adv* **1** **A2** used when something is not certain: *Someone, possibly Tom, had left the window open.* **2** **B1** used in polite questions: *Could I possibly borrow your computer?* **3** used with "can" or "could" for emphasis: *We'll do everything we possibly can to help.*

post[1] /poʊst/ *noun* **1** a long piece of wood or metal set into the ground at

one end: *I found the dog tied to a post.*
2 formal a job: *a teaching post*

post² /poʊst/ verb **B1** to leave a message on a website: *I posted a question about Mexican cooking.*

postage /ˈpoʊ·stɪdʒ/ noun [no plural]
money that you pay to send a letter or package: *airmail postage*

postcard /ˈpoʊstˌkɑrd/ noun **A2** a card with a picture on one side that you send without an envelope

poster /ˈpoʊ·stər/ noun **A2** a large, printed picture or notice that you put on a wall

post office /ˈpoʊst ˌɔf·ɪs/ noun
A2 a place where you can buy stamps and send letters and packages

postpone /poʊstˈpoʊn/ verb
B1 to arrange for something to happen at a later time: *The trip to the museum has been **postponed until** next week.*

pot /pɑt/ noun **B1** a round container, usually used for keeping things or cooking: *a flower pot* ○ *a **pot of** coffee* ○ *There's plenty of space in the kitchen for all your **pots and pans**.*
→ See **The Kitchen** on page C10

potato /pəˈteɪ·toʊ/ noun (plural **potatoes**)
A1 a round, white vegetable with brown skin that grows in the ground
→ See **Fruits and Vegetables** on page C8

potato chip /pəˈteɪ·toʊ ˌtʃɪp/ noun
A2 a very thin slice of potato that is fried until it is dry: *a bag of potato chips*

potential¹ /pəˈten·tʃəl/ adj possible: *A few **potential** buyers have been found.*

potential² /pəˈten·tʃəl/ noun [no plural]
qualities that allow someone or something to develop or succeed: *She has a lot of potential as a writer.*

potentially /pəˈten·ʃə·li/ adv possibly: *a potentially fatal disease* ○ *This crisis is potentially very serious.*

pottery /ˈpɑt·ər·i/ noun [no plural]
1 plates, bowls, etc. that are made from clay **2** the activity of making plates, bowls, etc. from clay

poultry /ˈpoʊl·tri/ noun [no plural]
chickens and other birds that people keep for meat and eggs

pounce /paʊns/ verb (present participle **pouncing**, past tense and past participle **pounced**) to suddenly move toward a person or animal that you want to catch

pound /paʊnd/ noun (written abbreviation **lb.**) **A2** a unit for measuring weight, equal to 16 ounces: *a pound of potatoes* ○ *The baby weighed only four pounds when she was born.*

pour /pɔr/ verb **pour**
1 **B1** to make a liquid flow from or into a container: *I poured the milk **into** a glass.*
2 **B1** to rain a lot: *We can't go out in this weather – it's pouring!*

poverty /ˈpɑv·ər· t̮i/ noun [no plural] the state of being very poor: *They live **in** poverty.*

powder /ˈpaʊ·dər/ noun [no plural]
B1 a dry substance made of many small, loose grains: *curry powder*
• **powdered** adj *powdered milk/sugar*

power /ˈpaʊ·ər/ noun **1** **B1** [no plural] energy, usually electricity, that is used to make light, heat, etc.: *nuclear power*
2 [no plural] control over people and things that happen: *He likes to have **power over** people.* **3** [no plural] political control in a country: *This government has been **in power** too long.*

powerful /ˈpaʊ·ər·fəl/ adj **1** **B1** able to control or influence people or things that happen: *My mother was a powerful influence on me.* **2** **B1** very strong: *a powerful weapon*
• **powerfully** adv

power plant /ˈpaʊ·ər ˌplænt/ noun
a place where electricity is produced

practical /ˈpræk·tɪ·kəl/ adj **1** relating to real situations: *They can offer practical help.* **2** able to be done successfully: *The plan really isn't practical.* **3** Someone who is practical knows what can be done successfully, and makes good decisions: *She has a lot of interesting ideas, but she's not very practical.* **4** good at repairing and making things

practically /'præk·tɪ·kli/ *adv* almost: *We see her practically every day.*

practice¹ /'præk·tɪs/ *verb* (present participle **practicing**, past tense and past participle **practiced**) **A1** to do something again and again in order to get better at it: *They're practicing for tomorrow's concert.* ○ *Did you practice your violin today?*

practice² /'præk·tɪs/ *noun* **1 A2** [no plural] the act of doing an activity again and again to get better at it: *We need a lot more practice before the performance.* **2** the things people do or how they do them: *business practices* ○ *the illegal practice of copying CDs* **3 be out of practice** to not do something well because you have not done it recently: *I didn't play very well today – I'm out of practice.* **4 in practice** used to say what really happens rather than what people think happens: *In practice, the new laws have not been effective.*

prairie /'preər·i/ *noun* a large flat area of land in North America that is usually covered in grass

praise¹ /preɪz/ *verb* (present participle **praising**, past tense and past participle **praised**) to say that someone or something is very good: *He praised the team's performance.*

praise² /preɪz/ *noun* [no plural] words that you say to show that you think someone or something is very good: *They deserve praise for their achievements.*

pray /preɪ/ *verb* **A2** to speak to a god in order to show your feelings or to ask for something: *We're praying for you.*

prayer /preər/ *noun* **1 B1** the words you say to a god: *Let's say a prayer for him.* **2** [no plural] the act of saying words to a god: *They stood in silent prayer.*

pre- /pri/ *prefix* before (a time or an event): *a pre-vacation haircut* ○ *to preheat the oven*

preach /pritʃ/ *verb* to talk to a group of people about a religious subject, usually in a church

preacher /'pri·tʃər/ *noun* someone who speaks about religious subjects in public, usually in a church

precaution /prɪ'kɔ·ʃən/ *noun* something that you do to stop bad things from happening in the future: *They called the doctor as a precaution.* ○ *He took the precaution of locking the door.*

precious /'preʃ·əs/ *adj* **1** very important to you: *His books are his most precious possessions.* **2** very valuable: *a precious metal*

precise /prɪ'saɪs/ *adj* **1** exact and accurate: *Her instructions were very precise.* **2 to be precise** used to give exact details about something: *We met in 2004 – on October 11th to be precise.*

precisely /prɪ'saɪs·li/ *adv* exactly: *He arrived at 6 o'clock precisely.*

predict /prɪ'dɪkt/ *verb* **B1** to say what you think will happen in the future: *Companies are predicting huge profits.*

predictable /prɪ'dɪk·tə·bəl/ *adj* happening or behaving in a way that you expect; not unusual or interesting: *The results were predictable.*

prediction /prɪ'dɪk·ʃən/ *noun* a statement of what you think will happen in the future: *I can't make any predictions about the final score.*

prefer /prɪ'fɜr/ *verb* (present participle **preferring**, past tense and past participle **preferred**) **1 A2** to like someone or something more than another person or thing: *I prefer dogs to cats.* ○ *She prefers watching tennis to playing.* **2 would prefer A2** used to say what you want or ask someone what he or she wants: *I'd prefer to eat alone.* ○ *Would you prefer red or white wine?*

preferable /'pref·ər·ə·bəl/ *adj* better or more suitable: *Buying a house is preferable to paying rent.*

preferably /'pref·ər·ə·bli/ *adv* used to show what you think is the best choice:

| æ cat | ɑ hot | e get | ɪ sit | i see | ɔ saw | ʊ book | u too | ʌ cut | ə about | ər mother | ɜr turn | ɔr for | aɪ my | aʊ how | eɪ say | ɔɪ boy |

Serve the pie with ice cream, preferably vanilla.

preference /ˈpref·ər·əns/ **noun**
a greater desire for one person or thing than another person or thing: *personal preferences* ∘ *We have white and red wine. Do you have a preference?*

prefix /ˈpri·fiks/ **noun** a group of letters that you add to the beginning of a word to make another word. In the word "unsafe," "un-" is a prefix.

pregnancy /ˈpreg·nən·si/ **noun** (plural **pregnancies**) the state of being pregnant: *a healthy pregnancy*

pregnant /ˈpreg·nənt/ **adj** 🔵 A pregnant woman has a baby growing inside her body: *She's five months pregnant.*

prejudice /ˈpredʒ·ə·dɪs/ **noun** a strong dislike of a group of people because they are a different race, sex, religion, etc.: *racial prejudice*

prejudiced /ˈpredʒ·ə·dɪst/ **adj**
not liking a group of people or treating them badly because they are a different race, sex, religion, etc.: *I think my boss is prejudiced against women.*

preparation /ˌprep·əˈreɪ·ʃən/ **noun**
1 [no plural] the things that you do to prepare for something: *Did you do much preparation for your interview?*
2 preparations plans or arrangements that you make to prepare for something: *We're making preparations for the trip.*

prepare /prɪˈpeər/ **verb** (present participle **preparing**, past tense and past participle **prepared**) **1** 🔵 to get someone or something ready for something in the future: ∘ *The students are preparing for their final exams.* **2** 🔵 to make food ready to be eaten: *I prepared lunch for the kids.*
3 prepare yourself 🔵 to make yourself ready to deal with a difficult situation: *Prepare yourself for a shock.*

prepared /prɪˈpeərd/ **adj 1** 🔵 ready for a situation: *I wasn't prepared for the cold.* **2** be prepared to do *something* to be willing to do something: *You should be prepared to work hard.*

preposition /ˌprep·əˈzɪʃ·ən/ **noun**
🔵 a word or group of words that is used before a noun or pronoun to show place, direction, time, etc. For example, "on" in "Your keys are on the table." is a preposition.

prescription /prɪˈskrɪp·ʃən/ **noun**
🔵 a piece of paper on which a doctor writes what medicine a sick person needs: *Antibiotics are available by prescription.*

presence /ˈprez·əns/ **noun** [no plural]
the fact of someone or something being in a place: *Your presence at the meeting would be appreciated.* ∘ *She signed the document in the presence of two witnesses.*

present[1] /ˈprez·ənt/ **adj** be present
🔵 to be in a particular place: *The whole family was present at the funeral.*

present[2] /ˈprez·ənt/ **present**
noun 1 the present
(also **the present tense**)
🔵 in grammar, the
form of a verb that is
used to show what
happens or exists now
2 🔵 something that you give to someone, usually on a special day: *a birthday present* **3** the present 🔵 the period of time that is happening now: *Let's talk about the present, not the past.*

present[3] /prɪˈzent/ **verb** to give something to someone, often at a formal ceremony: *They presented her with a medal.*

presentation /ˌprez·ənˈteɪ·ʃən/ **noun**
1 🔵 a talk giving information about something: *She gave an interesting presentation on the history of the city.* **2** a formal ceremony at which you give someone something **3** [no plural] the way you show something to people: *Presentation is important if you want people to buy your products.*

present participle /ˈprez·ənt ˈpɑr·tə·sɪp·əl/ **noun** in grammar, the form of a verb that ends with "-ing"

the present perfect /ˈprez·ənt ˈpər·fɪkt/ noun in grammar, the form of a verb that is used to show things that have happened in a period of time up to now. The sentence "I have never been to Canada" is in the present perfect.

preserve /prɪˈzɜrv/ verb (present participle **preserving**, past tense and past participle **preserved**) to keep something the same or stop it from being destroyed: *to preserving the rainforest*

presidency /ˈprez·ɪ·dən·si/ noun (plural **presidencies**) **1** the period when someone is president: *Her presidency lasted four years.* **2 the presidency** the job of being president: *He won the presidency*.

president /ˈprez·ɪ·dənt/ noun **1** B1 the highest political position in some countries, usually the leader of the government: *the president of the United States* **2** the person in charge of a company or organization

presidential /ˌprez·ɪˈden·ʃəl/ adj relating to the president of a country: *a presidential candidate*

press[1] /pres/ verb B1 to push something firmly: *Press the button to start the machine.* ○ *He pressed his face against the window.*

press[2] /pres/ noun **the press** newspapers and magazines, or the people who write them: *the national press*

pressure /ˈpreʃ·ər/ noun **1** [no plural] the act of trying to make someone else do something by arguing or persuading: *public/political pressure* ○ *Teachers are under pressure to work longer hours.* **2** difficult situations that make you feel worried or unhappy: *the pressures of work* **3** [no plural] the force that you produce when you push something

presume /prɪˈzum/ verb to think that something is probably true, although you are not certain: *I presume that you finished your homework.*

pretend /prɪˈtend/ verb to behave as if something is true when it is not: *I can't*

pretend that I like him. ○ *Were you just pretending to be interested?*

pretty[1] /ˈprɪt·i/ adv informal B1 fairly, but not very: *The traffic was pretty bad.* ○ *I'm pretty sure they'll accept the invitation.*

pretty[2] /ˈprɪt·i/ adj (comparative **prettier**, superlative **prettiest**) A2 nice to look at, attractive: *Your daughter is very pretty.* ○ *a pretty little garden*

prevent /prɪˈvent/ verb B1 to stop something from happening or to stop someone from doing something: *to prevent crime* ○ *Visitors were prevented from entering the building.*

> ❗ **Common mistake: prevent**
>
> **Prevent** should not be followed by "to do something."
> *We must prevent such a disaster from happening again.*
> ~~We must prevent such a disaster to happen again.~~

prevention /prɪˈven·ʃən/ noun [no plural] the act of stopping something from happening or stopping someone from doing something: *crime prevention* ○ *the prevention of diseases*

previous /ˈpri·vi·əs/ adj B1 existing or happening before this one: *the previous day/year* ○ *his previous marriage*

previously /ˈpri·vi·əs·li/ adv B1 before: *He previously worked as a teacher.*

prey /preɪ/ noun [no plural] an animal that is hunted and killed by another animal

price /praɪs/ noun A2 the amount of money that you pay to buy something: *high/low prices* ○ *The price of fuel has gone up again.*

priceless /ˈpraɪs·ləs/ adj very valuable: *a priceless antique/painting*

pride /praɪd/ noun [no plural] **1** a feeling of satisfaction at your achievements or the achievements of your family or friends: *She felt a great sense of pride as she watched him accept the award.* **2** the respect that you feel for yourself: *She has too much pride to accept any help.*

a
b
c
d
e
f
g
h
i
j
k
l
m
n
o
p
q
r
s
t
u
v
w
x
y
z

priest /prist/ noun **B1** someone who performs religious duties and ceremonies

primary /ˈpraɪ·mer·i/, /ˈpraɪ·mər·i/ adj most important: *Her primary responsibility is to train new employees.*

prime minister /ˌpraɪm ˈmɪn·əs·tər/ noun the leader of an elected government in some countries

primitive /ˈprɪm·ɪ·tɪv/ adj relating to a time long ago when people lived in a simple way without machines or a writing system: *primitive man*

prince /prɪns/ noun **1** **B1** the son of a king or queen, or one of their close male relatives: *Prince Edward* **2** the male ruler of a small country

princess /ˈprɪn·sɪs/ noun **1** **B1** the daughter of a king or queen, or one of their close female relatives **2** **B1** the wife of a prince

principal¹ /ˈprɪn·sə·pəl/ adj **B1** main, or most important: *Her principal reason for moving is to live closer to her mother.*
• **principally** adv *The magazine is aimed principally at women.*

principal² /ˈprɪn·sə·pəl/ noun the person in charge of a school

principle /ˈprɪn·sə·pəl/ noun **1** a belief about how you should behave: *He must be punished – it's a matter of principle.* **2 on principle** If you refuse to do something on principle, you refuse to do it because you think it is morally wrong: *She doesn't wear fur on principle.*

print¹ /prɪnt/ verb **1** **A2** to make writing or images on paper or other material with a machine: *The instructions are printed on the side of the box.* **2** to make books, newspapers, magazines, etc., usually in large quantities, using machines: *Fifty thousand copies of the book have been printed.*

print² /prɪnt/ noun **1** [no plural] words, letters, or numbers that are made on paper by a machine: *The print is so small in this book that I can hardly read it.* **2** a mark that is left on a surface where

someone has walked: *The dog left prints all over the kitchen floor.*

printer /ˈprɪn·tər/ noun **1** **A2** a machine that is connected to a computer which makes writing or images on paper: *a laser printer* → See **The Office** on page C12 **2** a person or company that prints books, newspapers, magazines, etc.

priority /praɪˈɔr·ɪ·ti/, /praɪˈɑr·ɪ·ti/ noun (plural **priorities**) something that is very important and that must be dealt with before other things: *My first priority is to find somewhere to live.*

prison /ˈprɪz·ən/ noun **B1** a place where criminals are kept as a punishment: *He's spent most of his life in prison.*

prisoner /ˈprɪz·ə·nər/ noun **B1** someone who is being kept in prison as a punishment

privacy /ˈpraɪ·və·si/ noun [no plural] the right to be alone and do things without other people seeing or hearing you: *I hate sharing a bedroom – I never get any privacy.*

private /ˈpraɪ·vɪt/ adj **1** **B1** only for one person or group and not for everyone: *You can't park here – this is private property.* **2** controlled by or paid for by a person or company and not by the government: *a private law firm* **3** **B1** If information or an emotion is private, you do not want other people to know about it: *This is a private matter – it doesn't concern you.* **4 in private** If you do something in private, you do it where other people cannot see or hear you: *I need to talk to you in private.*

privately /ˈpraɪ·vɪt·li/ adv in secret, or with only one or two other people present: *She spoke privately with the manager.*

private school /ˈpraɪ·vɪt ˌskul/ noun a school that you pay to go to

privilege /ˈprɪv·ə·lɪdʒ/ noun an advantage that only one person or group has, usually because of their position or because they are rich

prize /praɪz/ noun **A2** something valuable that is given to someone who wins a competition: *to win a prize* ○ *first/second prize*

pro /proʊ/ **noun the pros and cons** the advantages and disadvantages of something: *We discussed the pros and cons of buying a bigger house.*

probable /ˈprɑb·ə·bəl/ **adj** likely to be true or to happen: *The probable cause of death was heart failure.*

probably /ˈprɑb·ə·bli/ **adv** **A2** used to mean that something is very likely: *I'll probably be home by midnight.*

problem /ˈprɑb·ləm/ **noun** **1** **A1** a situation that causes difficulties: *health problems* ○ *I'm having problems with my computer.* ○ *Drugs have become a serious problem in the area.* **2 no problem** informal **A2** something that you say to mean you can or will do what someone has asked you to do: *"Can you get me to the airport by 11:30?" "No problem."* **3 no problem** informal **A2** something that you say when someone has thanked you for something: *"Thanks for taking me home." "No problem."* **4 have a problem with something/someone** informal to not like something or someone: *I'm having a problem with your bad attitude.*

procedure /prəˈsi·dʒər/ **noun** the official or usual way of doing something: *You must follow the correct procedure.*

proceed /prəˈsid/ **verb** formal to continue as planned: *His lawyers have decided not to proceed with the case.*

process /ˈprɑs·es/ **noun 1** a series of actions that you take in order to do something: *Buying a house can be a long and complicated process.* **2** a series of changes that happen naturally: *the process of growing old*

procession /prəˈsef·ən/ **noun** a line of people or cars that moves forward slowly as part of a ceremony or public event: *a funeral procession*

produce[1] /prəˈdus/ **verb** (present participle **producing**, past tense and past participle **produced**) **1** **B1** to make or grow something: *The factory produces about*

900 *cars a year.* **2** to cause a particular result: *Nuts produce an allergic reaction in some people.* **3** to control how a movie, play, program, or musical recording is made: *He produced some of the most famous shows on Broadway.*

produce[2] /ˈproʊ·dus/, /ˈprɑd·us/ **noun** [no plural] fruits or vegetables that are grown in large quantities to be sold: *fresh produce*

producer /prəˈdu·sər/ **noun 1** a company, country, or person that makes things or grows food: *Australia is one of the world's main producers of wool.* **2** someone who controls how a movie, program, play, or musical recording is made: *a movie/record producer*

product /ˈprɑd·əkt/ **noun** **B1** something that someone makes or grows so that he or she can sell it: *We have a new line of skin-care products.*

production /prəˈdʌk·ʃən/ **noun 1** [no plural] the process of making or growing something: *Sand is used in the production of glass.* **2** [no plural] the amount of something that is made or grown: *We need to increase production by 20%.* **3** a performance or series of performances of a play or show: *a school production of "Romeo and Juliet"* **4** [no plural] the control of how a movie, program, play, or musical recording is made: *She wants a career in TV production.*

productive /prəˈdʌk·tɪv/ **adj 1** having a good or useful result: *We had a very productive meeting and solved a lot of problems.* **2** producing a large amount: *a productive worker*

profession /prəˈfeʃ·ən/ **noun 1** **B1** a type of work that needs special training or education: *He's working in a restaurant, but he's a teacher by profession* (= he trained to be a teacher). **2** the people who do a type of work, considered as a group: *The medical profession is worried about the new drug.*

professional[1] /prəˈfeʃ·ə·nᵊl/ **adj 1** **B1** Someone is professional if he or she gets money for a sport or activity

that most people do as a hobby: *a professional athlete/musician* → Opposite **amateur adj 2 B1** showing skill and careful attention: *a professional attitude* **3** relating to a job that needs special training or education: *You should get some professional advice about your finances.*
• **professionally** adv *He's good enough at football to play professionally.*

professional[2] /prəˈfeʃ·ə·nᵊl/ noun someone who gets money for doing a sport or activity that most other people do as a hobby: *a golf professional*

professor /prəˈfes·ər/ noun
B1 a teacher in a university or college: *a history professor at Yale*

profile /ˈprou·faɪl/ noun **1** a short description of a person, organization, etc., giving the main details about them: *He updated his profile on the website.* **2** a side view of someone's face or head: *The picture shows him in profile.*

profit /ˈprɑf·ɪt/ noun money that you get from selling something for more than it cost you to buy or produce: *a profit of $4.5 million* ○ *It's very hard for a new business to make a profit in its first year.*

profitable /ˈprɑf·ɪ·t̬ə·bəl/ adj making a profit: *a profitable business*

program[1] /ˈprou·ɡræm/ noun **1 A2** a set of instructions that you put into a computer to make it do something: *to write a computer program* **2 A2** a show on television or radio: *a TV program* **3** a plan of events or activities with a particular purpose: *The church offers religious programs for teens.* **4** a thin book that you receive or buy at a concert, sports event, etc.

program[2] /ˈprou·ɡræm/ verb (present participle **programming**, past tense and past participle **programmed**) If you program a computer, you give it a set of instructions to do something.

programmer /ˈprou·ɡræm·ər/ noun someone who writes computer programs as a job

progress[1] /ˈprɑɡ·rəs/ noun [no plural] **1 B1** development and improvement of skills, knowledge, etc.: *technological progress* ○ *He has made good progress in French this year.* **2 in progress** happening or being done now: *Quiet please – exams in progress.* **3** movement toward a place

> **! Common mistake: progress**
>
> Remember that **progress** is not used with "a."
>
> *I have made great progress in speaking English.*
> ~~I have made a great progress in speaking English.~~

progress[2] /prəˈɡres/ verb **1** to improve: *Technology has progressed rapidly in the last 100 years.* **2** to continue gradually: *I began to feel more relaxed as the evening progressed.*

prohibit /prouˈhɪb·ɪt/ verb formal to say by law that you must not do something: *Smoking is prohibited on most flights.*

project[1] /ˈprɑdʒ·ekt/ noun **1 B1** a piece of school work that involves detailed study of a subject: *We're doing a class project on the environment.* **2** a planned piece of work that has a particular purpose: *The new building project will cost $45 million.*

projector /prəˈdʒek·tər/ noun a machine that shows movies, pictures, or words on a screen or a wall

prominent /ˈprɑm·ə·nənt/ adj **1** important or famous: *a prominent businessman* **2** very easy to see or notice: *a prominent nose*
• **prominently** adv

promise[1] /ˈprɑm·ɪs/ verb (present participle **promising**, past tense and past participle **promised**) **1 B1** to say that you will certainly do something or that something will certainly happen: *She promised to write to me every week.* ○ *Paul promised me that he'd cook dinner tonight.* **2 B1** to say that you will certainly give something to someone: *Her parents promised her a new car when she graduates from college.*

promise[2] /'prɑm·ɪs/ *noun* **B1** a statement that you will certainly do something: *I'm not sure I can do it so I won't* **make** *any* **promises**. ○ *I said I would take her swimming and I don't want to* **break** *my* **promise** (= not do what I said I would).

promote /prə'moʊt/ *verb* (present participle **promoting**, past tense and past participle **promoted**) **1** **B1** to give someone a more important job in the same organization: *She was just* **promoted** *to manager.* **2** to advertise something: *The band is promoting their new album.*

promotion /prə'moʊ·ʃən/ *noun* **1** activities that advertise something: *a sales promotion* **2** a move to a more important job in the same organization: *She* **got** *a* **promotion** *in her first year with the company.*

prompt /prɑmpt/ *adj* done or acting quickly and without waiting: *a prompt reply*
• **promptly** *adv*

pronoun /'proʊ·nɑʊn/ *noun* **B1** in grammar, a word that is used instead of a noun which has usually already been talked about. For example, the words "she," "it," and "mine" are pronouns.

pronounce /prə'nɑʊns/ *verb* (present participle **pronouncing**, past tense and past participle **pronounced**) **B1** to make the sound or sounds of a letter or word: *How do you pronounce his name?*

pronunciation /prə,nʌn·si'eɪ·ʃən/ *noun* **B1** the way words are pronounced: *There are two different pronunciations of this word.*

proof /pruf/ *noun* [no plural] a fact or a piece of information that shows something exists or is true: *She showed us her passport as* **proof of** *her identity.* ○ *My landlord asked for* **proof that** *I'm employed.*

propeller /prə'pel·ər/ *noun* a piece of equipment that turns around and moves a ship or plane move

proper /'prɑp·ər/ *adj* **B1** correct or suitable: *Please put those books back in their proper place.*

properly /'prɑp·ər·li/ *adv* **B1** correctly, or in a satisfactory way: *If she doesn't behave properly, she will have to leave.*

proper noun /'prɑp·ər 'nɑʊn/ *noun* a word or group of words that is the name of a person or place and always begins with a capital letter: *"New York" is a proper noun.*

property /'prɑp·ər·ti/ *noun* **1** **B1** [no plural] objects that belong to someone: *The police recovered a large amount of stolen property.* **2** (plural **properties**) a building or area of land: *Private property – no parking.*

prophet /'prɑf·ɪt/ *noun* someone sent by God to tell people what to do, or to say what will happen in the future

proportion /prə'pɔr·ʃən/ *noun* a part of a total number or amount: *Children make up a large* **proportion of** *the world's population.*

proposal /prə'poʊ·zəl/ *noun* **1** a suggestion for a plan: *a proposal to raise taxes* **2** an act of asking someone to marry you

propose /prə'poʊz/ *verb* (present participle **proposing**, past tense and past participle **proposed**) **1** to suggest a plan or action: *I* **propose that** *we delay our decision until we have more information.* **2** to ask someone to marry you: *He* **proposed to** *me on my birthday.* **3** **propose to do** *something* to intend to do something: *They propose to cross the desert by car.*

prosecute /'prɑs·ɪˌkjut/ *verb* to accuse someone of a crime in a court of law: *No one has been* **prosecuted for** *the murders.*

prospect /'prɑs·pekt/ *noun* the possibility that something might happen in the future: *Business groups are unhappy about the* **prospect of** *a tax increase.*

protect /prə'tekt/ *verb* **B1** to keep someone or something safe from something dangerous or bad: *It's important to* **protect** *your skin* **from** *the sun.*
• **protection** *noun* [no plural] *This coat doesn't provide any* **protection against** *the rain.*

a
b
c
d
e
f
g
h
i
j
k
l
m
n
o
p
q
r
s
t
u
v
w
x
y
z

| æ cat | ɑ hot | e get | ɪ sit | i see | ɔ saw | ʊ book | u too | ʌ cut | ə about | ər mother | ɜr turn | ɔr for | aɪ my | aʊ how | eɪ say | ɔɪ boy |

protected /prəˈtek·tɪd/ **adj** protected animals, plants, and land are kept safe by laws that stop them from harming or damaging them: *Tigers are a protected species.*

protective /prəˈtek·tɪv/ **adj** giving protection: *protective clothing*

protein /ˈproʊ·tin/ **noun** a substance found in foods such as meat and milk that is necessary for the body to grow and be strong

protest¹ /ˈproʊ·test/ **noun** an act of showing that you strongly disagree with something, often by somewhere and shouting, carrying signs, etc.: *a protest against the war*

protest² /prəˈtest/ **verb** to show that you disagree with something by standing somewhere, shouting, carrying signs, etc.: *They're on strike to protest the pay cuts.*

Protestant /ˈprɑt·ə·stənt/ **noun** a member of one of the Christian churches that separated from the Roman Catholic Church during the 16th century
• **Protestant adj**

protester /prəˈtes·tər/ **noun** someone who shows that he or she disagrees with something by standing somewhere, shouting, carrying signs, etc.

proud /praʊd/ **adj** **1** 🔒 feeling very happy about something you own or something you have done: *She was so proud of her son.* ○ *I'm very proud to be involved in this project.* **2** feeling that you are more important than you really are: *She's too proud to admit she is wrong.*
• **proudly adv**

prove /pruv/ **verb** (present participle **proving**, past tense and past participle **proved**) **1** 🔒 to show that something is true: *Can you prove that you weren't there?* ○ *He's desperately trying to prove his innocence.* **2** to show a particular result or quality after a period of time: *The operation proved to be a success.*

proverb /ˈprɑv·ɜrb/ **noun** a famous phrase or sentence that gives you advice: *an ancient Chinese proverb*

provide /prəˈvaɪd/ **verb** (present participle **providing**, past tense and past participle **provided**) 🔒 to give something to someone: *It's a new program that provides schools with free computers.*

provided /prəˈvaɪ·dɪd/ **conjunction** (also **providing**) only if: *He's welcome to come, provided that he behaves himself.*

provider /prəˈvaɪ·dər/ **noun** a person or company that gives or sells someone something that he or she needs: *an Internet service provider*

province /ˈprɑv·ɪns/ **noun** one of the large areas into which some countries are divided: *the Canadian province of Alberta*

provoke /prəˈvoʊk/ **verb** (present participle **provoking**, past tense and past participle **provoked**) to cause a strong and usually angry reaction: *Her statement provoked an angry response.*

psychiatrist /saɪˈkaɪ·ə·trɪst/ **noun** a doctor who treats people who have a mental illness

psychological /ˌsaɪ·kəˈlɑdʒ·ɪ·kəl/ **adj** relating to the human mind and feelings: *psychological problems*
• **psychologically adv** *Are you psychologically prepared for your new job?*

psychologist /saɪˈkɑl·ə·dʒɪst/ **noun** someone who studies the human mind and feelings

psychology /saɪˈkɑl·ə·dʒi/ **noun** [no plural] the study of the human mind and feelings: *He's studying psychology at college.*

pt. written abbreviation for pint: a unit for measuring liquid

public¹ /ˈpʌb·lɪk/ **adj** **1** public parks, bathrooms, transportation, etc. 🔒 parks, bathrooms, transportation, etc. that are for everyone to use: *Smoking should be banned in public places.* **2** public opinion, health, support, etc. the opinions, health, support, etc. of ordinary people: *Public opinion has turned against him.*

public² /ˈpʌb·lɪk/ **noun** **1** the (general) public all of the ordinary people in a

287   **pump**

particular place: *It's the job of the police to protect the members of the general public.* ○ *The public has a right to know about this.* **2 in public** where everyone can see you: *They shouldn't argue like that in public.*

• **publicly** adv *The company publicly apologized for the accident.*

publication /ˌpʌb·lɪˈkeɪ·ʃən/ noun
1 a book, newspaper, etc. in which information or stories are published: *Our latest publication is a magazine for teachers.* **2** [no plural] the act of making information or stories available to people in a printed form: *The book will be ready for publication in September.*

publicity /pəˈblɪs·ɪ·t̬i/ noun [no plural] advertising or information about someone or something in the newspaper, on television, etc.: *a publicity campaign*

public school /ˈpʌb·lɪk ˌskul/ noun a school that is free to go to because the government provides the money for it

public transportation /ˈpʌb·lɪk ˌtræns·pərˈteɪ·ʃən/ noun [no plural]
B1 a system of vehicles such as buses and trains that everyone can use

publish /ˈpʌb·lɪʃ/ verb **1 B1** to prepare and print a book, newspaper, magazine, article, etc. so that people can buy it: *This book is published by Harvard University Press.* **2 B1** to make information available to the public

publisher /ˈpʌb·lɪ·ʃər/ noun a company or person who prepares and prints books, newspapers, magazines, etc.

puck /pʌk/ noun a hard, round, flat object that players try to hit into a goal in the sport of hockey
→ See **Sports (1)** on page C15

pudding /ˈpʊd·ɪŋ/ noun a sweet, soft food that is made from milk, sugar, and eggs: *vanilla pudding*

puddle /ˈpʌd·ᵊl/ noun a pool of liquid on the ground, usually from rain

puff¹ /pʌf/ verb to breathe fast and with difficulty, usually because you have been running

puff² /pʌf/ noun a small amount of smoke, gas, powder, etc.: *a puff of smoke*

pull /pʊl/ verb **1 A2** to take hold of something and move it somewhere: *She pulled the door open.* ○ *Pull up your socks.* ○ *A child was pulling at his sleeve.*
2 pull *something* **off, out, up, etc.**
B1 to take hold of something and use physical effort to remove it from somewhere: *He pulled off his sweater.* ○ *I pulled the plug out.* **3 pull** *yourself* **along, up, etc.** to take hold of something and use effort to move your body: *She pulled herself up the stairs, holding onto the rail.*

pull

pullover /ˈpʊlˌoʊ·vər/ noun **B1** a warm piece of clothing that covers the top of your body and is pulled on over your head
→ See **Clothes** on page C5

pulse /pʌls/ noun the regular movement of blood through your body when your heart is beating: *The doctor **took** (=checked) my **pulse**.*

pump¹ /pʌmp/ noun **B1** a piece of equipment that forces liquid or gas to move somewhere: *a water pump*

pumps

gas pump

bicycle pump

| æ cat | ɑ hot | e get | ɪ sit | i see | ɔ saw | ʊ book | u too | ʌ cut | ə about | ər mother | ɜr turn | ɔr for | aɪ my | aʊ how | eɪ say | ɔɪ boy |

a

b

c

d

e

f

g

h

i

j

k

l

m

n

o

p

q

r

s

t

u

v

w

x

y

z

pump[2] /pʌmp/ **verb** to force liquid or gas to move somewhere: *Your heart pumps blood around your body.*

pump something up phrasal verb to fill something with air using a pump: *You should pump your tires up.*

pumpkin /ˈpʌmp·kɪn/ noun a large, round vegetable with thick, orange skin

pumpkin

punch[1] /pʌntʃ/ **verb** **1** to hit someone or something with your fist (=closed hand): *He punched me twice in the stomach.* **2 punch a hole in something** to make a hole in something with a special piece of equipment

punch[2] /pʌntʃ/ **noun** an act of hitting someone or something with your fist (=closed hand): *a punch in the nose*

punctual /ˈpʌŋk·tʃu·əl/ **adj** arriving at the right time and not late
• **punctually** adv

punctuation /ˌpʌŋk·tʃuˈeɪ·ʃən/ **noun** [no plural] **B1** the use of marks in writing so that people can see when a sentence begins and ends, that something is a question, etc.

puncture /ˈpʌŋk·tʃər/ **noun** a small hole made by a sharp object

punish /ˈpʌn·ɪʃ/ **verb** **B1** to make someone suffer because he or she has done something bad: *They must be severely punished for these crimes.*

punishment /ˈpʌn·ɪʃ·mənt/ **noun** an act of punishing someone: *He had to stay in his bedroom as a punishment for fighting.*

pupil /ˈpjuː·pəl/ **noun** **1** **A2** a person who is being taught, especially in a class: *The school has 410 pupils aged 6 to 11.* **2** the black, round part in the center of your eye

puppet /ˈpʌp·ɪt/ noun a toy in the shape of a person or animal that you can move with strings or by putting your hand inside: *a finger puppet*

puppet

puppy /ˈpʌp·i/ **noun** (plural **puppies**) **B1** a young dog

purchase[1] /ˈpɜr·tʃəs/ **verb** (present participle **purchasing**, past tense and past participle **purchased**) formal to buy something: *Tickets must be purchased two weeks in advance.*

purchase[2] /ˈpɜr·tʃəs/ **noun** formal **1** the act of buying something: *the illegal purchase of guns* **2** something that you buy: *He made a number of purchases.*

pure /pjʊr/ **adj** **1** **B1** A pure substance is not mixed with anything else: *pure gold* **2** **B1** clean and healthy: *pure air/ water* **3** complete or only: *Getting the job was pure luck.*

purely /ˈpjʊr·li/ **adv** only: *She married him purely for his money.*

purple[1] /ˈpɜr·pəl/ **adj** **A2** being a color that is a mixture of red and blue

purple[2] /ˈpɜr·pəl/ **noun** **A2** the color purple
→ See **Colors** on page C6

purpose /ˈpɜr·pəs/ **noun** **1** **B1** why you do something or why something exists: *The main purpose of the meeting is to discuss the future of the company.* **2 on purpose** **B1** If you do something bad on purpose, you wanted or planned to do it: *I didn't do it on purpose – it was an accident.*

purposely /ˈpɜr·pəs·li/ **adv** wanting to do something: *I wasn't purposely trying to hurt you.*

purr /pɜr/ **verb** If a cat purrs, it makes a soft sound in its throat to show pleasure.

purse /pɜrs/ **noun** **A2** a bag carried by a woman with her money, keys, etc. inside

pursue /pərˈsuː/ **verb** (present participle **pursuing**, past tense and past participle **pursued**) to try to do something over a period of time: *She decided to pursue a career in finance.*

push[1] /pʊʃ/ **verb** **1** **A2** to move someone or something by pressing them with your hands or body: *He pushed me out of the door.* ○ *Someone pushed him*

|oʊ go|aɪər **fire**|aʊər **hour**|eər **hair**|ɪər **ear**|ʊər **poor**|j **yet**|ʒ **measure**|ʃ **ship**|dʒ **judge**|tʃ **chin**|ð **that**|θ **thin**|ŋ **hang**|

into the river. → See picture at **pull 2** 🅑🅑 to press something: *If you push this button, your seat will go back.* **3** 🅑🅑 to move somewhere by moving someone or something away from you: *She pushed through the crowd.* **4** *push someone to do something* to try hard to make someone do something: *My parents have always pushed me to do well in school.* **5** *push yourself* to work very hard in order to achieve something: *She really pushed herself to pass her exams.*

push^2 /pʊʃ/ *noun* 🅑🅑 an act of moving someone or something by pressing them with your hands or body: *She gave him a little push toward the door.*

put /pʊt/ *verb* (present participle **putting**, past tense and past participle **put**) **1** 🅐🅐 to move something to a place or position: *Where did you put the keys?* ○ *She put her bag on the floor.* ○ *He put his arm around her.* **2** 🅐🅐 to write something: *I put the date of the party on my calendar.*

put *something* **away** *phrasal verb* 🅑🅑 to put something in the place where you usually keep it: *She folded the towels and put them away in the closet.*
→ See **Phrasal Verbs** on page C13

put *something* **back** *phrasal verb* 🅑🅑 to put something where it was before it was moved: *I put the book back on the shelf.*

put *something* **down** *phrasal verb* 🅑🅑 to put something that you are holding onto the floor or onto another surface: *I need to put my bag down for a minute – it's really heavy.*
→ See **Phrasal Verbs** on page C13

put *something* **off** *phrasal verb* 🅑🅑 to decide to do something at a later time: *I'll put off doing the laundry until tomorrow.*

put *something* **on** *phrasal verb* **1** 🅐🅐 to put clothes or shoes onto your body: *You'd better put your coat on – it's cold outside.* → See **Phrasal Verbs** on page C13 **2** 🅐🅐 to put makeup or cream onto your skin: *Put some sunscreen on before you go out.* **3** 🅐🅐 to put a CD, DVD, etc. into a machine so that you can hear or see it: *Do you mind if I put some music on?*

put *something* **out** *phrasal verb* 🅑🅑 to make something that is burning stop burning: *to put out a fire*

put *something* **up** *phrasal verb* 🅑🅑 to attach something to a wall or ceiling: *They put a few pictures up on the wall.*

put up with *someone/something* *phrasal verb* to accept something that is bad although you do not like it: *He's so rude! How do you put up with him?*

puzzle /ˈpʌz·əl/ *noun* **1** 🅐🅑 a game or activity in which you have to put pieces together or answer questions using skill: *a jigsaw puzzle* **2** a situation that is very difficult to understand: *Scientists have been trying to solve this puzzle for years.*

puzzled /ˈpʌz·əld/ *adj* confused because you do not understand something: *He had a puzzled look on his face.*

pyramid /ˈpɪr·ə·mɪd/ *noun* a shape with a square base and four triangular sides that meet to form a point at the top
→ See picture at **shape noun** (1)

Qq

Q, q /kju/ the seventeenth letter of the alphabet

qt. written abbreviation for **quart**: a unit for measuring liquid

quack /kwæk/ *noun* the sound made by a duck (= water bird)
• **quack** *verb*

quaint /kweɪnt/ *adj* attractive and different in an old-fashioned way: *a quaint little village*

qualification /ˌkwɑl·ə·fɪˈkeɪ·ʃən/ *noun* a skill or type of experience that prepares you to do a particular job or activity, or proof that you have this skill or experience: *What qualifications do you need for the teaching job?*

qualified /ˈkwɑl·əˌfɑɪd/ *adj* having the skills, qualities or experience that you need in order to do something: *I'm not really **qualified to** give you advice on that subject.*

qualify /ˈkwɑl·əˌfɑɪ/ *verb* (present participle **qualifying**, past tense and past participle **qualified**) **1** If you qualify for something, you are allowed to do it: *To **qualify for** the competition, you must be over 18.* **2** to succeed in getting into a competition: *Nigeria was the first team to **qualify for** the World Cup.*

quality /ˈkwɑl·ɪ·t̬i/ *noun* **1** [no plural] how good or bad something is: *good/high quality* ○ *The air quality in this area is terrible.* **2** [no plural] the fact of being very good or well made: *I was impressed by the quality of her work.* **3** (plural **qualities**) part of the character of someone or something: *Anthony has leadership qualities.*

quantity /ˈkwɑn·tɪ·t̬i/ *noun* (plural **quantities**) the amount or number of something: *A huge quantity of information is available on the Internet.*
→ See **Quantities** on page C14

quarrel /ˈkwɑr·əl/ *noun* an argument: *She walked out after **having a quarrel** with her sister.*

quart /kwɔrt/ *noun* (written abbreviation **qt.**) a unit for measuring liquid, equal to 32 ounces (2 U.S. pints)

quarter /ˈkwɔr·t̬ər/ *noun* **quarter**
1 (also **fourth**) one of four equal parts of something; 1/4: *We only finished a quarter of the pie.* **2** a period of 15 minutes before or after the hour: *It's **a quarter to** three (=2:45).* ○ *We're leaving at **a quarter after** six (= 6:15).* **3** a coin with a value of 25 cents (=25/100 of a dollar): *There are four quarters in a dollar.* **4** one of four time periods that a school or college year can be divided into. The summer quarter is not usually a necessary part of the school year.

queen /kwin/ *noun* **1** a female ruler in some countries: *Queen Elizabeth*

2 the wife of a king **3** a playing card that has a picture of a queen on it: *the queen of hearts*

query /ˈkwɪər·i/ *noun* (plural **queries**) a question: *I have a query about the last exercise.*

question¹ /ˈkwes·tʃən/ *noun* **1** a sentence or phrase that asks you for information: *Is it OK if I **ask** you a few **questions**?* ○ *He refused to **answer** my **question**.* **2** on a test or exam, a problem that tests a person's knowledge or ability: ***Answer** as many **questions** as you can.* **3** [no plural] doubt: *There is **no question** that the fire was an accident.* **4** a situation or problem that needs to be dealt with or considered: *Your article **raises the question** of human rights.*

> **! Common mistake: ask a question**
>
> Remember to use the verb **ask** with question.
> *We weren't allowed to ask any questions.*
> ~~We weren't allowed to make any questions.~~

question² /ˈkwes·tʃən/ *verb* **1** to ask someone questions: *Police are **questioning** the neighbors **about** the murder.* **2** to show or feel doubt about something: *I'm just **questioning whether** we need the extra staff.*

question mark /ˈkwes·tʃən ˌmɑrk/ *noun* a mark [?] used at the end of a question

questionnaire /ˌkwes·tʃəˈneər/ *noun* a set of questions that a lot of people are asked in order to gather information about a subject: *They asked visitors to **complete** a **questionnaire**.*

quick /kwɪk/ *adj* doing something fast or taking only a short time: *I tried to catch him but he was too quick for me.*

quickly /ˈkwɪk·li/ *adv* fast or in a short time: *I quickly shut the door.*

quiet¹ /ˈkwɑɪ·ɪt/ *adj* **1** making little or no noise: *Can you **be quiet**, please?*

We're trying to work. **2** **A2** lacking noise or activity: *I need some quiet time today.* **3** **B1** If someone is quiet, he or she talks very little: *a shy, quiet man*

quiet[2] /'kwaɪ·ɪt/ **noun** [no plural] a state in which there is little or no noise: *She needs some **peace and quiet**.*

quietly /'kwaɪ·ɪt·li/ **adv** **1** **B1** making little or no noise: *"Don't worry," she said quietly.* **2** **B1** doing something without much noise or activity: *He sat quietly, waiting for her to come home.*

quilt /kwɪlt/ **noun** a cover for a bed that is filled with feathers or other warm material

quit /kwɪt/ **verb** (present participle **quitting**, past tense and past participle **quit**) **1** **B1** to leave your job: *She recently quit her job to spend more time with her family.* **2** **B1** to stop doing something: *I gained weight after I quit smoking.*

quite /kwaɪt/ **adv** **1** **A2** to a large degree: *The two situations are quite different.* **2** a bit, a few, a lot, etc. **A2** a large amount or number: *There is quite a bit of mail for you here.* **3** not quite almost but not completely: *The colors don't quite match.*

❗ Common mistake: quiet or quite?

Be careful! These two words look very similar, but they are spelled differently and have completely different meanings.

Quiet means "making little or no noise."
  The house was very quiet without the kids around.

Quite means "to a large degree."
  It's quite cold today.

---

quiz /kwɪz/ **noun** (plural **quizzes**) **1** a short test on a subject in school: *a math quiz* **2** **A2** a game in which you answer questions: *a television quiz show*

quota /'kwoʊ·t̬ə/ **noun** a limited amount of something that is officially allowed: *an import quota*

quotation /kwoʊ'teɪ·ʃən/ **noun** a sentence or phrase that is taken out of a book, poem, or play: *a quotation from Shakespeare*

quote /kwoʊt/ **verb** (present participle **quoting**, past tense and past participle **quoted**) **1** to repeat what someone has said or written: *I was quoting from Marx.* ∘ *Witnesses were quoted as saying there were two robbers.* **2** to say how much a piece of work will cost before you do it

Rr

R, r /ɑr/ the eighteenth letter of the alphabet

rabbi /'ræb·aɪ/ **noun** a leader and teacher in the Jewish religion

rabbit /'ræb·ɪt/ **noun** **A2** a small animal with fur and long ears that lives in a hole in the ground

raccoon /ræ'kun/ **noun** a small gray animal with black marks like a mask on its face and a tail with black rings

race[1] /reɪs/ **noun** **1** **A2** a competition in which people run, ride, drive, etc. against each other in order to see who is the fastest: *a horse race* **2** one of the groups that people are divided into, having the same color skin or hair and other things that are the same: *people of many different races*

race[2] /reɪs/ **verb** (present participle **racing**, past tense and past participle **raced**) **1** **B1** to compete in a race: *I'll race you to the end of the road!* **2** to move somewhere very quickly: *I raced over to see what was the matter.* **3** to take someone somewhere very quickly: *Ambulances raced the injured to a nearby hospital.*

racial /'reɪ·ʃəl/ **adj** relating to people's race: *a racial minority*

racing /'reɪ·sɪŋ/ **noun** [no plural] an activity or sport in which people, animals, or vehicles race one another: *car racing*
→ See **Sports 1** on page C15

racism /ˈreɪ·sɪz·əm/ **noun** [no plural]
the belief that other races of people are
not as good as your own

racist /ˈreɪ·sɪst/ **noun** someone who believes that other races of people are not
as good as his or her own
• **racist** adj *a racist attack*

rack /ræk/ **noun** a type of shelf that
you can put things on or hang things
from: *a luggage rack*

rack

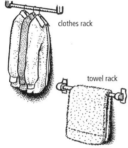

clothes rack

towel rack

racket /ˈræk·ɪt/ **noun** **1** **A2** a piece of
equipment that you use to hit a ball in
sports such as tennis
→ See **Sports 2** on page C16 **2** informal a
loud noise: *The neighbors were **making**
such **a racket**.*

radar /ˈreɪ·dɑr/ **noun** [no plural] a system
that uses radio waves to find out the
position of something you cannot see

radiation /ˌreɪ·diˈeɪ·ʃən/ **noun** [no plural]
a dangerous form of energy that comes
from certain substances: *high **levels of
radiation***

radiator /ˈreɪ·diˌeɪ·tər/ **noun** **1** a metal
piece of equipment that is filled with
hot water and is used to heat a room
2 a part of a car that makes the engine
cool

radio /ˈreɪ·diˌoʊ/ **noun** **1** **A1** a piece of
equipment used for listening to radio
broadcasts: *a car radio* **2 the radio**
A1 the programs that you hear when

you listen to the radio: *We heard him
speaking **on the radio** this morning.*
3 **B1** [no plural] a system of sending and
getting sound through the air: *local radio*

radioactive /ˌreɪ·di·oʊˈæk·tɪv/ **adj**
giving off radiation (= a harmful form of
energy): *radioactive waste*

radius /ˈreɪ·di·əs/ **noun** (plural **radii**)
the distance from the center of a circle
to its edge

rag /ræg/ **noun** a piece of old cloth that
you use to clean things

rage /reɪdʒ/ **noun** strong anger that
you cannot control: *a jealous rage*

raid[1] /reɪd/ **noun** a sudden attack on a
place by soldiers or police: *an air raid*

raid[2] /reɪd/ **verb** If soldiers or police
raid a place, they suddenly attack it.

rail /reɪl/ **noun** **1** a bar on the wall that
you hang things on: *a curtain rail*
2 **B1** [no plural] trains as a method of
transportation: *rail travel*

railing /ˈreɪ·lɪŋ/ **noun** a fence made
from posts and bars: *an iron railing*

railroad /ˈreɪlˌroʊd/ **noun** **1** **A2** the systems and organizations connected with
trains: *He worked on the railroad for much
of his life.* **2** the metal tracks that trains
travel on: *A railroad used to be where the
highway is now.*

railroad station /ˈreɪlˌroʊd ˌsteɪ·ʃən/
noun a train station

rain[1] /reɪn/ **noun** [no plural] **A1** water
that falls from the sky in small drops:
heavy rain

rain[2] /reɪn/ **verb** **it rains** **A1** If it rains,
water falls from the sky in small drops:
It was raining all weekend.

rainbow /ˈreɪn·boʊ/ **noun** a half circle
with seven colors that sometimes appears in the sky when the sun shines
through rain

raincoat /ˈreɪn·koʊt/ **noun** **A2** a coat
that you wear to keep yourself dry when
it is raining

raindrop /ˈreɪn·drɑp/ **noun** a single
drop of rain

rainforest /'reɪnˌfɒr·ɪst,/'reɪnˌfɑːr·ɪst/
noun **B1** a forest with a lot of tall trees
where it rains a lot: *a tropical rainforest*

rainy /'reɪ·ni/ **adj** (comparative **rainier**,
superlative **rainiest**) **B1** raining a lot: *a
rainy afternoon*

raise /reɪz/ **verb** (present participle **raising**,
past tense and past participle **raised**) **1** **B1** to
lift something to a higher position: *She
raised her hand.* **2** **B1** to make an
amount or level go up: *They have raised
taxes.* **3** to take care of a child until he
or she has become an adult **4** to collect
money from people in order to do a particular thing: *They held a sale to raise
money for charity.* **5** **raise a question,
subject, etc.** to start talking about a
subject that you want other people to
consider: *I'm going to raise the issue
with Sally at the meeting.*

raisin /'reɪ·zɪn/ **noun** a dried grape
(=small, round fruit)

rally /'ræl·i/ **noun** (plural **rallies**) **1** a large
public meeting in support of something:
an election/campaign rally **2** a car or
motorcycle race: *a rally driver*

ran /ræn/ past tense of run

ranch /ræntʃ/ **noun** a large farm where
animals are kept: *a cattle ranch*

random /'ræn·dəm/ **adj** by chance:
Winners will be chosen at random.

rang /ræŋ/ past tense of ring²

range /reɪndʒ/ **noun** **1** **B1** a group of
different things of the same general
type: *We discussed a wide range of subjects.* **2** the amount or number between a particular set of limits: *The
product is aimed at young people in the
18-25 age range.* **3** [no plural] the distance
from which things can be seen, heard,
or reached: *He was shot at close range
(=from very nearby).* **4** a line of hills or
mountains

rank /ræŋk/ **noun** a position in society
or in an organization, for example the
army: *He holds the rank of general.*

ransom /'ræn·səm/ **noun** the money
that is demanded for the return of someone who is being kept as a prisoner

rap /ræp/ **noun** [no plural] **A2** a type of
music in which the words are spoken
and there is a strong beat: *a rap artist*

rape /reɪp/ **verb** to force someone to
have sex when he or she does not want to
• **rape noun** *He was accused of rape.*

rapid /'ræp·ɪd/ **adj** happening or moving very quickly: *rapid change*
• **rapidly adv**

rare /reər/ **adj** **B1** very unusual: *a rare
disease* ◦ *It's very **rare** to see these birds
in England.*

rarely /'reər·li/ **adv** **B1** not often: *I
rarely see her these days.*

rash¹ /ræʃ/ **noun** a group of small, red
spots on the skin: *an itchy rash*

rash² /ræʃ/ **adj** done suddenly and
without thinking carefully: *a rash decision*

raspberry /'ræz·ber·i/ **noun** (plural
raspberries) a small, soft, red fruit
that grows on bushes

rat /ræt/ **noun**   **rat**
A2 an animal that
looks like a large
mouse and has a
long tail: *Rats carry
disease.*

rate /reɪt/ **noun**
1 how often some-
thing happens, or how many people
something happens to: *the birth rate*
◦ *the rate of unemployment* **2** a fixed
amount of money given for something:
rates of pay **3** the speed at which something happens: *the rate of progress*

rather /'ræð·ər/ **adv** **1** **B1** slightly: *I find
her books rather boring.* **2** **rather than**
B1 instead of: *He saw his music as a
hobby rather than a career.* **3** **would
rather** **B1** If you would rather do something, you would prefer to do that
thing: *I'd much rather go out for a meal
than stay at home and watch TV.* **4** used
to change something you have just said
and make it more correct: *The music, or
rather noise, from the party upstairs went
on all night.*

ration¹ /ˈræʃ·ən/ noun   the amount of something that you are allowed to have when there is little of it: *a food/gas ration*

ration² /ˈræʃ·ən/ verb   to give people only a small amount of something because there is little of it: *They might have to start rationing water.*

rational /ˈræʃ·ə·nəl/ adj   based on facts and not affected by someone's emotions or imagination: *a rational decision*

rattle¹ /ˈræt̬·əl/ verb (present participle **rattling**, past tense and past participle **rattled**)   to keep making a noise by knocking against something: *The wind blew hard, rattling the doors and windows.*

rattle² /ˈræt̬·əl/ noun   a toy that a baby shakes to make a noise

raw /rɔ/ adj   1 **B1** not cooked: *raw meat/vegetables*   2 in the natural state and not changed: *Oil is an important* **raw material**.

ray /reɪ/ noun   a narrow beam of light, heat, or energy: *the rays of the sun*

razor /ˈreɪ·zər/ noun   a piece of equipment with a sharp blade used for removing hair from the face, legs, etc.
→ See **The Bathroom** on page C1

razor blade /ˈreɪ·zər ˌbleɪd/ noun   a very thin, sharp blade that you put in a razor

Rd. (also **Rd**)   written abbreviation for road: *17 Shoreline Rd.*

re- /ri/ prefix   used to add the meaning "do again," especially to verbs: *redo* ○ *rewrite*

reach¹ /riʧ/ verb   1 **B1** to arrive somewhere: *We won't reach Miami until five or six o'clock.*   2 to stretch your arm and hand to touch or take something: *She* **reached for** *a cigarette.* ○ *He* **reached out** *and grabbed her arm.*   3 **can reach (something)** to be able to touch or take something with your hand: *Could you get that book down for me – I can't reach.*   4 **reach a decision, agreement, conclusion, etc.** to make a decision, agreement, conclusion, etc. about something: *She*

reached the conclusion that she couldn't help him.   5 to get to a particular level, situation, etc.: *The temperature could reach 90°F today.* ○ *He's reached the age of 95 with his mind still sharp.*   6 to speak to someone on the telephone: *You can reach him at home.*

reach² /riʧ/ noun [no plural]   1 **out of reach** too far away for someone to take hold of: *I keep the medicines up here, out of the children's reach.*   2 **be within reach** to be close enough for someone to take hold of: *The gun lay within reach.*   3 the distance that can be traveled, especially easily: *We live* **within easy reach** *of the station.*

react /riˈækt/ verb   to say, do, or feel something because of something else that has been said or done: *He* **reacted** *angrily* **to** *her comments.*

reaction /riˈæk·ʃən/ noun   1 something you say, feel, or do because of something that has happened: *What was his* **reaction to** *the news?*   2 **reactions** the ability to move quickly when something suddenly happens: *Drivers need to have quick reactions.*   3 an unpleasant feeling or illness caused by something you have eaten or used on your body: *Some people* **have a bad reaction to** *this drug.*

read /rid/ verb (past tense and past participle **read**)   1 **A1** to look at words and understand what they mean: *What was the last book you read?* ○ *I've been* **reading about** *Marilyn Monroe.*   2 **A2** to look at words that are written and say them aloud for other people to listen to: *Do you want me to* **read** *it* **to** *you?*
read something out phrasal verb   to read something and say the words so that other people can hear: *He read out the names of all the winners.*
read something over/through phrasal verb   to read something from the beginning to the end, especially to find mistakes: *I read over my essay to check for errors.*

reader /ˈri·dər/ noun   1 **B1** someone who reads: *She's a slow reader.*   2 **B1** a book containing a simple story for people who are learning to read or learning

295 reasonable

a language: *There are readers at different levels, from beginner to advanced.*

readily /ˈred·ᵊl·i/ adv **1** quickly and easily: *Information is readily available on the Internet.* **2** willingly and without stopping to think: *He readily agreed to help.*

reading /ˈri·dɪŋ/ noun [no plural]
A1 the activity or skill of getting information from books, newspapers, etc.: *I did a lot of reading over vacation.*

ready /ˈred·i/ adj **1** **A1** prepared for doing something: *Are you ready to go yet?* ○ *We're leaving at eight, so you have an hour to get ready.* **2** **A2** prepared and available to be eaten, drunk, used, etc.: *Is dinner ready?*

real /ˈri·əl, /ril/ adj **1** **A2** existing and not imagined: *He's not real you know, he's just a character in a book.* ○ *Romance is never like that in real life.* **2** **A2** not false: *real leather* **3** **B1** true and not pretended: *Is that your real name?* **4** being the most important or the main thing: *The real problem is money.* **5** used to emphasize a noun: *She was a real help.*

real estate /ˈri·əl əˌsteɪt/, /ˈril əˌsteɪt/ noun [no plural] land or buildings: *We're planning to buy some real estate in the city.*

real estate agent /ˈri·əl əˌsteɪt ˌer·dʒənt/ noun someone who sells buildings and land as his or her job

realistic /ˌri·əˈlɪs·tɪk/ adj **1** **B1** showing things and people as they really are, or making them seem to be real: *The scene in the movie where they find a dinosaur is very realistic.* **2** accepting the true facts of a situation: *Let's be realistic – we're not going to finish this by Friday.*

reality /riˈæl·ɪ·t̬i/ noun [no plural] the way things or situations really are and not the way you would like them to be: *Listening to music is my escape from reality.* ○ *He may seem charming but in reality he's actually quite unpleasant.*

realize /ˈri·əˌlaɪz/ verb (present participle **realizing**, past tense and past participle **realized**) **B1** to notice or understand something that you did not notice or

understand before: *I suddenly realized I'd met him before.*

really /ˈri·ə·li/, /ˈri·li/ adv **1** **A1** very or very much: *She's really nice.* ○ *I really don't want to go.* **2** **B1** used when you are saying what is true about a situation: *She tried to hide what she was really thinking.* **3** **A2** used to give particular importance to a verb: *You really shouldn't worry.* **4** **really?** **A2** used when you are surprised at what someone has just said: *"Apparently, he's leaving." "Really?"* **5** **not really** **B1** used for replying that something is not true in a way that is less strong than just 'no': *"Did you like him?" "Not really."*

rear¹ /rɪər/ noun **the rear** the back part of something: *the rear of the train*
• **rear** adj *a rear window*

rear² /rɪər/ verb If you rear children or young animals, you look after them until they are adults.

reason /ˈri·zən/ noun **1** **A2** the facts about why something happens or why someone does something: *Is there any particular reason why he doesn't want to come?* ○ *He left without giving a reason.* ○ *That was the reason for telling her.* **2** something that makes it right for you to do something: *I think we have reason to be concerned.*

> **⚠ Common mistake: reason**
>
> Be careful to choose the correct preposition.
> *That was the main reason for the trip.*
> ~~That was the main reason of the trip.~~

reasonable /ˈri·zə·nə·bəl/, /ˈriz·nə·bəl/ adj **1** **B1** big enough or large enough in number, although not very big or not many: *There were a reasonable number of people there.* **2** **B1** not expensive: *reasonable prices* **3** **B1** good enough but not the best: *The service in the restaurant is reasonable.* **4** fair and showing good judgment: *It's not reasonable to expect people to work those hours.* **5** based on facts that can be explained: *There must be a reasonable explanation for this.*

reasonably /ˈriːzənəbli/, /ˈrɪznəbli/ adv **1** in a fair way, showing good judgment: *Why can't we discuss this reasonably, like adults?* **2 reasonably good, well, etc.** good, well, etc. enough but not very good or very well: *I did reasonably well in school but not as well as my sister.* **3 reasonably priced** ⬛ available at a good price: *reasonably priced meals*

reassure /ˌriːəˈʃʊər/ verb (present participle **reassuring**, past tense and past participle **reassured**) to say something to stop someone from worrying: *He reassured me that I would be paid soon.*

rebel[1] /ˈrebəl/ noun someone who does not like authority and refuses to obey rules

rebel[2] /rəˈbel/ verb (present participle **rebelling**, past tense and past participle **rebelled**) to refuse to obey rules: *She rebelled against her family.*

rebellion /rəˈbeljən/ noun an act of fighting against the government of a country

rebuild /riːˈbɪld/ verb (past tense and past participle **rebuilt**) ⬛ to build something again after it has been damaged: *The cathedral was rebuilt after the fire.*

receipt /rɪˈsiːt/ noun ⬛ a piece of paper that proves that you have received goods or money: *Could I have a receipt?*

receive /rɪˈsiːv/ verb (present participle **receiving**, past tense and past participle **received**) ⬛ to get something that someone has given or sent to you: *Occasionally, he receives letters from fans.*

⚠ Common mistake: receive

People often spell **receive** wrong. Remember that the e comes before the i.

recent /ˈriːsənt/ adj ⬛ happening or starting from a short time ago: *a recent photo* ∘ *Sales have gone up in recent years.*

recently /ˈriːsəntli/ adv ⬛ not long ago: *Have you seen any good movies recently?*

reception /rɪˈsepʃən/ noun **1** ⬛ the place in a hotel or office building where people go when they arrive: *Ask for me at reception.* **2** a formal party to celebrate a special event or to welcome someone: *a wedding reception*

receptionist /rɪˈsepʃənɪst/ noun ⬛ someone who works in a hotel or office and answers the telephone and deals with visitors when they arrive: *a hotel receptionist*

recipe /ˈresəpi/ noun ⬛ a list of foods and a set of instructions telling you how to cook something: *a recipe for carrot cake*

reckless /ˈrekləs/ adj doing something dangerous and not caring about what might happen: *reckless driving*
• **recklessly** adv

recognition /ˌrekəgˈnɪʃən/ noun **1** the act of accepting that something is true or real: *There is a growing recognition of the size of the problem.* **2** [no plural] the act of remembering something or someone because you have seen that person or thing before: *I waved at her, but she showed no sign of recognition.*

recognize /ˈrekəgnaɪz/ verb (present participle **recognizing**, past tense and past participle **recognized**) **1** ⬛ to know someone or something because you have seen that person or thing before: *I recognized her from her picture.* **2** to accept that something is true or real: *Smoking is recognized as a leading cause of cancer.*

recommend /ˌrekəˈmend/ verb **1** ⬛ to say that someone or something is good or right for a particular purpose: *Can you recommend a good wine to go with this dish?* **2** to say that something should be done: *The report recommends that tourists avoid the region.*

⚠ Common mistake: recommend

People often spell **recommend** wrong. Remember that there is one c and two m's.

recommendation /ˌrekəmənˈdeɪʃən/ noun a suggestion that someone or something is good or right for a particular purpose: *I bought this book on Andy's recommendation.*

record[1] /'rek·ərd/ **noun** **1** 🅱 the best, biggest, longest, tallest, etc.: *He holds the world record in the marathon.* **2** 🅱 a song or music that has been recorded and that is available for the public to buy: *My favorite Beatles' record is "Love Me Do."* **3** information that is written on paper or stored on a computer so that it can be used in the future: *medical records* ○ *Our teacher keeps a record of our absences.* **4** A person's or company's record is the behavior or achievements of that person or company: *They have the best safety record of all the airlines.*

record[2] /rɪ'kɔrd/ **verb** 🅰2 to store sounds or pictures using electronic equipment, a camera, etc. so that you can listen to them or see them again: *They just recorded a new album.* ○ *I recorded that program for you.* **2** to write down information or store it on a computer so that it can be used in the future: *He recorded details of their conversation in his diary.*

record-breaking /'rek·ərd,breɪ·kɪŋ/ **adj** better, bigger, longer, etc. than anything else before: *record-breaking sales of the new DVD*

recorder /rɪ'kɔr·dər/ **noun** **1** a machine for storing sounds or pictures: *a digital video recorder* **2** a long, thin musical instrument that you play by blowing into it

recording /rɪ'kɔr·dɪŋ/ **noun** 🅱 sounds or moving pictures that have been recorded, or the process of recording: *a new system of digital recording*

recover /rɪ'kʌv·ər/ **verb** 🅱 to become healthy again after having been sick or hurt: *It takes a long time to recover from surgery.*

recovery /rɪ'kʌv·ə·ri/ **noun** [no plural] the process of feeling better again after having been sick or hurt: *She only had the operation last month but she's made a good recovery.*

recreation /,rek·ri'eɪ·ʃən/ **noun** activities that you do for enjoyment when you are not working: *The lake is great for all kinds of recreation.*
• **recreational adj**

recruit[1] /rɪ'krut/ **verb** to try to persuade someone to join an organization

recruit[2] /rɪ'krut/ **noun** someone who has recently joined an organization: *a new recruit*

recruitment /rɪ'krut·mənt/ **noun** [no plural] the act of persuading someone to join an organization: *graduate recruitment*

rectangle /'rek,tæŋ·gəl/ **noun** a shape with four 90° angles and four sides, with opposite sides of equal length and two sides longer than the other two

rectangular /rek'tæŋ·gjə·lər/ **adj** shaped like a rectangle: *a rectangular room*

recycle /ri'saɪ·kəl/ **verb** (present participle **recycling**, past tense and past participle **recycled**) 🅱 to use paper, glass, plastic, etc. again and not throw it away: *We recycle all our newspapers and bottles.*
• **recycling noun** [no plural] 🅱 *Our office has recycling bins (= containers for material to be recycled).*

red[1] /red/ **adj** (comparative **redder**, superlative **reddest**) **1** 🅰1 being the same color as blood: *a red shirt* **2** 🅰2 describes hair that is an orange-brown color: *Both children have red hair.* → See **Hair** on page C9 **3** red wine 🅰2 Red wine is made from dark purplegrapes: *a bottle of red wine* **4** go red If someone goes red, his or her face becomes red because he or she is embarrassed or angry: *He kissed her on the cheek and she went bright red.*

red[2] /red/ **noun** 🅰2 the color of blood → See **Colors** on page C6

redo /ri'du/ **verb** to do something again: *I messed up my homework and had to redo it.*

reduce /rɪ'du/ **verb** (present participle **reducing**, past tense and past participle **reduced**) 🅱 to make something less: *Prices have been reduced by 50 percent.*

reduction /rɪˈdʌk·ʃən/ noun   the act of making something less or smaller: *price reductions*

refer /rɪˈfɜr/ verb (present participle **referring**, past tense and past participle **referred**)

refer to *someone/something* phrasal verb **1** to talk or write about someone or something: *She didn't refer to her son at all.* **2** If writing or information refers to someone or something, it relates to that person or thing: *The sales figures refer to U.S. sales only.*

referee /ˌref·əˈri/ noun   someone who makes sure that players follow the rules during a sports event

reference /ˈref·ər·əns/ noun   **1** something you say or write about someone or something: *In his book he **makes** several **references** to his time in France.* **2** [no plural] the act of looking at something to get information: *Please keep this handout for future reference (= to look at in the future).* **3** a letter that is written by someone who knows you, to say if you are right for a job or position

reference book /ˈref·ər·əns ˌbʊk/ noun   a book, such as a dictionary, that you look at to find information

reflect /rɪˈflekt/ verb   **1** to show or be a sign of something: *The statistics reflect a change in people's spending habits.* **2** If a surface such as a mirror or water reflects something, you can see the image of that thing in the mirror, water, etc.: *He saw himself **reflected in** the store window.* **3** to think in a serious and careful way: *In prison, he had plenty of time to **reflect on** his crimes.*

reflection /rɪˈflek·ʃən/ noun   **1** the image of something in a mirror, on a shiny surface, etc.: *I saw my reflection in the window.* **2** a reflection of something something that is a sign or result of a particular situation: *His poor job performance is a reflection of his lack of training.*

reform[1] /rɪˈfɔrm/ noun   the process of making changes to improve a system, organization, or law: *political reform*

reform[2] /rɪˈfɔrm/ verb   to change a system, organization, or law in order to improve it: *Efforts have been made to reform the tax laws.*

refresh /rɪˈfreʃ/ verb   **1** to make you feel less hot or tired: *A cool shower will refresh you.* **2** to make the most recent information on an Internet page appear on your computer **3** refresh someone's memory to help someone remember something: *She reread her notes to refresh her memory.*

refreshed /rɪˈfreʃt/ adj   feeling less tired: *I felt refreshed after a good night's sleep.*

refreshing /rɪˈfreʃ·ɪŋ/ adj   **1** different and interesting: *It's refreshing to see a movie that's so original.* **2** making you feel less hot or tired: *a refreshing shower*

refreshments /rɪˈfreʃ·mənts/ plural noun   🔒 food and drinks that are given at a meeting, on a trip, etc.

refrigerator /rɪˈfrɪdʒ·əˌreɪ·t̬ər/ noun   a large container that uses electricity to keep food cold
→ See **The Kitchen** on page C10

refuge /ˈref·judʒ/ noun   a place where you are protected from danger: *a refuge for homeless people*

refugee /ˌref·jʊˈdʒi/ noun   someone who has been forced to leave his or her country, especially because of a war: *a refugee camp*

refund[1] /ˈri·fʌnd/ noun   🔒 an amount of money that is given back to you, especially because you are not happy with something you have bought: *The tour company gave us a **full refund**.*

refund[2] /rɪˈfʌnd/ verb   to give back money that someone has paid to you: *Your deposit cannot be refunded.*

refusal /rɪˈfju·zəl/ noun   an act of saying you will not do or accept something: *I was surprised by his **refusal** to admit his mistake.*

refuse[1] /rɪˈfjuz/ verb (present participle **refusing**, past tense and past participle

refused) 🔵 to say that you will not do or accept something: *I asked him to leave but he refused.* ○ *Cathy refuses to admit that she was wrong.*

refuse² /'ref·jus/ noun [no plural] formal things that no one needs that have been thrown away: *a pile of refuse*

regard¹ /rɪ'gɑrd/ verb to think of someone or something in a particular way: *She is generally regarded as one of the greatest singers of this century.*

regard² /rɪ'gɑrd/ noun [no plural] **1** respect or admiration for someone or something: *I have the greatest regard for her.* **2** in/with regard to something formal relating to something: *I am writing with regard to your letter of June 24.*

regarding /rɪ'gɑr·dɪŋ/ preposition formal 🔵 about or relating to: *I am writing to you regarding your application dated April 29.*

regardless /rɪ'gɑrd·ləs/ adv **regardless of something** despite something: *She'll do what she wants regardless of what we say.*

regards /rɪ'gɑrdz/ plural noun 🔵 friendly greetings: *Give my regards to your mother when you see her.*

regiment /'redʒ·ə·mənt/ noun a large group of soldiers

region /'ri·dʒən/ noun 🔵 a particular area in a country or the world: *the polar regions*

regional /'ri·dʒə·nᵊl/ adj relating to a particular area in a country or the world: *regional foods*

register¹ /'redʒ·ə·stər/ noun **1** an official list of names: *the class register* **2** a cash register

register² /'redʒ·ə·stər/ verb **1** 🔵 to put information about someone or something, especially a name, on an official list: *Students need to register for the class by the end of April.* **2** to show an amount on an instrument that measures something: *The earthquake registered 7.3 on the Richter scale.*

registration /ˌredʒ·ə'streɪ·ʃən/ noun [no plural] 🔵 the act of recording a name or information on an official list

regret¹ /rɪ'gret/ verb (present participle **regretting**, past tense and past participle **regretted**) **1** 🔵 to feel sorry about a situation, especially something that you wish you had not done: *If you don't tell her the truth you'll regret it later.* ○ *I really regret leaving school so young.* **2** formal used to say that you are sorry that you have to tell someone about a situation: *We regret that we cannot supply this information.*

regret² /rɪ'gret/ noun a feeling of sadness about a situation, especially something that you wish you had not done: *We married very young, but we've been really happy and I have no regrets.*

regular /'reg·jə·lər/ adj **1** 🔵 usual or normal: *I couldn't see my regular dentist.* **2** 🔵 happening or doing something often, especially at the same time every week, year, etc.: *a regular visitor to Dallas* **3** 🔵 informal being a standard size: *a burger and regular fries* **4** 🔵 following the usual rules or patterns in grammar: *"Talk" is a regular verb but "go" is not.* → Opposite **irregular** adj **5** repeated with the same amount of time or space between one thing and the next: *a regular pulse* ○ *Plant the trees at regular intervals.*

regularity /ˌreg·jə'lær·ɪ·t̬i/ noun [no plural] the fact that something happens again and again

regularly /'reg·jə·lər·li/ adv **1** 🔵 often: *Accidents occur regularly on this stretch of the road.* **2** 🔵 at the same time each day, week, month, etc.: *They meet regularly – usually once a week.*

regulation /ˌreg·jə'leɪ·ʃən/ noun an official rule that controls how something is done: *building regulations*

rehearsal /rɪ'hɜr·səl/ noun a time when people practice a play, dance, etc. in order to prepare for a performance

rehearse /rɪ'hɜrs/ verb (present participle **rehearsing**, past tense and past participle **rehearsed**) to practice a play, dance, etc. in order to prepare for a performance

a
b
c
d
e
f
g
h
i
j
k
l
m
n
o
p
q
r
s
t
u
v
w
x
y
z

reign[1] /reɪn/ noun a period of time when a king or queen rules a country: *the reign of Henry VIII*

reign[2] /reɪn/ verb to be the king or queen of a country: *Queen Victoria reigned for 64 years.*

rein /reɪn/ noun a long, thin piece of leather that helps you to control a horse: *Hold the reins in your left hand.*

reindeer /'reɪn.dɪər/ noun (plural **reindeer**) a type of deer with large horns that lives in northern parts of Europe, Asia, and North America

reject /rɪ'dʒekt/ verb **1** to refuse to accept or agree with something: *The United States government rejected the proposal.* **2** to refuse to accept someone for a job, program, etc.

rejection /rɪ'dʒek.ʃən/ noun **1** the act of refusing to accept or agree with something: *He was disappointed by their rejection of his suggestion.* **2** a letter that says you have not been successful in getting a job, a place at a university, etc.: *I've sent off ten applications but I've only gotten back rejections so far.*

relate /rɪ'leɪt/ verb (present participle **relating**, past tense and past participle **related**)
relate to someone/something phrasal verb to be connected to someone or something: *Please provide all information relating to the claim.*

related /rɪ'leɪ.tɪd/ adj **1** If two or more people are related, they belong to the same family: *Did you know that I'm related to Jackie?* **2** connected: *We discussed unemployment and related issues.* ○ *There's been an increase in crimes related to drugs.*

relation /rɪ'leɪ.ʃən/ noun **1** 🅱1 someone who belongs to the same family as you **2** **relations** the way in which two people or groups of people feel and behave toward each other: *Britain has good relations with Canada.* **3 in relation to something** compared with something: *Prices are too high in relation to salaries.* **4 in relation to something** about or

connected with something: *I'd like to ask you something in relation to what you said earlier.*

relationship /rɪ'leɪ.ʃən.ʃɪp/ noun **1** 🅱1 the way two people feel and behave toward each other: *He has a very good relationship with his older sister.* **2** 🅱1 a sexual or romantic friendship: *I'm not ready for a relationship right now.* **3** the way in which two things are connected: *the relationship between sunburn and skin cancer*

> **❗ Common mistake: have a relationship with someone**
>
> Be careful to use the correct preposition in this expression.
>
> *I have a good relationship with my parents.*
> ~~I have a good relationship to my parents.~~

relative /'rel.ə.tɪv/ noun 🅱1 someone in your family: *a party for friends and relatives*

relatively /'rel.ə.tɪv.li/ adv quite, when compared with other things or people: *I think you'll find the class relatively easy.*

relax /rɪ'læks/ verb 🅱1 to become happy and comfortable because nothing is worrying you, or to make someone do this: *I find it difficult to relax.*

relaxation /ˌriː.læk'seɪ.ʃən/ noun [no plural] 🅱1 the feeling of being relaxed: *He listens to music for relaxation.*

relaxed /rɪ'lækst/ adj **1** 🅱1 feeling happy and comfortable because nothing is worrying you: *She seemed relaxed and in control of the situation.* **2** 🅱1 A relaxed situation or place is comfortable and informal: *There was a very relaxed atmosphere at the party.*

relaxing /rɪ'læk.sɪŋ/ adj 🅱1 making you feel relaxed: *a relaxing bath*

release /rɪ'liːs/ verb (present participle **releasing**, past tense and past participle **released**) **1** to allow a prisoner to be free: *Six hostages were released shortly* *before noon.* **2** to make a record or movie ready for people to buy or see: *The album is due to be released in time for Christmas.*

relevant /'rel·ə·vənt/ *adj* related to or useful for what is happening or being talked about: *The website has all the **relevant information.***

reliable /rɪ'laɪ·ə·bəl/ **B1** able to be trusted or believed: *a reliable car* ∘ *reliable information*
→ Opposite **unreliable** *adj*

relief /rɪ'lif/ *noun* [no plural] the good feeling that you have when something bad stops or does not happen: *It was such a relief when the exams were over.*

relieve /rɪ'liv/ *verb* (present participle **relieving,** past tense and past participle **relieved**) to make pain or a bad feeling less bad: *Breathing exercises can help to relieve stress.*

relieved /rɪ'livd/ *adj* feeling happy because something bad did not happen: *I'm just **relieved that** she's safe and well.*

religion /rɪ'lɪdʒ·ən/ *noun* **B1** the belief in a god or gods, or a particular system of belief in a god or gods: *the Christian religion*

religious /rɪ'lɪdʒ·əs/ *adj* **1** relating to religion: *religious paintings* **2** having a strong belief in a religion: *He's a very religious man.*

reluctance /rɪ'lʌk·təns/ *noun* [no plural] the act of not wanting to do something

reluctant /rɪ'lʌk·tənt/ *adj* not wanting to do something: *I'm **reluctant to** spend all that money.*
• **reluctantly** *adv*

rely /rɪ'laɪ/ *verb* (present participle **relying,** past tense and past participle **relied**)
rely on *someone/something phrasal verb*
1 to need someone or something: *We rely too much on our cars.* **2** to trust someone or something: *I know I can rely on you to help me.*

remain /rɪ'meɪn/ *verb* **B1** to continue to be in the same state: *Despite the*

chaos around him, he remained calm.
2 to continue to exist when everything or everyone else has gone: *Only a few hundred of these animals remain today.*
3 formal to stay in the same place: *The doctor ordered him to **remain in** bed for a few days.*

remaining /rɪ'meɪ·nɪŋ/ *adj* continuing to exist when everything or everyone else has gone or everything has been done: *Mix in half the butter and save the remaining half for later.*

remains /rɪ'meɪnz/ *noun* **1** the parts of something that exist when other parts of it have gone: *the remains of a Buddhist temple* **2** formal someone's body after the person has died

remark[1] /rɪ'mɑrk/ *noun* something that you say: *He made a remark about her hair.*

remark[2] /rɪ'mɑrk/ *verb* to say something: *He remarked that she was looking thin.*

remarkable /rɪ'mɑr·kə·bəl/ *adj* very unusual in a way that you admire: *He has a remarkable memory.*

remarkably /rɪ'mɑr·kə·bli/ *adv* in a way that makes you feel surprised: *She is remarkably young-looking for 50.*

remedy /'rem·ə·di/ *noun* (plural **remedies**) **1** something that makes you better when you are ill: *a headache remedy* **2** something that stops a problem: *So what is the **remedy** for the traffic problem?*

remember /rɪ'mem·bər/ *verb* **1** **A1** to keep something in your mind, or bring it back into your mind: *I can't remember his name.* ∘ *I don't remember signing a contract.* ∘ *He suddenly **remembered that** it was her birthday.* **2 remember to do** *something* **A2** to not forget to do something: *Remember to take your passport.*

remind /rɪ'maɪnd/ *verb* **B1** to make someone remember something, or remember to do something: *Every time we meet he reminds me about the money he lent me.* ∘ *Will you remind me to buy some eggs?*

a b c d e f g h i j k l m n o p q r s t u v w x y z

a
b
c
d
e
f
g
h
i
j
k
l
m
n
o
p
q
r
s
t
u
v
w
x
y
z

remind *someone* **of** *something/someone* **phrasal verb** ③ to make someone think of something or someone else: *This song reminds me of our trip to Spain.*

⚠ Common mistake: remind or remember?

If you **remember** a fact or something from the past, you keep it in your mind, or bring it back into your mind.

I can't remember the name of the book.
Did you remember to bring the camera?

When you **remind** someone to do something, you make him or her remember it.

Can you remind me to call Anna tomorrow?
~~Can you remember me to call Anna tomorrow?~~

---

remote /rɪˈmoʊt/ **adj** far away: *a remote mountain village*

remote control /rɪˈmoʊt kənˈtroʊl/ **noun 1** ③ (also **remote**) a piece of equipment that is used to control something such as a television from a distance
→ See **The Living Room** on page C11
2 [no plural] the use of radio waves to control something such as a television from a distance

remotely /rɪˈmoʊt·li/ **adv not remotely interested, surprised, etc.** not at all interested, surprised, etc.: *I'm not remotely interested in football.*

removal /rɪˈmu·vəl/ **noun** [no plural] the act of taking something away or out of something: *stain removal ○ garbage removal*

remove /rɪˈmuv/ **verb** (present participle **removing**, past tense and past participle **removed**) **1** ③ to take something away: *An operation was needed to remove the bullets from his chest.* **2** to take something off: *She removed her jacket and hung it on a chair.*

rent¹ /rent/ **verb 1** ③ to pay money to live in a building that someone else

owns: *He rents an apartment in the city.* **2** ④ (also **rent out**) to allow someone to pay you money to live in your building: *He has a cabin that he rents to tourists.* **3** ④ to pay money to use something for a short time: *We could rent a car for the weekend.*

rent² /rent/ **noun** ④ the amount of money that you pay to live in a building that someone else owns

rep /rep/ **noun** informal someone whose job is to sell things for a company: *the company's New England sales rep*

repaid /rɪˈpeɪd/ past tense and past participle of repay

repair¹ /rɪˈpeər/ **verb** ④ to fix something that is broken or damaged: *I need to get my bike repaired.*

repair² /rɪˈpeər/ **noun** ③ something that you do to fix something that is broken or damaged: *The repairs cost me $150.*

repay /rɪˈpeɪ/ **verb** (present participle **repaying**, past tense and past participle **repaid**) to pay back money that you have borrowed: *to repay a loan*

repeat /rɪˈpit/ **verb** ④ to say or do something more than once: *He repeated the number. ○ The test must be repeated several times.*

repeated /rɪˈpi·t̬ɪd/ **adj** done or happening more than once: *He has refused repeated requests to be interviewed.*
• **repeatedly adv** *The victim was stabbed repeatedly with a knife.*

repetition /ˌrep·əˈtɪʃ·ən/ **noun** the act of saying or doing something more than once: *We don't want a repetition of last year's disaster.*

replace /rɪˈpleɪs/ **verb** (present participle **replacing**, past tense and past participle **replaced**) **1** ③ to get something new because the one you had before has been lost or damaged: *We'll have to replace this carpet soon.* **2** ③ to start using another thing or person instead of the one that you are using now: *We're thinking of replacing our old TV.* **3** to start to be used instead of the thing or

---

| ou go | aɪər **fire** | aʊər **hour** | eər **hair** | ɪər **ear** | ʊər **poor** | j **yet** | ʒ **measure** | ʃ **ship** | dʒ **judge** | tʃ **chin** | ð **that** | θ **thin** | ŋ **hang** |

person that is being used now: *This system will replace the old one.*

replacement /rɪˈpleɪs·mənt/ *noun*
a new thing or person in place of something or someone that was there before: *It's not going to be easy to find a replacement for you.*

replay /ˈriːpleɪ/ *noun* an occasion when something that is recorded is shown again, for example part of sports game on television

reply[1] /rɪˈplaɪ/ *verb* (present participle **replying**, past tense and past participle **replied**) **B1** to answer: *"I don't understand," she replied.* ○ *He didn't **reply to** my email.*

reply[2] /rɪˈplaɪ/ *noun* (plural **replies**)
B1 an answer: *Have you received a **reply to** your letter?*

report[1] /rɪˈpɔrt/ *noun* **B1** a description of an event or situation: *a police report*

report[2] /rɪˈpɔrt/ *verb* **1** to describe something that has just happened, especially on television, radio, or in a newspaper: *She **reported that** the situation had changed dramatically.* **2** **B1** to tell someone in authority that something has happened, especially an accident or crime: *He should have reported the accident immediately.*

reported speech /rɪˈpɔr·tɪd ˈspitʃ/ *noun* [no plural] speech or writing that is used to report what someone has said, but not using exactly the same words: *The sentence "He told me that he would like to go" is an example of reported speech.*

reporter /rɪˈpɔr·tər/ *noun* **B1** someone whose job is to discover information about news events and describe them on television, radio, or in a newspaper

represent /ˌrep·rɪˈzent/ *verb* **1** to officially speak for someone else because the person has asked you to: *The union represents over 200 employees.* **2** to be a sign or symbol of something: *The crosses on the map represent churches.*

representative /ˌrep·rɪˈzen·tə·t̬ɪv/ *noun* someone who speaks or does something officially for another person

reproduce /ˌri·prəˈdus/ *verb* (present participle **reproducing**, past tense and past participle **reproduced**) **1** to make a copy of something **2** formal If people, animals, or plants reproduce, they produce babies or young animals or plants.

reproduction /ˌri·prəˈdʌk·ʃən/ *noun*
1 [no plural] the process of producing babies or young animals and plants **2** a copy of something, especially a painting

reptile /ˈrep·təl/, /ˈrep·taɪl/ *noun*
an animal whose body is covered with scales (= pieces of hard skin), and whose blood changes temperature, for example a snake

republic /rɪˈpʌb·lɪk/ *noun* a country with no king or queen but with an elected government: *France is a republic.*

reputation /ˌrep·jəˈteɪ·ʃən/ *noun*
the opinion that people have about someone or something: *Both hotels have a good reputation.*

request[1] /rɪˈkwest/ *noun* **B1** the act of asking for something: *His doctor **made** an urgent **request for** a copy of the report.*

request[2] /rɪˈkwest/ *verb* **B1** to ask for something: *We requested more computers.*

require /rɪˈkwaɪər/ *verb* (present participle **requiring**, past tense and past participle **required**) **B1** to need something: *The job requires a high level of concentration.*

requirement /rɪˈkwaɪər·mənt/ *noun*
something that is needed: *college entrance requirements*

rescue[1] /ˈres·kju/ *verb* (present participle **rescuing**, past tense and past participle **rescued**) **B1** to save someone or something from a dangerous situation: *Fifty passengers had to be rescued from a sinking ship.*

rescue[2] /ˈres·kju/ *noun* **B1** the act of saving someone or something from a dangerous situation: *a rescue attempt*

research[1] /riˈsɜrtʃ/ *noun* [no plural]
B1 the study of a subject in order to discover new information: *She does research into language development.*

research[2] /rɪˈsɜrtʃ/ *verb* to study a subject in order to discover new information about it

• **researcher** *noun*

resemblance /rɪˈzem·bləns/ *noun*
the way in which two people or things appear similar: *There's a striking resemblance between the sisters.*

resemble /rɪˈzem·bəl/ *verb* (present participle **resembling**, past tense and past participle **resembled**) to look like or be like someone or something: *She resembles her father.*

resent /rɪˈzent/ *verb* to feel angry and upset about an unfair situation: *I resent having to work late.*

resentment /rɪˈzent·mənt/ *noun*
[no plural] a feeling of anger about an unfair situation

reservation /ˌrez·ərˈveɪ·ʃən/ *noun*
🔵 an arrangement that you make to have a seat on a plane, a room in a hotel, etc.: *I'd like to make a reservation for Friday evening.*

reserve[1] /rɪˈzɜrv/ *verb* (present participle **reserving**, past tense and past participle **reserved**) **1 🔵** to arrange to have a seat on a plane, a room in a hotel, etc.: *I'd like to reserve two seats on the 9:15 train to Baltimore.* **2 🔵** to not allow people to use something because it is only for a particular person or for a particular purpose: *This space is reserved for ambulances.*

reserve[2] /rɪˈzɜrv/ *noun* an amount of something that you keep until it is needed: *emergency cash reserves*

reservoir /ˈrez·ərˌvwɑr/ *noun* a place where water is kept before it goes to people's houses

residence /ˈrez·ɪ·dəns/ *noun* formal
a building where someone lives: *the mayor's official residence*

residence hall /ˈrez·ɪ·dəns ˌhɔl/ *noun*
(also **dorm**) a building where university or college students live

resident /ˈrez·ɪ·dənt/ *noun* someone who lives in a particular place: *We have had complaints from local residents.*

residential /ˌrez·ɪˈden·tʃəl/ *adj*
A residential area has only houses and not offices or factories.

resign /rɪˈzaɪn/ *verb* to officially tell your employer that you are leaving your job: *Mr Aitken has resigned from the company.*

resign *yourself* to *something* *phrasal verb* to make yourself accept something bad because you cannot change it: *He resigned himself to living alone.*

resignation /ˌrez·ɪgˈneɪ·ʃən/ *noun*
1 the act of telling your employer that you are leaving your job: *a letter of resignation* ∘ *I handed in my resignation yesterday.* **2** [no plural] the act of accepting something bad because you cannot change it

resist /rɪˈzɪst/ *verb* **1** to stop yourself from doing something that you want to do: *I can't resist eating chocolate.* **2** to refuse to accept something and try to stop it from happening: *The President is resisting calls for him to resign.* **3** to fight against someone or something that is attacking you: *British troops resisted the attack for two days.*

resistance /rɪˈzɪs·təns/ *noun* [no plural]
the act of disagreeing with a plan or idea and refusing to accept it: *resistance to political change*

resolution /ˌrez·əˈlu·ʃən/ *noun* a promise to yourself to do something: *My New Year's resolution is to get more exercise.*

resort /rɪˈzɔrt/ *noun* **1 🔵** a place where many people go for a vacation: *a ski resort* **2 last resort** something that you do because everything else has failed: *We can ask your mother for help, but only as a last resort.*

resource /ˈriˌsɔrs/, /rɪˈzɔrs/ *noun*
something that a country, person, or organization has that he, she, or it can use: *financial/natural resources*

respect[1] /rɪˈspekt/ *noun* **1 🔵** [no plural] polite behavior to someone, especially because the person is older or more important than you: *You should show more respect for your parents.* **2 🔵** [no plural] a feeling of admiration that you have for someone because of the person's knowledge, skill, or achievements: *She's an excellent teacher and I have the greatest **respect for** her.* **3 in this respect/ many respects** in a particular way, or in many ways: *The school has changed in many respects.*

respect[2] /rɪˈspekt/ verb **1 B1** to admire someone because the person knows a lot or has done good things: *I respect him **for** his honesty.* **2** If you respect someone's rights, customs, wishes, etc., you accept that the person is important and you don't do anything to change or harm him or her: *The agreement will respect the rights of both countries.*
• **respected** adj *He's a **highly respected** doctor.*

respectable /rɪˈspek·tə·bəl/ adj behaving well, in a way that most people think is right: *a respectable family*

respectful /rɪˈspekt·fəl/ adj showing respect for someone or something: *The children were polite and respectful.*

respond /rɪˈspɑnd/ verb to answer someone or react to something: *How quickly did the police **respond to** the call?*

response /rɪˈspɑns/ noun an answer or reaction to something that has been said or done: *I'm writing **in response to** your letter.*

responsibility /rɪˌspɑn·səˈbɪl·ɪ·t̬i/ noun (plural **responsibilities**) something that it is your job or duty to do: *It is your **responsibility to** make sure that your homework is done on time.*

responsible /rɪˈspɑn·sə·bəl/ adj **1 B1** having to do something as your duty: *I'm **responsible for** organizing the conferences.* **2** having caused something to happen, especially something bad: *Who was **responsible for** the accident?* **3** showing good judgment and able to be trusted: *He's hard-working and responsible.* **4** A responsible job is important because you have to make decisions that affect other people: *Being a teacher is a very responsible job.*

rest[1] /rest/ noun **1 the rest A2** the part of something that remains: *Do you want to spend **the rest of** your life with him?* **2 A2** a period of time when you relax or sleep: *You should try to **get some rest** before we leave.*

rest[2] /rest/ verb **1 B1** to relax or sleep because you are tired: *Pete's resting after his long drive.* **2** to put something on or against a surface: *She rested her head on his shoulder.*

restaurant /ˈres·tər·ənt, /ˈres·tə̩rɑnt/ noun **A1** a place where you can buy and eat a meal: *an Italian restaurant*

restful /ˈrest·fəl/ adj making you calm and relaxed: *restful music*

restless /ˈrest·ləs/ adj not able to be still (=stand or sit without moving)or relax because you are bored or nervous: *The audience was getting restless.*

restore /rɪˈstɔr/ verb (present participle **restoring**, past tense and past participle **restored**) **1** to make something good exist again: *We hope to restore peace in the region.* **2** to repair something old: *to restore antiques*

restrain /rɪˈstreɪn/ verb to stop someone doing something, sometimes by using force: *He became violent and had to be physically restrained.*

restrict /rɪˈstrɪkt/ verb to limit something: *new laws restricting the sale of guns* ○ *I **restrict** myself **to** two glasses of wine most evenings.*

restriction /rɪˈstrɪk·ʃən/ noun a rule or law that limits what people can do: *parking restrictions*

restroom /ˈrest·rum, /ˈrest̩rʊm/ noun **A2** a room with toilets that is in a public place

result[1] /rɪˈzʌlt/ noun **1 B1** something that happens or exists because something else has happened: *Most accidents are **the result of** human error.* **2 B1** information that you get from something such as an exam, a scientific experiment, or a medical test: *I finished my exams yesterday, but I won't **get the results***

until August. **3** 🔵 the score or number of votes at the end of a competition or election: *The election results will be known by Sunday.* ∘ *What was the result of this afternoon's game?*

result² /rɪˈzʌlt/ *verb*

result in *something* phrasal verb to be the reason something happens: *The improvements in training resulted in better performance.*

resume /rɪˈzuːm/ *verb formal* If an activity resumes, or if you resume it, it starts again: *The talks are due to resume today.*

résumé /ˈrez.ə.meɪ/ (also **resume**) *noun* 🔵 a document that describes your education and work experience, which you send to an employer that you want to work for

retain /rɪˈteɪn/ *verb* to continue to keep something: *The local authority will retain control of the school.*

retire /rɪˈtaɪər/ *verb (present participle* **retiring,** *past tense and past participle* **retired)** 🔵 to leave your job and stop working because you are old: *She retired from the company in 1990.*
• **retired** *adj* *Both my parents are retired.*

retirement /rɪˈtaɪər.mənt/ *noun [no plural]* **1** the period of your life after you have stopped working: *We wish you a long and happy retirement.* **2** the time when you leave your job and stop working, usually because you are old: *What is the normal retirement age in this country?*

retreat¹ /rɪˈtriːt/ *verb* the action of soldiers moving away from the enemy, especially to avoid fighting: *The army was forced to retreat.*

retreat² /rɪˈtriːt/ *noun* a move back by soldiers or an army, either because they have been defeated or in order to avoid fighting: *Enemy soldiers are in retreat.*

return¹ /rɪˈtɜːn/ *verb* **1** 🅰 to go or come back to a place where you were before: *She returned to America in 1954.* **2** 🅰 to give, send, or put something back where it came from: *I have to return the book by Friday.* **3 return to**

something to start doing an activity again or talking about something again: *I returned to work three months after Susie was born.* **4** to happen again or start to exist again: *You need to go to the doctor if the pain returns.*

return² /rɪˈtɜːn/ *noun* **1** 🔵 the act of going or coming back to a place where you were before: *On his return to Sydney, he started up a business.* **2** 🔵 *[no plural]* a key on a computer keyboard that is used to make the computer accept information: *Type in the password and press return.* **3 in return** in exchange for something or as a reaction to something: *I'd like to give them something in return for everything they've done for us.*

reunion /riˈjuːn.jən/ *noun* an occasion when people who have not met each other for a long time meet again: *We're having a family reunion next week.*

reuse /riˈjuːz/ *verb* to use something again: *Businesses are finding new ways to reuse materials.*

reveal /rɪˈviːl/ *verb* to tell someone a piece of secret information: *It was revealed in this morning's papers that the couple intend to marry.*

revenge /rɪˈvendʒ/ *noun [no plural]* something that you do to punish someone who has done something bad to you: *He was shot in revenge for the murder.*

Reverend /ˈrev.ər.ənd/ *adj (written abbreviation* **Rev.)** used as a title before the name of some Christian officials: *the Reverend Clive Jones*

reverse¹ /rɪˈvɜːs/ *verb (present participle* **reversing,** *past tense and past participle* **reversed)** to change a situation or change the order of things so that it becomes the opposite: *It is unlikely that the judge will reverse his decision.*

reverse² /rɪˈvɜːs/ *noun [no plural]* the method of controlling a vehicle that makes it go backwards: *To back up, put the car in reverse.*

review¹ /rɪˈvjuː/ *noun* 🔵 a piece of writing in a newspaper that gives an opinion about a new book, film, etc.: *a book review*

review² /rɪˈvju/ *verb* **1** to give your opinion about a book, film, television show, etc.: *He reviews movies for the Times.* **2** to study a subject before you take a test

revise /rɪˈvaɪz/ *verb* (present participle **revising**, past tense and past participle **revised**) to change something so that it is more accurate: *a revised edition of the book*

revision /rɪˈvɪʒ·ən/ *noun* [no plural] changes that is made to something, or the process of making these changes

revive /rɪˈvaɪv/ *verb* (present participle **reviving**, past tense and past participle **revived**) to become conscious again or make someone conscious again: *A police officer tried to revive her.*

revolt /rɪˈvoʊlt/ *noun* an act of trying to change a government, often using violence

revolting /rɪˈvoʊl·tɪŋ/ *adj* very unpleasant: *The food was revolting.*

revolution /ˌrev·əˈlu·ʃən/ *noun* **1** a change in the way that a country is governed, usually to a different political system and often using violence: *the French Revolution* **2** a very important change in the way that people do things: *This discovery caused a revolution in medicine.*

revolutionary /ˌrev·əˈlu·ʃə·ner·i/ *adj* **1** completely different from what was done before: *a revolutionary new medical treatment* **2** relating to a political revolution: *a revolutionary movement*

revolve /rɪˈvɑlv/ *verb* (present participle **revolving**, past tense and past participle **revolved**) to move in a circle around a central point: *A fan was revolving slowly.*

reward¹ /rɪˈwɔrd/ *noun* **1** 🔵 something good that you get because you have done something good: *There'll be a reward for whoever finishes first.* **2** 🔵 money given to someone for

helping to find something or for helping the police: *The police offered a reward for any information about the robbery.*

reward² /rɪˈwɔrd/ *verb* to give a reward to someone: *She was rewarded for her bravery.*

rewrite /riˈraɪt/ *verb* (past tense **rewrote**, past participle **rewritten**) to write something again in order to improve it: *I had to rewrite my essay.*

rheumatism /ˈru·məˌtɪz·əm/ *noun* [no plural] a disease in which there is pain in the joints (=parts of the body where bones connect)

rhino /ˈraɪ·noʊ/ *noun* short form of rhinoceros

rhinoceros /raɪˈnɑs·ər·əs/ *noun* a large animal from Africa or Asia that has thick skin and one or two horns on its nose

rhyme¹ /raɪm/ *verb* (present participle **rhyming**, past tense and past participle **rhymed**) If a word rhymes with another word, the end part of the words sound the same: *"Moon" rhymes with "June."*

rhyme² /raɪm/ *noun* **1** a short poem that has words that rhyme at the end of each line **2** a word that rhymes with another word

rhythm /ˈrɪð·əm/ *noun* a regular, repeating pattern of sound: *You need a sense of rhythm to be a good dancer.*
• **rhythmically** *adv*

rib /rɪb/ *noun* one of the curved bones in the chest

ribbon /ˈrɪb·ən/ *noun* a long, thin piece of cloth that is used for decoration

rice /raɪs/ *noun* [no plural] 🔴 small grains from a plant that are cooked and eaten
→ See **Food** on page C7

rich /rɪtʃ/ *adj* **1** 🔵 A rich person has a lot of money. ⬌ Opposite **poor** *adj* **2** Rich food has a lot of butter, cream, or eggs in it: *a rich sauce* **3** containing a lot of something that is important or valuable: *Oranges are rich in vitamin C.*

| æ cat | ɑ hot | e get | ɪ sit | i see | ɒ saw | ʊ book | u too | ʌ cut | ə about | ər mother | ɜr turn | ɔr for | aɪ my | aʊ how | eɪ say | ɔɪ boy |

rid /rɪd/ *adj* **1 get rid of** *something* **B1** to throw something away: *We have to get rid of some of those old books.* **2 get rid of** *something* to end something unpleasant: *I can't get rid of this headache.*

ridden /ˈrɪd.ᵊn/ the past participle of ride

riddle /ˈrɪd.ᵊl/ *noun* a strange and difficult question that has a clever and often funny answer

ride[1] /raɪd/ *verb* (present participle **riding**, past tense **rode**, past participle **ridden**) **A1** to travel by sitting on a horse, bicycle, or motorcycle and controlling it: *I ride my bike to work.*

ride[2] /raɪd/ *noun* **1 A2** a trip in a car or train, or on a bus: *a long bus ride* ○ *I'm getting a ride with Steve to the baseball game* (= he is driving me there). **2 B1** a trip riding a bicycle, motorcycle, or horse: *He went out for* **a ride on** *his bicycle.* **3 B1** a machine at a fair that moves people up and down, around in circles, etc. as they sit in it: *She wanted me to* **go on a ride** *with her.*

rider /ˈraɪ.dər/ *noun* **B1** someone who rides a horse, bicycle, or motorcycle

ridiculous /rɪˈdɪk.jə.ləs/ *adj* very silly: *It was a ridiculous suggestion.*

riding /ˈraɪ.dɪŋ/ *noun* [no plural] the sport or activity of riding horses: *She* **goes riding** *every Saturday.*

rifle /ˈraɪ.fᵊl/ *noun* a long gun that you hold against your shoulder when you shoot

right[1] /raɪt/ *adj* **1 A1** correct or true: *He only got half the answers right.* ○ *You're* **right about** *Alison – she's incredible!* ○ *"You came here in 2009, didn't you?" "That's right."* **2 A2** on or toward the side of your body that is to the east when you are facing north: *your right hand* **3 B1** suitable or best in a particular situation: *I'm not sure she's the right person for the job.* **4** fair or morally acceptable: *It isn't right to lie.* ○ *Someone had to tell him – you did the right thing.*

right[2] /raɪt/ *adv* **1 A1** to the right side: *Turn right after the bridge.* **2 A2** used at the beginning of a sentence to get someone's attention or to show you have understood someone: *Right, whose turn is it to clean up?* **3 B1** exactly in a place or time: *He's right here with me.* **4 right away/now** **B1** immediately: *Do you want to start right away?* ○ *I'm busy right now.* **5** correctly: *Nothing was going right.* **6** all the way: *Did you read it right through to the end?*

right[3] /raɪt/ *noun* **1 A2** [no plural] the right side of your body, or the direction toward this side: *You'll find her in the second room* **on the right.** **2** something that the law allows you to do: *the* **right to vote** **3** [no plural] morally good behavior: *She knows the difference between right and wrong.*

right[4] /raɪt/ *exclamation* **A2** informal used to express agreement with someone: *"Johnny, you climb up first." "Right!"*

right angle /ˈraɪt ˌæŋ.gəl/ *noun* an angle of the type that is in a square

right-hand /ˌraɪt ˈhænd/ *adj* **A2** on the right of something: *On* **the right-hand side** *you'll see a sign.*

right-handed /ˌraɪt ˈhæn.dɪd/ *adj* using your right hand to do most things

rigid /ˈrɪdʒ.ɪd/ *adj* **1** not able to change or be changed easily: *I found the rules a little too rigid.* **2** not able to bend or move easily: *a rigid structure*

rim /rɪm/ *noun* the edge of something round: *the rim of a cup*

rind /raɪnd/ *noun* the thick skin of fruits such as oranges and lemons and other foods, for example cheese

ring[1] /rɪŋ/ *noun* **1 A2** a round piece of jewelry that you wear on your finger: *a wedding ring* → See picture at **jewelry** **2** something that is the shape of a circle: *The children sat in a ring around the teacher.* **3** a sound a bell makes: *a doorbell ring* **4** an area with seats around it where people perform or compete: *a boxing ring*

ring[2] /rɪŋ/ *verb* (past tense **rang**, past participle **rung**) **B1** If something rings, it makes the sound of a bell, and if you ring a bell, you cause it to make a sound: *The phone's ringing.*

ringtone /ˈrɪŋ.toʊn/ *noun* the sound that a mobile phone makes

rink /rɪŋk/ *noun* a large flat surface where you can skate: *an ice rink*

rinse /rɪns/ *verb* (present participle **rinsing**, past tense and past participle **rinsed**) to wash something in clean water in order to remove dirt or soap: *Rinse the beans with cold water.*

riot /ˈraɪ.ət/ *noun* angry, violent behavior by a crowd of people

rip /rɪp/ *verb* (present participle **ripping**, past tense and past participle **ripped**) to tear quickly and suddenly: *She ripped her dress getting off her bike.* ○ *He ripped open the package.*

ripe /raɪp/ *adj* developed enough and ready to be eaten: *ripe bananas*

rip-off /ˈrɪp.ɔf/ *noun* informal something that costs too much money: *The drinks here are a complete rip-off.*

rise[1] /raɪz/ *verb* (present participle **rising**, past tense **rose**, past participle **risen**)
1 🔒 to move up: *The balloon rose slowly into the air.* **2** 🔒 When the sun or moon rises, it appears in the sky: *The sun rises in the East.* **3** to get bigger in level: *Prices rose by ten percent.* **4** to stand, especially after sitting: *He rose from his seat.*

rise[2] /raɪz/ *noun* an increase in the level of something: *a rise in temperature*

risk[1] /rɪsk/ *noun* **1** the possibility of something bad happening: *the risk of heart disease* **2 take a risk** to do something although something bad might happen because of it **3 at risk** being in a situation where something bad is likely to happen: *All houses within 100 yards of the sea are **at risk of** flooding*

risk[2] /rɪsk/ *verb* **1** If you risk something bad, you do something although that bad thing might happen: *I'd like to help you, but I can't risk losing my job.* **2** to

put something or yourself in danger: *He risked his life to save me.*

risky /ˈrɪs.ki/ *adj* dangerous because something bad might happen: *It's risky to buy a car without some good advice.*

rival /ˈraɪ.vəl/ *noun* someone or something that is competing against another person or thing: *political rivals*
• **rivalry** *noun* There is intense **rivalry between** the two teams.

river /ˈrɪv.ər/ *noun* 🔒 a long, natural area of water that flows across the land: *the River Thames*

road /roʊd/ *noun* **1** 🔒 a long, hard surface built for cars to drive on: *Be careful when you cross the road.* ○ *The journey takes about three hours **by road** (=in a car, bus, etc.).* **2 Road** 🔒 used in the name of a road as part of an address: *142 Park Road*

roar[1] /rɔr/ *verb* to make a loud, deep sound: *She **roared with laughter**.*

roar[2] /rɔr/ *noun* a loud, deep sound: *a lion's roar*

roast /roʊst/ *verb* 🔒 If you roast food, you cook it in an oven or over a fire: *Roast the lamb in a hot oven for 35 minutes.*
→ See picture at **cook**
• **roast** *adj* 🔒 *roast beef*

rob /rɑb/ *verb* (present participle **robbing**, past tense and past participle **robbed**) 🔒 to steal from a person or a place, often using violence: *to rob a bank*

robber /ˈrɑb.ər/ *noun* someone who steals: *a bank robber*

robbery /ˈrɑb.ər.i/ *noun* (plural **robberies**) the crime of stealing from a person or a place: *a bank robbery*

robe /roʊb/ *noun* **1** a piece of clothing like a long coat that you wear at home when you are not dressed **2** a long, loose piece of clothing that covers most of the body

robin /ˈrɑb.ɪn/ *noun* a bird with a red chest and dark back and wings

robot /ˈroʊ.bɑt/ *noun* a machine controlled by a computer that can move and do other things that people can do

| æ cat | ɑ hot | e get | ɪ sit | i see | ɔ saw | ʊ book | u too | ʌ cut | ə about | ɚ mother | ɝ turn | ɔr for | aɪ my | aʊ how | eɪ say | ɔɪ boy |

rock

rock[1] /rɑk/ noun **1** 🅱1 [no plural] the hard, natural substance that forms part of the Earth's surface **2** 🅱1 a large piece of rock or stone: *Huge waves were crashing against the rocks.* **3** 🅰2 [no plural] loud, modern music with a strong beat, often played with electric guitars and drums: *a rock band*

rock[2] /rɑk/ verb to move backwards and forwards or from side to side, or to make someone or something do this: *She rocked back and forth on her chair.* ○ *He gently rocked the baby to sleep.*

rocket /'rɑk·ɪt/ noun a tube-shaped vehicle for traveling in space

rocking chair /'rɑk·ɪŋ ˌtʃeər/ noun (also **rocker**) a chair built on two pieces of curved wood so that you can move forward and backward when you sit in it

rocky /'rɑk·i/ adj (comparative **rockier**, superlative **rockiest**) with lots of rocks: *a rocky beach*

rod /rɑd/ noun a thin, straight pole: *a fishing rod*

rode /roʊd/ past tense and past participle of ride

rodent /'roʊ·dənt/ noun an animal with long, sharp teeth, such as a mouse

rodeo /'roʊ·di·oʊ/ noun a public performance or competition in which people show how well they can ride cattle and wild horses, and catch cattle with ropes

role /roʊl/ noun **1** 🅱1 a part in a play or movie: *In his latest movie, he plays the role of a gangster.* **2** the job someone or something has in a particular situation: *Schools play an important role in society.*

role play /'roʊl ˌpleɪ/ noun an activity in which people pretend to be someone else, especially as part of learning a new skill: *a role-play activity*

roll[1] /roʊl/ verb **1** to move somewhere by turning in a circular direction, or to make something move this way: *The ball rolled through the goalkeeper's legs.* ○ *She rolled over onto her side.* **2** to turn something around itself to make the

shape of a ball or tube: *to roll a cigarette* **3** to move somewhere smoothly: *Tears rolled down her face.*

roll[2] /roʊl/ noun **1** something that has been turned around itself into a round shape like a tube: *a roll of toilet paper* **2** 🅱1 a small loaf of bread for one person

Rollerblades /'roʊ·lər,bleɪdz/ plural noun trademark boots with a single line of wheels on the bottom, used for moving across the ground
→ See **Sports 1** on page C15
• **Rollerblading** noun [no plural]

roller skate /'roʊ·lər ˌskeɪt/ noun a boot with wheels on the bottom, used for moving across the ground
• **roller skating** noun [no plural]

rolling pin /'roʊ·lɪŋ ˌpɪn/ noun a kitchen tool made of a long, thin, round piece of wood, used for making dough flat
→ See **The Kitchen** on page C10

romance /roʊ'mæns/ noun **1** 🅱1 an exciting relationship or love between two people, often a short one: *They had a brief romance.* **2** a story about love

romantic /roʊ'mæn·tɪk/ adj **1** 🅱1 relating to exciting feelings of love: *a romantic dinner for two* **2** 🅱1 relating to a story about love: *a romantic movie*

roof /ruf/, /rʊf/ noun 🅰2 the surface that covers the top of a building or vehicle: *He climbed onto the roof.*
→ See picture at **chimney**

room /rum/, /rʊm/ noun **1** 🅰1 a part of the inside of a building, that is separated from other parts by walls, floors, and ceilings: *a hotel room* **2** [no plural] space for things to fit into: *Is there enough room for all of us in your car?*

roommate /'rum,meɪt/, /'rʊm,meɪt/ noun **1** 🅰2 someone whom you share a room or apartment with: *He was my roommate in college.* **2** someone whom you share your home with

root /rut/ plural noun **1** the part of a plant that grows under the ground **2** roots where someone or something originally comes from: *He lives in London but his roots are in Ireland.*

rope /rəʊp/ noun very thick, strong string

rose[1] /rəʊz/ past tense and past participle of rise

rose[2] /rəʊz/ noun

rose

B1 a flower with a pleasant smell and thorns (=sharp points on the stem)

rot /rɒt/ verb (present participle **rotting**, past tense and past participle **rotted**) to become bad and soft because of being dead or old: *The fruit had been left to rot.* ○ *Sugar rots your teeth.*

rotate /rəʊˈteɪt/ verb (present participle **rotating**, past tense and past participle **rotated**) to turn in a circular direction, or to make something turn in a circular direction: *The handle rotates freely.*
• **rotation** noun *the rotation of the Earth*

rotten /ˈrɒtᵊn/ adj **1** old and bad: *rotten eggs* **2** informal very bad: *rotten weather*

rough /rʌf/ adj **1** **B1** A rough surface is not smooth: *rough hands* **2** **B1** not completely accurate but close: *Can you give me a rough idea of the cost?* **3** dangerous or violent: *Hockey can be a rough game.* **4** If the sea or weather is rough, there is a lot of strong wind and sometimes rain: *The boat sank in rough seas.* **5** difficult or unpleasant: *She's having a rough time at work.*

roughly /ˈrʌf.li/ adv **1** close to a particular number, although not exactly that number: *Sales have increased roughly 30% since last year.* **2** with force or violence: *He pushed us roughly out of the door.*

round /raʊnd/ adj **A2** in the shape of a circle or ball: *a round table* ○ *round eyes* → See picture at flat adj

round trip /ˌraʊnd ˈtrɪp/ noun a trip from one place to another and back to where you started: *I have a round trip of 45 miles to get to work.*
• **round-trip** adj *a round-trip ticket*

round-trip ticket /ˌraʊnd.trɪp ˌtɪk.ɪt/ noun a ticket that lets you travel to a place and back again

route /ruːt/ noun **B1** the roads you follow to get from one place to another place

routine /ruːˈtiːn/ noun **B1** the things that you do every day at the same time: *a daily routine*

row[1] /rəʊ/ noun **1** **B1** a straight line of people or things: *a row of trees* **2** **B1** a line of seats: *I was sitting in the front row.* **3** in a row one after another without a break: *He's just won the race for the fifth year in a row.*

row[2] /rəʊ/ verb to move a boat or move someone in a boat through the water using oars (=poles with flat ends)
• **rowing** noun [no plural]

rowboat /ˈrəʊ.bəʊt/ noun a small boat that is moved by pulling oars (=poles with flat ends) through the water

royal /ˈrɔɪ.əl/ adj relating to a queen or king and his or her family: *the British royal family*

royalty /ˈrɔɪ.əl.ti/ noun [no plural] the people in the royal family

rub /rʌb/ verb (present participle **rubbing**, past tense and past participle **rubbed**) to press your hand or a cloth on a surface and move it backwards and forwards: *He rubbed himself dry with a towel.* ○ *Rub the stain with a damp cloth.*

rubber /ˈrʌb.ər/ noun [no plural] a strong material that bends easily and is used to make tires, boots, etc.

rubber band /ˌrʌb.ər ˈbænd/ noun a thin circle of rubber used to hold things together

ruby /ˈruː.bi/ noun (plural **rubies**) a valuable bright red stone that is used in jewelry

rude /ruːd/ adj **B1** behaving in a way that is not polite and upsets other people: *a rude remark* ○ *He was very rude to me.* ○ *It would be rude to leave without saying goodbye.*
→ Opposite polite adj
• **rudely** adv
• **rudeness** noun [no plural]

a
b
c
d
e
f
g
h
i
j
k
l
m
n
o
p
q
r
s
t
u
v
w
x
y
z

rug /rʌg/ noun **rug**
B1 a soft piece of
material used to
cover the floor:
*The dog was lying
on the rug in front of
the fire.*
→ See **The Living
Room** on page C11

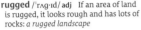

rugged /'rʌg·ɪd/ adj If an area of land
is rugged, it looks rough and has lots of
rocks: *a rugged landscape*

ruin¹ /'ru·ɪn/ verb to spoil or destroy
something: *They were late and the dinner was ruined.*

ruin² /'ru·ɪn/ noun **B1** the broken parts
that are left from an old building or
town: *Thousand of tourists wander
around these ancient ruins every year.*

rule¹ /rul/ noun **1 B1** an official statement about what you must or must not
do: *You can't smoke at school. It's **against
the rules** (= not allowed).* **2 B1** a basic
idea that explains how a system, such as
a language or science, works: *the rules of
grammar* **3** the usual way something is: *I
visit my parents once a week **as a rule**.*

rule² /rul/ verb (present participle **ruling**,
past tense and past participle **ruled**) to be in
control of somewhere, usually a coun-
try: *They were ruled for many years by a
dictator.*

ruler /'ru·lər/ noun **1** the leader of a
country **2 A2** a flat, straight stick that
is used to measure things
→ See **The Classroom** on page C4

rum /rʌm/ noun a strong, alcoholic
drink made from sugar

rumble /'rʌm·bəl/ verb (present participle
rumbling, past tense and past participle
rumbled) to make a deep, long sound:
*The smell of cooking made his stomach
rumble.*

rumor /'ru·mər/ noun something that a
lot of people are talking about although
they do not know whether it is true: *I
heard a rumor that you were leaving.*

run¹ /rʌn/ verb (present participle **running**,
past tense **ran**, past participle **run**) **1 A1** to

move on your feet at a faster speed
than walking: *He can run very fast.* ○ *I
run about three miles every morning.*
2 B1 to organize or control something:
She ran her own restaurant for five years.
3 If a piece of equipment is running, it
is switched on and working: *The engine
is running more smoothly now.* **4** If
trains or buses are running, they are
available to travel on: *The buses only run
until 11 p.m.* **5** If liquid runs somewhere, it flows: *Tears ran down her face.*
run away phrasal verb to secretly leave
a place because you are unhappy there:
He ran away from home as a child.
run out phrasal verb **B1** to finish, use,
or sell all of something so that there is
none left: *I almost **ran out of** money.*
run *someone/something* **over** phrasal
verb to hit someone or something with
a car, bus, etc. and hurt or kill the person or damage the thing: *He was run
over by a bus as he crossed the road.*

run² /rʌn/ noun **1 B1** the act of moving on your feet at a speed faster than
walking as a sport: *I think I'll go for a
run.* **2** in baseball, a single point: *They
lost by two runs.*

rung /rʌŋ/ the past participle of ring²

runner /'rʌn·ər/ noun **A2** someone
who runs: *a long-distance runner*

running /'rʌn·ɪŋ/ noun [no plural] **A2** the
sport of moving on your feet at a speed
faster than walking: *I **go running** three
times a week.*
→ See **Sports 1** on page C15

runny /'rʌn·i/ adj (comparative **runnier**,
superlative **runniest**) **1** A runny substance is more liquid than usual: *a
runny egg yolk* **2 runny nose** If you
have a runny nose, liquid is coming out
of your nose all the time

runway /'rʌn·weɪ/ noun a long piece of
ground that planes use to land on or to
start flying from

rural /'rʊər·əl/ adj relating to the country and not to towns: *a rural area*

rush¹ /rʌʃ/ verb to hurry or move
quickly somewhere: *We had to rush to
catch the bus.*

rush^2 /rʌʃ/ noun [no plural]   a situation in which you have to hurry or move somewhere quickly: *I'm sorry I can't talk now – I'm in a rush.*

rush hour /'rʌʃ ˌaʊər/ noun [no plural] the time when roads and trains are very busy because a lot of people are traveling to or from work: *I hate driving during rush hour.*

rust /rʌst/ noun [no plural]   a dark orange substance that gets on metal when it is wet
• **rust** verb

rustle /'rʌs·əl/ verb (present participle **rustling,** past tense and past participle **rustled**)   If things such as paper or leaves rustle, they move around and make a soft, dry sound: *Outside, the trees rustled in the wind.*

rusty /'rʌs·ti/ adj (comparative **rustier,** superlative **rustiest**)   Rusty metal has rust (=an orange substance) on its surface: *rusty nails*

rut /rʌt/ noun   **1** a long, deep track in a dirt road   **2 in a rut** in a bad situation in which you do the same things all the time: *He seems to be stuck in a rut.*

Ss

S, s /es/   the nineteenth letter of the alphabet

sack /sæk/ noun
a large, strong bag
used to carry or
keep things: *a sack
of potatoes*

sack

sacred /'seɪ·krɪd/
adj   relating to a
religion or considered to be holy:
sacred music

sacrifice^1 /'sæk·rəˌfɑɪs/ noun   **1** something good that you must stop having in order to achieve something: *Sometimes you have to **make sacrifices** to succeed.*   **2** an animal that is killed and offered to a god in a religious ceremony

sacrifice^2 /'sæk·rəˌfɑɪs/ verb (present participle **sacrificing,** past tense and past participle **sacrificed**)   **1** to stop having something good in order to achieve something: *There are thousands of men ready to **sacrifice** their lives **for** their country.*   **2** to kill an animal and offer it to a god in a religious ceremony

sad /sæd/ adj (comparative **sadder,** superlative **saddest**)   **1** 🅐 not happy at all: *I was very sad when our cat died.* ○ *a sad book*   **2** boring or not fashionable: *I cleaned the house on Saturday night, which is sad.*
• **sadness** noun [no plural]

saddle /'sæd·əl/ noun   **1** a leather seat that you put on a horse so that you can ride it   **2** a seat on a bicycle or motorcycle

sadly /'sæd·li/ adv   **1** in a sad way: *She shook her head sadly.*   **2** used to say that you are sorry something is true: *Sadly, the marriage ended.*

safari /sə'fɑr·i/ noun   a journey, usually to Africa, to see wild animals

safe^1 /seɪf/ adj   **1** 🅐 not dangerous: *a safe driver* ○ *Air travel is generally very safe.*   **2** 🅑 not hurt or in danger: *She said that all the hostages were safe.*
• **safely** adv 🅑 *Drive safely!*

safe^2 /seɪf/ noun   a strong metal box with locks where you keep money, jewelry, etc.

safety /'seɪf·ti/ noun [no plural]   a state of being safe from harm or danger: *road safety*

sag /sæg/ verb (present participle **sagging,** past tense and past participle **sagged**)   to sink or bend down: *Our mattress sags in the middle.*

said /sed/   past tense and past participle of say

sail^1 /seɪl/ verb   **1** 🅑 to control or travel in a boat or a ship that has an engine or sails: *We sailed to Barbados.* ○ *She sails her own boat.*   **2** When a boat or a ship sails, it travels on the water: *The boat **sailed along** the coast.*

a
b
c
d
e
f
g
h
i
j
k
l
m
n
o
p
q
r
s
t
u
v
w
x
y
z

sail[2] /seɪl/ **noun** a large piece of material that is fixed to a pole on a boat to catch the wind and make the boat move

sailing /'seɪ·lɪŋ/ **noun** [no plural] **A2** a sport using boats with sails: *We're **going** sailing next weekend.*

sailor /'seɪ·lər/ **noun** **B1** someone who sails ships or boats as his or her job or as a sport

saint /seɪnt/ **noun** a dead person who lived his or her life in a holy way

sake /seɪk/ **noun** **1 for the sake of** *someone* in order to help or please someone: *He asked her to stay for the sake of the children.* **2 for goodness sake!** something you say when you are angry about something: *For goodness sake, will you come here!?*

salad /'sæl·əd/ **noun** **A2** a cold mixture of vegetables that have not been cooked

salad

salary /'sæl·ə·ri/ **noun** (plural **salaries**) **B1** the money that you get, usually every month, for working

sale /seɪl/ **noun** **1** **A2** a time when a store sells things for less money than usual: *I bought this dress **on sale**.* **2 for sale** **A2** available to buy: *Is this painting for sale?* **3 on sale** **A2** available to buy in a store, on the Internet, etc.: *The DVD is now on sale.* **4** the act of selling something: *The sale of alcohol is now banned.* **5 sales** the number of items sold: *Our sales have doubled this year.*

salesclerk /'seɪlz,klɜrk/ **noun** someone whose job is selling things in a store

salesman /'seɪlz·mən/ **noun** (plural **salesmen**) **B1** a man whose job is selling things

saleswoman /'seɪlz,wʊm·ən/ **noun** (plural **saleswomen**) **B1** a woman whose job is selling things

salmon /'sæm·ən/ **noun** (plural **salmon**) **B1** a large, silver fish, or the pink meat of this fish

salon /sə'lɑn/ **noun** a shop where you can have your hair cut or have your appearance improved: *a hair salon*

salt /sɔlt/ **noun** [no plural] **A1** a white substance used to add flavor to food: *salt and pepper*

salty /'sɔl·ti/ **adj** (comparative **saltier**, superlative **saltiest**) tasting of or containing salt: *Is the soup too salty?*

salute[1] /sə'lut/ **noun** a sign of respect to someone of a higher rank in a military organization, often made by putting the right hand at the side of the head

salute[2] /sə'lut/ **verb** (present participle **saluting**, past tense and past participle **saluted**) to give a salute to someone of a higher rank in a military organization

same[1] /seɪm/ **adj** **1 the same** **A1** exactly alike: *He's **the same** age **as** me.* ○ *We work at the same speed.* **2 the same** **A1** not another different person, thing or situation: *My brother and I sleep in the same room.* **3 at the same time** **B1** If two things happen at the same time, they happen together: *We arrived at the same time.*

same[2] /seɪm/ **pronoun** **1 the same** **A2** exactly like: *People say I look **just the same as** my sister.* ○ *He looks **exactly the same** as he did ten years ago.* **2 the same** **B1** not another different thing or situation: *I'd do the same if I were in your situation.*

same[3] /seɪm/ **adv** **the same** in the same way: *We treat all our children the same.*

sample /'sæm·pəl/ **noun** a small amount of something that shows you what it is like: *She brought in some samples of her work.* ○ *The doctor took a blood sample.*

sand /sænd/ **noun** [no plural] **B1** a substance that is found on beaches, which is made from very small grains of rock

sandal /'sæn·dəl/ **noun** **B1** a light shoe with straps that you wear in warm weather

→ See **Clothes** on page C5

sandwich /'sænd·wɪtʃ/ noun **A1** two slices of bread with meat, cheese, etc. between them: *a cheese sandwich*
→ See **Food** on page C7

sandy /'sæn·di/ adj (comparative **sandier**, superlative **sandiest**) **B1** covered with sand: *a sandy beach*

sane /seɪn/ adj having a healthy mind
→ Opposite **insane** adj

sang /sæŋ/ past tense and past participle of sing

sank /sæŋk/ past tense and past participle of sink

sarcasm /'sɑr·kæz·əm/ noun [no plural] a way of using words that are the opposite of what you mean, in order to be unpleasant or to criticize something in a humorous way

sarcastic /sɑr·kæs·tɪk/ adj using sarcasm: *Are you being sarcastic?*

sat /sæt/ past tense and past participle of sit

satellite /'sæt·ᵊl·aɪt/ noun a piece of equipment that is sent into space around the Earth to get and send signals: *a weather satellite*

satellite dish /'sæt·ᵊl·aɪt ‚dɪʃ/ noun a round piece of equipment that is used for receiving television or radio signals

satin /'sæt·ᵊn/ noun [no plural] a smooth, shiny cloth

satisfaction /‚sæt·əs·fæk·ʃən/ noun [no plural] a good feeling because you have done something well: *job satisfaction*

satisfactory /‚sæt·əs·fæk·tə·ri/ adj good enough: *We hope to find a satisfactory solution to the problem.*
→ Opposite **unsatisfactory** adj

satisfied /'sæt·əs·faɪd/ adj **B1** happy because you have gotten what you wanted: *Are you satisfied with the new arrangement?*
→ Opposite **dissatisfied** adj

satisfy /'sæt·əs·faɪ/ verb (present participle **satisfying**, past tense and past participle **satisfied**) to please someone by giving him or her what he or she wants: *They*

sell 31 flavors of ice cream – enough to satisfy everyone!

Saturday /'sæt·ər·deɪ/ noun **A1** the day of the week after Friday and before Sunday

sauce /sɔs/ noun **A2** a liquid that you put on food to add flavor: *pasta with tomato sauce*

saucepan /'sɔs·pæn/ noun **B1** a metal pan with a long handle and a lid, used for cooking food
→ See **The Kitchen** on page C10

saucer /'sɔ·sər/ noun **B1** a small plate that you put under a cup
→ See picture at cup

sauna /'sɔ·nə/ noun a room that is hot and filled with steam where people sit to relax or feel healthy

sausage /'sɔ·sɪdʒ/ noun **A2** a mixture of meat and spices pressed into a long tube

sausages

save /seɪv/ verb (present participle **saving**, past tense and past participle **saved**) **1** **A2** (also **save up**) to keep money so that you can buy something with it in the future: *We've saved almost $2,900 for our wedding.* **2** **A2** to keep something to use in the future: *I've saved some food for you.* **3** save files, work, etc. **A2** to store work or information on a computer **4** **B1** to stop someone or something from being killed or destroyed: *He was badly injured, but the doctors saved his life.* **5** save money, space, time, etc. **B1** to reduce the amount of money, space, time, etc. that you have to use: *You'll save time by doing it yourself.* **6** save a goal to stop a player from scoring a goal

savings /'seɪ·vɪŋz/ plural noun money that you have saved, usually in a bank: *a savings account*

saw¹ /sɔ/ past tense and past participle of see

saw² /sɔ/ noun a tool with a sharp edge that you use to cut wood or other hard material

saxophone /ˈsæk·səˌfoʊn/ noun
a metal musical instrument that you
play by blowing into it and pressing keys

say /seɪ/ verb (present participle **saying**, past
tense and past participle **said**) **1** **A1** to speak
words: *"I'd like to go home," she said.*
○ *How do you say this word?* **2** **B1** to
tell someone about a fact or opinion: *He
said that he was leaving.* **3** **B1** to give
information in writing, numbers, or
signs: *My watch says one o'clock.*
4 **B1** to think or believe: *People say
that he's over 100.*

> **⚠ Common mistake: say or tell?**
>
> Say can refer to any type of speech.
> *"Good night," she said.*
> *She said she was unhappy.*
> *Jim said to meet him here.*
>
> Tell is used to report that someone
> has given information or an order.
> The verb **tell** is always followed by
> the person that the information or
> order is given to.
> *Alex told **me** about his new job.*
>
> Say is never followed by the person
> that the information or order is given
> to.
> *He told us to stay here.*
> ~~He said us to stay here.~~

saying /ˈseɪ·ɪŋ/ noun a famous phrase
that people use to give advice about life

scab /skæb/ noun a layer of dried blood
that covers a cut in the skin

scaffolding /ˈskæf·əlˌdɪŋ/ noun [no plural]
a temporary structure made of flat
boards and metal poles used to work on
a tall building

scale /skeɪl/ noun **1** the size or level of
something: *We don't yet know the scale
of the problem.* **2** the set of numbers,
amounts, etc. used to measure or compare the level of something: *How would
you rate her work **on a scale of** 1-10?*
3 a piece of equipment for measuring
weight: *a bathroom scale* → See **The
Bathroom** on page C1 **4** how the size of
things on a map, model, etc. relates to

the same things in real life: *a map with
a scale of one inch per mile* **5** a series of
musical notes that is always played in
order and that goes up from the first note
6 one of the flat pieces of hard material
that cover the skin of fish and snakes

scalp /skælp/ noun the skin on the top
of your head under your hair

scan /skæn/ verb (present participle
scanning, past tense and past participle
scanned) **1** to examine something with
a machine that can see inside an object
or body: *Airports use X-ray machines to
scan luggage for weapons.* **2** to use a
machine that copies words or pictures
from paper into a computer: *I scanned
the photos into my computer.* **3** to read
something quickly in order to understand the main meaning or to find a
particular piece of information:
*I scanned the travel brochures looking for
a cheap vacation.*

scandal /ˈskæn·dºl/ noun something
that shocks people because they think it
is very bad: *a political scandal*

scanner /ˈskæn·ər/ noun a piece of equipment that copies words or pictures from
paper into a computer

scar¹ /skɑr/ noun a permanent mark
left on the body from a cut or other
injury

scar² /skɑr/ verb (present participle **scarring**,
past tense and past participle **scarred**) to
cause a scar: *He was scarred for life by
the accident.*

scarce /skeərs/ adj rare, existing only
in small amounts: *scarce resources*

scarcely /ˈskeərs·li/ adv only just: *They
had scarcely finished eating when the
doorbell rang.*

scare¹ /skeər/ verb (present participle
scaring, past tense and past participle **scared**)
to frighten a person or animal: *Sudden
loud noises scare me.*

scare² /skeər/ noun **1** a sudden feeling
of fear or worry: *The earthquake gave us
a scare.* **2** a situation that worries or
frightens people: *a health scare*

scarecrow /'skeər,kroʊ/ **noun** a model of a person that is put in a field to frighten birds and stop them from eating the plants

scared /skeərd/ **adj** **B1** frightened or worried: *Robert's **scared** of heights.*

scarf /skɑrf/ **noun** (plural **scarves, scarfs**) **A2** a piece of cloth that you wear around your neck or head to keep warm or for decoration
→ See **Clothes** on page C5

scary /'skeər·i/ **adj** informal
B1 frightening: *a scary story*

scatter /'skæt̬·ər/ **verb** **1** to throw a lot of small objects over an area: *He scattered some flower seeds in the garden.* **2** to suddenly move away in different directions: *The crowd scattered at the sound of shots being fired.*

scene /sin/ **noun** **1** **B1** a short part of a movie, play, or book in which things happen in one place: *a love scene* **2** a view or picture of a place, event, or activity: *scenes of horror* **3** a place where a bad thing has happened: *the scene of the crime*

scenery /'si·nə·ri/ **noun** [no plural] **1** **B1** the attractive, natural things that you see in the countryside **2** the large pictures of buildings, countryside, etc. used on a theater stage

scent /sent/ **noun** **1** a nice smell: *the sweet scent of orange blossoms* **2** liquid with a nice smell that people put on their skin

schedule[1] /'skedʒ·ul/ **noun** **1** **A2** a list of the times and days of classes at a school, college, university, etc. **2** **B1** a list of times when buses, trains, etc. arrive and leave **3** a list of dates and times that shows when things will happen or a plan for them to happen: *a project schedule* ○ *Will the work be completed **on schedule** (=at the expected time)?*

schedule[2] /'skedʒ·ul/ **verb** to plan an event for a particular day or time: *I need to schedule a doctor's appointment.*

scheduled /'skedʒ·uld/ **adj** planned to happen at a particular time or on a

particular date: *The play will start half an hour later than the scheduled time.*

scheme /skim/ **noun** a plan for doing or organizing something, especially one that does not follow the usual rules: *a creative scheme for making money*

scholar /'skɑl·ər/ **noun** someone who has studied a subject and knows a lot about it: *a legal scholar*

scholarship /'skɑl·ər,ʃɪp/ **noun** an amount of money given to a person by an organization to pay for his or her education

school /skul/ **noun** **1** **A1** a place where children go to learn things: *I ride my bike to school.* **2** **A2** [no plural] the time that you spend at school: *I started school when I was five.* **3** a dance, language, riding, etc. school **A2** a place where you can study a particular subject: *She goes to a dance school every Saturday.* **4** **B1** informal any college or university

schoolchild /'skul,tʃaɪld/ **noun** (plural **schoolchildren**) **A2** a child who goes to school: *a bus full of schoolchildren*

schoolteacher /'skul,ti·tʃər/ **noun** someone who teaches children in a school

science /'saɪ·əns/ **noun** **1** **A2** [no plural] the study of the structure of natural things and the way that they behave **2** **B1** a particular type of science: *Chemistry, physics, and biology are all sciences.*

science fiction /'saɪ·əns ˈfɪk·ʃən/ **noun** [no plural] (also **sci-fi**) **B1** stories about life in the future or in other parts of the universe

scientific /ˌsaɪ·ən'tɪf·ɪk/ **adj** **B1** relating to science: *scientific experiments*
• **scientifically adv** *The theory has not been scientifically proven.*

scientist /'saɪ·ən·tɪst/ **noun** **B1** someone who studies science or works in science

scissors /'sɪz·ərz/ **plural noun** **A2** a tool for cutting paper, hair, etc. that you hold in your hand and that has two blades: *a pair of scissors*
→ See picture at **pair noun**

scold /skoʊld/ verb   to speak angrily to someone, especially a child, because he or she has done something wrong: *His mother **scolded** him **for** breaking a vase.*

scoop /skup/ noun   to remove something from a container using a spoon, your curved hands, etc.: *She scooped the ice cream into the dishes.*

scooter /ˈsku·t̬ər/ noun   **1** Ⓐ2 a small motorcycle   **2** a child's vehicle that has two wheels fixed to the ends of a long board and a long handle

score¹ /skɔr/ noun   Ⓑ1 the number of points someone gets in a game or test: *a high/low score ○ What's the score?*

score² /skɔr/ verb (present participle **scoring**, past tense and past participle **scored**)   Ⓑ1 to get points in a game or test: *The Giants scored just before halftime.*

scorn /skɔrn/ noun [no plural] formal   the belief that something is stupid

scorpion /ˈskɔr·pi·ən/ noun   a small, insect-like creature with a curved, poisonous tail

scowl /skaʊl/ verb   to look at someone angrily: *He **scowled at** me from behind his paper.*

• **scowl** noun

scramble /ˈskræm·bəl/ verb (present participle **scrambling**, past tense and past participle **scrambled**)   to move or climb quickly but with difficulty, often using your hands: *We scrambled up the hill.*

scrambled eggs /ˈskræm·bəld ˌegz/ plural noun   a dish of eggs that are mixed together then cooked: *a plate of scrambled eggs*

scrap /skræp/ noun   a small piece or amount of something: *He wrote his phone number on **a scrap of** paper.*

scrape /skreɪp/ verb (present participle **scraping**, past tense and past participle **scraped**)   **1** to damage the surface of something by rubbing it against something rough: *Jamie fell over and scraped his knee.*   **2** to remove something from a surface using a sharp edge: *I had to scrape the ice off the car.*

scratch¹ /skrætʃ/ verb   **1** to rub your skin with your nails: *My skin was so itchy, I was scratching all night.*   **2** to make a slight cut or long, thin mark with a sharp object: *The car door was scratched.*   **3** to rub a hard surface with a sharp object, often making a noise: *The dog is **scratching at** the door – he wants to be let in.*

scratch² /skrætʃ/ noun   **1** a slight cut or a long, thin mark made with a sharp object: *I've got all these scratches on my arm from the cat.*   **2 from scratch** from the beginning: *We didn't have any furniture of our own so we had to start from scratch.*

scream¹ /skrim/ verb   Ⓑ1 to make a loud, high noise with your voice because you are afraid or hurt: *someone was screaming in the street.*

scream² /skrim/ noun   Ⓑ1 an act of screaming: *We heard screams coming from their apartment.*

screech /skritʃ/ verb   to make an unpleasant, high, loud sound: *A car came screeching around the corner.*

screen /skrin/ noun   **1** Ⓐ2 the part of a television or computer that shows images or writing: *I spend most of my day working in front of a computer screen.*   **2** Ⓐ2 a large, flat surface where a movie or an image is shown   **3** movies: *She first appeared **on screen** in 1965.*

screw¹ /skru/ noun   a small, pointed piece of metal that you turn around and around to fasten things together

screw² /skru/ verb   **1** to fasten something with a screw: *You need to screw the cabinet to the wall.*   **2** to fasten something by turning it around until it is tight

screwdriver /ˈskruˌdraɪ·vər/ noun   a tool for turning screws

scribble /ˈskrɪb·əl/ verb (present participle **scribbling**, past tense and past participle **scribbled**)   to write or draw something quickly and without care: *She scribbled some notes in her book.*

scripture /'skrɪp·tʃər/ noun [no plural] the holy books of a religion

scroll /skroʊl/ verb to move text or an image on a computer screen so that you can look at the part that you want

scrub /skrʌb/ verb (present participle **scrubbing**, past tense and past participle **scrubbed**) to clean something by rubbing it hard with a brush or cloth: *She scrubbed the floor.*

sculpture /'skʌlp·tʃər/ noun **B1** a piece of art that is made from stone, wood, clay, etc.: *a wooden sculpture*

sea /si/ noun **1 A1** a large area of salt water; the ocean: *I'd like to live by the sea.* **2 Sea** a particular area of salt water: *the Black Sea*

seafood /'si·fud/ noun [no plural] animals from the sea that are eaten as food
→ See **Food** on page C7

seagull /'si·gʌl/ noun a gray and white bird that lives near the sea

seal[1] /sil/ noun an animal with smooth fur that eats fish and lives near the sea

seal[2] /sil/ verb to close an entrance or container so that air or liquid cannot enter or leave it: *She sealed the bottle.*

sea level /'si ˌlev·əl/ noun [no plural] the level of the sea's surface, used to measure the height of an area of land: *The town is 500 feet above sea level.*

seam /sim/ noun a line of sewing where two pieces of cloth have been joined together

search[1] /sɜrtʃ/ verb **1 B1** to try to find someone or something: *He searched in his pockets for some change.* **2 B1** to use a computer to find information, especially on the Internet: *I searched the Internet to find cheap flights to Cancun.*

3 If the police search a place or a person, they look to see if he, she, or it is hiding anything illegal, such as drugs: *Police are still searching the forest for the missing girl.*

search[2] /sɜrtʃ/ noun **1 B1** an attempt to find something or someone: *Police are continuing their search for the missing girl.* **2 B1** the act of looking for information with a computer, especially using the Internet: *We did a search for hotels in the city.* **3** the process of trying to find an answer to a problem: *the search for happiness*

the seashore /'si·ʃɔr/ noun [no plural] the area of land along the edge of the sea

seasick /'si·sɪk/ adj feeling sick because of the way a boat is moving

season /'si·zən/ noun **1 B1** one of the four periods of the year; winter, spring, summer, or fall **2 B1** a period of the year when a particular thing happens: *the holiday season* **3 in season** if vegetables or fruit are in season, they are available and ready to eat: *Fruit is cheaper when it's in season.*

seat[1] /sit/ noun **A2** something that you sit on: *Please, **have/take a seat** (=sit down).* ○ *a bus/car seat*

seat[2] /sit/ verb **be seated** to be sitting: *The director was seated on his chair.*

seat belt /'sit ˌbelt/ noun a strap that you fasten across your body when traveling in a car or plane
→ See **Car** on page C3

seaweed /'si·wid/ noun [no plural] a plant that grows in the sea

second[1] /'sek·ənd/ adj **1 A1** being the one after the first: *This is my second piece of cake.* **2 B1** used to show that only one thing is bigger, better, etc. than the thing mentioned: *St. Petersburg is Russia's second city.* **3** another: *Accept the invitation – you won't get a second chance.*

second[2] /'sek·ənd/ pronoun **B1** the one after the first: *You're second on the list.*

second[3] /'sek·ənd/ adv **B1** after one other person or thing in order or importance: *She came in second in the race.*

second[4] /'sek·ənd/ noun **1** Ⓐ2 one of the 60 parts a minute is divided into **2** Ⓑ1 informal a very short period of time: *I'll be back in just a second.*

second-class /'sek·ənd'klæs/ adj not as good or important as the best quality, person, service, etc.: *We are being treated like second-class citizens.*

secondhand /'sek·ənd'hænd/ adj, adv Ⓑ1 If something is secondhand, someone else had it or used it before you: *secondhand books*

second person /'sek·ənd 'pɜr·sən/ noun [no plural] in grammar, the form of a verb or pronoun that is used when referring to the person being spoken or written to: *"You" is a second-person pronoun.*

secret[1] /'si·krət/ adj Ⓑ1 If something is secret, other people are not allowed to know about it: *a secret meeting* ○ *I'll tell you, but you must keep it secret.*
• **secretly** adv Ⓑ1 *He secretly recorded their conversation.*

secret[2] /'si·krɪt/ noun **1** Ⓑ1 something that you tell no one about or only a few people: *I'm having a party for him but it's a secret.* ○ *Can you keep a secret?* **2** the best way of achieving something: *What's the secret of your success?* **3 in secret** without telling other people: *For years they met in secret.*

secretary /'sek·rɪ,ter·i/ noun (plural **secretaries**) **1** Ⓐ2 someone who works in an office, typing letters, answering the telephone, etc. **2** an official who is in charge of a large department of the government: *the Secretary of State*

section /'sek·ʃən/ noun Ⓑ1 one of the parts that something is divided into: *a non-smoking section in a restaurant* ○ *the business section of a newspaper*

secure /sɪ'kjʊər/ adj **1** not likely to fail or be lost: *a secure job* **2** safe from danger: *I don't feel that the house is secure.* **3** firmly fastened and not likely to fall: *Check that all windows and doors are secure.* **4** confident about yourself and the situation that you are in: *Children need to feel secure in order to do well.*

security /sɪ'kjʊər·ɪ·t̬i/ noun [no plural] **1** Ⓑ1 the things that are done to keep someone or something safe: *airport security* **2** Ⓑ1 protection from something failing or being lost: *job security*

see /si/ verb (present participle **seeing**, past tense **saw**, past participle **seen**) **1** Ⓐ1 to notice people and things with your eyes: *Have you seen Molly?* ○ *Turn the light on so I can see.* **2** Ⓐ1 to meet or visit someone: *I'm seeing Peter tonight.* **3** Ⓐ2 to watch a movie, television program, etc.: *Did you see that documentary last night?* **4** Ⓑ1 to understand something: *I see what you mean.* ○ *I don't see why I have to go.* **5** Ⓑ1 to find out information: *I'll just see what time the train gets in.* **6** to imagine or think about something or someone in a particular way: *She didn't see herself as brave.* **7 see you later, soon, tomorrow, etc.** Ⓐ1 used for saying goodbye to someone you are going to meet again later, soon, tomorrow, etc.: *I'll see you later!* **8 I'll/we'll see** used to say that you will make a decision about something later: *"Dad, can I have a guitar?" "We'll see."*

seed /sid/ noun a small round thing that a new plant can grow from

seek /sik/ verb (past tense and past participle **sought**) formal to try to find or get something: *I am seeking advice on the matter.*

seem /sim/ verb **1** Ⓑ1 to appear to be: *She seemed happy.* ○ *It seemed like a good idea at the time.* ○ *There doesn't seem to be any real solution.* **2 it seems…** used to say that something appears to exist or be true: *It seems that the banks close early here.* ○ *It seems to me that she's in the wrong job.*

seen /sin/ the past participle of see

seize /siz/ verb (present participle **seizing**, past tense and past participle **seized**) **1** to take hold of something quickly and firmly: *She seized my arm and pulled me toward her.* **2 seize a chance/opportunity** to do something quickly in order to use an opportunity: *You need to seize every opportunity.*

|oʊ go|ɑɑr fire|aʊər hour|eər hair|ɪər ear|ʊər poor|j yet|ʒ measure|ʃ ship|dʒ judge|tʃ chin|ð that|θ thin|ŋ hang|

seldom /'sel·dəm/ adv not often: *We seldom go out in the evenings.*

select /sə'lekt/ verb **B1** to choose someone or something: *We've selected three candidates.*

selection /sə'lek·ʃən/ noun a group of people or things that has been chosen: *We have a wide selection of furniture.*

self /self/ noun (plural **selves**) who you are as a person: *Lucy didn't seem her usual cheerful self today.*

self-confident /ˌself'kɑn·fɪ·dənt/ adj feeling sure about yourself and your abilities
• **self-confidence** noun [no plural]

self-control /ˌself·kən'troʊl/ noun [no plural] the ability to control your emotions, especially when you are angry or upset

self-defense /ˌself·dɪ'fens/ noun [no plural] actions you take to protect yourself from someone who is attacking you: *He used the gun in self-defense.*

self-employed /ˌself·ɪm'plɔɪd/ adj working for yourself and not for a company or other organization: *He is a self-employed builder.*

selfish /'sel·fɪʃ/ adj **B1** caring only about yourself and not other people
• **selfishly** adv
• **selfishness** noun [no plural]

self-service /ˌself'sɜr·vɪs/ adj **B1** A self-service restaurant or store is one in which you get food or things yourself.

sell /sel/ verb (past tense and past participle **sold**) **1** **A2** to give something to someone who gives you money for it: *He sold his guitar for $50.* ○ *I sold my bike to Claire.* **2** **A2** to offer something for people to buy: *Excuse me, do you sell newspapers?*

sell out phrasal verb to sell all of one thing in a store: *They'd sold out of the skirt I wanted by the time I got there.*

seller /'sel·ər/ noun **B1** someone who sells something: *a flower seller*

semester /sə'mes·tər/ noun **A2** one of two time periods that a school or college year can be divided into

semicircle /'sem·ɪˌsɜr·kəl/ noun half a circle

semicircle

semicolon /'sem·ɪˌkoʊ·lən/ noun a mark [;] used to separate parts of a sentence

semifinal /ˌsem·ɪ'fɑɪ·nəl/ noun one of the two games in a sports competition that are played to decide who will play in the final game

the Senate /'sen·ɪt/ noun one of the two parts of the government of the U.S., or of some states, that make laws

senator /'sen·ə·tər/ noun someone who has been elected to the Senate

send /send/ verb (past tense and past participle **sent**) **1** **A1** to arrange for something to go or be taken somewhere, especially in the mail: *I sent him a letter last week.* **2** to make someone go somewhere: *I sent him into the house to get some glasses.*

send something back phrasal verb **B1** to return something to the person who sent it to you, especially because it is damaged or not suitable: *I had to send the shirt back because it didn't fit me.*

send something off phrasal verb to send a letter, document, or package in the mail: *Have you sent off your application yet?*

senior¹ /'sin·jər/ adj **1** having a more important job or position than someone else: *a senior executive* → Opposite **junior** adj **2** older: *senior citizens* **3** relating to a student's fourth year of high school or college: *my senior year*

senior² /'sin·jər/ noun a student in his or her fourth year of high school or college: *a group of graduating seniors*

a
b
c
d
e
f
g
h
i
j
k
l
m
n
o
p
q
r
s
t
u
v
w
x
y
z

senior citizen /ˈsin·jər ˈsɪt·ə·zən/ *noun*
an older person, especially one who no longer works: *Museum entry is free for senior citizens.*

sensation /senˈseɪ·ʃən/ *noun* **1** a physical feeling, or the ability to physically feel things: *a burning sensation* ○ *Three months after the accident she still has no sensation in her right foot.* **2** a lot of excitement and interest: *Their affair* **caused a sensation.** **3** a strange feeling or idea that you cannot explain: *I had the odd **sensation that** someone was following me.*

sense[1] /sens/ *noun* **1** 🄱🄱 [no plural] the ability to make good decisions and do things that will not make problems: *He had the **good sense** to book a seat in advance.* **2** 🄱🄱 [no plural] a feeling or understanding about yourself or about a situation: *Living in the country gave us a great sense of freedom.* **3** a sense of humor 🄱🄱 the ability to understand funny things and to be funny yourself **4** one of the five natural abilities of sight, hearing, touch, smell, and taste: *I have a very poor **sense** of smell.* **5** the meaning of a word, phrase, or sentence **6** the ability to do something: *a sense of direction* ○ *good business sense* **7 make sense** to have a meaning or reason that you can understand: *He's written me this note but it doesn't make any sense.* **8 make sense** to be a good thing to do: *It makes sense to buy while prices are low.*

sense[2] /sens/ *verb* (present participle **sensing**, past tense and past participle **sensed**) to understand what someone is thinking or feeling without being told about it: *I **sense that** you aren't happy.*

sensible /ˈsen·sə·bəl/ *adj* 🄱🄱 showing the ability to make good decisions and do things that will not make problems: *That's a sensible decision.* ○ *Wouldn't it be more **sensible to** leave before the traffic gets bad?*
• **sensibly** *adv* *She eats sensibly.*

sensitive /ˈsen·sə·t̬ɪv/ *adj* **1** able to understand what people are feeling and behave in a way that does not upset

them: *I want a man who's kind and sensitive.* **2** often upset by the things people say or do: *She's **very sensitive about** her weight.* **3** able to react very quickly and easily: *He has a very sensitive nose.* **4** A sensitive subject or situation needs to be dealt with carefully in order to avoid upsetting people: *Religion is a sensitive issue.*

> **⚠ Common mistake: sensitive or sensible?**
>
> Remember that **sensible** does not mean "easily upset" or "able to understand what people are feeling." The word you need to express that is **sensitive**.
>
> *Don't criticize her too much. She's very sensitive.*

sent /sent/ past tense and past participle of **send**

sentence[1] /ˈsen·t̬ns/ *noun* **1** 🄰🄵 a group of words, usually containing a verb, that expresses a complete idea: *I wasn't able to complete my sentence.* **2** a punishment that a judge gives to someone who has committed a crime: *He got a three-year jail sentence.*

sentence[2] /ˈsen·t̬ns/ *verb* (present participle **sentencing**, past tense and past participle **sentenced**) to give a punishment to someone who has committed a crime: *He was sentenced to six years in prison.*

sentimental /ˌsen·t̬əˈmen·t̬ᵊl/ *adj* showing feelings such as sympathy, love, etc., especially in a silly way: *a sentimental song*

separate[1] /ˈsep·ər·ət/ *adj* **1** 🄱🄵 not joined or touching anything else: *Keep raw meat **separate from** other food.* **2** 🄱🄵 different: *Use a separate sheet of paper for the next exercise.* **3** not related: *He keeps his work and private lives separate.*
• **separately** *adv*

separate[2] /ˈsep·əˌreɪt/ *verb* (present participle **separating**, past tense and past participle **separated**) **1** to divide into parts, or to make something divide into parts: *I **separated** the class **into** three groups.*

2 to move apart, or to make people move apart: *I'll separate you two if you don't stop talking!* **3** to start to live in a different place from your husband or wife because the relationship has ended: *My parents separated when I was four.*

separation /ˌsep·ə'reɪ·ʃən/ **noun** [no plural] the fact of people or things being separate: *a long period of separation*

September /sep'tem·bər/ **noun** **A1** the ninth month of the year

sequence /'si·kwəns/ **noun** a group of related events or things that have a particular order: *We still don't know the sequence of events that led to his death.*

sergeant /'sɑr·dʒənt/ **noun** **1** an officer of low rank in the police **2** a soldier of middle rank in the army or air force

serial /'sɪər·i·əl/ **noun** a story that is told in separate parts over a period of time

series /'sɪər·iz/ **noun** (plural **series**) **1** many things or events of the same type that come one after the other: *a series of lectures* **2** **B1** a group of television or radio programs that have the same main characters or deal with the same subject: *a comedy series*

serious /'sɪər·i·əs/ **adj** **1** **B1** A serious problem or situation is bad and makes people worry: *a serious accident/illness* ○ *This is a serious matter.* **2** **B1** thinking or speaking honestly about something and not joking: *Are you **serious about** changing your job?* **3** **B1** A serious person is quiet and does not laugh often: *a serious child* **4** important and needing your complete attention: *That's an interesting offer – I'm going to give it some serious consideration.*
• **seriousness noun** [no plural]

seriously /'sɪər·i·əs·li/ **adv** **1** **B1** in a serious way: *Smoking can seriously damage your health.* **2** take *someone/something* seriously to believe that someone or something is important and that you should give attention to him or her: *The police have to take any terrorist threat seriously.*

sermon /'sɜr·mən/ **noun** a religious speech given by a priest in church: *to give a sermon*

servant /'sɜr·vənt/ **noun** someone who works and lives in someone else's house, especially in the past

serve /sɜrv/ **verb** (present participle **serving**, past tense and past participle **served**) **1** **A2** to give someone food or drink, especially in a restaurant or bar: *Are you still serving?* **2** **B1** to help customers and sell things to them in a store: *Are you being served?* **3** to do work that helps society: *to serve in the army* **4** to be useful as something: *The spare bedroom also **serves as** a study.* **5** to be in prison for a period of time

server /'sɜr·vər/ **noun** **B1** a computer that stores and manages programs and information used by other computers: *an Internet server*

service /'sɜr·vɪs/ **noun** **1** **B1** [no plural] the work that people who work in stores, restaurants, hotels, etc. do to help customers: *The food was good, but the service was awful.* **2** **B1** a system that supplies something that people need: *financial services* ○ *They **provide** a free bus **service** from the station.* **3** [no plural] the time you spend working for an organization: *He retired last week after 25 years' service.* **4** [no plural] extra money that is added to your check in a restaurant to pay the waiters: *Service not included.* **5** a religious ceremony: *Not many people **attended** the funeral **service**.*

session /'seʃ·ən/ **noun** **B1** a period during which you do one activity: *We're having a training session this afternoon.*

set¹ /set/ **verb** (present participle **setting**, past tense and past participle **set**) **1** **B1** to arrange a time when something will happen: *Should we **set a date** for the next meeting?* **2** **B1** to make a piece of equipment ready to be used: *He set the alarm for 7 a.m.* **3** **B1** When the sun sets, it moves down in the sky so that it cannot be seen. **4** **B1** If a book, play, or movie is set in a place or period of time, the

a
b
c
d
e
f
g
h
i
j
k
l
m
n
o
p
q
r
s
t
u
v
w
x
y
z

story happens there or at that time: *It's a historical adventure set in India in the 1940s.* **5 set** someone **free** to allow someone to leave prison **6 set fire to** something to make something start burning **7 set the table** to put plates, knives, forks, etc. on the table before you have a meal **8** If a liquid substance sets, it becomes solid.

set off phrasal verb **B1** to start a trip: *What time are you setting off tomorrow morning?*

set out phrasal verb **B1** to start a trip: *We had to set out early.*

set something **up** phrasal verb **B1** to start a company or organization: *He just set up his own company.*

set[2] /set/ noun **1 A2** a group of things that belong together: *a set of instructions* ○ *a set of keys* **2 B1** a television or radio: *a TV set*

settle /ˈset·ᵊl/ verb (present participle **settling**, past tense and past participle **settled**) **1** If you settle an argument, you stop the problem and stop arguing. **2** to start living somewhere that you are going to live for a long time: *Finally he settled in Vienna.* **3** to decide or arrange something: *It's settled. We're going to Spain.* **4** to relax into a comfortable position: *She settled herself into the chair.* **5 settle a check/bill** to pay the money that you owe

settle down phrasal verb **1** to start living in a place where you will stay for a long time, usually with a person you love: *Do you think he'll ever settle down and have a family?* **2** to become familiar with a place and to feel happy and confident in it: *She quickly **settled down in** her new job.*

settle in phrasal verb to begin to feel relaxed and happy in a new home or job: *Are you settling in OK?*

settlement /ˈset·ᵊl·mənt/ noun **1** an official agreement that finishes an argument: *a **peace settlement*** **2** a town or village that people build to live in after arriving from somewhere else

settler /ˈset·ᵊl·ər/ noun one of a group of people who build a place for themselves

to live after arriving from somewhere else: *the first European settlers in America*

seven /ˈsev·ən/ **A1** the number 7

seventeen /ˈsev·ənˈtin/ **A1** the number 17

seventeenth /ˈsev·ənˈtinθ/ 17th written as a word

seventh[1] /ˈsev·ənθ/ **A2** 7th written as a word

seventh[2] /ˈsev·ənθ/ noun one of seven equal parts of something; 1/7

seventies /ˈsev·ən·tiz/ plural noun **1 the seventies** the years from 1970 to 1979: *He wrote the book **in the seventies**.* **2 in your seventies** to be aged between 70 and 79: *He's **in his seventies**.*

seventy /ˈsev·ən·ti/ **A2** the number 70
• **seventieth** 70th written as a word

several /ˈsev·ər·əl/ pronoun, determiner **A2** some, but not a lot: *Several people have complained about the noise.*

severe /səˈvɪər/ adj **1** very bad: *a severe headache* ○ *severe weather conditions* **2** not kind or gentle: *a severe punishment* • **severely** adv *He was severely injured.*

sew /soʊ/ verb (past participle **sewn**) **B1** to join things together with a needle and thread: *I need to sew a button on my shirt.*

sewing /ˈsoʊ·ɪŋ/ noun [no plural] the activity of joining pieces of cloth together with a needle and thread

sewing machine /ˈsoʊ·ɪŋ məˌʃin/ noun a machine that joins pieces of cloth together with a needle and thread

sex /seks/ noun [no plural] **1 B1** the physical activity that people do to produce a baby or because it feels good: *How old were you when you **had sex** for the first time?* **2 B1** whether a person or animal is male or female: *Do you know what sex the baby is?*

sexual /ˈsek·ʃu·əl/ adj relating to sex: *sexual organs* ○ *sexual equality* • **sexually** adv

shade[1] /ʃeɪd/ noun **1 B1** [no plural] an area where there is no light from the sun and it is darker: *I'd prefer to sit in the shade.* **2** a color, especially when saying how dark or light it is: *a pale/dark shade of gray*

shade

shade   shadow

shade² /ʃeɪd/ **verb** (present participle **shading**, past tense and past participle **shaded**) to cover something in order to protect it from the sun: *He shaded his eyes with his hand.*

shadow /ˈʃæd·oʊ/ **noun** **B1** a dark area made by something that is stopping the light: *Our dog chases his own shadow.* → See picture at **shade noun**

shady /ˈʃeɪ·di/ **adj** (comparative **shadier**, superlative **shadiest**) A shady place is protected from the sun and is darker and cooler: *We found a shady spot to sit in.*

shake /ʃeɪk/ **verb** (present par-

shake

ticiple **shaking**, past tense **shook**, past participle **shaken**) **1** **B1** to make quick, short movements from side to side or up and down, or to make something or someone do this: *Shake the bottle.* **2** If you are shaking, your body makes quick short movements, because you are frightened or nervous: *He was shaking with nerves.* **3 shake hands** **B1** to hold someone's hand and move it up and down when you meet the person for the first time: *The two leaders smiled and shook hands*

for the photographers. **4 shake your head** to move your head from side to side to mean "no"

shaken /ˈʃeɪ·kən/ the past participle of shake

shall /ʃæl/ **verb** formal used with "I" or "we" instead of "will" or "should": *What shall we do?* ○ *Shall I cook dinner tonight?*

shallow /ˈʃæl·oʊ/ **adj** **1** not deep: *shallow water* → Opposite **deep adj** → See picture at **deep adj 2** not showing any interest in serious ideas

shame /ʃeɪm/ **noun** **1 what a shame** **A2** something you say about something that disappoints you: *What a shame that Joe couldn't come.* **2** [no plural] a bad feeling about something wrong that you have done

shampoo /ʃæmˈpu/ **noun** **A2** a liquid substance that you use to wash your hair
• **shampoo verb**

shape /ʃeɪp/ **noun** **1** **B1** the physical form of something made by the line around its outer edge: *a circular shape* ○ *I like the shape of the jacket.* **2 in good, bad, etc. shape** in good, bad, etc. health or condition: *She runs every day so she's in great shape.*

shapes

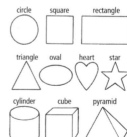

circle   square   rectangle

triangle   oval   heart   star

cylinder   cube   pyramid

-shaped /ʃeɪpt/ **suffix** used after nouns to mean "having a particular shape": *a heart-shaped cake*

share¹ /ʃeər/ **verb** (present participle **sharing**, past tense and past participle **shared**) **1** **A2** to have or use something at the same time as someone else: *She **shares***

a   b   c   d   e   f   g   h   i   j   k   l   m   n   o   p   q   r   **s**   t   u   v   w   x   y   z

a

b

c

d

e

f

g

h

i

j

k

l

m

n

o

p

q

r

s

t

u

v

w

x

y

z

a house **with** *Paul.* **2** A2 to divide something between two or more people: *We shared a pizza.* **3** B1 If two or more people or things share a feeling, quality, or experience, they both or all have the same feeling, quality or experience: *I don't share your views.*

share[2] /ʃeər/ *noun* **1** one of the equal parts that the value of a company is divided into when it is owned by a group of people: *We own shares in a number of companies.* **2** a part of something that has been divided: *When am I going to get my share of the money?*

shark /ʃɑrk/ *noun*
B1 a large fish with very sharp teeth

shark

sharp /ʃɑrp/ *adj*
1 B1 having a very thin edge or point that can cut things: *a sharp knife* ○ *sharp teeth* **2** sudden and very large: *a sharp rise in house prices* **3** quick to notice and understand things: *a sharp mind*

sharpen /ʃɑr·pən/ *verb* to make something sharper: *to sharpen a knife*

sharply /ʃɑrp·li/ *adv* quickly and suddenly: *Prices have risen sharply this week.*

shatter /ʃæt̬·ər/ *verb* to break into very small pieces: *The windshield shattered.*

shave /ʃeɪv/ *verb*
(present participle
shaving, past tense
and past participle
shaved) B1 to cut
hair off your face or
body: *He shaves
every day.*

shave

shaver /ʃeɪ·vər/ *noun* a piece of electrical equipment used to cut hair off the head or body
→ See **The Bathroom** on page C1

shaving cream /ʃeɪ·vɪŋ ˌkrim/ *noun* [no plural] a substance that you put on your face or legs before shaving to make the skin soft

she /ʃi/ *pronoun* A1 used when talking about a woman who has already been talked about: *"When is Ruth coming?" "She'll be here soon."*

shed[1] /ʃed/ *noun* a small building used to keep things such as tools: *a garden shed*

shed[2] /ʃed/ *verb* (present participle **shedding,** past tense and past participle **shed**) **shed leaves, skin, hair, etc.** to lose something because it falls off: *A lot of trees shed their leaves in the autumn.*

she'd /ʃid/ **1** short form of she had: *By the time I got there, she'd fallen asleep.* **2** short form of she would: *She knew that she'd be late.*

sheep /ʃip/ *noun* (plural sheep) A1 a farm animal whose skin is covered with wool: *a flock of sheep*

sheep

sheer /ʃɪər/ *adj* **1** used to say that a feeling or quality is very strong: *a look of sheer delight* ○ *sheer determination* **2** very steep: *a sheer cliff*

sheet /ʃit/ *noun* **1** B1 a large piece of cloth on a bed that you lie on or under **2 a sheet of paper, glass, metal, etc.** A2 a flat piece of paper, glass, etc.

sheet pan /ʃit ˌpæn/ *noun* a rectangular sheet of metal with low sides, used for baking food

shelf /ʃelf/ *noun* (plural **shelves**) A2 a board used to put things on, often attached to a wall: *Please put that book on the shelf over there.*
→ See **The Living Room** on page C11

shells

shell /ʃel/ *noun* the hard outer covering of some creatures and of eggs, nuts, or seeds: *a snail's shell*
→ See picture at **egg noun**

she'll /ʃil/ short form of she will: *She'll be away until Tuesday.*

shellfish /ʃel·fɪʃ/ *noun* [no plural] sea creatures that live in shells and are eaten as food

shelter[1] /ʃel·tər/ *noun* **1** a place that protects you from bad weather or danger: *a bomb shelter* **2** [no plural] protection from bad weather or danger: *We took shelter from the rain in a doorway.*

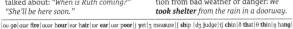

shelter² /ˈʃel·tər/ verb to go under a cover or inside a building to be protected from bad weather or danger: *The tree sheltered us from the rain.*

shepherd /ˈʃep·ərd/ noun someone whose job is to look after sheep

sheriff /ˈʃer·əf/ noun an elected official who makes people obey the law in a town or county

she's /ʃiz/ **1** short form of she is: *She's very nice.* **2** short form of she has: *She's been working very hard.*

shield¹ /ʃild/ noun a large, flat object that soldiers hold in front of their bodies to protect themselves

shield² /ʃild/ verb to protect someone or something from something bad: *She shielded her eyes from the sun.*

shift /ʃɪft/ noun **1** a change in something: *There has been a **shift in public** opinion on this matter.* **2** a period of work in a place such as a factory or hospital: *a night shift*

shin /ʃɪn/ noun the front part of a leg between the knee and the foot
→ See **The Body** on page C2

shine /ʃaɪn/ verb (present participle **shining**, past tense and past participle **shone**) **1** 🔵 to make bright light: *The sun was shining brightly through the window.* **2** to point a light somewhere: *The car's headlights shone right into my eyes.* **3** If a surface shines, it reflects light: *Her hair really shines.*

shiny /ˈʃaɪ·ni/ adj (comparative **shinier**, superlative **shiniest**) 🔵 A shiny surface is bright because it reflects light: *shiny, black shoes*

ship /ʃɪp/ noun 🔵 a large boat that carries people or things by sea

shirt /ʃɜrt/ noun 🔵 a piece of clothing worn on the top part of the body
→ See **Clothes** on page C5

shiver /ˈʃɪv·ər/ verb to shake because you are cold or frightened: *She shivered in the cold rain.*
• **shiver** noun

shock¹ /ʃɑk/ noun 🔵 a big, unpleasant surprise: *Her death came as a terrible shock to him.* **2** (also **electric shock**) a sudden, painful feeling that you get when electricity flows through your body

shock² /ʃɑk/ verb to surprise and upset someone: *Many people were shocked by the violent scenes in the movie.*

shocking /ˈʃɑk·ɪŋ/ adj 🔵 very bad and making you feel upset: *shocking news*

shoe /ʃu/ noun 🔵 a strong covering for the foot, often made of leather: *a pair of shoes*
→ See **Clothes** on page C5

shoelace /ˈʃu·leɪs/ noun a long, thin piece of material used to fasten shoes

shone /ʃoʊn/ past tense and past participle of shine

shook /ʃʊk/ past tense of shake

shoot¹ /ʃut/ verb (past tense and past participle **shot**) **1** 🔵 to hurt or kill a person or animal by firing a bullet from a gun: *He was **shot dead** in the incident.* **2** 🔵 to fire a bullet from a gun: *Don't shoot!* **3** 🔵 to try to score points in some sports by hitting, kicking, or throwing the ball toward the goal: *He shot from the middle of the field and managed to score.* **4** to move somewhere very quickly: *She shot out of the room.*

shoot² /ʃut/ noun a new branch or stem growing on a plant: *bamboo shoots*

shooting /ˈʃu·tɪŋ/ noun **1** an occasion when someone is injured or killed by a bullet from a gun: *There have been several shootings in the capital this week.* **2** [no plural] the sport of firing bullets from guns, sometimes to kill animals

shop¹ /ʃɑp/ verb (present participle **shopping**, past tense and past participle **shopped**) 🔵 to buy things: *I'm **shopping for** baby clothes.*

shop² /ʃɑp/ noun 🔵 a small store: *a gift shop*

shoplifting /ˈʃɑp·lɪf·tɪŋ/ noun [no plural] the act of taking things from a store without paying for them: *He was arrested for shoplifting.*
• **shoplifter** noun

a b c d e f g h i j k l m n o p q r s t u v w x y z

a
b
c
d
e
f
g
h
i
j
k
l
m
n
o
p
q
r
s
t
u
v
w
x
y
z

shopping /ˈʃɑp·ɪŋ/ **noun** [no plural]
A1 the activity of going to stores and buying things: *I love shopping.* ○ *I usually go shopping on Saturdays.*

shopping center /ˈʃɑp·ɪŋ ˌsen·tər/ **noun** a building where lots of stores have been built close together

shore /ʃɔr/ **noun** **B1** the area of land along the edge of the sea or a lake

short /ʃɔrt/ **adj** **1** **A1** having a small distance from one end to the other: *short, brown hair* ○ *short legs* → Opposite **long adj** → See **Hair** on page C9 **2** **A1** continuing for a small amount of time: *a short visit* → Opposite **long adj** **3** **A1** A short person is not as tall as most people. → Opposite **tall adj** **4** **A2** A short book or other piece of writing has not many pages or words: *It's a very short book – you'll read it in an hour.* **5** used to refer to a shorter form of a name or word: *Her name's Jo – it's short for Josephine.*

shortage /ˈʃɔr·tɪdʒ/ **noun** a situation in which there is not enough of something that is needed: *food shortages*

shortcut /ˈʃɔrtˌkʌt/ **noun** **1** a quicker way of getting somewhere or doing something: *I took a shortcut through the parking lot.* **2** a quick way to start or use a computer program

shorten /ˈʃɔr·tʰn/ **verb** to become shorter or to make something shorter: *Smoking shortens your life.* ○ *I need to get this skirt shortened.*

shortly /ˈʃɔrt·li/ **adv** **1** **B1** not long: *I got home at midnight and Jane arrived shortly afterward.* **2** soon: *Our plans for next year will be announced shortly.*

shorts /ʃɔrts/ **plural noun 1** **A2** a very short pair of pants that stop above the knees: *bike shorts* → See **Clothes** on page C5 **2** men's underwear

> **! Common mistake: shorts**
>
> Shorts is a plural word.
> *These shorts are too big for me.*

short-term /ˈʃɔrtˈtɜrm/ **adj** continuing only a short time into the future: *a short-term weather forecast*

shot¹ /ʃɑt/ past tense and past participle of shoot

shot² /ʃɑt/ **noun 1** the act of firing a bullet from a gun: *Three shots were fired.* **2** an attempt to score a point in sports such as soccer: *Good shot!*

should /ʃʊd/ **verb 1** **A2** used to say or ask what is the correct or best thing to do: *He should go to the doctor.* ○ *Should I apologize to her?* **2** **B1** used to say that you think something is true or that you think something will happen: *She should be feeling better by now.* ○ *The letter should arrive by Friday.* **3 why should/ shouldn't…?** used to ask or give the reason for something, especially when you are surprised or angry about it: *Why shouldn't I get a new car if I want one?*

shoulder /ˈʃoʊl·dər/ **noun** **B1** where your arm joins your body next to your neck: *He put his arm around my shoulder.* → See **The Body** on page C2

shouldn't /ˈʃʊd·ʰnt/ short form of should not: *I shouldn't have said that.*

should've /ˈʃʊd·əv/ short form of should have: *She should've finished by now.*

shout¹ /ʃaʊt/ **verb** **A2** to say something very loudly: *"Look out!" she shouted.* ○ *I was angry and I shouted at him.*

shout² /ʃaʊt/ **noun** **B1** a loud cry of anger, excitement, or fear: *He was woken by a loud shout.*

shovel /ˈʃʌv·əl/
noun
a tool used for digging that has a long handle and a wide, flat metal part at one end

shovel

show¹ /ʃoʊ/ **verb** (past participle **shown**)
1 **A1** to let someone look at something: *Show me your photos.* **2** **B1** to teach someone how to do something by explaining it or by doing it yourself: *She showed me how to use the new computer system.* ○ *Have you shown him what to do?* **3** **B1** to take someone to or around a place: *She showed me around the factory.*

4 **B1** to give information in a book, on a website, on a piece of equipment, etc.: *On this map, cities are **shown in gray**.* ◦ *The pictures show two types of phone.*
5 to prove that something is true: *Sales figures showed a significant increase last month.* **6** to express a feeling so that other people are able to notice it: *If she was upset, she certainly didn't show it.*

show off phrasal verb to try to make people notice you, especially in a way that is annoying: *Stop showing off!*

show up phrasal verb **B1** informal to arrive somewhere: *The party started at eight, but he didn't show up until nine-thirty.*

show /ʃoʊ/ noun **1** **A2** a television or radio program or a theater performance: *He has his own show on a local channel.* **2** a time at which a group of similar things are brought together for the public to see: *a fashion show* ◦ *a flower show*

shower[1] /ˈʃaʊ·ər/ noun **1** **A1** an act of washing your whole body while standing under a flow of water: *I **took a shower** and got dressed.* **2** **A2** a special area of a bathroom that you stand in to wash your whole body: *He's **in the shower**.* → See **The Bathroom** on page C1 **3** **B1** a short period of rain

shower[2] /ˈʃaʊ·ər/ verb to wash your body while standing under a flow of water: *I shower every morning.*

shower head /ˈʃaʊ·ər ˌhed/ noun **A1** a piece of bathroom equipment that you stand under to wash your whole body → See **The Bathroom** on page C1

shown /ʃoʊn/ past participle of show

shrank /ʃræŋk/ past tense of shrink

shred /ʃred/ noun a very small piece that has been torn from something: *She tore the letter to shreds.*

shrimp /ʃrɪmp/ noun (plural **shrimp**, **shrimps**) **B1** a small sea animal that you can eat, with a curved body and a shell

shrine /ʃraɪn/ noun a holy place where people go to pray

shrink /ʃrɪŋk/ verb (past tense **shrank**, past participle **shrunk**) to become smaller, or to make something smaller: *My shirt shrank in the wash.*

shrub /ʃrʌb/ noun a large plant that is smaller than a tree

shrug /ʃrʌɡ/ verb (present participle **shrugging**, past tense and past participle **shrugged**) to move your shoulders up and down to show that you do not care about something or that you do not know something: *I told him we weren't happy with it but he just shrugged his shoulders.*
• **shrug noun**

shrunk /ʃrʌŋk/ past participle of shrink

shudder /ˈʃʌd·ər/ verb to shake, usually because you are thinking of something bad: *She shuddered with horror.*
• **shudder noun**

shut[1] /ʃʌt/ verb (present participle **shutting**, past tense and past participle **shut**) **A2** to close something, or to become closed: *Shut the door.* ◦ *He lay back and shut his eyes.* ◦ *The door shut with a bang.*

shut (something) down phrasal verb **B1** If a computer or machine shuts down or someone shuts it down, it stops operating: *Make sure you shut down your computer before you leave.*

shut up phrasal verb informal to stop talking: *Just shut up and get back to work!*

shut[2] /ʃʌt/ adj **B1** closed: *Her eyes were shut, but she was still awake.*

shutter /ˈʃʌt·ər/ noun a wooden or metal cover on the outside of a window

shy /ʃaɪ/ adj **B1** not confident, especially about meeting new people: *He was too shy to say anything to her.*

sibling /ˈsɪb·lɪŋ/ noun someone's sister or brother: *He has four siblings – three brothers and a sister.*

sick /sɪk/ adj **1** **A2** ill: *He stayed home sick for most of last week.* **2 feel sick** **A2** to feel that the food or drink in your stomach will soon come up through your mouth **3 be sick** **B1** If you are

sick, food and drink comes up from your stomach and out of your mouth: *The baby was sick all down his shirt.*
4 be sick of *something* informal to be bored with or angry about something: *I'm sick of people telling me how to run my life.*

! Common mistake: sick or ill?

Sick is the word that is usually used to mean "not well."
He went home early because he felt sick.

Ill is a more formal word that is usually used to talk about someone whose sickness is more serious.
His father is seriously ill.

---

sickness /ˈsɪk·nəs/ *noun* [no plural]
1 illness or poor health **2** the feeling that the food or drink in your stomach will come up through your mouth: *motion sickness*

side /saɪd/ *noun* **1** **A2** one of the two parts that something would divide into if you drew a line down the middle: *I sleep on **the right/left side** of the bed.* **2** **A2** a flat, outer surface of an object, especially one that is not its top, bottom, front, or back: *The side of the car was badly scratched.* **3** **A2** one edge of something: *A square has four sides.* **4** **B1** the area next to something: *He stood by the side of the road, waiting for the bus.* **5** either of the two surfaces of a thin, flat object such as a piece of paper or a coin: *Write on both sides of the paper.* **6** one of the people or groups who are arguing, fighting, or competing: *Whose **side** is he **on**?* **7** one of the two areas of your body from under your arms to the tops of your legs: *She lay on her side.* **8** [no plural] a part of a situation that can be considered or dealt with separately: *She takes care of the financial side of things.* **9** [no plural] a part of someone's character: *She has a very practical side.* **10 from side to side** If something moves from side to side, it moves from left to right and back again repeatedly: *He shook his head from side to side.*

11 side by side If two things or people are side by side, they are next to each other: *We sat side by side on the couch.*

sidewalk /ˈsaɪd·wɔk/ *noun* **B1** a path with a hard surface by the side of a road that people walk on

sideways /ˈsaɪdˌweɪz/ *adv* in a direction to the left or right, not forward or backward: *He glanced sideways.*

sigh /saɪ/ *verb* to make a noise when you breathe out, often because you are sad: *He sighed deeply and sat down.*
• **sigh** *noun a sigh of relief*

sight /saɪt/ *noun* **1** **B1** [no plural] the ability to use your eyes to see: *Doctors managed to save his sight.* **2** the act of seeing someone or something: *The sight of so much blood shocked him.* **3** something that you see, especially something interesting: *the sights and sounds of the market* **4** used to talk about the area that it is possible for you to see: *I **caught sight of** (=suddenly saw) Tony in the crowd.* ○ *She kept **out of sight** (=hidden) behind a tree.* **5 the sights** **B1** the beautiful or interesting places in a city or country: *He took me around New York and showed me the sights.* **6 at first sight** the time when you first see or hear about something or someone: *It may, at first sight, seem a surprising choice.*

sightseeing /ˈsaɪtˌsi·ɪŋ/ *noun* [no plural] **A2** the activity of visiting interesting or beautiful places: *a sightseeing tour of London*

sightseer /ˈsaɪtˌsi·ər/ *noun* a person who goes sightseeing

sign[1] /saɪn/ *noun* **1** **A2** a symbol or message in a public place that gives information or instructions: *a road sign* ○ *a "no smoking" sign* **2** **B1** something that shows that something is happening: *Flowers are the first **sign of** Spring.* ○ *It's a **sign that** things are improving.* **3** **B1** a movement you make to give someone information or tell him or her what to do **4** a symbol that has a particular meaning: *a dollar sign*

sign[2] /saɪn/ *verb* **B1** to write your name on something to show that you wrote, painted, or created it or to show that you agree to it: *He signs his letters "Prof. James D. Nelson."*

sign up phrasal verb **B1** to arrange to do an organized activity: *I've **signed up** for a dance class.*

signal¹ /'sɪg·nəl/ noun **1** a movement, light, or sound that gives information, or tells people what to do: *Don't move until I give the signal.* **2** A series of electrical waves that are sent to a radio, television, cell phone, etc.: *My phone doesn't work here – there's no signal.*

signal² /'sɪg·nəl/ verb to make a movement that gives information or tells people what to do: *He **signaled for** them to be quiet.*

signature /'sɪg·nə·tʃər/ noun **B1** your name written in your own way, which is difficult for someone else to copy

significance /sɪg'nɪf·ɪ·kəns/ noun [no plural] the importance or meaning of something: *I still don't understand **the significance** of his remark.*

significant /sɪg'nɪf·ɪ·kənt/ adj important or large: *These measures will save a significant amount of money.*

• **significantly** adv *Prices have risen significantly (=a lot).*

silence /'saɪ·ləns/ noun **1** **B1** [no plural] a lack of sound: *The three men ate **in silence**.* **2** a period of time in which there is complete quiet or no speaking: *a long, uncomfortable silence*

silent /'saɪ·lənt/ adj **1** **B1** without any sound: *The building was dark and silent.* **2** without talking: *She said a silent goodbye to her old house.*

• **silently** adv *The snow fell silently all around them.*

silk /sɪlk/ noun [no plural] **B1** a type of cloth that is light and smooth: *a silk dress*

silky /'sɪl·ki/ adj (comparative **silkier**, superlative **silkiest**) soft and smooth, like silk: *a cat with silky gray fur*

silly /'sɪl·i/ adj (comparative **sillier**, superlative **silliest**) **1** **B1** not serious enough or

showing much intelligence: *Do I look silly in this hat?* ○ *It's silly to spend money on something you don't need.* **2** **B1** small and not important: *She gets upset over silly things.*

silver¹ /'sɪl·vər/ noun [no plural] **A2** a valuable, shiny, gray-white metal used to make jewelry: *silver and gold*

silver² /'sɪl·vər/ adj **1** **A2** made of silver: *a silver necklace* **2** **A2** being the color of silver: *a silver sports car*

silverware /'sɪl·vər,wear/ noun [no plural] knives, forks, and spoons

similar /'sɪm·ə·lər/ adj **B1** Something that is similar to something else has many things the same, although it is not exactly the same: *The two houses are remarkably similar.*

similarity /ˌsɪm·əˈlær·ɪ·ti/ noun (plural **similarities**) the fact of two things or people being similar, or a way in which they are similar: *There are a number of **similarities between** the two systems.*
→ Opposite **difference** noun

simmer /'sɪm·ər/ noun to cook something so that it is very hot, but does not boil, or to be cooked in this way: *The soup needs to simmer for another hour.*

simple /'sɪm·pəl/ adj **1** **A2** not difficult to do or to understand: *It's very simple to use.* **2** **B1** not complicated: *a simple life* ○ *a simple black dress (=dress without decoration)* **3** used to describe the one important fact, truth, etc.: *We didn't go swimming for the simple reason that the water was too cold.*

simplicity /sɪm'plɪs·ɪ·ti/ noun [no plural] the quality of being simple

simplify /'sɪm·plə,faɪ/ verb (present participle **simplifying**, past tense and past participle **simplified**) to make something easier to do or understand: *We need to simplify the instructions.*

simply /'sɪm·pli/ adv **1** in a way that is not complicated or hard to understand: *simply prepared food* ○ *He explained it as simply as he could.* **2** used to emphasize what you are saying: *We simply*

a
b
c
d
e
f
g
h
i
j
k
l
m
n
o
p
q
r
s
t
u
v
w
x
y
z

don't have the time. **3** only: *A lot of people miss this opportunity simply because they don't know about it.*

sin /sɪn/ *noun* something that is against the rules of a religion: *the sin of pride*

since¹ /sɪns/ *adv, preposition* **A2** from a time in the past until a later time or until now: *They've been waiting since March.* ∘ *The factory has been closed since the explosion.*

> **⚠ Common mistake: since or for?**
>
> When you talk about the beginning of a period of time, use **since**.
> *I have lived here since 2006.*
> When you talk about a length of time, use **for**.
> *I have lived here for five years.*
> ~~I have lived here since five years.~~

---

since² /sɪns/ *conjunction* **1** **B1** from a time in the past until a later time or until now: *I've known Tom since he was seven.* **2** **B1** because: *Since we had a few minutes to wait, we had some coffee.*

sincere /sɪnˈsɪər/ *adj* honest and saying what you really feel or believe: *He seems to be sincere.*

sincerely /sɪnˈsɪər·li/ *adv* **1** in a sincere way: *I sincerely hope that this never happens again.* **2** *Sincerely (yours)* formal **B1** used at the end of formal letters

sing /sɪŋ/ *verb* (past tense **sang**, past participle **sung**) **A1** to make musical sounds with your voice: *They all sang "Happy Birthday" to him.*

singer /ˈsɪŋ·ər/ *noun* **A2** someone who sings: *a jazz singer*

singing /ˈsɪŋ·ɪŋ/ *noun* [no plural] **A2** the activity of singing: *He is popular for both his singing and his acting.*

single /ˈsɪŋ·ɡəl/ *adj* **1** **A2** not married: *He's young and single.* **2** **A2** for only one person: *a single bed* **3** **B1** raising your children alone: *a single mother* **4** **B1** used to make the word "every" stronger: *I call him **every single** day.*

∘ *He could hear every single word we said.* **5** only one: *There was a single light in the corner of the room.*

singular /ˈsɪŋ·ɡjə·lər/ *adj* **A2** The singular form of a word is used to talk about one person or thing: *"Woman" is the singular form of "women."*

the singular /ˈsɪŋ·ɡjə·lər/ *noun* **A2** the form of a word for one person or thing and no more

sink¹ /sɪŋk/ *verb* (past tense **sank**, past participle **sunk**) **1** **B1** to go down or make something go down under the surface of water and not come back up: *The Titanic sank after hitting an iceberg.* → See picture at **float verb** (1) **2** **B1** to go down, or make something go down, into something soft: *My feet keep sinking into the sand.*

sink² /sɪŋk/ *noun* **A2** a bowl that is fixed to the wall in a kitchen or bathroom that you wash dishes, your hands, etc. in → See **The Bathroom** on page C1

sip /sɪp/ *verb* (present participle **sipping**, past tense and past participle **sipped**) to drink, taking only a small amount at a time: *She sipped her champagne.*
• **sip** *noun* *He **took a sip of** his coffee and then continued.*

sir /sɜr/ *noun* **1** **B1** You call a man "sir" when you are speaking to him politely: *Excuse me, sir, is this seat taken?* **2** *Dear Sir* a way of beginning a formal letter to a man whose name you do not know

siren /ˈsaɪ·rən/ *noun* a piece of equipment that makes a loud sound as a warning: *a police siren*

sister /ˈsɪs·tər/ *noun* **A1** a girl or woman who has the same parents as you: *an older/younger sister* ∘ *my **little sister** (= younger sister)* ∘ *my **big sister** (= older sister)*

sister-in-law /ˈsɪs·tər·ɪnˌlɔ/ *noun* (plural **sisters-in-law**) the woman married to someone's sibling, or the sister of someone's husband or wife: *She and her sister-in-law are good friends.*

sit /sɪt/ **verb** (present participle **sitting**, past tense and past participle **sat**) **1** **A1** to be in a position with the weight of your body on your bottom and the top part of your body up, for example, on a chair: *Emma was* **sitting on** *a stool.* ∘ *The children* **sat at** *the table by the window.* **2** **A2** (also **sit down**) to move your body into a sitting position after you have been standing: *She sat down on the grass.*

sit up phrasal verb to move your body to a sitting position after you have been lying down: *I sat up and opened my eyes.*
→ See **Phrasal Verbs** on page C13

site /saɪt/ **noun** **1** **A2** short form of website **2** **B1** an area that is used for something or where something happens: *a building site* **3** the place where something important happened in the past: *the site of a battle*

situated /ˈsɪtʃ·uˌeɪ·t̬ɪd/ **adj** formal
be situated in, on, by, etc. **B1** to be in a particular place: *a hotel situated on Lake Huron*

situation /ˌsɪtʃ·uˈeɪ·ʃən/ **noun** **B1** the set of things that are happening at a particular time and place: *the current political situation* ∘ *He's* **in** *a difficult situation.*

six /sɪks/ **A1** the number 6

sixteen /ˈsɪksˈtin/ **A1** the number 16

sixteenth /ˈsɪksˈtinθ/ 16th written as a word

sixth[1] /sɪksθ/ **A2** 6th written as a word

sixth[2] /sɪksθ/ **noun** one of six equal parts of something; 1/6

sixties /ˈsɪks·tiz/ **plural noun**
1 the sixties the years from 1960 to 1969: *The Beatles became famous* **in the sixties.** **2 be in your sixties** to be aged between 60 and 69: *Many people retire* **in their sixties.**

sixty /ˈsɪks·ti/ **A2** the number 60
• **sixtieth** 60th written as a word

size /saɪz/ **noun** **1** **A2** how big or small something is: *It's an area about the size of Florida.* ∘ *The size of some of those trees*

is incredible. **2** **A2** one of the different measurements in which things, for example, clothes, food, etc. are made: *What size shoes do you take?*

skate[1] /skeɪt/ **noun** **1** **A2** (also **roller skate**) a boot with wheels on the bottom, used for moving across the ground: *a pair of skates* **2** **A2** (also **ice skate**) a boot with a metal part on the bottom, used for moving across ice
→ See **Sports 1** on page C15

skate[2] /skeɪt/ **verb** (present participle **skating**, past tense and past participle **skated**) **B1** to move using skates
• **skater noun**
• **skating noun** [no plural]

skateboard /ˈskeɪtˌbɔrd/ **noun** **A2** a board with wheels on the bottom, which you stand on and move forward by pushing one foot on the ground
• **skateboarding noun** [no plural] **A2** *Is skateboarding allowed in the park?*
→ See **Sports 1** on page C15

skeleton /ˈskɛl·ɪ·t̬ən/ **noun** the structure made of all the bones in the body of a person or animal: *the skeleton of a dog*

sketch[1] /skɛtʃ/ **noun** a simple picture that you draw quickly: *He did a quick sketch of the cat.*

sketch[2] /skɛtʃ/ **verb** to draw a sketch: *I sketched a map for him on a scrap of paper.*

ski[1] /ski/ **noun** (plural **skis**) **B1** one of a pair of long, thin pieces of wood or plastic that you wear on the bottom of boots to move over snow

ski[2] /ski/ **verb** **B1** to move over snow wearing skis
• **skiing noun** [no plural] **A2** *I'd like to go skiing in Vermont.*
→ See **Sports 1** on page C15

skid /skɪd/ **verb** (present participle **skidding**, past tense and past participle **skidded**) If a vehicle skids, it slides along a surface and you cannot control it: *The car skidded on ice and hit a tree.*

skill /skɪl/ **noun** **B1** the ability to do an activity or job well, especially because

a
b
c
d
e
f
g
h
i
j
k
l
m
n
o
p
q
r
s
t
u
v
w
x
y
z

you have done it many times: *You need good computer skills for this job.*

skilled /skɪld/ adj having the abilities needed to do an activity or job well: *a highly skilled (= very skilled) photographer* ○ *He has become **skilled in** dealing with the media.*

skillful /ˈskɪl·fəl/ adj good at doing something: *a skillful artist*
• **skillfully** adv

skin /skɪn/ noun **1** [B1] the outer layer of a person or animal's body: *dark skin* **2** the outer layer of a fruit or vegetable: *a banana skin*

skinny /ˈskɪn·i/ adj (comparative **skinnier**, superlative **skinniest**) very thin

skip /skɪp/ verb (present participle **skipping**, past tense and past participle **skipped**) **1** to not do something that you usually do: *I think I'll skip lunch today.* **2** to move forward, jumping quickly from one foot to the other: *She watched her daughter skipping down the street.*

skirt /ˈskɜrt/ noun **A1** a piece of women's clothing that hangs from the waist and has no legs
→ See **Clothes** on page C5

ski slope /ˈski ˌsloʊp/ noun an area of land on a hill or mountain where people can ski

skull /skʌl/ noun the bones in your head

sky /skaɪ/ noun (plural **skies**) **A2** the area above the Earth where you can see clouds, the sun, the moon, etc.: *a beautiful, blue sky*

skyscraper /ˈskaɪˌskreɪ·pər/ noun a very tall building

slab /slæb/ noun a thick, flat piece of something, especially stone: *a slab of concrete*

slack /slæk/ adj loose or not tight: *Suddenly the rope became slack.*

slam /slæm/ verb (present participle **slamming**, past tense and past participle **slammed**) to close with great force, or to make something close with great force: *Kate heard the front door slam.*

slang /slæŋ/ noun [no plural] informal language

slant[1] /slænt/ verb to slope in a particular direction: *Pale sunlight slanted **through** the curtain.*

slant[2] /slænt/ noun a position that is sloping: *The road is **on a slant**.*

slap[1] /slæp/ verb (present participle **slapping**, past tense and past participle **slapped**) to hit someone with the flat, inside part of your hand: *She slapped him across the face.*

slap[2] /slæp/ noun a hit with the flat, inside part of your hand

slash /slæʃ/ verb, noun the mark [/]

slaughter[1] /ˈslɔ·tər/ verb **1** to kill an animal for meat **2** to kill a lot of people in a very cruel way

slaughter[2] /ˈslɔ·tər/ noun [no plural] a situation in which a lot of people or animals are killed in a cruel way

slave[1] /sleɪv/ noun someone who is owned by someone else and has to work for them: *He treats his mother like a slave.*

slave[2] /sleɪv/ verb (present participle **slaving**, past tense and past participle **slaved**) informal to work very hard: *Giorgio was **slaving away at** his homework.*

slavery /ˈsleɪ·və·ri/ noun [no plural] the practice of having slaves

sled /sled/ noun a vehicle that is used for traveling on snow

sleep[1] /slip/ verb (past tense and past participle **slept**) **A1** to be in the state of rest when your eyes are closed, your body is not active, and your mind is unconscious: *We slept in a hotel last night.* ○ *Did you sleep well?*

sleep in phrasal verb to sleep longer in the morning than you usually do

sleep[2] /slip/ noun **1** [no plural] the state you are in when you are sleeping, or a period of time when you are sleeping: *You need to go home and **get some sleep**.* ○ *It took me ages to **get to sleep** (= to succeed in sleeping).* **2** [B1] a period

|oʊ go|ɑɪɑr fire|ɑʊɑr hour|eər hair|ɪər ear|ʊər poor|j yet|ʒ measure|ʃ ship|dʒ judge|tʃ chin|ð that|θ thin|ŋ hang|

of sleeping: *You need a good night's sleep* (= a night when you sleep well).
3 go to sleep 🔒 to begin to sleep: *Babies often go to sleep after they are fed.*

sleeping bag /ˈsli·pɪŋ ˌbæɡ/ *noun* a long bag made of thick material that you sleep inside

sleepless /ˈslip·ləs/ *adj* **sleepless night** a night when you are not able to sleep

sleepy /ˈsli·pi/ *adj* (comparative **sleepier**, superlative **sleepiest**) 🔒 feeling tired and wanting to go to sleep: *The heat made me sleepy.*

sleet /slit/ *noun* [no plural] a mixture of snow and rain
• **sleet** *verb* ***It was sleeting*** *when I looked outside.*

sleeve /sliv/ *noun* **1** 🔒 the part of a jacket, shirt, etc. that covers your arm: *He rolled up his sleeves to do the dishes.*
→ See picture at **jacket** **2 have something up your sleeve** *informal* to have a secret plan

slender /ˈslen·dər/ *adj* thin in an attractive way: *long, slender fingers*

slept /slept/ past tense and past participle of sleep

slice¹ /slaɪs/ *noun* 🅰️🅱️ a flat piece of food that has been cut from a larger piece: *a slice of bread/cake*
→ See **Quantities** on page C14

slice² /slaɪs/ *verb* (present participle **slicing**, past tense and past participle **sliced**) (also **slice up**) to cut food into flat pieces: *Could you slice the tomatoes?*

slide¹ /slaɪd/ *verb* (present participle **sliding**, past tense and past participle **slid**) to move smoothly over a surface: *My car slid on the ice.*

slide² /slaɪd/ *noun* a large object that children climb and slide down as a game

slight /slaɪt/ *adj* small and not important: *slight differences in color*

slightly /ˈslaɪt·li/ *adv* a little: *Tickets cost slightly more on the weekend.*

slim /slɪm/ *adj* (comparative **slimmer**, superlative **slimmest**) 🅰️🅱️ thin in an attractive way: *She's tall and slim.*

slime /slaɪm/ *noun* [no plural] a thick, sticky liquid that is unpleasant to touch

slimy /ˈslaɪ·mi/ *adj* (comparative **slimier**, superlative **slimiest**) covered in slime

sling /slɪŋ/ *noun* a piece of cloth that you wear around your neck and put your arm into when it is hurt

slip¹ /slɪp/ *verb* (present participle **slipping**, past tense and past participle **slipped**)
1 🔒 to slide by accident and fall or almost fall: *She slipped on the ice and broke her ankle.* **2** to slide out of the correct position: *The photo slipped out of the frame.* **3** to go somewhere quietly or quickly: *She slipped out of bed and tiptoed to the door.*

slip up *phrasal verb* to make a mistake

slip² /slɪp/ *noun* **1** a small piece of paper: *He wrote the number on a slip of paper.* **2** a small mistake **3 a slip of the tongue** a mistake made by using the wrong word

slipper /ˈslɪp·ər/ *noun* a soft, comfortable shoe that you wear in the house

slippery /ˈslɪp·ə·ri/ *adj* If something is slippery, it is difficult to hold or walk on because it is smooth or wet: *Be careful – the floor is slippery.*

slit¹ /slɪt/ *noun* a long, thin cut or hole in something

slit² /slɪt/ *verb* (present participle **slitting**, past tense and past participle **slit**) to make a long, thin cut in something: *She slit open the envelope.*

slogan /ˈsloʊ·ɡən/ *noun* a short phrase that is easy to remember and is used to make people notice something: *an advertising slogan*

slope¹ /sloʊp/ *noun* a surface or piece of land that is high at one end and low at the other: *The house is at the top of a steep slope.*

slope² /sloʊp/ *verb* (present participle **sloping**, past tense and past participle **sloped**) to be high at one end and low at the other: *The field slopes down to the river.*

sloppy /ˈslɑp·i/ *adj* (comparative **sloppier**, superlative **sloppiest**) not done carefully:

a
b
c
d
e
f
g
h
i
j
k
l
m
n
o
p
q
r
s
t
u
v
w
x
y
z

His work was sloppy and full of spelling mistakes.

slot /slɑt/ *noun* a long, thin hole that you put something into, especially money

slot machine /'slɑt məˌʃin/ *noun* a machine that you put money into in order to try to win more money

slow[1] /sloʊ/ *adj* **1** 🅰1 moving, happening, or doing something without much speed: *He's a slow reader.* → Opposite **fast adj** **2** If a clock is slow, it shows a time that is earlier than the correct time.

slow[2] /sloʊ/ *verb*
slow (something) down *phrasal verb* to become slower or to make something become slower: *Slow down, Claire, you're walking too fast!*

slowly /'sloʊ-li/ *adv* 🅰2 at a slow speed: *Could you speak more slowly, please?*

slug /slʌg/ *noun* a small, soft creature with no legs that moves slowly and eats plants
→ See picture at **snail**

slum /slʌm/ *noun* a poor and crowded area of a city: *He grew up in the slums of Mexico City.*

slump /slʌmp/ *verb* **1** If a price, value, or amount slumps, it goes down suddenly: *Sales have slumped by 50%.* **2** to fall or sit down suddenly because you feel tired or weak: *She slumped back in her chair, exhausted.*

smack /smæk/ *verb* to hit something hard against something else: *I smacked my head on the door frame.*

small /smɔl/ *adj* **1** 🅰1 little in size or amount: *We teach the children in small groups.* → Opposite **big adj, large adj** **2** 🅰1 A small child is very young: *a woman with three small children* **3** 🅰2 not important or serious: *a small mistake*

smart /smɑrt/ *adj* 🅱1 intelligent: *Rachel is one of the smartest kids in the class.*

smash /smæʃ/ *verb* to break into a lot of pieces with a loud noise, or to make

something break into a lot of pieces with a loud noise: *The plate smashed on the floor.*

smear[1] /smɪər/ *verb* to spread a thick liquid or sticky substance over something: *His shirt was smeared with paint.*

smear[2] /smɪər/ *noun* a dirty mark: *There was a smear of blood on her face.*

smell[1] /smel/ *verb* **1** 🅱1 to have a particular quality that people notice by using their nose: *That soup smells delicious.* ○ *Her lotion smells like roses.* **2** 🅱1 to notice something by using your nose: *I think I can smell something burning.* **3** 🅱1 to have a bad smell: *Your running shoes really smell!* **4** to have the ability to notice or discover that a substance is present by using your nose: *Humans can't smell as well as dogs can.*

smell[2] /smel/ *noun* **1** 🅱1 the quality that something has which you notice by using your nose: *The smell of roses filled the room.* **2** [no plural] the ability to notice smells: *Smoking can affect your sense of smell.* **3** a bad smell: *I wish I could get rid of that smell in the bathroom.*

smelly /'smel-i/ *adj* (comparative **smellier**, superlative **smelliest**) having a bad smell: *smelly feet*

smile[1] /smaɪl/ *verb* (present participle **smiling**, past tense and past participle **smiled**) 🅱1 to make the corners of your mouth go up so that you look happy or friendly: *She smiled at me.*

smile[2] /smaɪl/ *noun* 🅱1 an expression on your face that makes the corners of your mouth go up so that you look happy or friendly: *He gave me a big smile and wished me good luck.*

smog /smɑg,ˌ/smɔg/ *noun* [no plural] air pollution in a city that is a mixture of smoke, gases, and chemicals

smoke[1] /smoʊk/ *noun* [no plural] 🅱1 the gray or black gas that is made when something burns

smoke[2] /smoʊk/ *verb* (present participle **smoking**, past tense and past participle **smoked**) **1** 🅰1 to breathe smoke into

---

| ou **go** | aɪər **fire** | aʊər **hour** | eər **hair** | ɪər **ear** | ʊər **poor** | j **yet** | ʒ **measure** | ʃ **ship** | dʒ **judge** | tʃ **chin** | ð **that** | θ **thin** | ŋ **hang** |

your mouth from a cigarette: *Do you mind if I smoke?* **2** to make or send out smoke: *The pot on the stove is smoking!*

smoker /ˈsmoʊ·kər/ *noun* someone who smokes cigarettes

smoking /ˈsmoʊ·kɪŋ/ *noun* [no plural] **A1** the activity of smoking cigarettes

smolder /ˈsmoʊl·dər/ *verb* to burn slowly, producing smoke but no flames: *The fire was still smoldering the next morning.*

smooth /smuð/ *adj* **1** **B1** having a regular surface that has no holes or lumps in it: *soft, smooth skin* → Opposite **rough adj** **2** A substance that is smooth has no lumps in it: *Mix the butter and sugar together until smooth.* **3** happening without any sudden movements: *The plane made a smooth landing.*

smoothly /ˈsmuð·li/ *adv* **go smoothly** to happen without any problems: *The picnic went smoothly until it rained.*

smother /ˈsmʌð·ər/ *verb* to kill someone by covering his or her face with something so that he or she cannot breathe

smudge¹ /smʌdʒ/ *noun* a dirty mark: *a smudge of ink*

smudge² /smʌdʒ/ *verb* (present participle **smudging**, past tense and past participle **smudged**) If ink, paint, etc. smudges, or if it is smudged, it becomes dirty or not clear because someone has touched it: *Be careful that you don't smudge the drawing.*

smuggle /ˈsmʌɡ·əl/ *verb* (present participle **smuggling**, past tense and past participle **smuggled**) to take something into or out of a place in an illegal or secret way: *He was arrested for smuggling drugs onto the plane.*

• **smuggler** *noun* *drug smugglers*

snack /snæk/ *noun* **A2** a small amount of food

snack bar /ˈsnæk ˌbɑr/ *noun* a place where you can buy a small meal such as a sandwich

snag /snæɡ/ *noun* informal a problem

snail /sneɪl/ *noun* a small creature with a long, soft body and a round shell

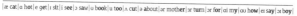

snake /sneɪk/ *noun* **A2** a long, thin creature with no legs that slides along the ground

snap¹ /snæp/ *verb* (present participle **snapping**, past tense and past participle **snapped**) **1** If something long and thin snaps, it breaks making a short, loud sound, and if you snap it, you break it, making a short, loud sound: *The twigs snapped as we walked on them.* **2** to say something suddenly in an angry way: *Mom snapped at us when she saw the mess.* **3** If an animal snaps, it tries to bite someone.

snap something up *phrasal verb* informal to buy or get something quickly: *The dress was on sale, so I snapped it up.*

snap² /snæp/ *noun* **1** a sudden, short, loud sound like something breaking: *I heard a snap as I sat on the pencil.* **2** a small metal fastener used on clothes

snarl /snɑrl/ *verb* **1** to speak angrily: *"Go away!" he snarled.* **2** If an animal snarls, it shows its teeth and makes an angry sound.

snatch /snætʃ/ *verb* to take something or someone quickly and suddenly: *Bill snatched the phone from my hand.*

sneak /snik/ *verb* to go somewhere quietly because you do not want anyone to hear you: *I sneaked into his bedroom while he was asleep.*

sneaker /ˈsni·kər/ *noun* **A2** a soft sports shoe

sneeze /sniz/ *verb* (present participle **sneezing**, past tense and past participle **sneezed**) When you sneeze, air suddenly comes out through your nose and mouth: *He had a cold and was sneezing a lot.*

• **sneeze** *noun*

sniff /snɪf/ verb **1** to breathe air in through your nose in a way that makes a noise: *Sally has a cold – she keeps sniffing and sneezing.* **2** to breathe air in through your nose in order to smell something: *She sniffed the flowers.*
• **sniff** noun

snob /snɑb/ noun someone who thinks he or she is better than other people

snooze /snuz/ verb (present participle **snoozing**, past tense and past participle **snoozed**) informal to sleep for a short time, especially during the day: *Grandpa was snoozing in his chair.*
• **snooze** noun [no plural] informal *You look tired – why don't you take a snooze?*

snore /snɔr/ verb (present participle **snoring**, past tense and past participle **snored**) to breathe in a very noisy way while you are sleeping
• **snore** noun

snorkel[1] /ˈsnɔr·kəl/ noun a tube that you use to breathe when you are swimming underwater

snorkel[2] /ˈsnɔr·kəl/ verb (present participle **snorkeling**, past tense and past participle **snorkeled**) to swim using a snorkel
• **snorkeling** noun [no plural] *We went snorkeling in Key West.*

snow[1] /snoʊ/ noun [no plural] **A1** soft white pieces of frozen water that fall from the sky when the weather is cold: *Children were playing in the snow.*

snow[2] /snoʊ/ verb **it snows** **A2** If it snows, snow falls from the sky: *It snowed all day yesterday.*

snowball /ˈsnoʊˌbɔl/ noun a ball made from snow that children throw at each other

snowboard /ˈsnoʊˌbɔrd/ noun **B1** a large board that you stand on to move over snow
→ See **Sports 1** on page C15

snowboarding /ˈsnoʊˌbɔr·dɪŋ/ noun [no plural] **A2** a sport in which you stand on a large board and move over snow
→ See **Sports 1** on page C15

snowflake /ˈsnoʊˌfleɪk/ noun a small piece of snow that falls from the sky

snowman /ˈsnoʊˌmæn/ noun (plural **snowmen**) a figure of a person made of snow

snowplow /ˈsnoʊˌplaʊ/ noun a vehicle used for removing snow from roads and railroads

snowy /ˈsnoʊ·i/ adj (comparative **snowier**, superlative **snowiest**) snowing or covered with snow: *a cold, snowy day*

so[1] /soʊ/ adv **1** **A2** used before an adjective or adverb to make that adjective or adverb stronger: *I was so tired when I got home.* ○ *I love her so much.* ○ *I was so upset that I couldn't speak.* **2** **A2** used to give a short answer to a question to avoid repeating a phrase: *"Is Ben coming to the party?" "I hope so."* **3** **A2** used at the beginning of a sentence to connect it with something that was said or happened previously: *So, here we are again.* **4** **and so on** **A2** used after a list of things to show that you could add other similar things: *I want to buy postcards, souvenirs, and so on.* **5** **or so** **B1** used after a number or amount to show that it is not exact: *"How many people were at the party?" "Fifty or so, I guess."* **6** **So (what)?** used to say that you do not think something is important, especially in a rude way: *"She might tell Emily." "So what?"* **7** **so did we, so have I, so is mine, etc.** **B1** used to say that someone else also does something or that the same thing is true about someone or something else: *She likes football and so do I.*

so[2] /soʊ/ conjunction **1** **A2** used to say that something is the reason why something else happens: *I was tired so I went to bed.* ○ *Greg had some money so he bought a bike.* **2** **so (that)** **B1** in order to make something happen or be possible: *He put his glasses on so that he could see the television better.*

soak /soʊk/ verb **1** to put something in a liquid for a period of time: *Soak the bread in the milk.* **2** to make something very wet: *The rain soaked my clothes.*

soaking /ˈsoʊ·kɪŋ/ adj completely wet: *My clothes were soaking wet.*

soap /soup/ *noun* **1** [no plural] a substance that you use to wash yourself: *a bar of soap* → See **The Bathroom** on page C1 **2** [B1] (also **soap opera**) a television program about the lives of a group of people that is shown every day or every week

soar /sɔr/ *verb* **1** to go up to a high level very quickly: *House prices have soared.* **2** to move quickly and smoothly in the sky: *The birds were soaring high above.*

sob /sɑb/ *verb* (present participle **sobbing**, past tense and past participle **sobbed**) to cry in a noisy way
• **sob** *noun*

sober /'sou·bər/ *adj* Someone who is sober is not drunk.

so-called /'sou'kɔld/ *adj* used to show that you think a word that is used to describe someone or something is wrong: *My so-called friend stole money from me.*

soccer /'sɑk·ər/ *noun* [no plural]
[A2] a game in which two teams of eleven people kick a ball and try to score goals: *a soccer ball*
→ See picture at **ball**
→ See **Sports 2** on page C16

sociable /'sou·ʃə·bəl/ *adj* Someone who is sociable likes being with people and meeting new people.

social /'sou·ʃəl/ *adj* **1** [B1] relating to the things you do with other people for enjoyment when you are not working: *I have a very busy social life.* **2** relating to society and the way people live: *social problems*

socialize /'sou·ʃə·laɪz/ *verb* (present participle **socializing**, past tense and past participle **socialized**) to spend time enjoying yourself with other people: *Students can socialize with teachers at the café.*

social networking /'sou·ʃəl 'net·wɜr·kɪŋ/ *noun* [no plural] [B1] the activity of communicating with other people who have similar interests using a website that provides this service: *a social networking site*

social worker /'sou·ʃəl ˌwɜr·kər/ *noun* someone whose job is to help people who have problems because they are poor, old, have difficulties with their family, etc.

society /sə'saɪ·ɪ·t̬i/ *noun* [B1] [no plural] a large group of people who live in the same country or area and have the same laws, traditions, etc.: *Racism is still a problem in modern society.*

sock /sɑk/ *noun* something that you wear on your foot inside your shoe: *a pair of black socks*
→ See **Clothes** on page C5

socket /'sɑk·ɪt/ *noun* the place on a wall where you connect electrical equipment to the electricity supply

soda /'sou·də/ *noun* **1** (also **soda pop**) a sweet drink with bubbles: *a can of soda* **2** [no plural] (also **soda water**) water with bubbles in it that you mix with other drinks

sofa /'sou·fə/ *noun* [A2] a large, comfortable seat for more than one person
→ See **The Living Room** on page C7

soft /sɔft/ *adj* **1** [A2] not hard, and easy to press: *a soft cushion* ○ *Cook the onion until it's soft.* → Opposite **hard** *adj* **2** [A2] smooth and pleasant to touch: *soft hair/ skin* → Opposite **rough** *adj* **3** [B1] A soft sound is very quiet: *He spoke in a soft voice.* **4** [B1] A soft color or light is not bright: *soft yellow paint* → Opposite **bright** *adj* **5** too kind: *You're too soft to be a police officer.*
• **softness** *noun* [no plural]

soft drink /'sɔft 'drɪŋk/ *noun* [A2] a cold, sweet drink that does not have alcohol in it

soften /'sɔ·fən/ *verb* to become softer or to make something become softer: *Heat the butter until it softens.*

softly /'sɔft·li/ *adv* [B1] in a quiet or gentle way: *"Are you OK?" she asked softly.*

software /'sɔft·wear/ *noun* [no plural] [A2] programs that you use to make a computer do different things: *educational software*

a
b
c
d
e
f
g
h
i
j
k
l
m
n
o
p
q
r
s
t
u
v
w
x
y
z

Common mistake: software

Remember you cannot make **software** plural. Do not say "softwares."
The software was already installed.

soggy /ˈsɒg·i/ adj (comparative **soggier**, superlative **soggiest**) very wet and soft, when this is not what is wanted: *soggy cereal*

soil /sɔɪl/ noun [no plural] the top layer of earth that plants grow in

solar /ˈsoʊ·lər/ adj relating to the sun: *solar power*

sold /soʊld/ past tense and past participle of sell

soldier /ˈsoʊl·dʒər/ noun **B1** a person in an army

sole[1] /soʊl/ adj only: *the sole survivor of the car crash*

sole[2] /soʊl/ noun the bottom part of your foot that you walk on

solely /ˈsoʊl·li/ adv only, and not involving anyone or anything else: *I bought it solely for that purpose.*

solemn /ˈsɑl·əm/ adj serious or sad: *solemn music*

solid[1] /ˈsɑl·ɪd/ adj **1** hard and firm without holes or spaces, and not liquid or gas: *solid ground* ○ *solid food* **2** strong and not easily broken or damaged: *solid furniture*

solid[2] /ˈsɑl·ɪd/ noun a substance or object that is not a liquid or a gas

solo[1] /ˈsoʊ·loʊ/ adj, adv done alone by one person only: *a solo performance* ○ *to fly solo*

solo[2] /ˈsoʊ·loʊ/ noun a piece of music for one person or one instrument: *a trumpet solo*

solution /səˈlu·ʃən/ noun **B1** the way to stop a problem: *There's no easy solution to this problem.*

solve /sɑlv/ verb (present participle **solving**, past tense and past participle **solved**) **B1** to find the answer to something or to stop

a problem: *We have solved the problem.* ○ *The police have still not solved the crime.*

some /sʌm/ pronoun, determiner
1 **A1** used to mean an amount of something without saying exactly how much or how many: *You'll need a pair of scissors and some glue.* ○ *I can't eat all of these apples, would you like some?* ○ *Could I have some more paper, please?*
2 **A1** used to mean a part of a larger amount or number of something and not all of it: *Some people don't eat meat.* ○ *Some of the children were frightened.*
3 a large amount or number of something: *It will be some time before I see you again.*

Common mistake: some or any?

Be careful not to confuse these two words. Any is used in questions and negative sentences.
Do you have any friends in Canada? I don't have any money.
Some is used in positive sentences.
I have some friends in Canada.
Sometimes some is used in questions, especially when the speaker thinks that the answer will be "yes."
Do you have some money I could borrow?
The same rules are true for something/anything and someone/anyone.
I didn't see anything I wanted to buy. I saw someone I knew at the party.

somebody /ˈsʌm·bɑd·i/, /ˈsʌm·bʌd·i/ pronoun **A2** another word for someone

somehow /ˈsʌm·haʊ/ adv **1** **B1** in a way that you do not know or do not understand: *Don't worry, we'll fix it somehow.* ○ *Somehow they managed to get in.* **2** for a reason that is not clear: *It was my birthday, but somehow I felt sad.*

someone /ˈsʌm·wʌn/ pronoun (also **somebody**) **1** **A1** used to mean "a person" when you do not know who the person is, or when it is not important

|oʊ go|aɪər fire|aʊər hour|eər hair|ɪər ear|ʊər poor|j yet|ʒ measure|ʃ ship|dʒ judge|tʃ chin|ð that|θ thin|ŋ hang|

who he or she is: *There's someone at the door.* ○ *Will someone please answer the phone?* **2 someone else** a different person: *Sorry, I thought you were talking to someone else.*

someplace /ˈsʌmˌpleɪs/ adv **B1** used to refer to a place when you do not know where it is or when it is not important where it is: *They live someplace in the South.*

something /ˈsʌm·θɪŋ/ pronoun **1 A1** used to mean a thing when you do not know what it is or when it is not important what it is: *As soon as I walked in, I noticed that something was missing.* ○ *We know about the problem and we're trying to do something about it.* ○ *There's something else (=another thing) that I wanted to tell you.* **2 or something (like that)** used to show that what you have just said is only an example or that you are not certain about it: *Why don't you go to a movie or something?*

sometime /ˈsʌmˌtaɪm/ adv used to mean a time when you do not know exactly what it is or when it is not important what it is: *We'll plan it for sometime before June.* ○ *You should come over and visit sometime.*

sometimes /ˈsʌmˌtaɪmz/ adv **A1** on some occasions but not always or often: *He does cook sometimes, but not very often.* ○ *Sometimes I feel so lonely.*

somewhat /ˈsʌmˌhwɑt/, /ˈsʌmˌhwʌt/ adv a little: *We were somewhat disappointed with the food.*

somewhere /ˈsʌmˌhweər/ adv **A2** used to mean a place when you do not know exactly where it is, or when it is not important exactly where it is: *They had difficulties finding somewhere to live.* ○ *He comes from somewhere near Chicago.* ○ *Can you think of somewhere else (=a different place) we could go?*

son /sʌn/ noun **A1** someone's male child: *They have two sons.*

song /sɔŋ/ noun **A2** words that go with a short piece of music: *a love song* ○ *to sing a song*

son-in-law /ˈsʌn·ɪnˌlɔ/ noun (plural **sons-in-law**) the husband of someone's child: *Our daughter and son-in-law live close to us.*

soon /sun/ adv **1 A2** after a short period of time: *We need to leave soon.* ○ *It's too soon to make a decision.* **2 as soon as B1** at the same time or a very short time after: *They want it as soon as possible.* **3 sooner or later** used to say that you do not know exactly when something will happen, but you are sure that it will happen: *Sooner or later they'll realize that their plan is not going to work.*

soot /sʊt/ noun [no plural] a black powder made when coal, wood, etc. is burned

soothe /suð/ verb (present participle **soothing**, past tense and past participle **soothed**) **1** to make something feel less painful: *I had a long, hot bath to soothe my aching muscles.* **2** to make someone feel calm or less worried: *to soothe a crying baby*

soothing /ˈsu·ðɪŋ/ adj making you feel calm or in less pain: *soothing music*

sophomore /ˈsɑf·əˌmɔr/ noun a student in his or her second year of high school or college: *We met when we were sophomores.*
• **sophomore** adj *my sophomore year*

sore /sɔr/ adj **B1** painful, especially when touched: *a sore throat* ○ *Her eyes were red and sore.*

sorry /ˈsɑr·i/ adj (comparative **sorrier**, superlative **sorriest**) **1 (I'm) sorry A1** something that you say to be polite when you have done something wrong: *Sorry I'm late.* ○ *Oh, I'm sorry. I didn't see you there.* **2 A2** used to show that you are sad about a person or situation: *I was sorry to hear about your brother's accident.* **3 feel sorry for someone B1** to feel sympathy for someone because he or she is in a difficult situation: *I feel so sorry for them – their dog just died.* **4** used to politely disagree or refuse to do something: *I'm sorry, I don't agree with you.* **5** used to say that you wish something in the past had been different: *I'm sorry that I ever met him.*

| æ cat | ɑ hot | e get | ɪ sit | i see | ɔ saw | ʊ book | u too | ʌ cut | ə about | ər mother | ɑr turn | ɔr for | aɪ my | aʊ how | eɪ say | ɪ boy |

a b c d e f g h i j k l m n o p q r **s** t u v w x y z

a
b
c
d
e
f
g
h
i
j
k
l
m
n
o
p
q
r

s

t
u
v
w
x
y
z

sort¹ /sɔrt/ *noun*   **1** 🅐🅱 a type of something: *We both like the same **sort of** music.* ○ *What **sort of** job do you want?*   **2** all **sorts of** 🅐🅱 many different types of something   **3** that **sort of** thing 🅑🅱 used to show that what you have just said is only an example from a larger group of things: *He likes sketching, painting, that sort of thing.*   **4** sort of used to describe something approximately: *The sweater is a sort of pale blue color.*

sort² /sɔrt/ *verb*   to put things into different groups or types or into an order: *The names are sorted alphabetically.*

sort something **out** *phrasal verb* to organize or arrange things that are messy: *I need to sort out all my bills.*

sought /sɔt/   past tense and past participle of seek

soul /soʊl/ *noun*   **1** 🅐🅱 a type of popular music that expresses deep feelings, originally performed by African Americans   **2** the part of a person that is not his or her body, which some people believe continues to exist after the person dies

sound¹ /saʊnd/ *noun*   🅐🅱 something that you hear: *I could **hear** the **sounds** of the city through the open window.* ○ *She stood still, not **making a sound**.*

sound² /saʊnd/ *verb*   **1** sound good, interesting, strange, etc. 🅐🅱 to seem good, interesting, strange, etc. from what you have heard or read: *Your job sounds really interesting.*   **2** sound like/ as if/as though 🅑🅱 to seem like something, from what you have heard or read: *That sounds like a really good idea.* ○ *It sounds like you have a sore throat.*   **3** sound angry, happy, rude, etc. to seem angry, happy, rude, etc. when you speak: *He sounded really sad on the phone.*

sound³ /saʊnd/ *adj*   good or safe and able to be trusted: *sound advice*

sound⁴ /saʊnd/ *adv*   sound **asleep** in a deep sleep

soundly /ˈsaʊnd·li/ *adv*   sleep **soundly** to sleep well

soundtrack /ˈsaʊndˌtræk/ *noun*   the music used in a movie

soup /sup/ *noun* [no plural]   🅐🅱 a hot, liquid food, made from vegetables, meat, or fish: *chicken soup*
→ See **Food** on page C7

sour /saʊər/ *adj*   🅑🅱 having a sharp taste like a lemon, and not sweet: *These plums are a little sour.*

source /sɔrs/ *noun*   where something comes from: *Oranges are a good **source of** vitamin C.*

south, South /saʊθ/ *noun* [no plural]   **1** 🅐🅱 the direction that is on your right when you face toward the rising sun: *The stadium is to the south of the city.*   **2** the south 🅐🅱 the part of an area that is farther toward the south than the rest: *It's drier in the south of the state.*
• south *adj* 🅐🅱 *the south side of the house* ○ *South America*
• south *adv* 🅐🅱 *We drove south.*

southeast, Southeast /ˌsaʊθˈist/ *noun* [no plural]   **1** 🅑🅱 the direction between south and east   **2** the southeast 🅑🅱 the southeast part of a country
• southeast *adj, adv*

southeastern, Southeastern /ˌsaʊθˈis·tərn/ *adj*   in or from the southeast

southern, Southern /ˈsʌð·ərn/ *adj*   in or from the south part of an area: *the southern half of the country*

the South Pole /ˈsaʊθ ˈpoʊl/ *noun* [no plural]   the point on the Earth's surface that is farthest south

southwest, Southwest /ˌsaʊθˈwest/ *noun* [no plural]   **1** 🅑🅱 the direction between south and west   **2** the southwest 🅑🅱 the southwest part of a country
• southwest *adj, adv*

southwestern, Southwestern /ˌsaʊθˈwes·tərn/ *adj*   in or from the southwest

souvenir /ˌsu·vəˈnɪər/ *noun*   🅑🅱 something that you buy or keep to remember a special time or vacation: *I kept the ticket as a **souvenir** of my trip.*

sow /soʊ/ *verb* (past participle **sown**)   to put seeds into the ground

---

|oʊ go|aɪər **fire**|aʊər **hour**|eər **hair**|ɪər **ear**|ʊər **poor**|j **yet**|ʒ measure|ʃ **ship**|dʒ **judge**|tʃ **chin**|ð **that**|θ **thin**|ŋ **hang**|

space /speɪs/ noun **1** 🅰️ an empty area that is free to be used: *a parking space* ○ *We need more open spaces for children to play in.* ○ *There wasn't enough space for everyone.* **2** 🅱️ [no plural] the area outside the Earth: *space travel*

spacecraft /'speɪs.krɑːft/ noun (plural **spacecraft**) a vehicle that can travel outside the Earth and into space

spaceman /'speɪs.mæn/ noun (plural **spacemen**) a man who travels into space

spaceship /'speɪs.ʃɪp/ noun a vehicle used for travel in space

spade /speɪd/ noun a tool used for digging that has a long handle and a wide, flat metal part at one end

spades /speɪdz/ plural noun one of the four suits (=groups) of playing cards: *the ten of spades*

spaghetti /spəˈɡet·i/ noun [no plural] long, thin pieces of pasta

spam /spæm/ noun [no plural] emails that you do not want, usually advertisements

span¹ /spæn/ noun the period of time that something exists or happens: *an average life span of seventy years*

span² /spæn/ verb (present participle **spanning**, past tense and past participle **spanned**) to continue for a particular amount of time: *Her acting career spanned almost forty years.*

spare¹ /speər/ adj **1** 🅱️ If something is spare, it is extra and not being used: *a spare tire* ○ *spare cash* **2 spare time** 🅰️ time when you are not working: *I enjoy gardening in my spare time.*

spare² /speər/ verb (present participle **sparing**, past tense and past participle **spared**) to give time or money to someone: *I have to go soon, but I can spare a few minutes.*

spark /spɑːrk/ noun a very small, bright piece of burning material: *The fire was caused by a spark from a cigarette.*

sparkle /'spɑːr·kəl/ verb (present participle **sparkling**, past tense and past participle

sparkled) to shine brightly because of reflected light: *a lake sparkling in the sun*

sparkling /'spɑːrk·lɪŋ/ adj **1 sparkling water/wine** 🅱️ water or wine with bubbles in it: *Would you like still or sparkling water?* **2** shining brightly because of reflected light

sparrow /'spær·oʊ/ noun a small, brown bird

spat /spæt/ past tense and past participle of spit

speak /spiːk/ verb (present participle **speaking**, past tense **spoke**, past participle **spoken**) **1** 🅰️ to say something using your voice: *She speaks very quietly.* ○ *There was complete silence – nobody spoke.* **2 speak English, French, German, etc.** 🅰️ to be able to say things in English, French, German, etc.: *Do you speak English?* **3 speak with someone** to talk to someone: *Could I speak with Mr. Davis, please?*

speak up phrasal verb to say something in a louder voice so that people can hear you: *Could you speak up, please? I can't hear you.*

⚠ Common mistake: speak or talk?

Remember that you **speak** a language. You do not "talk" it.

She speaks Chinese.
~~She talks Chinese.~~

---

speaker /'spiː·kər/ noun **1** 🅰️ the part of a radio, CD player, etc., that the sound comes out of **2** 🅱️ someone who makes a speech to a group of people: *a guest speaker* **3** 🅱️ someone who can speak a particular language: *He's a fluent Russian speaker.*

spear /spɪər/ noun a long weapon with a sharp point at one end used for hunting

special /'speʃ·əl/ adj **1** 🅰️ better or more important than usual things: *I'm cooking something special for her birthday.* **2** 🅱️ different from normal things, or used for one purpose: *You*

a b c d e f g h i j k l m n o p q r **s** t u v w x y z

need to use a special kind of paint on metal. **3 special attention/treatment** treatment that is better than usual

specialist /'speʃ·ə·lɪst/ noun someone who has a lot of knowledge, or skill in a particular subject: *a software specialist* ○ *He's a specialist in sports injuries.*

specialize /'speʃ·ə‚laɪz/ verb (present participle **specializing**, past tense and past participle **specialized**) to spend most of your time studying one subject or doing one type of business: *She works for a company specializing in business law.*

specially /'speʃ·ə·li/ adv **B1** for one purpose: *I bought the camera specially for this trip.*

species /'spi·ʃiz/ noun (plural **species**) a group of plants or animals that are the same in some way: *a rare species of bird*

specific /spɪˈsɪf·ɪk/ adj **1** particular and not general: *I asked you for a specific reason.* ○ *Do you need to leave at a specific time?* **2** exact or containing details: *Could you be more specific about the problem?*

specifically /spɪˈsɪf·ɪk·li/ adv **1** for one reason, purpose, etc.: *This website is specifically for children.* **2** exactly or in detail: *I specifically told them that I don't eat meat.*

specify /'spes·ə‚faɪ/ verb (present participle **specifying**, past tense and past participle **specified**) to say or describe something in an exact way: *They didn't specify what color they wanted.*

specimen /'spes·ə·mən/ noun an animal, plant, etc. used as an example of its type, especially for scientific study: *This is one of the museum's finest specimens.*

speck /spek/ noun a very small amount of something: *a speck of dirt*

spectacular /spek'tæk·jə·lər/ adj **B1** very good or exciting: *a spectacular view*
• **spectacularly** adv *a spectacularly beautiful country*

spectator /'spek‚teɪ·tər/ noun someone who watches an event, sport, etc.: *The stadium can hold up to 60,000 spectators.*

sped /sped/ past tense and past participle of speed

speech /spitʃ/ noun **1 B1** [no plural] someone's ability to talk, or an example of someone talking: *His speech was very slow and difficult to understand.* **2** a formal talk that someone gives to a group of people: *I had to make a speech at my brother's wedding.*

speed[1] /spid/ noun **B1** how fast something moves or happens: *He was traveling at a speed of 90 mph.*

speed[2] /spid/ verb (past tense and past participle **sped**) **1** to move somewhere or happen very fast: *The three men jumped into a car and sped away.* **2 be speeding** to be driving faster than you are allowed to
speed up phrasal verb to move or happen faster: *Can you try to speed up a little please?*

speed limit /'spid ‚lɪm·ɪt/ noun the fastest speed that a car is allowed to travel on a particular road: *I never break the speed limit.*

speedometer /spɪˈdɑm·ɪ·ţər/ noun a device in a vehicle that shows how fast the vehicle is moving
→ See Car on page C3

spell[1] /spel/ verb **1 A2** to write or tell someone the letters that are used to make a word: *How do you spell that?* **2** If you can spell, you know how to write the words of a language correctly: *She spelled my name wrong.*

spell[2] /spel/ noun **1** a period of time: *We are expecting rain and cold spells this week.* **2** magic words that are supposed to make a person or thing change shape, disappear, etc.: *The witch cast a spell that turned the boy into a frog.*

spelling /'spel·ɪŋ/ noun **1 A2** the letters that are used to write a word: *There are two possible spellings of this word.* ○ *spelling mistakes* **2** [no plural] someone's ability to spell words: *My spelling is terrible.*

spend /spend/ verb (past tense and past participle **spent**) **1 A2** to use money to buy or pay for something: She **spends** a lot **on** clothes. ○ How much did you spend? **2** A2 to use time doing something or being somewhere: He spent 18 months working on the project. ○ He's planning to **spend** some time at home with his family.

spice /spaɪs/ noun B1 a substance made from a plant, which is used to give a special taste to food: herbs and spices

spicy /'spaɪ·si/ adj (comparative **spicier**, superlative **spiciest**) B1 containing strong flavors from spices: spicy food

spider /'spaɪ·dər/ noun B1 a creature with eight long legs that catches insects in a web (=structure like a net)

spike /spaɪk/ noun a long, thin piece of metal, wood, etc. with a sharp point at one end

spiky /'spaɪ·ki/ adj (comparative **spikier**, superlative **spikiest**) B1 covered with spikes or having that appearance: spiky hair → See Hair on page C9

spill /spɪl/ verb B1 to pour liquid somewhere where you do not want it, by accident: I spilled wine all over the carpet.

spin /spɪn/ verb (present participle **spinning**, past tense and past participle **spun**) **1** If something spins or you spin something, it turns around and around quickly: The car **spun across** the road. **2** to make thread by twisting together cotton, wool, etc.

spinach /'spɪn·ɪtʃ/ noun [no plural] B1 a vegetable with large, dark green leaves

spine /spaɪn/ noun a long line of bones in a person's or animal's back

spiral /'spaɪ·rəl/ noun
a shape made by a curve turning around and around a central point: a spiral staircase

spiral

spirit /'spɪr·ɪt/ noun **1** the way people think and feel about something: a **spirit of** optimism ○ Everyone **got into the spirit of** the celebration (=they all celebrated). **2** The part of a person that is not his or her body, which some people believe continues to exist after they die

3 in good, high, low, etc. **spirits** feeling good, excited, unhappy, etc.: The whole class was in good spirits that day.

spiritual /'spɪr·ɪ·tʃu·əl/ adj relating to deep feelings and beliefs, especially religious beliefs: a spiritual leader

spit /spɪt/ verb (present participle **spitting**, past tense and past participle **spat**) to force out the liquid in your mouth: He took a mouthful of coffee and then spat it out.

spite /spaɪt/ noun **1 in spite of** something B1 although something exists or happens: In spite of a bad storm, the plane landed safely. **2** [no plural] a feeling of anger toward someone that makes you want to upset them: She broke his toy **out of spite**.

spiteful /'spaɪt·fəl/ adj said or done to upset someone: That was a very spiteful thing to do.

splash¹ /splæʃ/ verb **1** If a liquid splashes or you splash a liquid, drops of it fall on something: She splashed some cold water on her face. **2** to move in water so that drops of it go in all directions: The children splashed around in the puddles.

splash² /splæʃ/ noun **1** a drop of liquid that has fallen on something, or the mark made by it: There were several small splashes of paint on the carpet. **2** the sound of something falling into or moving in water

splinter /'splɪn·tər/ noun a small, sharp piece of wood, glass, etc., that has broken from a larger piece: I have a splinter in my finger.

split /splɪt/ verb (present participle **splitting**, past tense and past participle **split**) **1** to share something by dividing it into smaller parts: The cost of the wedding will be **split between** the two families. **2** If something splits or you split it, it tears so that there is a long, thin hole in it: My pants split when I sat down.

split up phrasal verb B1 If two people split up, they end their relationship: She **split up with** her boyfriend.

spoil /spɔɪl/ verb B1 to stop something from being enjoyable or successful: The picnic was spoiled by the bad

a
b
c
d
e
f
g
h
i
j
k
l
m
n
o
p
q
r
s
t
u
v
w
x
y
z

a
b
c
d
e
f
g
h
i
j
k
l
m
n
o
p
q
r
s
t
u
v
w
x
y
z

weather. **2** If you spoil a child, you let him or her have anything he or she wants, which usually has a bad effect on his or her behavior.

spoke /spouk/ past tense of speak

spoken /'spou·kən/ past participle of speak

spokesman /'spouks·mən/ **noun** (plural **spokesmen**) a man who is chosen to speak officially for a group or organization

spokesperson /'spouks‚pɜr·sən/ **noun** (plural **spokespeople**) someone who is chosen to speak officially for a group or organization

spokeswoman /'spouks‚wum·ən/ **noun** (plural **spokeswomen**) a woman who is chosen to speak officially for a group or organization

sponge /spʌndʒ/ **noun** a piece of a soft substance full of small holes, which is used for washing things

sponge

sponsor[1] /'spɑn·sər/ **noun** a person or organization that gives money to support an activity, event, etc.: *The show's producers are looking for new sponsors.*

sponsor[2] /'spɑn·sər/ **verb** to give money to support an activity, event, etc.: *The festival was sponsored by a software company.*

spoon /spun/ **noun** **A2** an object with a handle and a round, curved part at one end, used for eating and serving food: *knives, forks, and spoons*

spoonful /'spun·ful/ **noun** the amount of something that can be held on a spoon: *Add a spoonful of sugar.*

sport /spɔrt/ **noun** **A1** a game or activity that people do to keep healthy or for enjoyment, often competing against each other: *winter sports ○ team sports*

sports /spɔrts/ **plural noun** **1** **B1** used especially before another noun to say that something is connected with sports: *sports equipment* **2** all types of physical activity that people do to keep

healthy or for enjoyment: *She is really good at sports.*

sports car /'spɔrts ‚kɑr/ **noun** a fast car, often with only two seats and an open roof

sportsman /'spɔrts·mən/ **noun** (plural **sportsmen**) a man who is good at sports

sportswoman /'spɔrts‚wum·ən/ **noun** (plural **sportswomen**) a woman who is good at sports

sporty /'spɔr·ți/ **adj** (comparative **sportier**, superlative **sportiest**) good at sports

spot[1] /spɑt/ **noun** **1** **B1** a small, round mark that is a different color than the surface it is on: *There was a spot of blood on her shirt.* **2** a place: *We found a good spot to park the car.*

spot[2] /spɑt/ **verb** (present participle **spotting**, past tense and past participle **spotted**) to see or notice something or someone: *She spotted the mistake and fixed it.*

spotless /'spɑt·ləs/ **adj** very clean: *Her house is spotless.*

sprain /spreɪn/ **verb** to hurt part of your body by twisting it: *I slipped on the ice and sprained my ankle.*

sprang /spræŋ/ past tense of spring

spray[1] /spreɪ/ **noun** liquid in a container that forces it out in small drops: *spray paint*

spray[2] /spreɪ/ **verb** to force liquid out of a container in many small drops: *She sprayed a little perfume on her wrists.*

spread /spred/ **verb** (past tense and past participle **spread**) **1** to arrange something so that it covers a large area: *He spread the cards **out** on the table.* **2** to affect a larger number of people: *The virus is spread by rats.* **3** to move a soft substance across a surface so that it covers it: *Mom **spread** some butter **on** the bread.* **4** to tell information to a lot of people: *News of his death spread quickly.*

spring[1] /sprɪŋ/ **noun** **1** **A2** the season of the year between winter and summer, when the weather becomes warmer and plants start to grow again **2** a piece of metal which curves around and around: *bed springs* **3** a place where water comes out of the ground: *hot springs*

spring² /sprɪŋ/ verb (past tense **sprang**, past participle **sprung**) to jump or move somewhere suddenly: *The cat sprang onto the sofa.*

sprinkle /'sprɪŋ·kəl/ verb (present participle **sprinkling**, past tense and past participle **sprinkled**) to gently drop small pieces of something over a surface: *Sprinkle the pasta with cheese.*

sprinkle

sprout /spraʊt/ verb If a plant sprouts, or if it sprouts something, it begins to make leaves, flowers, etc.: *The seeds I planted are just beginning to sprout.*

sprung /sprʌŋ/ past participle of spring

spun /spʌn/ past tense of spin

spy¹ /spaɪ/ noun (plural **spies**) **B1** someone who secretly tries to find information about a person, country, etc.

spy² /spaɪ/ verb (present participle **spying**, past tense and past participle **spied**) to see someone or something, often from a long way away: *I spied her walking down the street.*

spy on *someone* phrasal verb to secretly watch someone: *He spied on her through the keyhole.*

squad /skwɑd/ noun **1** a group of people who have special skills to deal with particular problems: *a bomb squad* **2** a sports team: *the American soccer squad*

square¹ /skweər/ noun **1** **A2** a shape with four equal sides and four 90° angles → See picture at **shape** noun **2** **A2** an open area with buildings around it, often in the center of a town: *Times Square*

square² /skweər/ adj **A2** having the shape of a square: *a square room*

squash¹ /skwɑʃ/ noun **B1** a large vegetable that grows along the ground.

Some types of squash have hard skin and many seeds in the middle.

squash² /skwɑʃ/ verb to press something into a flat shape: *I stepped on a spider and squashed it.*

squeak /skwik/ verb to make a short, high sound: *His shoes squeaked loudly as he walked.*
• **squeak** noun

squeal /skwil/ verb to make a loud, high sound, often because of fear or excitement: *She squealed with delight.*
• **squeal** noun *squeals of laughter*

squeeze /skwiz/ verb (present participle **squeezing**, past tense and past participle **squeezed**) to press something firmly: *She squeezed his hand and said goodbye.*

squid /skwɪd/ noun (plural **squid**) a sea creature with a long body and ten long arms

squirrel /'skwɜr·əl/ noun a small animal with a thick, furry tail that climbs trees and eats nuts

squirrel

St. 1 written abbreviation for street: *42 Orchard St.* **2** written abbreviation for saint: *St. Patrick*

stab /stæb/ verb (present participle **stabbing**, past tense and past participle **stabbed**) to push a knife into someone: *He was stabbed several times in the chest.*

stable¹ /'steɪ·bəl/ adj **1** not likely to change or end suddenly: *a stable relationship* **2** fastened or safe and not likely to move: *Be careful! That chair isn't very stable.*

stable² /'steɪ·bəl/ noun a building where horses are kept

stack¹ /stæk/ noun a neat pile of things: *a stack of books/CDs*

stack

stack² /stæk/ verb to put things in a neat pile: *Can you help me stack these chairs?*

a
b
c
d
e
f
g
h
i
j
k
l
m
n
o
p
q
r
s
t
u
v
w
x
y
z

stadium /ˈsteɪ·di·əm/ noun **A2** a very large building with seats around an open area in the middle, used for playing and watching sports or for other events such as music shows: *a football stadium*

staff /stæf/ noun [no plural] **A2** the people who work for an organization: *The company has over 500 staff members.*

stage /steɪdʒ/ noun **1 A2** the raised area in a theatre where actors perform: *He's on stage for most of the play.* **2** a period of development, or a particular time in a process: *an early stage in his career* ○ *Our project is in its final stages.*

stagger /ˈstæg·ər/ verb to walk as if you might fall

stain[1] /steɪn/ noun a dirty mark on something that is difficult to remove: *a blood stain* ○ *a stain on the carpet*

stain[2] /steɪn/ verb to leave a dirty mark on something that is difficult to remove, or to become dirty in this way: *I spilled my wine and stained my pants.*

staircase /ˈsteər‚keɪs/ noun a set of stairs and the structure around them: *a spiral staircase*

stairs /steərz/ noun **A2** a set of steps from one level in a building to another: *to go up/down the stairs*

stale /steɪl/ adj old and not fresh: *stale bread*

stalk /stɔk/ noun the main stem of a plant

stall /stɔl/ noun **stall**
1 a small space that has walls, a door, and usually an open top: *a horse stall* ○ *a shower stall* **2** a small space with a table and an open front from which things are sold: *a market stall*

stamp[1] /stæmp/ noun **1 A2** a small piece of paper that you buy and stick onto a letter before you mail it **2** a tool for putting a special ink mark on something, or the mark made by it: *a stamp in a passport*

stamp[2] /stæmp/ verb **1** to make a mark on something with a tool that you put ink on and press down: *She stamped the date on the invoice.* **2** to put your foot down on the ground hard and quickly, often to show anger: *"No!" she shouted, stamping her foot.*

stand[1] /stænd/ verb (present participle **standing**, past tense and past participle **stood**) **1 A2** to be in a vertical position on your feet: *We stood there for an hour.* ○ *He's standing over there, next to Karen.* **2 A2** (also **stand up**) to rise to a vertical position on your feet from sitting or lying down: *I get dizzy if I stand up too quickly.* ○ *Please stand when the bride arrives.* → See **Phrasal Verbs** on page C13 **3** to be in or to put something in a particular place or position: *The tower stands in the middle of a field.* ○ *She stood the umbrella by the door.* **4 can't stand someone/something** informal **B1** to hate someone or something: *I can't stand him – he is so rude!* ○ *She can't stand doing housework.*

stand for *something* phrasal verb If a letter stands for a word, it is used to mean it: *TMI stands for "too much information."*

stand out phrasal verb **1** to be very easy to see or notice: *The bright blue letters really stand out on the page.* **2** to be much better than other similar things or people: *One candidate stood out from the rest.*

stand up for *something/someone* phrasal verb to defend or support a particular idea or a person who is being criticized or attacked: *We should all stand up for our rights.*

stand[2] /stænd/ noun a small store with an open front or a table from which things are sold: *a lemonade stand*

standard[1] /ˈstæn·dərd/ noun **1** a level of quality, especially a level that is good enough: *a high standard of service* ○ *low safety standards* ○ *His work was below standards* (= not good enough). **2** a level of behavior, especially a level that is good enough: *high moral standards* **3 standard of living** how much money and comfort someone has: *a low/high standard of living*

standard² /ˈstæn.dərd/ *adj* usual and not special: *standard practice*

standby /ˈstænd.baɪ/ *noun* **be on standby** to be ready to do something or to be used if needed: *Some passengers were on standby for the flight.*

stank /stæŋk/ past tense of stink

staple /ˈsteɪ.pəl/ *noun* a small piece of wire that you put through pieces of paper to join them together

stapler /ˈsteɪ.plər/ *noun* a piece of equipment used for putting staples through paper

star¹ /stɑːr/ *noun* **1** 🅐🅑 a ball of burning gases that you see as a small point of light in the sky at night **2** 🅐🅑 a famous singer, actor, sports person, etc.: *a pop star* **3** 🅐🅑 a shape that has five or more points
→ See picture at **shape** *noun*

stars

star² /stɑːr/ *verb* (present participle **starring**, past tense and past participle **starred**) 🅑🅑 to be the main person in a movie, play, etc.: *a movie starring Julia Roberts*

stare /steər/ *verb* (present participle **staring**, past tense and past participle **stared**) to look at someone or something for a long time and not move your eyes: *Sean was staring at me.*
• **stare** *noun*

start¹ /stɑːrt/ *verb* **1** 🅐🅑 to begin doing something: *Maria started to laugh.* ○ *We start working at nine o'clock.* **2** 🅑🅑 to begin to happen or to make something

begin to happen: *The fire started in the kitchen.*

start (something) off *phrasal verb* 🅑🅑 to begin by doing something, or to make something begin by doing something: *She started off her essay with a quote from the book.*

start² /stɑːrt/ *noun* 🅑🅑 the beginning of something: *Our teacher checks who is in class at the start of each day.* ○ *Ivan has been involved in the project from the start.*

startle /ˈstɑːr.t̬əl/ *verb* (present participle **startling**, past tense and past participle **startled**) to suddenly surprise or frighten someone: *The sound startled me.*

starve /stɑːrv/ *verb* (present participle **starving**, past tense and past participle **starved**) to become ill or die because you do not have enough food: *Many people have starved to death in parts of Africa.*
• **starvation** *noun* [no plural] *Children were dying of starvation.*

starving /ˈstɑːr.vɪŋ/ *adj* **1** dying because there is not enough food: *starving people* **2** informal very hungry: *I'm absolutely starving.*

state¹ /steɪt/ *noun* **1** the condition that something or someone is in: *the state of the economy* ○ *Ben was in a state of shock after the fire.* **2** (also **State**) one of the parts that some countries are divided into: *Alaska is the largest state in the U.S.* **3 the state** the government of a country: *financial help from the state*

state² /steɪt/ *verb* (present participle **stating**, past tense and past participle **stated**) to officially say or write something: *The medical report stated that he was mentally ill.*

statement /ˈsteɪt.mənt/ *noun* something that someone says or writes officially: *The government is expected to make a statement later today.*

station /ˈsteɪ.ʃən/ *noun* **1** 🅐🅑 a place where trains or buses stop so that you can get on or off them: *Dad met me at the station.* **2** a company that shows or sends out television or radio programs: *a classical music station*

stationery /'steɪ·ʃə·ner·i/ noun [no plural]
things that you use for writing, such as
pens and pencils

statistics /stə'tɪs·tɪks/ noun [no plural]
the subject that involves collecting and
studying numbers to show information

statue /'stætʃ·u/
noun **B1** a model
that looks like a
person or animal,
usually made from
stone or metal

statue

stay¹ /steɪ/ verb
1 A1 to continue to
be in a place, job,
etc. and not leave:
*The weather was
bad so we stayed home.*   **2 A2** to spend
a short period of time in a place: *We
stayed in a hotel.*   **3 B1** to continue to
be in a particular state: *The supermarket
stays open late.*

stay behind phrasal verb **B1** to not
leave a place when other people leave it:
*He stayed behind after class to speak to
the teacher.*

stay in phrasal verb **B1** to stay in your
home: *Let's stay in tonight and watch a
movie.*

stay out phrasal verb to not come home
at night, or to go home late: *Our cat usually stays out at night.* ○ *My mom won't
let me stay out late.*

stay² /steɪ/ noun **B1** a period of time
that you spend in a place: *Did you enjoy
your stay in Tokyo?*

steady /'sted·i/ adj (comparative **steadier**,
superlative **steadiest**) **1** happening at a
gradual, regular rate: *a steady improvement*   **2** still and not shaking: *You need
steady hands to be a dentist.*   **3** not
changing: *She drove at a steady speed.*
• **steadily** adv

steak /steɪk/ noun **A2** a thick, flat piece
of meat or fish

steal /stil/ verb (past tense **stole**, past participle **stolen**) **A2** to secretly take something that belongs to someone else:
*Burglars broke into the house and stole a
computer.*

steam /stim/ noun [no plural]
the gas that water makes
when you heat it

steam

steel /stil/ noun [no plural]
a very strong metal made
from iron, used for mak-
ing knives, machines, etc.

steep /stip/ adj
B1 A steep slope, hill, etc. goes up or
down very quickly: *The hill was too steep
to drive up.*
• **steeply** adv

steer /stɪər/ verb   to control the direction of a car, boat, etc.: *I tried to steer the
boat away from the bank.*

steering wheel /'stɪər·ɪŋ ˌhwil/ noun
a wheel that you turn to control the direction of a vehicle
→ See **Car** on page C3

stem /stem/ noun   the long, thin part of
a plant that the leaves and flowers grow on

step¹ /step/ noun **1 B1** one of the
movements you make with your feet
when you walk: *She took a few steps forward.*   **2 B1** one of the surfaces that
you walk on when you go up or down
stairs   **3** one of the things that you do
to achieve something: *This meeting is
the first step toward a peace agreement.*

step² /step/ verb (present participle **stepping**,
past tense and past participle **stepped**)
1 B1 to move somewhere by lifting
your foot and putting it down in a different place: *She stepped carefully over
the dog.*   **2 B1** to put your foot on or in
something: *I accidentally stepped on her
foot.*

stepfather /'step.fɑ·ðər/ noun   the man
who has married your mother but is not
your father

stepmother /'step.mʌð·ər/ noun
the woman who has married your father
but is not your mother

stereo /'ster·iˌoʊ/ noun   a piece of equipment for playing CDs, listening to the
radio, etc. that has two speakers (= parts
where sound comes out): *a car stereo*
→ See **The Living Room** on page C11

stern /stɜrn/ adj very serious and not friendly or funny: *a stern face*

stew /stu/ noun food made of vegetables and meat cooked together in liquid: *beef stew*

stick¹ /stɪk/ verb (past tense and past participle **stuck**) **1** 🔵 to become joined to something else or to make something become joined to something else, for example with a substance like glue: *The book got wet and the pages all stuck together.* ○ *She had stuck a lot of photos on her wall with tape.* **2** informal to put something somewhere: *You can stick your bag under the table.* **3** If you stick something sharp somewhere, you push it into something: *She stuck the needle into his arm.* **4** to become fixed in one position and not be able to move: *This drawer is stuck – I can't open it.*

stick out phrasal verb to go past the surface or edge of something: *That hat makes her ears stick out.*

stick *something* out phrasal verb to make part of your body come forward from the rest of your body: *The boy stuck his tongue out at her.*

stick to *something* phrasal verb to do what you say you will do or what you plan to do, and not change: *It's hard to stick to a diet.*

stick together phrasal verb If people stick together, they support and help each other: *My family always sticks together in bad times.*

stick up phrasal verb to point up above a surface and not lie flat: *Your hair's sticking up.*

stick² /stɪk/ noun **1** 🔵 a long, thin piece of wood **2** walking, hockey, etc. stick 🔵 a long, thin piece of wood that you use when you are walking, playing hockey, etc.

sticky /ˈstɪk-i/ adj (comparative **stickier**, superlative **stickiest**) 🔵 made of or covered with a substance that can stick to other things: *sticky fingers* ○ *sticky candy*

stiff /stɪf/ adj **1** hard and difficult to bend: *stiff paper* **2** If a part of your body is stiff, it hurts and does not move as easily as it should: *stiff muscles*

still¹ /stɪl/ adv **1** 🔵 used to say that something is continuing to happen now: *He's still here if you want to talk to him.* ○ *Do you still play basketball?* **2** 🔵 used to show that you did not expect something to happen: *He didn't study, but he still passed the test.* **3** used to say that something continues to be possible: *We can still catch the train if we leave now.*

still² /stɪl/ adj stand, stay, sit, etc. still 🔵 to stand, stay, sit, etc. without moving: *Sit still so I can brush your hair.*

sting¹ /stɪŋ/ verb (past tense and past participle **stung**) If an insect, plant, etc. stings you, it causes pain by putting poison into your skin: *He was stung by a wasp.*

sting² /stɪŋ/ noun painful skin that you get when an insect, plant, etc. puts poison into your skin: *a wasp/bee sting*

stink¹ /stɪŋk/ verb (present participle **stinking**, past tense **stank**, past participle **stunk**) to smell very bad: *Wow, that bathroom stinks!*

stink² /stɪŋk/ noun a very bad smell

stir /stɜr/ verb (present participle **stirring**, past tense and past participle **stirred**) **1** 🔵 to mix food or liquid by moving a spoon around and around in it: *Stir the mixture until it is smooth.* **2** to move slightly: *The baby stirred in its sleep.*

stitch /stɪtʃ/ noun a short line of thread that is sewn through a piece of material

stock /stɑk/ noun **1** [no plural] all the things that you can buy in a store **2** in stock/out of stock available or not available in a store: *Sorry, we don't have that size in stock.* **3** an amount of something that is ready to be used: *grain stocks* **4** a share of the value of a company, which people can buy: *I buy stock in high-tech companies.*

stocking /ˈstɑk-ɪŋ/ noun a very thin piece of clothing that covers a woman's foot and leg: *a pair of stockings*
→ See Clothes on page C5

a
b
c
d
e
f
g
h
i
j
k
l
m
n
o
p
q
r
s
t
u
v
w
x
y
z

stole /stoʊl/ past tense of steal

stolen /'stoʊ·lən/ past participle of steal

stomach /'stʌm·ək/ noun **1 A2** the part of your body where food is digested **2** the front part of your body just below your chest
→ See **The Body** on page C2

stomachache /'stʌm·ək,eɪk/ noun **A2** pain in your stomach

stone /stoʊn/ noun **1 B1** [no plural] a hard, natural substance that is found in the ground: *a stone wall* **2 B1** a small rock or piece of rock **3 B1** a hard, valuable substance that is often used in jewelry: *precious stones*

stood /stʊd/ past tense and past participle of stand

stool /stul/ noun a seat that does not have a back or arms

stool

stoop¹ /stup/ verb to bend the top half of your body forward and down: *He stooped to pick up the letter off the floor.*

stoop² /stup/ noun a set of steps leading up to the front door of a house

stop¹ /stɑp/ verb (present participle **stopping**, past tense and past participle **stopped**) **1 A1** to finish doing something: *Stop laughing – it's not funny.* ○ *He started to say something and then stopped.* **2 A2** If a bus, train, etc. stops at a particular place, it lets people get on and off: *Does this train stop at Union Station?* **3 A2** to stop a journey or an activity for a short time: *We stopped at a café for lunch.* **4 B1** to not move any more, or make someone or something not move any more: *A car stopped outside the house.* **5 B1** to not continue to operate, or to make something not continue to operate: *My watch stopped.* **6 B1** to prevent something from happening or prevent someone from doing something: *This program will help you stop smoking.* **7** to make something end: *We must find a way to stop the war.*

stop² /stɑp/ noun **1 A1** a place where a bus or train stops so that people can get on or off: *We need to get off at the next stop.* **2 B1** the act of stopping an activity or trip, or a period of time when you stop: *We made a stop to get lunch.* **3 put a stop to something** to end something bad: *We must put a stop to the violence.*

stop sign /'stɑp ,saɪn/ noun a sign that tells traffic to stop before moving on. It is red and has eight sides and the word "stop" in white letters on it.

store¹ /stɔr/ noun **B1** a building or part of a building where you can buy things: *a grocery store* ○ *She works at a men's clothing store.*

store² /stɔr/ verb (present participle **storing**, past tense and past participle **stored**) **1** to put something somewhere and not use it until you need it: *Store the wine in a dark, cool place.* **2** to keep information on a computer: *All the data is stored on the hard drive.*

storm /stɔrm/ noun **A2** very bad weather with a lot of rain or snow and strong wind: *Strong storms will move through Chicago this evening.*

stormy /'stɔr·mi/ adj (comparative **stormier**, superlative **stormiest**) If it is stormy, the weather is bad with a lot of wind and rain: *a stormy night*

story /'stɔr·i/ noun (plural **stories**) **1 A2** a description of a series of real or imaginary events that people read for enjoyment: *a horror story* ○ *She reads stories to the children every night.* **2** a level of a building: *a three-story house*

stove /stoʊv/ *noun* a piece of equipment used to cook food over gas flames or electric heat
→ See **The Kitchen** on page C10

straight[1] /streɪt/ *adj* **1** **A2** not curved or bent: *a straight road* ○ *straight hair*
→ See **Hair** on page C9   **2** in a position that is level or vertical: *That shelf is not straight.*   **3** honest: *a straight answer*

straight[2] /streɪt/ *adv* **1** **A2** in a straight line: *Drive straight ahead for one block and turn right.*   **2** **B1** without pausing or delaying: *Please come straight home after school.*   **3** **sit up/stand up straight** to sit or stand with your body vertical

straighten /ˈstreɪ·tᵊn/ *verb* **1** to become straight or to make something straight **2** to put things in the right places and in good order

strain[1] /streɪn/ *noun* **1** the feeling of being worried and nervous about something: *The strain of the divorce was too much for her.*   **2** pressure put on something by a bad situation or by too much weight or force: *Their arguments were putting a strain on their marriage.*

strain[2] /streɪn/ *verb* **1** to try hard to do something, usually to see or hear something: *I had to strain to hear the music.*   **2** to hurt part of your body by using it too much: *I think I strained a muscle.*

strainer /ˈstreɪ·nər/ *noun* a kitchen tool with a handle on one end and a part shaped like a bowl and made of wire at the other, used for separating pieces of food from liquids
→ See **The Kitchen** on page C10

strait /streɪt/ *noun* a narrow area of sea that connects two large areas of sea: *the straits of Florida*

strand /strænd/ *noun* a thin piece of hair, thread, rope, etc.: *She tucked a strand of hair behind her ear.*

stranded /ˈstræn·dɪd/ *adj* not able to leave a place: *We were stranded at the airport for ten hours.*

strange /streɪndʒ/ *adj* **1** **A2** unusual or not expected: *It's strange that she hasn't*

called. ○ *What a strange-looking dog.*
2 **B1** A strange person or place is one that you are not familiar with: *I was lost and alone in a strange city.*
• **strangely** *adv* She's been acting really strangely (= in an unusual way) lately.

stranger /ˈstreɪn·dʒər/ *noun* **B1** someone you have never met before

strangle /ˈstræŋ·gəl/ *verb* (present participle **strangling**, past tense and past participle **strangled**) to kill someone by pressing his or her throat

strap[1] /stræp/ *noun* a thin piece of material used to fasten two things together or to carry something: *a watch strap* ○ *I want a bag with a shoulder strap.*

strap[2] /stræp/ *verb* (present participle **strapping**, past tense and past participle **strapped**) to fasten something using a strap

strategy /ˈstræt·ə·dʒi/ *noun* (plural **strategies**) a plan that you use to do something: *a sales strategy*

straw /strɔ/ *noun* **1** [no plural] the long, dried stems of plants such as wheat (= plant for grain), often given to animals **2** a thin plastic or paper tube that you use for drinking through

strawberry /ˈstrɔˌber·i/ *noun* (plural **strawberries**) **B1** a small, red fruit with small, brown seeds on its surface

stray /streɪ/ *adj* A stray animal is lost or has no home: *a stray dog*

streak /strik/ *noun* a thin line or mark: *She has dark hair with streaks of gray.*

stream /strim/ *noun* **1** **B1** a small river **2** a stream of *something* a line of people or cars moving in the same direction: *a constant stream of traffic*

street /strit/ *noun* **1** **A1** a road in a town or city that has houses or other buildings: *We live on the same street.*
2 Street **A1** used in the name of a street as part of an address: *25 Maple Street*

streetlight /ˈstritˌlaɪt/ *noun* a light on a tall post next to a street
→ See picture at **light** *noun*

| æ cat | ɑ hot | e get | ɪ sit | i see | ɔ saw | ʊ book | u too | ʌ cut | ə about | ər mother | ɜr turn | ɔr for | ɑɪ my | aʊ how | eɪ say | ɔɪ boy |

a b c d e f g h i j k l m n o p q r s t u v w x y z

strength 354

strength /streŋkθ/ *noun* **1** [no plural] the quality of being strong: *A good boxer needs skill as well as strength.* **2** [no plural] the power that an organization, country, etc. has: *economic strength* **3** a good quality or ability: *We all have our strengths and weaknesses.*

strengthen /ˈstreŋkθən/ *verb* to become stronger or make something become stronger: *These exercises strengthen the leg muscles.*

stress¹ /stres/ *noun* **1** 🅱 feelings of worry caused by difficult situations such as problems at work: *work-related stress* ○ *She's been under a lot of stress recently.* **2** [no plural] a greater force you use to say one part of a word or phrase: *In the word "blanket," the stress is on the first syllable.*

stress² /stres/ *verb* **1** to show that something is important: *I stressed that they should not arrive late.* **2** to say one part of a word or phrase more strongly than the rest of it: *In the word "table," you should stress the first syllable.*

stressed /strest/ *adj* (also **stressed out**) **1** 🅱 worried and not able to relax: *Tanya is really stressed about her exams.* **2** A stressed part of a word or phrase is said more strongly than the rest of it.

stressful /ˈstresfəl/ *adj* 🅱 making someone worry a lot: *a stressful job*

stretch /stretʃ/ *verb* **1** to become longer or wider, or to pull something so that it becomes longer or wider: *If you stretch a rubber band too far, it will snap.* **2** to make your body or part of your body straighter and longer: *Stretch your arms above your head.* **3** to cover a large area: *The fields stretched away into the distance.*

stretcher /ˈstretʃ·ər/ *noun* a flat structure covered with cloth that is used to carry someone who is hurt

strict /strɪkt/ *adj* **1** 🅱 A strict person makes sure that children or people working for him or her behave well and

does not allow them to break any rules: *a strict teacher* ○ *My parents were very **strict with** us.* **2** If a rule, law, etc. is strict, it must be obeyed: *She gave me strict instructions to be there by ten.* **3** always behaving in a particular way because of your beliefs: *She's a strict vegetarian.*

strictly /ˈstrɪkt·li/ *adv* **1** exactly or correctly: *That's not strictly true.* **2** done for a particular person or purpose: *Her visit is strictly business.* **3** used to emphasize that something is not allowed: *The use of cameras is strictly forbidden.*

strike¹ /straɪk/ *verb* (present participle **striking**, past tense and past participle **struck**) **1** 🅱 formal to hit someone or something: *Two climbers were struck by falling rocks.* ○ *His car went out of control and struck a tree.* **2** If a thought or idea strikes you, you suddenly think of it: *It struck me that Jane was probably unhappy.* **3** If a group of workers strike, they stop working for a period of time to try to force their employer to give them more money or to improve their working situation: *Bus drivers are threatening to strike.* **4** If a clock strikes, a bell rings to show what the time is.

strike² /straɪk/ *noun* 🅱 a period of time when a group of workers stop working, to try to force their employer to give them more money or to improve their working situation: *Teachers are planning to go on strike next month.*

string /strɪŋ/ *noun* **1** very thin rope used for tying things: *a ball of string* **2** a piece of wire that is part of a musical instrument: *guitar strings*

strip¹ /strɪp/ *verb* (present participle **stripping**, past tense and past participle **stripped**) to remove all your clothes, or to remove all someone else's clothes: *She stripped and jumped into the pool.*

strip² /strɪp/ *noun* a long, thin piece of something: *a strip of paper*

stripe /straɪp/ *noun* 🅱 a long, straight area of color: *His shirt was white with blue stripes.*

striped /straɪpt/ adj with a pattern of stripes: *a striped shirt*

stroke¹ /strouk/ verb (present participle **stroking**, past tense and past participle **stroked**) to gently move your hand over a surface: *She stroked the cat's fur.*

stroke² /strouk/ noun **1** a serious medical condition in the brain that makes you suddenly unable to move part of your body **2** a movement that you make something with your hand, a pen, brush, etc.: *a brush stroke* **3** a style of swimming **4** a stroke of luck something good that happens to you by chance

stroll /stroul/ verb to walk somewhere in a slow and relaxed way: *They strolled along the beach.*
• **stroll** noun *We took a stroll around the neighborhood.*

stroller /'strou·lər/ noun a chair on wheels that is used to move small children

strong /strɔŋ/ adj **1** A2 A strong person or animal is physically powerful: *Are you strong enough to lift this table by yourself?* → Opposite **weak** adj **2** B1 A strong object does not break easily or can support heavy things: *a strong box* **3** B1 If a taste, smell, etc. is strong, it is very easy to notice: *There's a strong smell of smoke outside.* **4** B1 produced using a lot of power: *a strong kick* ○ *Her voice was clear and strong.* **5** B1 Strong relationships last for a long time, and are not easily damaged: *During the crisis their marriage remained strong.* **6** of a good quality or level and likely to be successful: *a strong team* ○ *a strong economy* **7** A strong feeling, belief, or opinion is felt in a very deep and serious way: *a strong sense of pride* **8** If a person is strong or has a strong personality, he or she is confident and deals with problems well: *All my aunts were strong women.*

strongly /'strɔŋ·li/ adv very much or in a very serious way: *They are strongly opposed to higher taxes.*

struck /strʌk/ past tense and past participle of strike

structure /'strʌk·tʃər/ noun **1** the way that parts of something are arranged or put together: *a cell's structure* ○ *grammatical structure* **2** a building or something that has been built

struggle¹ /'strʌg·əl/ verb (present participle **struggling**, past tense and past participle **struggled**) **1** to try very hard to do something difficult: *He's struggling to pay off his debts.* **2** to fight someone when he or she is holding you: *She struggled to get away from them.*

struggle² /'strʌg·əl/ noun **1** the act of trying very hard to do something difficult: *It was a real struggle to stay awake during the movie.* **2** a difficult or long fight between people: *their struggle for independence*

stubble /'stʌb·əl/ noun [no plural] short hair that grows where something has not recently shaved
→ See **Hair** on page C9

stubborn /'stʌb·ərn/ adj never changing your ideas, plans, etc. even when you should
• **stubbornly** adv

stuck¹ /stʌk/ past tense and past participle of stick

stuck² /stʌk/ adj **1** not able to move anywhere: *We were stuck at the airport for twelve hours.* **2** not able to continue reading, answering questions, etc. because something is too difficult: *I keep getting stuck on difficult words.*

student /'stu·dənt/ noun A1 someone who is studying at a school or college: *a law student*
→ See **The Classroom** on page C4

studies /'stʌd·iz/ plural noun A2 the work that you do while you are at a college or university: *I'm enjoying my studies a lot more this year.*

studio /'stu·di·ou/ noun **1** B1 a room where television or radio programs or musical recordings are made **2** B1 a company that makes movies or a place where movies are made: *a major movie studio* **3** a room where an artist or photographer works

---

æ cat | ɑ hot | e get | ɪ sit | i see | ɔ saw | ʊ book | u too | ʌ cut | ə about | ər mother | ɜr turn | ɔr for | ɑɪ my | ɑʊ how | eɪ say | ɔɪ boy

a
b
c
d
e
f
g
h
i
j
k
l
m
n
o
p
q
r
s
t
u
v
w
x
y
z

study[1] /ˈstʌd·i/ verb (present participle **studying**, past tense and past participle **studied**) **1** 🔵 **A1** to learn about a subject, usually at school or in college: *I studied biology before going into medicine.* **2** to look at something very carefully: *He studied his face in the mirror.* **3** to examine a subject in detail in order to discover new information: *Researchers have been studying how babies learn to speak.*

study[2] /ˈstʌd·i/ noun **1** [no plural] the activity of learning about a subject, usually at a school or college: *the study of English literature* **2** 🔵 **B1** (plural **studies**) a room in a house where you can read, write, etc. **3** (plural **studies**) a piece of work that examines a subject in detail in order to find new information: *For years, studies have shown the link between smoking and cancer.*

stuff[1] /stʌf/ noun [no plural] informal 🔵 **B1** used to mean a substance or a group of things, ideas, actions, etc., without saying exactly what they are: *There's some sticky stuff on the carpet.* ∘ *Can I leave my stuff at your house?* ∘ *That kind of stuff (= that behavior) makes me mad.*

stuff[2] /stʌf/ verb **1** to quickly push something into a small space: *He stuffed his clothes into a bag and left.* **2** to completely fill a container or a hole with something: *an envelope stuffed with money* ∘ *To stuff a turkey, follow these steps.* **3** **stuffed up** informal If you or your nose is stuffed up, you cannot breathe through it.

stuffing /ˈstʌf·ɪŋ/ noun [no plural] **1** a substance that is used to fill a hollow object: *a toy bear's stuffing* **2** a type of food made from pieces of bread, vegetables, and spices that is cooked inside a large piece of meat: *turkey stuffing*

stuffy /ˈstʌf·i/ adj (comparative **stuffier**, superlative **stuffiest**) hot, with no clean air: *a stuffy room*

stumble /ˈstʌm·bəl/ verb (present participle **stumbling**, past tense and past participle **stumbled**) to step badly and almost fall over: *Rachel stumbled on the rocks.*

stump /stʌmp/ noun the short part of something that is left after most of it has been removed: *a tree stump*

stung /stʌŋ/ past tense and past participle of sting

stunk /stʌŋk/ past participle of stink

stunt /stʌnt/ noun **1** an exciting and dangerous action that is usually done by a skilled person for a movie: *an actor who does his own stunts* **2** something that is done to get people's attention: *We thought she had been kidnapped, but it was just a stunt.*

stupid /ˈstu·pɪd/ adj 🔵 **B1** not at all intelligent, or very silly: *That's a stupid thing to say.* ∘ *Don't be stupid!*
• **stupidly** adv *I stupidly left my key inside the room.*

stupidity /stuˈpɪd·ə·ti/ noun [no plural] behavior that is very silly or shows you do not think about your actions: *I can't believe the stupidity of these people!*

sturdy /ˈstɜr·di/ adj (comparative **sturdier**, superlative **sturdiest**) very strong and solid: *sturdy walking boots*

stutter /ˈstʌt·ər/ verb to repeat the first sound of a word many times when you talk, usually because you have a speech problem: *"C-c-can we g-go now?" she stuttered.*
• **stutter** noun

style /staɪl/ noun **1** 🔵 **B1** a way of doing something that is typical of a particular person, group, place, or period: *a style of painting* **2** 🔵 **B1** a way of designing hair, clothes, furniture, etc.: *She had her hair cut in a really nice style.*

stylish /ˈstaɪ·lɪʃ/ adj 🔵 **B1** fashionable and attractive

sub /sʌb/ noun short form of submarine: a type of long sandwich
→ See **Food** on page C7

subject /ˈsʌb·dʒɪkt/ noun **1** 🔵 **A1** an area of knowledge studied in school: *Chemistry is my favorite subject.* **2** 🔵 **B1** what someone is writing or talking about: *The subject of the program was mental health.*

3 **B1** in grammar, the person or thing that does the action described by a verb. In the sentence "Bob called me yesterday," "Bob" is the subject.

submarine /ˈsʌb·məˌrin/ noun a boat that travels under water

substance /ˈsʌb·stəns/ noun a solid, liquid, or gas: *a dangerous substance*

substitute[1] /ˈsʌb·stɪˌtut/ noun someone who takes the place of someone else: *a substitute teacher*

substitute[2] /ˈsʌb·stɪˌtut/ verb to use one person or thing instead of another person or thing: *You can substitute pasta for the rice in this recipe.*

subtitles /ˈsʌbˌtɑɪ·t̬lz/ plural noun words shown at the bottom of a movie or television screen to explain what is being said: *It's a French film with English subtitles.*

subtle /ˈsʌt̬·əl/ adj not obvious or easy to notice: *a subtle change*

subtract /səbˈtrækt/ verb to take one number away from another number: *You need to subtract 25% from the final figure.*
• **subtraction** noun

suburb /ˈsʌb·ɚb/ noun an area where people live outside a city: *a suburb of New York*
• **suburban** adj *a suburban area*

subway /ˈsʌbˌweɪ/ noun **A1** a system of trains that is built under a city: *a subway station* ○ *the New York subway*

succeed /səkˈsid/ verb **B1** to do something good that you have been trying to do: *He finally succeeded in passing his exams.*
→ Opposite **fail** verb

> ⚠ **Common mistake: succeed**
>
> Remember that **succeed** is often followed by the preposition **in**, plus "doing something." It is not used with "to do something."
> *Two prisoners succeeded in escaping.*
> ~~Two prisoners succeeded to escape.~~

success /səkˈses/ noun **1** **B1** [no plural] the fact of achieving something good

that you have been trying to do: *Her success is due to hard work and determination.*
→ Opposite **failure** noun **2** **B1** something that has a good result or that is very popular: *His first movie was a great success.*
→ Opposite **failure** noun

successful /səkˈses·fəl/ adj **1** **B1** having a good result: *The operation was successful.* **2** very popular: *a successful book* **3** having achieved a lot or made a lot of money through your work: *a successful businesswoman*
• **successfully** adv

such /sʌtʃ/ pronoun, determiner **1** **A2** used to make an opinion stronger: *She's such a nice person.* ○ *It's such a shame that he's leaving.* **2** like the person or thing you were just talking about: *It's difficult to know how to treat such cases.* **3 such as** **A2** for example: *She can't eat dairy products, such as milk and cheese.*

suck /sʌk/ verb to have something in your mouth and use your tongue, lips, etc. to pull on it: *I was sucking on a mint.* ○ *Martha still sucks her thumb.*

sudden /ˈsʌd·ᵊn/ adj **1** done or happening quickly and not expected: *a sudden change* ○ *His sudden death was a great shock to us all.* **2 all of a sudden** quickly and in a way that was not expected: *All of a sudden she got up and walked out.*

suddenly /ˈsʌd·ᵊn·li/ adv **B1** quickly and when not expected: *I suddenly realized who she was.*

sue /su/ verb (present participle **suing**, past tense and past participle **sued**) to take legal action against someone and try to get money from him or her because he or she has harmed you: *She's threatening to sue the company for age discrimination.*

suede /sweɪd/ noun [no plural] leather that has a slightly rough surface

suffer /ˈsʌf·ɚ/ verb **1 suffer from something** **B1** to have an illness: *She suffers from depression.* **2** to feel pain or sadness and worry: *I can't bear to see animals suffering.* **3** to experience something bad: *Many people in this country have suffered discrimination.*

suffering /ˈsʌf·ə·rɪŋ/ noun [no plural] a feeling of pain or sadness or worry: *human suffering*

sufficient /səˈfɪʃ·ənt/ adj enough: *She didn't have sufficient time to answer all the questions.*

suffix /ˈsʌf·ɪks/ noun a group of letters that you add to the end of a word to make another word. In the word "slowly," "-ly" is a suffix.

sugar /ˈʃʊg·ər/ noun [no plural] **A1** a very sweet substance used to give flavor to food and drinks: *coffee with milk and sugar*

suggest /səˈdʒest/ verb **1** **B1** to say an idea or plan for someone else to consider: *I suggest that we park the car here.* ∘ *He suggested having the meeting at his house.* **2** **B1** to say that someone or something is suitable for something: *Can you suggest a good hotel?*

suggestion /səˈdʒes·tʃən/ noun **B1** an idea or plan that someone suggests: *Philip made a few suggestions.*

suicide /ˈsuː·əˌsɑɪd/ noun the act of deliberately killing yourself: *He committed suicide after a long period of depression.*

suit /suːt/ noun **1** **A2** a jacket and pants or a jacket and skirt that are made from the same material: *She wore a dark blue suit.* **2** one of the four types of card in a set of playing cards, each having a different shape printed on it: *The four suits in a pack of cards are hearts, spades, clubs, and diamonds.*

suitable /ˈsuː·t̬ə·bəl/ adj **B1** acceptable or right for someone or something: *What is a suitable time to call?* ∘ *This movie is suitable for children.*
→ Opposite **unsuitable** adj
• **suitably** adv *He was suitably dressed for an interview.*

suitcase /ˈsuːtˌkeɪs/ noun **A2** a rectangular case with a handle that you use for carrying clothes when you are traveling
→ See picture at **luggage**

sulk /sʌlk/ verb to look unhappy and not speak to anyone because you are angry about something: *He's upstairs sulking in his bedroom.*

sum[1] /sʌm/ noun **B1** an amount of money: *a large sum of money*

sum[2] /sʌm/ verb (present participle **summing**, past tense and past participle **summed**)
sum (something/someone) up phrasal verb to describe briefly the most important facts or details of something: *The book can be summed up as pleasant but not very useful.*

summarize /ˈsʌm·əˌrɑɪz/ verb (present participle **summarizing**, past tense and past participle **summarized**) to describe briefly the main facts or ideas of something: *The report summarizes the main points of the argument.*

summary /ˈsʌm·ə·ri/ noun (plural **summaries**) a short description that gives the main facts or ideas about something: *He gave a brief summary of what happened.*

summer /ˈsʌm·ər/ noun **A1** the warmest season of the year, between spring and fall: *We usually go away in the summer.*

summit /ˈsʌm·ɪt/ noun the top of a mountain: *We hope to reach the summit before night.*

summon /ˈsʌm·ən/ verb formal to officially order someone to come to a place: *He was summoned to a meeting.*

sun /sʌn/ noun [no plural] **1 the sun** the large, bright star that shines in the sky during the day and gives light and heat to the Earth **A1** the light and heat that comes from the sun: *I can't sit in the sun for too long.*

sunbathe /ˈsʌnˌbeɪð/ verb (present participle **sunbathing**, past tense and past participle **sunbathed**) **B1** to sit or lie in the sun so that your skin becomes darker
• **sunbathing** noun [no plural]

sunburn /ˈsʌnˌbɜrn/ noun [no plural] painful, red skin that you get from being in the sun too long

• **sunburned** adj *I got sunburned when I fell asleep in the sun.*

Sunday /'sʌn·deɪ/ noun **A1** the day of the week after Saturday and before Monday

sung /sʌŋ/ the past participle of sing

sunglasses /'sʌnˌɡlæs·ɪz/ plural noun **A2** dark glasses that you wear to protect your eyes from the sun
→ See **Clothes** on page C5

sunk /sʌŋk/ past participle of sink

sunlight /'sʌn·laɪt/ noun [no plural] the light from the sun

sunny /'sʌn·i/ adj (comparative **sunnier**, superlative **sunniest**) **A2** bright because of light from the sun: *a lovely sunny day*

sunrise /'sʌn·raɪz/ noun **B1** the time when the sun appears in the morning and the sky becomes light

sunscreen /'sʌnˌskrin/ noun a substance that protects your skin in the sun

sunset /'sʌnˌset/ noun **B1** the time when the sun disappears in the evening and the sky becomes dark

sunshine /'sʌnˌʃaɪn/ noun [no plural] **B1** the light from the sun: *Let's sit over there in the sunshine.*

suntan /'sʌnˌtæn/ noun (also **tan**) darkened skin you get from being in the sun: *suntan oil*
• **suntanned** adj (also **tanned**)

super[1] /'su·pər/ adj, adv informal very good: *We had a super time.*

super[2] /'su·pər/ noun short form of supervisor: someone whose job is to take care of an apartment building

superb /sʊ'pɜrb/ adj excellent: *a superb restaurant*

superior /sʊ'pɪər·i·ər/ adj better than other things: *This car is far superior to the others.*
→ Opposite **inferior** adj

superlative /sʊ'pɜr·lə·t̬ɪv/ noun **A2** the form of an adjective or adverb that is used to show that someone or

something has more of a particular quality than anyone or anything else. For example "best" is the superlative of "good" and "slowest" is the superlative of "slow."

supermarket /'su·pərˌmar·kɪt/ noun **A1** a large store that sells food, drinks, things for the home, etc.

supernatural /ˌsu·pər'nætʃ·ər·əl/ adj Supernatural events cannot be explained by science: *People thought that cats had supernatural powers.*

superstition /ˌsu·pər'stɪʃ·ən/ noun a belief that particular actions or objects are lucky or unlucky

supervise /'su·pərˌvaɪz/ verb (present participle **supervising**, past tense and past participle **supervised**) to watch a person or activity and make certain that everything is done correctly, safely, etc.: *Students must be supervised by a teacher at all times.*

supervision /ˌsu·pər'vɪʒ·ən/ noun [no plural] the act of watching a person or activity to make certain that everything is done correctly or safely: *He needs constant supervision.*

supervisor /'su·pərˌvaɪ·zər/ noun someone who supervises

supper /'sʌp·ər/ noun **A2** a meal that you eat in the evening: *What are we having for supper?*

supply[1] /sə'plaɪ/ verb (present participle **supplying**, past tense and past participle **supplied**) to give things that people want or need, often over a long period of time: *This lake **supplies** the whole town **with** water.*

supply[2] /sə'plaɪ/ noun (plural **supplies**) an amount of something that is ready to be used: *a supply of water* ○ *food supplies*

support[1] /sə'pɔrt/ verb **1** **B1** to help and encourage someone, often when he or she is having problems: *My family has always supported me in my career.* **2** **B1** to take care of someone by paying for his or her food, clothes, etc.: *He has four children to support.* **3** to agree with an idea, group, or person: *Do you support the governor's proposal?* **4** to hold the weight of someone or something: *That ladder doesn't look strong enough to support you.* **5** to give encouragement or money to someone or something because you want him, her, or it to succeed: *I think it's important to support local businesses.*

support[2] /səˈpɔrt/ *noun* [no plural]
1 **B1** help or encouragement given to someone when he or she is having problems: *You have my full support if you decide to apply for the job.* **2** **B1** the money someone needs in order to buy food and clothes, and pay for somewhere to live: *He is dependent on his father for support.* **3** agreement with an idea, group, or person: *There's a lot of public support for the new law.*

suppose /səˈpoʊz/ *verb* (present participle **supposing,** past tense and past participle **supposed**) **1** **A2** to think that something is probably true: *I suppose he feels angry with her.* **2** **I suppose (so)** **B1** used to show agreement to something when you do not really want to: *I suppose you're right.* "*Can I come with you?*" "*I suppose so.*" **3** **be supposed to do** *something* **B1** to be expected to do something, especially when this does not happen: *He was supposed to be here by nine.* **4** **be supposed to be** *something* to be expected to be something, especially because of a rule, agreement, etc.: *The children are supposed to be at school by 8 a.m.* **5** **be supposed to be** *something* to be considered by many people to be something: *The scenery is supposed to be fantastic.*

sure[1] /ʃʊər/ *adj* **1** **A2** certain: *I'm sure that he won't mind.* ○ *I'm sure about the second answer.* → Opposite **unsure** adj **2** **make sure (that)** **A2** to take action so that you are certain that something happens, is true, etc.: *Make sure that you close all the windows before you leave.* **3** **for sure** **B1** without any doubts: *I think he's from Korea but don't know for sure.* **4** **be sure of** *something* to be confident that something is true: *He'll*

win this year – I'm sure of it. **5** **be sure of** *yourself* to be confident of your own abilities, qualities, etc.: *She seems a bit more sure of herself since she got a job.*

sure[2] /ʃʊər/ *adv* **A2** used to show agreement: "*Do you want to come swimming with us?*" "*Sure.*"

surely /ˈʃʊərli/ *adv* used to show surprise that something has happened or is going to happen: *Surely he didn't say that, did he?*

surf /sɜrf/ *verb* **1** **surf the Internet/Net/Web** **A2** to look at information on the Internet by moving from one page to another **2** **B1** to ride on a wave in the sea using a special board
• **surfing** *noun* [no plural] **A2** *Let's go surfing this afternoon.*

surface /ˈsɜrfəs/ *noun* **1** the top or outside part of something: *the Earth's surface* ○ *The sun was reflected on the surface of the water.* **2** [no plural] what someone or something seems to be like when you do not know much about him or her: *On the surface, he seemed very pleasant.*

surfboard /ˈsɜrfbɔrd/ *noun* a long piece of wood or plastic that you use to ride on waves in the sea

surfer /ˈsɜrfər/ *noun* someone who surfs

surgeon /ˈsɜrdʒən/ *noun* a doctor who cuts people's bodies and removes or repairs part of them

surgery /ˈsɜrdʒəri/ *noun* [no plural] medical treatment in which a doctor cuts your body open and removes or repairs something: *She has had surgery for the problem.* ○ *heart surgery*

surname /ˈsɜrneɪm/ *noun* the name that you and people in your family all have: *His surname is Walker.*

surprise[1] /sərˈpraɪz/ *noun* **1** **A2** something that you did not expect to happen: *I didn't know that my parents were coming – it was a lovely surprise.* ○ *a surprise party* **2** [no plural] the feeling that you get when something happens that you did not expect: *He agreed to everything, much to my surprise.*

surprise[2] /sərˈpraɪz/ verb (present participle **surprising**, past tense and past participle **surprised**) **B1** to make someone feel surprise: *I didn't tell her I was coming home early – I thought I'd surprise her.*

surprised /sərˈpraɪzd/ adj **A2** feeling surprise because something has happened that you did not expect: *I'm surprised to see you here.* ○ *She wasn't surprised at his decision.*

surprising /sərˈpraɪzɪŋ/ adj **B1** not expected and making someone feel surprised: *That was a surprising decision.*

surprisingly /sərˈpraɪzɪŋli/ adv **B1** used to say that something surprises you: *a surprisingly good meal* ○ *Surprisingly, they accepted our offer.*

surrender /səˈrendər/ verb to stop fighting because you know the other side will win: *Rebel troops are refusing to surrender.*
• **surrender** noun [no plural]

surround /səˈraʊnd/ verb **B1** to be or go everywhere around something or someone: *The house is surrounded by a large yard.* ○ *The police have surrounded the building.*

surrounding /səˈraʊndɪŋ/ adj in a position around something: *a city and its surrounding areas*

surroundings /səˈraʊndɪŋz/ plural noun the place where someone or something is and the things that are in it: *Have you gotten used to your new surroundings?*

survey /ˈsɜrveɪ/ noun an examination of people's opinions or behavior done by asking people questions: *A recent survey showed that 58% of people do not exercise enough.*

survival /sərˈvaɪvəl/ noun [no plural] the state of continuing to live, especially after a dangerous situation: *Flood victims had to fight for survival.*

survive /sərˈvaɪv/ verb (present participle **surviving**, past tense and past participle **survived**) to continue to live after almost dying because of an accident, illness, etc.: *No one survived the plane crash.*

survivor /sərˈvaɪvər/ noun someone who continues to live after almost dying because of an accident, illness, etc.: *Rescuers have given up hope of finding any more survivors.*

suspect[1] /ˈsʌspekt/ noun someone who may have done a crime: *He's a suspect in the murder case.*

suspect[2] /səˈspekt/ verb **1** to think that someone may have done a crime or done something else that is bad: *He was suspected of drug dealing.* **2** to think that something is probably true: *They suspected that he was lying.*

suspend /səˈspend/ verb **1** to stop something from happening for a short time: *The game was suspended because of bad weather.* **2** to hang something from somewhere: *A light bulb was suspended from the ceiling.*

suspenders /səˈspendərz/ plural noun a pair of straps that hold up a pair of pants, which are attached to the waist of the pants and stretch over your shoulders

suspense /səˈspens/ noun [no plural] the feeling of excitement that you have when you are waiting for something to happen: *What's your answer then? Don't keep me in suspense.*

suspicion /səˈspɪʃən/ noun **1** a belief that someone has done something wrong: *They were arrested on suspicion of drug dealing.* **2** an idea that something may be true: *I had a suspicion that he might like her.*

suspicious /səˈspɪʃəs/ adj **1** making you feel that something is wrong or that something bad is happening: *suspicious behavior* ○ *I called police after noticing a suspicious-looking package.* **2** not trusting someone: *Many of them remain suspicious of journalists.*
• **suspiciously** adv *His shoes were suspiciously clean (=the fact that they were clean made me suspicious).*

swallow /ˈswɑloʊ/ verb to move your throat in order to make food or drink go down: *These tablets are too big to swallow.*

swam /swæm/ the past tense of **swim**

swamp /swɒmp/ noun   an area of very wet, soft land

swan /swɒn/ noun   a large, white bird with a long neck that lives on lakes and rivers

swan

swap /swɒp/ verb (present participle **swapping**, past tense and past participle **swapped**)   to give something to someone and get something from them in return: *Would you mind if Dave swapped places with you for a while?*
• swap noun *We'll do a swap.*

sway /sweɪ/ verb   to move slowly from one side to the other: *The trees swayed gently in the wind.*

swear /sweər/ verb (past tense **swore**, past participle **sworn**)   **1** to use rude language about sex, the body, etc.: *He was sent home because he swore at the teacher.* **2** to promise: *I swear I won't tell anyone.*

swear word /ˈsweər ˌwɜrd/ noun   a rude word about sex, the body, etc.

sweat¹ /swet/ verb   to make liquid through your skin because you are hot: *I'd been running and I was sweating.*

sweat² /swet/ noun [no plural]   the liquid that is on your skin when you are hot: *The sweat was running down his face.*

sweater /ˈswet·ər/ noun **A2** a warm piece of clothing that covers the top of your body and is pulled on over your head
→ See **Clothes** on page C5

sweatshirt /ˈswet·ʃɜrt/ noun **B1** a piece of clothing made of soft cotton that covers the top of your body

sweaty /ˈswet·i/ adj (comparative **sweatier**, superlative **sweatiest**)   covered in sweat: *He was hot and sweaty from running.*

sweep /swip/ verb (past tense and past participle **swept**)   **1** to clean the floor using a brush: *I just swept that floor!* **2** to push or carry something with force: *Many trees were swept away in the flood.*

sweet¹ /swit/ adj   **1** **A1** with a taste like sugar: *The sauce was too sweet.* **2** **A2** attractive, often because of being small: *Look*

at that sweet little puppy! **3** **B1** kind: *It was really sweet of you to come.*

sweet² /swit/ noun **A2** a small piece of sweet food; candy: *Sweets are bad for your teeth.*

sweet potato /ˈswit pəˌteɪ·toʊ/ noun   a brown or orange vegetable with yellow or orange flesh that tastes slightly sweet

swell /swel/ verb (past participle **swollen**)   to get bigger: *One side of his face had swollen up where he'd been stung.*

swelling /ˈswel·ɪŋ/ noun   a part of your body that has become bigger because of illness or injury: *The doctor gave me drugs to reduce the swelling in my ankle.*

swept /swept/   past tense and past participle of sweep

swerve /swɜrv/ verb (present participle **swerving**, past tense and past participle **swerved**)   to change direction suddenly, especially when you are driving a car: *He swerved to avoid a cyclist and hit another car.*

swift /swɪft/ adj   happening or moving quickly: *a swift response*
• swiftly adv

swim¹ /swɪm/ verb (present participle **swimming**, past tense **swam**, past participle **swum**) **A1** to move through water by moving your body: *I learned to swim when I was about five years old.*
• swimming noun [no plural] **A2** *I usually go swimming about twice a week.*
→ See **Sports 1** on page C15

swim² /swɪm/ noun **A2** a time when you swim: *I went for a swim before breakfast.*

swimmer /ˈswɪm·ər/ noun   a person who swims: *I'm not a very strong swimmer*

swimming pool /ˈswɪm·ɪŋ ˌpul/ noun **A1** an area of water that has been made for people to swim in

swimming trunks /ˈswɪm·ɪŋ ˌtrʌŋks/ plural noun   a piece of clothing that boys and men wear to go swimming
→ See **Clothes** on page C5

swimsuit /ˈswɪm·sut/ noun   a piece of clothing that girls and women wear to go swimming

swing¹ /swɪŋ/ **verb** (present participle **swinging**, past tense and past participle **swung**) to move smoothly backward and forward, or to make something do this: *She swings her arms when she walks.*

swing² /swɪŋ/ **noun** a chair hanging on two ropes that children sit on and swing backward and forward

switch¹ /swɪtʃ/ **verb** to change from one thing to another: *He just switched jobs.*

switch (something) off phrasal verb
🔵 to turn off a light, television, etc. by using a switch: *Did you switch the computer off?*

switch (something) on phrasal verb
🔵 to turn on a light, television, etc. by using a switch: *Could you switch on the light?*

switch² /swɪtʃ/ **noun** **1** 🔵 a small object that you push up or down with your finger to turn something electrical on or off **2** a change: *There has been a switch in policy.*

swollen¹ /ˈswoʊ·lən/ the past participle of swell

swollen² /ˈswoʊ·lən/ **adj** bigger than usual: *a swollen wrist* ○ *swollen rivers*

sword /sɔrd/ **noun** a weapon with a long, metal blade and a handle, used especially in the past

sword

swore /swɔr/ the past tense of swear

sworn /swɔrn/ the past participle of swear

swum /swʌm/ the past participle of swim

swung /swʌŋ/ past tense and past participle of swing

syllable /ˈsɪl·ə·bəl/ **noun** a word or part of a word that has one vowel sound: *"But" has one syllable and "apple" has two syllables.*

syllabus /ˈsɪl·ə·bəs/ **noun** (plural **syllabuses, syllabi**) a list of the subjects that are included in a course

symbol /ˈsɪm·bəl/ **noun** a sign or object that is used to mean something: *A heart shape is the symbol of love.*

symbolic /sɪmˈbɑl·ɪk/ **adj** representing something else: *The blue in the flag is symbolic of the ocean.*

sympathetic /ˌsɪm·pəˈθet̬·ɪk/ **adj** showing that you understand and care about someone's problems: *My boss is very sympathetic about my situation.*
• **sympathetically adv** *All requests for help will be treated sympathetically.*

> ⚠ **Common mistake:**
> **sympathetic**
>
> Be careful not to use **sympathetic** when you simply want to say that someone is **nice**, **friendly**, or **kind**. Remember that if someone is **sympathetic**, he or she understands your problems.

sympathy /ˈsɪm·pə·θi/ **noun** [no plural] an act of showing that you understand and care about someone's problems: *You have my sympathy – it's horrible having a bad cold.*

symptom /ˈsɪmp·təm/ **noun** a physical feeling or problem that shows that you have a particular illness: *A sleeping problem is often a **symptom of** some other illness.*

synagogue /ˈsɪn·ə·ɡɑɡ/ **noun** a building in which Jewish people pray

synonym /ˈsɪn·ə·nɪm/ **noun** a word that means the same as another word

syringe /səˈrɪndʒ/ **noun** a piece of medical equipment used to push liquid into or take liquid out of someone's body

syringe

syrup /ˈsɪr·əp/ **noun** [no plural] a very sweet liquid made from sugar and water

system /ˈsɪs·təm/ **noun** **1** 🔵 a set of connected pieces of equipment that work together: *We have an alarm system at home.* **2** a way or method of doing things: *the American legal system* ○ *the public transportation system*

Tt

T, t /tiː/ the twentieth letter of the alphabet

table /'teɪ·bəl/ *noun*

table

tablecloth

1 **A1** a piece of furniture with four legs, used for eating at, putting things on, etc.: *The plates are on the table.* ○ *the kitchen table*

→ See **The Living Room** on page C11

2 **B1** an arrangement of facts or numbers in a special order: *The table below shows the results of the experiment.*

3 set the table **B1** to put plates, knives, forks, etc. on the table to prepare for a meal: *Can you set the table for me, please?*

tablecloth /'teɪ·bəl·klɔθ/ *noun* a piece of material that covers a table

table tennis /'teɪ·bəl ˌten·ɪs/ *noun* [no plural] (usually **Ping-Pong**) a game in which two or four people hit a small ball over a low net on a large table

tabloid /'tæb·lɔɪd/ *noun* a small newspaper with a lot of pictures and short, simple news stories

tackle¹ /'tæk·əl/ *verb* (present participle **tackling**, past tense and past participle **tackled**) **1** to try to stop a problem: *We must find new ways to tackle crime.* **2** to try to catch someone or knock someone down, especially in a game like football

tackle² /'tæk·əl/ *noun* an attempt to catch someone or knock someone down, especially in a game like football

tacky /'tæk·i/ *adj* (comparative **tackier**, superlative **tackiest**) informal cheap and of bad quality: *tacky souvenirs*

tact /tækt/ *noun* [no plural] the ability to talk to people about difficult subjects without upsetting them

tactful /'tækt·fəl/ *adj* careful not to say or do anything that could upset someone

tactless /'tækt·ləs/ *adj* not being careful about saying or doing something that could upset someone

tag /tæg/ *noun* a small piece of paper or plastic with information on it that is fastened to something: *a price tag*

tail /teɪl/ *noun* the long, narrow part that sticks out from the back of an animal's body: *The dog is happy to see you – he's **wagging** his tail.*

tail

tail light /'teɪl ˌlaɪt/ *noun* either of the two red lights on the back of a vehicle

→ See **Car** on page C3

tailpipe /'teɪl·paɪp/ *noun* the pipe at the end of a vehicle that carries gases away from the engine

→ See **Car** on page C3

take /teɪk/ *verb* (present participle **taking**, past tense **took**, past participle **taken**) **1** **A1** to get and carry something with you when you go somewhere: *I always **take** an umbrella **with** me.* **2** **A1** to go somewhere with someone, often paying for that person: *We're **taking** the kids **to** the circus on Saturday.* **3 take a picture, photograph, etc.** **A1** to photograph someone or something: *I took some great pictures of the kids.* **4** **A2** to travel somewhere by using a bus, train, car, etc.: *He takes the bus to work.* **5** **A2** used to tell someone which road to go on or which turn to take in order to get somewhere: *Take State St. down the hill to the traffic light.* **6** **A2** to do an exam or test: *When are you taking your driving test?* **7** **A2** If something takes a particular amount of time, or a particular quality, you need that amount of time or that quality in order to be able to do it: *It took me three days to get here.* **8** **A2** to swallow or use medicine: *Take two pills, three times a day.* **9** **B1** to remove something without asking someone: *someone took my coat!* **10** **B1** to get hold of something and move it: *He reached across and took the glass from her.* **11** **B1** used with some nouns to say that someone performs an action: *I need to take a shower.*

○ *Take a look at this.* **12** 🇬🇧 to study a subject: *He's taking chemistry and physics.* **13** 🇬🇧 to accept something: *So, are you going to take the job?* **14 take care of** *someone/something* 🇬🇧 to care for someone or something: *Don't worry, I can take care of myself.* **15 take it easy** 🇬🇧 to relax and not use too much energy: *You'll need to take it easy after your surgery.* **16 take advantage of** *something* 🇬🇧 to use something good in a situation to help you: *You should take advantage of the student discount on movie tickets.*

take *something* **away** phrasal verb
1 🇬🇧 to remove one number from another number: *If you take 4 away from 12 you get 8.* **2** to remove something: *A waiter came to take our plates away.*

take *something* **back** phrasal verb 🇬🇧 to return something to the place where you got it: *Did you take those books back to the library?*

take *something* **off** phrasal verb 🇦🇺 to remove something: *If you're hot, take your jacket off.*
→ See **Phrasal Verbs** on page C13

take off phrasal verb 🇦🇺 If a plane takes off, it begins to fly.

take *someone* **out** phrasal verb 🇬🇧 to go somewhere with someone and pay for that person: *Our boss took us out for lunch.*

take *something* **out** phrasal verb
1 🇬🇧 to remove something from somewhere: *He reached into his bag and took out a book.* **2** 🇬🇧 to buy food in a restaurant to eat somewhere else: *Is that to eat here or take out?*

take *something* **up** phrasal verb **1** 🇬🇧 to start doing a particular job or activity: *I've taken up knitting.* **2** to fill an amount of space or time: *This desk takes up too much room.* ○ *My children take up most of my time.*

takeoff /ˈteɪk.ɒf/ noun the moment when a plane leaves the ground and begins to fly

takeout /ˈteɪk.aʊt/ noun [no plural] a meal that you buy in a restaurant but eat elsewhere

tale /teɪl/ noun a story about exciting events, sometimes one that is not true:

My grandfather told us tales about his time as a pilot in the war.

talent /ˈtæl.ənt/ noun 🇬🇧 a natural ability to do something: *She showed an early talent for drawing.*

talented /ˈtæl.ən.tɪd/ adj 🇬🇧 showing natural ability in a particular area: *a talented young musician*

talk[1] /tɔːk/ verb 🇬🇧 to say things to someone: *We were just talking about Jack's new girlfriend.* ○ *I was talking to Adam.*

> **⚠ Common mistake: talk about or talk of?**
>
> After **talk** we normally use **about**.
> *We talked about politics.*
> ~~We talked of politics.~~

talk[2] /tɔːk/ noun **1** 🇬🇧 a conversation about a particular subject: *I had a long talk with Chris about going to college.* **2** a speech to a group of people about a particular subject: *She gave a talk about Internet safety at the school.*

talkative /ˈtɔː.kə.tɪv/ adj A talkative person talks a lot.

talk show /ˈtɔːk ʃoʊ/ noun a television or radio program in which people are asked questions about themselves: *I saw her on a talk show last week.*

tall /tɔːl/ adj **1** 🇦🇺 being higher than most other people or things: *He's tall and thin.* ○ *It's one of the tallest buildings in the city.* → Opposite **short** adj **2** 🇦🇺 used to describe or ask how high someone or something is: *How tall is she?* ○ *He's almost 6 feet tall.*

the Talmud /ˈtæl.mʊd/ noun the collection of Jewish laws and traditions relating to religious and social matters

tame[1] /teɪm/ adj If an animal is tame, it is not wild and not frightened of people.

tame[2] /teɪm/ verb (present participle **taming**, past tense and past participle **tamed**) to make a wild animal tame

tan /tæn/ noun (also **suntan**) brown skin you get from being in the sun

tangerine /ˌtæn·dʒəˈrin/ *noun* a fruit like a small orange

tangled /ˈtæŋ·ɡəld/ *adj* (also **tangled up**) twisted together in a messy way: *The wires are all tangled.*

tank /tæŋk/ *noun* **1** a large container for keeping liquid or gas: *a water tank* **2** a large, strong military vehicle with a gun on it

tanker /ˈtæŋ·kər/ *noun* a ship or truck used to carry large amounts of liquid or gas: *an oil tanker*

tank top /ˈtæŋk ˌtɑp/ *noun* a light shirt with no sleeves and a curved neck, often worn under another shirt
→ See **Clothes** on page C5

tap /tæp/ *verb* (present participle **tapping**, past tense and past participle **tapped**) to hit or touch something gently: *I tapped her on the shoulder to get her attention.*

tape¹ /teɪp/ *noun* **1** a long, thin piece of plastic that is used to store sound, pictures, or information, or a plastic box containing it: *I've got the game on tape.* **2** [no plural] a thin piece of plastic that has glue on one side and is used for sticking things together: *clear tape*
→ See **The Classroom** on page C4

tape² /teɪp/ *verb* (present participle **taping**, past tense and past participle **taped**) **1** to record something onto tape: *Their conversations were taped by the police.* **2** to stick something somewhere using tape

tape measure /ˈteɪp ˌmeʒ·ər/ *noun* a long, thin piece of cloth or metal used to measure length

tar /tɑr/ *noun* [no plural] a thick, black substance that is sticky when hot and is used to cover roads

target /ˈtɑr·ɡɪt/ *noun* **1** something or someone that you attack, shoot at, try to hit, etc.: *It's very difficult to hit a moving target.* **2** something that you are trying to do: *I'm hoping to save $3,000 by June – that's my target.*

tart /tɑrt/ *noun* a small pastry with a sweet, often fruit filling and usually no top: *a berry tart*

tartan /ˈtɑr·tᵊn/ *noun* cloth with a pattern of different colored squares and crossing lines

task /tæsk/ *noun* a piece of work, especially something unpleasant: *Our first task is to clean off these shelves.*

taste¹ /teɪst/ *noun* **1** 🅱1 the flavor of a particular food in your mouth: *a bitter taste* ○ *It has a very strong taste.* **2** [no plural] the ability to feel different flavors in your mouth: *When you have a cold you often lose your sense of taste.* **3** the particular things you like, such as styles of music, clothes, decoration, etc.: *I don't like his taste in music.*

taste² /teɪst/ *verb* (present participle **tasting**, past tense and past participle **tasted**) **1** taste funny, good, sweet, etc. 🅱1 If food tastes a particular way, it has that flavor: *This sauce tastes strange.* **2** 🅱1 to put food or drink in your mouth to find out what its flavor is like: *I always taste food while I'm cooking it.*

tasty /ˈteɪ·sti/ *adj* (comparative **tastier**, superlative **tastiest**) 🅱1 Food that is tasty has a nice flavor and is good to eat.

tattoo /tæˈtu/ *noun* a picture on someone's skin that is put on using ink and a needle

tattoo

taught /tɔt/ past tense and past participle of teach

tax /tæks/ *noun* 🅱1 money that you have to pay to the government from what you earn or when you buy things: *They're raising the tax on cigarettes.*

taxi /ˈtæk·si/ *noun* 🅰1 a car with a driver whom you pay to take you somewhere: *I'll take a taxi to the airport.*

taxi stand /ˈtæk·si ˌstænd/ *noun* a place where you can go to get a taxi

tea /ti/ *noun* 🅰1 a hot drink that you make by pouring water onto dried leaves: *Would you like a cup of tea or coffee?*

teabag /ˈti·bæg/ *noun* a small paper bag with dried leaves inside, used for making tea

teach /tiːtʃ/ verb (past tense and past participle **taught**) **1** 🅐🅘 to give classes in a particular subject at a school, university, etc.: *He teaches history.* **2** 🅐🅩 to show or explain to someone how to do something: *My dad taught me to drive.* **3** 🅑🅘 If a situation teaches you something, it gives you new knowledge or helps you to understand something: *The experience taught him to be more careful.*

teacher /'tiː·tʃər/ noun 🅐🅘 someone whose job is to teach in a school, college, etc.: *a science teacher*
→ See **The Classroom** on page C4

teaching /'tiː·tʃ·ɪŋ/ noun [no plural] 🅑🅘 the job of being a teacher: *He decided to go into teaching (= become a teacher).*

team /tiːm/ noun **1** 🅐🅩 a group of people who play a sport or game together: *a football team* **2** 🅑🅘 a group of people who work together to do something: *a management team*

teapot /'tiː·pɑt/ noun a container used for making and serving tea
→ See **The Kitchen** on page C10

tear¹ /teər/ verb (present participle **tearing**, past tense **tore**, past participle **torn**) **1** 🅑🅘 to pull paper, cloth, etc. into pieces, or to make a hole in it by accident: *The nail tore a hole in my skirt.* **2 be torn between** *something* and *something* to be unable to decide between two choices: *I'm torn between the apple pie and the chocolate cookie.*

tear

tear *something* **up** phrasal verb to tear something into a lot of small pieces: *He tore up her photograph.*

tear² /teər/ noun a hole in a piece of cloth, paper, etc. where it has been torn

tear³ /tɪər/ noun 🅑🅘 a drop of water that comes from your eye when you cry: *I was in tears (= crying) by the end of the movie.* ○ *She burst into tears (= started crying) when she heard the news.*

tease /tiːz/ verb (present participle **teasing**, past tense and past participle **teased**) to laugh at someone or say bad things to someone: *They were teasing Dara about her new haircut.*

teaspoon /'tiː·spuːn/ noun a small spoon that is used for mixing drinks and measuring small amounts of food

technical /'tek·nɪ·kəl/ adj **1** relating to the knowledge, machines, or methods used in science and industry: *We're having a few technical problems.* **2** relating to practical skills and methods that are used in a particular activity: *As a dancer she had great technical skill.*

technician /tek'nɪʃ·ən/ noun someone whose job involves practical work with scientific or electrical equipment: *a computer technician*

technique /tek'niːk/ noun 🅑🅘 a particular way of doing something: *It's a new technique for taking blood samples.*

technological /ˌtek·nə'lɑdʒ·ɪ·kəl/ adj relating to or involving technology: *technological developments*

technology /tek'nɑl·ə·dʒi/ noun [no plural] 🅑🅘 knowledge, equipment, and methods that are used in science and industry: *computer technology*

teddy bear /'ted·i ˌbeər/ noun a soft toy bear

tedious /'tiː·di·əs/ adj boring: *a tedious job*

teenage /'tiːnˌeɪdʒ/ adj 🅑🅘 aged between 13 and 19, or right for people of that age: *a teenage daughter* ○ *teenage magazines*

teenager /'tiːnˌeɪ·dʒər/ noun 🅐🅩 someone who is between 13 and 19 years old

teens /tiːnz/ noun [plural] **be in your teens** to be aged between 13 and 19: *Her youngest daughter is still in her teens.*

teeth /tiːθ/ plural of **teeth** **tooth**

telephone¹ /'tel·əˌfoʊn/ noun (also **phone**) 🅐🅩 a piece of equipment that is used

a
b
c
d
e
f
g
h
i
j
k
l
m
n
o
p
q
r
s
t
u
v
w
x
y
z

to talk to someone who is in another place: The **telephone rang** and she hurried to pick it up. ○ Could you **answer the telephone**?

telephone[2] /ˈtel·əˌfoʊn/ verb (present participle **telephoning**, past tense and past participle **telephoned**) (also **phone**) formal **A2** to speak to someone by telephone

telescope /ˈtel·əˌskoʊp/ noun a piece of equipment in the shape of a tube, used to make things that are far away look bigger

telescope

television /ˈtel·əˌvɪʒ·ən/ noun (also **TV**) **1 A1** a piece of equipment in the shape of a box with a screen on the front, used for watching programs: Richard turned the television on. **2 A1** [no plural] the programs that are shown on a television: I mostly **watch television** in the evening. **3 B1** [no plural] the system or business of making and broadcasting programs for television: a television channel/network

tell /tel/ verb (past tense and past participle **told**) **1 A1** to say something to someone, usually giving them new information: He **told** me **about** his new school. **2 tell** someone **to do** something **A2** to order someone to do something: I told you to stay here. **3 can tell** to know something from what you hear, see, etc.: You could tell that he was tired.
tell someone **off** phrasal verb to tell someone that the person has done something wrong and that you are angry about it: Darren **got told off** for talking in class.
→ See **Phrasal Verbs** on page C13

teller /ˈtel·ər/ noun someone who works at a bank and helps customers put money in or take money out

temper /ˈtem·pər/ noun **1** If a person has a temper, he or she becomes angry very easily: He has a really **bad temper**. **2 lose your temper (with** someone**)** to suddenly become angry: I lost my temper with the kids this morning.

temperature /ˈtem·pər·ə·tʃər/ noun **1 A2** how hot or cold something is: Last

night the temperature dropped to below freezing. **2 have a temperature A2** to be hotter than usual because you are ill

temple /ˈtem·pəl/ noun **B1** a building where people in some religions go to pray: a Buddhist temple

temporary /ˈtem·pəˌrer·i/ adj **B1** existing or happening for only a short time: a temporary job
• **temporarily** adv

tempt /tempt/ verb to make someone want to have or do something that he or she should not: Can I tempt you to go shopping?

temptation /tempˈteɪ·ʃən/ noun a feeling that you want to do or have something, although you know you should not

ten[1] /ten/ **A1** the number 10

ten[2] /ten/ noun a ten-dollar bill: Could I borrow a ten?

tenant /ˈten·ənt/ noun someone who pays money to live in a room, house, etc.

tend /tend/ verb **tend to do** something to often do a particular thing: I tend to wear dark colors.

tendency /ˈten·dən·si/ noun (plural **tendencies**) something that someone often does, or something that often happens: She **has a tendency** to talk for too long.

tender /ˈten·dər/ adj **1** kind and gentle: a tender kiss **2** Tender meat or vegetables are soft and easy to cut.
• **tenderly** adv He kissed her tenderly on the cheek.
• **tenderness** noun [no plural]

tennis /ˈten·ɪs/ noun [no plural] **A1** a sport in which two or four people hit a small ball to each other over a net: a tennis ball
→ See picture at **ball**
→ See **Sports 2** on page C16

tennis shoe /ˈten·ɪs ˌʃu/ noun a soft sports shoe
→ See **Clothes** on page C5

tense[1] /tens/ adj **1** nervous and not able to relax: The students looked tense as they *waited for their test scores.* **2** A tense situation makes you feel nervous.

tense² /tens/ *noun* **B1** in grammar, the form of a verb that shows the time at which an action happened. For example, "I sing" is in the present tense and "I sang" is in the past tense.

tension /'ten·ʃən/ *noun* **1** a feeling of fear or anger between people or countries who do not trust each other: *There are increasing* **tensions between** *the two countries.* **2** [no plural] a feeling that you are nervous, worried, and not relaxed: *You could feel the tension in the room as we waited for our test scores.*

tent /tent/ *noun*
B1 a structure for sleeping in made of cloth attached to metal poles: *It only took twenty minutes to* **put the tent up** (= make it ready to use).

 tent

tenth¹ /tenθ/ 10th written as a word

tenth² /tenθ/ *noun* one of ten equal parts of something; 1/10; 0.1

term /tɜrm/ *noun* **1** **B2** a word or phrase that is used to mean a particular thing: *a* **legal/scientific/medical** *term* **2** a fixed period of time: *a prison term* ○ *Senators serve a six-year term.* **3** **A2** one of the periods of time that a school or college year is divided into: *The fall term starts September 7.* **4** **in the short/long term** over a period of time that continues for a short time or a long time into the future: *In the short term we do not expect an improvement in sales.*

terminal /'tɜr·mə·nᵊl/ *noun* a building where you can get onto an plane, bus, or ship

terms /tɜrmz/ *plural noun* **1** the rules of an agreement **2** **in…terms** used to explain which part of a situation you mean: *In financial terms, the project was not a success.* **3** **come to terms with something** to accept a sad situation: *He still hasn't come to terms with his brother's death.*

terrace /'ter·əs/ *noun* a flat area outside a house, restaurant, etc. where you can sit

terrible /'ter·ə·bəl/ *adj* **A2** very bad: *a terrible accident* ○ *The weather was terrible.*

terribly /'ter·ə·bli/ *adv* **1** **B1** very: *She was terribly upset.* **2** very badly: *I slept terribly last night.*

terrific /tə'rɪf·ɪk/ *adj* **B1** excellent: *I thought she looked terrific.*

terrified /'ter·ə·faɪd/ *adj* **B1** very frightened: *I'm* **terrified of** *flying.*

terrify /'ter·ə·faɪ/ *verb* to make someone feel very frightened: *Snakes terrify me.*

terrifying /'ter·ə·faɪ·ɪŋ/ *adj* very frightening: *It was a terrifying experience.*

territory /'ter·ə·tɔr·i/ *noun* (plural **territories**) **1** land that is owned or controlled by a particular country: *Canadian territory* **2** an area that an animal or person thinks belongs to him or her: *Cats like to protect their territory.*

terror /'ter·ər/ *noun* [no plural] a feeling of being very frightened

terrorism /'ter·ə,rɪz·əm/ *noun* [no plural] the use of violence for political purposes, for example putting bombs in public places: *an act of terrorism*

terrorist /'ter·ə·rɪst/ *noun* someone who is involved in terrorism: *a terrorist attack*

test¹ /test/ *noun* **1** **A1** a set of questions to find out how much someone knows or how well someone can do something: *a driving test* ○ *You have to* **take a test.** **2** **B1** a short medical examination of part of your body or of something such as blood that is taken from your body: *a blood test* ○ *The doctors have done some tests to find out what's wrong with her.*

test² /test/ *verb* **1** **B1** to give someone a set of questions in order to find out how much the person knows or how well the person can do something: *You'll be* **tested on** *all the subjects we've studied this term.* **2** to do a medical examination of part of someone's body: *I'm going to get my hearing tested.*

a
b
c
d
e
f
g
h
i
j
k
l
m
n
o
p
q
r
s
t
u
v
w
x
y
z

testify /ˈtes.tə.faɪ/ **verb** (present participle **testifying**, past tense and past participle **testified**) to give information and answer questions in a court of law: *The victim didn't testify at the trial.* ○ *The baseball player testified that he had used drugs.*

testimony /ˈtes.tə.moʊ.ni/ **noun** (plural **testimonies**) a statement that something is true, given in a court of law: *In her testimony, the victim described the attack.* ○ *The jury heard testimony for nearly three months.*

text[1] /tekst/ **noun 1** **A2** a message in writing sent from one cell phone to another: *I sent her a text.* **2** **B1** [no plural] the written words in a book, magazine, etc., not the pictures: *a page of text*

text[2] /tekst/ **verb** **A2** to send a text from a cell phone: *Text me when you get there.*

textbook /ˈtekst.bʊk/ **noun** **A2** a book about a particular subject, written for students: *a chemistry textbook*
→ See **The Classroom** on page C4

text message /ˈtekst ˌmes.ɪdʒ/ **noun** **A2** a message in writing sent from one cell phone to another

texture /ˈteks.tʃər/ **noun** the way that something feels when you touch it: *wood with a rough texture*

than /ðæn/ **preposition, conjunction** **A1** used to compare two different things or amounts: *Susannah's car is bigger than mine.* ○ *It cost less than I expected.*

> **⚠ Common mistake: than or then?**
>
> **Warning:** Choose the right word!
> These two words look similar, but they are spelled differently and have completely different meanings.
> To talk about a particular time or about what happened next, don't say **than**, say **then**.
> ~~I did the dishes and than I went to bed.~~
> *I did the dishes and then I went to bed.*

thank /θæŋk/ **verb** **A2** to tell someone that you are happy about something he or she has given you or done for you: *I need to thank her for her present.*

thanks /θæŋks/ **exclamation** informal **1** **A1** used to tell someone that you are happy about something he or she has given you or done for you: *Can you pass me the book? Thanks very much.* ○ *Thanks for all your help.* **2** no, thanks **A2** used to refuse someone's offer: *"Would you like a cup of coffee?" "No, thanks."*

thank you[1] /ˈθæŋk ju/ **exclamation 1** **A1** used to tell someone that you are happy about something he or she has given you or done for you: *Thank you very much for the birthday card.* ○ *"I can babysit on Friday." "Oh, thank you!"* **2** no, thank you **A2** used to politely refuse someone's offer: *"Would you like something to eat?" "No, thank you."*

thank you[2] /ˈθæŋk ju/ **noun** **B1** something that you say or do in order to show that you are happy that someone has done something for you or given you something: *I'd like to say a big thank you to everyone for all your help.* ○ *a thank-you letter*

that[1] /ðæt/ **determiner 1** **A1** used to mean something or someone that has already been talked about or seen: *Did you see that woman in the post office?* ○ *How much is that dress?* **2** **A1** used to mean something or someone that is not near you: *Have you seen that man over there?*

that[2] /ðæt/ **pronoun 1** **A1** used to mean something that has already been talked about or seen: *That looks heavy.* **2** **A1** used to mean something that is not near you: *What's that in the corner?* **3** **A2** used to make a connection with an earlier statement: *My train was cancelled. That's why I'm late.* **4** that's it used to say that something is correct: *You need to push the two pieces together. That's it.*

> **⚠ Common mistake: that's**
>
> Remember that **that's** is always written with an apostrophe.

that³ /ðæt/ **conjunction 1 A2** used after some verbs, nouns, and adjectives to start a new part of a sentence: *He said that he'd collect it later.* **2 B1** used instead of "who" or "which" in the middle of a sentence: *Have you eaten all the cake that I made yesterday?*

thaw /θɔ/ **verb** to become warmer and softer or change to liquid: *Allow the meat to thaw before cooking it.*

the /ðə/, /ði/ **determiner 1 A1** used before nouns to mean things or people that have already been talked about or are already known: *Please pass the salt.* ○ *I'll pick you up at the station.* **2 A1** used before nouns when only one of something exists: *the Eiffel Tower* ○ *the world* **3** used before some adjectives to make them into nouns: *a home for the elderly* **4** used before numbers that refer to dates: *Thursday the 29th of April*

theater /'θi·ə·t̬ər/ **noun 1 A2** a building with a stage where people go to watch plays and shows: *the Apollo Theater* **2** (also **movie theater**) a building where people go to watch movies

theft /θeft/ **noun** the action or crime of stealing something: *car theft*

their /ðeər/ **determiner A1** belonging to or relating to them: *It was their problem, not mine.*

theirs /ðeərz/ **pronoun A2** the things that belong or relate to them: *I think she's a friend of theirs.*

them /ðem/ **pronoun A1** the group of people, animals, or things that have already been talked about: *I'm looking for my keys – have you seen them?*

theme /θim/ **noun** the subject of a book, movie, speech, etc.: *"Good versus evil" is a common theme in his stories.*

theme park /'θim ˌpɑrk/ **noun** a park with different types of entertainment, such as machines to ride on, that is often based on one idea

themselves /ðəm'selvz/, /ˌðem'selvz/ **pronoun 1 A2** used to show that the people who do the action are also the

people who are affected by it: *They were enjoying themselves at the party.* **2** (all) **by themselves A2** alone or without anyone else's help: *The kids made breakfast all by themselves.* **3** used to give more attention to the word "them": *They paid for the wedding themselves.*

then /ðen/ **adv 1 A1** at that time: *Call me tomorrow – we'll talk about it then.* **2 A1** next, or after something has happened: *Add the eggs, then mix until smooth.* **3 A2** so or because of that: *Take a nap now, then you won't be tired this evening.*

theory /'θɪər·i/ **noun** (plural **theories**) an idea or set of ideas that explains something: *Darwin's theory of evolution*

therapy /'θer·ə·pi/ **noun** (plural **therapies**) the treatment of mental or physical illness without using an operation: *He's in therapy* (= being treated) *for depression.*

there¹ /ðeər/ **pronoun there is, are, was, etc. A1** used to show that something exists or happens: *There are three schools in the town.* ○ *Is there any milk?*

there² /ðeər/ **adv 1 A1** in or at a particular place: *We live in Dallas because my wife works there.* **2 A1** used when you are pointing at something in order to make someone look somewhere: *My car is there, next to the red one.* **3 A2** used when you are giving something to someone: *There is your boarding pass – have a good trip.* ○ *"Can I have a pen?" "There you are."*

therefore /'ðeər.fɔr/ **adv B1** for that reason: *She is under 18 and therefore cannot vote this year.*

thermometer /θər'mɑm·ɪ·t̬ər/ **noun** a piece of equipment that shows how hot or cold something is

thermometer

Thermos /'θɜr·məs/ **noun** trademark a special container that keeps drinks or other liquids hot or cold: *a Thermos of coffee*

Thermos

| æ cat | ɑ hot | e get | ɪ sit | i see | ɔ saw | ʊ book | u too | ʌ cut | ə about | ər mother | ɜr turn | ɔr for | ɑɪ my | ɑʊ how | eɪ say | ɔɪ boy |

these /ðiz/ **pronoun, determiner**
A1 plural of this: *Are these your sunglasses?* ○ *Take these dishes to the kitchen, please.*

thesis /ˈθiːsɪs/ **noun** (plural **theses**) a long piece of writing that you do as part of a college degree (=course of study): *I wrote my thesis on Spanish literature.*

they /ðeɪ/ **pronoun**   **1 A1** used as the subject of the verb when meaning a group of people, animals, or things that have already been talked about: *I saw Kate and Nick yesterday – they came over for dinner.*   **2 B1** used to refer to a person when you want to avoid saying "he" or "she" or when you do not know if the person is male or female: *If anybody comes, they can wait in the hall.*   **3** people in general: *They say that money can't buy happiness.*

they'd /ðeɪd/   **1** short form of they had: *They'd just left when I arrived.*   **2** short form of they would: *They'd like to take us out to dinner.*

they'll /ðeɪl/   short form of they will: *They'll be in Miami next week.*

they're /ðeər/   short form of they are: *They're both from Washington.*

they've /ðeɪv/   short form of they have: *They've been waiting for you.*

thick /θɪk/ **adj**   **thick**
1 B1 Something that is thick is larger than usual between its opposite sides: *a thick layer of snow*
→ Opposite **thin adj**
2 10 inches, 2 feet, etc.
thick being 10 inches, 2 feet, etc. thick: *a piece of wood 6 in. thick.*   **3** growing very close together and in large amounts: *thick, dark hair*   **4** Thick smoke, cloud, or fog is difficult to see through: *Thick black smoke was pouring out of the chimney.*

thief /θif/ **noun** (plural **thieves**)   **B1** someone who steals things: *a car thief*

thigh /θaɪ/ **noun**   the top part of your leg above your knee
→ See **The Body** on page C2

thin /θɪn/ **adj** (comparative **thinner**, superlative **thinnest**)   **1 A2** Something that is thin is smaller than usual between its opposite sides: *a thin slice of meat* → See picture at **thick adj** → Opposite **thick adj**   **2 A2** A thin person or animal has very little fat on his or her body.   **3** A thin substance or liquid has a lot of water in it: *thin soup*

thing /θɪŋ/ **noun**   **1 A1** used to mean an object without saying its name: *I need to get a few things at the supermarket.*   **2 A2** a fact about or characteristic of someone or something: *The best thing about the wedding was the food.*   **3 a thing** **B1** used instead of "anything" in order to emphasize what you are saying: *I don't have a thing to wear.*   **4** used to refer to an idea or comment: *I just want to forget the whole thing.*   **5** used to refer to an activity or event: *Meeting Nina was the best thing that's ever happened to me.*   **6 thing to do/say** something that is done or said: *What a silly thing to do.*

things /θɪŋz/ **plural noun**   **1 A1** the objects that you own: *I'll just get my things and then I'll be ready.*   **2 B1** what is happening, especially in your life: *How are things with you?*

think /θɪŋk/ **verb** (past tense and past participle **thought**)   **1 A1** to believe that something is true, or to expect that something will happen, although you are not sure: *I think we've met before.* ○ *Do you think it's going to rain?*   **2 A1** to have an opinion about something or someone: *What did you think of the show?*   **3 B1** to use the brain to plan something, solve a problem, understand a situation, etc.: *He thought for a few seconds before answering.*

think about/of *someone/something* **phrasal verb 1 A2** to consider doing something: *I'm thinking of moving to San Francisco.*   **2 B1** to remember someone or something: *I was just thinking about you when you called.*

think *something* **over phrasal verb** to consider an idea or plan carefully before making a decision: *I'll think it over and give you an answer next week.*

think *something* **through** phrasal verb to carefully consider the possible results of doing something: *It sounds like a good idea, but we need to think it through.*

> ⚠ **Common mistake: think about** or **think of?**
>
> **Think about** someone/something means to have thoughts in your mind about a person or thing, or to consider something.
> *I was thinking about my mother.*
> ~~I thought the question before answering.~~
> *I thought about the question before answering.*
> **Think of/about** something/someone also means to have an opinion about something or someone.
> *What do you think of/about the color?*
> ~~What do you think the color?~~
> **Think of doing something** means to consider the possibility of doing something.
> *We are thinking of having a party.*
> ~~We are thinking to have a party.~~

third¹ /θɜrd/ **A2** 3rd written as a word

third² /θɜrd/ noun one of three equal parts of something; 1/3

the third person /ˈθɜrd ˈpɜr·sən/ noun [no plural] the form of a verb or pronoun that is used when referring to the person or thing being spoken about or described: *"She" is a third-person pronoun.*

thirst /θɜrst/ noun [no plural] the feeling that you want to drink something

thirsty /ˈθɜr·sti/ adj (comparative **thirstier**, superlative **thirstiest**) **A2** wanting or needing a drink: *I felt really hot and thirsty after my run.*

thirteen /ˈθɜrˈtin/ **A1** the number 13

thirteenth /ˈθɜrˈtinθ/ 13th written as a word

thirties /ˈθɜr·tiz/ plural noun **1** the thirties the years from 1930 to 1939: *Our house was built in the thirties.* **2** be in your thirties to be aged between 30 and 39: *My brother is in his thirties.*

thirty /ˈθɜr·ti/ **A2** the number 30
• **thirtieth** 30th written as a word

this¹ /ðɪs/ determiner **1** **A1** used to mean something that you have already talked about: *Most people don't agree with this decision.* **2** **A1** used to mean something or someone that is near you or that you are pointing to: *How much does this CD cost?* **3** **A1** used to mean the present week, month, year, etc. or the one that comes next: *I'll see you this evening.*

this² /ðɪs/ pronoun **1** **A2** used to mean something that you have already talked about: *When did this happen?* **2** **A2** used to mean someone or something that is near you or that you are pointing to: *This is my girlfriend, Beth.* **3** **A2** used to refer to something that is happening or something that you are doing: *This is how you prepare the fish.*

> ⚠ **Common mistake: this/that** or **these/those?**
>
> Remember **this** and **that** are used before a singular noun. **These** and **those** are used before a plural noun.
> *Look at this photo.*
> *Look at these photos.*
> *Can you pass me that book, please?*
> *Can you pass me those books, please?*

thorn /θɔrn/ noun a small, sharp point on the stem of a plant

thorough /ˈθɜr·oʊ/, /ˈθʌr·oʊ/ adj careful and covering every detail: *The police did a thorough investigation of the crime.*

thoroughly /ˈθɜr·ə·li/, /ˈθʌr·ə·li/ adv **1** very carefully: *Wash the fruit thoroughly.* **2** very, or very much: *We thoroughly enjoyed ourselves.*

those /ðoʊz/ pronoun, determiner **A1** plural of that: *These apples look much nicer than those.* ∘ *I want those shoes.*

though¹ /ðoʊ/ conjunction **1** **B1** used before a fact or opinion that makes the other part of the sentence surprising: *Though she's small, she's really strong.*

a
b
c
d
e
f
g
h
i
j
k
l
m
n
o
p
q
r
s
t
u
v
w
x
y
z

a
b
c
d
e
f
g
h
i
j
k
l
m
n
o
p
q
r
s
t
u
v
w
x
y
z

○ *Natasha didn't call, **even though** she said she would.* **2** but: *They're coming next week, though I don't know when.*

though² /ðoʊ/ *adv* used especially at the end of a sentence to add a fact or opinion to what you have just said: *Okay, I'll come. I'm not staying late though.*

thought¹ /θɔt/ past tense and past participle of think

thought² /θɔt/ *noun* **1** 🄱🄱 an idea or opinion: *What are your thoughts on the subject?* **2** [no plural] the activity of thinking: *Give the offer some thought, and call me tomorrow.*

thoughtful /ˈθɔt·fəl/ *adj* kind and always thinking about how you can help other people: *Thank you for the card – it was very thoughtful of you.* ○ *She's a very thoughtful person.*

thousand /ˈθaʊ·zənd/ **1** 🄰🄰 the number 1,000: *There were over **a thousand** people in the audience.* ○ *There are **one thousand** grams in a kilogram.* **2 thousands** informal a lot: *Thousands of homes were destroyed by the storm.*

thousandth¹ /ˈθaʊ·zəndθ/,/ˈθaʊ·zənθ/ 1000th written as a word

thousandth² /ˈθaʊ·zənθ/ *noun* one of a thousand equal parts of something; 1/1000; .001: *a thousandth of a second*

thread /θred/ *noun* a long, thin piece of cotton, wool, etc. that is used for sewing: *a needle and thread*

threat /θret/ *noun* a statement that you will harm or punish someone if that person does not not do what you want: *a death threat*

threaten /ˈθret·ᵊn/ *verb* to tell someone that you will do something bad to him or her if he or she does not do what you want: *He **threatened to** call the police.*

three /θri/ 🄰🄰 the number 3

threw /θru/ past tense of throw

thrill /θrɪl/ *noun* a strong feeling of excitement and pleasure: *Winning the game was a big thrill.*

thrilled /θrɪld/ *adj* very excited and pleased: *She was thrilled with your present.*

thriller /ˈθrɪl·ər/ *noun* 🄱🄱 a book or movie with an exciting story, often about crime

thrilling /ˈθrɪl·ɪŋ/ *adj* very exciting: *It was a thrilling game.*

throat /θroʊt/ *noun* **1** 🄱🄱 the back part of your mouth and the part inside your neck: *a sore throat* **2** the front of your neck: *He grabbed her by the throat.*
→ See **The Body** on page C2

through /θru/ *preposition* **1** 🄰🄰 from one end or side of something to the other: *The Mississippi River flows through New Orleans.* **2** 🄱🄱 from the beginning to the end of something: *He worked through the night.* **3** 🄱🄱 because of someone or something, or with someone's help: *She got the job through hard work.* **4** from one time until another time: *The store is open Monday through Friday.*

throughout /θru'aʊt/ *adv, preposition* **1** in every part of a place: *The disease spread quickly throughout the country.* **2** during the whole of a period of time: *He yawned throughout the performance.*

throw /θroʊ/ *verb* (past tense **threw**, past participle **thrown**) 🄰🄰 to make something move through the air by pushing it out of your hand: *Amy **threw** the ball **to** the dog.*

throw something away *phrasal verb* 🄱🄱 to get rid of something that you do not want any more: *He read the magazine and then threw it away.*
→ See **Phrasal Verbs** on page C13

throw

|oʊ go|aɪər fire|ɑʊər hour|eər hair|ɪər ear|ʊər poor|j yet|ʒ measure|ʃ ship |dʒ judge|tʃ chin|ð that|θ thin|ŋ hang|

thud /θʌd/ *noun* the sound that is made when something heavy falls: *There was a thud as he fell on the floor.*

thug /θʌg/ *noun* a bad person who behaves violently

thumb /θʌm/ *noun* **B1** the short, thick finger on the side of your hand
→ See **The Body** on page C2

thumbtack /ˈθʌm.tæk/ *a pin with a wide, flat top, used for fastening pieces of paper to a wall*

thump /θʌmp/ *verb* to hit something and make a noise: *The dog's tail thumped on the floor.*

thunder /ˈθʌn.dər/ *noun* [no plural] **B1** the loud noise in the sky that you hear during a storm: *The thunder and lightning scared the kids.*

thunderstorm /ˈθʌn.dər.stɔrm/ *noun* **A2** a storm that has thunder (= loud noise) and lightning (= sudden flashes of light in the sky)

Thursday /ˈθɜrz.deɪ/ *noun* **A1** the day of the week after Wednesday and before Friday

thus /ðʌs/ *adv* formal **1** used to say what happened as a result: *The guard fell asleep, thus allowing the prisoner to escape.* **2** in this way: *They limit the number of people allowed into the forest, thus preventing damage to the trails.*

tick[1] /tɪk/ *noun* the sound that a clock or watch makes every second

tick[2] /tɪk/ *verb* If a clock or watch ticks, it makes a sound every second.

ticket /ˈtɪk·ɪt/ *noun*   **ticket**
1 **A1** a small piece of paper that shows you have paid to do something, for example travel on a bus, watch a movie, etc.: *a lottery ticket ○ plane tickets ○ a **ticket machine** (= where you can buy tickets)* **2** an official notice that says you must pay a fine because you have parked in an illegal place, driven too fast, etc.: *I got a **ticket** for speeding.*

ticket office /ˈtɪk·ɪt ˌɔ·fɪs/ *noun* a place where you can buy a ticket

tickle /ˈtɪk·əl/ *verb* (present participle **tickling**, past tense and past participle **tickled**) to touch someone lightly with your fingers, in order to make him or her laugh

tide /taɪd/ *noun* the regular rise and fall in the level of the sea: *high/low tide*

tidy /ˈtɑɪ·di/ *adj* (comparative **tidier**, superlative **tidiest**) **A2** having everything in the right place and arranged in a good order: *Her room was clean and tidy.*

tie[1] /tɑɪ/ *verb* (present participle **tying**, past tense and past participle **tied**) **1** **B1** to fasten something with string, rope, etc.: *She gave me a pretty box tied with a red ribbon.* **2** **B1** to make a knot in a piece of string, rope, etc.: *She tied his shoelaces.* → Opposite **untie** verb

tie *something* up phrasal verb to fasten something together using string, rope, etc.

tie

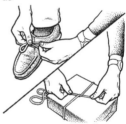

tie[2] /tɑɪ/ *noun* **A2** a long, thin piece of cloth that a man wears around his neck with a shirt
→ See **Clothes** on page C5

tiger /ˈtɑɪ·gər/ *noun* **B1** a large wild cat that has yellow fur with black lines on it

tight /tɑɪt/ *adj* **1** **B1** fitting your body very closely: *a tight skirt* → Opposite **loose** adj **2** firm and difficult to move: *Make sure the knot is tight.* **3** strongly controlled and obeying all rules completely: *They kept tight control of the budget.*
• **tightly** adv

a

b

c

d

e

f

g

h

i

j

k

l

m

n

o

p

q

r

s

t

u

v

w

x

y

z

tighten /ˈtaɪ.ᵊn/ verb to become tighter or to make something become tighter: *His hand tightened around her arm.*

tights /taɪts/ plural noun **A2** a piece of women's clothing made of very thin material that fits tightly over the legs and bottom

tile[1] /taɪl/ noun one of the flat, square pieces that are used for covering roofs, floors, or wallsnd

tile[2] /taɪl/ verb (present participle **tiling**, past tense and past participle **tiled**) to cover a surface with tiles: *a tiled bathroom*

till /tɪl/ preposition, conjunction **A2** until: *The supermarket is open till midnight.*

tilt /tɪlt/ verb to move into a position where one end or side is higher than the other: *I tilted my chair back and put my feet up.*

time[1] /taɪm/ noun **1** **A1** a particular point in the day or night: *What time is it?* ○ *What time do you leave for work in the morning?* **2** **A2** [no plural] Time is what we measure in minutes, hours, days, etc.: *He wants to **spend** more time with his family.* **3** **A2** a period of minutes, hours, years, etc.: *I lived in Florida for a long time.* **4** **A2** an occasion when something happens: *How many times have you been to Chicago?* **5 all the time** **A2** very often: *We go swimming all the time.* **6 have time** **A2** to have enough time to do something: *I never have time to eat breakfast.* **7 it's time for/to do something** **B1** used to say that something should happen or be done now: *It's time to get up.* **8 on time** **B1** not early or late: *I got to school on time.* **9 in time** **B1** early or at the right time: *We arrived **in time to** catch the train.* **10 at the same time** **B1** If two things happen at the same time, they happen together: *We arrived at the same time.* **11 two, three, four, etc. times** **B1** used to say how much bigger, better, worse, etc. one thing is than another thing: *Their house is three times larger than ours.* **12 in no time** very soon: *We'll be home in no time.* **13 at times**

sometimes: *At times, I wish I didn't have to work.* **14 from time to time** sometimes, but not often: *We go to the beach from time to time.* **15 take your time** to do something without hurrying: *The test will be difficult – take your time.*

time[2] /taɪm/ verb (present participle **timing**, past tense and past participle **timed**) to measure how long it takes for something to happen: *Have you timed the trip from New York to Philadelphia?*

times /taɪmz/ preposition used to say that one number is multiplied by another number: *Two times three is six.*

timetable /ˈtaɪmˌteɪ·bəl/ noun a list of dates and times that shows when things will happen

timid /ˈtɪm·ɪd/ adj shy and easily frightened: *a timid little boy*
• **timidly** adv

tin /tɪn/ noun a metal container with a lid that you keep food or other substances in: *a cookie tin*

tiny /ˈtaɪ·ni/ adj (comparative **tinier**, superlative **tiniest**) **B1** very small: *a tiny baby*

tip[1] /tɪp/ noun **1** the end of something long and narrow: *the tips of your fingers* **2** **B1** a piece of useful advice: *gardening tips* **3** **B1** an extra amount of money that you give to someone such as a driver to thank him or her for a service: *We left a big tip.*

tip[2] /tɪp/ verb (present participle **tipping**, past tense and past participle **tipped**) **1** to move so that one side is higher than the other side: *The table tipped over and all the drinks fell on the floor.* **2** to make the contents of a container fall out by turning the container over: *She tipped out the contents of her purse onto the table.* **3** to give an extra amount of money to someone such as a driver to thank him or her for a service: *We left a big tip.*

tiptoe[1] /ˈtɪpˌtoʊ/ noun **on tiptoe** standing on your toes

tiptoe[2] /ˈtɪpˌtoʊ/ verb (present participle **tiptoeing**, past tense and past participle **tiptoed**) to walk quietly on your toes

tire /taɪər/ *noun* a thick, round piece of rubber filled with air that fits around a wheel: *My bike has a **flat tire** (= a tire with no air in it).*
→ See **Car** on page C3

tired /taɪrd/ *adj* **1 A1** feeling that you want to rest or sleep: *I'm too tired to go out tonight.* ○ *He was **tired out** (= very tired) by the end of the day.* **2** tired of doing *something* **B1** bored or angry about something that has happened too often: *I'm tired of listening to her problems.*
• **tiredness** *noun* [no plural]

tiring /taɪərɪŋ/ *adj* **B1** making you feel tired: *a long and tiring day*

tissue /tɪʃ·u/ *noun* **1 B1** a soft piece of paper that you use for cleaning your nose **2** the material that animals and plants are made of: *human brain tissue*

title /taɪtᵊl/ *noun* **1 B1** the name of a book, movie, etc. **2** a word such as "Dr.," "Mrs.," etc. that is used before someone's name

to¹ /tə/ *A1* **1** used with a verb to make the infinitive: *I want to learn Spanish.* **2** used to give the reason for doing something: *I'm going out to get some milk.*

to² /tu/, /tʊ/, /tə/ *preposition* **1 A1** in the direction of something: *I ran to the door.* **2 A2** used to show who gets something: *Could you give these keys to Pete?* **3** from… to… *A2* used to give information about periods of time and distances: *The museum is open from Monday to Saturday.* ○ *The bus goes from Austin to Houston.* **4 A1** used to say "before" the hour when you are saying what time it is: *It's five to three.* **5 B1** used to say who is treated in a particular way, or who or what is affected by something: *She was very kind to us.*

toad /toʊd/ *noun* a small, brown animal with long back legs for swimming and jumping

toast /toʊst/ *noun* [no plural] **A2** bread that has been heated to make it brown: *a slice of toast*

toaster /toʊ·stər/ *noun* a machine that heats bread so that it becomes brown
→ See **The Kitchen** on page C10

tobacco /təˈbæk·oʊ/ *noun* [no plural] dried leaves that are inside cigarettes

today /təˈdeɪ/ *noun* [no plural], *adv* **1 A1** this day, or on this day: *It's Jack's birthday today.* ○ *Today is Friday.* **2 A1** the period of time that is happening now, or in this period of time: *More young people travel today than in the past.*

toddler /tɒd·lər/ *noun* a child who has just learned to walk

toe /toʊ/ *noun* **A2** one of the five separate parts at the end of your foot
→ See **The Body** on page C2

toenail /toʊˌneɪl/ *noun* one of the hard, flat parts on top of the end of your toes: *I need to cut my toenails.*

together /təˈɡeð·ər/ *adv* **1 A1** with each other: *They live together.* **2 A1** in the same place or close to each other: *We all sat together.* **3 B1** at the same time: *We can deal with both problems together.*

toilet /tɔɪ·lɪt/ *noun* **A1** a bowl that you sit on or stand near when you get rid of waste substances from your body
→ See **The Bathroom** on page C1

toilet paper /tɔɪ·lɪt ˌpeɪ·pər/ *noun* [no plural] paper used for cleaning your body after you have used the toilet
→ See **The Bathroom** on page C1

told /toʊld/ past tense and past participle of tell

tolerate /tɒl·əˌreɪt/ *verb* to accept or allow something although you do not like it: *We will not tolerate racism of any kind.*

tomato /təˈmeɪ·toʊ/ *noun* (plural **tomatoes**) **A1** a soft, round, red fruit eaten in salads or as a vegetable
→ See **Fruits and Vegetables** on page C8

tomb /tum/ *noun* a place where a dead person is buried

tombstone /tum·stoʊn/ *noun* a stone that shows the name of a dead person who is buried under it

tomorrow /təˈmɑr·oʊ/ *noun* [no plural], *adv* **1 A1** the day after today or on the day after today: *It's my birthday tomorrow.* **2 A1** the future, or in the future: *the children of tomorrow*

a
b
c
d
e
f
g
h
i
j
k
l
m
n
o
p
q
r
s
t
u
v
w
x
y
z

| æ cat | ɑ hot | e get | ɪ sit | i see | ɔ saw | ʊ book | u too | ʌ cut | ə about | ər mother | ɜr turn | ɔr for | aɪ my | aʊ how | eɪ say | ɔɪ boy |

ton /tʌn/ noun (plural **tons, ton**) **1** a unit for measuring weight, equal to 2,000 pounds **2** a ton/tons informal **B1** a lot of something: Wow, you have **tons of space** in your apartment.

tone /toʊn/ noun the quality of a sound, especially of someone's voice: I knew by her **tone of voice** that she was serious.

tongue /tʌŋ/ noun **B1** the soft thing inside your mouth that you use for tasting and speaking

tonight /tə'naɪt/ noun [no plural], adv **A1** the night of this day, or during the night of this day: We're going to a movie tonight.

too /tu/ adv **1** too small, heavy, much, etc. **A1** used before adjectives and adverbs to mean that something is more than allowed, necessary, possible, etc.: It's too late. ○ The movie was too long. **2** also: Do you know Jason too? **3** not too **A2** used before adjectives and adverbs to mean "not very": I didn't play too well today.

took /tʊk/ past tense of take

tool /tul/ noun a piece of equipment that you use with your hands in order to help you do something

tooth /tuθ/ noun (plural **teeth**) **A1** one of the hard, white things in your mouth that you use for biting: You should **brush** your **teeth** twice a day.

toothache /'tuθ,eɪk/ noun [no plural] **A2** a pain in one of your teeth

toothbrush /'tuθ,brʌʃ/ noun **A2** a small brush that you use to clean your teeth
→ See picture at **brush noun**

toothpaste /'tuθ,peɪst/ noun [no plural] **B1** a substance that you use to clean your teeth
→ See **The Bathroom** on page C1

top¹ /tɑp/ noun **1** **A2** the highest part of something: They were waiting for him **at the top of** the stairs. **2** **B1** a piece of women's clothing worn on the upper

part of the body **3** the lid or cover of a container, pen, etc.: Put the top back on the bottle.

top² /tɑp/ adj **1** **B1** at the highest part of something: I can't reach the top shelf. **2** **B1** the best, most important, or most successful: He's one of the country's top athletes.

topic /'tɑp·ɪk/ noun **B1** a subject that you talk or write about

the Torah /'toʊ·rə/, /'tɔr·ə/ noun the first five books of the Jewish bible, or all of the Jewish law and tradition

tore /tɔr/ past tense of tear

torn /tɔrn/ past participle of tear

tornado /tɔr'neɪ·doʊ/ noun (plural **tornados, tornadoes**) (also **twister**) an extremely strong wind that blows in a circle

torrent /'tɔr·ənt/, /'tɑr·ənt/ noun a torrent of something a lot of something bad: a torrent of cruel words

torrential /tə'ren·ʃəl/ adj Torrential rain is very heavy rain.

tortoise /'tɔr·təs/ noun a slow animal with a thick, hard shell

tortoise

shell

torture¹ /'tɔr·tʃər/ verb (present participle **torturing**, past tense and past participle **tortured**) to cause someone extreme pain, often in order to make that person tell you something

torture² /'tɔr·tʃər/ noun **1** an act of causing someone extreme pain **2** a very unpleasant experience: I had to spend the night in the airport – it was torture!

toss /tɔs/ verb to throw something somewhere carelessly: He read the letter quickly, then tossed it into the trash.

total¹ /'toʊ·t̬əl/ adj **1** **B1** including everything: The total cost of the work was $800. **2** extreme or complete: The whole evening was a total disaster.

total² /'toʊ·t̬əl/ noun **B1** the amount you get when you add smaller amounts together: The total came to $762.

totally /ˈtoʊ·tᵊl·i/ adv **B1** completely: *They look totally different.*

touch¹ /tʌtʃ/ verb **1** **A1** to put your hand on something: *Don't touch that pan – it's hot.* **2** If two things touch, they are so close to each other that there is no space between them: *These two wires should not touch.* **3** to feel pleased because someone has been kind to you: *I was deeply touched by her letter.*

touch² /tʌtʃ/ noun **1** the act of putting your hand on something: *I felt the touch of his hand on my face.* **2** [no plural] the ability to feel things by putting your hand on them: *It was cold to the touch* (= when I touched it). **3 get in touch** **B1** to contact someone: *I've been trying to get in touch with her.* **4 keep/stay in touch** **B1** to often speak to someone or write to him or her **5 lose touch** to stop speaking with someone or writing to him or her: *We've lost touch over the years.*

tough /tʌf/ adj **1** difficult: *Starting a new job can be tough.* **2** not easily damaged, cut, etc.: *tires made of tough rubber* **3** strong and not afraid of violence: *a tough guy* **4** describes food that is difficult to cut or eat: *tough steak*

tour¹ /tʊər/ noun **A2** a visit to and around a place, area, or country: *a tour of Europe*

tour² /tʊər/ verb **B1** to travel around a place for pleasure: *to tour Athens*

tour guide /ˈtʊərˌɡaɪd/ noun **A2** someone whose job is to show visitors a place or area: *Our tour guide explained the church's history.*

tourism /ˈtʊərˌɪz·əm/ noun [no plural] **B1** the business of providing services for tourists

tourist /ˈtʊər·ɪst/ noun **A2** someone who visits a place for pleasure and does not live there

tournament /ˈtʊər·nə·mənt/ noun **B1** a competition: *a tennis tournament*

tow /toʊ/ verb to pull a car, boat, etc.: *His car was towed away by the police.*

toward /tɔrd/ preposition **1** **B1** in the direction of someone or something: *She stood up and walked toward me.* **2** near to a time or place: *Your seats are toward the back of the theater.* ○ *It's getting toward lunchtime.*

towards /tɔrdz/ preposition **B1** another form of toward

towel /taʊ·əl/ noun **A2** a soft piece of cloth or paper that you use for drying yourself: *a bath towel*
→ See **The Bathroom** on page C1

tower /ˈtaʊ·ər/ noun **B1** a very tall, narrow building, or part of a building: *a church tower*

town /taʊn/ noun **1** **A1** a place where people live and work that is smaller than a city: *Colby is a small town in Kansas.* **2** **A2** the central area of a town where the stores are: *I usually go into town on Saturdays.* ○ *Let's meet in town.*

toxic /ˈtɑk·sɪk/ adj poisonous: *toxic chemicals/waste*

toy /tɔɪ/ noun **A2** an object for children to play with: *a toy car*

trace¹ /treɪs/ verb (present participle **tracing**, past tense and past participle **traced**) to find someone or something that was lost: *The police are trying to trace the missing woman.*

trace² /treɪs/ noun proof that someone or something was in a place: *There was no trace of her anywhere.*

track¹ /træk/ noun **1** **B1** a narrow path or road: *We followed a dirt track off the main road.* **2** **B1** a path, often circular, used for races: *a race track* **3** the long metal lines that a train travels along **4** a mark or line of marks left on the ground or on another surface by an animal, person, or vehicle that has moved over it: *The hunters followed the tracks of the deer.* **5** one song or piece of music on a CD, record, etc. **6 lose track** to not know what is happening to someone or something any more: *I lost track of how much we spent.*

track² /træk/ verb to follow a person or animal: *Scientists are tracking the wildlife in the valley.*

tractor /'træk·tər/ noun a strong vehicle with large back wheels used on farms for pulling things

trade¹ /treɪd/ noun **1** 🔵 [no plural] the buying and selling of large numbers of things, especially between countries: *a trade agreement* **2** a type of business: *the tourist trade* **3** someone's job: *He's a builder by trade.*

trade² /treɪd/ verb (present participle **trading**, past tense and past participle **traded**) to buy and sell things, especially between countries: *Do you trade with Asia?*

tradition /trə'dɪʃ·ən/ noun a custom or way of behaving that has continued for a long time in a group of people: *strong family traditions ○ cultural traditions*

traditional /trə'dɪʃ·ə·nᵊl/ adj 🔵 following the customs or ways of behaving that have continued in a group of people for a long time: *traditional farming methods*
• **traditionally** adv

traffic /'træf·ɪk/ noun [no plural] 🔵 the cars, trucks, etc. on a road: *Sorry we're late – we got stuck in traffic.*

traffic jam /'træf·ɪk ˌdʒæm/ noun 🔵 a line of cars, trucks, etc. that are moving slowly or not at all

traffic light /'træf·ɪk ˌlaɪt/ noun 🔵 a set of red, green, and yellow lights that is used to stop and start traffic
→ See picture at **light** noun

tragedy /'trædʒ·ɪ·di/ noun (plural **tragedies**) something very sad that happens, usually involving death: *the tragedy of their daughter's death*

tragic /'trædʒ·ɪk/ adj very sad, often involving death: *a tragic accident*
• **tragically** adv

trail /treɪl/ noun **1** a line of marks that someone or something leaves behind as he, she, or it moves: *a trail of muddy footprints* **2** a path through a wild or rural area, such as a forest: *a nature trail*

trailer /'treɪ·lər/ noun **1** a container with wheels that can be pulled by a car

or a truck **2** a structure that is pulled by a vehicle that people stay in when they are on vacation **3** another word for **mobile home**

train¹ /treɪn/ noun 🔵 a long, thin vehicle that travels along metal tracks and carries people or goods: *I take the train to work every day.*

train² /treɪn/ verb **1** 🔵 to practice a sport or exercise in order to prepare for a competition **2** to learn the skills you need to do a job: *He was trained as a mechanic.* **3** to teach someone how to do something, usually a skill that is needed for a job: *We train all our staff in first aid.*

trainer /'treɪ·nər/ noun 🔵 someone who teaches people how to do a skill well, especially for a job or sport: *a fitness trainer*

training /'treɪ·nɪŋ/ noun [no plural] **1** 🔵 the process of learning a skill: *computer training* **2** 🔵 the process of preparing for a sport or competition: *weight training*

train station /'treɪn ˌsteɪ·ʃən/ noun a place where trains stop so that you can get on or off them: *We have to be at the train station by 11.*

traitor /'treɪ·tər/ noun someone who does something that harms his or her country, especially by helping its enemies

trample /'træm·pᵊl/ verb (present participle **trampling**, past tense and past participle **trampled**) to walk on something, usually damaging it: *She shouted at the boys for trampling on her flowers.*

transfer /træns'fɜr/, /'træns·fɜr/ verb (present participle **transferring**, past tense and past participle **transferred**) 🔵 to move someone or something from one place to another: *She was transferred to a closer hospital.*
• **transfer** noun *I'm hoping for a transfer to the Atlanta office.*

transform /træns'fɔrm/ verb to change something completely, usually to improve it: *You've transformed this house!*
• **transformation** noun

transitive /ˈtræn·sɪ·tɪv/ *adj* A transitive verb always has an object. In the sentence "I'll make a drink," "make" is a transitive verb.

translate /trænsˈleɪt/, /trænzˈleɪt/ *verb* (present participle **translating**, past tense and past participle **translated**) **B1** to change words from one language to another: *We were asked to translate a short story.*
• **translator** *noun* a Japanese translator

translation /trænsˈleɪ·ʃən/, /trænzˈleɪ·ʃən/ *noun* **B1** something that has been changed from one language to another

transparent /trænˈspær·ənt/ *adj* If a substance or material is transparent, you can see through it: *transparent plastic*

transport[1] /ˈtræns·pɔrt/ *noun* [no plural] **B1** short form of transportation

transport[2] /trænsˈpɔrt/ *verb* to move people or things from one place to another using a vehicle

transportation /ˌtræns·pərˈteɪ·ʃən/ *noun* [no plural] **1** **B1** a vehicle or system of vehicles, such as buses, trains, planes, etc., for getting from one place to another: *A lot of cities don't have good **public transportation**.* **2** the act of moving people or things from one place to another: *the transportation of live animals*

trap[1] /træp/ *noun* a piece of equipment for catching animals: *a mouse trap*

trap[2] /træp/ *verb* (present participle **trapping**, past tense and past participle **trapped**) **1** If someone or something is trapped, that person or thing cannot escape from a place or situation: *The car turned over, trapping the driver underneath.* **2** to catch an animal using a trap

trash /træʃ/ *noun* [no plural] **1** **B1** things that you throw away because you do not want them: *a **trash can** (= a container for trash)* **2** *informal* something that is of bad quality: *Why are you reading that trash?*

travel[1] /ˈtræv·əl/ *verb* (present participle **traveling**, past tense and past participle **traveled**) **1** **A1** to make a trip: *I spent a year traveling around Asia.* **2** **B1** If

light, sound, or news travels, it moves from one place to another: *News of the accident traveled fast.*

travel[2] /ˈtræv·əl/ *noun* [no plural] **B1** the activity of travel: *space travel*

travel agency /ˈtræv·əl ˌeɪdʒ·ən·si/ *noun* (plural **travel agencies**) a business that makes travel arrangements for people

travel agent /ˈtræv·əl ˌeɪdʒ·ənt/ *noun* **B1** someone whose job is making travel arrangements for people

traveler /ˈtræv·ə·lər/ *noun* **B1** someone who is traveling

traveler's check /ˈtræv·ə·lərz ˌtʃek/ *noun* a special piece of paper that you exchange for the money of another country

tray /treɪ/ *noun* a flat object with higher edges, used for carrying food and drinks

treasure /ˈtreʒ·ər/ *noun* [no plural] a collection of gold, silver, jewelery, and valuable objects: *buried treasure*

treat[1] /trit/ *verb* **1** to behave toward someone in a particular way: *He treats her really badly.* ◦ *They **treat** her **like** one of their own children.* **2** to give medical care to someone who is sick or hurt: *He's being **treated for** cancer.*

treat[2] /trit/ *noun* something special that you buy or do for someone else: *a birthday treat* ◦ *As a special treat I'm taking him out for dinner.*

treatment /ˈtrit·mənt/ *noun* **1** something that you do to try to cure an illness or injury: *She's receiving treatment for a lung infection.* **2** [no plural] the way you behave toward someone: *There have been complaints about the treatment of prisoners.*

treaty /ˈtri·ți/ *noun* (plural **treaties**) a written agreement between two or more countries: *a peace treaty*

tree /tri/ *noun*
A1 a tall plant with a thick stem that has branches coming from it and leaves

tree

branch

trunk

tremble /'trem·bəl/ **verb** (present participle **trembling**, past tense and past participle **trembled**) to shake slightly, especially because you are frightened or cold

tremendous /trə'men·dəs/ **adj 1** very good: *I think she's doing a tremendous job.* **2** very large, great, strong, etc.: *a tremendous amount of money*

• **tremendously** adv

trend /trend/ **noun** ⬛ a general development or change in a situation: *I'm not familiar with the latest trends in teaching.*

trendy /'tren·di/ **adj** (comparative **trendier**, superlative **trendiest**) informal fashionable at the moment: *She has some trendy new glasses.*

trial /'traɪ·əl/ **noun 1** a legal process to decide if someone has done a crime: *The two men are now on trial for attempted murder.* **2** a test of something new to find out if it is safe, works correctly, etc.: *The drug is currently undergoing trials.*

triangle /'traɪ·æŋ·gəl/ **noun** a flat shape with three sides

→ See picture at **shape noun**

• **triangular** adj

tribe /traɪb/ **noun** a group of people who live together, usually in areas far away from cities, and who still have a traditional way of life: *Native American tribes*

• **tribal** adj *a tribal council*

tribute /'trɪb·jut/ **noun** something that you do or say to show that you respect and admire someone: *The concert was organized as a tribute to the singer who died last year.*

trick[1] /trɪk/ **noun 1** ⬛ something you do to deceive someone, or to make someone look stupid: *It's not nice to play tricks on people.* **2** ⬛ something that is done to entertain people and that seems to be magic: *a card trick*

trick[2] /trɪk/ **verb** to deceive someone: *They tricked him into signing the papers.*

trickle /'trɪk·əl/ **verb** (present participle **trickling**, past tense and past participle **trickled**) If liquid trickles somewhere,

it flows slowly and in a thin line: *The sweat trickled down her back.*

• **trickle noun** *a trickle of blood*

tricky /'trɪk·i/ **adj** (comparative **trickier**, superlative **trickiest**) difficult: *a tricky question*

tried /traɪd/ past tense and past participle of **try**

trigger /'trɪg·ər/ **noun** the part of a gun that you pull when you shoot

trillion /'trɪl·jən/ the number 1,000,000,000,000

trim /trɪm/ **verb** (present participle **trimming**, past tense and past participle **trimmed**) to cut a small amount from something: *I had my hair trimmed.*

trip[1] /trɪp/ **noun** ⬛ an occasion when you travel to visit a place and come back again: *a trip to the grocery store* ○ *a long business trip*

trip[2] /trɪp/ **verb** (present participle **tripping**, past tense and past participle **tripped**) to lose your balance or fall because your foot hits against something when you are moving: *She tripped over the cat.*

triple[1] /'trɪp·əl/ **adj** having three parts of the same type, or happening three times: *a triple world champion*

triple[2] /'trɪp·əl/ **verb** to increase three times (= used to show the difference in amount of two things, by multiplying one of them by the stated number) in size or amount, or to make something do this: *Sales have tripled in the past year.*

triumph /'traɪ·əmf/ **noun** an important success: *The bridge is a triumph of engineering.*

• **triumph verb** *The Giants triumphed over the Rangers, 4 games to 1.*

trivial /'trɪv·i·əl/ **adj** small and not important: *a trivial problem*

troops /trups/ **plural noun** soldiers: *How many troops have been sent overseas?*

trophy /'troʊ·fi/ **noun** (plural **trophies**) a prize, such as a silver cup, that you get for winning a competition

tropical /'trɑp·ɪ·kəl/ **adj** from or in the hottest parts of the world: *a tropical climate*

the tropics /'trɒp.ɪks/ *plural noun*
the hottest parts of the world

trot /trɒt/ *verb* (present participle **trotting**, past tense and past participle **trotted**)
to walk with quick, short steps: *The little boy trotted along behind his father.*

trouble¹ /'trʌb.əl/ *noun* **1** **B1** problems: *We had trouble finding somewhere to park.* **2** **the trouble with someone/something** used to say what is wrong with someone or something: *The trouble with a white floor is that it gets dirty so quickly.* **3** [no plural] a problem with a machine or part of your body: *back trouble* ∘ *car trouble* **4** **B1** [no plural] a situation in which you have done something wrong and will be punished: *They got into trouble with the police.*

> **❗ Common mistake: trouble or problem?**
>
> **Problem** means "a situation that causes difficulties and that needs to be dealt with." You can talk about **a problem** or **problems**.
> *Tell me what the problem is.*
> *There's a problem with the engine.*
> *He's having a few problems at work.*
> **Trouble** means "problems, difficulties, or worries" and is used to talk about problems in a more general way. **Trouble** is almost always uncountable, so do not use a before it.
> *We had some trouble while we were on vacation.*
> *He helped me when I was in trouble.*
> *I had trouble with the car last night.*
> ~~I had a trouble with the car last night.~~

trouble² /'trʌb.əl/ *verb* (present participle **troubling**, past tense and past participle **troubled**) to make someone worry: *The situation has been troubling me for a while.*

truck /trʌk/ *noun* **B1** a large road vehicle for carrying things from place to place → See picture at **vehicle**

true /truː/ *adj* **1** **A2** based on facts and not imagined: *a true story* ∘ *Is it true that* they're getting married? **2** **B1** real: *true love* **3** **come true** **B1** If a dream or hope comes true, it really happens.

truly /'truː.li/ *adv* used to say that something is sincere or honest: *I truly believe that he is innocent.*

trumpet /'trʌm.pɪt/ *noun* **B1** a metal musical instrument that you play by blowing into it

trumpet

trunk /trʌŋk/ *noun* **1** the thick stem of a tree that the branches grow from → See picture at **tree** **2** the long nose of an elephant **3** a closed space at the back of a car where you can store things → See **Car** on page C3

trunks /trʌŋks/ *plural noun* (also **swimming trunks**) a piece of clothing that boys and men wear for swimming → See picture at **Clothes** on page C5

trust¹ /trʌst/ *verb* **1** **B1** to believe that someone is good and honest and will not harm you: *My sister warned me not to trust him.* **2** **trust someone to do something** to be sure that someone will do the right thing: *I trust them to make the right decision.*

trust² /trʌst/ *noun* [no plural] the belief that you can trust someone or something: *a marriage based on love and trust*

truth /truːθ/ *noun* **the truth** **B1** the real facts about a situation: *Do you think he was **telling the truth**?*

truthful /'truːθ.fəl/ *adj* honest and not containing or telling any lies: *a truthful answer*
• **truthfully** *adv*
• **truthfulness** *noun* [no plural]

try¹ /traɪ/ *verb* (present participle **trying**, past tense and past participle **tried**) **1** **A2** to make an effort to do something: *I tried to open the window but couldn't.* **2** **B1** to do, test, taste, etc. something to discover if it works or if you like it: *I tried that recipe you gave me last night.*

try something on *phrasal verb* **A2** to put on a piece of clothing to see if it fits you: *Could I try this dress on, please?*

| a |
| b |
| c |
| d |
| e |
| f |
| g |
| h |
| i |
| j |
| k |
| l |
| m |
| n |
| o |
| p |
| q |
| r |
| s |
| **t** |
| u |
| v |
| w |
| x |
| y |
| z |

try² /traɪ/ *noun* (plural **tries**) an occasion when you make an effort to do something or test something to see if it will work

T-shirt /ˈtiː.ʃɜːrt/ *noun* (also **tee shirt**) **A1** a piece of cotton clothing for the top part of the body with short sleeves and no collar

→ See **Clothes** on page C5

tub /tʌb/ *noun* **1** a container that you fill with water and sit in to wash your body: *She filled the tub with hot water for her bath.* **2** a small, plastic container with a lid, used for keeping food: *a tub of ice cream*

tube /tuːb/ *noun* **1** **B1** a long, thin container for a soft substance that you press to get the substance out: *a tube of toothpaste* → See picture at **container** **2** a pipe made of glass, plastic, metal, etc., especially for liquids or gases to flow through

tuck /tʌk/ *verb* to push a loose piece of clothing or material in place: *Tuck your shirt in.*

Tuesday /ˈtuːz.deɪ/ *noun* **A1** the day of the week after Monday and before Wednesday

tug /tʌɡ/ *verb* (present participle **tugging**, past tense and past participle **tugged**) to pull something suddenly and strongly: *Tom tugged at his mother's arm.*

tulip /ˈtuː.lɪp/ *noun* a brightly colored, bell-shaped flower that grows early in the spring

tulip

tumble /ˈtʌm.bəl/ *verb* (present participle **tumbling**, past tense and past participle **tumbled**) to suddenly fall: *He tumbled down the stairs.*

tummy /ˈtʌm.i/ *noun* (plural **tummies**) informal stomach

tuna /ˈtuː.nə/ *noun* (plural **tuna**) **1** a large sea fish **2** **B1** [no plural] the meat of a tuna

tune /tuːn/ *noun* **B1** a series of musical notes that are nice to listen to: *He was humming a tune.*

tunnel /ˈtʌn.ᵊl/ *noun* **tunnel** **B1** a long, covered road under the ground or through a mountain: *The train went into the tunnel.*

turkey /ˈtɜːr.ki/ *noun* **1** a bird that looks like a large chicken **2** **B1** [no plural] the meat of a turkey

turn¹ /tɜːrn/ *verb* **1** **A2** to change direction when you are moving, or to make a car do this: *Turn left at the traffic lights.* ∘ *I turned the car into the drive.* **2** **B1** to move your body so that you are facing a different direction: *Ricky turned and saw Sue standing in the doorway.* **3** **B1** to move a page in a book or magazine in order to see the next one: *I offered to turn the pages for the pianist.* ∘ *Turn to page 35.* **4** to move around a central point in a circle, or to make something do this: *Turn the steering wheel as quickly as you can.* **5 turn blue, cold, etc.** to become blue, cold, etc.: *The sky turned black and it started to rain.*

turn *something* **down** *phrasal verb* **1** **B1** to reduce the level of sound or heat that a machine produces: *Could you turn the radio down, please?* **2** to refuse an offer or request: *They offered me the job, but I turned it down.*

turn (*someone/something*) **into** *someone/something phrasal verb* **B1** to change and become someone or something different, or to make someone or something do this: *The farmland is turning into a desert.* ∘ *They want to turn the offices into apartments.*

turn *something* **off** *phrasal verb* **A2** to move the switch on a machine, light, etc. so that it stops working: *How do you turn the computer off?*

→ See **Phrasal Verbs** on page C13

turn *something* **on** *phrasal verb* **A2** to move the switch on a machine, light, etc. so that it starts working: *Ben turned the TV on.*

→ See **Phrasal Verbs** on page C13

turn out *phrasal verb* to happen in a particular way or to have a particular

result, especially an unexpected one:
How did the recipe turn out?

turn *something* **up** phrasal verb **B1** to
increase the level of sound or heat that
a machine produces: *Can you turn the
heat up, please?*

turn² /tɜrn/ noun **1 B1** the time when
you can or must do something, usually
before or after someone else: *You'll have
to be patient and wait your turn.*
2 take turns If two or more people take
turns, one person does something, then
another person does something, etc.:
Mom and Dad take turns cooking. **3** a
change in the direction in which you
are moving or facing: *a right/left turn*
4 B1 a bend or corner in a road, river,
etc.: *Take the next turn on the right.*

turn signal /'tɜrn ˌsɪɡ·nᵊl/ noun one of
the lights on a vehicle that flash to show
which direction the driver intends to
turn
→ See **Car** on page C3

turtle /'tɜr·t̬ᵊl/ noun an animal with
four legs and a hard shell that lives
mainly in water

tusk /tʌsk/ noun one of the two long,
pointed teeth that come out of the
mouth of some animals

tutor /'tu·t̬ər/ noun a teacher who
works privately with one student, usually to review what the student learned
in class: *a private tutor*
• **tutor** verb

TV /'ti'vi/ noun **A1** television: *What's on
TV tonight?*
→ See **The Living Room** on page C11

tweezers /'twi·zərz/
plural noun a small
tool with two narrow
pieces of metal joined
at one end, used for
picking up very
small things

tweezers

twelfth¹ /twelfθ/ 12th written as a
word

twelfth² /twelfθ/ noun one of twelve
equal parts of something; 1/12

twelve /twelv/ **A1** the number 12

twenties /'twen·ti̬z/ plural noun **1 the
twenties** the years from 1920 to 1929:
She was born in the twenties. **2 be in
your twenties** to be aged between 20
and 29: *I think he's in his twenties.*

twenty¹ /'twen·ti̬/ **A1** the number 20
• **twentieth** 20th written as a word

twenty² /'twen·ti̬/ noun a twenty-dollar
bill: *The ATM only gives you twenties.*

twice /twaɪs/ adv **A2** two times: *I've
been there twice.*

twig /twɪɡ/ noun a small, thin branch
on a tree

twilight /'twaɪˌlaɪt/ noun [no plural]
the time in the evening when it starts to
become dark, or the time in the morning when it starts to become light

twin /twɪn/ noun **B1** one of two children who are born to the same mother
at the same time

twinkle /'twɪŋ·kəl/ verb (present participle
twinkling, past tense and past participle
twinkled) If light twinkles, it shines
and seems to be quickly flashing on and
off: *The lights of the town twinkled in the
distance.*

twist¹ /twɪst/ verb **1** to turn something
using your hand: *She twisted the ring
around on her finger.* **2** to bend and
turn something many times and change
its shape: *The wheels of the bike had been
twisted in the accident.* **3** If a road, river,
etc. twists, it has a lot of bends in it.

twist² /twɪst/ noun **1** the act of twisting
something **2** a bend in a river, road, etc.

twitch /twɪtʃ/ verb If a part of your body
twitches, it suddenly makes a slight
movement: *His face twitched nervously.*
• **twitch** noun

two /tu/ **A1** the number 2

tying /'taɪ·ɪŋ/ the present participle of tie

type¹ /taɪp/ noun **A1** a group of people
or things that have similar qualities:
They sell over 20 different types of cheese.
○ *Illnesses of this type are very common in
children.*

a b c d e f g h i j k l m n o p q r s t u v w x y z

| æ cat | ɑ hot | e get | ɪ sit | i see | ɔ saw | ʊ book | u too | ʌ cut | ə about | ər mother | ɜr turn | ɔr for | ɑɪ my | ɑʊ how | eɪ say | ɔɪ boy |

type² /taɪp/ **verb** (present participle **typing**, past tense and past participle **typed**) **B1** to write something using a keyboard
• **typing noun** [no plural]

typical /ˈtɪp·ɪ·kəl/ **adj** **B1** having all the qualities you expect a particular person, object, place, etc. to have: *typical German food* ○ *This style of painting is typical of Monet.*

typically /ˈtɪp·ɪ·kli/ **adv** **1** **B1** used for saying that what usually happens: *Schools in the area typically start at 8:30.* **2** used for saying that something is typical of a person, thing, place, etc.: *His reply was typically frank.*

U u

U, u /ju/ the twenty-first letter of the alphabet

ugly /ˈʌɡ·li/ **adj** (comparative **uglier**, superlative **ugliest**) **B1** bad to look at: *an ugly city*

uh exclamation /ʌ/ something that you say while you are thinking about what to say next: *She has some, uh, good qualities.*

ulcer /ˈʌl·sər/ **noun** a painful, infected area on your skin or inside your body: *a mouth ulcer*

ultimate /ˈʌl·tə·mət/ **adj** better, worse, or greater than all similar things: *Climbing Mount Everest is the ultimate challenge.*

um /ʌm/ **exclamation** something that you say while you are thinking about what to say next: *Well, um, I don't know.*

umbrella /ʌmˈbrel·ə/ **noun** **A2** a thing that you hold above your head to keep yourself dry when it is raining

umpire /ˈʌm·paɪər/ **noun** someone whose job is to watch a sports game and make sure that the players obey the rules: *a baseball umpire*

the UN /ˈjuˈen/ **noun** abbreviation for the United Nations

unable /ʌnˈeɪ·bəl/ **adj** **B1** be unable to do something **B1** to not be able to do something: *Some days he is unable to get out of bed.*

unacceptable /ˌʌn·əkˈsep·tə·bəl/ **adj** too bad to be accepted or allowed to continue: *That kind of behavior is completely unacceptable.*

unanimous /juˈnæn·ə·məs/ **adj** agreed by everyone: *The jury was unanimous in finding him guilty.*

unattractive /ˌʌn·əˈtræk·tɪv/ **adj** bad to look at: *I felt old and unattractive.*

unaware /ˌʌn·əˈwear/ **adj** not knowing about something: *He seems totally unaware of the problem.*

unbearable /ʌnˈbear·ə·bəl/ **adj** very painful or unpleasant: *The heat was almost unbearable.*
• **unbearably adv**

unbelievable /ˌʌn·bɪˈli·və·bəl/ **adj** **B1** extremely bad or good and making you feel surprised: *It's unbelievable how lucky she is.*

uncertain /ʌnˈsɜr·tən/ **adj** not sure or not able to decide about something: *We're a little uncertain about what we're doing this weekend.*

uncle /ˈʌŋ·kəl/ **noun** **A2** the brother of someone's mother or father, or the husband of someone's aunt: *My uncle taught me how to fish.*

unclear /ʌnˈklɪər/ **adj** not easy to understand: *It is unclear how many people have lost their homes in the disaster.*

uncomfortable /ʌnˈkʌm·fər·tə·bəl/, /ʌnˈkʌmf·tər·bəl/ **adj** **1** **B1** not making you feel comfortable and pleasant: *These shoes are really uncomfortable.* **2** slightly embarrassed, or making you feel slightly embarrassed: *an uncomfortable silence*
• **uncomfortably adv** *It was uncomfortably hot in the room.*

uncommon /ʌnˈkam·ən/ **adj** unusual: *It's not uncommon for people to get sick when they travel (= it often happens).*

unconscious /ʌnˈkɑn·ʃəs/ adj in a state as though you are sleeping, for example because you have been hit on the head: *She was **knocked unconscious**.*

uncontrollable /ˌʌn·kənˈtroʊ·lə·bəl/ adj not possible to control: *uncontrollable anger*

uncountable noun /ʌnˈkɑʊn·tə·bəl ˈnɑʊn/ noun **B1** a noun that does not have a plural form and cannot be used with "a" or "one": *"Music" is an uncountable noun.*

uncover /ʌnˈkʌv·ər/ verb to discover something that had been secret or hidden: *The inspectors uncovered evidence of corruption.*

under /ˈʌn·dər/ preposition **1 A1** below something: *She pushed her bag under the table.* **2 A2** less than a number, amount, or age: *You can buy the whole system for just under $2,000.*

under- /ˈʌn·dər/ prefix **1** not enough: *undercooked potatoes* **2** below: *underwear*

underage /ˌʌn·dərˈeɪdʒ/ adj younger than the legal age when you are allowed to do something: *underage drinking*

undergo /ˌʌn·dərˈgoʊ/ verb (past tense **underwent**, past participle **undergone**) to experience something, especially a change or medical treatment: *He is undergoing surgery for a heart problem.*

undergraduate /ˌʌn·dərˈgrædʒ·u·ət/ noun a student at a college or university who has not yet received a bachelor's degree

underground /ˌʌn·dərˈgrɑʊnd/ adj, adv under the surface of the ground: *an animal that lives underground*

undergrowth /ˈʌn·dərˌgroʊθ/ noun [no plural] short plants and bushes that grow around trees

underline /ˈʌn·dərˌlaɪn/ verb **B1** to draw a line under a word or words: *All the technical words have been underlined in red.*

underneath /ˌʌn·dərˈniθ/ adv, preposition under something: *I found her shoes underneath the bed.*

underpants /ˈʌn·dərˌpænts/ plural noun **B1** a piece of clothing that you wear next to your skin, under your pants

understand /ˌʌn·dərˈstænd/ verb (past tense and past participle **understood**) **1 A1** to know the meaning of something that someone says: *She didn't understand so I explained it again.* **2 A2** to know why or how something happens or works: *We still don't fully understand how the brain works.* **3 B1** to know how someone feels or why he or she behaves in a particular way: *I don't understand James sometimes.*

understandable /ˌʌn·dərˈstæn·də·bəl/ adj An understandable feeling or action is one that you would expect in the situation: *It's understandable that he's angry.*

understanding[1] /ˌʌn·dərˈstæn·dɪŋ/ noun [no plural] knowledge about a subject, situation, etc.: *We now have a better understanding of this disease.*

understanding[2] /ˌʌn·dərˈstæn·dɪŋ/ adj showing sympathy for someone's problems: *Fortunately, my girlfriend is very understanding.*

understood /ˌʌn·dərˈstʊd/ past tense and past participle of understand

underwater /ˌʌn·dərˈwɔt·ər/ adj, adv under the surface of water, or used there: *an underwater camera*

underwear /ˈʌn·dərˌweər/ noun [no plural] **B1** the clothes that you wear next to your skin, under your other clothes

underwent /ˌʌn·dərˈwent/ past tense of undergo

undid /ʌnˈdɪd/ past tense of undo

undo /ʌnˈdu/ verb (present participle **undoing**, past tense **undid**, past participle **undone**) to open something that is fastened: *I undid my belt.*

undone /ʌnˈdʌn/ adj not fastened or tied: *Her shoelaces were undone.*

undoubtedly /ʌnˈdɑʊ·t̬ɪd·li/ adv used to say that something is true: *She is undoubtedly good at her job.*

undress /ʌnˈdres/ verb **B1** to remove your clothes or someone else's clothes

a
b
c
d
e
f
g
h
i
j
k
l
m
n
o
p
q
r
s
t
u
v
w
x
y
z

| æ cat | ɑ hot | e get | ɪ sit | i see | ɔ saw | ʊ book | u too | ʌ cut | ə about | ər mother | ɜr turn | ɔr for | aɪ my | ɑʊ how | eɪ say | ɔɪ boy |

• **undressed** adj *I got undressed and went to bed.*

uneasy /ʌnˈiː·zi/ adj (comparative **uneasier,** superlative **uneasiest**) worried because you think something bad might happen: *I feel a little **uneasy about** her traveling alone.*

unemployed /ˌʌn·ɪmˈplɔɪd/ adj **B1** not having a job: *I've been unemployed for six months.*

unemployment /ˌʌn·ɪmˈplɔɪ·mənt/ noun [no plural] **1 B1** the number of people who are unemployed: *high/low unemployment* **2** the fact of being unemployed: *A long period of unemployment can lead to financial trouble.* **3** money that the government pays to unemployed people who are looking for jobs: *He's **on unemployment.***

uneven /ʌnˈiː·vən/ adj not level or smooth: *an uneven floor*
• **unevenly** adv

unexpected /ˌʌn·ɪkˈspek·tɪd/ adj **B1** Something that is unexpected surprises you because you did not know it was going to happen: *His death was completely unexpected.*
• **unexpectedly** adv

unfair /ʌnˈfeər/ adj **B1** not treating people in an equal way: *an unfair system*
• **unfairly** adv

unfashionable /ʌnˈfæʃ·ə·nə·bəl/ adj not fashionable at a particular time

unfasten /ʌnˈfæs·ən/ verb to open something whose parts are fastened together: *to unfasten a seat belt*

unfit /ʌnˈfɪt/ adj not suitable or good enough: *The food was judged **unfit for** human consumption.*

unforgettable /ˌʌn·fərˈget·ə·bəl/ adj **B1** Something that is unforgettable is so good, interesting, etc. that you remember it for a long time: *Seeing Niagara Falls was an **unforgettable experience.***

unfortunate /ʌnˈfɔr·tʃə·nət/ adj bad and causing problems: *an unfortunate mistake*

unfortunately /ʌnˈfɔr·tʃə·nət·li/ adv **A2** used to say that you wish something was not true or that something had not

happened: *I'd love to come, but unfortunately I have to work.*

unfriendly /ʌnˈfrend·li/ adj (comparative **unfriendlier,** superlative **unfriendliest**) **B1** not friendly

unfurnished /ʌnˈfɜr·nɪʃt/ adj If a room, apartment, etc. is unfurnished, there is no furniture in it.

ungrateful /ʌnˈɡreɪt·fəl/ adj not thanking someone who has done something good for you

unhappy /ʌnˈhæp·i/ adj (comparative **unhappier,** superlative **unhappiest**) **1 A2** sad: *an unhappy childhood* **2 B1** not satisfied: *Alex was **unhappy with** his test scores.*
• **unhappiness** noun [no plural]

unhealthy /ʌnˈhel·θi/ adj (comparative **unhealthier,** superlative **unhealthiest**) **1 B1** likely to damage your health: *Eating too much is unhealthy.* **2** looking ill: *She looks pale and unhealthy.*

unhelpful /ʌnˈhelp·fəl/ adj not wanting to help someone: *The taxi driver was rude and unhelpful.*

uniform /ˈjuː·nɪˌfɔrm/ noun **A2** a special set of clothes that are worn by people who do a particular job or by the students at some schools: *a school uniform*
○ *a nurse's uniform*

unimportant /ˌʌn·ɪmˈpɔr·t²nt/ adj **B1** not important: *an unimportant opinion*

uninhabited /ˌʌn·ɪnˈhæb·ɪ·t̬əd/ adj If a place is uninhabited, no one lives there: *an uninhabited island*

uninterested /ʌnˈɪn·trə·stəd/ adj **B1** not interested: *He's completely **uninterested in** politics.*

uninteresting /ʌnˈɪn·trə·stɪŋ/ adj **B1** not interesting in comparison with other things: *His later work is uninteresting in comparison with his first novel.*

union /ˈjuːn·jən/ noun **1 B1** (also **trade union**) an organization that represents people who do a particular job: *a teachers' union* **2** two or more countries, groups, etc. that join together to make one country, group, etc.

| ou go | ɑɚ **fire** | ɑʊɚ **hour** | eɚ **hair** | ɪɚ **ear** | ʊɚ **poor** | j **yet** | ʒ **measure** | ʃ **ship** | dʒ **judge** | tʃ **chin** | ð **that** | θ **thin** | ŋ **hang** |

unique /juˈnik/ **adj 1** different from everyone and everything else: *Everyone's fingerprints are unique.* **2** unusual and special: *a unique opportunity*

unit /ˈju·nɪt/ **noun 1** a measure used to express an amount or quantity: *The ounce is a **unit of weight**.* **2 B1** a single, complete thing that is part of a larger thing: *a textbook with ten units*

unite /juˈnaɪt/ **verb** (present participle **uniting**, past tense and past participle **united**) to join together as a group, or to make people join together as a group: *We need a leader who can unite the party.*

the United Nations /juˈnaɪ·t̬ɪd ˈneɪ·ʃənz/ **noun** an international organization that tries to stop world problems in a peaceful way

universal /ˌju·nəˈvɜr·səl/ **adj** relating to everyone in the world, or to everyone in a particular group: *Kittens and puppies have an almost universal appeal.*
• **universally adv** *It's a style of music that is universally popular.*

the universe /ˈju·nəˌvɜrs/ **noun** **B1** everything that exists, including stars, space, etc.

university /ˌju·nəˈvɜr·sɪ·t̬i/ **noun** (plural **universities**) **A2** a place where students study at a high level to get a degree (= type of qualification): *the University of Maryland*

unkind /ʌnˈkaɪnd/ **adj** **B1** slightly cruel: *an unkind remark*

unknown /ʌnˈnoʊn/ **adj 1 B1** not known: *The cause of his death is unknown.* **2** not famous: *an unknown actor*

unleaded /ʌnˈled·ɪd/ **adj** Unleaded fuel does not contain lead (= a metal).

unless /ənˈles/ **conjunction** **B1** except if: *I won't call you unless there are problems.*

unlike /ʌnˈlaɪk/ **preposition** different from someone or something

unlikely /ʌnˈlaɪk·li/ **adj** (comparative **unlikelier**, superlative **unlikeliest**) **B1** not expected to happen: *It's **unlikely that** I'll come to the party.*

unload /ʌnˈloʊd/ **verb** to remove things from a vehicle: *Can you help me unload the car?*

unlock /ʌnˈlɑk/ **verb** to open something that is locked using a key

unlucky /ʌnˈlʌk·i/ **adj** (comparative **unluckier**, superlative **unluckiest**) **B1** having or causing bad luck: *Some people think it's unlucky to walk under ladders.*

unmarried /ʌnˈmær·id/ **adj** not married

unmistakable /ˌʌn·məˈsteɪ·kə·bəl/ **adj** Something that is unmistakable is very obvious and cannot be confused with anything else: *an unmistakable look of disappointment*

unnatural /ʌnˈnætʃ·ər·əl/ **adj** not normal or right: *an unnatural interest in death*

unnecessary /ʌnˈnes·əˌser·i/ **adj** **B1** not needed: *Don't take any unnecessary car trips in this weather.*

unofficial /ˌʌn·əˈfɪʃ·əl/ **adj** not said or done by the government or someone in authority: *The President made an unofficial visit to Paris* (= not representing the government).
• **unofficially adv**

unpack

unpack /ʌnˈpæk/ **verb** **B1** to take things out of a bag, box, etc.: *Bella unpacked her suitcase.*

unpaid /ʌnˈpeɪd/ **adj 1** An unpaid debt, tax, etc. has not been paid. **2** involving work for which you are not paid: *an unpaid position*

unpleasant /ʌnˈplez·ənt/ **adj** **B1** not enjoyable or pleasant: *an unpleasant experience*

unplug /ʌnˈplʌg/ **verb** (present participle **unplugging**, past tense and past participle **unplugged**) to stop a piece of electrical equipment from being connected to an electricity supply by pulling its plug out of the wall

unpopular /ʌnˈpɑp·jə·lər/ adj   disliked by most people: *an unpopular idea*

unpredictable /ˌʌn·prɪˈdɪk·tə·bəl/ adj   changing so much that you do not know what will happen next: *unpredictable weather conditions*

unreasonable /ʌnˈri·zə·nə·bəl/ adj   not fair: *unreasonable demands*

unreliable /ˌʌn·rɪˈlɑɪ·ə·bəl/ adj   not able to be trusted or depended on: *The trains were noisy, dirty, and unreliable.*

unsafe /ʌnˈseɪf/ adj   dangerous: *The building is unsafe.*

unsatisfactory /ˌʌn·sæt·əsˈfæk·tə·ri/ adj   not good enough to be acceptable: *Many school buildings are in an unsatisfactory condition.*

unstressed /ʌnˈstrest/ adj   An unstressed part of a word or phrase is said less strongly than the rest of it.

unsuccessful /ˌʌn·səkˈses·fəl/ adj   not achieving what was wanted or planned: *an unsuccessful attempt*
• **unsuccessfully** adv

unsuitable /ʌnˈsu·t̬ə·bəl/ adj   not acceptable or right for someone or something: *My parents considered the movie unsuitable for children.*

unsure /ʌnˈʃʊər/ adj   not certain, or having doubts: *I'm a little **unsure about** what to do.*

unsympathetic /ˌʌn·sɪmˈpɑˈθet̬·ɪk/ adj   showing that you do not understand or care about someone's problems: *I told him I had a cold but he was completely unsympathetic.*

untie /ʌnˈtɑɪ/ verb
(present participle
untying, past tense
and past participle
untied)   to unfasten a knot or something that has been tied with a knot: *I untied my shoelaces and kicked off my shoes.*

untie

until /ənˈtɪl/ preposition, conjunction (also **till,** /tɪl/)   **1** A1 continuing to happen before a particular time or event and then stopping: *We'll be performing this show until the end of the month.* ○ *We walked until it got dark.*   **2** A2 as far as: *Drive west until you get to a traffic light and then turn right.*   **3** not until B1 not before a particular time or event: *The store doesn't open until seven.*

untrue /ʌnˈtru/ adj   false: *Everything she said about me is untrue.*

unusual /ʌnˈju·ʒu·əl/ adj   A2 different and not ordinary, often in a way that is interesting: *an unusual name*

unwanted /ʌnˈwɑn·tɪd/ adj   not desired or needed: *unwanted advice*

unwelcome /ʌnˈwel·kəm/ adj   not wanted: *an unwelcome visitor*

unwell /ʌnˈwel/ adj   ill: *I was feeling unwell.*

unwilling /ʌnˈwɪl·ɪŋ/ adj   not wanting to do something: *Many people are unwilling to accept change.*

unwind /ʌnˈwɑɪnd/ verb (past tense and past participle **unwound**) informal   to relax, especially after working: *Music helps me to unwind.*

unwise /ʌnˈwɑɪz/ adj   stupid and likely to cause problems: *an unwise decision*
• **unwisely** adv

unwrap /ʌnˈræp/ verb (present participle **unwrapping,** past tense and past participle **unwrapped**)   to remove the paper, cloth, etc. that is covering something: *She carefully unwrapped the present.*

up¹ /ʌp/ adv, preposition   **1** A2 toward or in a higher place: *He ran up the stairs.* ○ *She looked up and smiled at me.*   **2** A1 to or toward a position that is vertical or as straight as possible: *He stood up.* ○ *She sat up.*   **3** to a greater degree, amount, volume, etc.: *Can you turn up the heat?*   **4** used to say that someone completes an action or uses all of something: *I used up all my money.* ○ *Eat up the rest of your dinner.*   **5** up the road, street, etc. A2 along or farther along the street, road, etc.: *They live just up the road.* **6 go, walk, etc. up to someone/ something** **B1** to walk directly toward someone or something until you are next to that person or thing: *He came straight up to me and introduced himself.* **7 up to 10, 20, etc. B1** any amount under 10, 20, etc.: *We can invite up to 65 people.* **8 up to/till/until B1** until a particular time: *You can call me up till midnight.* **9 be up to someone B1** If an action or decision is up to someone, that person is responsible for doing or making it: *I can't decide for you. It's up to you.* **10 be up to something** informal **B1** to be doing or planning something bad: *What are you two up to?*

up² /ʌp/ *adj* **B1** not in bed: *Is she up yet?*

upbringing /ˈʌpˌbrɪŋ·ɪŋ/ *noun* [no plural] the way that your parents take care of you and the things that they teach you when you are growing up: *She had a very strict upbringing.*

update¹ /ˈʌpˌdeɪt/, /ˌʌpˈdeɪt/ *verb* (present participle **updating**, past tense and past participle **updated**) **B1** to add new information: *We just updated our website.*

update² /ˈʌpˌdeɪt/ *noun* a new form of something that existed at an earlier time: *a software update*

upgrade /ˌʌpˈgreɪd/ *verb* (present participle **upgrading**, past tense and past participle **upgraded**) to get something that is newer and better: *I really should upgrade my computer.*
• **upgrade** *noun*

uphill /ˈʌpˈhɪl/ *adv* toward the top of a hill: *We walked half a mile uphill.*

upload /ˈʌpˌloʊd/ *verb* to copy computer information, usually from a single computer to the Internet

upon /əˈpɑn/ *preposition* formal on: *Her anger had no effect upon him.*

upper /ˈʌp·ər/ *adj* **B1** at a higher position: *an upper floor* ∘ *the upper lip*

uppercase /ˈʌpˌərˌkeɪs/ *noun* [no plural] letters of the alphabet that are written as capitals, such as A, B, C
• **uppercase** *adj*

upright /ˈʌpˌraɪt/ *adj* straight up or vertical: *Please return your seats to their upright position.*

upset¹ /ˌʌpˈset/ *adj* **A2** sad or worried because something bad has happened: *They had an argument and she's still **upset about it.***

upset² /ˌʌpˈset/ *verb* (present participle **upsetting**, past tense and past participle **upset**) **1** to make someone feel sad or worried: *The phone call clearly upset her.* **2** to cause problems for something: *The bad weather upset our vacation plans.*

upside down

upsetting /ʌpˈset·ɪŋ/ *adj* making you sad or worried: *I found the movie very upsetting.*

upside down /ˈʌpˌsaɪd ˈdaʊn/ *adv* turned so that the part that is usually at the top is now at the bottom: *Turn the jar **upside down** and shake it.*

upstairs /ˈʌpˈsteərz/ *adv* **A2** on or to a higher level of a building: *He ran upstairs to answer the phone.*
• **upstairs** *adj* **B1** *an upstairs bedroom*

up-to-date /ˌʌp·təˈdeɪt/ *adj* **B1** modern, and using the most recent technology or knowledge

upward /ˈʌp·wərd/ *adv* toward a higher place or level: *House prices have started moving upward again.*

upwards /ˈʌp·wərdz/ *adv* another form of upward

urban /ˈɜr·bən/ *adj* belonging or relating to a city or town: *urban areas*

urge¹ /ɜrdʒ/ *verb* (present participle **urging**, past tense and past participle **urged**) **urge someone to do something** to try to persuade someone to do something: *His parents urged him to go to college.*

urge² /ɜrdʒ/ *noun* a strong wish or need: *I felt a powerful urge to slap him.*

urgent /ˈɜː·dʒənt/ **adj** **B1** very important and needing you to take action immediately: *an urgent message*
• **urgently adv** **B1** *I urgently need to speak to you.*

us /ʌs/ **pronoun** **A1** used after a verb or preposition to mean the person who is speaking or writing and one or more other people: *She gave us all a present.*

use¹ /juːz/ **verb** (present participle **using**, past tense and past participle **used**) **1** **A1** If you use something, you do something with it for a particular purpose: *Can I use your pen?* ∘ *She uses her car for work.* **2** **B1** to take an amount from a supply of something: *These light bulbs use less electricity.*
use something up phrasal verb to finish an amount of something: *someone used up all the eggs.*

use² /juːs/ **noun** **1** **A2** [no plural] the act of using something, or the state of something being used: *Guests have free use of the hotel swimming pool.* **2** **B1** a purpose for which something is used: *Can you find a use for this box?* **3** **B1** one of the meanings of a word, or the way that a particular word is used: *Can you list all the uses of the word "point"?* **4** **be no use** used to say that trying to do something has no effect: *It's no use talking to him – he won't listen.*

used¹ /juːst/ **adj** **be used to something/doing something** **B1** If you are used to something, you have done it or had it many times before: *He's used to working long hours.* **get used to something/doing something** **B1** to become familiar with something or someone: *You get used to getting up early after a day or two.*

used² /juːzd/ **adj** owned by someone else before you: *a used car*

used to /ˈjuːst tu/ **modal verb** **used to do/be something** **B1** If something used to happen or exist, it happened often or existed in the past but it does not happen now: *I used to go out every night when I was a student.* ∘ *Monica used to live in Iowa.*

⚠ Common mistake: used to and be used to

You use the phrase **used to** with a verb for talking about a situation or regular activity in the past.

My dad used to smoke when he was younger.
I used to live in Ohio, but now I live in Alaska.

When you make **used to** + **verb** into a question or negative using the verb **do**, the correct form is **use to**.

My dad didn't use to smoke.
Where did you use to live?
~~Where did you used to live?~~

The expression **be used to something/doing something** is for talking about something that you have done or experienced a lot before.

I don't mind the heat. I'm used to hot weather.
He's not used to working long hours.
~~He's not use to working long hours.~~

---

useful /ˈjuːs·fəl/ **adj** **A2** helping you to do or get something: *useful information*

useless /ˈjuːs·ləs/ **adj** **B1** If something is useless, it does not work well or has no effect: *This umbrella is useless – there's a big hole in it.*

user /ˈjuː·zər/ **noun** **B1** someone who uses a product, machine, or service: *a new service for Internet users*

usual /ˈjuː·ʒu·əl/ **adj** **1** **B1** normal and happening most of the time: *I went to bed at my usual time.* ∘ *This winter has been much colder than usual.*
→ Opposite **unusual** **A2** **2 as usual** **A2** in the way that happens most of the time: *As usual, Nick was the last to arrive.*

usually /ˈjuː·ʒu·ə·li/ **adv** **A2** in the way that happens most often: *I usually get home at about six o'clock.*

utensil /juˈten·səl/ **noun** a tool that you use for doing jobs in the house, especially cooking: *wooden cooking utensils*

utter /ˈʌt·ər/ **adj** complete: *She dismissed the article as utter nonsense.*

---

utterly /ˈʌt·ər·li/ adv   completely: *The new rule is utterly ridiculous.*

Vv

V, v /viː/   the twenty-second letter of the alphabet

vacancy /ˈveɪ·kən·si/ noun (plural **vacancies**)   1 a room that is not being used in a hotel: *Do you have any vacancies?*   2 a job that is free for someone to do: *There are a few vacancies in the art department.*

vacant /ˈveɪ·kənt/ adj   1 Somewhere that is vacant is not being used: *a vacant building*   2 A vacant job is free for someone to do.

vacation /veɪˈkeɪ·ʃən/ noun 🔵 a period of time when you are not at home but are staying somewhere else for enjoyment: *We're **taking a vacation** to Florida.*

vaccinate /ˈvæk·sə·neɪt/ verb (present participle **vaccinating**, past tense and past participle **vaccinated**)   to give someone a substance to stop him or her from getting a disease: *Babies are **vaccinated against** childhood diseases.*
• **vaccination** noun

vaccine /vækˈsiːn/ noun   a substance that you take into your body to avoid getting a disease: *the flu vaccine*

vacuum /ˈvæk·juːm/ verb   to clean something using a vacuum cleaner

vacuum cleaner /ˈvæk·juːm ˌkliː·nər/ noun   an electric machine that cleans floors by sucking up dirt

vagina /vəˈdʒaɪ·nə/ noun   the part of a woman's body that connects her outer sex organs to the place where a baby grows

vague /veɪɡ/ adj   not clear or certain: *I have a vague idea of where the hotel is.*
• **vaguely** adv *I vaguely (=slightly) remember meeting her.*

vain /veɪn/ adj   too interested in your own appearance and thinking you are very attractive

valid /ˈvæl·ɪd/ adj   A valid ticket or document is legally acceptable: *The ticket is valid for three months.*
→ Opposite **invalid** adj

valley /ˈvæl·i/ noun 🔵 an area of low land between hills or mountains

valuable /ˈvæl·juː·ə·bəl/, /ˈvæl·jə·bəl/ adj   1 🔵 Valuable objects could be sold for a lot of money: *valuable paintings*   2 Valuable information, help, advice, etc. is very helpful.

value¹ /ˈvæl·juː/ noun   1 🔵 the amount of money something could be sold for: *Cars go down in value quickly.*   2 🔵 [no plural] how useful or important something is: *a document of great historical value*

value² /ˈvæl·juː/ verb (present participle **valuing**, past tense and past participle **valued**)   1 If you value something or someone, that thing or person is very important to you: *I always value his opinion.*
2 to judge how much money something could be sold for: *The ring was **valued at** $1,000.*

valve /vælv/ noun   something that opens and closes to control the flow of liquid or gas

vampire /ˈvæm·paɪər/ noun   in stories, a dead person who bites people's necks and drinks their blood

van /væn/ noun 🔵 a vehicle that is used for carrying things but that is smaller than a truck
→ See picture at **vehicle**

vandalism /ˈvæn·dᵊl·ɪz·əm/ noun [no plural]   the crime of damaging things in public places

vandalize /ˈvæn·dᵊl·aɪz/ verb (present participle **vandalizing**, past tense and past participle **vandalized**)   to damage things in public places

vanilla /vəˈnɪl·ə/ noun [no plural]   a substance that is used to give flavor to some sweet foods: *vanilla ice cream*

a
b
c
d
e
f
g
h
i
j
k
l
m
n
o
p
q
r
s
t
u
v
w
x
y
z

vanish /ˈvæn·ɪʃ/ **verb** to disappear suddenly: *The sun vanished behind the trees.*

vanity /ˈvæn·ɪ·t̬i/ **noun** [no plural] too much pride in your appearance or achievements

vapor /ˈveɪ·pər/ **noun** [no plural] many small drops of liquid in the air that look like a cloud

varied /ˈveər·id/ **adj** having many different types of things: *a long and varied career*

variety /vəˈrɑɪ·ɪ·t̬i/ **noun** **1** 🅱1 [no plural] a lot of different activities, situations, people, etc.: *I need more variety in my life.* **2 a variety of *something/someone*** 🅰2 many different types of things or people: *Ben has done a variety of jobs.* **3** (plural **varieties**) a different type of something: *a new variety of potato*

various /ˈveər·i·əs/ **adj** 🅰2 many different: *They have offices in various parts of the country.*

varnish[1] /ˈvɑr·nɪʃ/ **noun** a clear liquid that you paint onto wood to protect it

varnish[2] /ˈvɑr·nɪʃ/ **verb** to put varnish on a surface

vary /ˈveər·i/ **verb** (present participle **varying**, past tense and past participle **varied**) If things of the same type vary, they are different from each other: *Car prices vary greatly from state to state.*

vase /veɪs/, /veɪz/, /vɑz/ **noun** 🅱1 a container that you put flowers in

vast /væst/ **adj** very big: *a vast amount of money*

vegetable /ˈvedʒ·tə·bəl/, /ˈvedʒ·ə·tə·bəl/ **noun** 🅰1 a plant or part of a plant that you eat, for example a potato, onion, etc.
→ See **Fruits and Vegetables** on page C8

vegetarian /ˌvedʒ·ɪˈteər·i·ən/ **noun** 🅱1 someone who does not eat meat or fish

vehicle /ˈvi·ɪ·kəl/ **noun** 🅱1 something such as a car or bus that takes people from one place to another

vehicle

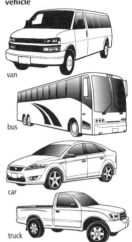

van

bus

car

truck

veil /veɪl/ **noun** a thin piece of material that covers a woman's face

vein /veɪn/ **noun** **1** one of the tubes in your body that carries blood to your heart **2 in the same vein** in the same style of speaking or writing

velvet /ˈvel·vɪt/ **noun** [no plural] cloth that has a thick, soft surface on one side: *a black velvet jacket*

ventilate /ˈven·t̬ᵊlˌeɪt/ **verb** (present participle **ventilating**, past tense and past participle **ventilated**) to let air come into and go out of a room or building
• **ventilation** noun [no plural] *a ventilation system*

venue /ˈven·ju/ **noun** a place where a sports game, musical performance, etc. happens

verb /vɜrb/ **noun** 🅰2 a word or group of words that refers to an action, state, or experience. For example, the words "arrive," "make," "be," and "feel" are verbs.

vase

---

verdict /ˈvɜr·dɪkt/ noun a decision in a court of law saying whether someone has done a crime: *a guilty verdict*

verse /vɜrs/ noun **1** one of the parts that a song or poem is divided into: *I only know the first verse.* **2** [no plural] words that are in the form of poetry: *The story was told in verse.*

version /ˈvɜr·ʒən/ noun one form of something that has many forms: *I saw the original version of the movie.*

versus /ˈvɜr·səs/ preposition used to say that one team or person is competing against another: *Tomorrow's game is the Lions versus the Chargers.*

vertical /ˈvɜr·tɪ·kəl/ adj pointing straight up from a surface: *a vertical line*
→ See picture at **horizontal**

very /ˈver·i/ adv **1** **A1** used to make an adjective or adverb stronger: *She was very pleased.* ◦ *Thank you very much.*
2 not very good, tall, happy, etc. **A1** not good, happy, etc.: *The movie wasn't very good.*

vest /vest/ noun a piece of clothing with buttons at the front and no sleeves, that you wear over a shirt
→ See **Clothes** on page C5

vet /vet/ noun **B1** someone whose job is to give medical care to animals that are hurt or sick

via /ˈvaɪ·ə/, /ˈvi·ə/ preposition **1** **B1** going through or stopping at a place on the way to another place: *This flight goes to Dallas via Atlanta.* **2** **B1** using a particular machine, system, or person to send or receive something: *Reports are coming in via satellite.*

vibrate /ˈvaɪ·breɪt/ verb (present participle **vibrating**, past tense and past participle **vibrated**) to shake with small, quick movements: *The music was so loud that the floor was vibrating.*
• **vibration** noun

vice /vaɪs/ noun something bad that someone often does: *Smoking is his only vice.*

vice president /ˈvaɪs ˈprez·ɪ·dənt/ noun the person who is a rank lower than the president of a country or company

vicious /ˈvɪʃ·əs/ adj violent and dangerous: *a vicious attack on a child*

victim /ˈvɪk·təm/ noun someone who has been hurt or killed: *the victim of a crime* ◦ *flood victims*

victory /ˈvɪk·tə·ri/ noun (plural **victories**) an act of winning a fight or competition: *Phoenix had a 135-114 victory over Denver.*

video /ˈvɪd·i·oʊ/ noun **A2** a recording of a movie, TV program, etc. that you can watch on a television or computer: *You can get the movie on video.*

video game /ˈvɪd·i·oʊ ˌɡeɪm/ noun **A2** a game in which you make pictures move on a screen

view /vju/ noun **1** **A2** the things that you can see from a place: *There was a lovely view of the lake from the bedroom window.* **2** **B1** your opinion: *We have different views on education.* ◦ *In her view this is wrong.* **3** [no plural] how well you can see something from a place: *We had a great view of the procession.*

viewer /ˈvju·ər/ noun someone who watches a television program

vigorous /ˈvɪɡ·ər·əs/ adj showing or needing a lot of physical energy: *vigorous exercise*
• **vigorously** adv *He nodded his head vigorously.*

village /ˈvɪl·ɪdʒ/ noun **A1** a very small town in the country: *She is from a small village in Greece.*

villain /ˈvɪl·ən/ noun a bad person in a movie, book, etc.

vine /vaɪn/ noun a plant that grapes (=small, green or purple fruit used for making wine) grow on

vinegar /ˈvɪn·ɪ·ɡər/ noun [no plural] a sour liquid that is used in cooking, often made from wine

vineyard /ˈvɪn·jərd/ noun an area of land where someone grows grapes (=small, green or purple fruit) for making wine

violence /ˈvaɪ·ə·ləns/ noun [no plural] the act of hurting or killing someone else: *Many people were killed in the violence.*

a b c d e f g h i j k l m n o p q r s t u **v** w x y z

a
b
c
d
e
f
g
h
i
j
k
l
m
n
o
p
q
r
s
t
u
v
w
x
y
z

violent /ˈvaɪ·ə·lənt/ **adj** **1** involving violence: *I don't like violent movies (=movies that show violence).* **2** likely to hurt or kill someone else: *a violent criminal* **3** sudden and causing damage: *a violent storm*

• **violently adv**

violin /ˌvaɪ·əˈlɪn/ **noun** **A2** a wooden musical instrument that you hold against your neck and play by moving a stick across strings

violin

VIP /ˌviˈaɪˈpi/ **noun** abbreviation for very important person: someone who is famous or powerful and is treated in a special way

virtual /ˈvɜr·tʃu·əl/ **adj** **1** almost a particular thing or quality: *They played the game in virtual silence.* **2** using computer images and sounds to make you think something is real: *an online virtual museum*

virtually /ˈvɜr·tʃu·ə·li/ **adv** almost: *They're virtually the same.*

virtue /ˈvɜr·tʃu/ **noun** **1** a useful quality: *The great virtue of having a small car is that you can park it easily.* **2** a good quality that someone has: *Patience is not among his virtues.*

virus /ˈvaɪ·rəs/ **noun** **1** a very small thing that causes illnesses, or an illness that it causes **2** **B1** a program that is secretly put onto a computer in order to destroy the information that is stored on it

visa /ˈvi·zə/ **noun** **B1** an official mark in your passport (=book showing where you come from) that allows you to enter or leave a particular country

visible /ˈvɪz·ə·bəl/ **adj** able to be seen: *The fire was visible from two miles away.* → Opposite **invisible adj**

vision /ˈvɪʒ·ən/ **noun** **1** an idea or image in your mind of what something could be like in the future: *a vision of a better society* **2** [no plural] the ability to see: *He has poor vision in his left eye.*

visit[1] /ˈvɪz·ɪt/ **verb** **1** **A1** to go somewhere to see someone or a place: *Did you visit St. Petersburg while you were in Russia?* ◦ *We have friends coming to visit this weekend.* **2** **A2** to look at a website: *Visit our website!*

visit[2] /ˈvɪz·ɪt/ **noun** **B1** an occasion when you go to see a place or a person: *the President's visit to Hong Kong*

visitor /ˈvɪz·ɪ·tər/ **noun** **A2** someone who visits a person or place: *The museum attracts large numbers of visitors.*

visual /ˈvɪʒ·u·əl/ **adj** relating to seeing: *The movie has dramatic visual effects.*

vital /ˈvaɪ·t²l/ **adj** necessary: *Tourism is vital to the country's economy.*

vitamin /ˈvaɪ·tə·mɪn/ **noun** one of a group of natural substances in food that you need to be healthy: *Oranges are full of vitamin C.*

vivid /ˈvɪv·ɪd/ **adj** **1** Vivid descriptions or memories produce strong, clear images in your mind: *He gave a very vivid description of life in Caracas.* **2** A vivid color is very bright.

• **vividly adv** *I vividly remember my first day at work.*

vocabulary /voʊˈkæb·jə·ler·i/ **noun** (plural **vocabularies**) **A2** words: *Reading helps to widen your vocabulary.* ◦ *Computing has its own special vocabulary.*

voice /vɔɪs/ **noun** **B1** the sounds that you make when you speak or sing: *I could hear voices in the next room.* ◦ *Jessie has a beautiful singing voice.*

voice mail /ˈvɔɪs ˌmeɪl/ **noun** [no plural] an electronic telephone answering system

volcano /vɑlˈkeɪ·noʊ/ **noun** (plural **volcanoes**, **volcanos**) a mountain with a large hole at the top, which sometimes explodes

volcano

• **volcanic adj** *volcanic ash*

volleyball /ˈvɑl·iˌbɔl/ **noun** [no plural] **A2** a game in which two

teams use their hands to hit a ball over
a net
→ See **Sports 2** on page C16

volt /voʊlt/ *noun*   a unit for measuring
the force of an electric current

volume /ˈvɑl·jum/, /ˈvɑl·jəm/ *noun*
1 🅱1 [no plural] the level of sound made
by a television, radio, etc.: *Could you
turn the volume down?* **2** [no plural] the
amount of space inside an object **3** a
book, especially one of a set: *a new dictionary in two volumes*

voluntary /ˈvɑl·ənˌter·i/ *adj*   done,
made, or given willingly, without being
forced or paid to do it: *Participation in
the study is voluntary.*
• **voluntarily** *adv* She left voluntarily.

volunteer[1] /ˌvɑl·ənˈtɪər/ *verb*   to offer
to do something without being asked to
do it: *Rob volunteered to babysit.*

volunteer[2] /ˌvɑl·ənˈtɪər/ *noun*   someone
who works without being paid, especially
doing work that involves helping people: *a Red Cross volunteer*

vomit[1] /ˈvɑm·ɪt/ *verb*   If someone vom-
its, the food or liquid that was in his or
her stomach comes up and out of his or
her mouth.

vomit[2] /ˈvɑm·ɪt/ *noun* [no plural]   the food
or liquid that comes from your mouth
when you vomit

vote[1] /voʊt/ *verb* (present participle **voting**,
past tense and past participle **voted**)
🅱1 to choose someone or something in
an election or meeting by marking an
official piece of paper or putting your
hand up: *Who did you vote for?* ○ *The
town council voted to reject new taxes.*

vote[2] /voʊt/ *noun*   🅱1 an act of choosing someone or something in an election or meeting by marking an official
piece of paper or putting your hand up:
He lost the election by twenty votes.

voter /ˈvoʊ·t̬ər/ *noun*   someone who
votes or who is officially allowed to vote

vowel /ˈvaʊ·əl/ *noun*   🅱1 a speech
sound that you make with your lips and

teeth open, shown in English by the letters "a," "e," "i," "o," or "u"

voyage /ˈvɔɪ·ɪdʒ/ *noun*   a long trip, especially by ship or in space: *He was a
young sailor on his first voyage.*

vs. *preposition*   abbreviation for versus:
used to say that one team or person is
competing against another: *the Raiders
vs. the Bears*

vulnerable /ˈvʌl·nər·ə·bəl/ *adj*   easy to
hurt or attack: *The troops are in a vulnerable position.*

vulture /ˈvʌl·tʃər/ *noun*   a large bird
with no feathers on its head or neck
that eats dead animals

W w

W, w /ˈdʌb·əl.ju/   the twenty-third letter
of the alphabet

wade /weɪd/ *verb* (present participle **wading**,
past tense and past participle **waded**)   to walk
through water: *He waded across the river.*

wag /wæg/ *verb* (present participle **wagging**,
past tense and past participle **wagged**)   If a dog
wags its tail, it moves it from side to side.

wage /weɪdʒ/ *noun* (also **wages**)   🅱1 the
amount of money a person regularly
gets for his or her job: *hourly wages*

wail /weɪl/ *verb*   to cry loudly because
you are very sad: *"I can't find my mom!"
she wailed.*

waist /weɪst/ *noun*   the part around the
middle of your body where you wear a
belt
→ See **The Body** on page C2

wait[1] /weɪt/ *verb*   **1** 🅰1 to stay in a
place until someone or something arrives: *I'm waiting for Harry.* ○ *How long
did you wait for a taxi?* **2 can't wait**
informal 🅰2 used to say how excited you
are about something that you are going
to do: *I can't wait to see him.* **3 wait a**

a *b* *c* *d* *e* *f* *g* *h* *i* *j* *k* *l* *m* *n* *o* *p* *q* *r* *s* *t* *u* *v* *w* *x* *y* *z*

| æ cat | ɑ hot | e get | ɪ sit | i see | ɔ saw | c ? | u book | u too | ʌ cut | ə about | ər mother | ɜr turn | ɔr for | aɪ my | aʊ how | eɪ say | ɔɪ boy |

minute/second **B1** said in order to interrupt someone, or to get his or her attention or when you have suddenly thought of something important: *Now, wait a minute – I don't agree with that.*
4 keep *somebody* waiting **B1** to be late so that someone has to wait for you: *I'm sorry that I kept you waiting.*

⚠️ **Common mistake: wait or expect?**

When you **wait**, you stay somewhere until a person or thing arrives or is ready.
I waited twenty minutes for the bus.
She's waiting for her test results.
When you **expect** something, you think that it will happen.
I'm expecting the bus to arrive in about five minutes.
She expected to do well on the test.
~~She waited to do well on the test.~~

---

wait² /weɪt/ *noun* [no plural] the act of staying in a place until someone or something arrives or someone or something is ready for you: *We had a long wait at the airport.*

waiter /ˈweɪ·tər/ *noun* **A1** a man who works in a restaurant, bringing food to customers

waiting room /ˈweɪ·tɪŋ ˌrum/, /ˈweɪ·tɪŋ ˌrʊm/ *noun* a room in which people wait for something, for example to see a doctor

waitress /ˈweɪ·trəs/ *noun* **A1** a woman who works in a restaurant, bringing food to customers

wake /weɪk/ *verb* (present participle **waking**, past tense **woke**, past participle **woken**) (also **wake up**) **A1** to stop sleeping or to make someone else stop sleeping: *I just woke up. ○ Could you wake me up before you go?*
→ See **Phrasal Verbs** on page C13

walk¹ /wɔk/ *verb* **A1** to move forward by putting one foot in front of the other and then repeating the action: *She walks to school. ○ We walked twenty miles.*

walk² /wɔk/ *noun* **A2** a trip that you make by walking, often for enjoyment: *He took the dog for a walk.*

walking /ˈwɔ·kɪŋ/ *noun* [no plural] **A2** the activity of going for a walk: *I love walking on the beach.*

wall /wɔl/ *noun* **1 A1** one of the sides of a room or building: *There were several paintings on the wall.* **2 A1** a structure made of brick or stone that divides areas that are owned by different people: *a garden wall*

wallet /ˈwɑl·ɪt/ *noun* **A2** a small, flat container for paper money and credit cards (=plastic cards used for paying with)

wallpaper /ˈwɑlˌpeɪ·pər/ *noun* [no plural] paper, usually with a pattern, that you decorate walls with
• **wallpaper** *verb*

walnut /ˈwɔl·nət/ *noun* a nut that is in two halves inside a brown shell

wander /ˈwɑn·dər/ *verb* to walk slowly around a place without any purpose: *They wandered around the town.*

want /wɑnt/ *verb* **1 A1** to feel that you would like to have something: *He wants a new car. ○ Who wants ice cream?* **2 A1** to feel that you would like something to happen: *I want you to be happy. ○ I don't want to talk about it.*

war /wɔr/ *noun* **A2** fighting, using soldiers and weapons, between two or more countries, or two or more groups inside a country: *They've been at war for the past five years.*

ward /wɔrd/ *noun* a room in a hospital: *the cancer ward*

wardrobe /ˈwɔr·droʊb/ *noun* **B1** the clothes that a person has

warehouse /ˈweərˌhaʊs/ *noun* a large building for keeping things that are going to be sold

warfare /ˈwɔrˌfeər/ *noun* [no plural] fighting in a war, especially using a particular type of weapon: *chemical warfare*

warm¹ /wɔrm/ *adj* **1 A1** having a temperature between cool and hot: *It's nice* *and warm in here.* ○ *Are you warm enough?* **2 A2** Warm clothes or covers keep your body warm: *a warm sweater* **3 B1** friendly: *a warm welcome*

warm² /wɔrm/ **verb** to become warm or to make something become warm: *I'll warm the soup.*

warm up *phrasal verb* to do gentle exercises before a sport: *They were warming up before the match.*

warm (someone/something) up *phrasal verb* to become warmer or to make someone or something warmer: *A hot drink will warm you up.*

warmly /'wɔrm·li/ **adv** in a friendly way

warmth /wɔrmθ/ **noun** [no plural] **1** the heat that is made by something: *the warmth of the fire* **2** the quality of being friendly: *There was no warmth in his eyes.*

warn /wɔrn/ **verb** **B1** to tell someone that something bad may happen in the future: *I warned you that it would be cold, but you still wouldn't wear a coat.*

warning /'wɔr·nɪŋ/ **noun** **B1** something that tells or shows you that something bad may happen: *All cigarette packs have a warning.*

was /wʌz/, /wʌz/ /wʌz/ **verb** the past tense of be, used with "I," "he," "she," and "it": *He was young.*

wash¹ /wɑʃ/ **verb** **1 A1** to make something clean using water and soap: *Dad was washing the dishes.* **2 A1** to clean part of your body with water and soap: *Have you washed your hands?*

wash up *phrasal verb* **A1** to wash your hands, especially before a meal: *It's time to wash up for dinner.*

wash² /wɑʃ/ **noun** **A2** clothes, sheets, etc. that are being washed together: *Your jeans are in the wash.*

washer /'wɑʃ·ər/ **noun** **B1** a machine that washes clothes

washing machine /'wɑʃ·ɪŋ mə,ʃin/ **noun** **A2** a machine that washes clothes

wasn't /'wɑz·ənt/, /'wʌz·ənt/ short form of was not: *I wasn't hungry this morning.*

wasp /wɑsp/ **noun** a flying insect with a thin body that is black and yellow
→ See picture at **insect**

waste¹ /weɪst/ **noun** **1 B1** a bad use of something useful, such as time or money: *Meetings are a waste of time.* ○ *They throw away tons of food – it's such a waste.* **2** [no plural] things that are not wanted: *household waste*

waste² /weɪst/ **verb** (present participle **wasting**, past tense and past participle **wasted**) **B1** to use too much of something or use something badly: *Why waste money on things you don't need?*

waste³ /weɪst/ **adj** **B1** Waste material is no longer needed and can be gotten rid of: *waste paper*

wastebasket /'weɪst,bæs·kɪt/ **noun** a container that is used for paper that you want to get rid of

watch¹ /wɑtʃ/ **verb** **1 A1** to look at something for a period of time: *The kids are watching TV.* ○ *I watched him as he arrived.* **2** to be careful about something: *She has to watch what she eats.*

watch out *phrasal verb* used to tell someone to be careful: *Watch out! There's a car coming!*

watch² /wɑtʃ/ **noun** **1 A1** a small clock on a strap that you fasten around your arm **2** [no plural] an act of watching or giving attention to something or someone: *We're keeping a close watch on the situation.*

watch

water¹ /'wɔ·t̬ər/ **noun** [no plural] **A1** the clear liquid that falls from the sky as rain and that is in seas, lakes, and rivers: *hot/cold water* ○ *a drink of water*

water² /'wɔ·t̬ər/ **verb** to pour water over plants

waterfall /'wɔ·t̬ər,fɔl/ **noun** **B1** a stream of water that falls from a high place, often to a pool below

watermelon /'wɔt̬·ər,mel·ən/ **noun** a large, round, green fruit that is pink inside with a lot of black seeds
→ See **Fruits and Vegetables** on page C8

waterproof /ˈwɔ·tər·pruf/ **adj**   Waterproof material or clothing does not let water through: *a waterproof sleeping bag*

watt /wɑt/ **noun**   a unit for measuring electrical power: *a 60-watt light bulb*

wave[1] /weɪv/ **verb** (present participle **waving**, past tense and past participle **waved**) **1** 🔵 to put your hand up and move it from side to side in order to attract someone's attention or to say goodbye: *Wave goodbye to Grandma.* ○ *She waved at him.* **2** to move from side to side in the air or make something move this way: *The long grass waved in the breeze.*

wave[2] /weɪv/ **noun** **1** 🔵 a line of higher water that moves across the surface of the sea or a lake: *I could hear the waves crashing against the rocks.* **2** the act of waving your hand: *She gave a little wave as the train left.* **3** the pattern in which some types of energy, such as sound, heat, and light, are spread or carried: *radio waves*

wave

a wave   she's waving

wavy /ˈweɪ·vi/ **adj** (comparative **wavier**, superlative **waviest**)   not straight but with slight curves: *wavy hair*
→ See **Hair** on page C9

wax /wæks/ **noun** [no plural]   a solid substance that becomes soft when warm and melts easily, often used to make candles

way /weɪ/ **noun** **1** 🟢 how you do something: *I need to find a way to help him.* ○ *We looked at different ways of solving the problem.* **2** 🟢 the route you take to get from one place to another: *Is there another way out of here?* ○ *I should buy a newspaper on the way home.* **3** 🔵 a particular choice, opinion, belief, or action, especially from among several possibilities: *I don't like the way she dresses.* **4** 🔵 a direction something faces or travels in: *This bus is going the wrong way.* **5** 🔵 an amount of space or time: *We're a long way from home.* ○ *Summer vacation is still a long way off.* **6** by the way 🟢 used when you say something new or on a different subject: *Oh, by the way, I forgot to buy the milk.* **7** way of life 🔵 the way in which a person lives: *Stealing became a way of life for him.* **8** no way! informal 🔵 certainly not: "*Will you lend me some money?*" "*No way!*" **9** be on her, my, its, etc. way to be arriving soon: *She just called – she's on her way.* **10** get in the way to stop someone from doing or continuing with something: *Don't let computer games get in the way of your studies.* **11** be under way to be already happening: *Building work is already under way.* **12** give way If something gives way, it falls because it is not strong enough to support the weight on top of it: *Suddenly the ground gave way under me.* **13** in a way/in many ways used to say that you think something is partly true: *In many ways, she was right.* **14** make your way to move somewhere, often with difficulty: *We made our way through the store to the main entrance.* **15** get/have your own way to get what you want, although it upsets other people: *She cries until she gets her own way.*

we /wi/ **pronoun** **1** 🟢 used as the subject of the verb when the person speaking or writing is referring to himself or herself and one or more other people: *My wife and I both play golf and we love it.* **2** 🔵 used to refer to people generally: *The world we live in today is very different.*

weak /wik/ **adj** **1** 🔵 not physically strong: *He felt too weak to sit up.* **2** 🔵 of a low quality or level: *She reads well but her spelling is weak.* → Opposite **strong adj** **3** likely to break and not able to support things: *a weak bridge* **4** A weak drink has little taste or contains little alcohol:

weak coffee **5** not powerful, or not having a strong character: *a weak leader*
• **weakly** adv

weaken /ˈwiː·kən/ **verb** to become less strong or powerful, or to make someone or something less strong or powerful: *Another war would weaken the economy.*

weakness /ˈwiːk·nəs/ **noun** **1** [no plural] a lack of strength or power: *Asking for help is not a sign of weakness.* **2** a part or quality of something or someone that is not good: *What do you think are your weaknesses as a manager?*

wealth /welθ/ **noun** [no plural] a large amount of money or property that someone has

wealthy /ˈwel·θi/ **adj** (comparative **wealthier**, superlative **wealthiest**) rich: *a wealthy businesswoman*

weapon /ˈwep·ən/ **noun** a gun, knife, or other object used to kill or hurt someone: *nuclear weapons*

wear /weər/ **verb** (past tense **wore**, past participle **worn**) **1** **A1** to have a piece of clothing, jewelry, etc. on your body: *I wear jeans all the time.* ○ *She wears glasses.* **2** to become thin and damaged after being used a lot, or to make this happen: *The carpet has worn thin.*

wear off phrasal verb If a feeling or the effect of something wears off, it gradually stops: *The anesthetic is starting to wear off.*

wear *someone* **out phrasal verb** to make someone very tired: *All this walking is wearing me out.*

wear *something* **out phrasal verb** **B1** to use something so much that it is damaged and cannot be used any more: *He's already worn out two pairs of shoes.*

weather /ˈweð·ər/ **noun** [no plural] **A1** the temperature or conditions outside, for example if it is hot, cold, sunny, etc.: *bad/good weather*

weather forecast /ˈweð·ər ˌfɔr·kæst/ **noun** **B1** a description of what the weather will be like for the next few hours, days, etc.: *Have you heard the **weather forecast for** tomorrow?*

weave /wiv/ **verb** (present participle **weaving**, past tense **wove**, past participle **woven**) to make cloth by crossing threads under and over each other by hand or on a machine

web /web/ **noun** **1** **B1** a type of net made by a spider (= creature with eight legs) to catch insects: *a spider web* **2 the Web** **A2** part of the Internet that consists of all the connected websites (= pages of text and pictures)

webcam /ˈweb.kæm/ **noun** **B1** a camera that records moving pictures and sounds and allows these to be shown on the Internet as they happen

web page /ˈweb ˌpeɪdʒ/ **noun** **A2** a part of a website that can be read on a computer screen

website /ˈweb.saɪt/ **noun** **A1** an area on the Web where information about a particular subject, organization, etc. can be found

we'd /wid/ **1** short form of we had: *We'd better not be late.* **2** we would: *We'd like to help you.*

wedding /ˈwed.ɪŋ/ **noun** **B1** an official ceremony at which two people get married: *We're going to a wedding on Saturday.*

Wednesday /ˈwenz.deɪ/ **noun** **A1** the day of the week after Tuesday and before Thursday

weed[1] /wid/ **noun** a wild plant that you do not want in your garden

weed[2] /wid/ **verb** to remove wild plants from a garden where they are not wanted

week /wik/ **noun** **1** **A1** a period of seven days: *last week* ○ *I have three meetings this week.* **2** **A1** the five days from Monday to Friday when people usually go to work or school: *I don't go out much during the week.*

weekday /ˈwik.deɪ/ **noun** **A2** one of the five days from Monday to Friday when people usually go to work or school

weekend /ˈwik.end/ **noun** Saturday and Sunday, the two days in the week

a b c d e f g h i j k l m n o p q r s t u v w x y z

when many people do not work: *Are you doing anything this weekend?*

weekly /'wik·li/ adj, adv **A2** happening once a week or every week: *a weekly newspaper*

weep /wip/ verb (past tense and past participle **wept**) to cry tears

weigh /weɪ/ verb **1 weigh 8 ounces, 100 pounds, 4 tons, etc. B1** to have a weight of 8 ounces, 100 pounds, 4 tons, etc.: *Annie weighs 145 pounds.* **2** to measure how heavy someone or something is: *Can you weigh these apples for me?*

weight /weɪt/ noun [no plural] **1 B1** how heavy someone or something is: *He's about average in height and weight.* **2** the quality of being heavy: *The shelf collapsed under the weight of the books.* **3 lose weight** If someone loses weight, he or she becomes lighter and thinner: *You look thinner – did you lose weight?* **4 gain weight** If someone gains weight, he or she becomes heavier and fatter: *I gained a lot of weight after I lost my job.*

weird /wɪərd/ adj very strange: *I had a really weird dream last night.*

welcome[1] /'wel·kəm/ noun, exclamation **1 A2** said to someone who has just arrived somewhere: *Welcome home!* ○ *Welcome to Dallas.* **2 you're welcome A2** said as a polite answer when someone thanks you for doing something: *"Thanks a lot for helping!" "You're welcome."* **3 B1** If you are welcome, people are happy that you are there: *You will always be welcome here.* **4 be welcome to do something B1** used to tell someone that he or she can certainly do something, if he or she wants to: *Anyone who is interested is welcome to come.*

welcome[2] /'wel·kəm/ verb (present participle **welcoming**, past tense and past participle **welcomed**) **1 B1** to say hello to someone who has arrived in a place: *Both families were there to welcome us.* **2** to be happy about something and want it to happen: *The decision was welcomed by everybody.*

welcome[3] /'wel·kəm/ noun **B1** the act of saying hello to someone who arrives

somewhere: *He was given a warm welcome by his fans.*

welfare /'wel·feər/ noun [no plural] **1** someone's welfare is his or her health and happiness: *He is concerned about the welfare of homeless people.* **2** money or help that a government gives to people who are poor or do not have jobs: *welfare payments*

well[1] /wel/ adj (comparative **better**, superlative **best**) **A1** healthy: *You look well!* ○ *I'm not very well.*

well[2] /wel/ adv **1 A1** in a good way: *I thought they played well.* ○ *He's doing well in school.* **2 A2** in a complete way or as much as possible: *I know him very well.* **3 well done! A1** used to tell someone how happy you are about his or her success: *"I scored three goals!" "Well done!"* **4 as well A2** also: *Are you going to invite Steve as well?* **5 as well as something A2** in addition to something: *They have lived in California as well as Oregon.* **6 oh well B1** used to say that a situation cannot be changed although it might be disappointing: *Oh well, you'll have plenty of other chances to find a job.* **7 all is well B1** everything is in a good or acceptable state: *I hope all is well with Zack.* **8 may/might as well** used to say that it is better to do something, even though it is not a lot better: *It's not raining, so we might as well take a walk.*

well[3] /wel/ exclamation **A1** something you say before you start speaking: *"Are you with us?" "Well, I'm not sure."*

well[4] /wel/ noun a deep hole in the ground from which you can get water, oil, or gas

we'll /wil/ short form of we will: *We'll be home on Friday.*

well behaved /'wel bɪ'heɪvd/ adj behaving in a polite and quiet way: *The children are polite and well behaved.* ○ *a well-behaved child*

well dressed /'wel 'drest/ adj **B1** wearing attractive, good-quality clothes: *a well-dressed woman* ○ *Their kids are always well dressed.*

well known /ˈwel ˈnoʊn/ **adj**
A2 famous: *She is well known for her photography.* ○ *a well-known actor*

well off /ˈwel ˈɔf/ **adj** having a lot of money: *Her parents are really well off.* ○ *a well-off family*

well paid /ˈwel ˈpeɪd/ **adj** If you are well paid or have a well-paid job, you earn a lot of money.

went /went/ past tense of go

wept /wept/ past tense and past participle of weep

were /wɜr/ past tense of be, used with "you," "we," and "they": *They were happy.*

we're /wɪr/ short form of we are: *Hurry! We're late!*

weren't /ˈwɜrnt/, /ˈwɜr·ənt/ short form of were not: *They weren't there.*

west, West /west/ **noun** [no plural]
1 **A2** the direction that you face to see the sun go down: *Which way is west?*
2 the west **A2** the part of an area that is farther toward the west than the rest: *The west of the state has a lot of farms.*
3 the West the countries of North America and western Europe
• **west adj** **A2** *the west shore of the lake* ○ *West Virginia*
• **west adv** **A2** *We drove west.*

western, Western /ˈwes·tɚn/ **adj 1** in or from the west part of an area: *western Connecticut* **2** related to the countries of North America and western Europe: *a Western diplomat*

wet /wet/ **adj** (comparative **wetter**, superlative **wettest**) **1** **A2** covered in water or another liquid: *a wet towel* **2** **A2** raining: *a wet and windy day* **3** **B1** not dry yet: *wet paint*

we've /wiv/ short form of we have: *We've been waiting for you.*

whale /hweɪl/ **noun**
B1 a very large animal that looks like a fish and lives in the sea

whale

wharf /hwɔrf/ **noun** a structure built

next to water where boats stop and things are taken on and off

what /hwʌt/, /hwɑt/ **pronoun, determiner**
1 **A1** used to ask for information about something: *What's (= what is) this?* ○ *What time is it?* **2** **A1** informal used when you have not heard what someone has said and you want him or her to repeat it. Some people think this use is not polite: *"Would you like more coffee, Tom?" "What?"* **3** **B1** used to refer to something without giving it a name: *I heard what he said.* ○ *Do you know what I mean?* **4** informal used to ask what someone wants when he or she calls your name: *"Jenny?" "What?"* **5 what about...?** **A2** used to suggest something: *What about asking Andy to help?* **6 what a/an...** **B1** used to give your opinion: *What an awful day!* **7 what if...?** **B1** used to ask about something that could happen in the future, especially something bad: *What if I miss the plane?* **8 what... for?** used to ask about the reason or the purpose for something: *What are these tools for?* ○ *What are you doing that for?*

> **⚠ Common mistake: what**
>
> When you have not heard what someone has said and you want him or her to repeat it, you can say **What?**, but this is not polite. It is better to say **Excuse me?** or **Pardon?**.
>
> *"It's ten o'clock." "Excuse me/Pardon?" "I said it's ten o'clock."*

whatever /hwʌtˈev·ɚr/, /hwɑtˈev·ɚr/ **adv, pronoun, determiner 1** **B1** anything or everything: *He eats whatever I put in front of him.* **2** used to say that what happens is not important because it does not change a situation: *Whatever happens I'll still love you.*

wheat /hwit/ **noun** [no plural] a plant whose grain is used for making flour, or the grain itself

wheel /hwil/ **noun** **A2** a circular object attached under a vehicle so that it moves smoothly over the ground: *My bike needs a new front wheel.*

a
b
c
d
e
f
g
h
i
j
k
l
m
n
o
p
q
r
s
t
u
v
w
x
y
z

æ cat | ɑ hot | e get | ɪ sit | i see | ɔ saw | ʊ book | u too | ʌ cut | ə about | ɚ mother | ɜr turn | ɔr for | aɪ my | aʊ how | eɪ say | ɔɪ boy |

wheelchair /'hwiːl.tʃeər/ noun
B1 a chair with wheels used by someone who cannot walk

when[1] /hwen/ adv **A1** used to ask at what time something happened or will happen: *When is your birthday?* ○ *When did he leave?*

when[2] /hwen/ conjunction **A2** used to say at what time something happened or will happen: *I found it when I was cleaning out the closet.* ○ *We'll go when you're ready.*

whenever /hwen'ev.ər/ conjunction
B1 every time or at any time: *You can go whenever you want.*

where[1] /hweər/ adv **A1** used to ask about the place or position of someone or something: *Where does she live?* ○ *Where are my car keys?*

where[2] /hweər/ conjunction **A2** at, in, or to a place or position: *I know where to go.*

whereas /hweər'æz/ conjunction
used to compare things that are different: *You eat a big lunch, whereas I have a sandwich.*

wherever /hweər'ev.ər/ conjunction
1 B1 in or to any place or every place: *You can sit wherever you like.* **2 wherever possible** every time it is possible: *We try to use natural fabrics wherever possible.*

whether /'hweð.ər/ conjunction
1 B1 used to talk about a choice between two or more possibilities: *I didn't know **whether or not** to go.* **2 B1** if: *I wasn't sure whether you'd like it.*

which /hwɪtʃ/ pronoun, determiner
1 A2 used to ask or talk about a choice between two or more things: *Which of these do you like best?* ○ *Which way is it to the station?* **2 B1** used to give more information about something: *The book, which includes a map, gives you all the information you need about Venice.*

> **!** Common mistake: **which**
>
> People often spell **which** wrong. Remember that there is an h after the w.

while[1] /hwaɪl/ conjunction **1 A2** during the time that: *I can't talk to anyone while I'm driving.* **2 B1** used to compare two different facts or situations: *Tom is very confident, while Katy is shy and quiet.*

while[2] /hwaɪl/ noun **a while B1** a period of time: *I'm going out for a while.*

whimper /'hwɪm.pər/ verb to make quiet crying sounds because of fear or pain: *The dog was whimpering with pain.*

whine /hwaɪn/ verb (present participle **whining**, past tense and past participle **whined**) to complain in an annoying way: *She's always whining about something.*

whip[1] /hwɪp/ noun a long piece of leather attached to a handle and used to hit an animal or person

whip[2] /hwɪp/ verb (present participle **whipping**, past tense and past participle **whipped**) **1** to hit a person or animal with a whip **2** to make a food such as cream more solid by mixing it hard with a kitchen tool

whirl /hwɜrl/ verb to move or make something move quickly around and around

whisker /'hwɪs.kər/ noun one of the long, stiff hairs that grow around the mouths of animals such as cats

whiskey /'hwɪs.ki/ noun a strong alcoholic drink made from grain

whisper /'hwɪs.pər/ verb to speak very quietly so that other people cannot hear: *She whispered something to the girl sitting next to her.*
• **whisper** noun

whisper

whistle[1] /'hwɪs.əl/ verb (present participle **whistling**, past tense and past participle **whistled**) to make a sound by breathing air out through a small hole made with your lips: *someone whistled at her as she walked past.*

whistle[2] /'hwɪs.əl/ noun **1** a small, simple instrument that makes a high sound when you blow through it: *The referee* ***blew*** *the* ***whistle*** *to end the game.* **2** the sound made by someone or something whistling

white[1] /hwaɪt/ *adj* **1** (A1) being the color of snow or milk: *a white T-shirt* ○ *white walls* **2** (A2) White wine is a light yellow color. **3** (B1) Someone who is white has skin that is pale in color.

white[2] /hwaɪt/ *noun* **1** (A2) the color of snow or milk → See **Colors** on page C6 **2** the part of an egg that is white when it is cooked: *Mix the egg whites with the sugar.* → See picture at **egg noun**

whiteboard /ˈhwaɪtˌbɔrd/ *noun* a large white board that teachers write on → See **The Classroom** on page C4

> **⚠ Common mistake: who or that?**
>
> Use **that** to refer to a thing.
> *The restaurant that is next to the park is good.*
> ~~The restaurant who is next to the park is good.~~
> Use **who** to refer to a person.
> *The boy who is wearing the red coat is named Paul.*
> ~~The boy which is wearing the red coat is named Paul.~~
> Sometimes it is possible to use no word instead of **that** or **who is**.
> *The boy wearing the red coat is named Paul.*
> *The restaurant next to the park is good.*

who /hu/ *pronoun* **1** (A1) used to ask about someone's name or which person or group someone is talking about: *Who told you?* ○ *Who's that?* **2** (A2) used to show which person or group of people you are talking about: *There's the officer who helped me.* **3** (B1) used to give more information about someone: *My brother, who's (= who is)sixteen, just got his driver's license.*

who'd /hud/ **1** short form of who had: *I read about a man who'd sailed around the world.* **2** who would: *Who'd like to go?*

whoever /huˈev·ər/ *pronoun* **1** the person who: *Whoever broke the window will have to pay for it.* **2** used to ask who a person is when you are surprised: *Whoever is calling at this hour?*

whole[1] /hoʊl/ *adj* (A2) complete, including every part: *She spent the whole afternoon studying.*

whole[2] /hoʊl/ *noun* **1** the whole of *something* (B1) all of something: *She went to every class for the whole of the semester.* **2** on the whole (B1) generally: *On the whole we're very happy.* **3** as a whole when considered as a group and not in parts: *The population as a whole is getting healthier.*

who'll /hul/ short form of who will: *Who'll be at your party?*

wholly /ˈhoʊl·li/ *adv* completely: *The news was wholly unexpected.*

whom /hum/ *pronoun formal* used instead of "who" as the object of a verb or preposition: *I just saw a woman with whom I used to work.* ○ *That's the man whom I met last week.*

who's /huz/ **1** short form of who is: *Who's your new friend?* **2** short form of who has: *Who's been using my computer?*

whose /huz/ *pronoun, determiner* **1** (B1) used to ask whom something belongs to or whom someone or something is connected with: *Whose gloves are these?* ○ *Whose car should we use?* **2** (B1) used for adding information about a person or thing just mentioned: *The story was about a man whose family came from Russia.* ○ *It was an old house whose owner had died.*

why /hwaɪ/ *adv* **1** (A1) used to ask or talk about the reasons for something: *Why didn't you call me?* ○ *I wonder why he didn't come.* **2** why don't you…? (A2) used to make a suggestion: *Why don't you come with us?* ○ *Why don't you give it a try?* **3** why not? (B1) used to agree with something that someone has suggested: *"Let's get some ice cream." "Sure, why not?"*

wicked /ˈwɪk·ɪd/ *adj* **1** very bad and morally wrong: *a wicked joke* **2** very informal very good: *They sell some wicked clothes.*

wide¹ /waɪd/ adj   **1** A2 measuring a long distance or longer than usual from one side to the other: *a wide road* ○ *I have very wide feet.*   **2** 5 miles, 3 inches, etc. wide B1 having a distance of 5 miles, 3 inches, etc. from one side to the other: *The swimming pool is 15 feet wide.*   **3** a wide range, selection, etc. B1 a lot of different types of thing: *They sell a wide range of books and magazines.*

wide² /waɪd/ adv   **1** wide apart/open as far apart or open as possible: *The window was wide open.*   **2** wide awake completely awake: *The baby is still wide awake.*

widely /ˈwaɪd·li/ adv   including a lot of different places, people, subjects, etc.: *He has traveled widely.*

widen /ˈwaɪ·dᵊn/ verb   to become wider or make something become wider: *The road is widened to two lanes.*

widespread /ˈwaɪdˈspred/ adj   affecting or including a lot of places, people, etc.: *This is a widespread problem.*

widow /ˈwɪd·oʊ/ noun   a woman whose husband has died

widower /ˈwɪd·oʊ·ər/ noun   a man whose wife has died

width /wɪdθ/, /wɪtθ/ noun   the distance from one side of something to the other side: *a width of 10 feet*
→ See picture at **length**

wife /waɪf/ noun (plural **wives**)   A1 the woman that someone is married to

wig /wɪg/ noun   a covering of hair that you wear on your head

wild /waɪld/ adj   **1** A2 A wild animal or plant lives or grows in its natural place and not where people live: *a wild dog* ○ *wild flowers*   **2** not controlled: *a wild party* ○ *wild dancing*

wildlife /ˈwaɪldˌlaɪf/ noun [no plural]   B1 animals, birds, and plants in the place where they live

will¹ /wɪl/ verb   A2 used to talk about what is going to happen in the future, especially things that you are certain about: *Claire will be five next month.* ○ *I'll see him on Saturday.* ○ *She'll have a great time.*   **2** A1 used to talk about when someone or something is willing or able to do: *Ask Susie if she will take them.* ○ *The car won't start.*   **3** A2 used to ask someone to do something: *Will you give me her address?* ○ *Will you give that to Tony when you see him, please?*

will² /wɪl/ noun   **1** the power to control your thoughts and actions: *She has a very strong will.* ○ *He lacks the will to win.*   **2** what someone wants: *She was forced to marry him against her will.*   **3** a piece of paper that says who will get your money, house, and things when you die: *She left me money in her will.*

willing /ˈwɪl·ɪŋ/ adj   **1** be willing to do something B1 to be happy to do something: *He's willing to lend us some money.*   **2** wanting to do something: *willing volunteers*
→ Opposite **unwilling** adj
• **willingly** adv *I willingly agreed to help.*
• **willingness** noun [no plural]

win¹ /wɪn/ verb (present participle **winning**, past tense and past participle **won**)   **1** A2 to get the most points in a competition or game: *The Mets won the game.*   **2** A2 to get a prize in a game or competition: *He won $500.* ○ *She won a gold medal at the Olympics.*   **3** B1 to get the most votes in an election: *Who do you think will win the election?*   **4** to be successful in a war, fight, or argument: *This is a war that no one can win.*

⚠ Common mistake: win or beat?

You **win** a game or competition.
Who do you think will win the game?
You **beat** someone, or a team you are playing against.
We beat both teams.
~~We won both teams.~~

---

win² /wɪn/ noun   success or victory in a game or competition: *The Jets have only had three wins this season.*

a b c d e f g h i j k l m n o p q r s t u v w x y z

wind¹ /wɪnd/ noun **A1** a natural, fast movement of air: *The wind blew her hat off.*

wind² /waɪnd/ verb (past tense and past participle **wound**) **1** to turn or twist something long and thin around something else several times: *She wound the rope around the tree.* **2** If a river, road, etc. winds somewhere, it bends a lot and is not straight: *The path winds along the edge of the bay.*

windbreaker /ˈwɪndˌbreɪ·kər/ noun a light jacket
→ See **Clothes** on page C5

window /ˈwɪn·doʊ/ noun **window**
1 **A1** a space in the wall of a building or car that has glass in it, used for letting light and air inside and for looking through: *Open the window if you're too hot.*
2 **B1** a separate area on a computer screen showing information, which you can move around

windowsill /ˈwɪn·doʊˌsɪl/ noun a shelf formed by the bottom part of the frame of a window

windshield /ˈwɪndˌʃild/ noun **B1** the window at the front end of a car, bus, etc. → See **Car** on page C3

windshield wiper /ˈwɪndˌʃild ˌwaɪ·pər/ noun one of two long parts that move against a car's window to remove rain → See **Car** on page C3

windsurfing /ˈwɪndˌsɜr·fɪŋ/ noun [no plural] **B1** a sport in which you sail across water by standing on a board and holding onto a large sail
• **windsurfer** noun

windy /ˈwɪn·di/ adj (comparative **windier**, superlative **windiest**) **A2** with a lot of wind: *a windy day*

wine /waɪn/ noun **A1** an alcoholic drink that is made from the juice of grapes (=small green or purple fruit): *a glass of wine*

wing /wɪŋ/ noun **1** **B1** one of the two parts that a bird or insect uses to fly

2 one of the two long, flat parts at the sides of a plane that make it stay in the sky

wings

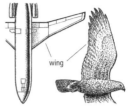

wing

wink¹ /wɪŋk/ verb **wink** to quickly close and then open one eye, in order to be friendly or to show that something is a joke: *She smiled and winked at me.*

wink² /wɪŋk/ noun an act of winking at someone: *He gave me a friendly wink.*

winner /ˈwɪn·ər/ noun **A2** someone who wins a game, competition, or election: *the winners of the World Series*

winter /ˈwɪn·tər/ noun **A1** the coldest season of the year, between fall and spring: *We went skiing last winter.*

wipe¹ /waɪp/ verb **wipe** (present participle **wiping**, past tense and past participle **wiped**) to clean or dry something by moving a cloth across it: *She wiped her hands on the towel.*

wipe² /waɪp/ noun **1** an act of cleaning or drying something with a cloth: *I'll give the table a wipe.* **2** a thin cloth or piece of paper used for cleaning: *baby wipes*

wire /waɪər/ noun **1** thin, metal thread, used to fasten things or to make fences, cages, etc. **2** a long, thin piece of metal thread, usually covered in plastic, that carries electricity: *electrical wires*

|æ cat|ɑ hot|e get|ɪ sit|i see|ɔ saw|ʊ book|u too|ʌ cut|ə about|ər mother|ɜr turn|ɔr for|aɪ my|aʊ how|eɪ say|ɔɪ boy|

a b c d e f g h i j k l m n o p q r s t u v **w** x y z

wisdom /ˈwɪz·dəm/ **noun** [no plural]
the ability to use your knowledge and
experience to make good decisions

wise /waɪz/ **adj** **B1** having or showing
the ability to make good judgments,
based on a deep understanding and experience of life: *a wise leader* ○ *I think we
made a wise choice.* → Opposite **unwise adj**
• **wisely adv**

wish[1] /wɪʃ/ **verb** **1 wish (that)** **B1** to
want a situation that is different from
the one that exists: *I wish that I didn't
have to go to work.* ○ *I wish he would
leave.* **2 wish someone** luck, success,
etc. **B1** to say that you hope someone
will be lucky, successful, etc.: *I wished
him luck for his test.* **3 wish to do
something** formal to want to do something: *I wish to speak to the manager.*

wish[2] /wɪʃ/ **noun** **1** what you want to do
or what you want to happen: *It was her
wish to go to Paris again.* **2 best wishes**
A2 something you say or write at the
end of a letter: *Best wishes, Pete*

wit /wɪt/ **noun** [no plural]   the ability to say
things that are funny and smart

witch /wɪtʃ/ **noun**   in stories, a woman
who has magical powers

with /wɪθ/, /wɪð/ **preposition** **1** **A1** used
to say that people or things are in a
place together or are doing something
together: *Will you play a game with me?*
○ *Hang your coat up with the others.*
2 **A1** having or including something: *a
house with a swimming pool* ○ *a woman
with brown eyes* **3** **A2** using something: *Eat with a fork, not with your fingers.* **4** **B1** used to describe the way
someone does something: *He plays with
great enthusiasm.* **5** **B1** used to say
what fills, covers, etc. something: *a
bucket filled with water* ○ *shoes covered
with mud* **6** because of something: *She
was trembling with fear.* **7** relating to
something or someone: *There's something wrong with the car.*

withdraw /wɪθˈdrɔː/, /wɪðˈdrɔː/ **verb** (past
tense **withdrew**, past participle **withdrawn**)
1 to take money out of a bank account:

She withdrew $50. **2** to remove some-
thing, especially because of an official
decision: *He has threatened to withdraw
his support.*

withdrawal /wɪθˈdrɔː·əl/, /wɪðˈdrɔː·əl/ **verb**
1 the act of taking money out of a bank
account: *I'd like to make a cash withdrawal.* **2** the act of removing something, especially because of an official
decision: *the withdrawal of troops*

within /wɪðˈɪn/, /wɪθˈɪn/ **preposition**
1 **B1** before a particular period of time
has finished: *The ambulance arrived
within ten minutes.* **2** **B1** less than a
particular distance from something: *She
has always lived within 20 miles of New
York.* **3** inside an area, group, or system: *There's a pharmacy within the hospital building.*

without /wɪðˈaʊt/, /wɪθˈaʊt/ **preposition**
1 **A2** not having, using, or doing something: *I did the test without any problems.*
○ *I can't see without my glasses.* **2** **A2** not
with someone: *You can start the meeting
without me.*

witness[1] /ˈwɪt·nəs/ **noun**   someone who
sees an accident or crime: *The police are
looking for witnesses to the shooting.*

witness[2] /ˈwɪt·nəs/ **verb**   to see something happen, especially an accident or
crime: *Did anyone witness the attack?*

witty /ˈwɪt̬·i/ **adj** (comparative **wittier**, superlative **wittiest**)   using words in a funny
and smart way: *a witty writer*

wives /waɪvz/   plural of wife

wizard /ˈwɪz·ərd/ **noun**   in stories, a
man who has magical powers

wobble /ˈwɑb·əl/ **verb** (present participle
wobbling, past tense and past participle
wobbled)   If something wobbles, it
moves from side to side, often because
it is not on a flat surface: *The ladder
started to wobble.*
• **wobbly adj** (comparative **wobblier**, superlative **wobbliest**) *a wobbly chair*

woke /woʊk/   past tense of wake

woken /ˈwoʊ·kən/   past participle of wake

wolf /wʊlf/ *noun* (plural **wolves**) a wild animal like a large dog: *Wolves hunt in packs.*

woman /ˈwʊm·ən/ *noun* (plural **women**) **A1** an adult female person: *a 30-year-old woman*

womb /wum/ *noun* the part inside a woman's body where a baby grows

won /wʌn/ past tense and past participle of win

wonder[1] /ˈwʌn·dər/ *verb* **1 B1** to want to know something or to try to understand the reason for something: *I wonder what he's making for dinner.* **2 I/we wonder if…** **B1** used to politely ask someone for something or to suggest something: *I wonder if you could help me?*

wonder[2] /ˈwʌn·dər/ *noun* **1** [no plural] surprise and admiration: *The boys gazed in wonder at their new baby sister.* **2 no wonder** used to say that you are not surprised about something: *No wonder she failed the test – she didn't study for it.*

wonderful /ˈwʌn·dər·fəl/ *adj* **A2** very good: *We had a wonderful time in Florida.* • **wonderfully** *adv* *You've all been so wonderfully helpful.*

> **⚠ Common mistake: wonderful**
>
> People often spell **wonderful** wrong. Remember that there is only one **l**.

won't /woʊnt/ short form of will not: *I won't be home before midnight.*

wood /wʊd/ *noun* **A2** the hard material that trees are made of: *a piece of wood*
→ See **Quantities** on page C14

wooden /ˈwʊd·ən/ *adj* **A2** made of wood: *a wooden chair*

woods /ˈwʊdz/, /ˈwʊds/ *plural noun* **A2** a large area of trees growing closely together: *We went for a walk in the woods.*

wool /wʊl/ *noun* [no plural] **1** the soft, thick hair on a sheep **2 A2** thick thread or material that is made from the hair of a sheep: *a wool suit*

word /wɜrd/ *noun* **1 A1** a group of letters or sounds that mean something: *"Hund" is the German word for "dog."* **2 have a word with** *someone* to talk to someone for a short time: *I'll have a word with the neighbors about the noise.* **3 in other words** used to explain what something means in a different way: *He said he's too busy. In other words, he isn't interested.* **4 word for word** using the exact words that were originally used: *She repeated what he said word for word.* **5 not believe, understand, say, etc. a word** **B1** to not believe, understand, say, etc. anything: *I don't believe a word he says.*

wore /wɔr/ past tense of wear

work[1] /wɜrk/ *verb* **1 A1** to do a job that you get money for: *Helen works for a computer company.* ○ *He works as a waiter in an Italian restaurant.* **2 A2** If a machine or piece of equipment works, it is not broken: *The refrigerator isn't working.* **3 B1** If something works, it is successful: *Her plan to get rid of me didn't work.*

work *something* **out** *phrasal verb* to calculate an amount: *I'm trying to work out the total cost.*

work out *phrasal verb* **1 B1** to do exercises to make your body stronger
→ See **Phrasal Verbs** on page C13 **2** If a problem or difficult situation works out, it gradually becomes better: *I hope everything works out for you.*

work[2] /wɜrk/ *noun* **1 A1** [no plural] something you do to get money: *Has she found any work yet?* **2 A1** [no plural] the place where you go to do your job: *He had an accident at work.* **3 A2** [no plural] the activities that you do at school, for your job, etc.: *Do you have a lot of work to do?* **4 A2** a painting, book, piece of music, etc.: *the complete works of Shakespeare* **5 B1** [no plural] the effort needed to do something: *Painting that room was hard work.* **6 get to work** to start doing something: *I need to get to work on my essay.*

a
b
c
d
e
f
g
h
i
j
k
l
m
n
o
p
q
r
s
t
u
v
w
x
y
z

a
b
c
d
e
f
g
h
i
j
k
l
m
n
o
p
q
r
s
t
u
v
w
x
y
z

> ⚠ **Common mistake: work, job, or occupation?**
>
> **Work** is something you do to earn money. Remember that this noun is uncountable.
>
> *She enjoys her work in the hospital.*
> *He's looking for work.*
> ~~He's looking for a work.~~
>
> **Job** is used to talk about the particular work activity that you do.
>
> *He's looking for a job in computer programming.*
> *Teaching must be an interesting job.*
> ~~Teaching must be an interesting work.~~
>
> **Occupation** is a formal word that means the job that you do. It is often used on forms. See also: **career** and **profession**.

worker /'wɜr·kər/ *noun* **1 A2** someone who works for a company or organization but does not have a powerful position: *an office worker* **2 a quick, slow, good, etc. worker B1** someone who works quickly, slowly, well, etc.: *He's a slow worker, but he is very thorough.*

working /'wɜr·kɪŋ/ *adj* [always before noun] **1 B1** relating to your job: *good working conditions* **2 a working man, woman, etc.** someone who has a job: *a working mother* **3 a working knowledge of something** knowledge about something that is good enough to be useful: *She has a working knowledge of Russian.*

workman /'wɜrk·mən/ *noun* (plural **workmen**) a man who does a physical job such as building

workout /'wɜrk·aʊt/ *noun* **B1** a series of exercises that you do to make your body strong and healthy: *I do a daily workout at the gym.*

worksheet /'wɜrk·ʃit/ *noun* a piece of paper with questions and exercises for students

workshop /'wɜrk·ʃɑp/ *noun* **1** a place where people make or repair things **2** a meeting where people learn about

something by discussing it and doing practical exercises

world /wɜrld/ *noun* **1 the world A1** the Earth and all the people, places, and things on it: *Everest is the highest mountain in the world.* ∘ *She has traveled all over the world.* **2 B1** the people and things that are involved in a particular activity or subject: *the world of politics* **3 your world A2** your life and experiences: *His whole world fell apart when she left.*

world-famous /'wɜrld'feɪ·məs/ *adj* known by people everywhere in the world: *The Taj Mahal is a world-famous monument.*

worldwide /'wɜrld'waɪd/ *adj, adv* in all parts of the world: *ten million copies have been sold worldwide.* ∘ *a worldwide success*

the World Wide Web /'wɜrld ˌwaɪd 'web/ *noun* part of the Internet that consists of all the connected websites (=pages of text and pictures)

worm /wɜrm/ *noun* a small creature with a long, thin, soft body and no legs

worn /wɔrn/ past participle of wear

worn out /'wɔrn 'aʊt/ *adj* **1** very tired: *I was worn out after all that dancing.* **2** damaged after being used too much: *a worn-out carpet*

worried /'wɜr·id/, /'wʌr·id/ *adj* **A2** unhappy because you are thinking about bad things that might happen: *She's really **worried about** her son.* ∘ *I'm **worried that** she'll tell Maria.*

worry¹ /'wɜr·i/, /'wʌr·i/ *verb* (present participle **worrying**, past tense and past participle **worried**) **1 A1** to think about problems or bad things that might happen: ***Don't worry** – she'll be all right.* ∘ *She's always **worrying about** something.* **2** to make someone anxious because of problems or unpleasant things that might happen: *It **worries** me **that** he hasn't called yet.*

> **❗ Common mistake: worry about** something or someone
>
> Be careful to use the correct preposition after this verb.
>
> *They were worried about the weather.*
> ~~*They were worried for the weather.*~~

worry² /ˈwɜr·i/, /ˈwʌr·i/ noun (plural **worries**) **B1** a problem that makes you feel unhappy: *money worries*

worrying /ˈwɜr·i·ɪŋ/, /ˈwʌr·i·ɪŋ/ adj making you feel anxious: *It's a very worrying situation.*

worse¹ /wɜrs/ adj **1** **A2** comparative of bad: more unpleasant, difficult, etc.: *The exam was* ***worse than*** *I expected.* ○ *We'll have to stop the game if the rain* ***gets*** *any* ***worse***. **2** **B1** more ill: *The drugs aren't working – he just seems to be* ***getting worse***.

worse² /wɜrs/ adv **B1** comparative of badly: *He was treated much worse than I was.*

worship /ˈwɜr·ʃɪp/ verb (present participle **worshipping**, past tense and past participle **worshipped**) **1** to show respect for a god by saying prayers **2** to love and respect someone very much: *She worshipped her mother.*
• **worship** noun [no plural] *a place of worship* (= a religious building)

worst¹ /wɜrst/ adj **A2** superlative of bad: the most unpleasant, difficult, etc.: *What's the worst job you've ever had?*

worst² /wɜrst/ adv superlative of badly: *San Francisco was the worst hit by the earthquake.*

worst³ /wɜrst/ noun **the worst** **B1** the most unpleasant or difficult thing, person, or situation: *I've made mistakes in the past, but this is definitely the worst.*

worth¹ /wɜrθ/ adj **1** **be worth something** **B1** to have a particular value, especially in money: *Our house is worth about $300,000.* **2** **be worth it** **B1** to be useful or enjoyable despite needing a lot of effort: *It was a long climb up the mountain, but the view was worth it.*

3 **be worth doing, seeing, trying, etc.** **B1** to be useful or enjoyable to do, see, try, etc.: *It's not as good as his last book, but it's definitely worth reading.*

> **❗ Common mistake: be worth doing** something
>
> When **worth** is followed by a verb, the verb is always in the **-ing** form.
>
> *Do you think it's worth asking Patrick first?*
> ~~*Do you think it's worth to ask Patrick first?*~~

worth² /wɜrθ/ noun **1 a month's, year's, etc. worth of** *something* the amount of something that can be done or used in a month, year, etc.: *The prize was a year's worth of free groceries.* **2 $20, $100, etc. worth of** *something* the amount of something that you can buy for $20, $100, etc.: *I'd like $20 worth of gas, please.*

worthless /ˈwɜrθ·ləs/ adj having no value in money

worthwhile /ˈwɜrθˈhwaɪl/ adj useful and enjoyable, despite needing a lot of effort: *It's a difficult class, but it's really worthwhile.*

worthy /ˈwɜr·ði/ adj (comparative **worthier**, superlative **worthiest**) deserving respect or support: *a worthy cause*

would /wʊd/ /wəd/ verb **1** **B1** used to say what might happen if something else happens: *What would you do if you lost your job?* **2** **B1** used as the past form of "will": *Lottie promised that she would help.* ○ *The car wouldn't start this morning.* **3** **B1** used to talk about a situation that you can imagine happening: *It would be fun to go to New York.* **4** **would like/love** *something* **A1** used to say politely that you want something: *I'd (= I would) like a cup of coffee, please.* **5** **would you...?** used to politely ask someone something: *Would you like a drink?*

wouldn't /ˈwʊd·ənt/ short form of would not: *She wouldn't let us watch TV.*

a
b
c
d
e
f
g
h
i
j
k
l
m
n
o
p
q
r
s
t
u
v
w
x
y
z

wound[1] /waʊnd/ past tense and past participle of wind[2]

wound[2] /wund/ noun an injury

wound[3] /wund/ verb to hurt someone, especially with a knife or gun: *He was badly wounded in the attack.*
• **wounded** adj *a wounded animal*

wove /woʊv/ past tense of weave[2]

woven /ˈwoʊ·vən/ past participle of weave[2]

wow /waʊ/ **exclamation** informal
A2 something that you say to show surprise, excitement, admiration, etc.: *Wow! Look at that car!*

wrap /ræp/ verb (present participle **wrapping**, past tense and past participle **wrapped**) (also **wrap up**) **B1** to cover something or someone with paper, cloth, etc.: *to wrap a present* ○ *They wrapped him in a blanket.*
→ Opposite **unwrap** verb

wrapping paper /ˈræp·ɪŋ ˌpeɪ·pər/ noun [no plural] decorated paper used for covering presents: *a roll of wrapping paper*

wreath /riθ/ noun (plural **wreaths**) a large ring of leaves or flowers used as a decoration

wreck /rek/ verb to destroy something completely: *The explosion wrecked several cars.*

wreckage /ˈrek·ɪdʒ/ noun [no plural] the parts that remain of a car, ship, or plane that has been destroyed: *Two survivors were pulled from the wreckage.*

wrench[1] /rentʃ/ verb to pull something violently away from a fixed position: *The phone had been wrenched off the wall.*

wrench[2] /rentʃ/ noun a tool with a round end that is used to turn nuts and bolts (= metal objects used to fasten things together)

wrestle /ˈres·əl/ verb (present participle **wrestling**, past tense and past participle **wrestled**) to fight with someone by holding the person and trying to push him or her to the ground

wrestling /ˈres·lɪŋ/ noun [no plural] a sport in which two people fight and try to push each other to the ground
• **wrestler** noun

wriggle /ˈrɪg·əl/ verb (present participle **wriggling**, past tense and past participle **wriggled**) to twist your body or move part of your body with short, quick movements: *She wriggled her toes in the warm sand.*

wring /rɪŋ/ verb (past tense and past participle **wrung**) (also **wring out**) to twist a cloth or piece of clothing with your hands to remove water from it: *He wrung out his socks and hung them up to dry.*

wrinkle /ˈrɪŋ·kəl/ noun a small line on your face that you get when you grow old
• **wrinkled** adj *a wrinkled face*

wrinkles

wrist /rɪst/ noun the part of your body between your hand and your arm

write /raɪt/ verb (present participle **writing**, past tense **wrote**, past participle **written**)
1 **A1** to make words, letters, or numbers on a surface using a pen or pencil: *Write your name at the top of the page.* **2** **A2** to send someone a letter: *I wrote her a letter last week.* **3** **B1** to create a book, story, article, etc. or a piece of music: *He's writing a book on Russian literature.*

write *something* **down** phrasal verb
B1 to write something on a piece of paper so that you do not forget it: *Did you write Joe's phone number down?*

writer /ˈraɪ·tər/ noun **B1** someone whose job is writing books, stories, articles, etc.

writing /ˈraɪ·tɪŋ/ noun [no plural]
1 **A1** the skill or activity of producing words on a surface: *Speaking and writing are important parts of learning a language.* **2** **A2** words that have been written or printed: *The writing was too small to read.* **3** **B1** the way that someone writes: *You have very neat writing.* **4** the activity or job of creating books, stories, or articles **5 in writing** in the form of an official letter or document: *Please confirm your reservation in writing.*

> ⚠ **Common mistake: writing**
>
> Remember that the -ing form of **writing** has only one t.

written[1] /ˈrɪt-ᵊn/ past participle of write

written[2] /ˈrɪt-ᵊn/ adj expressed in writing, or involving writing: *a written exam* ○ *written instructions*

wrong[1] /rɒŋ/ adj **1 A1** not correct: *the wrong answer* ○ *We're going the wrong way.* **2 be wrong A2** to think or say something that is not correct: *You were **wrong about** the party – it's today, not tomorrow.* **3 B1** If something is wrong, there is a problem: *What's wrong?* ○ *There's something **wrong with** my computer.* **4 get** *something* **wrong B1** to produce an answer or result that is not correct, or to say or write something that is not correct: *I got most of the answers wrong.* ○ *The newspapers got the story completely wrong.* **5** morally bad: *It's wrong to tell lies.* **6** not suitable: *I think she's **wrong for** this job.*

wrong[2] /rɒŋ/ adv **1 A2** in a way that is not correct: *He always says my name wrong.* **2 go wrong B1** to develop problems: *Something went wrong with my computer.*

wrong[3] /rɒŋ/ noun behavior that is not morally right: *She's old enough to know the difference between right and wrong.*

wrongly /ˈrɒŋ·li/ adv in a way that is not correct: *The letter was wrongly addressed.*

wrote /roʊt/ past tense of write

wrung /rʌŋ/ past tense and past participle of wring

WWW noun abbreviation for World Wide Web: the part of the Internet that consists of all the connected websites

X x

X, x /eks/ **1** the twenty-fourth letter of the alphabet **2** used to show that an answer is wrong **3** used to mean a kiss at the end of a letter **4** used to mean an unknown person or thing

Xmas /ˈkrɪs·məs/ noun [no plural] informal used as a short way of writing "Christmas" (= a Christian holiday), mainly on signs or cards: *Merry Xmas!*

X-ray[1] /ˈeks.reɪ/ noun a photograph that shows the inside of your body: *They **took an X-ray** of his leg.*

X-ray[2] /ˈeks.reɪ/ verb to take a photograph that shows the inside of something

Y y

Y, y /waɪ/ the twenty-fifth letter of the alphabet

yacht /jɑt/ noun a large boat with sails used for pleasure or in racing: *a luxury yacht*

yacht

yam /jæm/ noun an orange vegetable with yellow flesh that tastes slightly sweet

yard /jɑrd/ noun (written abbreviation **yd.**) **1 B1** a unit for measuring length, equal to 3 feet **2 A2** an area of land in front of or behind a house: *the front yard*

yawn /jɒn/ verb to take a deep breath with your mouth wide open, because you are tired or bored: *She yawned and looked at her watch.*
• **yawn** noun

yd. written abbreviation for yard: a unit for measuring length

yeah /jeə/ **exclamation** informal spoken
A2 yes: *Yeah, I agree.*

year /jɪər/ **noun** **1 A1** a period of twelve
months, or 365 or 366 days, especially
from January 1 to December 31: *He
joined the company a year ago.* **2 be ...
years old A1** to be a particular age: *Her
son is six years old.* **3 A2** the part of
the year, in a school or university, during
which courses are taught: *the school
year* ∘ *She's in her senior year of college.*
4 years B1 a long time: *I haven't seen
Linda for years.*

yearly /ˈjɪər·li/ **adj, adv** happening once
a year or every year: *a yearly fee*

yeast /jist/ **noun** [no plural] a substance
used to make bread rise and to make
beer and wine

yell /jel/ **verb** to shout something very
loudly: *The policeman **yelled at** them to
stop.*
• **yell noun**

yellow[1] /ˈjel·oʊ/ **adj** **A1** being the same
color as a lemon or the sun: *a bright yellow tablecloth*

yellow[2] /ˈjel·oʊ/ **noun** **A2** the color yellow → See **Colors** on page C6

yes exclamation **1 A1** used to agree
with something, or to give a positive answer to something: *"Can I borrow your
pencil?" "Yes, of course."* ∘ *"Coffee?" "Yes,
please."* **2 A1** used as an answer when
someone calls you: *"Jack!" "Yes?"*
3 A2 used when you are disagreeing
with a negative statement: *"I'm not a
very good cook." "Yes, you are – you cook
really well!"*

yesterday /ˈjes·tər.deɪ/ **noun** [no plural],
adv A1 the day before today: *I went to
see the doctor yesterday.* ∘ *Yesterday was
my birthday.*

yet[1] /jet/ **adv** **1 A2** before now or before
that time: *Have you read his book yet?*
∘ *"Has he called?" "No, not yet."*
2 A2 now or as early as this time: *I don't
want to go home yet.* **3 the best, worst,
etc. yet** the best, worst, etc. until now:
That was my worst score yet.

yet[2] /jet/ **conjunction** **B1** used to connect two words, phrases, or clauses when
the second part adds something surprising to the first part: *Her solution was simple yet effective.* ∘ *The price of the house
was low, yet no one wanted to buy it.*

yield /jild/ **verb** **1** to make or provide
something: *to yield a profit* **2 yield to
demands, pressure, etc.** to be forced to
do something

yoga /ˈjoʊ·gə/ **noun** [no plural] **B1** a set of
exercises for the mind and body, based
on the Hindu religion: *She does yoga
three times a week.*

yogurt /ˈjoʊ·gərt/ **noun** a thick, liquid
food with a slightly sour taste that is
made from milk
→ See **Food** on page C7

yolk /joʊk/ **noun** the round, yellow part
in the middle of an egg
→ See picture at **egg noun**

you /ju/ju/, /jə/ **pronoun** **1 A1** used to
mean the person or people you are talking to: *I love you.* ∘ *You said I could go
with you.* **2 A2** people generally: *You
learn to relax as you get older.*

you'd /jud/ **1** short form of you had: *You'd
better go home now.* **2** you would: *I assume you'd like some lunch.*

you'll /jul/ short form of you will: *I hope
you'll come again.*

young[1] /jʌŋ/ **adj** **A1** having lived or
existed for only a short time; not old:
young people

young[2] /jʌŋ/ **noun** [no plural] **1 the
young** young people generally: *It's the
kind of music that appeals mainly to the
young.* **2 something's young** an animal's babies

your /jʊər/, /jɔr/, /jɑr/ **determiner**
1 A1 belonging or relating to the person or people you are talking to: *Can I
borrow your pen?* ∘ *It's not your fault.*
2 B1 belonging or relating to people in
general: *You never stop loving your children.*

you're /jʊər/ short form of you are: *You're
my best friend.*

yours /jʊərz/, /jɔrz/ *pronoun* **1** A2 the things that belong or relate to the person or people you are talking to: *Is this pen yours?* **2 Yours truly, sincerely, etc.** B1 used just before your name at the end of a polite or formal letter

yourself /jʊərˈself/, /jɔrˈself/ *pronoun* **1** A2 used to show that it is you who is affected by an action: *Don't cut yourself with that sharp knife.* **2** used to give more attention to the word "you": *Did you make the dress yourself?* **3 by yourself/yourselves** A2 alone or without anyone else's help: *I'm amazed that you managed to move those boxes all by yourself.* **4** used when both the subject and object of the verb are "you," and "you" is also being used to refer to people generally: *You tell yourself that everything's all right, but you know it's not really.*

youth /juθ/ *noun* formal **1** a young man: *gangs of youths* **2** B1 young people generally: *the youth of today* **3 someone's youth** the period of time when someone is young: *I was very shy in my youth.* **4** [no plural] the quality of being young

youth hostel /ˈjuθ ˌhɑsˈtºl/ *noun* a cheap, simple hotel, especially for young people who are traveling around

you've /juv/ short form of you have: *If you've finished your work, you can go.*

yuck /jʌk/ *exclamation* informal used to say that something looks or tastes very bad

yummy /ˈjʌm·i/ *adj* (comparative **yummier,** superlative **yummiest**) informal If food or drink is yummy, it tastes very good.

Zz

Z, z /zi/ the twenty-sixth and last letter of the alphabet

zebra /ˈzi·brə/ *noun* an animal like a horse with black and white lines

zero /ˈzɪər·oʊ/ A2 the number 0

zigzag /ˈzɪɡˌzæɡ/ *noun* a line that changes direction from left to right and back again at sharp angles

zip /zɪp/ *verb* (present participle **zipping,** past tense and past participle **zipped**) (also **zip up**) to fasten something with a zipper: *He zipped up his jacket.*

ZIP code /ˈzɪp ˌkoʊd/ *noun* a set of numbers that go after someone's address in the U.S.

zipper /ˈzɪp·ər/ *noun* a thing for fastening clothes, bags, etc. consisting of two rows of very small parts that connect together

zone /zoʊn/ *noun* B1 an area where a particular thing happens: *an earthquake zone* (= where earthquakes happen often)

zoo /zu/ *noun* A1 a place where wild animals are kept and people come to look at them

zucchini /zuˈki·ni/ *noun* (plural **zucchini, zucchinis**) a long, green vegetable that is white inside

a
b
c
d
e
f
g
h
i
j
k
l
m
n
o
p
q
r
s
t
u
v
w
x
y
z

Irregular Verbs

This list gives the infinitive form of the verb, its past tense, and then the past participle.

Infinitive	Past Tense	Past Participle	Infinitive	Past Tense	Past Participle
arise	arose	arisen	feed	fed	fed
be	was/were	been	fall	fell	fallen
bear	bore	borne	feel	felt	felt
beat	beat	beaten	fight	fought	fought
become	became	become	find	found	found
begin	began	begun	flee	fled	fled
bend	bent	bent	fling	flung	flung
bet	bet	bet	fly	flew	flown
bid	bid	bid	forbid	forbade	forbidden
bind	bound	bound	forecast	forecast	forecasted
bite	bit	bitten	foresee	foresaw	foreseen
bleed	bled	bled	forget	forgot	forgotten
blow	blew	blown	forgive	forgave	forgiven
break	broke	broken	freeze	froze	frozen
breed	bred	bred	get	got	gotten
bring	brought	brought	give	gave	given
broadcast	broadcast	broadcast	go	went	gone
build	built	built	grind	ground	ground
burst	burst	burst	grow	grew	grown
buy	bought	bought	hang	hung	hung
cast	cast	cast	have	had	had
catch	caught	caught	hear	heard	heard
choose	chose	chosen	hide	hid	hidden
cling	clung	clung	hit	hit	hit
come	came	come	hold	held	held
cost	cost	cost	hurt	hurt	hurt
creep	crept	crept	keep	kept	kept
cut	cut	cut	kneel	knelt	knelt
deal	dealt	dealt	know	knew	known
dig	dug	dug	lay	laid	laid
draw	drew	drawn	lead	led	led
dream	dreamed, dreamt	dreamed, dreamt	leave	left	left
			lend	lent	lent
drink	drank	drunk	let	let	let
drive	drove	driven	lie	lay	lain
eat	ate	eaten	light	lit	lit

Infinitive	Past Tense	Past Participle	Infinitive	Past Tense	Past Participle
lose	lost	lost	slide	slid	slid
make	made	made	slit	slit	slit
mean	meant	meant	sow	sowed	sown
meet	met	met	speak	spoke	spoken
mistake	mistook	mistaken	speed	sped	sped
misunderstand	misunderstood	misunderstood	spend	spent	spent
			spin	spun	spun
mow	mowed	mown	spit	spat	spat
outgrow	outgrew	outgrown	split	split	split
overhear	overheard	overheard	spread	spread	spread
oversleep	overslept	overslept	spring	sprang	sprung
overtake	overtook	overtaken	stand	stood	stood
pay	paid	paid	steal	stole	stolen
put	put	put	stick	stuck	stuck
quit	quit	quit	sting	stung	stung
read	read	read	stink	stank	stunk
rebuild	rebuilt	rebuilt	strike	struck	struck
repay	repaid	repaid	swear	swore	sworn
rewind	rewound	rewound	sweep	swept	swept
ride	rode	ridden	swell	swelled	swollen
ring	rang	rung	swim	swam	swum
rise	rose	risen	swing	swung	swung
run	ran	run	take	took	taken
say	said	said	teach	taught	taught
see	saw	seen	tear	tore	torn
seek	sought	sought	tell	told	told
sell	sold	sold	think	thought	thought
send	sent	sent	throw	threw	thrown
set	set	set	undergo	underwent	undergone
sew	sewed	sewn	understand	understood	understood
shake	shook	shaken	undo	undid	undone
shed	shed	shed	unwind	unwound	unwound
shine	shone	shone	upset	upset	upset
shoot	shot	shot	wake	woke	woken
show	showed	shown	wear	wore	worn
shrink	shrank	shrunk	weave	wove	woven
shut	shut	shut	weep	wept	wept
sing	sang	sung	win	won	won
sink	sank	sunk	wind	wound	wound
sit	sat	sat	withdraw	withdrew	withdrawn
sleep	slept	slept	wring	wrung	wrung
			write	wrote	written

Essential phrasal verbs

Phrasal verbs are verbs that have two or three words. For example, **look up** and **come from** are phrasal verbs. In this section you will find the most important phrasal verbs. Try to learn them, starting with those marked A1, then A2, then B1.

add something **up** **B1**
to put two or more numbers together to get a total:
Have you added up all the figures?

base something **on** something **B1**
If you base something on facts or ideas, you use those facts or ideas to develop it:
This book is based on a true story.

believe in something **B1**
to be certain that something exists:
Do you believe in ghosts?

belong to someone **A2**
If something belongs to you, you own it:
This necklace belonged to my grandmother.

belong to something **B1**
to be a member of an organization:
We belong to the same health club.

blow (something) **away** **B1**
If something blows away, or if the wind blows something away, that thing moves because the wind blows it:
The letter blew away and I had to run after it.

blow (something) **down** **B1**
If something blows down, or if the wind blows something down, that thing falls to the ground because the wind blows it:
The wind blew our fence down last night.

blow something **out** **B1**
to stop a flame burning by blowing on it:
Emma blew out the candle.

blow something **up** **B1**
to destroy something with a bomb:
Terrorists blew up an office building.
2 to fill something with air:
blowing up balloons

break down **B1**
If a car or machine breaks down, it stops working:
My car broke down on the way to work.

break into something **B1**
to get into a building or car using force, usually to steal something:
Someone broke into the office and stole some computers.

break up
1 **B1** to stop having a relationship:
He just broke up with his girlfriend.

bring something **back** **B1**
to return from somewhere with something:
Look at what I brought back from my trip.

bring someone **up** **B1**
to take care of a child until he or she becomes an adult:
Her grandparents brought her up.

call (someone) **back** **B1**
to telephone someone a second time, or to telephone someone who telephoned you earlier:
I'll call back later.

call someone **up** **B1**
to telephone someone:
Call Paul up and ask what he's doing tonight.

care for someone **B1**
to provide for the needs of someone
who is young, old, or ill:
*The children are being cared for by a
relative.*

carry on **B1**
to continue doing something:
*We will carry on with the game unless
it rains.*

carry something **out** **B1**
to do or complete something, especially
something that you have said you
would do or that you have been told
to do:
*The hospital is carrying out tests to find
out what's wrong with her.*

catch up
1 **B1** to reach the same level or quality
as someone or something else:
*She's doing extra work to catch up with
the rest of the class.*
2 to learn and discuss the newest facts
about something:
*Let's go out for lunch – I want to catch up
on all your news.*
3 to reach someone or something that
is in front of you by moving faster:
We soon caught up with the car in front.

check in **B1**
to show your ticket at an airport so they
can give you your seat number

check in/check into something **B1**
to say who you are when you arrive at a
hotel so that you can be given a key for
your room:
Please check in at the reception desk.

check out **B1**
1 to leave a hotel after paying
2 to go to an area to pay for the things
you have chosen to buy in a store or on
a website:
*I had already checked out when I
remembered we were out of milk.*
3 to borrow a book, CD, etc. from a
library:
You can check out up to six items at a time.

come along **B1**
to go somewhere with someone:
*We're going to the zoo. Do you want to
come along?*

come back **A2**
to return to a place:
We just came back from vacation.

come from something **A1**
to be born, gotten from, or made
somewhere:
She comes from Poland. ○ *Milk comes
from cows.*

come in **A2**
to enter a room or building:
Come in and have a seat.

come on **B1**
said to encourage someone to do
something, especially to hurry or try
harder:
Come on, the taxi's waiting.

come out
1 **B1** If a book, movie, etc. comes out,
it becomes available for people to buy
or see:
When does their new album come out?
2 **B1** If the sun, the moon, or a star
comes out, it appears in the sky:
It will warm up when the sun comes out.

come over **A2**
to visit someone at his or her house:
*You should come over for dinner
sometime.*

complain of something **B1**
to tell other people that something is
making you feel sick:
*She's been complaining of a headache
all day.*

consist of something **B1**
to be made from something:
The dessert consisted of fruit and cream.

cut something **up** **B1**
to cut something into pieces

deal with something **B1**
to do something to make a situation work or to solve a problem:
How will we deal with the issue of immigration?

depend on someone/something
1 B1 to need the help of someone or something:
Our economy depends on the car industry.
2 to be affected by someone or something:
What you buy depends on how much you can spend.
3 to trust someone or something and know that he, she, or it will help you or do what you want or expect:
You can always depend on her in a crisis.

eat out **B1**
to eat at a restaurant:
Let's eat out tonight.

end up **B1**
to finally be in a particular place or situation:
He ended up in prison.

fall down **B1**
to fall onto the ground:
The wall is in danger of falling down.

fall over **B1**
to fall to the ground from a standing position:
My glass fell over and spilled.

fill something **in/out** **A2**
to write all the information that is needed on a document:
Please fill out this form.

fill (something) **up** **B1**
to become full, or to make something become full:
The restaurant soon filled up with people.

find (something) **out** **A2**
to get information about something:
Did you find out Ruby's phone number?

get along
1 A2 If two or more people get along, they like each other and are friends:
Karen and Dianne don't get along.
2 B1 to manage or deal with a situation:
How are you getting along in your new job?

get around **B1**
to move from place to place:
The subway makes it easy to get around New York City.

get at something **B1**
to be able to reach or get something:
Put the cake on a high shelf where the kids can't get at it.

get back **A2**
to return to a place after you have been somewhere else:
We got back home late last night.

get something **back** **B1**
to be given something again that you had before:
Don't lend him money – you'll never get it back.

get in
1 B1 to succeed in entering a place, especially a building:
The thieves got in through the bathroom window.
2 B1 to arrive at a place at a particular time:
My train gets in at 9:45 p.m.
3 B1 to succeed in being chosen or elected:
He wanted to go to Princeton but he didn't get in.

get off (something) **A2**
to leave a bus, train, plane, or boat:
We should get off at the next stop.

get on (something) **A2**
to go onto a bus, train, plane, or boat:
I think we got on the wrong bus.

get out **B1**
to move out of a car:
Stop at the corner so I can get out.

get together **B1**
to meet in order to do something or spend time together:
A few of us are getting together next week for a barbecue.

get (someone) **up** **A1**
to wake up and get out of bed, or to make someone do this:
I had to get up at five o'clock this morning.

give something **away**
1 **B1** to give something to someone without asking for payment:
They're giving away a CD with this magazine.
2 to tell people something secret, often without intending to:
The party was supposed to be a surprise, but Sharon gave it away.

give something **back** **A2**
to give something to the person who gave it to you:
Did she give you those books back yet?

give in **B1**
to finally agree to do something that someone wants:
We won't give in to terrorists' demands.

give something **out** **B1**
to give something to a lot of people:
He gave out copies of the report.

give up **B1**
to accept that you cannot continue trying to do something:
You'll never guess the answer – do you give up? ○ I had to give up halfway through the race.

give up something
1 **B1** If you give up something bad, such as smoking, you stop doing it or having it:
I gave up drinking two years ago.
2 **B1** to stop doing an activity or piece of work before you have completed it, usually because it is too difficult:
I've given up trying to help her.

3 **B1** to stop doing a regular activity or job:
Are you going to give up work when you have your baby?

go away
1 **B1** to leave a place:
Just go away and leave me alone.
2 **B1** to leave your home in order to spend time in a different place:
We're going away for a few weeks in the summer.

go back **B1**
to return to a place where you were or where you have been before:
When are you going back to Las Vegas?

go down
1 **B1** to become lower in level:
Profits have gone down by about 2%.
2 **B1** When the sun goes down, it moves down in the sky until it cannot be seen anymore:
I sat and watched the sun go down.

go for something **B1**
to choose something:
I don't know whether to go for the fish or the steak for dinner.

go in **A2** to enter a place:
I looked in the window but I didn't go in.

go off
1 **B1** to leave a place and go somewhere else:
She went off with Laurie.
2 **B1** If a light or machine goes off, it stops working:
The heating goes off at ten o'clock.
3 If a bomb or gun goes off, it explodes or fires.
4 If something that makes a noise goes off, it suddenly starts making a noise:
His car alarm goes off every time it rains.

go on
1 **B1** to last for a particular period of time:
The speech seemed to go on forever.
2 to continue doing something:
We can't go on living like this.
3 **B1** to happen:
What's going on?

go out
1 (A1) to leave a place in order to go somewhere else:
Are you going out tonight?
2 (B1) If two people go out together, they have a romantic relationship with each other:
Tina is going out with Peter.
3 (B1) If a light or something that is burning goes out, it stops producing light or heat:
I'm sorry – I let the fire go out.

go up (B1)
to become higher in level:
House prices keep going up.

grow up (A2)
to become older or an adult:
She grew up in Texas.

hand something **in** (B1)
to give your finished work to a teacher:
Have you handed your history essay in yet?

hand something **out** (B1)
to give something to all the people in a group:
The teacher handed out worksheets to the class.

hang around *informal* (B1)
to spend time somewhere, usually doing little:
A lot of teenagers hang around at the mall.

hang on *informal* (B1)
to wait for a short time:
Hang on – I'm coming.

hang out *informal* (B1)
to spend a lot of time in a place or with someone:
I was hanging out with my friends last night.

hang up (B1)
to finish talking on the telephone

hang something **up** (B1)
to put something such as a coat somewhere where it can hang:
You can hang up your jacket over there.

hear from someone (B1)
to get a letter, telephone call, or other message from someone:
Have you heard from Helena recently?

hold on *informal* (B1)
to wait:
Hold on! Let me check my calendar.

hold something/someone **up** (B1)
to make something or someone slow or late:
Sorry I'm late. I got held up in traffic.

hurry up (B1)
to start moving or doing something more quickly:
Hurry up! We're going to be late.

join in (something) (B1)
to do an activity with other people:
We're playing cards. Would you like to join in?

keep someone **in** (B1)
to make someone stay inside, sometimes as a punishment:
She kept the children in because it was so cold.

keep (someone/something) **off** something (B1)
to not go onto an area, or to stop someone or something from going onto an area:
Keep off the grass.

keep on doing something (B1)
to continue to do something, or to do something again and again:
She kept on asking me questions.

keep (someone/something) **out** (B1)
to not go into a place, or to stop someone or something from going into a place:
Keep out of the kitchen until lunch is ready.

keep something **up** (B1)
to not allow something that is good, strong, etc. to become less good, strong, etc.:
Keep up the good work!

key something **in** 🅱1
to put information into a computer using a keyboard:
Key in your name and password.

laugh at someone/something 🅱1
to show that you think someone or something is stupid:
The other children laughed at him because of his strange clothes.

leave someone/something **behind** 🅰2
to leave a place without taking someone or something with you:
We were in a hurry and I left my keys behind.

lie down 🅰2
to move into a position in which your body is flat, usually in order to sleep or rest:
I'm not feeling well – I'm going to lie down.

look around (something) 🅱1
to visit a place and look at the things in it:
She spent the afternoon looking around the neighborhood.

look forward to something
1 🅱1 to feel happy and excited about something that is going to happen:
I'm really looking forward to seeing him.
2 *formal* used at the end of a formal letter to say you hope to hear from or see someone soon, or that you expect something from them:
I look forward to hearing from you.

look out! 🅱1
something you say when someone is in danger:
Look out – there's a car coming!

look something **up** 🅱1
to look at a book or computer in order to find information:
I looked it up on the Internet.

move in 🅱1
to begin living in a new home:
We're moving in next week.

move out 🅱1
to stop living in a particular home:
He moved out when he was only 18.

pass something **on**
1 🅱1 to tell someone something that someone else has told you:
Did you pass on my message to him?
2 🅱1 to give something to someone else:
Will you pass the book on to Lara when you're done with it?

pay someone/something **back** 🅱1
to pay someone the money that you owe him or her:
Has he paid you back the money he owes you?

pick something/someone **up**
1 🅰2 to lift something or someone by using your hands:
He picked his coat up off the floor.
2 🅰2 to go somewhere in order to get someone or something:
Can you pick me up from the airport?

pick something **up** 🅰2
to learn a new skill or language by practicing it, not by studying it:
When you live in a country you soon pick up the language.

put something **away** 🅱1
to put something in the place where you usually keep it:
She folded the towels and put them away.

put something **back** 🅱1
to put something where it was before it was moved:
I put the book back on the shelf.

put something **down** 🅱1
to put something that you are holding onto the floor or onto another surface:
You can put your suitcase down in the hall.

put something **off** 🅱1
to decide to do something at a later time:
I'll put off doing the laundry until tomorrow.

put something **on**
1 **A2** to put clothes or shoes onto your body:
You'd better put your coat on – it's cold outside.
2 **A2** to put makeup or cream onto your skin:
Put some sunscreen on before you go out.
3 **A2** to put a CD, DVD, etc. into a machine so that you can hear or see it:
Do you mind if I put some music on?

put something **out** **B1**
to make something that is burning stop burning:
to put out a fire

put something **up** **B1**
attach something to a wall or ceiling:
They put a few pictures up on the wall.

remind someone **of** something/someone **B1**
to make someone think of something or someone else:
This song reminds me of our trip to Spain.

run out
1 **B1** to finish, use, or sell all of something so that there is none left:
I almost ran out of money.

send something **back** **B1**
to return something to the person who sent it to you, especially because it is damaged or not suitable:
I had to send the shirt back because it didn't fit me.

set off **B1**
to start a trip:
What time are you setting off tomorrow morning?

set out **B1**
to start a trip:
We had to set out early.

set something **up** **B1**
to start a company or organization:
He set up his own company.

show up **B1** *informal*
to arrive somewhere:
The party started at eight, but he didn't show up until nine-thirty.

shut (something) **down** **B1**
If a computer or machine shuts down or someone shuts it down, it stops operating:
Make sure you shut down your computer before you go.

sign up **B1**
to arrange to do an organized activity:
I've signed up for evening classes at Central Community College.

split up **B1**
If two people split up, they end their relationship:
She split up with her boyfriend.

start (something) **off** **B1**
to begin by doing something, or to make something begin by doing something:
She started off her essay with a quote from the book.

stay behind **B1**
to not leave a place when other people leave it:
He stayed behind after class to speak to the teacher.

stay in **B1**
to stay in your home:
Let's stay in tonight and watch a movie.

switch (something) **off** **B1**
to turn off a light, television, etc. by using a switch:
Did you switch the computer off?

switch (something) **on** **B1**
to turn on a light, television, etc. by using a switch:
Could you switch on the light?

take something **away**
1 to remove something:
A waiter came to take our plates away.
2 **B1** to remove one number from another number:
If you take 4 away from 12 you get 8.

take something **back** (B1)
to return something to the place where
you got it:
*Did you take those books back to the
library?*

take something **off** (A2)
to remove something:
If you're hot, take your jacket off.

take off (A2)
If a plane takes off, it begins to fly.

take someone **out** (B1)
to go somewhere with someone and pay
for that person:
Our boss took us out for a meal.

take something **out** (B1)
1 to remove something from
somewhere:
*He reached into his bag and took out
a book.*
2 to buy food in a restaurant to eat
somewhere else:
Is that to eat here or take out?

take something **up**
1 (A2) to start doing a particular job
or activity:
I've taken up knitting.
2 to fill an amount of space or time:
This desk takes up too much room. ○ *My
children take up most of my time.*

think about/of someone/something
1 (A2) to consider doing something:
I'm thinking of moving to San Francisco.
2 (B1) to remember someone or
something:
*I was just thinking about you when you
called.*

throw something **away** (B1)
to get rid of something that you do not
want any more:
*He read the magazine and then threw
it away.*

try something **on** (A2)
to put on a piece of clothing to see if
it fits you:
Could I try this dress on, please?

turn something **down**
1 (B1) to reduce the level of sound or
heat that a machine produces:
Could you turn the radio down, please?
2 to refuse an offer or request:
*They offered me the job, but I turned it
down.*

turn (someone/something) **into**
someone/something (B1)
to change and become someone
or something different, or to make
someone or something do this:
The farmland is turning into a desert.
○ *They want to turn the offices into
apartments.*

turn something **off** (A2)
to move the switch on a machine, light,
etc. so that it stops working:
How do you turn the computer off?

turn something **on** (A2)
to move the switch on a machine, light,
etc. so that it starts working:
Ben turned the TV on.

turn something **up** (B1)
to increase the level of sound or heat
that a machine produces:
Could you turn the heat up, please?

wash up (A1)
to wash your hands, especially before
a meal:
It's time to wash up for dinner.

wear something **out** (B1)
to use something so much that it is
damaged and cannot be used any more:
He's already worn out two pairs of shoes.

work out
1 If a problem or difficult situation
works out, it gradually becomes better:
I hope everything works out for you.
2 (B1) to do exercises to make your body
stronger

write something **down** (B1)
to write something on a piece of paper
so that you do not forget it:
Did you write Joe's phone number down?

Countries, regions, and continents

This list shows the spellings and pronunciations of countries, regions, and continents. Each name is followed by its related adjective. Most of the time you can use the adjective to talk about a person who comes from each place. However, in some cases you must use a special word, which is shown after the adjective (for example, **Finn** is the word for a person from **Finland**). Sometimes the word shown ends in **-man**. This word can only be used to refer to a man; the word for a woman ends in **-woman** (for example, **Frenchman**, **Frenchwoman**).

To talk about more than one person from a particular place, add **-s**, except for:
· words ending in **-ese** or **-s**, which remain the same (**Chinese**, **Swiss**);
· words ending in **-man** or **-woman** which change to **-men** and **-women** (**Irishman**, **Irishmen**; **Irishwoman**, **Irishwomen**).

This list is for reference only. Inclusion does not imply or suggest status as a sovereign nation.

Name	Adjective/Person
Afghanistan /æfˈɡæn·əˌstæn/	Afghan /ˈæf·ɡæn/
Africa /ˈæf·rɪ·kə/	African /ˈæf·rɪ·kən/
Albania /ælˈbeɪ·ni·ə/	Albanian /ælˈbeɪ·ni·ən/
Algeria /ælˈdʒɪər·i·ə/	Algerian /ælˈdʒɪər·i·ən/
Central America /ˈsen·trəl əˈmer·ɪ·kə/	Central American /ˈsen·trəl əˈmer·ɪ·kən/
North America /ˈnɔrθ əˈmer·ɪ·kə/	North American /ˈnɔrθ əˈmer·ɪ·kən/
South America /ˈsaʊθ əˈmer·ɪ·kə/	South American /ˈsaʊθ əˈmer·ɪ·kən/
Andorra /ænˈdɔr·ə/	Andorran /ænˈdɔr·ən/
Angola /æŋˈɡoʊ·lə/	Angolan /æŋˈɡoʊ·lən/
Antarctica /æntˈɑrk·tɪ·kə/	Antarctic /æntˈɑrk·tɪk/
Antigua and Barbuda /ænˈti·ɡə ənd bɑrˈbju·də/	Antiguan /ænˈti·ɡən/, Barbudan /bɑrˈbju·dən/
The Arctic /ˈɑrk·tɪk/	Arctic /ˈɑrk·tɪk/
Argentina /ˌɑr·dʒənˈti·nə/	Argentine /ˈɑr·dʒənˌtaɪn/, Argentinian /ˌɑr·dʒənˈtɪn·i·ən/
Armenia /ɑrˈmi·ni·ə/	Armenian /ɑrˈmi·ni·ən/
Asia /ˈeɪ·ʒə/	Asian /ˈeɪ·ʒən/
Australasia /ˌɔ·strəˈleɪ·ʒə/	Australasian /ˌɔ·strəˈleɪ·ʒən/
Australia /ɔˈstreɪl·jə/	Australian /ɔˈstreɪl·jən/
Austria /ˈɔ·stri·ə/	Austrian /ˈɔ·stri·ən/
Azerbaijan /ˌæz·ər·baɪˈdʒɑn/	Azerbaijani /ˌæz·ər·baɪˈdʒɑ·ni/; *Person:* Azeri /əˈzeər·i/

The Bahamas /bəˈhɑ·məz/   Bahamian /bəˈheɪ·mi·ən/
Bahrain /bɑˈreɪn/   Bahraini /bɑˈreɪ·ni/
Bangladesh /ˌbæŋ·gləˈdeʃ/   Bangladeshi /ˌbæŋ·gləˈdeʃ·i/
Barbados /bɑrˈbeɪ·dəs/   Barbadian /bɑrˈbeɪ·di·ən/
Belarus /ˌbel·əˈrus/   Belorussian /ˌbel·əˈrʌʃ·ən/
Belgium /ˈbel·dʒəm/   Belgian /ˈbel·dʒən/
Belize /bəˈliz/   Belizean /bəˈli·zi·ən/
Benin /beˈnin/   Beninese /ˌben·ɪˈniz/
Bhutan /buˈtɑn/   Bhutanese /ˌbu·təˈniz/
Bolivia /bəˈlɪv·i·ə/   Bolivian /bəˈlɪv·i·ən/
Bosnia-Herzegovina
  /ˈbɑz·ni·əˌhɜr·tsə·gouˈvi·nə/   Bosnian /ˈbɑz·ni·ən/
Botswana /bɑtˈswɑ·nə/   Botswanan /bɑtˈswɑ·nən/;
    Person: Motswana /mɑtˈswɑ·nə/

Brazil /brəˈzɪl/   Brazilian /brəˈzɪl·jən/
Britain /ˈbrɪt·ᵊn/   British /ˈbrɪt·ɪʃ/;
    Person: Briton /ˈbrɪt·ᵊn/
Brunei /bruˈnaɪ/   Bruneian /bruˈnaɪ·ən/
Bulgaria /bʌlˈgeər·i·ə/   Bulgarian /bʌlˈgeər·i·ən/
Burkina Faso /bərˈki·nə ˈfas·ou/   Burkinabe /bərˈki·nəˌbeɪ/
Burma /ˈbɜr·mə/   Burmese /ˈbɜrˈmiz/
Burundi /bəˈrundi/   Burundian /bəˈrun·di·ən/
Cambodia /kæmˈbou·di·ə/   Cambodian /kæmˈbou·di·ən/
Cameroon /ˌkæm·əˈrun/   Cameroonian /ˌkæm·əˈru·ni·ən/
Canada /ˈkæn·ə·də/   Canadian /kəˈneɪ·di·ən/
Cape Verde /ˌkeɪp ˈvɜrd/   Cape Verdean /ˌkeɪp ˈvɜr·di·ən/
The Caribbean /ˌkær·əˈbi·ən/,   Caribbean /ˌkær·əˈbi·ən/,
  /kəˈrɪb·i·ən/   /kəˈrɪb·i·ən/
The Central African Republic   Central African
  /ˈsen·trəl ˈæf·rɪ·kən rɪˈpʌb·lɪk/   /ˈsen·trəl ˈæf·rɪ·kən/
Chad /tʃæd/   Chadian /ˈtʃæd·i·ən/
Chile /ˈtʃɪl·i/   Chilean /ˈtʃɪl·i·ən/
China /ˈtʃaɪ·nə/   Chinese /tʃaɪˈniz/
Colombia /kəˈlʌm·bi·ə/   Colombian /kəˈlʌm·bi·ən/
Comoros /ˈkɑm·əˈrouz/   Comoran /kəˈmɔr·ən/
The Democratic Republic of Congo   Congolese /ˌkɑŋ·gəˈliz/
  /ˌdem·əˈkræt·ɪk rɪˈpʌb·lɪk əv ˈkɑŋ·gou/
The Republic of Congo   Congolese /ˌkɑŋ·gəˈliz/
  /rɪˈpʌb·lɪk əv ˈkɑŋ·gou/
Costa Rica /ˌkɔs·tə ˈri·kə/   Costa Rican /ˌkɔs·tə ˈri·kən/
Côte d'Ivoire /ˌkout diˈvwar/   Ivorian /aɪˈvɔr·i·ən/
Croatia /krouˈeɪ·ʃə/   Croatian /krouˈeɪ·ʃən/;
    Person: Croat /ˈkrou·æt/
Cuba /ˈkju·bə/   Cuban /ˈkju·bən/
Cyprus /ˈsaɪ·prəs/   Cypriot /ˈsɪp·ri·ət/
The Czech Republic /ˈtʃek rɪˈpʌb·lɪk/   Czech /tʃek/
Denmark /ˈden·mɑrk/   Danish /ˈdeɪ·nɪʃ/;
    Person: Dane /deɪn/

Djibouti /dʒɪˈbuˌti/

Djiboutian /dʒɪˈbuˌtiˌən/

Dominica /ˌdɑˈmɪnˌɪˌkə/

Dominican /dəˈmɪnˌɪˌkən/

The Dominican Republic
  /dəˈmɪnˌɪˌkən rɪˈpʌbˌlɪk/

Dominican /dəˈmɪnˌɪˌkən/

East Timor /ˈist ˈtiˌmɔr/

East Timorese /ˈist ˌtiˌmɔˈriz/

Ecuador /ˈekˌwəˌdɔr/

Ecuadorian /ˌekˌwəˈdɔrˌiˌən/

Egypt /ˈiˌdʒɪpt/

Egyptian /ɪˈdʒɪpˌʃən/

El Salvador /ˌel ˈsælˌvəˌdɔr/

Salvadoran /ˌsælˌvəˈdɔrˌən/

England /ˈɪŋˌglənd/

English /ˈɪŋˌglɪʃ/;
  Person: Englishman /ˈɪŋˌglɪʃˌmən/

Equatorial Guinea
  /ˌekˌwəˈtɔrˌiˌəl ˈgɪnˌi/

Equatorial Guinean
  /ˌekˌwəˈtɔrˌiˌəl ˈgɪnˌiˌən/

Eritrea /ˌerˌɪˈtreɪˌə/

Eritrean /ˌerˌɪˈtreɪˌən/

Estonia /eˈstouˌniˌə/

Estonian /eˈstouˌniˌən/

Ethiopia /ˌiˌθiˈouˌpiˌə/

Ethiopian /ˌiˌθiˈouˌpiˌən/

Europe /ˈjuərˌəp/

European /ˌjuərˌəˈpiˌən/

Fiji /ˈfiˌdʒi/

Fijian /fiˈdʒiˌən/

Finland /ˈfɪnˌlənd/

Finnish /ˈfɪnˌɪʃ/; *Person:* Finn /fɪn/

France /fræns/

French /frentʃ/;
  Person: Frenchman /ˈfrentʃˌmən/

Gabon /gæˈbɔn/

Gabonese /ˌgæbˌəˈniz/

Gambia /ˈgæmˌbiˌə/

Gambian /ˈgæmˌbiˌən/

Georgia /ˈdʒɔrˌdʒə/

Georgian /ˈdʒɔrˌdʒən/

Germany /ˈdʒɜrˌməˌni/

German /ˈdʒɜrˌmən/

Ghana /ˈgɑˌnə/

Ghanaian /gɑˈneɪˌən/

Great Britain /ˌgreɪt ˈbrɪtˌ³n/

British /ˈbrɪtˌɪʃ/;
  Person: Briton /ˈbrɪtˌ³n/

Greece /gris/

Greek /grik/

Greenland /ˈgrinˌlənd/

Greenland /ˈgrinˌlənd/; *Person:*
  Greenlander /ˈgrinˌlənˌdər/

Grenada /grəˈneɪˌdə/

Grenadian /grəˈneɪˌdiˌən/

Guatemala /ˌgwɑˌtəˈmɑˌlə/

Guatemalan /ˌgwɑˌtəˈmɑˌlən/

Guinea /ˈgɪnˌi/

Guinean /ˈgɪnˌiˌən/

Guinea-Bissau /ˌgɪnˌiˌbɪˈsaʊ/

Guinea-Bissauan /ˌgɪnˌiˌbɪˈsaʊˌən/

Guyana /gaɪˈænˌə/

Guyanese /ˌgaɪˌəˈniz/

Haiti /ˈheɪˌti/

Haitian /ˈheɪˌʃən/

Honduras /hɑnˈdʊərˌəs/

Honduran /hɑnˈdʊərˌən/

Hungary /ˈhʌŋˌgərˌi/

Hungarian /hʌŋˈgeɑrˌiˌən/

Iceland /ˈaɪsˌlənd/

Icelandic /aɪsˈlænˌdɪk/; *Person:*
  Icelander /ˈaɪsˌlənˌdər/

India /ˈɪnˌdiˌə/

Indian /ˈɪnˌdiˌən/

Indonesia /ˌɪnˌdəˈniˌʒə/

Indonesian /ˌɪnˌdəˈniˌʒən/

Iran /ɪˈrɑn/

Iranian /ɪˈreɪˌniˌən/

Iraq /ɪˈrɑk/

Iraqi /ɪˈrɑˌki/

Ireland /ˈaɪərˌlənd/

Irish /ˈaɪˌrɪʃ/;
  Person: Irishman /ˈaɪˌrɪʃˌmən/

Israel /ˈɪzˌriˌəl/

Israeli /ɪzˈreɪˌli/

Italy /ˈɪtˌ³lˌi/

Italian /ɪˈtælˌjən/

Jamaica /dʒəˈmeɪˌkə/

Jamaican /dʒəˈmeɪˌkən/

Japan /dʒəˈpæn/

Japanese /ˌdʒæp·əˈniz/

Jordan /ˈdʒɔr·dən/

Jordanian /dʒɔrˈdeɪ·ni·ən/

Kazakhstan /kəˌzakˈstɑn/

Kazakh /kəˈzak/

Kenya /ˈken·jə/

Kenyan /ˈken·jən/

Kiribati /ˌkɪər·əˈbæs/

Kiribati /ˌkɪər·əˈbæs/

North Korea /ˈnɔrθ kəˈri·ə/

North Korean /ˈnɔrθ kəˈri·ən/

South Korea /ˈsaʊθ kəˈri·ə/

South Korean /ˈsaʊθ kəˈri·ən/

Kuwait /kuˈweɪt/

Kuwaiti /kuˈweɪ·ti/

Kyrgyzstan /ˌkɪər·gɪˈstɑn/

Kyrgyz /ˈkɪər·gɪz/

Laos /laʊs/

Laotian /leɪˈoʊ·ʃən/

Latvia /ˈlæt·vi·ə/

Latvian /ˈlæt·vi·ən/

Lebanon /ˈleb·ə·nən/

Lebanese /ˌleb·əˈniz/

Lesotho /ləˈsu·tu/

Basotho /bəˈsu·tu/;
Person: Mosotho /məˈsu·tu/

Liberia /laɪˈbɪər·i·ə/

Liberian /laɪˈbɪər·i·ən/

Libya /ˈlɪb·i·ə/

Libyan /ˈlɪb·i·ən/

Liechtenstein /ˈlɪk·tənˌstaɪn/

Liechtenstein /ˈlɪk·tənˌstaɪn/;
Person: Liechtensteiner /
ˈlɪk·tənˌstaɪ·nər/

Lithuania /ˌlɪθ·uˈeɪ·ni·ə/

Lithuanian /ˌlɪθ·uˈeɪ·ni·ən/

Luxembourg /ˈlʌk·səmˌbɜrg/

Luxembourg /ˈlʌk·səmˌbɜrg/;
Person: Luxembourger
/ˈlʌk·səmˌbɜr·gər/

The Former Yugoslav Republic of
Macedonia /ˈfɔr·mər ˈju·gəˌslav
rɪˈpʌb·lɪk əv ˌmæs·əˈdoʊ·ni·ə/

Macedonian /ˌmæs·əˈdoʊ·ni·ən/

Madagascar /ˌmæd·əˈgæs·kər/

Malagasy /ˌmæl·əˈgæs·i/

Malawi /məˈlɑ·wi/

Malawian /məˈlɑ·wi·ən/

Malaysia /məˈleɪ·ʒə/

Malaysian /məˈleɪ·ʒən/

The Maldives /ˈmɔl·divz/

Maldivian /mɔlˈdi·vi·ən/

Mali /ˈmɑ·li/

Malian /ˈmɑ·li·ən/

Malta /ˈmɔl·tə/

Maltese /mɔlˈtiz/

The Marshall Islands
/ˈmɑr·ʃəl ˈaɪ·ləndz/

Marshallese /ˌmɑr·ʃəˈliz/

Mauritania /ˌmɔr·ɪˈteɪ·ni·ə/

Mauritanian /ˌmɔr·ɪˈteɪ·ni·ən/

Mauritius /mɔˈrɪʃ·əs/

Mauritian /mɔˈrɪʃ·ən/

Mexico /ˈmek·sɪˌkoʊ/

Mexican /ˈmek·sɪ·kən/

Micronesia /ˌmaɪ·krəˈni·ʒə/

Micronesian /ˌmaɪ·krəˈni·ʒən/

Moldova /mɔlˈdoʊ·və/

Moldovan /mɔlˈdoʊ·vən/

Monaco /ˈmɑn·əˌkoʊ/

Monégasque /ˌmɑn·eɪˈgæsk/

Mongolia /mɑŋˈgoʊ·li·ə/

Mongolian /mɑŋˈgoʊ·li·ən/

Montenegro /ˌmɑn·təˈni·groʊ/

Montenegrin /ˌmɑn·təˈni·grən/

Morocco /məˈrɑk·oʊ/

Moroccan /məˈrɑk·ən/

Mozambique /ˌmoʊ·zæmˈbik/

Mozambican /ˌmoʊ·zæmˈbi·kən/

Myanmar /mjanˈmɑr/

Burmese /bɜrˈmiz/

Namibia /nəˈmɪb·i·ə/

Namibian /nəˈmɪb·i·ən/

Nauru /nɑˈu·ru/

Nauruan /nɑˈu·ru·ən/

Nepal /nəˈpɔl/

Nepalese /ˌnep·əˈliz/

The Netherlands /ˈneð·ər·ləndz/

Dutch /dʌtʃ/;
Person: Dutchman /ˈdʌtʃ·mən/

New Zealand /ˌnu ˈzi·lənd/

Nicaragua /ˌnɪk·əˈrɑg·wə/

Niger /niˈʒeər/

Nigeria /naɪˈdʒɪər·i·ə/

Northern Ireland
  /ˈnɔr·ðərn ˈaɪər·lənd/

Norway /ˈnɔr·weɪ/

Oman /oʊˈmɑn/

Pakistan /ˈpæk·ɪˌstæn/

Palau /pəˈlaʊ/

Palestine /ˈpæl·əˌstaɪn/

Panama /ˈpæn·əˌmɑ/

Papua New Guinea
  /ˈpæp·u·ə nu ˈɡɪn·i/

Paraguay /ˈpær·əˌɡwaɪ/

Peru /pəˈru/

The Philippines /ˈfɪl·əˌpinz/

Poland /ˈpoʊ·lənd/

Portugal /ˈpɔr·tʃə·ɡəl/

Qatar /ˈkɑ·tɑr/

Romania /roʊˈmeɪ·ni·ə/

Russia /ˈrʌʃ·ə/

Rwanda /ruˈɑn·də/

St Kitts and Nevis
  /ˌseɪnt ˈkɪts ənd ˈni·vɪs /

St Lucia /seɪnt ˈlu·ʃə/

St Vincent and the Grenadines
  /ˌseɪnt ˈvɪn·sənt ənd ðə ˈɡren·əˌdinz/

Samoa /səˈmoʊ·ə/

San Marino /ˌsæn məˈri·noʊ/

São Tomé and Príncipe
  /ˌsaʊ təˈmeɪ ənd ˈprɪn·səˌpeɪ/

Saudi Arabia /ˌsaʊ·di əˈreɪ·bi·ə/

Scandinavia /ˌskæn·dəˈneɪ·vi·ə/

Scotland /ˈskɑt·lənd/

Senegal /sen·ɪˈɡɔl/

Serbia /ˈsɜr·bi·ə/

The Seychelles /seɪˈʃelz/

Sierra Leone /siˈer·ə liˈoʊn/

Singapore /ˈsɪŋ·əˌpɔr/

Slovakia /sloʊˈvɑ·ki·ə/

Slovenia /sloʊˈvi·ni·ə/

New Zealand /ˌnu ˈzi·lənd/; *Person:*
  New Zealander /ˌnu ˈzi·lən·dər/

Nicaraguan /ˌnɪk·əˈrɑg·wən/

Nigerien /niˈʒeər·i·ən/

Nigerian /naɪˈdʒɪər·i·ən/

Northern Irish /ˈnɔr·ðərn ˈaɪ·rɪʃ/;
  Person: Northern Irishman /
  ˈnɔr·ðərn ˈaɪ·rɪʃ·mən/

Norwegian /nɔrˈwi·dʒən/

Omani /oʊˈmɑ·ni/

Pakistani /ˌpæk·ɪˈstæn·i/

Palauan /pəˈlaʊ·ən/

Palestinian /ˌpæl·əˈstɪn·i·ən/

Panamanian /ˌpæn·əˈmeɪ·ni·ən/

Papua New Guinean
  /ˈpæp·u·ə nu ˈɡɪn·i·ən/

Paraguayan /ˌpær·əˈɡwaɪ·ən/

Peruvian /pəˈru·vi·ən/

Philippine /ˈfɪl·əˌpin/; *Person:* Filipino
  /ˌfɪl·əˈpi·noʊ/, Filipina /ˌfɪl·əˈpi·nə/

Polish /ˈpoʊ·lɪʃ/; *Person:* Pole /poʊl/

Portuguese /ˌpɔr·tʃəˈɡiz/

Qatari /kɑˈtɑr·i/

Romanian /roʊˈmeɪ·ni·ən/

Russian /ˈrʌʃ·ən/

Rwandan /ruˈɑn·dən/

Kittsian /ˈkɪt·si·ən/,
  Nevisian /niˈvɪs·i·ən/

St Lucian /seɪnt ˈlu·ʃən/

Vincentian /vɪnˈsen·ʃən/

Samoan /səˈmoʊ·ən/

Sanmarinese /ˌsæn·mær·əˈniz/

São Tomean /ˌsaʊ təˈmeɪ·ən/

Saudi /ˈsaʊ·di/

Scandinavian /ˌskæn·dəˈneɪ·vi·ən/

Scottish /ˈskɑt·ɪʃ/; *Person:* Scot /
  skɑt/, Scotsman /ˈskɑts·mən/

Senegalese /ˌsen·ɪ·ɡəˈliz/

Serbian /ˈsɜr·bi·ən/;
  Person: Serb /sɜrb/

Seychelles /seɪˈʃelz/;
  Person: Seychellois /ˌseɪ·ʃelˈwɑ/

Sierra Leonean /siˈer·ə liˈoʊ·ni·ən/

Singaporean /ˌsɪŋ·əˈpɔr·i·ən/

Slovak /ˈsloʊ·vɑk/

Slovenian /sloʊˈvi·ni·ən/;
  Person: Slovene /sloˈvin/

The Solomon Islands
/ˈsɑl·ə·mən ˈaɪ·ləndz/
Somalia /səˈmɑ·li·ə/
South Africa /ˌsaʊθ ˈæf·rɪ·kə/
Spain /speɪn/

Sri Lanka /ˌsri ˈlɑŋ·kə/
Sudan /suˈdæn/
Suriname /ˌsʊər·əˈnɑ·mə/
Swaziland /ˈswɑ·ziˌlænd/
Sweden /ˈswi·dən/

Switzerland /ˈswɪt·sər·lənd/
Syria /ˈsɪər·i·ə/
Taiwan /ˌtaɪˈwɑn/
Tajikistan /təˈdʒɪ·kəˌstɑn/
Tanzania /ˌtæn·zəˈni·ə/
Thailand /ˈtaɪ·lænd/
Tibet /tɪˈbet/
Togo /ˈtoʊ·goʊ/
Tonga /ˈtɑŋ·gə/
Trinidad and Tobago
/ˈtrɪn·ɪˌdæd ənd təˈbeɪ·goʊ/

Tunisia /tuˈnɪ·ʒə/
Turkey /ˈtɜr·ki/
Turkmenistan /tɜrkˈmen·əˌstæn/
Tuvalu /tuˈvɑ·lu/
Uganda /juˈgæn·də/
Ukraine /juˈkreɪn/
The United Arab Emirates
/juˈnaɪ·tɪd ˈær·əb ˈem·ər·ɪts/
The United Kingdom (UK)
/juˈnaɪ·tɪd ˈkɪŋ·dəm/
The United States of America (USA)
/juˈnaɪ·tɪd ˈsteɪts əv əˈmer·ɪ·kə/
Uruguay /ˈjʊər·əˌgwaɪ/
Uzbekistan /ʊzˈbek·əˌstæn/
Vanuatu /ˌvɑ·nuˈɑ·tu/
Vatican City /ˈvæt·ɪ·kən ˈsɪt·i/
Venezuela /ˌven·əˈzweɪ·lə/
Vietnam /viˌetˈnɑm/
Wales /weɪlz/

Western Sahara /ˈwes·tərn səˈhær·ə/
Yemen /ˈjem·ən/
Zambia /ˈzæm·bi·ə/
Zimbabwe /zɪmˈbɑb·weɪ/

Solomon Islander
/ˈsɑl·ə·mən ˈaɪ·lən·dər/
Somali /səˈmɑ·li/
South African /ˌsaʊθ ˈæf·rɪ·kən/
Spanish /ˈspæn·ɪʃ/;
Person: Spaniard /ˈspæn·jərd/
Sri Lankan /ˌsri ˈlɑŋ·kən/
Sudanese /ˌsu·dənˈiz/
Surinamese /ˌsʊər·ə·nəˈmiz/
Swazi /ˈswɑ·zi/
Swedish /ˈswi·dɪʃ/;
Person: Swede /swid/
Swiss /swɪs/
Syrian /ˈsɪər·i·ən/
Taiwanese /ˌtaɪ·wəˈniz/
Tajik /təˈdʒik/
Tanzanian /ˌtæn·zəˈni·ən/
Thai /taɪ/
Tibetan /tɪˈbet·ᵊn/
Togolese /ˌtoʊ·gəˈliz/
Tongan /ˈtɑŋ·gən/
Trinidadian /ˌtrɪn·ɪˈdæd·i·ən/

Tunisian /tuˈnɪ·ʒən/
Turkish /ˈtɜr·kɪʃ/; Person: Turk /tɜrk/
Turkmen /ˈtɜrk·men/
Tuvaluan /tuˈvɑ·lu·ən/
Ugandan /juˈgæn·dən/
Ukrainian /juˈkreɪ·ni·ən/
Emirati /em·əˈrɑ·ti/

British /ˈbrɪt·ɪʃ/;
Person: Briton /ˈbrɪt·ᵊn/
American /əˈmer·ɪ·kən/

Uruguayan /ˌjʊər·əˈgwaɪ·ən/
Uzbek /ˈuz·bek/
Vanuatuan /ˌvɑ·nuˈɑ·tu·ən/
Vatican /ˈvæt·ɪ·kən/
Venezuelan /ˌven·əˈzweɪ·lən/
Vietnamese /viˌet·nəˈmiz/
Welsh /welʃ/;
Person: Welshman /ˈwelʃ·mən/

Sahrawian /sɑˈrɑ·wi·ən/
Yemeni /ˈjem·ə·ni/
Zambian /ˈzæm·bi·ən/
Zimbabwean /zɪmˈbɑb·wi·ən/

Prefixes

ante- before or in front of

anti- **1** opposed to or against **2** preventing or destroying

auto- **1** operating without being controlled by humans **2** self

bi- two

centi-, cent- hundred

co- with or together

contra- against or opposite

de- to take something away

dis- not, or the opposite of

e- electronic, usually relating to the Internet

eco- relating to the environment

en- **1** used to form verbs that mean ªto put into or onto somethingº **2** used to form verbs that mean ªto cause to be somethingº

ex- from before

extra- outside of, or in addition to

geo- of or relating to the Earth

ill- in a way that is bad or not suitable

in-, il-, im-, ir- not

inter- between or among

intra- within

kilo- a thousand

micro- very small

mid- in the middle of

milli- a thousandth

mini- small

mis- not or badly

mono- one or single

multi- many

non- not, or the opposite of

out- more than or better than

over- too much

photo- connected with or produced by light

post- after or later than

pre- before or earlier than

pro- supporting

psycho- of the mind or mental processes

re- again

self- of or by yourself or itself

semi- half or partly

sub- **1** under or below **2** less important or a smaller part of a larger whole

super- extremely, or more than usual

trans- **1** across **2** showing a change

tri- three

un- not, or the opposite of

under- **1** not enough **2** below

Suffixes

-able, -ible changes a verb into an adjective meaning "able to be"

-al 1 changes a noun into an adjective meaning "relating to" **2** changes a verb into a noun meaning "the action of (the verb)"

-an, -ian 1 makes a noun meaning "a person of or from" **2** makes an adjective meaning "belonging to" or "like"

-ance, -ancy makes a noun meaning "an action, condition, or characteristic"

-ation, -ion changes a verb into a noun meaning "the action, or the result of the action of (the verb)"

-ed makes an adjective meaning "having" or "typical of"

-en changes an adjective into a verb meaning "to become" or "to make something become"

-ence, -ency makes a noun meaning "an action, condition, or characteristic"

-er, -or changes a verb into a noun meaning "someone who does (something)"

-ful 1 changes a noun into an adjective meaning "full of" **2** changes a noun into an adjective meaning "having a particular characteristic"

-hood makes a noun meaning "the state of"

-ian 1 makes a noun meaning "a person who does something" **2** makes an adjective meaning "belonging to"

-ible, -able changes a verb into an adjective meaning "able to"

-ical changes a noun ending in *-y* or *-ics* to an adjective meaning "relating to"

-ing makes an adjective meaning "making someone feel something"

-ion, -ation changes a verb into a noun meaning "the action, or the result of the action (of the verb)"

-ish 1 makes an adjective meaning "slightly" or "approximately" **2** makes an adjective meaning "similar to"

-ist 1 makes a noun meaning "a person who does something" **2** makes a noun and an adjective meaning "someone with a particular set of beliefs"

-ive changes a verb into an adjective meaning "having a particular characteristic or effect"

-ize changes an adjective into a verb meaning "to cause to be or become"

-less changes a noun into an adjective meaning "without"

-like changes a noun into an adjective meaning "similar to"

-ly 1 changes an adjective into an adverb meaning "in this way" **2** makes an adjective and an adverb meaning "every" **3** changes a noun into an adjective meaning "like"

-ment changes a verb into a noun meaning "the action or its result"

-ness changes an adjective into a noun meaning "the characteristic or condition"

-ology makes a noun meaning "the study of"

-or, -er change a verb into a noun meaning "someone who does something"

-ous changes a noun into an adjective meaning "having that characteristic"

-ship makes a noun meaning "in the condition" or "having the characteristic"

-ward(s) makes an adverb meaning "toward the direction"

-y changes a noun into an adjective meaning "having a lot of"

Notes

Notes

Notes

Notes

Notes

Notes